Pierre Tim Böhn

Residential Segregation as Part (

Geschichte
History

Band/Volume 153

LIT

Pierre Tim Böhm

Residential Segregation as Part of Imperial Policies

A Transnational Analysis for the Case of Windhoek

LIT

Cover Image: Reproduction by permission of National Archives
of Namibia

This book is printed on acid-free paper.

D 17

Bibliographic information published by the Deutsche Nationalbibliothek
The Deutsche Nationalbibliothek lists this publication in the Deutsche
Nationalbibliografie; detailed bibliographic data are available on the Internet at
http://dnb.d-nb.de.
ISBN 978-3-643-91027-1 (pb)
ISBN 978-3-643-96027-6 (PDF)
Zugl.: Darmstadt, Technische Universität, Diss., 2016

A catalogue record for this book is available from the British Library.

© LIT VERLAG GmbH & Co. KG Wien,
Zweigniederlassung Zürich 2018
Klosbachstr. 107
CH-8032 Zürich
Tel. +41 (0) 44-251 75 05
E-Mail: zuerich@lit-verlag.ch   http://www.lit-verlag.ch
Distribution:
In the UK: Global Book Marketing, e-mail: mo@centralbooks.com
In North America: Independent Publishers Group, e-mail: orders@ipgbook.com
In Germany: LIT Verlag Fresnostr. 2, D-48159 Münster
Tel. +49 (0) 2 51-620 32 22, Fax +49 (0) 2 51-922 60 99, e-mail: vertrieb@lit-verlag.de
e-books are available at www.litwebshop.de

Residential Segregation as Part of Imperial Policies – A Transnational Analysis for the Case of Windhoek (1914-1945)

Table of contents

List of figures

List of tables

List of abbreviations

ADSWA: Amtsblatt für das Schutzgebiet Deutsch-Südwestafrika
ARD: Arbeitsgemeinschaft der öffentlich-rechtlichen Rundfunkanstalten der Bundesrepublik Deutschland
CIAM: Congrès Internationaux d'Architecture Moderne
DKG: Deutsche Kolonialgesellschaft
DS: Der Städtebau – Monatsschrift
DSWA: Deutsch-Südwestafrika (as part of South West Africa's German colonial period)
GLRPC: Greater London Regional Planning Committee
IFHTP: International Federation for Housing and Town Planning
NAN: National Archives of Namibia, Windhoek
NS: National Socialist/National Socialism
NSDAP: Nationalsozialistische Deutsche Arbeiterpartei
RPNY: Regional Plan of New York and its Environs
RT: Reichstag
SWA: South West Africa (as part of the South African Mandated period)
TPR: The Town Planning Review
VPLA: Votes and Proceedings of the Legislative Assembly of South West Africa
ZDF: Zweites Deutsches Fernsehen

Acknowledgements

Of course, it was a long way until this work made it into this printed version. At this point I would like to express my gratitude to those who have helped me during the preparation of this PhD dissertation in their individual ways, may it be through their encouragement, critical and constructive advice, hints at relevant literature or simply with consoling words if something did not progress as expected. In this respect, a lot of people have helped me over the past more than three years.

First and foremost I am deeply indebted to Professor Dr Dieter Schott who has been a superb supervisor. I very much appreciated his helpful feedback and support in both terms: content and formality. Although I am just a spatial planner and not part of the historians' community proper, he was willing to take care of an interdisciplinary work from our first meeting in January 2013. Back then he did not let himself be confused by my indeed very ambitious, though equally wholly sketchy grasp about my topic and research setup. With a lot of patience he has asked the right questions and pointed to certain boundaries that opened my eyes to the essential elements.

Merci beaucoup to Professor Dr Jean-Michel Roux from our Mundus Urbano partner university at Grenoble, who did not doubt for a second to accept the position to be my second supervisor. I am equally indebted to Professor Dr Mikael Hård who early on indicated his willingness to be my second supervisor at the Department of History.

It is then necessary to address my thanks to Professor Dr Annette Rudolph-Cleff who – as my boss at Mundus Urbano – gave me the liberty to work on such an exotic topic. Her PhD colloquia gave me constructive feedback to readjust my work at an early stage. But I would also like to thank her and Professor Dr Constanze Petrow for regarding my application to the *IPID4all*-programme at the Faculty of Architecture with favour. Without the relevant travel grant, my research at the National Archives of Namibia in Windhoek would have been shortened and less productive. I am therefore grateful to DAAD as sponsoring institution of this programme too. Special thanks to Technische Universität Darmstadt's URBANgrad and its team. Discussing with the other members of this graduate school was not just inspiring but comforting at the same time, since every PhD student was suffering similar problems at one stage or another.

I then need to thank Professor Dr Lauren Uğur who confirmed my choice of the topic when I felt insecure and whose work ethic and brilliant thoughts inspired me during our time together at Mundus Urbano. These thanks further extend to my colleagues Anaïs De Keijser and Edith Subtil. In addition, Dr Mada Mevissen was an extremely helpful counsellor. She kept me on track and opened a lot of perspectives on how to stay focused on the things that really matter.

Then, of course, this work would have been impossible to write without the relevant sources, books and archival files. I therefore express my special thanks to the National Archives of Namibia and their chief archivist Werner Hillebrecht with his team members Dalbert, Hanna and Irene who patiently retrieved all requested files, even if they were hiding in the remotest corners of the archives. I am equally indebted to PD Dr Helge Svenshon at the University Library at Technische Universität Darmstadt as well as to the University Libraries at Ruhr-Universität Bochum, Technische Universität Dortmund, Universität Duisburg-Essen and Johann Wolfgang Goethe-Universität Frankfurt where the remnants of the former Deutsche Kolonial Gesellschaft are preserved.

For this final printed version I need to thank Veit Hopf at LIT-Verlag and Fotios (Jude) Apokis who gave his feedback on the work's language. And a big hug to my husband Georg for his patience while revising the work.

At the end I almost lack the right words to express the gratitude to my parents. I just want to commend their deep sympathy and encouragement during the past five years in Darmstadt, as well as to thank them for their understanding whenever I was unable to visit them. Besides, my father did a fantastic job in the transliteration of Joseph Eppeler's manuscript in 'the German handwriting' during our month-long stay in Windhoek. Thankfully, my mother was able to bear our long absence. Staying there, after someone had broken into the house while we were just sitting on the plane to Namibia, made her suffer a full month of nightmares that she kept to herself: Danke für's Tapferbleiben!

Abstract

Windhoek, the capital city of South West Africa or modern Namibia, has drawn some attention by historians and planners. So far their focus was almost exclusively either on the city's period under German colonial rule or on apartheid after the Second World War, with the subsequent Namibian struggle for independence toward a post-apartheid future. This PhD dissertation by contrast addresses the developments during the interwar decades covering the years 1914 to 1945. Although it is thematically centred on residential segregation it does contextualise policies and administrative actions within broader interwar debates about challenges the city faced. Many of those challenges such as housing shortages or anticipated traffic congestion resemble similar trends, which other towns of similar size around the globe experienced.

Based on as yet untapped archival sources from the National Archives of Namibia, this work illustrates the goals and regulatory frameworks in place to replicate the typical colonial idea of a Dual City in Windhoek. Here, as elsewhere in the colonial environment, administrative offices were guided by the aim to create two separate realms for European and indigenous populations. The built exclusion was just the most obvious form. Its proponents used stereotypical arguments like the spread of infectious diseases for justification, despite contradictory opinions among the administration itself and medical proof that made the occurrence of tropical diseases at Windhoek highly improbable. In the face of the coloniser's limited powers to enforce all regulations, opportunities for indigenous contestation and consented administrative exemptions from the rules revealed traces of a Hybrid City that has evolved during the interwar years. As some findings suggest that there was no predetermined path to apartheid rules, this work does link frameworks for the implementation of segregation in the built environment with complementary wider rules in the social and economic realms. Particular attention will therefore be paid to the acquisition and use of land and the transformation of the related legal system as a crucial element for segregation.

In an attempt to come up with a different perspective on the coloniser-colonised dichotomy, this PhD follows a transnational approach on colonial history as outlined by Pierre-Yves Saunier and tries to visualise the flow of ideas across borders. Three cycles of international exchange are covered, ranging from inner European debates among leading planning traditions to the bi-directional discourse between the metropole and the colonies as well as among various colonial entities themselves. A thorough analysis of two leading planning journals for the German and British tradition (*Der Städtebau* and *The Town Planning Review*) reveals the most frequently discussed urban challenges and the reception of colonial developments at the metropole. These trends are complemented by a visualisation of the journals' international coverage whilst, at the other geographical end, municipal archival sources serve to illustrate Windhoek's reception of foreign influences. Based on Stephen Ward's theoretical framework on the so-called diffusion of planning ideas, the sources shed some light on dominant foreign ideas. The work does also take into consideration the individual stakeholders in order to see what difference the "men on the spot" could actually make. As a result of this work, the planning networks are described and emphasis is laid on the continuities in policies from German to South African rule.

Keywords: Colonial history, Namibia, sanitation, segregation, South West Africa, transnational history, urban planning, Windhoek

Zusammenfassung

Windhoek, Hauptstadt Südwestafrikas bzw. des heutigen Namibia, hat durchaus die Aufmerksamkeit von Historikern und Planern erhalten. Allerdings ist die bisherige Forschung überwiegend auf die Phase unter deutscher Kolonialherrschaft oder auf die Apartheid-Regelungen nach dem Zweiten Weltkrieg, sowie die daraus erwachsenden namibischen Bemühungen um Unabhängigkeit von Südafrika und eine Zukunft nach der Abschaffung der Rassentrennung fokussiert. Diese Dissertation beschäftigt sich im Gegensatz dazu mit den Entwicklungen in der Zwischenkriegsphase von 1914 bis 1945. Obwohl die Arbeit ihren Schwerpunkt auf wohnungsbezogene Segregation legt, werden die dazugehörigen Politiken und das Verwaltungshandeln in den größeren Kontext zeitgenössischer Debatten gestellt, mit denen die Stadt konfrontiert wurde. In zahlreichen Fällen ergeben sich dabei Gemeinsamkeiten mit jenen Herausforderungen, die auch andere Städte ähnlicher Größe weltweit zu bewältigen hatten.

Auf der Grundlage bislang unberücksichtigter Quellen aus dem Nationalarchiv in Namibia zeichnet diese Arbeit die Zielstellungen und einschlägige rechtliche Rahmenbedingungen nach, mit deren Hilfe die typische Kolonialvorstellung einer „Dual City" in Windhoek umgesetzt werden sollte. Hier, wie auch in anderen Kolonien, verfolgten Verwaltungsstellen das Motiv, zwei voneinander getrennte Einheiten jeweils für die europäische und die indigene Bevölkerung zu errichten. Die indigene Absonderung in der gebauten Umwelt stellte hierbei nur die offensichtlichste Form dar. Befürworter dieses Konzeptes nutzten stereotype Begründungsmuster wie die mögliche Ausbreitung ansteckender Krankheiten, obwohl diese

Position weder innerhalb der Verwaltung unumstritten war noch durch Vertreter der medizinischen Behörden unterstützt wurde. Im Gegenteil belegen zeitgenössische Untersuchungen das weitgehend fehlende Vorkommen tropischer Krankheiten in Windhoek. Angesichts der beschränkten Möglichkeiten innerhalb der Kolonialverwaltung, alle formulierten Regelungen tatsächlich auch umsetzen und deren Einhaltung kontrollieren zu können, ergaben sich für die indigene Bevölkerung Möglichkeiten zum Widerstand. Darüber hinaus erteilte die Verwaltung selbst Ausnahmeerlasse von manchen Regeln, sodass sich innerhalb der analysierten Periode Spuren einer „Hybrid City" entwickeln konnten. Insofern legen manche Quellen den Schluss nahe, dass der Weg zur Apartheid während der Zwischenkriegszeit noch nicht festgeschrieben war. Über die gebaute Umwelt hinaus berücksichtigt diese Arbeit u.a. auch soziale und ökonomische Rahmenbedingungen, wobei insbesondere in den Bodenrechten und den Veränderungen der damit verbundenen Rechtssysteme ein zentrales Element in der Schaffung der Segregation liegt.

Um einen neuen Blickwinkel auf den Gegensatz zwischen Kolonisierern und Kolonisierten zu eröffnen, folgt diese Dissertation dem transnationalen Ansatz in Kolonialgeschichte wie er jüngst von Pierre-Yves Saunier formuliert worden ist. Dabei wird der grenzüberschreitende Ideenaustausch aufgezeigt, der sich im Wesentlichen in drei Kreisläufe einteilen lässt: zunächst geht es um die innereuropäischen Debatten, die unter den führenden Planungstraditionen angestoßen werden. Der zweite Kreislauf besteht aus den Wechselbeziehungen zwischen Metropole und Kolonien, während unter den Kolonien selbst der dritte Zyklus etabliert wird. Durch eine detaillierte Analyse zweier führender Planungszeitschriften für die deutsche und die britische Planungstradition (*Der Städtebau* und *The Town Planning Review*) werden die häufig diskutierten städtebaulichen Herausforderungen sowie die Wahrnehmung kolonialer Entwicklungsthemen in der Metropole herausgefiltert. Diese grundsätzlichen Themen werden durch eine Visualisierung der internationalen Berichterstattung in den Zeitschriftenbeiträgen ergänzt und gleichermaßen auf der Basis von kommunalem Archivmaterial für die Perspektive Windhoeks gespiegelt. Anhand dieser Dokumente kann die Aufnahmebereitschaft und der Einfluss ausländischer Ideen auf die Stadtentwicklung analysiert werden, wofür insbesondere Stephen Wards theoretischer Rahmen herangezogen wird. Darüber hinaus wird beispielhaft die Rolle individueller Akteure untersucht, um die Entscheidungsspielräume der sogenannten „men on the spot" darzustellen. Insgesamt ergibt die Arbeit ein umfassendes Bild von den zeitgenössischen Netzwerken innerhalb der mit Stadtplanung befassten Akteure, wodurch auch gewisse Kontinuitäten zwischen der deutschen und südafrikanischen Verwaltung sichtbar werden.

Schlagwörter: Gesundheitspflege, Kolonialgeschichte, Namibia, Segregation, Stadtplanung, Südwestafrika, transnationale Geschichte, Windhoek

1. Introduction to the work

This chapter provides a brief overview on related recent academic research activities and relevant debates on imperial policies with a focus on their links to residential segregation, as well as to the selected case study of Windhoek in modern days Namibia. The second subchapter will then explain the work's research methodology and its key research questions.

1.1 State of research

From a rather general viewpoint one has to acknowledge the vast body of literature that is already available on colonial history. Therefore, one might be tempted to assume all questions have been investigated and everything has been said about this part of our global memory. This argument might sound reasonable at first instance but – among other reasons – *national specificities, different theoretical frameworks or new sources* prove it wrong.

Imperial and colonial history

As this work's concept is based on the inclusion of different imperial policies, it is necessary to highlight the different significance that is attributed to colonial history and its narrative in national contexts. In contrast to France or Great Britain[1], leading authors in Germany sometimes feel obliged to admit that, in face of the country's short-lived official colonial record, which lasted for slightly more than three decades[2], it forms a small niche only. Jürgen Zimmerer recently described the retrospective German perception with the term of "colonial amnesia", under which the national memory showed some signs of relief for not being burdened with colonial questions and remnants, as is the case in France or the UK.[3] He takes up one position of the interwar years, where yet in the immediate aftermath of the

---

[1] Cooper refers to both countries' long colonial tradition in historiography, though they mostly made a clear distinction between domestic events and the foil of colonial history "out there" (Cooper, Frederick, *Kolonialismus denken: Konzepte und Theorien in kritischer Perspektive*, Frankfurt/New York: Campus 2012: 282).

[2] The first contracts guaranteeing German state intervention to safeguard national imperial interests and which in turn have led to the official proclamation of "Protectorates", were signed in 1884. Depending on the respective colonial entity's situation during the First World War, German rule de facto ended at varying dates and de jure once the Peace Treaty at Versailles had been signed by all parties involved (Gründer, Horst, *Geschichte der deutschen Kolonien*, Paderborn *et al.*: Schöningh/UTB 2012: 85-235, 253-77).

[3] Zimmerer, Jürgen, *Kolonialismus und kollektive Identität: Erinnerungsorte der deutschen Kolonialgeschichte*, Frankfurt: Campus 2013: 9.

loss of all colonial possessions, the German sentiment was extremely diverse and hovered between some revisionist voices fantasising about the "People without Space" (Volk ohne Raum), as formulated by Hans Grimm in his popular 1926 novel[4], and the rather mainstream idea expressed by Thomas Mann in his 1927 statement.

> "Ich glaube, dass die Ereignisse uns gelehrt haben, unsere Freiheit von kolonialem Gepäck als einen Vorteil zu empfinden."[5]

For the most part of its postcolonial period, historians paid little attention to Germany's former overseas territories. Many publications only appeared out of personal interest in the topic or in face of particular 'anniversaries' which form waves of interest. Sebastian Conrad has summarised those cyclical waves in their transition from politically motivated revisionist works, which neglected international research during Weimar Republic, with critical reflections on the impacts of imperialism in the 1960s and 70s in both German states, before the topic almost fell away until the mid-1990s. According to Conrad, globalisation and the new turns in postcolonial studies then sparked a new German interest in the colonies.[6] This new interest was much more open and critical in nature, as Winfried Speitkamp has exemplified for the context of colonial memorials in Germany and the commemoration of colonial agents in street names.[7] Research at the local level has triggered a new perspective on the country's colonial past, though Speitkamp deplores that almost no attention is paid to those results. From the viewpoint of the foreign historian's community, Pierre-Yves Saunier nevertheless acknowledged those recent efforts made to review German history in its international context.[8] Over the last decade scholarly literature has been notably complemented by a rather constant supply of publications written to appeal to a wide audience such as TV documentaries[9] on the subject. Although much attention is still drawn towards Ger-

---

[4] Conrad, Sebastian, *Deutsche Kolonialgeschichte*, München: C.H. Beck 2008: 117-8. Similar in Speitkamp, Winfried, *Deutsche Kolonialgeschichte*, Stuttgart: Reclam 2005: 9-12.

[5] Cited in Knopp, Guido [Ed.], *Das Weltreich der Deutschen: Von kolonialen Träumen, Kriegen und Abenteuern*, München/Zürich: Pendo 2010: 23. "I believe, that the events have taught us to regard our liberty from colonial luggage as an advantage" (author's translation).

[6] Conrad 2008: 8-14.

[7] Speitkamp, Winfried, *Kolonialdenkmäler*. In: Zimmerer, Jürgen [Ed.]: Kein Platz an der Sonne: Erinnerungsorte der deutschen Kolonialgeschichte. Frankfurt: Campus 2013: 418-21.

[8] Saunier, Pierre-Yves, *Transnational History*, Houndsmill: Palgrave Macmillan 2013: 2.

[9] E.g.: "Das Weltreich der Deutschen" (German Empire, 2010) on public television network ZDF or, more specific, "Namibia: Eine Heimat – Zwei Welten" (Namibia: One home – two worlds, 2015) on public television network ARD.

man activities in the colonies, different perspectives, for example from colonised descendants in the metropole, are meanwhile equally well received.[10]

The thematic foci have shifted throughout the decades. Whilst early works were concentrating on the diplomatic and political backgrounds, trying to reconstruct the motives in the foreign-policy agenda that eventually favoured colonial interventions, research then started to shed light on specific stakeholders such as politicians[11] and the administration[12], missionaries[13] or the heterogeneous settler community. Once the political motives were evaluated in a supposedly sufficient way, the question of the colonies' economic relevance for their "mother country" turned out to be of pivotal interest. At the occasion of the Centennial of the 'acquisition' of first colonial possessions, Francesca Schinzinger has submitted a work, that analysed the economic impacts of the colonies on Germany.[14] Herein she tried to verify the main historic arguments used to justify the colonial engagement from an economic standpoint, such as, a) supply of the mother country with commodities, and b) creation of potential sales markets for exports. In this respect Schinzinger's contribution reflected overall research interests in the 1980s, when Anthony King highlighted the underlying interrelations between colonial cities and the world economy.[15] As Conrad has pointed out, the debate on globalisation proved to be a milestone creating new ideas and interest connected to colonial history since the mid-1990s. The range of works addressing this issue includes scholarly textbooks such as the one by Reinhard Wendt[16], as well as books like Christoph Marx's[17] which rather cater to the popular taste. Throughout the historical analysis, continuous attention was paid to military interventions and the wars

---

[10] Examples with personal references to the interwar period are among others Massaquoi, Hans Jürgen, *"Neger, Neger, Schornsteinfeger!:" meine Kindheit in Deutschland*, Bern *et al.*: Fretz und Wasmuth 1999 and Michael, Theodor, *Deutsch sein und schwarz dazu: Erinnerungen eines Afro-Deutschen*, München: Dtv 2015.

[11] For Bismarck's role e.g. Riehl, Axel T.G., *Der "Tanz um den Äquator": Bismarcks antienglische Kolonialpolitik und die Erwartung des Thronwechsels in Deutschland 1883 bis 1885*, Berlin: Duncker und Humblot 1993.

[12] E.g.: Bley, Helmut, *Kolonialherrschaft und Sozialstruktur in Deutsch-Südwestafrika 1894-1914*, Hamburg : Leibniz-Verlag 1968.

[13] E.g.: De Vries, Johannes Lucas, *Namibia : Mission und Politik : 1880-1918*, Neukirchen-Vluyn : Neukirchener Verlag 1980.

[14] Schinzinger, Francesca, *Die Kolonien und das Deutsche Reich: Die wirtschaftliche Bedeutung der deutschen Besitzungen in Übersee*, Stuttgart: Franz Steiner Verlag 1984.

[15] King, Anthony D., *Colonialism, Urbanism and the Capitalist World Economy*. 1989.

[16] Wendt, Reinhard, *Vom Kolonialismus zur Globalisierung. Europa und die Welt seit 1500*, Paderborn *et al.*: Schöningh/UTB 2007.

[17] Marx, Christoph, *Pelze, Gold und Weihwasser. Handel und Mission in Afrika und Amerika*, Darmstadt: Primus 2008.

that have been fought across Germany's colonial possessions. Two of the most recent works have been released in commemoration of the genocide against the major Namibian ethnic groups of Herero and Nama carried out between 1904 and 1908.[18] From the German perspective, the atrocities of this war have long been played down despite their devastating effects on the Indigenous population.[19] Later they have also served to identify a potential historic starting point that could be linked to the later extermination of the Jewish community in Nazi-Germany as Hannah Arendt has tried to explain.[20] In fact it took more than a century and another 'anniversary' – in this case the Centennial of the formal German surrender to South Africa's Union Defence Forces on 9 July 1915 – until a key politician in Germany officially classified these historic events as genocide.[21]

Colonial urban history

Entering the more specific arena, a lot of works have either exclusively, or at least in parts, addressed the thematic field of urban and architectural development in former German colonies. None of the exclusive studies covered town planning in South West Africa (SWA) or Windhoek in particular. They dealt with the Chinese city of Qingdao[22], architectural patterns in Cameroon[23] and Togo[24], or the devel-

---

[18] Olusoga, David/Erichsen, Caspar W., *The Kaiser's Holocaust: Germany's Forgotten Genocide*, London: Faber and Faber 2010; Zimmerer, Jürgen/Zeller, Joachim [Eds.], *Völkermord in Deutsch-Südwestafrika: Der Kolonialkrieg (1904-1908) in Namibia und seine Folgen*, Augsburg: Weltbild [2003] 2011.

[19] Due to inaccuracies and neglect in terms of statistics, the exact numbers remain disputed but Wallace refers to conservative estimations according to which more than half of the Herero community of 60,000 to 100,000 before the war died. One third of the Nama community's 20,000 members are assumed to have died (Wallace, Marion, *Geschichte Namibias: Von den Anfängen bis 1990*, Basel/Frankfurt: Basler Afrika Bibliographien/Brandes 2015: 274-5). Zimmerer equally points to this uncertainty (Zimmerer, Jürgen, *Deutsche Herrschaft über Afrikaner: Staatlicher Machtanspruch und Wirklichkeit im kolonialen Namibia*, Münster *et al.*: LIT-Verlag 2001: 40). German casualties by contrast were meticulously recorded at 1,741 – 1,525 officers and soldiers, 92 marines, 124 civilians (Bravenboer, Brenda, *Windhoek: Capital of Namibia*, Windhoek: Gamsberg Macmillan 2004: 63). Gründer and Knopp both mention almost 1,500 victims out of more than 14,000 soldiers due to a mix of casualties during combats and in consequence of illnesses (Gründer 2012: 132; Knopp 2010: 90).

[20] Gründer 2012: 137.

[21] Website Zeit-Online. The article nevertheless points to the formal apology by Heidemarie Wieczorek-Zeul, then Federal Minister for Economic Cooperation and Development, at the Centennial of the genocide's outbreak in 2004 without using the term.

[22] Warner, Torsten, *Planung und Entwicklung der deutschen Stadtgründung Qingdao (Tsingtau) in China: Der Umgang mit dem Fremden*, Hamburg 1996.

[23] Lauber, Wolfgang [Ed.], *Deutsche Architektur in Kamerun 1884-1914: Deutsche Architekten und Kameruner Wissenschaftler dokumentieren die Bauten der deutschen Epoche in Kamerun/Afrika*, Stuttgart: Krämer 1988.

4

opment of the East African cities of Dar es Salaam, Tanga and Tabora.[25] Of course this is not to say that nothing has been researched with respect to urban SWA or nowadays Namibia. The information is scattered in rather small pieces, that in most cases form minor parts of either comprehensive accounts on the history of Namibia, or are descriptions of the urban environment under which other social scientists and historians explain their research frameworks. With regards to their specificities in design Walter Peters has investigated the traces of German architecture for the whole of colonial SWA[26], whilst urban development and town planning have only been covered as subchapters of some recent works. Although Jakob Zollmann focused on the colonial police forces and the limitations of German colonial rule in SWA, he devoted a small section to urban planning and segregation.[27] It is necessary to illustrate how segregation was embedded into and formed part of a social construction in interwar years. This construction intended to create a society which privileged the White[28] German ethnic community, as has been investigated by Jürgen Zimmerer in his PhD dissertation.[29] In his work he uncovers the concepts and tools implemented by the German colonial administration in order to attain virtually full control over property, and to subjugate the Indigenous population who should eventually be exploited as cheap labour reserve. Zimmerer illustrated the continuities in terms of the administrative staff members involved behind the scenes as well as the legal frameworks, court rulings or taxation system that should have helped to impose the German will on the so-called "Territory" of SWA. Just like Zollmann after him, he nonetheless emphasised the limitations of the enforcement. This still perspective focusing on the machinery of colonial power was complemented soon after by a book edited by Frank Becker, offering a specific look at the matter through the lens of policies of race in German colonialism and their impact on racial intermarriage.[30] Becker has made transparent how the colonial administration tried to influence social norms and habits, that went

---

[24] Lauber, Wolfgang [Ed.], *Deutsche Architektur in Togo 1884-1914: Ein Vorbild für ökologisches Bauen in den Tropen*, Stuttgart: Krämer 1993.

[25] Becher, Jürgen, *Dar es Salaam, Tanga und Tabora: Stadtentwicklung in Tansania unter deutscher Kolonialherrschaft 1885-1914*, Stuttgart: Franz Steiner Verlag 1997.

[26] Peters, Walter, *Baukunst in Südwestafrika 1884-1914: Die Rezeption deutscher Architektur in der Zeit von 1884 bis 1914 im ehemaligen Deutsch-Südwestafrika (Namibia)*, Windhoek: SWA Wissenschaftliche Gesellschaft 1981.

[27] Zollmann, Jakob, *Koloniale Herrschaft und ihre Grenzen: Die Kolonialpolizei in Deutsch-Südwestafrika 1894-1915*, Göttingen/Oakville, CT: Vandenhoeck & Ruprecht 2010: 215-37.

[28] The last section of this chapter explains the use of language with reference to colonial categorisations such as White or Indigenous.

[29] Zimmerer, Jürgen: *Deutsche Herrschaft über Afrikaner: Staatlicher Machtanspruch und Wirklichkeit im kolonialen Namibia*, Münster, Hamburg, Berlin, London: LIT-Verlag 2001.

[30] Becker, Frank [Ed.], *Rassenmischehen – Mischlinge – Rassentrennung. Zur Politik der Rasse im deutschen Kolonialismus*, Stuttgart: Franz Steiner Verlag 2004.

beyond limits originally set by the mother country. One of the means to enforce the Indigenous population's subjugation and to impose the German taxation system, were so-called "Native pass tokens" to be worn clearly visible by all Indigenous people. For South Africa, where a very similar and complex system of passes existed, Carl H. Nightingale describes it as direct legacy of the country's slavery era.[31] For the context of SWA Gordon McGregor illustrates the sheer variety of such tokens[32], which underscores the colonial administration's attempts to achieve total control. Those social studies on the colonial environment created an extremely important foundation, upon which my investigations on residential segregation can be built. They help to understand the complexity of the matter, and to bear in mind that segregation in town planning was eventually contributing to those socially constructed concepts of division, making them in turn clearly visible as a spatial expression in the built environment. On the other side, these works remind us that planning was just one discriminatory element within in a larger administrative context.

Colonial Namibia and Windhoek

Comprehensive historic descriptions, such as the one by Udo Kaulich for the period of German colonial rule, help to make sense of the administrative framework in place.[33] Going beyond the German period – and in a way more ambitious than Kaulich's work – Briton Marion Wallace has published a historic reference book.[34] In her attempt she covers Namibia's rich but often neglected pre-colonial history, though the focus of her work still remains on the long colonial period under German, British/South African and South African rule, until the country has eventually gained independence on 21st March 1990. Based on her extensive analysis Wallace underscores the remaining gaps in historical research on Namibia. She explicitly deplores the low interest in the country at an international level, which – in her opinion – is expressed in the few number of experts in Namibian history. But she does equally deplore the paucity of Indigenous narratives despite some efforts to stimulate home-grown historic research.[35] In the immediate aftermath of inde-

---

[31] Nightingale, Carl H., *Segregation: A Global History of Divided Cities*, Chicago/London: University of Chicago Press 2012: 250.

[32] McGregor, Gordon D. L., *The Native Pass Tokens of German South West Africa*, Windhoek: Namibia Scientific Society 2013.

[33] Kaulich, Udo, *Die Geschichte der ehemaligen Kolonie Deutsch-Südwestafrika: 1884-1914: Eine Gesamtdarstellung*, Frankfurt am Main: Peter Lang 2001.

[34] Wallace 2015. For this PhD thesis I rely on Wallace's German edition due to the minor corrections and additions that have been made in comparison to the original English version from 2011.

[35] Wallace 2015: 2-18.

6

pendence, historical research experienced a short boom period due to the now easy and non-bureaucratic access to the National Archives, which were (and remain) open to everyone. Nonetheless, Wallace sketches the imbalance between foreign and Indigenous contributions on the country's history that remains dominated by the European and North American scholarly community. In year 28 of independence, historical research still does not belong to Namibia's priorities, and most of the works addressing the country's past are hence written by foreigners like Wallace or me. The same applies to the research that has been conducted on the impact of segregation and later apartheid on Windhoek's urban development. South African-born David Simon focused his PhD on aspects of the city's prospective transition to postcolonial days through the lens of geography[36], and much of his early research on Namibia is concentrating on the South African period after the Second World War.[37] Though tourism is often associated with geographical research, Lukas Breitwieser has presented some astonishing results from the historian's perspective on development of SWA as a tourist destination in interwar years.[38] He shows how Windhoek and the Territory were put on the map before tourism played a significant role in the country's economy usually associated with the 1970s. More than a decade after Namibia's independence, Frenchwoman Elisabeth Peyroux has conducted her research on post-apartheid urban patterns in Windhoek during the immediate transitional period – before and after Namibia gained political independence from South Africa.[39] Parallel to Peyroux's contribution a rather general and non-reflective overview on Windhoek's history has been prepared by Brenda Bravenboer[40], although the latter work appears as a rather random collection of snippets and anecdotes on the city, its buildings and inhabitants with a preponderance of White narratives.

The decades from the First to the Second World War are largely left untouched in historical scholarship. This has been confirmed to me by Werner Hillebrecht, who is working at the National Archives of Namibia since 1992, and who has worked

[36] Simon, David, *Aspects of Urban Change in Windhoek, Namibia, during the transition to independence*, Oxford: PhD dissertation at Linacre College 1983.
[37] E.g. Simon, David, *The End of Apartheid? Some Dimensions of Urban Poverty in Windhoek*, Cape Town: Conference paper 1984.
[38] Breitwieser, Lukas, *"We are going to put South West Africa on the map this time." The homogenisation and differentiation of Namibian tourist spaces*, 2012.
[39] Peyroux, Elisabeth, *Windhoek, capitale de la Namibie: changement politique et recomposition des périphéries*, Paris/Johannesburg : Karthala 2004.
[40] Bravenboer 2004.

on the country's literary and scholarly memory before his appointment to Africa, through his bibliographical collections of theses on the country.[41]

Despite the original intention to focus on those days' African perspective on Windhoek's town planning, the outcome will remain extremely limited for two reasons: firstly oral sources for the time period in question are unfortunately lost, as Zollmann has already explained as part of his research efforts half a decade earlier.[42] On the other hand, the few traceable remarks and comments in the archival files need to be treated with particular caution that goes beyond the historian's critical review of primary sources. Here it has to be taken into account that those remarks have been produced as part of the official administrative documents and are based on interpreter's work. Therefore it can be argued, these findings bear the label of being biased. In face of those limitations, this PhD dissertation will nonetheless be able to contribute new insights based on archival files that have so far either been neglected[43] in previous academic research, or because those files have, in exceptional cases, just returned from South Africa as part of the still ongoing repatriation efforts.

Theoretical contexts

This work is inextricably embedded into the larger theoretical frameworks that have gained new dynamics over the past couple of years. It is essential to acknowledge the complexity of colonial history within its historic context as well as regarding its retrospective reception. Several authors have referred to the close interrelations between imperialism and colonialism, and a full body of theories has been developed, from Karl Marx and Friedrich Engels's[44] economic reflections to King's contextualisation with specific attention paid to (world) cities.[45] Such theo-

---

[41] E.g. Hillebrecht, Werner, *Namibia in Hochschulschriften: A Bibliography on all Aspects of Namibian concern including German Colonial Policy and International Law 1851-1984*, Basel: Basler Afrika-Bibliographien 1985; idem, *Central Register of Theses on Namibia: 1992 Edition*, Windhoek: National Archives of Namibia 1992. Hillebrecht's statement can further be verified by an inspection of all issues of the *Journal of Namibian Studies*, that have been published since its first volume appeared in 2007. Despite its reputation as the only international journal exclusively devoted to Namibian research, and as being transdisciplinary in outlook, colonial urban planning has played, at best, a marginal role here.

[42] Zollmann 2010: 26.

[43] Instead of the Governor's and District Office's files this work is based on files of the Municipality of Windhoek.

[44] Marx, Karl/Engels, Friedrich, *Manifest der Kommunistischen Partei*, Stuttgart: Reclam [1872] 2010.

[45] E.g. King, Anthony D. 1989; idem, *Global Cities: Post-Imperialism and the Internationalization of London*, London: Routledge 1990; idem, *Spaces of Global Cultures: Architecture Urbanism Identity*, London: Routledge 2005.

ries were extensively compiled and compared by historian Wolfgang Mommsen based on their various lenses through which to look at imperialism and colonial relationships[46], and Herfried Münkler has submitted an example of their application on a collection of historic cases from the viewpoint of political sciences.[47] Though imperialism and colonialism are often regarded as "two sides of the same coin", the interests in and purpose of colonies[48] varied as much as did the approaches on how to organise colonial possessions. These circumstances had direct implications on the Indigenous population as Horst Gründer has (briefly) summarised for the German colonial policies.[49] Confronted with the language and contents of some of the historic files, one may not weigh these findings based on modern standards of political correctness or ethical and moral values. Frederick Cooper has therefore produced a remarkable work, in which he tries to give some advice on how to carefully revise the subject of colonialism from a current historian's viewpoint.[50] This PhD dissertation is largely inspired by Cooper's pivotal critical reflections that, among many other things, encourage a multi-disciplinary approach and support the notion of cyclical waves in colonial interests. The most important impact lies in his approach to question the validity of both, 'modernity' which has stereotypically been used as a label for driving forces behind the colonial projects in those days and the 'territorial' idea in colonial endeavours. Cooper is convinced that the Eurocentric idea of 'progress', which would have permeated from a centre to its periphery, is inappropriate.[51] At this point he creates an interesting contradiction, or at least tension, to Stephen Ward's theoretical framework on the so-called 'diffusion' of planning ideas which is based on this very narrative.[52] Nonetheless Ward's works form another major source of inspiration and his value is twofold: beyond his theoretical concept he has done extensive research at

---

[46] Mommsen, Wolfgang J., *Imperialismustheorien: Ein Überblick über die neueren Imperialismusinterpretationen*, Göttingen: Vandenbroeck & Ruprecht 1987.

[47] Münkler, Herfried, *Imperien: Die Logik der Weltherrschaft – vom Alten Rom bis zu den Vereinigten Staaten*, Berlin: Rowohlt 2007.

[48] Osterhammel, Jürgen/Jansen, Jan C., *Kolonialismus. Geschichte, Formen, Folgen*, München: C.H. Beck 2012: 7-18. At this stage the differentiation between 'colonisation' and 'colony' is omitted.

[49] Gründer 2012: 237-42.

[50] Cooper 2012.

[51] Cooper 2012: 23.

[52] E.g. Ward, Stephen V., *Re-examining the International Diffusion of Planning*. In: Freestone, Robert [Ed.]: Urban Planning in a Changing World: The Twentieth Century Experience. London: E&FN Spon 2000; idem, *Transnational Planners in a Postcolonial World*. In: Healey, Patsy; Upton, Robert [eds.]: Crossing Borders: International Exchange and Planning Practice. London/New York: Routledge 2010.

comparing British and German urban history.[53] Both approaches by Ward to cross national boundaries and to analyse how this crossing goes on, eventually fit with Cooper's critique at territoriality in colonial history.

Cooper characterises empire as an exceptional category of spatial systems that in fact crossed borders but remained self-contained in its operations.[54] In face of such a complex topic like town planning in the colonial context, it seems very appealing to reconsider the appropriateness of national confines for their analysis. Pierre-Yves Saunier's comments,

> "[t]ransnational history implies adjusting the space of our research to the questions we tackle, instead of squeezing our questions into national containers."[55]

Rather than focusing on national networks and how planning acted within this setup, the focus should be on town planning and how it evolved, irrespective of national borders. Besides Cooper, other authors have highlighted the artificial nature of borders under colonial circumstances too.[56]

It is in this context that a last cornerstone needs to be introduced. Saunier's approach to history through the lens of transnationality responds to the multifarious links that exist in colonial history, and that can neglect national or language borders.[57] Despite the fact that transnational history as such is still a very young approach[58], and Saunier himself expressed his uncertainty about its long-term qualities or its potential as a temporary fashion, it has already produced some promising results – especially with regards to colonial history and town planning: Liora Bigon and Yossi Katz used it for their edited analysis of the garden city movement's emulation in Palestine and Africa[59], whereas Luce Beeckmans and Johan Lagae contributed another example with their transnational research on Kinshasa's

---

53 E.g. Ward, Stephen V., *Planning the Twentieth-Century City. The Advanced Capitalist World*, Chichester: Wiley 2002; idem, *What did the Germans ever do for us? A Century of British Learning About and Imagining Modern Planning*, 2010.
54 Cooper 2012: 176.
55 Saunier 2013: 120.
56 E.g. Zimmerer 2001.
57 Saunier 2013.
58 Nevertheless transnational scientific exchange of ideas has already been investigated in the early 1990s as Bigon has pointed out (Bigon, Liora, *Transnational Networks of Administrating Disease and Urban Planning in West Africa: the Inter-Colonial Conference on Yellow Fever, Dakar, 1928*, Dordrecht: Springer Science+Business Media 2013: 109).
59 Bigon, Liora/Katz, Yossi [Eds.], *Garden Cities and Colonial Planning: Transnationality and Urban Ideas in Africa and Palestine*, Manchester: University Press 2014.

syndrome-planning.[60] In order to produce further results, which do also include less investigated colonial powers, Beeckmans explicitly encouraged research that includes former German colonies.[61]

The background of these larger theoretical frameworks needs to be focused upon the question of the colonial city's development and how planning attempted to or indeed did enforce residential segregation. In accordance with official policies to spatially separate the European population from the Indigenous one in the majority of colonial cities, authors first followed the "dual city" concept in their analyses. Janet Abu-Lughod has contributed some blueprint examples for such analyses with her detailed empirical research on Cairo[62] and Rabat.[63] Gwendolyn Wright has submitted one standard work[64] that is mentioned in virtually all Anglophone accounts in the context of French colonial urbanism. Though Wright's work has been complemented by Zeynep Çelik with regards to Algiers a couple of years later[65], it reflects the scarcity of (English) publications on French developments in colonial urbanism, as has been deplored very recently by Ambe Njoh.[66] He therefore encourages further research to cross language and regional borders in African history.[67] Despite the chronological fact of just six years lying between Wright's and Çelik's publications, both works are substantially different in their approach: whilst Wright uncritically replicated the Eurocentric philosophy of the dual city with its modernisation paradigm, Çelik has her focus on the question of Indigenous contestations. This shift refects a general transition – or turn – in historical sciences, which incorporate a more critical perspective on colonial urban history

---

[60] Beeckmans, Luce/Lagae, Johan, *Kinshasa's Syndrome-Planning in Historical Perspective: From Belgian Colonial Capital to Self-Constructed Megalopolis*. In: Silva, Carlos Nunes [Ed.]: Urban Planning in Sub-Saharan Africa: Colonial and Post-Colonial Planning Cultures. New York/London: Routledge 2015.
[61] Beeckmans, Luce, *Editing the African city: reading colonial planning in Africa from a comparative perspective*, London 2013.
[62] Abu-Lughod, Janet L., *Tale of Two Cities: The Origins of Modern Cairo*, Cambridge 1965.
[63] Abu-Lughod, Janet L., *Rabat: Urban Apartheid in Morocco*, Princeton: University Press 1981.
[64] Wright, Gwendolyn, *The Politics of Design in French Colonial Urbanism*, Chicago/London: University of Chicago Press 1991.
[65] Çelik, Zeynep, *Urban Forms and Colonial Confrontations: Algiers Under French Rule*, Berkeley: University of California Press 1997.
[66] Njoh, Ambe J., *French Colonial Urbanism in Africa*. In: Silva, Carlos Nunes [Ed.]: Urban Planning in Sub-Saharan Africa: Colonial and Post-Colonial Planning Cultures. New York/London: Routledge 2015.
[67] One of the few exceptions is Bigon's PhD dissertation comparing residential segregation in British Lagos and French Dakar (Bigon, Liora, *A History of Urban Planning in two West African Colonial Capitals: Residential Segregation in British Lagos and French Dakar (1850-1930)*, Lewiston: Edwin Mellen 2009).

since the mid-1990s. The dual city concept was then regarded with a growing scepticism and perceived as a kind of prolongation of colonial attitudes that neglected the Indigenous perspective and historic attempts of contestation. Brenda Yeoh has contributed as one of the first authors to this criticism through her comprehensive work on Singapore.[68] Therein she did not just question the validity and stability of power relations between colonisers and colonised as one of oppressors and oppressed, which became emblematic through the branding of spaces. Instead, she pointed to the artificial character of racial groups in colonial administration. Her approach was inspired by David Simon, who had – besides his already mentioned works on Namibia – contributed to southern African urban analysis, and encouraged a critical viewpoint on power relations in urban development. But Yeoh in turn inspired others to follow her approach, as Libby Porter has done with regards to Australasia and Canada.[69] Porter's work can be considered a turning point, for she does meticulously present the complicity of planning in colonialism and illustrates, how colonial elements in planning language still prevail. Instead, Porter calls for a stronger inclusion of Indigenous perspectives and rights in planning regimes. All these critical works and reflections supported the evolution and emanation of the "hybrid city" concept.

Virtually all works on colonial cities do either implicitly or explicitly build on the distinction of otherness as foundation for all forms of segregation. In this context Edward Said has published a ground-breaking work that reflected on the artificial and imagined character of "Orientalism" on European societies.[70] It contained a dichotomy between "European" community and "the other," although the latter was stigmatised as somehow fascinating but culturally less developed, valued and, hence, inferior and potentially dangerous to the superior "Europeans." Urs Bitterli has further contributed to this debate in the German-speaking community.[71] Although he underscored the significance and positive results of an interdisciplinary look at those cultural encounters, he still adhered to a rather un-reflected use of colonial terminology like "Savages" to describe Indigenous communities. A more balanced and detailed analysis on how Africans have been perceived in Germany's

---

[68] Yeoh, Brenda S.A., *Contesting Space: Power Relations and the Urban Built Environment in Colonial Singapore*, Oxford *et al.*: Oxford University Press 1996.
[69] Porter, Libby, *Unlearning the Colonial Cultures of Planning*, Farnham/Burlington: Ashgate 2010.
[70] Said, Edward, *Orientalism*, London: Penguin [1977] 2003.
[71] Bitterli, Urs, *Die "Wilden" und die "Zivilisierten": Grundzüge einer Geistes- und Kulturgeschichte der europäisch-überseeischen Begegnung*, München: C.H. Beck 1991.

colonial debates in parliament and the media has been compiled by Michael Schubert.[72]

In terms of fascination for the "other", Saunier has argued that "human zoos" were a key component for interwar colonial encounters and served as a means to underpin the racial divide in the colonial mission.[73] It does not come as a surprise that "human zoos" (Völkerschau) received some attention in historical research, which tried to investigate the European imagination of Black daily life, and what impact those events had on the public perception, as Hilke Thode-Arora did for the then famous Hagenbeck Völkerschau.[74] In her description she also points to the potential threat to public health in terms of infectious diseases that these exhibitions allegedly posed to both, "exhibited" people and visitors.[75] Susann Lewerenz pursued a different perspective in her analysis of the *Deutsche Afrika-Schau* which toured NS-Germany from 1936 to 1940.[76] She focused on the show's attempted exploitation by authorities and party organisations for political purposes, in order to convey the state propaganda of colonial revisionism. Similar to the already mentioned forms of syndrome-planning in Africa, it was in this overall context that public health concerns and medical recommendations were exploited in order to justify a system of spatial separation. This system should prevent the spread of infectious diseases which were usually attributed to the Indigenous population alone. A minimum distance of varying extent, labelled as "cordon sanitaire"[77] or "zone neutre"[78], should safeguard the colonisers' health in the first instance, and as a secondary priority that of the colonised too. Robert Home has investigated how

---

[72] Schubert, Michael, *Der schwarze Fremde: Das Bild des Schwarzafrikaners in der parlamentarischen und publizistischen Kolonialdiskussion in Deutschland von den 1870er bis in die 1930er Jahre*, Stuttgart: Franz Steiner Verlag 2003.

[73] Saunier 2013: 87.

[74] Thode-Arora, Hilke, *Hagenbeck: Tierpark und Völkerschau*. In: Zimmerer, Jürgen [Ed.]: Kein Platz an der Sonne: Erinnerungsorte der deutschen Kolonialgeschichte. Frankfurt: Campus 2013.

[75] The greatest danger was eventually posed by tuberculosis which affected many African people. Thode-Arora 2013: 248.

[76] Lewerenz, Susann, *Die Deutsche Afrika-Schau (1935-1940): Rassismus, Kolonialrevisionismus und postkoloniale Auseinandersetzungen im nationalsozialistischen Deutschland*, Frankfurt am Main *et al.*: Peter Lang 2006.

[77] Scholz, Wolfgang, *Stadtplanung in Afrika – Über den Umgang mit dem schwindenden Einfluss der Planung auf die Siedlungsentwicklung*, Dortmund 2002: 77.

[78] Beeckmans, Lagae 2015: 203-9.

British planning regulations prepared by colonial officer Lord Frederick Lugard have been turned into a potential blueprint solution beyond its origins in Nigeria.[79]

International conferences played a central role in their dissemination at both levels: town planning and tropical medicine. How well-connected the planning community between First and Second World War was, can be realised through the intense debates on new design trends for housing. Renzo Riboldazzi revealed those links through his investigations on the *International Federation of Housing and Town Planning* (IFHTP)[80], whereas Alan Mabin and Mark Oranje have shed some light on the 1938 town planning conference in Johannesburg that indicated a certain shift in the development of new planning concepts towards the colonial entities.[81] In terms of tropical medicine Bigon summarised some exemplary results regarding the 1928 Yellow Fever Conference at Dakar, which indicate the significance of transnational networks in those days and their promotion of residential segregation.[82] Through her reference to Helen Tilley's work, Bigon did demonstrate the applicability of the transnational approach to medical history, where an intense exchange of ideas dominated the interwar period in tropical medicine.[83]

All those segregationist attempts were embedded into the broader coeval concepts of 'modernisation' and 'progress' and therefore usually labelled as 'mission civilisatrice' or 'civilising mission', in order to disseminate the colonisers' perceived cultural and technological advances to the colonial entities. Pointing to early intentions Conrad has summarised such efforts in conjunction with missionary and cultural activities.

> "Emanzipation war durchaus beabsichtigt, aber eine Gleichstellung war nicht intendiert: perfekte "Eingeborene", nicht jedoch schwarze Europäer waren das Ziel der Zivilisierungsmission."[84]

---

[79] Home, Robert, *Colonial Urban Planning in Anglophone Africa*. In: Silva, Carlos Nunes [Ed.]: Urban Planning in Sub-Saharan Africa: Colonial and Post-Colonial Planning Cultures. New York/London: Routledge 2015.

[80] Riboldazzi, Renzo, *The IFHTP Discourse on Urbanism in Colonial Africa between the Wars*. In: Silva, Carlos Nunes [Ed.]: Urban Planning in Sub-Saharan Africa: Colonial and Post-Colonial Planning Cultures. New York/London: Routledge 2015.

[81] Mabin, Alan/Oranje, Mark: *The 1938 Johannesburg 'Town Planning Exhibition and Congress': Testament, Monument and Indictment*. In: Freestone, Robert; Amati, Marco [Eds.]: Exhibitions and the Development of Modern Planning Culture. Farnham/Burlington: Ashgate 2014.

[82] Bigon 2013.

[83] Bigon 2013: 105.

[84] Conrad 2008: 74. "Emancipation was indeed intended but this did not include formal equality: perfect 'Natives', but no Black Europeans were the civilising mission's goal" (author's translation)

14

Infrastructure projects played a significant role in this context and were considered as symbol for modernisation and mirror of social progress. Railways were emblematic for this development and have drawn the attention of historians, as was the case for the Constantinople-Baghdad-line, either written for a general audience like by Wolfgang Korn[85], or as part of a comprehensive scholarly research as conducted by Dirk van Laak.[86] These investments mirrored similar modernisation projects in Europe and Karl Ditt has described, how they were vying for attention and resources of potential investors in the 'mother countries.' As Ditt has concluded for the British context, colonial investments seemed more lucrative than domestic ones and in consequence hampered the extension and improvement of electricity grids in the UK.[87] This is one example of how the colonies made a direct impact on the imperial centre, and in this case created a backlog – for example in comparison to Germany, where banks then concentrated on the home markets – that was still felt in the 1920s.[88]

1.2 Research design

As Wallace has already pointed out[89], there remain many chapters in Namibia's history book that still need to be written. And though she has particularly the post-Second World War period in mind[90], research on Namibia's previous colonial past yet calls for additions. This PhD project is intended to contribute to fill part of this gap by addressing colonial town planning in Windhoek between 1914 and 1945. During those years three external powers ruled the city[91] and therefore contributed to the transnational setup. Emphasis will be laid on residential segregation and traces of German impacts that persisted into the South African mandate period.

---

[85] Korn, Wolfgang, *Schienen für den Sultan: Die Bagdadbahn: Wilhelm II., Abenteurer und Spione*, Köln: Komet 2012.

[86] Van Laak, Dirk, *Imperiale Infrastruktur: Deutsche Planungen für eine Erschließung Afrikas 1880 bis 1960*, Paderborn: Schöningh 2004: 150-64.

[87] Ditt, Karl, *Zweite Industrialisierung und Konsum: Energieversorgung, Haushaltstechnik und Massenkultur am Beispiel nordenglischer und westfälischer Städte 1880-1939*, Paderborn: Schöningh 2011: 126.

[88] Ditt 2011: 132.

[89] Wallace 2015: 3.

[90] Wallace 2015: 6-7.

[91] German rule until the surrender in 1915, British/South African martial law until 1920 and South African rules as part of the League of Nations' Mandate thereafter.

Theoretical and transnational standpoint

As Libby Porter's cautions[92], accepting my personal background being a male White European from Germany, raised in Christian values, educated as spatial planner and trained as civil servant in building administration, may well inhibit looking at the matter through the lens of the Indigenous perspective. Nevertheless, my argument seeks to this viewpoint in order to have a careful and inquisitive look at the administrative machinery and mechanisms in place to impose residential segregation as part of Windhoek's town planning. Although this work is thus interdisciplinary by nature with its inclusion of planning, legal, social and economic aspects, a primary approach is historical. Under these circumstances, Cooper's warnings about the 'yardsticks' by which historical actions should be measured will be taken to heart.[93] It is fruitless to judge documents of their day based on their insensitive language but necessary to see them as revealing in their own way. Though Jürgen Osterhammel and Jan Jansen have emphasised the notion of territoriality's significance as introduced by the colonial powers into the African context[94], it is essential to bear its limitations in mind. Through his detailed analysis of the German police forces in the territory of *Deutsch-Südwestafrika* (DSWA), Zollmann has demonstrated how fragile the imposition of European will and the enforcement of those alien concepts and rules to the African context remained.[95] German laws could be imposed in more or less strict terms within the demarcated confines of the so-called 'police zone'[96], and though Windhoek was the best staffed village in imperial Germany as regards its ratio between police officers and European inhabitants, it was impossible to enforce all laws and regulations.[97] This environment of aspired perfection, yet to a certain extent imagined colonial control with its loopholes in practice, defines the context of this research. In agreement with Yeoh, colonial cities will for the matter of this research be considered as a distinct category, which does not fit the pre-industrial vs. industrialised city dichot-

---

[92] L. Porter 2010: 11-8.
[93] Cooper 2012: 379-94.
[94] Osterhammel, Jansen 2012: 76-7.
[95] Zollmann 2010: 213-340.
[96] Some African kingdoms along the northern border region with Angola were able to defend their autonomy in German colonial times. As Wolfgang Werner explains, their territories were not part of the police zone whilst German officials claimed authority for all other areas along railway lines and main roads which should be policed accordingly (Werner, Wolfgang, *Landreform und Landrechte in Namibia*. In: Hess, Klaus A.; Becker, Klaus J. [Eds.]: Vom Schutzgebiet bis Namibia 2000. Göttingen/Windhoek: Klaus Hess Verlag 2002: 217).
[97] Zollmann 2010: 218.

16

omy often referred to in the colonial context[98]; Katrina Gulliver has taken a similar position very recently.[99] Besides, this move opens the opportunity to better reflect on potential forms of contestation, which can be carried out in unconscious means of daily routines. Zollmann's identification of limitations in colonial police powers actually confirms Yeoh's position, according to which the colonial influence depended on the colonised people's readiness to accept such impositions.[100] Such a view breaks with the classical notion of the colonised as passive victims of colonial oppression. Nonetheless, these forms of resistance in daily life may not lead to an underestimation of the most important option to exercise power in urban development: the access to and ownership of land. It was in this context that the colonial regime had a tremendous impact on the autochthonous population: the economic distribution of the most important urban asset did change profoundly; either voluntarily or by various means of force, and the consequences are to be felt up until today.[101] And with the land, the names have in many cases changed as well, inscribing the new power into space. As Porter has formulated[102], this expression of power to put a place on the map is a very important feature that needs to, and will be, critically reflected within this work.

Despite local and colonial specificities, Windhoek's town planning – just like in other colonial cities – was heavily influenced by external ideas. Planning ideas travelled as kind of ideological backpack, either in physical terms with their planners as well as in books and journals, or as mere ideas through various forms of interaction at conferences, exhibitions, etc. These exchanges created a complex system of interrelations and dependencies, and it is necessary to explain how this system has evolved, and what impact it has on the case study. The international circulation of planning ideas, as sketched in Saunier's publication on transnational history[103], will be investigated within this work. His approach represents another version of what Ward labels as 'diffusion' in his description of the planning profession's evolution.[104] For the context of Windhoek three overlapping circulation strands among the planning profession are addressed: a) the one among the major European planning traditions; b) the exchange between metropole and colonial entity; c) the flow among and between colonial entities.

---

[98] Yeoh 1996: 1.

[99] Gulliver, Katrina, *The Colonial City as a frame of historical analysis*, published online 2015 (https://unsw.academia.edu/KatrinaGulliver retrieved on 19.11.2015).

[100] Yeoh 1996: 14.

[101] For the South African context for example: Commey, Pusch, *Landless blacks: Why the impasse continues*, London/Paris 2014.

[102] L. Porter 2010: 91.

[103] Saunier 2013: 58-79.

[104] Ward 2000: 40-60.

The sources

During the interwar period the planning profession matured as a self-contained discipline in responding to the volatile environment in political, economic and social terms.[105] In order to understand the relevant matters in interwar urban development, a comparative analysis of two leading planning journals for the full interwar period will provide "first-hand" impressions of main interwar urban driving forces. Albers has already expressed the relevance of *Der Städtebau* in his 1975 historical overview on the planning profession's evolution in Germany[106], and it will be complemented by its British counterpart *The Town Planning Review* here. Both journals are analysed in quantitative and qualitative terms. In order to assess the potential impact and recognition of German colonies on the debate, before they had been handed over according to the Treaty of Versailles, the scope of analysis additionally covers some pre-First World War years, and spans from 1910 to 1945.

The comparative journal analysis serves three key interests: firstly it helps to identify the most urgent challenges in those days town planning; secondly it evaluates the relevant international ideas; whereas its final third aim is to trace the coverage and impact of colonial cities on the planning debate. Based on this analysis, they help to create a sound framework of the historic debates and schools of thought in planning. Wherever feasible, less frequently cited planning opinions of those years will be included, in order to round off the overall picture.

In addition to the journal analysis and a review of relevant secondary literature, this work relies on archival sources for the case study of Windhoek. Both, the remnants of the former *Deutsche Kolonialgesellschaft* (DKG) with its archives and library, which are today preserved at the university library of Frankfurt, as well as the National Archives of Namibia (NAN) at Windhoek were consulted. In contrast to previous research on SWA as delineated above (see 1.1), the focus is here on the Municipality of Windhoek and files specifically referring to her. Amongst many other documents Official Gazettes, administrative files, photos or maps were considered, although most of the latter are in such a dilapidated condition which renders their reproduction impossible. As already stated, all these documents are biased by the ruling coloniser's view on the state of affairs and they will be treated as

---

[105] Albers, Gerd, *Entwicklungslinien im Städtebau: Ideen, Thesen, Aussagen 1875-1945: Texte und Interpretationen*, Düsseldorf: Bertelsmann Fachverlag 1975: 17-9, 174-263. Albers has split his analysis on this period in two sections, i.e. 1915 to 1930 and 1930 to 1945.

[106] Albers 1975: 13, 17. Albers' hint drew some attention to that specific source for my work. He excluded the journal from further investigation for workload reasons and focused on historic books instead.

such. In face of the international links that might be revealed in the archival sources and as part of the journal analysis, references to other settler colonies, also in the French context, will be made, where deemed appropriate.

Research questions

There are three research questions that remained almost unaltered throughout the preparation of this work, and they therefore constitute its core guidelines.

Although economic aspects and public health concerns supposedly dominate the historical reflections on colonial urbanism at the rather general level, it is my intention to shed some light on potential similarities between European and colonial urban debates. This is relevant as most planners and persons in charge of planning matters were either European by origin or had been educated at one of the institutions in these countries. To investigate the impact of this origin and socialisation on their work where, as a consequence, certain ideas and habits permeated into the colonial context. Therefore this dissertation addresses the question:

> How did the European urban planning debate impact on the development of colonial cities between 1914 and 1945?

The question is in its very nature a broad-based one to define the scope of relevant historic key challenges and schools of thought that made their way to the colonies. It will help to trace the individual topic's significance for both contexts, and illustrate potential direct references between the debates in Europe and the colonies.

At the next level, those interrelations in terms of planning ideas travelling between the two spheres at the perceived metropole and the periphery form the background to further elaborate on the social implications they induced. In my research setup it seems important to demonstrate how, either directly or subconsciously, class distinctions and social attitudes were translated into the colonial context. I want to investigate the assumption that planners and administrations were well familiar with those stereotypical categorisations that had already been used towards slum-dwellers in the European context before the First World War. Now they applied this debate and its arguments to colonial cities, where the hierarchical system grew in complexity, since it was not limited to the distinctions created by social classes among the European communities anymore. It was instead complemented by the African Indigenous communities, which in turn transformed interwar tendencies of social segregation into patterns of segregation along racially defined lines. The hierarchy had to reflect both, the power relations between colonisers and colonised, as well as the social distinctions among both communities. As part of my work I intend to have a closer look at this adaptation, although it does not come as a surprise that the emphasis remained on the colonisers' social distinctions: on one hand, the debate was nourished by a constant fear of an evolving European *lumpenproletariat*, who would have posed a danger to the imagined superior European role in the colonies. Such a low-rank, White social group had the potential to undermine the civilising mission's goals. On the other hand there existed the constant imagination of African people as inherently diseased, thereby constituting a potential threat to public health. In an attempt to dissect these overlapping systems of social stratification, the work tries to investigate the following aspect:

> What kind of similarities and differences did the European planning debate produce in the colonial context with regards to residential segregation?

Through the definition of the third research question my analysis follows the transnational approach in colonial history. Here the work pursues two objectives: firstly, it serves as a rather general attempt to better reflect the existing international circulation of ideas during interwar years. It seems necessary to analyse the main sources of information that impacted on SWA and to see the extent of metropolitan influence as well as other colonial entities' impact on Windhoek. It is the intention to figure out, if and where the local planning community was able to negotiate its own development goals and strategies or to what extent it had to rely on foreign examples and to bow to external forces. Secondly, it is intended to go further into the details of Windhoek's residential planning and the impact international networks had on it. The question therefore is:

> To what extent has there been international exchange of ideas for the case study of Windhoek, and how did it impact on planning residential segregation?

Here the numerous links to other colonial administrations as well as to the metropole are discussed. The results are contextualised in Ward's theoretical framework and will reflect its limitations for the case of SWA, where several planning traditions were used as sources of reference.

Statement on language

At this stage I feel obliged to make a few comments on the terminology and language used in my PhD dissertation. First of all I do support gender equality and whenever I am using certain professions like planner, historian, etc. they are usually not meant as a reference to a certain sex, even if most following explanations do concentrate on male planners. This does only reflect the historic environment, since it is not my intention to offend female readers.

Similarly I am forced to use certain terms like "Negro" or "Native" in many contexts. This has nothing to do with my personal opinion but is a result of their use in historic documents. Substituting them with other terms or expressions would usually seem advisable in order not to offend other readers and to comply with current forms of political correctness. However, and here I am fully in line with Cooper, the ban on these words reflects our current 'yardsticks' which are intended to avoid pejorative undertones. To transfer these yardsticks would just represent the application of superficial cosmetics to a completely different mind-set. I will therefore use those terms without specific indications like apostrophes in order to give a correct account of the historic circumstances as reported in the files. Yet in order to reflect and remind the artificial character of the racial distinctions made in interwar debates, terms like Black, White, Indigenous or Native are written with capital letters.

Taking account the overlapping developments in the thematic fields of colonial and urban history, I need to make a distinction in terms of my use of the words "metropole" and "metropolis." Wherever I am referring to the relationships between imperial/colonial powers in their European territories I use the term *metropole*, which is complemented by colonial overseas territories. By contrast, in the context of urban development and the growth of cities I use *metropolis*, when I refer to large cities and the historic contrast and critique they sparked as opposed to the countryside.

2. Theoretical contexts

This chapter tries to summarise the main theoretical concepts, which have made a significant impact on this PhD dissertation. It starts with a subchapter (see 2.1) on the rather general context of transnationality in history, which is followed by some brief reflections on colonial history and a collection of the most relevant theories on imperialism, into which colonial history is embedded. In the following subchapter (see 2.2) concepts and elements of colonial cities are debated and put into the context of the circulation of planning ideas, as laid down in Ward's concept. The last subchapter (see 2.3) is devoted to the issue of residential segregation and considers its social component as originating from European debates, as well as its implementation in the colonial context. It is linked to the question of how the colonisers have imagined and perceived the colonised "Other," as discussed in Said's foundational work on "Orientalism."

2.1   Transnational aspects of imperial and colonial history

The perspective this work takes on colonial history is embedded in recent scholarly developments. In 2008 Sebastian Conrad has therefore underscored the impact of the latest turns.

> "Zu den innovativsten Anregungen der *postcolonial studies* gehört der Vorschlag, die Geschichte von Kolonisierern und Kolonisierten innerhalb eines zusammenhängenden analytischen Feldes zu betrachten."[1]

Conrad is pointing to the difficulties that arise, if colonial history is considered in too small categories at both, the spatial level as well as with regards to contents. He instead supports the idea to analyse the circulations that occurred at various levels of colonial and postcolonial history in order to recognise their side-effects on both, colony and metropole.[2] His statement can be related to the concepts of transnational history, as drafted in general terms by Pierre-Yves Saunier half a decade later, or for the specific context of planning by Anthony King, who has presented his ideas almost one decade earlier than Saunier. Due to King's scepticism and critique at the interpretation of cities as the product of one national narrative, his ideas will resonate throughout the following theoretical subchapters as well.

---

[1] Conrad 2008: 86. "Among the most innovative stimulations of *postcolonial studies* belongs the suggestion to regard the history of colonisers and colonised in the space of one comprehensive analytical field." (author's translation, emphasis in original).
[2] Conrad 2008: 86-96.

Concepts of transnational history

The main idea of transnational history is based on the continuous experience underscored by its key proponents, that certain developments cannot be fully grasped if they are only addressed by frameworks of national narratives or too stringent thematic concepts. According to King this is particularly true for the complex and at several levels intertwined urban environment. Cities play a key role as gatew not just for capital but mainly for ideas and people who migrate swiftly across borders. This has had direct implications on the circulation of planning ideas at large, like Mikael Hård and Thomas Misa have analysed for technical infrastructures and subsequently labelled as "hidden integration"[3], and for tools in colonial contexts. It is nonetheless imperative to recognise such circulations as bidirectional links; similar to the sender recipient relationship the circulation of planning ideas depended on the ability of a sender's – in my case the colonising powers – willingness and ability to disseminate its ideas. But it was equally relevant if the recipient were open to those ideas and how they impacted on the receiving society. As a reaction, King has formulated his expectations for a transnational theoretical framework.

> "The adoption, modification or refusal of ideas and practices of urban planning between different nation states, whether in colonial or non-colonial situations, requires a framework for spatial analysis which extends beyond a single, or even two or three nation states and also acknowledges the uneven distributions of power between them." [4]

Of course questions in the urban disciplines are special in their own way, and it may seem advisable to go one step back to the general level, in order to start with the definition of a potential overarching framework. Here, King identifies the need for,

> "[..] a framework for understanding transnational economic and political processes in which some nation states, at different historical times, exercise some hegemonic influence within the system of states or territories as a whole." And he further details: "We also need a framework, however, that, while acknowledging these economic and political processes, also recognizes the social and cultural dimensions of urban life and the way these, together, bring about spatial and material changes."[5]

---

[3] Hård, Mikael/Misa, Thomas, *Modernizing European Cities: Technological Uniformity and Cultural Distinction*, Cambridge: MIT Press 2010: 4.
[4] King 2005: 89.
[5] King 2005: 89.

Almost as a reply to these drafted expectations, Saunier has developed a theoretical framework, whose approach provides the tools to deal with such general questions, and which allows for their interpretation in specific spatial contexts at the same time.

Saunier's concept of transnational history

In his approach to explain and justify the concept of transnational history Saunier basically agrees with Cooper, when he argues that national history and its assumed dominance are not carved in stone. As Cooper explains they only dominated historical narratives since the fall of last formal empires[6], therefore for Saunier it makes sense to regard national history through the lens of a larger framework. Taking the past two decades into consideration, Saunier rather concedes two opposing trends with respect to national history: one of them tries to renationalise history like in countries of the former Soviet bloc; whilst the US and Germany turned to the opposite direction and experienced a more open approach to reconsider their respective history. The latter trend forms part of the basis for transnational history, and this work in particular, as it means, "writing a history with nations that is not a history of nations."[7] It therefore matches with the purpose of transnational approaches which originated from the social sciences, and tried to encourage research beyond traditional boundaries of territories and scales.[8] This notion is important to Saunier for he does not consider transnational history as a new discipline, and though its periodisation is not fixed, he suggests focusing on the last 200 to 250 years. The history of empires and colonisation was therefore one of the first sub-disciplines in historical sciences where transnational approaches were applied, and they created some fresh ideas as well as new results since the late 1980s. Saunier in this context refers to research trying to combine colonised, colonisers and territories as Brenda Yeoh has later done for contestations in colonial Singapore.[9] Labelled as "new imperial history", these approaches have helped to describe colonial relations as one of mutual coproduction that was not limited to the categorisations of dominance and resistance. Nevertheless, Saunier remarks that these transnational experiments remained limited and did not form part of the mainstream agenda back in the late 1980s.[10]

---

[6] Cooper 2012: 31.
[7] Saunier 2013: 8.
[8] Saunier 2013: 16.
[9] Yeoh 1996.
[10] Saunier 2013: 30.

For the concept of transnational history Saunier identifies *connections* and *circulations* to be the fundamental elements that create their results in form of *relations*. Such a system qualifies as *macro theory* in Anthony King's argumentation, as it helps to explain larger phenomena which all too often tend to be focused on national entities.[11] He complains, "[.] the context is too often seen as the system of states."[12] Daniel Rodgers has exemplified such connections in his analysis of social politics and how these have crossed the Atlantic.[13]

Saunier calls travel, trade and transplantation as the metaphorical "sites" for *connections*, for they induce linkages between different parts of the world or beliefs, etc.[14] Furthermore, the individual person serves as what is called *intermediaries* to disseminate ideas, gather new experiences and carry them to other places. Here Saunier conveys the idea of concepts figuratively seeping into new contexts and the adoption of new tools, as will be elaborated for Ward's diffusion concept in the planning profession (see 2.2). In case these activities are carried out as bi-directional passage at a small scale, for example among family members or participants of a conference, Saunier uses the term *circuit*.[15] The same situation is described by King who uses *micro theorisation* at small-scale level as his equivalent to circuits, and whose concept includes the group of *transmigrants*, de facto representing Saunier's intermediaries. According to King, transmigrants live and commute between their extended families who are spread over different countries, and can therefore be characterised by their maintenance of, "[...] many different racial, national and ethnic identities."[16] Following both authors it is in these families or at conferences that the applicability of transnational concepts becomes tangible, since they are susceptible to such networks in contrast to national approaches, where they do not play a significant role and remain a marginal phenomenon.

Another means of communication is created by infrastructures which eventually establish connections too[17]; Mikael Hård and Andrew Jamison have published an analysis with regards to the cultural appropriation of technology and technical infrastructures.[18] For the description of circulations as a larger system for ex-

---

[11] King 2005: 90-1.
[12] King 2005: 91.
[13] Rodgers, Daniel, *Atlantic Crossings : Social Politics in a Progressive Age*, Cambridge: Harvard University Press 1998.
[14] Saunier 2013: 40.
[15] Saunier 2013: 43-6.
[16] King 2005: 92.
[17] Saunier 2013: 50.
[18] Hård, Mikael/Jamison, Andrew, *Hubris and Hybrids : A Cultural History of Technology and Science*, New York/London : Routledge 2005.

change, Saunier draws on the image of a riverine system and equals its fullest extent to a catchment area. Two historic examples may help to explain the range of circulations. In a much secluded system like National Socialist (NS) Germany, where the exchange of ideas and technology would have contradicted the intended national entity's containment from the rest of the world as part of autarky policies, this technology transfer happened, as Saunier mentions with regard to the "patent for processing synthetic oil"[19] that had been sold to Fascist Spain. At the other end of the range stands the extensive research in social sciences and geography that has entered the historian's interest through the investigation of obvious forms of mobility, like capital, people or political ideas. Saunier is excited about recent research activities which now tend to cover "less visible or even clandestine circulations."[20] In this respect Saunier refers to a study by Kapil Raj, who argues that scholarly knowledge, such as legal knowledge, has not been invented and then moved from one place to another. It developed through interaction and the subsequently initiated circulation.[21] Saunier remarks,

> "[c]irculation is a creative process that affects the items that circulate; as a result, historians need to follow closely the trajectory of an item to capture the different usages and appropriations."[22]

This appropriation is not just a matter of spatiality. Saunier does equally underscore the importance of time or *duration* in order to detect the impact, ideas and knowledge can make. Basically, two levels of duration need to be differentiated in this context. Firstly, there is duration meant as a kind of stability within certain circulations. The product may stay the same as Saunier has illustrated with reference to coffee but the regions where the beans are actually grown or processed may change over time. He does point to the complete disappearance of such circulations as was the case with guano. On the other hand, duration can be used to illustrate the timespan it takes until a certain idea or knowledge 'arrives', and *de facto* impacts on a debate in different regions or communities. Saunier has based this on the example of translations. The time it takes for translation does influence the impact an idea or concept may have on a debate. Under the assumption that there are limited alternatives to spread the idea through relay translation, it may reach a country with a delay of several years or more. This fact becomes clearer with refer-

---

[19] Saunier 2013: 58.
[20] Saunier 2013: 59.
[21] Saunier 2013: 64.
[22] Saunier 2013: 63.

ence to Jürgen Habermas and his concepts of public sphere.[23] The reception of ideas with such a delay or *duration* will be completely different from what would have happened, if the idea had been available at more or less the same time like in its original community. And this impact does affect both elements: the receiving community will be in a different state of development when the idea arrives here; but the idea itself will presumably be interpreted through a different lens. Therefore the idea of duration does play a role for the circulation of planning ideas as well.

The results of connections and circulations are subsumed under the *relations* they establish, irrespective of whether or not the intermediaries are aware of their disseminating function. Nowadays certain terms like borrowing, imitation, adaptation and translation, which indicate a ubiquitous reference to the flow of ideas, are used in the context of several historical, planning and related disciplines.[24] Nevertheless Saunier recollects one of the earliest examples in Michel Espagne and Michael Werner's study on cultural transfers that has covered the mobility of books, authors and ideas in philology, literature and philosophy between France and Germany over roughly one century, starting in the late 18th century. Both authors have collaboratively conducted and amended their study in the 1980s, and Saunier emphasises the side-effects this study had, once its approach left the original confines and had been applied to other contexts and entities beyond the national ones.[25] The study on cultural transfers is noteworthy, as it seems to have contained similar backgrounds and processes like the work on diffusion processes in planning by Ward. Espagne and Werner have critically reviewed then used country-specific analytical frameworks for scholarly research, and which Saunier has ascribed with the characteristic to be a key feature since the Second World War. Saunier argues that national rivalry and competition, also between the political blocs, played a significant role for most part of the 20th century. This trend dominated at confer-

---

[23] Habermas, Jürgen, *Strukturwandel der Öffentlichkeit: Untersuchungen zu einer Kategorie der bürgerlichen Gesellschaft*, Frankfurt am Main: Suhrkamp [1962] 2006. Although he published his work in 1962 and it initiated a lot of debates in Germany, it took almost three decades before a translation into English appeared in 1989 (Habermas, Jürgen, *The Structural Transformation of the Public Sphere: An Inquiry into a Category of Bourgeois Society*, Cambridge: MIT Press [1989] 1991). This translation made it popular among the British scholarly community (Crossley, Nick/Roberts, John Michael [Eds.], *After Habermas: new perspectives on the public sphere*: Oxford: Blackwell 2004).
[24] Saunier 2013: 90. Other examples can be found in Anderson, Warwick, *Introduction: Postcolonial Technoscience*, London *et al.* 2002 or Sahlin, Kerstin/Wedlin, Linda, *Circulating Ideas: Imitation, Translation and Editing.* In: Greenwood, Royston, *et al.* [Eds.]: The SAGE Handbook of Organizational Institutionalism. Los Angeles, London, New Delhi, etc.: Sage 2013.
[25] Saunier 2013: 81.

ences and exhibitions, which have usually been organised as opportunities for open international exchange.[26] Due to the Nazi regime, in the German context such trends for a nationalisation of research did start earlier and can be extended for some more years, when autarky policies attempted to cut the scientific community off from the international exchange.

It is necessary to pay attention to some additional features of the relations established by connections and circulations. For the context of colonial relations, Saunier highlights what he calls "asymmetry" as one of their key characteristics, although he attributes them with reciprocity as an inevitable part of such relations. Based on the example of the USA until mid-20th century, he explains how the dominant power did not just export "her" ideas and values but the metropolitan society was *de facto* affected by reflections from the colonised societies too.[27] Concepts of racial segregation were a pronounced example for extensive exchange of ideas and concepts in late 19th and early 20th century, as Saunier mentions to protect images of White supremacy.[28]

Based on the above stated assumptions and ideas, this work uses circulation as implied in a circulatory regime as its general description for the flow of (planning) ideas in which colonial urban development was contextualised. It will therefore be the aim of this work to make such circulation visible within Windhoek's catchment area, and to uncover the several tributaries – this means metropolitan and other colonial sources – from which the city drew its input. The case study-based description of these circulations will be complemented by circuits that were established by conferences and excursions, either among European planning traditions or with regard to the colonial context as laid down in those days' planning journals.

All of them can be part of a *formation* in Saunier's sense that is centred on residential segregation: With formations he opens the opportunity to elaborate on a topic with so-called 'disjointed elements' that actually do not fit with traditional approaches, either because their spatial contexts are dissociated or because they try to link unconventional themes. Furthermore, formations can be split into a number of sub-categories of which two are applicable to the case of Windhoek. First it covers what is called *topical region*, a kind of thematic domain squeezed in and operating between various national territories but on a clearly demarcated topic like transnational links of Latin American meat production. Instead of meat production the topical region for my work is residential segregation as means to implement

---

[26] Saunier 2013: 85-6.
[27] Saunier 2013: 87-9.
[28] Saunier 2013: 91-2.

racial and social separation.[29] On the other hand, my work uses the *territory* for a specific delimitation of reference spaces under investigation. Saunier highlights the significance of war affected regions, which have changed hands many times during the course of history and form detached enclaves of exceptional legal frameworks. His example of Alsace-Lorraine serves well to illustrate the overlapping persistence of different national legislation within one region. This continuity over time is equally important to Anthony King who refers, amongst others, to Istanbul as being emblematic for a city's transnational nature.[30] Despite its immobility in geographical terms, Istanbul incorporates many ruptures and transformations over the course of the city's rich history, which had been caused by external intruders in their respective pursuit of imperial rule. Under such circumstances, and in face of the postcolonial influence that multinational firms exercise on the cityscape, King takes a very critical stance if urban histories are exclusively engrossed by one nation. He concludes that,

> "[…] the idea of the city being the sole product of a single, geographically bounded 'society' enclosed behind the borders of the nation state, [is] increasingly suspect (if, indeed, the idea ever had credibility before)."[31]

Besides, cities are considered by Saunier as territories of particular interest due to their 'gateway' functions in trade, politics, culture or migration. Lynn Hollen Lees dissects the various networks through which cities operate and communicate with each other. She therefore agrees with King's sceptical views on urban history as the affair of one single nation only.

> "Urban ties do not stop at national borders. Communications via water – and now air and electricity – allow cities to forge tight links round the world. Indeed, before the era of the railway, it was far easier to get from Hull to Hamburg than to either Leicester or Manchester. Cities, particularly the large ones and those with access to the sea, have for centuries participated in a network system whose organisational logic is not territorial and geometric but maritime and irregular."[32]

As a reaction to this focus of research efforts on seaports, Saunier argues in favour of smaller and remotely located towns as potential objects for transnational history.[33] In face of its historic and geographical specificities as integral part of mandat-

---

[29] Saunier 2013: 106-8.
[30] King 2005: 82.
[31] King 2005: 83.
[32] Lees, Lynn Hollen, *Urban Networks*. In: Daunton, Martin [Ed.]: The Cambridge Urban History of Britain – Volume III: 1840-1950. Cambridge: Cambridge University Press 2000: 90.
[33] Saunier 2013: 112-5.

ed SWA and as remote small town, Windhoek blends into the supportive arguments for a *formation*. Just like in Alsace-Lorraine, the city can help to demonstrate how different legal systems remained valid in SWA once South Africa took administrative responsibility. It is here at the small-scale level that Saunier's concept blends with King's position; to him there lies a kind of "missing historical dimension"[34] in the deliberate investigation of relatively small regions as opposed to nation states. Therefore, a transnational focus on Windhoek and its prevailing legal system is in line with such demands.

Despite the already on-going research activities, there still remain spatial confines, where King deems further investigations based on transnational approaches necessary. Those gaps comprise of the very micro level of single dwellings and the impact that the transplantation or, "transcultural adaptation of residential forms in places other than their native habitus"[35] have made on them.

Cooper's reflections on colonial history

It is necessary to briefly contextualise, what elements of and perspectives on how colonial history will be considered for my research, before the relevant interrelations between imperialism and colonialism are laid down for this work.

As has already been mentioned in the previous chapter, Cooper's reflections on colonial history form a major source of inspiration for this work. First of all he rejects the idea of colonialism as a kind of distinct category that stands apart and can be regarded as one foil to European history, which can in turn be switched off if deemed inappropriate.[36] Just like Saunier, he tries to question colonialism's boundaries in historical sciences, and he asks for a reconsideration of the multifaceted relations it has actually created over time and spaces. Through such a shift in perspectives it would in his opinion become apparent, how colonialism represents a cohesive part of history. This work is intended to follow this shift. Furthermore, Cooper is convinced of the additional insights an interdisciplinary approach can generate, as long as this approach goes beyond a superfluous interpretation of the other discipline(s) involved.[37] Further, Cooper is equally careful when it comes to certain concepts like 'globalisation' or 'identity.' For him analysis needs to fill such

_____

[34] King 2005: 91.
[35] King 2005: 92.
[36] Cooper 2012: 20.
[37] Cooper 2012: 23.

artificial terms or categories with new life, which for example comprises of a thorough investigation of interactions beyond territorial borders.[38]

Cooper critically reflects on nation states and the role they allegedly play in political history. Their pre-eminence in the execution of power was solidified after the fall of the last formal empires in the 1960s, when the competition between national and imperial entities ended.[39] On one side Cooper points out, how some constructions of historical narratives emphasise a national tradition although they should be contextualised as part of an imperial tradition. He refers to Philipp Ther's views on German history in late 19th century, where the imperial element in its European territories as well as overseas played an important role.[40] For the decades before the dissolution of the last empires it might have seemed appropriate, as Cooper argues, to consider every attempt to contest imperial power as a struggle for national self-determination irrespective of the 'real' intentions behind every such move made back in the 1940s and 1950s. Cooper takes this as an example for the retrospective construction of history, where the rise of nation states seems to prove every previous move to be nationalistic in character.[41] How far from reality such a position in some cases was becomes apparent with regards to one example he uses from within the French empire; subjects of the French colonies were often guided by the desire to receive equal rights and benefits like citizens in the French metropole. They were not fighting for nationalism and sovereignty but for recognition of their rights to better living standards *within* the imperial context – actually as late as the 1950s.[42]

This dispute touched the very foundations of imperialism in the colonial environment and the emphasis that has been laid on the human rather than the spatial dimension of this concept. Among the Western interpretation of colonialism it was used as justification to label certain people as 'exploitable' due to their alleged inability to organise themselves and who in turn might be controlled by the 'advanced' European nations under the framework of their imperial projects. Cooper argues that this human level of colonial empires was one of the two possible sides of colonialism and where the spatial one of planting new cities for a growing population, as done in ancient Greece, represented the other side.[43] In the long run, the dominance of colonialism's human level allowed for the establishment of social

---

[38] Cooper 2012: 27-9.
[39] Cooper 2012: 31.
[40] Cooper 2012: 301-2.
[41] Cooper 2012: 43-4.
[42] Cooper 2012: 50.
[43] Cooper 2012: 56-9.

hierarchies within the empires and it created a notion of inclusion or exclusion based on the subject's respective location. This leads Cooper to identify a characteristic of imperialism; historically empires tended to incorporate subdued foreign people and territory into *one* political entity, potentially sharing common moral and ethical values.[44] This tendency links to another important conclusion Cooper draws in relation to the empire's borders. Instead of a demarcation of closed entities he takes up the notion of permeable borders enabling circulation which fitted with the empire's dependency on an exchange of goods, ideas and staff for its viability.[45]

Imperial legacies in planning language

Beyond his specific comments on the colonial and imperial content, Cooper's work provides a critical eye on the use of certain terms and linguistic styles. In his chapter on identity jointly produced with Rogers Brubaker, they make the argument that the term "identity" as analytical category is unnecessary and does not produce added value, even if it is applied in research.[46] Cooper in his careful position does therefore match with Libby Porter's critical analysis of persisting colonial elements in modern planning language already mentioned in the introduction, which will be contextualised with regards to residential segregation (see 2.3). Furthermore, Cooper critically reflects on the inappropriate use of "globalisation" without the term's proper definition. In his argumentation he points to its current interpretation to convey the idea of growth to unprecedented levels in global economic relations. He questions the validity of this image by contrasting those developments with the vast quantities of labour migrants in the century following 1815 as well as the world's economic interconnectedness at its previous all-time high in 1913.[47] The situation can, in his opinion, be compared to the undefined use of the term "modernisation" during the 1950s and 1960s. Here, Cooper is unclear whether its use was dominated by Eurocentric criteria, or if it was based on an idealised image of what US American society should be.[48]

In addition, "modernity" is another term reviewed by Cooper as having a significant impact on colonial history. Of course, there is the narrative of 'modernity' in its Western interpretation, which has been used as stereotypical argument by imperial ideologists to justify European rule over Africa. In this case it was based on assumed European merits as being 'advanced' and therefore able but at the same

---

[44] Cooper 2012: 62, 176.
[45] Cooper 2012: 102.
[46] Cooper 2012: 145.
[47] Cooper 2012: 166.
[48] Cooper 2012: 169-70.

time obliged, to help the 'backward' African people in their transformation into a perceived modern society.[49] In opposition to such understanding, Cooper quotes John and Jean Comaroff with their extremely flexible definition of modernity as something colourless, inodorous and flavourless, amongst others. To them, modernity does not represent an analytical category but what they call an 'ideological formation.'[50] Nonetheless, with reference to arts, Cooper suggests two still opposing but more appropriate definitions: modernity can therefore either be a category in motion and subsequently changing over time, where modern elements cover the last 50 years, or modernity is based on the compliance with a particular set of criteria.[51] Both versions of modernity are still flexible, whilst Cooper emphasises a major continuity when he refers to the effects of the persisting regime of property rights in Western democracies.[52] This latter continuity is of relevance to the colonial context, where the imperial powers tried to implement such durable systems based on their experiences in the metropole.

Lastly, the question of alternative modernities remains unresolved, since their formulation underscores the potential contestation of Western notions of modernity as has happened in Japan. Cooper argues that the notion of an alternative modernity remains void, if there is neither a definition of what the alternative represents nor a proof for modernity itself.[53] Just as Cooper has illustrated the ambiguity in modernity's definition, which formed a key motivation for colonial projects, there was a great variety of aims affiliated with imperial projects at large, as they differed over time among northern and southern European empires.[54] It is therefore necessary to get an overview of the different kinds of imperialism that existed, and how they have been interpreted in theoretical frameworks.

Theories on imperialism

Colonialism cannot be fully grasped without having a look at its links and overall setup within imperialism, for both are explicitly described by some authors as two sides of the same coin. Martin Legassick has underscored the inextricable nexus between imperialism, capitalism and segregation in his analysis of early 20th century

---

[49] Cooper 2012: 197.
[50] Cooper 2012: 220.
[51] Cooper 2012: 203.
[52] Cooper 2012: 219.
[53] Cooper 2012: 222-3.
[54] Cooper 2012: 273.

South Africa.[55] Furthermore under the Cold War dichotomy Harold Wolpe concluded,

"[r]acial ideology in South Africa must be seen as an ideology which sustains and reproduces capitalist relations of production."[56]

This thesis pays attention to the key theories that were used to justify the colonial interventions in political, economic and socio-cultural terms. It illustrates the historic distinctions made between the perceived 'civilised' European metropole and the 'uncivilised' colonial periphery that would have to serve its colonisers in various ways.

As I am dealing with theories on imperialism for a dissertation focusing on the interwar period only, I need to make some remarks about the following section's scope in the first place; it is not my intention to reflect on all theories that were produced and influential over the past century. There are too many authors who have already contributed specific collections from various disciplinary viewpoints. Instead, I will briefly summarise those theories that can be interpreted as background canvas towards the subjugation, exploitation, and discrimination of the colonised peoples. This section aims to contextualise the overall setup of imperial policies and how these theories translated into commonly accepted standpoints that were either implicitly or explicitly in favour of residential segregation.

My summary is largely based on two authors who have contributed by presenting retrospective analyses on this subject, and which complement each other in terms of their viewpoints and the time periods covered. First I draw on the theoretical frameworks as described by Wolfgang Mommsen from a historian's perspective.[57] His publication is comprehensive in its meticulous collection of relevant theories but due to its date of publication in 1987, the discussions are heavily influenced by the then still prevalent Cold War outlook. Furthermore, Mommsen's work uses a different language when he refers to debates on neo-colonialism in 'third world' countries characterised as being 'under-developed.' I will show that these deficiencies do nevertheless not diminish the quality of his analysis. The second main source used in this section is a publication by Herfried Münkler who takes a look

---

[55] Legassick, Martin, *British Hegemony and the Origins of Segregation in South Africa, 1901-14*. In: Beinart, William; Dubow, Saul [Eds.]: Segregation and Apartheid in Twentieth Century South Africa. New York: Routledge 1995.
[56] Wolpe, Harold, *Capitalism and Cheap Labour Power in South Africa: From Segregation to Apartheid*. In: Beinart, William; Dubow, Saul [Eds.]: Segregation and Apartheid in Twentieth Century South Africa. New York: Routledge [1977] 1995: 87.
[57] Mommsen 1987.

at imperialism through the lens of political sciences.[58] His work, published in 2007, does then cover more than the first decade after the end of the Cold War confrontation. Münkler's contributions help to round off the theoretical discussions on imperialism with regards to one of its main historical justifications, which is based on considerations of political power in a Machiavellian sense and the reason of state.

At the general level, and as a starting point, Johan Galtung has differentiated five forms of imperialism (economic, political, military, communicational, and cultural) which are explicitly or implicitly included in those theoretical frameworks covered by Mommsen.[59] He himself uses a different approach to sort the myriad ways on how to synthesise imperialism, and basically describes them as an ideological challenge or rivalry between both political blocs of the Cold War confrontation. Where feasible, he mixes these discussions with references to relevant contributions in chronological order. As a result, Mommsen identifies theories on imperialism which cover a pronounced political or economic stance – as has been done in what he calls the 'classical perspectives' – and which are complemented by the equally classic Marxist-Leninist views. In addition to these, further notions are contained in some (then) new Western interpretations as well as theories of neo-colonialism, underdevelopment and 'dependencia.' Both classical and recent categories can be interpreted as answers to the ideological challenges caused by the Cold War decades too.

Political imperialism

Irrespective of the Cold War dichotomy, the political interpretation of imperialism proved to be important for the construction of colonial empires. Mommsen attributes Heinrich Friedjung with the original definition of imperialism in the personal rule of a monarch over several territories regardless of their exact geographical locations. In this interpretation imperialism had nothing in common with the question of direct or indirect rule over colonial possessions and dependencies, as later emphasised in the domination by modern industrialised countries. Mommsen highlights how latter interpretations based on the expansionist politics of nation states beyond their borders – with the aim to eventually form global empires – represent a rather common theory on imperialism.[60]

---

[58] Münkler 2007.
[59] Mommsen 1987: 120.
[60] Mommsen 1987: 7-8.

36

In the political arena of the interwar period such theories of imperialism played a significant role, either because it was lamented that nation states, which did not attempt to build a global empire would be doomed to subsequent degradation into second class political entities, or because they were guided by a nationalistic imperialism based on racial and biological determinants.[61] Mommsen underscores the consensus among European nations about the former theory in particular, where empire building received widespread public support after the 1884-5 Berlin Conference up until the First World War – coinciding with the period commonly labelled as "Scramble for Africa." He is supported in his interpretation by Münkler who links this quest for colonial possessions to Social Darwinism.[62]

Economic and social imperialism

Besides politics, economic theories on imperialism played an equally important role for the debate and were, for social motives, in many cases linked to criticism questioning the capitalist order. Labelled as 'social imperialism', colonial projects were regarded as safety valve to release some of the pressure that demography and pauperism created, and which particularly became manifest in industrialised European cities. In this respect, Mommsen uses the jingoism during the Boer War as one example to demonstrate this link between developments at the metropole and the perceived colonial periphery. This had already been criticised by John Hobson in 1901, who argued that the need for social reform in the metropole was over ridden with the colonial perspective. On one hand, he and many other authors regarded *under-consumption* as a pressing issue that affected vast parts of the poor British labour force without realistic prospects for substantial improvements of their individual economic situation. On the other hand, these authors saw no intentions for a change by the affluent minority who instead made profitable investments overseas and labelled them with the nationalistic aim to 'secure' colonial export markets. The risks attached to such investments, however, were not borne by the wealthy elite but by the commonwealth.[63] In this sense the existing social disparities in major European industrialising countries, imperialism was used as a common national goal to unify the people by the prospects, which colonial entities were expected to provide for the metropole in many ways – ranging from export markets to settler colonies.

Some scholarly activities have tried to link such theoretical concepts with developments on the ground. According to their conclusions and despite the above-

---

[61] Mommsen 1987: 8-10.
[62] Münkler 2007: 66.
[63] Mommsen 1987: 12-8.

mentioned stimuli for nationalistic popular support in mass media, influential key stakeholders, for example in finance, remained very reserved and selected their colonial investment projects carefully – based on the expected return on investment only. For Great Britain this attitude has nonetheless led to a substantial capital drain towards her colonies that was in turn not available for investments in domestic trade, as Tomlinson has illustrated in the context of settler colonies.[64] Based on his research on colonial infrastructures, van Laak has confirmed this socio-economic standpoint and refers to such views on imperialism as widespread.[65] Ditt has stressed the subsequent scarcity of financial resources to improve the electrical infrastructure in the UK.[66] Hence it becomes apparent, how imperialism was at the same time intertwined with historic social and economic challenges as well as political considerations 'at home' and abroad. Media coverage and other lobbying activities created a rather pro-colonial environment that should at least partially divert public attention and financial resources from improvements for needy parts of the population in Europe towards potential benefits in the colonies.

Nevertheless, according to Mommsen, Hobson's critique at the turn of the century was not intended to overthrow the capitalist order. Instead, Hobson's theoretical position pursued a different goal and can be considered a strong voice in support of social reform, aiming to redistribute purchasing power among the population in Europe, and as a voice in favour of free trade imperialism. Based on its nexus between capital investments and imperial policies on one hand, as well as for its analysis of the political milieu with a dominant wealthy upper-class trying to impose its particular interests upon the broad public on the other hand, Mommsen underscores the value of Hobson's work.[67] Of course it was not the only theory addressing social and economic imperialism but it played a significant role in interwar debates. The theory also demonstrates the close interrelation between imperial debates and the colonial context at the political, economic and social levels.

---

[64] Tomlinson, B.R., *Economics and Empire: The Periphery and the Imperial Economy*. In: Porter, Andrew [Ed.]: The Oxford History of the British Empire: Volume III The Nineteenth Century. Oxford/New York: Oxford University Press 1999. The importance of classical tropical colonies decreased since the 19th century and colonies labelled as 'Neo-Europes' (including the US, Canada, Australia, New Zealand, South Africa and half of Latin America) accumulated 56% of all British investments from 1865 to 1914 worth £1.6 billion as compared to only 33% or £945 million in the 'Tropics' (including India, the second half of Latin America as well as remaining countries in Africa, Asia and the Pacific) (Tomlison 1999: 59).
[65] Van Laak 2004: 405.
[66] Ditt 2011: 126.
[67] Mommsen 1987: 12-8.

Another important theoretical framework, which further elaborated the impact of certain pressure groups, was drafted by Joseph Schumpeter, whose contributions to this PhD dissertation can be traced at several levels. He did in parts influence Ward's analysis on the flow of planning ideas as will be discussed below (see 2.2). Here in this context, however, Mommsen classifies Schumpeter's work as a landmark – despite some assumed deficiencies in relation to an expected clear separation between free trade and imperialism – for it was ground-breaking in the attention it paid to the typical behaviour of specific social groups; this was particularly the case for the ruling elite. In Mommsen's opinion it hence heralded later sociological interpretations of imperialism. Whilst the Leninist approach assumed capitalism as kind of evolving system, often referred to as passing through different 'stages of maturity', Schumpeter specifically rejected Lenin's idea of imperialism as being the highest form of capitalist world order. On the contrary, in his argumentation imperialism was just a manifestation of the antecedent social structures in decay as they presented themselves in pre-Great War decades. These decades characterised by protective tariffs in many European countries, with the prominent exception of the UK, and structures of monopoly-capitalism in some businesses, seemingly favoured imperialistic tendencies among the elite. In Schumpeter's theory however such tendencies would become obsolete in a capitalism that was based on economic competition and they therefore represented a transitional period on the way to a final assertion of capitalism. He was convinced this trend would be paralleled by the development of a broad-based democracy, which would in turn reduce the potential impact of the ruling elite.[68]

Free trade imperialism

A last theoretical foil persisted and influenced the debate in interwar years and more recent times; the theory of free trade imperialism. As Mommsen indicates with regards to the Cold War dichotomy, one decisive innovation in its theoretical elaboration among 'Western' traditions has been submitted by John Gallagher and Ronald Robinson in their publication *The Imperialism of Free Trade*.[69] Particular attention was paid to the British Empire and its forms of intervention to protect its trade activities. This kind of symbiotic relation is usually subsumed under the slogan "The flag follows the trade."[70] Gallagher and Robinson went further as presented by Mommsen to describes these interventions as *informal imperialism*, which can in turn be recognised as an interpretation of imperialism as transitional phenomenon similar to Marxist-Leninist views.

---

[68] Mommsen 1987: 21-6.
[69] Mommsen 1987: 70-5.
[70] Mommsen 1987: 75.

However, despite Mommsen's view, this reported progress at the theoretical front of ideological Cold War confrontations, the question of informal imperialism points to fuzziness in definitions that has been addressed from the viewpoint by political sciences approaches. The mechanisms of informal imperialism as summarised by Mommsen are vague enough to be equally transferred to the context of Münkler's debate on the differentiation between what constitutes an empire and a hegemon.[71] Informal imperialism with its very concise power demonstrations only where free trade interests invite them, shows similarities to a hegemon. In a simplistic way, free trade could be interpreted as the (economic) regulatory framework commonly agreed on, and contraventions would subsequently be punished by the dominating hegemonic power. This interpretation suffers by limiting only to the economic dimensions of imperial relations but it already demonstrates some of the difficulties in generating precise definitions across the different disciplines. Mommsen for example is not satisfied with the use of informal imperialism unless this term and its theory without further critical elaboration.

Preliminary conclusions on imperialism

It can be concluded that the abovementioned theories on imperialism basically reflect two levels of interrelation with the colonial context. What all of these theories basically had in common was a more or less pronounced dichotomy between an assumed centre at the European metropole and a periphery, supposedly created by the colonies.[72] On one side the theories mirrored rivalries and debates of a predominant metropolitan focus. The political and economic motives contained in colonial projects can be interpreted as attempts to demonstrate nationalistic power in a system inspired by Social Darwinism. In conjunction with prevalent jingoism, imperialism should help to 'secure' additional export markets in order to absorb European excess production as part of free trade imperialism and avoid the need to address the social dimension of pauperism in the industrialised cities with their demographic trends. The colonies should instead serve as valve for social pressures without the need to initiate large-scale social reforms in the metropoles themselves. Beyond this inner-European level, on the other side, the theories can be interpreted as an expression and emphasis of assumed contrasts between colonisers and colonised, which extended beyond cultural terms. In the colonial environment, Rosa Luxemburg's image of the country's wealth lying in the hands of a small ruling elite bolstered by military power, resembles the classic opposition between European colonisers and African colonised. Additionally, it links them to the fre-

---

[71] Münkler 2007: 67-77.
[72] Münkler 2007: 41-50.

quently referred to motive of the 'civilising mission' summarised as the "White Man's Burden" by Rudyard Kipling in his 1899 appeal.[73] A key space where these various theories could be applied to and become manifest were the colonial cities.

2.2 Colonial cities and their planning

The attempt to define colonial cities is extremely challenging. Two overlapping layers contribute to this difficulty. On one side there is the complexity of the colonial environment, and on the other it has to do with the specific elements and functions that characterise a colonial city.

Definitions of cities in general

Although this question of delimitation is essential, one has to acknowledge the plurality of potential definitions. A comparison with the European context might help to understand the diversity of what might be considered a city which in turn may be transferred to the colonial context. Some cities are historically defined by the rights conferred to them by royal or clerical powers, or as a consequence of their trading activities. Cities can alternatively be defined on a descriptive basis as is usually done in geography.[74] Here then the physiognomy and compactness of a cityscape plays a significant role in their distinction from rural areas, or they do qualify by the quantity and quality of their functions[75] and/or prevailing lifestyles. Jürgen Bähr and Ulrich Jürgens point to the identification of characteristic functional neighbourhoods serving as Central Business District (CBD), industrial or residential areas. Of particular interest to them are the theories and descriptions by Walter Christaller, whose idea of a city's 'centrality' is based on the range of those goods and services offered here in relation to its surrounding tributary area.[76] This relation can be summarised by the city's respective function within regional hierarchies and its so-called 'excess significance', or what Christaller calls 'Bedeutungsüberschuss'. Due to their formulation in interwar years the theories' reception in the planning community will be addressed later (see 3.3.7).

In contrast to such descriptive approaches there exist normative derivatives of this theory, which try to define cities by the infrastructure they are supposed to provide as is characteristic of spatial planning. Central Place Concepts were popular among

---

[73] Ferguson, Niall, *Empire: How Britain Made the Modern World*, London: Penguin 2004: 380.
[74] Bähr, Jürgen/Jürgens, Ulrich, *Stadtgeographie II: Regionale Stadtgeographie*, Braunschweig: Westermann 2005: 22-5.
[75] King, Leslie J., *Central Place Theory*, Beverly Hills *et al.*: Sage [1984] 1985: 15.
[76] King [1984] 1985: 30-2.

41

the planning community during their heydays in the 1970s, setting standards for the facilities to be kept available at cities classified at certain functional levels as Hans Heinrich Blotevogel summarises.[77] Another frequently used alternative is the normative definition by size, although the sizes of threshold populations vary according to the country's overall size and respective administrative definitions. Bähr and Jürgens refer to a UN-report published after the turn of the millennium according to which the minimum population in Germany is set at 2,000 whilst Spain just requires 200 as opposed to 10,000 in Switzerland and Senegal or 50,000 in Japan.[78]

Characteristics of colonial cities

For the colonial context the situation can be summarised as being equally diverse. Following Osterhammel and Jansen, and as a first classification, old cities such as traditional Mughals' Delhi can be separated from relatively young ones planned in the late 19th or early 20th century like Nairobi or New Delhi.[79] This distinction is particularly relevant for the African context, where – in the eyes of the colonial powers – traces of pre-colonial towns were virtually non-existent. In their descriptions urban life only 'appeared' with the arrival of Europeans on the 'continent without history.' In a similar way well-known French historian Catherine Coquery-Vidrovitch summarises her experiences.

> "Combien de fois ai-je entendu au cours de ma carrière: 'Vous étudiez l'histoire africaine ? Mais qu'en sait-on avant l'arrivée des Européens ? Il y a donc des sources ?'"[80]

Earlier traces of genuinely African urbanity, for example with Windhoek in Namibia[81] or ancient settlements like the palace city of Great-Zimbabwe in Zimbabwe[82], were more or less deliberately neglected. Furthermore, Njoh has pointed to

---

[77] Blotevogel, Hans Heinrich [Ed.], *Fortentwicklung des Zentrale-Orte-Konzepts*, Hannover: Akademie für Raumforschung und Landesplanung 2002: 10-23.
[78] Bähr, Jürgens 2005: 25-6.
[79] Osterhammel, Jansen 2012: 96-7.
[80] Coquery-Vidrovitch, Catherine, *Petite histoire de l'Afrique : L'Afrique au sud du Sahara de la préhistoire à nos jours*, Paris : La Découverte 2011: 6. "How many times during my career have I heard: 'You study African history? But how can anyone know about it prior to the Europeans' arrival? Are there yet some sources?'" (author's translation). In this respect Coquery-Vidrovitch describes how the French view on African history has changed, notably since the 1960s (Coquery-Vidrovitch 2011: 5-31).
[81] The pre-German origins of Windhoek are up until today neglected – yet among official city representatives as Matheus Shikongo's foreword to Bravenboer's publication proved, despite his function as Mayor (Bravenboer 2004: vi).
[82] Bähr, Jürgens 2005: 284-5.

42

the difficulties with reference to North African cities, where their rich urban history presented a serious obstacle to the French '*mission civilisatrice*.'[83] Such older parts of the urban fabric, as exemplified in the Casbah as part of the traditional city centres, were later explicitly integrated into the Eurocentric concept of the dual city (for the concept's significance regarding residential segregation see 2.3). Following Benjamin Stanley with the imperial viewpoint, in Algiers, the Casbah represented the idealised though backward Indigenous living environment and it was therefore separated from the newly constructed European quarters.[84] Çelik has illustrated this tense relationship with particular reference to Le Corbusier's fascination for and interpretation of Islamic culture.[85] The idea of a dual city went beyond the built environment and did also represent a dichotomy between the colonised Indigenous and the colonisers' spheres in social or legal aspects, where their asymmetry of power became manifest. European quarters were intended to demonstrate imperial cultural 'advances' to the local population as well as serve as expressions of domination over those subjugated territories.

Besides historic roots, the cities were inevitably embedded into and contributed to the structure of their respective colonial entity in functional terms. One example within the German empire may serve to illustrate this relation. Qingdao was Germany's Chinese leasehold and, as an exception to the rule, directly governed by the Navy Office (Reichsmarineamt). Its prime function was bolstered by the military base it formed in the Far East but it was likewise supposed to form a bridgehead to the vast Chinese market. Despite some efforts to exploit the coalfields in the vicinity, which eventually turned out to be of lower quality and quantity than expected, the city itself was intended to serve as a showpiece for German imperial and colonial ambitions. Qingdao should demonstrate German cultural achievements, underscore the country's political agenda and help to initiate substantial trade. As Gründer states a "German Hong Kong" was intended.[86] Hence it conceptually followed a different development path in comparison to the African possessions, which had mostly been administered 'on the spot.' The local colonial administration first fell under the supervision of the Ministry of Foreign Affairs' Colonial Office, before the latter was turned into the autonomous and responsible ministry in 1907. Although there were some aspirations for DSWA as a settler colony where, in the long run, a considerable yet limited export market could evolve, the main focus was on the exploitation and use of the territories' natural wealth to the

---

[83] Njoh 2015: 97.
[84] Stanley, Benjamin W., *An historical perspective on the viability of urban diversity: lessons from socio-spatial identity construction in nineteenth-century Algiers and Cape Town*, 2012: 83.
[85] Çelik, Zeynep, *Le Corbusier, Orientalism, Colonialism*, 1992.
[86] Gründer 2012: 215-6.

benefit of the mother country's economy. Schinzinger demonstrated the marginal overall economic care of the colonies.[87]

Cultural facilities had to fit with the economic ambitions too, despite their goal of underscoring the 'progress' that European nations epitomised in their own thinking (see 2.3 and 3.3.2). In contrast to Qingdao, where a university had been founded as part of the showpiece efforts[88], educational facilities in the African colonial cities played a lesser role and in none of them any kind of higher education's facility was founded. The only exceptions were laboratories for experimental tests in agriculture and horticulture like at Neudamm in DSWA; those institutes were expected to contribute to the colonies' economic progress towards self-sufficiency and to their ability to deal with occurring diseases.[89] Basic education for the Indigenous population remained very limited and in many cases provided by missionaries (see below) whilst the European community had access to facilities comparable in standard to those at the metropole, with the already mentioned exception of higher education.

Imperial imprints on colonial cities

As mentioned for the case of Qingdao, colonial cities can be differentiated based on the particular functions they served in the respective colonial project. They were bridgeheads for trade and logistics, administrative centres, served military purposes, originated from railway workshops, or complemented mining and agricultural activities, to list a small collection. Naturally, their respective geographical and climatic locations made them more or less advantageous for certain functions, as Wright has identified within French policies for Morocco. Here, two categories of cities were maintained, with the first one for coastal cities which served administrative and cultural purposes (as was the case in Rabat), or had commercial and industrial functions (as in Casablanca). The second category comprised of the country's hinterland cities, which were made to serve their two coastal counterparts. Wright argued that the coastal cities maintained close links to France and served as look-out towards the 'admired' mother country.[90] Climatic conditions proved pivotal where environments were less favourable to European customs. This is why hill-top stations were preferred, either as permanent residences, as was

---

[87] Schinzinger 1984: 123-7.
[88] Gründer provides a list of all faculties and affiliated institutes (Gründer 2012: 234).
[89] Bigon has in this context pointed out how reluctant the Pasteur Institute at Paris was to recognise its Senegalese branch at Saint-Louis and later Dakar as scientific institution at eye level. This reluctance was evidenced by the lower quality equipment and fewer human resources available to the colonial institutions (Bigon 2013: 107).
[90] Wright 1991: 95.

the case in Cameroon under German rule, where the major administrative cluster was not located at the coastal city of Duala but at the hill-top settlement of Buea some 1,100 metres above sea level.[91] Or where the colonial administration was moved temporarily, as practiced in British India, where the staff members relocated from Calcutta and Delhi to Simla in the mountains of Himachal Pradesh more than 2,000 metres above sea level during summer times.[92]

Anthony King has therefore concluded that the concept of the colonial city remains a "slippery" one, depending on the geographical and social lenses through which to look at them. In accordance with authors like Meera Kosambi and Jyoti Hosagrahar he remarks,

> "[…] any attempt to construct 'snapshot' categories, frozen in one point of time, conceals changes over both space *and* time. This applies equally to notions of 'the colonial city' or the less precise concept of 'colonial urbanism' which might extend from between ten to three hundred years."[93]

He offered a categorisation of colonial cities based on their functions.

> "We should also note the equally important distinction between colonial capitals, colonial port cities and other locations such as hill stations and mobile bases."[94]

Regardless of those different roles each colonial city primarily played, there were some characteristics which all of them had in common, irrespective of their geographical location or the ruling imperial power. In virtually all cases, architectural and urban patterns were drawn from their respective mother countries. Instead, they usually formed a new hybrid style where local and external elements were combined. Wright has, to mention one example, meticulously illustrated for the case of Morocco, how French design was merged with what French representatives interpreted as vernacular architectural patterns. Under Hubert Lyautey, Resident-General of Morocco from 1912 to 1925, architects and planners were keen to better adapt themselves to Islamic traditions. By this move, these planners as representatives of French civil administration wanted to avoid what they regarded as 'previous mistakes' made under former military administration in 19th century Algeria. Despite these good intentions they still created 'their' own interpretation of

---

[91] Speitkamp 2005: 112.
[92] Ferguson 2004: 180-4.
[93] King 2005: 86-7, emphasis in original.
[94] King 2005: 87.

vernacular architecture. Wright emphasised the links between such styles and those historic reports, that were influential as part of the fascination for Orientalism.[95]

In Morocco, town planning sought to play a larger role which encompassed social and economic goals. As Wright has summarised, Lyautey pursued two seemingly contradictory key goals: first he tried to preserve what he and his compatriots interpreted as 'traditional' architectural and cultural elements; secondly he attempted to 'modernise' Morocco.[96] Similar patterns of an amalgamated architectural language can be found in Southern Africa, where veranda architecture served as interpretation and mediation between European blueprints and local conditions. SWA served as an example of such mixed veranda architecture, although German stylistic elements collided with the evolution of a vernacular style. The critique that was directed at the imposition of German blueprints will be investigated further for Windhoek (see 4.2.1).

Colonial representations in the built environment

Aside from such merely aesthetical aspects, Cooper has carved out and summarised the symbolic intentions of colonial architecture.

> "Indeed, the tenuous nature of colonial control made the mask of city planning and urban architecture all the more important as a symbol of hegemony. Colonial planning served not to integrate – or even to give the illusion of integration – but to emphasize distinctiveness and domination."[97]

Winfried Speitkamp further substantiated this thought that spatially contributed to the built colonial imprint on cities as a manifestation of the colonisers' power. He refers to the trio consisting of administrative, religious and military buildings, which were typically constructed at prominent places, and he explicitly quotes Windhoek as a role model example.[98] Those three elements did constitute the main driving forces behind the development of colonial towns and cities, and these institutions have tried to dominate the new colonial possessions. To a certain extent, their buildings can therefore be interpreted as visible signs of colonialism.

Barracks formed the essential pre-requirement to ensure the colonial rule exercised by foreign powers. The elevated site of those compounds should provide for the opportunity to monitor the local population as well as potential intruders. Despite

---

[95] Wright 1991: 108-11.
[96] Wright 1991: 85.
[97] Cooper, Frederick, *Struggle for the City: Migrant Labor, Capital, and the State in Urban Africa*, Beverly Hills/ London/New Delhi: Sage 1983: 27.
[98] Speitkamp 2005: 118-9.

their self-perception as superior rulers, the European colonisers were still afraid of their opponents, and took precautions for potential civil unrest among the colonised population. In times of crises, the barracks and military outposts provided shelter for European civilians.[99] *Administrative buildings*, on the other hand, were the spatial expression of an attempt to orderly subjugate and exploit the colonial entities. The bureaucratic machinery employed behind the scenes was working at these premises and needed to look impressive to the Indigenous population. Though *churches* usually represented the tallest buildings in colonial cities[100], they were not just the spiritual symbols of the new ruling elite but represented the mediating efforts of the missionaries. In accordance with the Gospel, the latter provided help to the local population, and were in many cases the only institution, where basic education would be made accessible to a broader section of the poor African population, though by no means to all, and with a comparatively limited curricula.

In contrast to all other German colonies, there existed no government schools for the African population in DSWA; here 'Native schools' were exclusively maintained by the Missionary Societies, whilst state-funded schools and boarding houses remained privileged for the White community. Anyhow the colonial administration granted missionary schools few subsidies for their efforts to disseminate the German language and the 'preparation' of future Indigenous labourers.[101] On the other side, the missionaries represented and were perceived as agents of the European colonial idea too, since they had sided with the colonial administration during riots or warfare against the colonised population. Zimmerer exemplified this double-edged position during the Namibian War, when the intimidated Herero and Nama population was forced to go into hiding in order to avoid their extermination by starvation or German imprisonment. Missionaries were able to convince many of them to leave the guerrilla-like vagrancy behind and to seek protection under the clergyman's supervision. The missionaries breached their promise though and handed all Africans over to the colonial police forces after a while.[102] Further, Missionary Societies were substantial land owners and therefore actively involved in many colonial businesses, drawing more suspicions from the Indigenous population of being accomplices with the colonial regime – despite the societies often pursuing their own agenda, such as agricultural businesses or to preach the gospel.

---

[99] Home 2015: 54.
[100] Njoh considers the construction of the Cathedral of Sacre Cœur in Muslim Casablanca, completed in 1930, a deliberate French provocation in face of the fact that the city just had a limited Christian parish and did not represent the seat of a bishop (Njoh 2015: 98).
[101] Zimmerer 2001: 243-50.
[102] Zimmerer 2001: 42-55.

The merchants were equally a stakeholder of the colonial setup and impacted the shape of many colonial cities. In addition to the barracks, administrative and religious facilities they contributed to other typical infrastructures in the municipalities like railway stations, port facilities, cold stores, abattoirs or horse racing tracks. Although Osterhammel and Jansen consider the last one to be merely an attribute of British colonialism[103], it was one of the key leisure time facilities in Windhoek under German rule too.

Symbolic meanings of colonial spaces

Public spaces like streets, squares or parks played an important role in the context of symbolisms. Colonial administrations were eager to provide their cities with such conveniences, which were perceived as typical standards with reference to the metropoles. Wide, paved streets and pavements in regular patterns were one component that would be complemented by street lighting, telephone wires (and poles) as well as other piped infrastructures. How important the provision of such urban amenities was in terms of the perception of a colonial city's self-esteem, will be analysed for the context of Windhoek (see 4.2.3). In addition to the abundant gardens in European residential quarters, the urban fabric of central areas was interspersed with public parks and/or tree lined squares. This composition intentionally made the colonial rule tangible, and underscored the respective power's will.

From the European perspective, *monuments* played a significant role in the domination of African spaces – but for their self-assurance as well. Therefore the monuments' sites were carefully chosen: they were either placed prominently in one of the parks, or on a square if they commemorated a colonial pioneer or battle. Niall Ferguson refers to Delhi and the memorial's elevated position for those soldiers killed during the "Indian Mutiny" in 1857-8[104], whilst Speitkamp similarly refers to the equestrian monument (Reiterdenkmal) in Windhoek, devoted to the German losses during the Namibian War of 1904-1908.[105] Despite their similarity in location, there is an important difference between both monuments. The first one listed a considerable number of Indian soldiers who had fought alongside the British, whereas the victims commemorated through in Windhoek exclusively depicted White soldiers. In colonies like South West or East Africa, memorials had a different connotation than in the metropole, as Speitkamp has highlighted.[106] In almost no case did they commemorate a monarch or leading political figure from the

---

[103] Osterhammel, Jansen 2012: 96.
[104] Ferguson 2004: 149-50.
[105] Speitkamp 2005: 122.
[106] Speitkamp 2005: 119-22.

mother country, except for Bismarck, but rather they memorialised anonymous German soldiers or early colonial (administrative) representatives.

For the last category, the inscriptions usually offered a direct interpretation of the way the Germans wanted to be viewed by the Indigenous population. In so far as the memorials were intended as symbols for the colonisers' domination, authority and power, they symbolically represented a break with how the African community traditionally passed on historic events to the next generation which was predominantly through oral narratives. Osterhammel and Jansen stress the symbolic quality behind those monuments and how they were politically charged in the colonial context. For both authors it was understandable that French troops tried to dismantle and repatriate 'their' memorials from Algiers back to France during their retreat in 1962.[107] For the German context, Speitkamp has documented that memorials commemorating the colonies did originally not play a significant role in the metropole. This changed in interwar years under the shadow of the Treaty of Versailles and the loss of all colonial "possessions." As Speitkamp points out, most of these interwar initiatives were organised by former staff members of the colonial administration and armed forces, though their public support remained limited.[108]

In a similar sense, but at more abstract level, colonial cities bear a symbolic dimension where they could be interpreted as 'outpost of civilisation' in some of the remotest places of the world. Under this umbrella they disseminate elements of 'modernity' and 'progress' from an imagined centre towards its periphery. Cities were turned into showpieces of European lifestyle, whose symbolic value went far beyond colonial cities or towns. The idea can be illustrated by the developments around Delhi under British rule. With the colonial administration's decision to make the city the new capital of British India it appropriated the historic authority of the 'Old' Mughal dynasty. The British tried to maintain some traditional social elements like the so-called Durbar, an assembly originally celebrated at the Mughal's Court. Nonetheless, it was adapted to a completely different context and intended as kind of public tribute paid to the British royal family as the new emperor.[109]

The British administration regarded the 'New' Delhi project as an expression of 'their' imperial power and dominance over the colonial territory. Considering India's size an intervention in Delhi shows little effect and confirms Cooper's posi-

---

[107] Osterhammel, Jansen 2012: 120-3.
[108] Speitkamp 2013: 409-13.
[109] Darwin, John, *After Tamerlane: The Rise and Fall of Global Empires, 1400 – 2000*, London: Penguin 2008: 262-9, 346-7.

tion on limited imperial power demonstrations.[110] At the same time the new city did incite reactions among wealthier parts of the autochthonous population. To them, the British activities created an impetus to modernise their own neighbourhoods with the means they had. Such local activities exemplify Anthony King's idea of various modernities.[111]

The autochthonous population contested the imperial power and resisted its position as passive spectators. Instead they made their claim to 'imagination' and 'ownership' of the colonial city and attempted to be part of the urban lifestyle. According to Speitkamp colonial cities offered additional (economic) options to local residents which were later restricted by segregationist policies.[112] Indigenous claims to the city contested the European notion of urbanity, a characteristic for the African colonial context as will be explored in the following subchapter. Actions by the colonisers always induced reactions from the colonised side and created a kind of iterative loop. Osterhammel and Jansen consequently describe colonial cities as "central spaces for interaction and conflict."[113]

This not only affected the colonial cities but made its impact on the metropole too. European cities like London or Berlin incorporated the colonial legacy in many ways and are mirrors of colonial cities. Anja Laukötter exemplifies this idea that the closer colonial administrations and affiliated institutes were constructed to important governmental offices, the more prestige can be attributed to a country's colonial aspirations. Laukötter describes the ethnological museum's location in late Wilhelminian Berlin, and the ensuing debates about the museum's relocation from city centre to the suburb of Dahlem as diminishing prestige and significance for the colonial aspirations in public awareness.[114]

Imperial considerations on colonial cities

Representations of the colonial experience were well received at the metropole but one golden rule had to be followed; the colonial project had to be sustained by colonial revenues, and not be a burden to the metropolitan taxpayers. Great Britain resembled France's approach during the 1920s, where both refused a "development" strategy in order to improve colonial infrastructures and to make their ex-

---

[110] Cooper 2012: 261.
[111] King 2005: 87.
[112] Speitkamp 2005: 113.
[113] Osterhammel, Jansen 2012: 96.
[114] Laukötter, Anja, *Das Völkerkundemuseum.* In: Zimmerer, Jürgen [Ed.]: Kein Platz an der Sonne: Erinnerungsorte der deutschen Kolonialgeschichte. Frankfurt: Campus 2013: 234-5.

ploitation more efficient in the long run.[115] Whilst such closer ties with the metropole had deliberately been rejected from European side, the effects of the Great Depression made themselves inevitably felt in the colonial context too. According to Cooper, the effects offered the opportunity to divert attention, and initiated a reconsideration of socio-political priorities and interests that should primarily benefit the metropole. It led to certain changes and privileges accrueing the urban areas to the detriment of the rural ones.[116] Scarce resources were used for improvements in the colonial cities rather than in remote agricultural areas. The impacts of such effects will be addressed for Windhoek (see 4.1).

The construction of the built environment in colonial cities was coordinated and structured through planning regimes. In some cases, the plans were centrally drafted by the colonial administration at the metropole and without sufficient cultural empathy or consideration of local circumstances. This was the case for Algeria under French military administration, when the Ministry of War took direct responsibility for the preparation of urban plans.[117] Similar mechanisms were in place for Germany's West African colonial territories, where all relevant plans for administrative buildings were drawn at desks in Berlin.[118] It was not just the plans that were exported to the German colonies but in many cases building materials were imported from Europe, and Speitkamp argues that the combination of these approaches underscored German claims and domination in the African context.

Such impositions of European architectural and urban aesthetics did not go without criticism by those days' experts, as Wright has demonstrated based on the Algerian experiences. For Morocco the key colonial administrative staff members sought to avoid earlier mistakes, and adapted their plans to vernacular patterns and local expectations – or what they interpreted as such. In his way, Hubert Lyautey transformed the urban landscape of many Moroccan cities with the aid of his chief planner Henri Prost, one of the key figures in colonial urban planning. In 1913 he was offered the position as kind of master planner in French Morocco, a position he held for ten years, and Wright emphasises his progressive ideas which were based on his comparative assessment of urban planning legislation in several European countries. In total he drew the master plans for nine major cities in the country, and the Architecture and Urbanism Department he led in the colony is the first of its kind in the French speaking world.[119] In Casablanca he formulated

---

[115] Cooper 2012: 307. For the British context Darwin 2008: 269.
[116] Cooper 2012: 308.
[117] Wright 1991: 92.
[118] Speitkamp 2005: 119.
[119] Wright 1991: 98.

the building instructions called *police des constructions* that were intended to regulate and harmonise the city's building standards in terms of materials, street layout and public health[120] – basic principles which are still valid in modern planning. Despite Wright's work being overlayed with notions of the dual city (see 2.2 and 2.3), she points to the idea of "de novo" planning, or *tabula rasa*, for the African colonial context.

> "For the French, Morocco offered a chance to create *de novo* a vision of the contemporary metropolis as a clean, efficient, and elegant setting."[121]

Colonial cities could be used as an experimental environment in contrast to the many formal restrictions in place at the metropole.[122] This is not to say there were no planning regulations in the colonial entities. Building codes and zoning developed along the emergence of many colonial cities but these regulations were a result of European intervention and not a reflection of vernacular traditions. Local planners were employed to lead and supervise the construction of new towns and cities based on recent developments and fashions in the metropole. However, *local* in this context does in most cases only refer to their work desks as being situated in the colonial territories themselves but it does not indicate their affiliation with the local population. Although some of these White planners might have been born and raised overseas, they were well familiar and embedded into the coloniser's way of thinking and habits, due to their education in metropolitan institutes. Lord Lugard can be considered as representative among the British administration, likewise for Gottlieb Redecker with the German administration in DSWA. Both have played a significant role for colonial urban planning, as will be explained later. Regardless of whether colonial developments were prepared locally or in the mother countries, they demonstrate the existing links between countries at the metropole and colonial entities at the perceived periphery.

Stephen Ward's diffusion concept for planning ideas

For the argument, Ward's concept of diffusion will be interpreted in conjunction with transnational history and the circulation of ideas, as promoted by King and Saunier. Ward's terminology like *diffusion*, *imposition* or *borrowing* references to Joseph

---

[120] Wright 1991: 105.

[121] Wright 1991: 88, emphasis in original. Tomlinson offers another interpretation of some colonies like South Africa as, "[…] 'empty' in the sense that the native peoples were ultimately unable to mount an effective resistance to capitalist colonization." His emphasis is on the impact of agriculture creating a form of what he calls ecological imperialism (Tomlinson 1999: 56).

[122] Hård, Misa 2010: 7.

52

Schumpeter's innovation theory. This section will summarise the main ideas behind Ward's concept but for the rest of this argument I will follow Saunier's less biased terms of 'circulation' and 'flow.'

First of all the general approach behind Ward's diffusion concept, is applicable to three different settings: the historic exchange of ideas among European traditions; the imperial context of White settler dominions; and subjugated colonial territories alike (see figure 1).[123] He edges different experiences around the world inform diffusion of planning ideas.

Figure 1: Transnational circulation of planning ideas

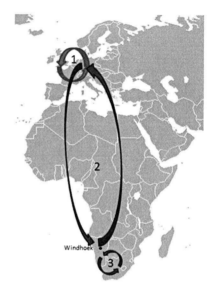

> "These cases underline the general point that diffusion needs to be understood as highly variable, rather than as a single, uniform process."[124]

Tracing 20th century developments he highlights three foci about diffusion: the mechanisms of diffusion; how the ideas or tools have changed during their diffusion; and under what circumstances did it take place. His approach is less depending on the impacts made by influential planning personalities, or by diffusion's interpretation as part of Western imperialism's hegemony. However, power relations play a significant role helping to disseminate certain planning tools to particular professional communities to narrow down the sources available to its subjugated entity. Ward differentiates between two groups of *diffusion* – the 'borrowed' and the 'imposed'. Each of them comprises of three types, which allows differences in the relationship between what he calls 'importing' and 'exporting' countries. In case where the importing country is able to deliberately select those ideas and tools it would like to include within its planning regime, then this relation can be described as *borrowing* in Ward's sense, whilst the opposite case of *imposition*

---

[123] Ward 2000: 42-3.
[124] Ward 2000: 43.

is characterised by a strong exporting country enforcing its planning system in foreign contexts.[125]

This classification as summarised in Table 1, offers the opportunity to address both planning ideas among European traditions as well as between metropoles and the colonial entities. These interactions are key subjects for examination in this PhD dissertation.

Within the **European context** Ward has identified three major planning traditions – the British, French and German.[126] Considering their political capabilities as well as their contributions to the planning profession, he classifies the diffusion of ideas among them as *synthetic borrowing*. All traditions kept close contacts with their counterparts and were usually well aware of advances the others had made. They could then filter these new ideas and check, whether they would fit into their own existing system.

> "Before 1914, for example, Britain borrowed heavily from German town extension, zoning and organic approaches to urban design. In turn, the Germans (having already borrowed British public health innovations) looked admiringly on British housing design and, above all, the garden city."[127]

As all the aforementioned planning traditions were already well developed, Ward stresses how skilfully they adopted new and relevant elements, which would in turn improve their own existing system. The respective planning communities subsequently used those elements to create something genuinely innovative that, "might themselves be diffused elsewhere."[128]

---

[125] Ward 2000: 43-5.
[126] Ward 2000: 41.
[127] Ward 2000: 45.
[128] Ward 2000: 46.

Table 1: Ward's typology of diffusion

Type	Indigenous Role	External Role	Typical Mechanisms	Potential for Distinctiveness	Characteristic Examples
Synthetic borrowing	Very high	Very low	Indigenous planning movements plus wide external contacts	Very high	Major countries of Western Europe and USA
Selective borrowing	High	Low	External contact with innovative planning traditions	High	Smaller countries of Western Europe
Undiluted borrowing	Medium	Medium	Indigenous deference to innovative external planning traditions	Fairly low	Dominions of British Empire, Japan and some European examples
Negotiated imposition	Low	High	Dependence on external planning tradition(s)	Low	Aid-dependent countries
Contested imposition	Very low	Very high	High dependence on one external planning tradition	Low	'Enlightened' colonial planning
Authoritarian imposition	None	Total	Total dependence on one external planning tradition	None	Newly subjugated territories

A less sophisticated relation is described by *selective borrowing*, where the adoption of external ideas is not used to create something specifically new. Instead, the receiving country is selecting some parts of other ideas for its own system without further theoretical reflection. Nevertheless, they can play a role as intermediaries in the diffusion of planning ideas among competing major traditions.

> "More generally, Belgium (along with Switzerland) apparently played significant parts in moving British and German urban reformist ideas into the Francophone world."[129]

The last version of voluntary adoption is called *undiluted borrowing*, and takes place in an environment where Indigenous planners are virtually non-existent. Ward emphasises the unequal relationship while the receiving country is still in control of the diffusion process.

> "The clearest examples of undiluted borrowing have undoubtedly been the white settled Dominions of the British Empire, whose early encounters with twentieth century planning came largely through the prism of British experience."[130]

The British influence in the dominions remained strong over a long period; although Ward is eager to mention similar cases in strong planning traditions like France, where the reconstruction of Reims after the First World War rested on the shoulders of US-American George Ford.[131] Accordingly Ford's plans drew much of the planning community's attentionas illustrated in *Der Städtebau*[132] and *The Town Planning Review*[133].

Such forms of voluntary reception are contrasted by diffusion through *imposition*, where the power balance tends to be reversed and the relationship is characterised by subordination at the receiving end of the diffusion process. The first one is labelled *negotiated imposition* is typically a result of postcolonial circumstances. As the word 'negotiated' indicates, it leaves space for the importing country to make its own decisions, although the options to choose from are usually very limited. Such limitation is for example a consequence of contractual conditions attached to (development) aid, or the number of exporting countries willing to exchange ideas with the importing one. Most receiving countries falling under this category do not have the resources to maintain their own functioning planning administration, and rely on the imported ideas, tools and the technical staff. He therefore concludes,

---

[129] Ward 2000: 48.
[130] Ward 2000: 49.
[131] Ward 2000: 50.
[132] DS (1920) 11/12: no author: 119; DS (1921) 1/2: De Fries: 21.
[133] TPR (1921) March: Holliday: 5-11.

"[a]lthough at the technical level, the export of foreign planning aid is now being undertaken more sensitively than ever before, with growing emphasis on indigenous expertise, the wider sense of imposition remains very strong."[134]

One level below is the *contested imposition*, where the environment is typically a colonial one without a democratic government and a specific planning community that could react to the diffused ideas. Ward explains the means and loopholes for Indigenous contestation are through simple disobedience, which could become more or less violent, depending on the degree the colonisers' were intruding into traditional local customs.[135] Those patterns of broad-based local opposition to colonial plans did occur and are illustrated by the following example.

"Thus in Indo-China, enlightened *urbanisme* could not tame the rising indigenous challenge to the colonizers in major cities such as Saigon and Hanoi. Around Moroccan cities such as Casablanca, burgeoning indigenous *bidonvilles* (shack communities) were soon challenging the colonial process."[136]

In fact, these *bidonvilles* were challenging the colonial plans through their mere physical existence rather than through explicit statements or petitions. The type of diffusion process with the least opportunities for Indigenous needs and expectations to be recognised is called *authoritarian imposition*. It can be considered as stereotypical of exploitative colonial environments, where the colonisers intended to create a symbol for their own dominance regardless of local conditions.

"Thus the early planning of Algeria, though skilfully undertaken by French military engineers, was a heavy handed exercise of imperial power, without concession to indigenous society or culture [...]. Similar charges have been laid against the British, especially in the most grandiose exercises in imperial planning such as New Delhi [..]"[137]

Modes of diffusion were predetermined by the power relations that exist among exporting and receiving countries. There is room for impact by a single exceptional planner to make in this process, if the circumstances grant such freedom for intervention. However, Ward argues that options for individual alterations are limited or virtually non-existent in colonial domains. As part of my research, I will apply Ward's concept to the case of SWA, and Windhoek in particular, in order to verify to what extent the general colonial setup dominates, or if the individual planning agent was able to make a difference.

---

[134] Ward 2000: 52.
[135] Ward 2000: 53.
[136] Ward 2000: 54, emphases in original.
[137] Ward 2000: 55.

Nevertheless, Carlos Silva argues that urban planning was no simple extension of colonial powers, and he calls this perception an oversimplification.[138] Instead, colonial cities were central places for exchange between colonised and colonisers, as Osterhammel and Jansen summarise.

> "Zentrale Experimentierfelder und Bühnen kolonialer Symbolpolitik waren die Städte. Hier fielen die staatlichen Machtzentren und die wichtigsten Interaktions-räume „pluraler" Kolonialgesellschaften zusammen. Städten galt daher in besonderem Maße die Aufmerksamkeit der Kolonialherren."[139]

Land tenure

Therefore it is necessary to focus on one invisible but extremely relevant agent of these "interactions" in the colonial setup, which became manifest in the issue of land tenure. Without proper systems to organise and manage land rights, all attempts for building codes and zoning would have remained void, and the symbols of colonial dominance would have been hard to enforce. More or less sophisticated attempts for land survey and the preparation of cadastre were characteristic of many colonial regimes like the British one as stated by Niall Ferguson.

> "We should never forget that as important as the telegraph in the technology of domination was the theodolite."[140]

Based on the maps created, colonial administrations on one hand knew 'their' territory and were able to prepare planning decisions, on the other hand they provided the basis for the land's future subdivision into individual plots. Land subsequently became part of trading goods, in many cases introducing a new feature[141], since African societies were characterised by a far less individualised ownership system. Land was instead used collectively to raise cattle or other livestock. Hence, it was in the domain of land that a clash of different cultures and habits became apparent. With the spread of a European understanding of land rights, the prevailing system did change significantly, and its persisting legacy can be counted as one root cause

---

[138] Silva, Carlos Nunes, *Introduction*, New York/London: Routledge 2015: 3.

[139] Osterhammel, Jansen 2012: 121, emphasis in original. "Cities were central experimental grounds and arenas for colonial symbolism. It was here, that state centres of power coincided with the most important spaces for interaction within "plural" colonial societies. Therefore, cities have received particular attention by the colonial rulers." (author's translation).

[140] Ferguson 2004: 171.

[141] E.g. Ferguson 2004: xxiii, 51; Gründer 2012: 163-6; Knopp: 47-8; Krüger, Gesine, *Das Goldene Zeitalter der Viehzüchter: Namibia im 19. Jahrhundert*. In: Zimmerer, Jürgen; Zeller, Joachim [Eds.]: Völkermord in Deutsch-Südwestafrika: Der Kolonialkrieg (1904-1908) in Namibia und seine Folgen. Augsburg: Weltbild 2011: 25.

58

for the socio-economic inequalities that are tangible in many of today's postcolonial countries. This legacy underscores the relevance for an analysis of those historic circumstances.

Basically two levels of land acquisition can be differentiated in the colonial context. The first one implies the imperial will to demarcate its territorial expansion, for example through signing treaties which did not only include the transfer of vast swaths of land but which were linked to diplomatic concessions that could be interpreted as mutual support among allies too. Examples were the establishment of protectorates as predecessors for a formal colonial intervention, as has happened under German rule. From the European perspective, these treaties were supposed to confer full control over the territory from the colonised to the colonisers. The latter should exercise all relevant powers and govern the country as if it were in Europe. Those negotiations were prone to misinterpretations due to the varying connotations of key terms like land tenure. Gesine Krüger illustrates Germany's early colonial days in DSWA, when Maharero (here called Kahimemua), Samuel Maharero's father, rejected a German offer for an alliance in 1888. The oral narration of this encounter sheds some light on the different interpretation of the words 'land' and 'soil.'

> "<Die Deutschen kamen und sagten Kahimemua, dass sie Land wollten. ‚Gut', sagte Kahimemua, [‚]bringt Gefäße, Eimer und Körbe und wir werden euch Land geben.' Behälter wurden gebracht und Kahimemua ließ sie mit Erdreich füllen. ‚Da habt ihr', sagte er zu den Deutschen, ‚hier ist Land für euch.' Die Deutschen wurden wütend und sagten, dass sie keine Erde wollten, die man in Gefäße füllen kann, sondern dass sie unsere Erde, unser Land wollten.>"[142]

Another example of unequal treaties and unfair acquisition of land can be traced to the respective unit, by which the acquired land was measured. Apparently, the Germans under merchant Adolf Lüderitz used a trick in their negotiations about Angra Pequeña, what later became known as Lüderitz Bay in DSWA. They acquired a coastal strip of 20 miles towards the interior but instead of the common English mile (c. 1.6 km) the Germans were referring to Geographical miles (c. 7.4 km), hence cheating on their African partners with the consent of those missionar-

---

[142] Cited in: Krüger 2011: 25. "<The Germans came and told Kahimemua they would like to have land. 'Well', said Kahimemua [']bring containers, buckets and baskets and we will give you your land.' Containers were brought and Kahimemua had them filled with earth. 'Take it' he said to the Germans, 'here is your land.' The Germans became angry and said they did not want soil to be filled in pots, but that they wanted our soil, our land.>" (author's translation).

ies present who were interpreting.[143] Aside from the private acquisition of land by merchants and colonial societies, governments got involved in the appropriation of land. The British approach was inspired by the idea of *terra nullius* or unclaimed property that could immediately, and without complication, be used for settlement purposes[144]; such swaths of land were usually recognised as crown land.

The second level of land acquisition is based on individual, small-scale ownership for private persons. These persons were able to acquire their own subdivided plot by sale or on leasehold terms, either from larger investors like Lüderitz or from the Government. In many cases the colonial administration granted subsidies for settlers willing to buy or they received land under favourable conditions.[145] Those conditions remained applicable as long as the settlers complied with some preconditions concerning their willingness to start construction on the plot, open their business or cultivating farms of sufficient size. All these plots were meticulously surveyed and then recorded in land registers.[146] Fences became the typical demarcation of property boundaries, representing a new element in the African context.

Many of the new farms and businesses received new names to make the ruling power more apparent. In this respect the colonisers' actions reflect Michel Foucault and his theories on power and the appropriation of space.[147] Power shows its productive elements and inscribes itself through the repetition of those new names in what social scientist Andrea Seier describes as "Wahrheitsritual" (ritual of truth).[148] Later forms of residential segregation are inextricably interwoven with the matter of land tenure and turned out to be the consequence of such early unequal acquisition: Knopp refers to the example of Samuel Maharero in his function as reputable Chief of the Herero community.[149] Historic descriptions depict him as being overwhelmed by his re-presentational duties which required him to hand out presents to his guests. Aside from his allegedly excessive alcohol consumption, this informed his trade relation with the local German business of Wecke & Voigts from where he ordered his supplies. Once he was highly indebted to this company,

---

[143] Wallace 2015: 183.

[144] Osterhammel, Jansen 2012: 11.

[145] Knopp 2010: 47.

[146] For 1902 Werner estimates that only 38% of the land was still in African hands before its final erosion until the completions of the Native reserve system in 1926 (Werner 2002: 217).

[147] Foucault, Michel, *Security, Territory, Population: Lectures at the College De France, 1977-78*, Basingstoke *et al.*: Palgrave Macmillan 2009.

[148] Seier, Andrea, *Macht*. In: Kleiner, Marcus S. [Ed.] (2001): Michel Foucault: Eine Einführung in sein Denken. Frankfurt: Campus 2001: 101.

[149] Knopp 2010: 49-50.

he was forced to pay in land for his mix of official and private debts, despite this land actually belonging to his community. As a result, he sold several valuable farms, some of which are still owned by this very company. Here, as elsewhere in DSWA and beyond, in addition to the physical loss of those farms, their sale also curtailed the future economic basis of the African population and made them dependent on other sources of income.[150] I will refer to this relation with regards to the particular circumstances in Windhoek (see 4.3.1).

2.3 Residential segregation

As Nightingale has summarised, the term 'segregation' was used over a long period of time and for various contexts such as chemistry or medicine.[151] It made its way into the urban context in the 1890s, when the spread of a Bubonic Plague epidemic starting in Hong Kong almost culminated in what Nightingale calls "segregation mania."[152] Administrations across the colonies tended to racialize the disease and therefore tried to isolate infected persons at some distance from European quarters or even offshore. Robert Home, who based his reflection on Saul Dubow, traced back the term 'segregation' meant as "physical separation of races"[153] until 1908. Dubow discovered the term's use during the opening of the 1902 Cape parliament.[154] Its use was vigorously advocated based on investigations with regards to the spread of plague in colonial Calcutta, conducted by Dr William Simpson during the late 1890s. He later advised several British administrations in Africa, and suggested the physical separation due to "native dirty health practices."[155] Home, sees the origins of segregation linked to British formulations of town planning legislation drafted during a first peak of debates in the years before the *Housing, Town Planning, Etc., Act 1909* was enacted. Though Stephen Ward argues that, "the actual term 'town planning' was coined, almost certainly, in 1905"[156], it illustrates how both phenomena actually refer to and complement each other, not just in chronologic terms. Despite such overlaps Nightingale stresses the difference between

---

[150] Zimmerer 2001: 63.

[151] Nightingale 2012: 159.

[152] Nightingale 2012: 160.

[153] Home 2015: 59.

[154] Dubow, Saul, *The Elaboration of Segregationist Ideology*. In: Beinart, William; Dubow, Saul [Eds.]: Segregation and Apartheid in Twentieth Century South Africa. New York: Routledge 1995: 147-8.

[155] Home 2015: 59.

[156] Ward, Stephen V., *Planning and Urban Change*, London *et al*.: Sage 2004: 2.

segregation's significance as catchword and ideology on one hand and its actual implementation on the other hand.[157]

Residential segregation might seem to be a relatively young phenomenon at first sight but its history in fact goes far beyond its etymological definition. Osterhammel and Jansen refer to explicit segregationist policies in some French African colonies applied in the 1880s[158], although they are usually associated with attempted assimilation. Singapore's foundation under Thomas Stamford Raffles in 1819 marked another earlier example where a separate European section developed quickly which was further protected by cantonments.[159] Nevertheless, it is helpful and advisable to have a look beyond the (biologically determined) racial divide[160], in order to understand the complexity of segregationist matters as echoed in the colonial context through exising social hierarchies and habits.

Historically separation played an important role between various religious communities, which left its imprint on the urban fabric, for example in form of the well-known different quarters in Jerusalem's historic Old City.[161] For the colonial context of the Namibian case study this history did not create a basis for substantial spatial disputes.

Another layer of distinctions are social hierarchies often made visible through the proximity of subjects to their ruling monarch[162], or with regard to the accommodation of social classes in modern industrial cities. Particularly the latter one seems to be of certain relevance for this work, bearing the circulation of planners and ideas to the colonial context. As part of their European experience, planners and other administrative staff members were familiar with the differentiations made in industrialising cities, where the socio-economic background had a strong impact in terms of accommodation. This link to the historic European debates is intended to complement my colonial investigations, where – despite a lot of research that has

---

[157] Nightingale 2012: 160-1.

[158] Osterhammel, Jansen 2012: 96.

[159] Turnbull, Constance Mary, *A History of Singapore, 1819-1988*, Oxford/New York: Oxford University Press 1989.

[160] Cooper refers to the controversies about the spreading idea of racial immutability in face of the abolition of slavery and which led to various forms of "scientific racism", debated since the 18th century. Although the debate covered pro and contra arguments at the beginning, negative tendencies dominated since the 19th century (Cooper 2012: 298).

[161] Wasserstein, Bernard, *Divided Jerusalem: The Struggle for the Holy City*, London: Profile Books 2002.

[162] Hofrichter, Hartmut [Ed.], *Stadtbaugeschichte von der Antike bis zur Neuzeit*, Braunschweig: Vieweg 1995: 76-95.

already been conducted on segregation – Silva very recently came to the conclusion that,

> "[t]he racist character of colonial urban policies continues to be a controversial issue that seems to require further research, comparison and debate."[163]

Silva's comment on the current state of research represents a reminder of Paul Maylam's 1995 statement, when he conceded that though there were a growing number of journal articles published on segregation in South Africa, "[…] it is perhaps surprising how few books have come out of this urban research."[164] Maylam argues publication's focused on case studies rather than comparative or synthesising works.

Even though I do not intend to question the racial divide's relevance for colonial policies, I would like to view them in conjunction with some ideas and viewpoints that might have (subconsciously) influenced the administrative activities in the colonies. Maynard Swanson described the interrelations between metropole and colonies as follows.

> "That the responses to outcast London were not identical in origin or conception nor directly linked with the question of racial segregation in South Africa should not obscure their interest as analogues to the subject of the present article. Moreover, it is reasonable to expect that the European background formed a major source of inspiration for the white response to social problems in Africa."[165]

Therefore class distinctions in Europe impacted on the planning profession. The "slum myth" with its inherent connotation of working class people living in such areas as being lazy and diseased is remarkable, as it formed a crucial basis for similar comparisons in the colonial context. I will shed light on some of the key motives for segregation and on what basis people were categorised before I reflect on the recent academic concept of hybrid cities.

The European background

As a consequence of the Industrial Revolution and manifestations of unfettered capitalism in the Global North, many European cities were in a stage of rapid transformation roughly since the mid-nineteenth century. Labelled as 'shock-city',

---

[163] Silva 2015a: 3.
[164] Maylam, Paul, *Explaining the Apartheid City: 20 Years of South African Urban Historiography*, 1995: 20-1.
[165] Swanson, Maynard W., *The Sanitations Syndrome: Bubonic Plague and Urban Native Policy in the Cape Colony, 1900-1909*, New York: Routledge [1977](1995): 27.

the early example par excellence, Manchester[166] made social divisions between poor working class people and the affluent upper class bourgeoisie drastically visible. Similar trends affected cities like Barmen and Elberfeld in Germany, though at a significantly lesser extent. Those poorer parts of the population were confronted with the limitations of their economic resources, which limited the kind of accommodation available to them and eventually led to severe overcrowding. Urban-rural migration and population growth, exacerbated this urban challenge. For the British context, Eric Hopkins compares the poorest people's situation at the outbreak of the First World War with those circumstances in mid-19th century.

> "The standard of living of the typical unskilled labourer was undoubtedly still very low, and may not have improved at all since the 1850s. His diet had always been poor, and much of the cheapest food by 1914 was of a worse quality than before. [...] The standard of living of the very poor in the city slums was therefore as bad as it had ever been, and this remained the greatest social failure of what was otherwise an age of improvement for the working classes."[167]

On the other hand, a small group of wealthier citizens and administrative staff members were able to afford larger dwellings located at preferred areas of the cities. In addition, they had the financial means to use, as one of the first customers, those developing new modes of transportation to commute between their homes and workplaces. What is important is the social interpretation and stigmatisation that evolved around it. Richard Dennis unveils the direct linguistic links, that were used to describe housing conditions in notoriously deprived neighbourhoods such as London's East End as paralleling colonial territories.

> "The East End was treated as a subject for exploration, 'darkest England' paralleling 'darkest Africa', or apocalyptically, as in references to 'the city of dreadful night', 'the inferno' or 'the people of the abyss'."[168]

Further he points out, how the inhabitants were stripped of their human nature and categorised as lower class subjects.

> "The sub-human nature of slum-dwellers was implied by allusions to 'rookeries' and 'dens', and it was assumed that physical and moral decay went hand-in-hand."[169]

---

[166] Schott, Dieter, *Europäische Urbanisierung (1000 – 2000): Eine umwelthistorische Einführung*, Köln *et al.*: Böhlau 2014: 202-8.

[167] Hopkins, Eric, *A Social History of the English Working Classes: 1815-1945*, London *et al.*: Hodder and Stoughton 1990: 207.

[168] Dennis, Richard, *Modern London*. In: Daunton, Martin [Ed.]: The Cambridge Urban History of Britain – Volume III 1840-1950. Cambridge: Cambridge University Press 2000: 112.

The "Slum Myth"

It is necessary to deconstruct the artificial nature of the category "slum." In this context Alan Mayne and Tim Murray have contributed although their research remains almost exclusively limited to the Global North and settler colonies.[170]

> "Slums are constructions of the imagination: a stereotype that was fashioned in the early nineteenth century by bourgeois entertainers and social reformers, and that obscured and distorted the varied spatial forms and social conditions to which it was applied. Historians have perpetuated this slum myth."[171]

Mayne and Murray demonstrate how the term 'slum' permeated the debate about working class neighbourhoods, thereby mixing dramatic fiction and realities; both authors use the word 'tunnel vision' to illustrate the intensity of those preconceived ideas in some historians' descriptions. Here the historic class-based viewpoints do play a pre-eminent role. Life in those 'slums' did show the same range of emotions as in well-to-do neighbourhoods but working class areas were interpreted as something inferior merely based on bourgeois etiquette.[172] Ellen Ross has investigated, how hundreds or sometimes thousands of middle class women visited London's deprived neighbourhoods since the 1860s in order to 'serve the poor.'[173] According to her findings, those activities were supported by prominent names like Eleanor Marx or Marie Hilton, and how such philanthropic organisations in the metropole already heralded, or rather incorporated, elements of the later "civilising mission" in the colonies. Ross in particular emphasises the role language played to denounce the inferiority of slum dwellers and the subsequent necessity for social welfare activities. Those early accounts of and encounters with supposed slums were constantly attributed with negative stereotypes confronted with accusations of laziness, drunkenness or the like.

Ross's description of those voluntary activities by women are emblematic for the prevalent class distinctions that heavily impacted the debates revolving slums. When those middle class ladies visited one of the deprived neighbourhoods to help inhabitants and to talk to them, this did usually not happen at an equitable level but

---

[169] Dennis 2000: 112.
[170] Mayne, Alan/Murray, Tim [Eds.], *The Archaeology of Urban Landscapes: Explorations in Slumland*, Cambridge: Cambridge University Press 2001.
[171] Mayne, Murray 2001: 1.
[172] Mayne, Murray 2001: 3.
[173] Ross, Ellen, *Slum journeys: ladies and London poverty 1860 – 1940*. In: Mayne, Alan; Murray, Tim [Eds.]: The Archaeology of Urban Landscapes: Explorations in Slumland. Cambridge: Cambridge University Press 2001: 11.

carried the notion of what Ross calls a "mistress-servant relation."[174] She refers to difficulties resulting from differences in voice and accent that made communication across social boundaries challenging for both sides. Whilst women performed their tasks mostly on voluntary basis and with certain insecurities, their male counterparts were well aware of their official tasks, for example as health inspectors. This situation did only change slightly in the last years before the First World War, when female nursing inspectors within London County Council (LCC) were vested with an officially recognised position. Ross quotes a 1908 statement by an LCC health inspector of foster homes.

> "English people do not like official inspection, especially in matters concerning their private domestic lives. Where capable, tactful and educated women Inspectors [sic] are employed to visit the homes, this objection would easily be overcome, and the nurse-mothers would welcome these visits."[175]

Health inspections were deemed necessary by upper class representatives but not just to lay the very basic foundations for what was considered a 'proper' daily life. The full extent rather covered a domestic civilising mission, which was intended to encourage the evolution of an 'advanced man' free of vice in the long run, of course based on bourgeois criteria. It was nonetheless fiercely disputed in historic debates as to whether or not slum dwellers were 'born' inferior elements of society, or if there were a correlation between the living environment and their inhabitants' social capabilities. Paul Belford quotes the 1899 report of Sheffield's Medical Officer, where the latter admitted that for, "the vast majority the influence of better surroundings does … act in the most beneficial manner."[176] A comprehensive and constant fight by authorities against the perceived working class problems of laziness, drunkenness and immoral tendencies was initiated, especially since slum-dwellers were considered as carriers of infectious diseases. The latter threat did (subconsciously) motivate the more affluent parts of the population to move to healthy and green suburbs, and to physically leave the overcrowded and potentially dangerous central areas behind. Throughout the interwar period the availability of

---

[174] Ross 2001: 14-5.

[175] Cited in Ross 2001: 14. It is interesting to note that a clear distinction among the European community was made, since Morris Knowles deemed such inspections absolutely imperative for Slavs in his recommendations on future US-American housing schemes. He thus made them second class people in face of their East European origins (Knowles, Morris, *Industrial Housing*, New York/London: McGraw-Hill Book Company 1920: 379-80).

[176] Cited in Belford, Paul, *Work, space and power in an English industrial slum: 'the Crofts', Sheffield, 1750 – 1850*. In: Mayne, Alan; Murray, Tim [Eds.]: The Archaeology of Urban Landscapes: Explorations in Slumland. Cambridge: Cambridge University Press 2001, 108.

new transportation means turned the search for a better place to stay into a mass phenomenon, and further exacerbated the social inequality.[177]

During the Second World War, class-related ties remained relatively durable according to Hopkins's research[178], and it was considered appropriate and more suitable to send working class children from Blitz-affected cities to families of similar social backgrounds at the countryside. Better prospects for social integration and, again, hygiene arguments were then used as justification. Some of the limited wartime inter-class contacts conveyed a stereotypical middle and upper classes' pejorative view on working class offspring. Hopkins quotes the owner of a large country house with the words,

> "I had little dreamt that English children could be so completely ignorant of the simplest rules of hygiene, and that they would regard the floors and carpets as suitable places upon which to relieve themselves."[179]

Similar real or imagined stories of backwardness seemed to support their position.

Comparison to the colonial context

Similar to the European context, the history of African social distinctions in fact predates the colonial era, as Catherine Coquery-Vidrovitch has summarised for existing traditions in sub-Saharan Africa.[180] Although such distinctions were usually not based on skin colour, she argues that a complex system defining the affiliation of individual persons, or groups of persons, to groups of similar status was in place. The system did equally contain a differentiation between what was labelled "civilised" and "savages." According to Coquery-Vidrovitch, one group comprised of chiefs, the educated or Muslims, whilst the other encompassed foreigners, socially excluded or supposedly inferior people. It was a system that clearly demarcated one's 'own' community from the 'Others', and therefore shows a similarity with the perception of 'otherness' as defined by Edward Said.[181] Many of those ethnic groups formulated a code of social hierarchies with more or less strict rules, depending on the respective region, which were complemented by various degrees of kinship and respect for lineage. This helps one to understand the complex

---

[177] Lenger, Friedrich, *Metropolen der Moderne: Eine europäische Stadtgeschichte seit 1850*, München: Beck 2013: 319-31.
[178] Hopkins 1990: 259.
[179] Hopkins 1990: 259.
[180] Coquery-Vidrovitch 2011: 72-7.
[181] Said [1977] 2003.

background of some of Africa's conflicts up until modern times, which cannot be fully attributed to colonial interventions only.[182]

These existing systems interacted with the ideas, habits and legal concepts, which the European colonisers brought with them. Over time African and European distinctions amalgamated and a rather complex system of social differentiation evolved, although the distinctions' origins were still traceable. The familiar distinctions between representatives of administrative authorities and the 'bourgeois' etiquette on one side and the working classes on the other, as defined from the Eurocentric viewpoint, categorised the colonial society in African as well as in other overseas colonies. Further, roles were distributed along skin colours, leading to a differentiation between racial interpretations of communities. Although social distinctions among the respective ethnic groups still played a role, they were less pronounced in comparison to interracial relations. With regards to ethnic groups, the European community rather underscored the opposition of her "own" community as compared to "the Other" – a phenomenon that was furthermore characterised by rejection and fascination alike.

How imperial powers treated 'their' colonial subjects differently, in comparison between India and Africa is discussed by Peter Burroughs.[183] Indian princes and local authorities were incorporated into British structures which helped to extend the Empire's grip on the colony. On the other hand, this collaboration did symbolise British appreciation and respect for Indian culture, which was far less pronounced in the African environment. For the British side, Africa was a place of 'no culture' and Nightingale presents,

"[…] a completely separate origin and an unchangeably inferior physical and moral makeup from whites."[184]

This neglect of African culture goes hand in hand with the Eurocentric view as the continent without history, a view that only changed over the second half of the 20th century. [185]

---

[182] Coquery-Vidrovitch in this case refers to the conflict lines between 'Arabs' and 'Africans' in Sudan or Zanzibar, or between Tutsi and Hutu in Rwanda and Burundi (Coquery-Vidrovitch 2011: 76-7).
[183] Burroughs, Peter, *Imperial Institutions and the Government of Empire*. In: Porter, Andrew [Ed.]: The Oxford History of the British Empire: Volume III The Nineteenth Century. Oxford/New York: Oxford University Press 1999.
[184] Nightingale 2012: 86.
[185] Coquery-Vidrovitch 2011: 5-31.

Many of the stereotypes used to describe working class conditions in Europe were transferred to the African context and African population. In his case study analysis of the plague epidemic in turn of the century Nairobi, Godwin Murunga has outlined what the European perspective on the autochthonous African population was.[186] Murunga points out that Black people were seen as "inherently diseased"[187] and therefore racial segregation was deemed necessary to accommodate them at specific sites called Locations, already before the epidemic had actually broken out. However, after the spread of plague started, it,

> "[…] was used to create an environment of fear and this environment became the basis on which settlers in Nairobi hardened their demand for segregation after 1907."[188]

In Nairobi and elsewhere in Africa, the fear of a potential transmission of diseases was used to justify racial segregation, not just as temporary precaution but as a permanent divisive line across the cities.[189] This happened in the face of state-of-the-art research in tropical medicine with malaria.[190] Maynard Swanson linked the frequent use of 'infection' by those days' British officials in the context of race relations to the "sanitation syndrome".[191] "Urban apartheid" was a consequence of this syndrome, with recommendations in 1914 for a minimum distance of 300 yards (c. 274 metres) of open land between European and African or Asian houses.[192] Other examples in the literature illustrate such: Lord Lugard recommended 440 yards (c. 400 metres) for Nigeria[193], whilst Winfried Speitkamp mentions one kilometre for the case of Duala[194], and Wolfgang Scholz refers to two kilometres for his blueprint example of a colonial African city.[195] All these examples show the rather arbitrary nature of sanitary belts as those distances exceed the radius a mos-

---

[186] Murunga, Godwin R., *"Inherently Unhygienic Races": Plague and the Origins of Settler Dominance in Nairobi: 1899-1907*. In: Salm, Steven J.; Falola, Toyin [Eds.]: African Urban Spaces in Historical Perspective. Rochester, NY: University of Rochester Press 2005: 98-130.
[187] Murunga 2005: 99.
[188] Murunga 2005 : 100.
[189] Nightingale 2012: 172.
[190] Lees, Andrew/Lees, Lynn Hollen, *Cities and the making of modern Europe: 1750-1914*, Cambridge: Cambridge University Press 2007: 275. Similar debates are presented by Carl H. Nightingale for decision makers at the British Colonial Office, where Command Paper No. 1,922 published in 1923 rejected the idea of segregation between Indians and Whites in Kenya to be essential for health reasons (Nightingale 2012: 188-9).
[191] Swanson 1977.
[192] Lees, Lees 2007: 275.
[193] Bigon 2013: 108.
[194] Speitkamp 2005: 113.
[195] Scholz 2002: 77.

quito can cover without favourable winds.[196] Lees and Lees summarise, how the eradication of anopheles mosquitoes and mosquitoes in general had been discussed as an alternative solution in fighting malaria by 1900 but for racist motives, segregation was the prime solution.[197] This solution was only bypassed for reasons of convenience, as Nightingale describes for the case of Sierra Leone and Freetown's hill station in 1904.

> "Later, servants were allowed into the bungalows themselves, though with instructions to make their quarters 'mosquito-proof.' Thus officials backhandedly admitted that the wisest antimalarial policy involved segregating mosquitoes from people, not blacks from whites."[198]

Considering these inconsistencies in colonial policies, Gwendolyn Wright offers a different interpretation of the sanitary belt's function. In French colonial policies there were usually no rules for a strict racial segregation imposed but Wright does still establish an interesting transnational link between the metropole and the colonies. Despite open criticism of the British segregationist approach by French officials, Wright highlights the similarities between Henri Prost's "district of *non edificandi*"[199] in Moroccan cities and Georges-Eugène Haussmann's zone of fortifications surrounding Paris. Prost, who worked in Morocco for one decade starting in 1913, supposedly drew his inspiration from the French capital where he had worked on a study about the fortifications zone with the Musée Social. According to Wright he wanted this zone to separate and protect two cultural spheres, serve as public open space similar to his later regional plans for Paris, and to function as concentration area for military purposes.[200] The width of all those greenbelts used in Morocco varied and made use of the respective topography.

> "The open zones of *non edificandi* had clear aesthetic and social purposes, marking the distinctions between the two parts of a city, setting off two scales of construction, two cultures, and two periods of history – at least in the eyes of the French. The term *cordon sanitaire* suggests the health precautions inherent in this familiar colonial policy of separation. In an off-guard moment Prost once acknowledged that the no-man's-land existed as well "for military reasons," allowing the rapid mobilization of French troops in the event of violence."[201]

---

[196] Bigon 2013: 108.
[197] Lees, Lees 2007: 275.
[198] Nightingale 2012: 176.
[199] Wright 1991: 145, emphasis in original.
[200] Wright 1991: 144-7.
[201] Wright 1991: 145, emphases in original.

Aside from sanitation aspects, the spatial divisions served European security concerns, and were supposedly meant to separate colonisers and colonised. A resemblance with Haussmann's Paris was claimed by Niall Ferguson for the context of British India, where the so-called "Indian Mutiny" at Lucknow in 1857-8 resulted in a new urban structure – here and beyond. Robert Napier totally transformed Lucknow, and its inhabitants had to pay for it. His whole approach reminds of Haussmann's work in Paris with its broad boulevards but it did also encompass new barracks, a fortress and a new railway station, as well as segregated living quarters.[202] What such these transformations eventually created, were two separate sections within colonial cities culminating in the dual city concept. Lord Lugard laid similar foundations with his *Township Ordinance 1917* for Nigeria.[203] Janet Abu-Lughod published results on Cairo[204] and Rabat[205], for which she explicitly linked the segregation aspect with the idea of urban apartheid. She acknowledges they remained inconsistent even within one imperial tradition, if one compares several colonial entities and their respective rules. Abu-Lughod argues that French policies in Morocco have laid the foundations for segregation and apartheid in the colonies themselves – and in contrast to ideas at the metropole. Local stakeholders used a careful wording of relevant laws to support segregation and, more importantly, European colonists were provided with exclusive access to high-quality neighbourhoods in the built urban environment further substantiating their advantageous economic position. Abu-Lughod describes two layers of rifts running through Morocco, one between coastal and hinterland cities, and the other within all cities themselves. In virtually all cities there were those new neighbourhoods built for Europeans and equipped with all, if not luxurious amenities, whereas the Indigenous quarters remained in dilapidated condition. A new 'caste' or social group has been superimposed onto the existing hierarchy, and both parts of the city were, "coexisting but not interpenetrating."[206]

Municipal administrations were the ideal agents to implement racial segregation.[207] Such dual cities did not mean the existence of two separate city structures but that the European one would become the dominant structure, exploiting and subordinating the pre-existing Moroccan structures.[208] The autochthonous population's role was disadvantaged in economic and legal terms. This conveys a Eurocentric

---

[202] Ferguson 2004: 179-80.
[203] Bigon 2013: 108.
[204] Abu-Lughod 1965.
[205] Abu-Lughod 1981.
[206] Abu-Lughod 1981: 151.
[207] Abu-Lughod 1981: xvii.
[208] Abu-Lughod 1981: 151.

view on the Indigenous population as passive victims of colonisation and colonial oppression.[209] Abu-Lughod criticises French scholarship on Morocco's urban development at the beginning of the 20th century which did not take into consideration those alterations to the Islamic city carried out throughout the 19th century in face of the growing influence of global economies and the competing European powers. As she explains, French scholars rather tried to mark those cities as 'static' and 'traditional' units, although her findings suggest many implications on cities like Sala/Salé neighbouring Rabat, where a new wealthy local elite started to dominate the city's affairs.[210]

Motives for segregation

The categorisations of *static*, *traditional*, *Savages* or *Natives* of Indigenous communities depicted the characteristics attributed by Europeans. Those days' ideas of colonial powers were interspersed with the awareness of their own superiority which created a kind of responsibility towards the colonised peoples. Urs Bitterli describes the idea of missionary efforts to spread the Gospel, where self-proclaimed 'advanced' civilisations applied a secular trusteeship over what they considered to be 'inferior' and less developed communities. Bitterli points to traces "An Essay on Colonization" published by Swede Carl Berns Wadström[211], who drew a line between 'civilised' and 'uncivilised' nations in 1795. The former nations would have to perform duties similar to those of parents taking care of their children's education. This motive remained one main impetus for the following colonial projects and subsequent European civilising missions. Frederick Cooper similarly identifies the origins of France's "mission civilisatrice" in late 19th century's Third Republic. The colonial administration's secular version had to fulfil its tasks with very scarce means, in particular teachers, physicians and engineers to carry out the projected tasks. Hence were they unable to match the church's missionary activities to spread the Word of God in their reach, and over-optimistic civilising goals frustrated by French policies for the interwar period.[212]

According to Cooper, both French and British colonialists instead focused on less expensive policies during interwar years and were satisfied with their rule over subjugated "traditional" societies without the construction of costly infrastructures. This attitude did bear another advantage; alleged Indigenous backwardness could in turn be used as another pretext to physically separate and exclude them from

---

[209] Yeoh 1996: 14.
[210] Abu-Lughod 1981: 86-7.
[211] Bitterli 1991: 296.
[212] Cooper 2012: 247-8.

amenities available to the 'superior' colonisers, at least until they would be at a comparable cultural level. Similar to the European working classes, where the bourgeoisie pursued its long-term goal to 'educate' the subordinate social elements, French colonial policies comprised of cultural assimilationist elements. For the case of Algiers Zeynep Çelik refers to three different housing types, designed by Tony Socard to match with the individual level of cultural assimilation to the French colonisers.[213] Yet the situation in North Africa varied from the setting in sub-Saharan regions and at this point it seems to be essential to mention two reasons for this difference. British and German colonial policies did usually not consider Africans to be part of the urban community; due to their assumed cultural backwardness they were believed to be 'unfit' for urban life and had to be kept at some distance from the cities. Winfried Speitkamp reports on the preferred paternalist view of European colonisers on Indigenous residents of cities basically as migrant labourers. Only a minority of African residents lived there for a limited time period and they then kept strong ties to their local communities. They sent remittances back home to support their dependant relatives who had to pay for their taxes in cash, whilst the migrant labourers received food in return from their rural relatives. After a certain time period they would return home, supporting Maylam's conclusion about the colonial expression, "that black people were essentially aliens in urban areas."[214] This fact leads Speitkamp to the assumption that colonial urbanisation and urban life did not destroy traditional ties and societal structures but it transformed them.[215] Coquery-Vidrovitch estimates the typical ratio between European and African populations in colonial cities to be between six to ten Africans per European. These numbers varied and mostly depended on the available jobs that were created in relation to the present White population. As well many African workers were accompanied by their families, thus further enlarging the Indigenous population. This fact was nonetheless usually ignored by official statistics.[216]

Coquery-Vidrovitch points out how South Africa in Cape Town and the Cape Colony enacted legislation which prevented Black people from entering White settlements. For the Cape Province Bill Freund was able to trace separate African

---

[213] Çelik 1997: 116. There existed plans for so-called *evolved*, *artisan* and *traditional* courtyard houses.
[214] Maylam 1995: 22.
[215] Speitkamp 2005: 115.
[216] Coquery-Vidrovitch, Catherine, *Introduction: African Urban Spaces: History and Culture*. In: Salm, Steven J.; Falola, Toyin [Eds.]: African Urban Spaces in Historical Perspective. Rochester, NY: University of Rochester Press 2005, xxx.

quarters as far back as to the 1840s[217] and his findings were predated by Maylam.[218] Both authors are therefore in line with Abu-Lughod, who portrays South Africa as exceptional in its consequent application of segregation. Abu-Lughod equally emphasises that virtually every colonial practice embodied more or less subtle racist undertones, though some had not been expressed as clearly as in the case of South Africa.[219] François-Xavier Fauvelle-Aymar presents the origins of legislation on segregation, and mentions the *Native Labour Regulation Act 1911* as one of the first laws limiting the Indigenous population's freedom of mobility.[220] Germany's colonial policies held an intermediary position between French assimilation and British racial divide, although DSWA can be considered exceptional due to its background as the empire's only settler colony of any significance. Here, legislation in neighbouring South Africa was assiduously assessed, notably after the shock of the Namibian War 1904-8.

This dichotomy (mainly) between Black and White populations fitted with the idea of the dual city concept. It reached its definitional and explanatory limits as soon as a person did not fit into either of these rigid categories. Pierre-Yves Saunier has illustrated this for migrant labourers of mixed ancestry at the diamond fields around Lüderitz Bay in DSWA.

> "The number of mixed-race Cape Colony workers involved in the migration eventually challenged the racial system of German South West Africa from the in-between of empires, with Cape Colony workers using the British consular system to have their 'white' rights recognised."[221]

As King points out, colonial cities played a vital role to form identities at various levels, from the individual person and local communities to nation states. He asks for a specific framework that makes interdependencies between identity, built environment and segregation traceable.

> "We also need a framework that recognizes the role that existing spatial, built, or even remembered environments play in the formation of identity, whether we think of this at the level of the individual, the community, the city, or any other larger or smaller unit, including the nation state. [...] The obvious examples here are the role of spatial segregation in contributing to the (involuntary) construction of race, eth-

---

[217] Freund, Bill: *The African City: A History*, Cambridge *et al.*: Cambridge University Press, 2007: 109.
[218] Maylam 1995: 23.
[219] Abu-Lughod 1981: xvii.
[220] Fauvelle-Aymar, François-Xavier, *Histoire de l'Afrique du Sud*, Paris : Points 2013: 380-403, here 385.
[221] Saunier 2013: 53, emphasis in original.

74

nic, caste or class consciousness; or the nature of, and access to, public space in the construction of gendered and sexualized subjects [...]"[222]

Determination of 'racial' belonging

The mentioned racial system symbolised a shift in German policies, which switched from a cultural definition of ethnic distinctions to a biological one, and where one single drop of Indigenous blood made the difference and subsequently excluded a person from the White community. Due to the uncertainties attached, Cooper underscores how the White colonial administration and society had to constantly renew and reassert its differentiation between coloniser and colonised. The threat of Indigenised Whites, who were supposedly 'drawn into' the inferior realms of African life (in German coined as "verkaffern") received particular attention, and such private details as sexual intercourse and interracial marriage were made subject to official prohibitive legislation.[223] The European community had to defend her own superiority by fostering metropolitan traditions through a clear rejection of African cultural practices. The abovementioned legislation was supposed to keep the White community free from Black 'intruders' but it likewise worked vice versa. Cooper reflects on the colonisers' attention paid to the 'reproduction' of future Indigenous workers; a matter that he reports to have been left to the rural areas before migrant labourers became subjects of thorough surveillance at enclosed camps close to the colonial cities. Anthony King equally criticises the 'coloniser-colonised' binary and its cracks around the question of half-castes.

King contributes to the debate, when he refers colonial cities such as Calcutta and Delhi as spaces for alternative lifestyle.[224] Such a view enables a different perspective on colonial cities as spaces of opportunities, which were not exclusively limited to the European community but open to the local population, and contest the narrative of White supremacy

Hybrid cities

Though residential segregation has officially been enforced, several authors regard the dual city concept as inadequate framework to properly reflect the full complexity of colonial cities. As William Bissell illustrates in the case of Zanzibar,

---

[222] King 2005: 90.
[223] Cooper 2012: 96-7.
[224] King 2005: 87-8. This reference focuses on the perspective of the colonised people, to whom such cities represented a space to be conquered by the, "emerging indigenous bourgeoisie" to put it in King's words (King 2005: 87).

"[i]f duality often characterized the forms of appearance of colonial urbanism, its actualization was marked by incompleteness and inconsistency."[225]

As a reply to the complexity of colonial cities, a group of authors developed the concept of hybrid cities. Here both supposedly separated spheres actually overlapped and the Indigenous population found its ways and means to contest the colonisers. For Bissell such an interpretation offers the opportunity to deconstruct traditional parallel narratives in (post)colonial history of colonisers' and colonised. Such a concept reveals several limitations in colonial rule and the dual city project as guiding policy, where too many agents with varying interests were at work.[226] Although Cooper classifies 'hybridity' as favourite word or buzzword in postcolonial studies, he traces some of its earliest records back to antiquity to the Roman Empire considered as an example of hybrid structures, where foreign elements of subjugated peoples tended to be incorporated in architectural terms as well as in culture.[227] Therefore, colonisers' and colonised cultures represented something fluid and in transition, as Çelik illustrates for the case of colonial Algiers.

"The ethnographic scholarship (which focused on rural habitat) and the artistic tradition (which focused on most apparent forms and fantasies) both overlooked the transformations in indigenous houses caused by the French presence. [...] The much revered purity of the Algerian house was disappearing fast, leaving in its place a hybridity characteristic of all aspects of a colonized culture."[228]

She challenges the dual city's dichotomy when she concludes,

"[t]he architecture of colonialism reveals levels of ambivalence and hybridity while persistently maintaining the overriding theme of difference."[229]

The metropole in the aftermath of the First World War expressed a somewhat shaken self-perception among the Allied imperial powers, for they had to rely on the support of their overseas colonies and non-White troops in order to win the war – a motive that was to prove more important with the upcoming the Second World War. The Senegalese soldiers fighting alongside the French army demanded recognition as equal citizens.[230] With her research on architectural design and confrontations in the Algerian context, Çelik delivered an urban exemplification of

---

[225] Bissell, William Cunningham, *Between Fixity and Fantasy: Assessing the Spatial Impact of Colonial Urban Dualism*, London: Sage 2011: 225.
[226] Bissell 2011.
[227] Cooper 2012: 264.
[228] Çelik 1997: 108.
[229] Çelik 1997: 6.
[230] Cooper 2012: 288-9.

76

Cooper's statement that a clear differentiation between rights for people at the imperial centres in Europe and those 'outside' its borders.[231] The latter had to 'prove their personal transformation' in order to be eligible to the same rights, in other words demonstrating their cultural assimilation, and Cooper underscores how the expectations towards such social climbers increased over time. For the context of Algeria French citizenship would only be granted to Christian settlers and Jews, whilst Muslims obtained those rights on a case-to-case basis, and only if they dropped their traditional Islamic rights in civil law.[232] This led to a shift in French policies during the 1920s, when granting citizenship to colonial subjects was more or less stopped and replaced by the "myth" of the Empire as new umbrella for a collection of different cultures, living side by side.[233] This solution was considered financially and politically viable, since the imperial powers did not intend to spend substantial domestic resources from the metropole in the colonies.

In the colonial cities one has to acknowledge the factual limitations of colonial powers. Where administrations tried to set certain boundaries for both communities in the dual city dichotomy, while local stakeholders simply ignored or resisted them whenever deemed inappropriate or inconvenient. Descendants of mixed ancestry are just one example of where the realms of colonised and colonisers intermingled in reality, despite legal and/or social bans. Similarly, a strict separation of the communities would have meant a voluntary curtailment of conveniences from the European perspective, such as the services of domestic servants.

Fascination for 'the Other' represented a strong impetus for European attempts to 'preserve' Indigenous quarters, such as in French North Africa. At the occasion of the 1931 International Congress on Urbanism in the Colonies, organised during the Colonial Exposition at Paris, Henri Prost perhaps paternalistically, demanded the preservation of historic Indigenous monuments and quarters in the colonial cities. Although segregation was in this case intended for their protection, those 'preserved' areas should be vacated by their inhabitants, since the areas received a new function and were envisaged as museums and shops, offering the background canvas to demonstrate to Europeans what local traditions and crafts looked like in their 'realistic' environment. These efforts were the forerunners of tourism in the long run[234] unintentionally creating a hybrid structure of encounters between both communities.

---

[231] Cooper 2012: 60.
[232] Cooper 2012: 286-7.
[233] Cooper 2012: 288-9.
[234] Çelik 1997: 40.

Another description of interracial relations in colonial cities is Yeoh's work on Singapore.[235] She gives an explanation on how to read subtle forms of contestation in everyday life that remained untraceable under the colonial administration's racially biased radar. Yeoh lists,

"[a]ctions ranging from riots and strikes to everyday acts of non-compliance, evasion, and the refusal to change 'customary' practices or adopt innovations introduced by the authorities which were recorded in colonial and municipal annals as irrational behaviour, apathy, ignorance, or superstition could be reread from a different perspective, avoiding the racist assumption which often underlay colonial discourse."[236]

All these activities took place in spite of colonial attempts to enforce racial segregation, specifically in its residential version. But Yeoh's work illustrates the power imbalances between colonised and colonisers. Aside from broad-based civil disobedience, she emphasises the role English-educated members played as advocates of the Chinese community, in order to defend their traditions and habits in the built environment against colonial interferences. They wrote petitions or articles in journals and they made representation to colonial or municipal committees.[237] It can be summarised,

"[i]n colonial societies, conceptual domination is occasionally inscribed in the legal code, but more often than not, mediated through institutional practices."[238]

Yeoh tries to reverse the usual interpretation of power relations, when she states that the degree of colonial influence depended on the willingness of the colonised people to accept those impositions. They had means to defend certain territories, regimes and the habits of their own traditions. Hence, Yeoh concludes that those two mentioned aspects of domination and making use of the city had different consequences for the shape of the urban landscape. There existed one symbolic layer, more or less directly inscribed into the built environment, and with clearly attributed representative functions like colonial administrative or commercial buildings. The other layer consisted of indirect colonial attempts to transform customary life through amenities such as sewerage systems, parks and demarcated streets.[239] Nevertheless, the creation of segregationist patterns was not the result of

---

[235] Yeoh 1996.
[236] Yeoh 1996: 20.
[237] Yeoh 1996: 314.
[238] Yeoh 1996: 12.
[239] Yeoh 1996: 14-8.

the colonial administration alone but depended on the collaboration of various stakeholders 'on the ground.' Yeoh gives some examples when she argues that,

> "[…] an institutional framework putting into effect a social technology for planning, orchestrating, and controlling the organization and shaping of urban space had to be created. The components of such a framework varied between the cities of different colonial powers, and included the church (particularly in the Latin American colonies of Spain and Portugal), trading companies (such as the British and Dutch East India Companies), the military (particularly in the laying out of army cantonments) and the local state or municipality."[240]

Nightingale has analysed the British East India Company's accumulation and exchange of knowledge on infrastructure improvements such as the restructuring of Calcutta over the first half of the 19th century.[241] He underscores the circulation of experiences between London and colonial Calcutta. The network of philosopher Jeremy Bentham's followers illustrates how innovations in urban layouts moved back and forth between the metropole and the colony. Some of the ideas created in India reached London and they impacted the developments at both ends, not just in terms of the built environment but in social relations too. Referring to Bentham's followers, Nightingale remarks,

> "[i]n their enthusiasm, they blurred some of the lines between race politics in the colonies and class politics in Britain."[242]

Libby Porter focused her investigations on the local state and the dominant role planning at the general level, and planning language in particular, played as accomplices of colonial rule.[243] Though her work does not directly address residential segregation, it illustrates the exclusionary character of planning to demonstrate colonial power which still persists today as part of the colonial legacy. Focusing on British White settler colonies, Porter dissects how planning ideas travelled around the globe and further disseminated the coloniser's perspective. [244] Her work made planning's inherent segregationist character as expressed by its prevalent values, habits and expectations transparent. It is necessary to acknowledge this coloniser's narrative in planning, before a critically reflected, more balanced narrative can evolve as part of a piecemeal process. Porter coalesced the negative role that planning typically played for the Indigenous population's life. She argues,

---

[240] Yeoh 1996: 17.
[241] Nightingale 2012: 90-4.
[242] Nightingale 2012: 92.
[243] L. Porter 2010.
[244] L. Porter 2010: 43.

"[i]n the context of settler states this has meant that planning has been, and remains, integrally involved in dispossession."[245]

Linking her argument to Foucault's ideas concerning the production of space, this kind of dispossession is in her opinion embedded in the opposition of two extremely different modes of production, and where the European version was able to dominate the Indigenous one. Due to the similarity of SWA as settler colony, her findings can be transferred and applied to the Territory's case too.

Porter's statements on New Zealand in the context of colonial land acquisition and attempts for 'improvements' wrap up many concerns raised in this review.

> "All of this effort and work in implementing and building spatial cultures into lands not yet European, however, continued to strike up against the lived reality that these were lands already owned and occupied. Far from being a straightforward or clean affair, colonialism is violent, messy, incomplete, and contradictory."[246]

The following chapters are intended to verify the applicability of this statement to the case of Windhoek from a transnational perspective. Prior to this I will look at historical colonial planning debates at the metropole through a journal analysis.

---

[245] L. Porter 2010: 51.
[246] L. Porter 2010: 65.

3. Urban debates - Analysis of historic urban development and planning issues based on a journal evaluation (1910-1945)

Following Saunier's thoughts on transnational history, this chapter is devoted to the analysis of interwar debates on urban development and planning. It comprises analysis and comparison of two planning journals, in order to acquire an understanding of frequently discussed subjects as well as the exchange of ideas among major planning traditions in Europe. The analysis basically serves two purposes, as it first helps to outline the **key topics** discussed, whilst it does secondly identifies **relevant interrelations** between urban development and planning among the European metropoles and with "their" colonial territories. In accordance with Ward[1], the analysis is based on journals representing two of the major planning traditions of those years: for the British context it is *"The Town Planning Review"* and for the German context *"Der Städtebau - Monatsschrift"*.

After an introduction related to the methodological approach (see 3.1 and 3.2), I will present the frequently covered topics (see 3.3). This section is structured according to the analysis results and will give an overview of the most pressing interwar urban debates. The analysis will be complemented by several excursuses, for example on metropolitan reform movements that have subsequently impacted on the colonial environment and which are not mentioned in the journals. These excursuses are intended to better reflect on the overarching context. The chapter does address prevalent social hierarchies, tendencies for class-based segregation, the impact technology and infrastructures have made on cities and their inhabitants' lives. I will use these debates as a link between the metropole andhow similar ideas and concepts were applied to the colonial environment. A specific subchapter will shed light on the quantitative results including the journals' internationality and their coverage of the colonial context and its reception at the metropole (see 3.4).

3.1 Selection criteria for the comparison of planning journals

The decision to analyse *The Town Planning Review* and *Der Städtebau* from among potential journals was made according to four selection criteria. They had to be

---

[1] Aside from Germany and Great Britain, Ward also considers France and the US to form the "major traditions" (Ward 2002: 81-125).

comparable in terms of their *contents*, the *editorial focus* and their overall *structure* as well as regarding their *frequency* of publication. These criteria help to achieve the overall goal of this analysis, as it is intended to compare the results represented in these journals illustrating both, similarities and differences in the planning profession's debate in the United Kingdom, Germany, and beyond national borders.

Hall's summary of the planning profession's evolution as published in 2000 indicates its move towards a distinguishable discipline at the eve of the First World War.[2] Started by Gerd Albers a quarter century earlier in 1975[3] and furthered by Anthony Sutcliffe[4] – the selected journals had to reflect this new standard and self-perception. It underscores the profession's transition from an occupational domain dominated by architects towards a self-contained job profile. Specialised journals focusing exclusively on architectural, technical, legal or aesthetical perspectives were not considered suitable to reflect this change. Instead, the journal's contents had to represent the comprehensive mixture, comprising of administrative or legal issues as well as technical, social and economic questions in urban development at large. In addition to this interdisciplinary background, the selected journals served as a forum to disseminate theoretical debates and to share best practice examples in public administration. Planning relies on the opportunity to discuss different stakeholder's opinions, weighing their arguments, and openness to new ideas. Journals which were either too theoretical / sophisticated or rather superficial in their reports, and did not offer space for discussion, were not suitable for the intended kind of analysis.

The journals in question needed to have a multiplier effect on the larger debate, for which they served as a mouthpiece among the planning community. In order to have such an effect, it required a certain level of editorial professionalism and sufficient reputation in terms of quality. Both selected journals drew a lot of the reputation from their editors and freelance authors contributing articles. For *The Town Planning Review* the list of editors starts in 1910 with Stanley Adshead, who was at the same time appointed as first professor for "Town Planning and Civic Art" at the University of Liverpool's School of Architecture. This professorship was based on a donation by William Lever[5], and – following the university's administrative rules – the journal was initiated as part of the required publications to share the

---

[2] Hall, Peter, *The Centenary of Modern Planning*, London: E&FN Spon 2000: 20 et seqq.
[3] Albers 1975: 16-8.
[4] Sutcliffe, Anthony, *Towards the Planned City: Germany, Britain, the United States and France 1780-1914*, Oxford: Blackwell 1981.
[5] Lever also signed responsible for the model village Port Sunlight close to his new soap factory founded in 1888. Ward 2002: 33.

results of on-going research activities with the interested public.[6] Hereby the foundation was laid for state-of-the-art scholarly articles as part of the regular publications in *The Town Planning Review*. Further contributions came from renowned experts such as Patrick Abercrombie, John Clarke, Wesley Dougill, and Barry Parker, to mention just a few. *Der Städtebau*, on the other hand, was not attached to a university but published as for-profit journal since 1904 under the patronage of changing publishing houses throughout its existence. Nonetheless, it was able to receive contributions from equally renowned authors like its British counterpart. Represented besides the (honorary) founders Camillo Sitte and Theodor Goecke were, amongst others, Werner Hegemann, Robert Schmidt, or Fritz Schumacher.

During the interwar period both journals established themselves among the leading journals for urban planning in their respective language area. Subscriptions to *Der Städtebau*, are reported to have doubled by late 1925 after its relaunch following its interruption in 1923-4.[7] Over the first half of the interwar period the journals served as a platform to present different ideas and to initiate open debates about those ideas' potential advantages and disadvantages for urban development. For the German journal changing political circumstances did not go unnoticed and left an imprint on the editorial focus and style during the second half of the interwar period. Soon after the National Socialists had come into power, they replaced Werner Hegemann with Friedrich Paulsen as *Der Städtebau's* editor-in-chief starting with its April-issue in 1933. From then on the journal abandoned its liberal tradition and was at least subject to self-censorship, if not direct propaganda. *Der Städtebau* decided to be fully in line with the regime's intentions, and Paulsen's articles contained a mix of nationalistic opinions as well as a spirit of Germanic superiority instead. The journal became part of the move for 'Gleichschaltung' (forcible-coordination) that took hold of the whole country, streamlining Germany according to NS intentions. This rupture, in turn, meant a change in the selection of topics for publication as well as the opinion they represented, which reduced *Der Städtebau's* scholarly standing. The British planning community did lose interest in German planning. As Stephen Ward summarised in retrospect, the only achievement that could still attract British attention was the construction of motorways since autobahns remained a propaganda success to the NS regime.[8] In contrast to conferences *The Town Planning Review* did not cover this topic.

Beyond these questions of contents, the journals needed to show a certain level of comparability in terms of their editorial structure, frequency of publication, and

---

[6] TPR (1910) April: no author: 1.
[7] DS (1925) 9/10: no author: no page.
[8] Ward 2002: 94.

number of pages. In terms of structure both are similarly arranged, with editorial forewords in some issues, usually followed by several longer articles on current planning affairs, and concluded by a variety of abstracts on passing events, news, competitions and book reviews. Another requirement affects the continuity of publication which should be ensured at least for the full interwar years from 1919 to 1939, and preferably covers wartimes too. In order to compare potential references to Germany's colonial cities before the country had lost all colonial possessions according to the Treaty of Versailles they should cover a few years before the outbreak of the First World War as well. Interruptions or reduced frequencies, for example due to shortages in paper supply during wartimes, have been anticipated and are taken into consideration. With regards to the criterion of frequency, whereas *The Town Planning Review* was originally published as quarterly journal, *Der Städtebau* was a monthly journal. Since all statistics of the analysis are only produced at an annual basis – as will be described in the section below – the difference is insignificant though. The same applies to wartimes, when the British journal's publishing activities had been impacted and were limited to one (extended) issue per year. Unfortunately, *Der Städtebau* ceased to publish in 1923 and 1924, due to then financial turmoil in Germany.

In conclusion, *The Town Planning Review* and *Der Städtebau* complied with this set of formal criteria. The publications are in their vast majority still available, either electronically (as is the case for *The Town Planning Review*) or as hard copies scattered at different university libraries across Germany in case of *Der Städtebau*. The collection for this journal remains incomplete for two reasons: in a few cases a single edition or just a few pages within were missing; the 1937 volume of *Der Städtebau* I was unable to retrieve a copy[9] and had to exclude it from detailed analyses. The focus is on the years from 1910 to 1939 plus the two wartime volumes of *The Town Planning Review* for 1942 and 1943 into account. Whilst there are no volumes for the German perspective, at least the British journal provides insights into wartime planning debates.

---

[9] At Bochum's Ruhr-University library this volume was officially listed and I saw the gap on the shelf. Despite careful attempts to retrieve it by several staff members over more than a week, they were unable to locate the book and reported it as lost.

3.2 Methodological approach towards the journal evaluation

As already indicated in the previous section, the analysis of both planning journals serves two fundamental goals. First it helps to trace the most relevant interwar urban developments and planning ideas in the European context, which formed the background canvas to what planners were confronted with in interwar years. Secondly, it follows Saunier's approach to transnational history and serves to describe the international setup for exchange among planners. Attention is paid to the developments in European and colonial cities, and their relations with the metropoles and other colonial entities.

Although the topic of this work deals with policies aimed to implement residential segregation in faraway Windhoek, with all its individual peculiarities and local circumstances, it is crucial to bear in mind that planning in the colonial context was not detached from developments in the major planning traditions of the Northern hemisphere. The vast majority of colonial planners had at least been educated in European institutions before they graduated from them. They either became members of the immediate colonial administrative system or started working on behalf of other interested (private) stakeholders. This circulation of staff members familiar with urban problems through the lens of European cities led to a paradoxical situation. These planners were trained to address urban problems based on values and tools developed for this specific societal context but their work desks would be thousands of kilometres away. Planners took with them experiences, mind-sets and standards of evaluation developed under different social, legal, political and economic networks of European to the colonial cities, where they mostly applied them often regardless of their (in)appropriateness for this context. In addition to these direct human links, planning ideas were travelling through the printed word – either as legal documents, direct commands, personal letters, and reports reflecting on one of the international city conferences – or eventually as journals.

These journals and other means of communication represented an important link for established colonial planners and staff members 'on the spot' to the latest urban trends. Some planners did not have the chance or permission for personal travels to the European heartlands. Examples from London, Paris or Berlin were the blueprints and yardsticks of what the future of colonial cities should look like from the administrative perspective, though such attempts to copy amenities usually remained limited in their availability to the imperial ruling elite. Then up-to-date statistical reports, like those cited by Paul Barth in 1926, suggest that the colonies' European communities were assiduous readers and recipients of reports and news from "home" as demonstrated by the amount of postal items dispatched to SWA.[10] A specific overview on Windhoek administration's main sources of information is given below (see 4.2.2), and in retrospect Brenda Bravenboer similarly hints at the city's various growing library collections.[11]

Key questions addressed in the journal analysis

The analysis will help summarise the most relevant challenges in urban development and planning based on the following questions: *What were the frequently discussed urban problems from their viewpoint and which ones were in turn considered as less important? What kind of potential solutions were discussed?* This overall picture is necessary to reflect the urgency of certain topics and decisions taken, also with regards to similar developments in Windhoek, and helps to identify key positions and schools of thought then articulated among the planning community. Additionally, my analysis can create an image that varies from retrospective perceptions as given in secondary literature. In the following subchapters I will first summarise the historic findings based on the results of my journal analysis before I give further contextualisation with current descriptions.

Following the identification of those general debates, the second layer of the analysis is dedicated to the matter of internationality and searches for examples of direct links within the planning profession. At this stage, my work will focus on the question: *How open to foreign ideas and international debates was the coverage in the respective planning journals?* I analyse the ratio between domestic and foreign topics or case studies covered and list the countries referred. Were the authors only focusing on the major planning traditions in Ward's sense, or did they include contributions from smaller countries too? It is my goal to trace articles on international matters like congresses, exhibitions or direct comparisons between different national policies or planning approaches. The investigation of those international links does then focus on specific developments in colonial cities. Were colonial cities covered at all? If so, what colonial cities are included and how many times are they referred? In case of the British Empire did *The Town Planning Review* exclusively focus on White settlement colonies like Australia or on the other colonial domains, or if the

---

[10] Barth, Paul, *Südwest-Afrika*, Windhoek: John Meinert 1926: 136-7. For 1924 Paul Barth referred to statistics which recorded more than 3.4 million postal items as delivered to the 20,000 European inhabitants in SWA.

[11] Bravenboer 2004: 73, 243. During the last 12 years of German rule, Windhoek's Public Library collected almost 2,900 books. The *Scientific Society of South West Africa* gathered a collection of 8,000 scientific journals since the 1920s. Bravenboer's figures are supported by an estimation of 2,200 volumes in the library's annual report for 1910 (NAN SVW B.9.c, sheet 14).

reports included both categories. In what style have these reports been written? And, last, what conclusions were drawn in the metropoles from the developments at the perceived periphery? Were these contributions written in a sentiment of fascination and curiosity for the "Other" world "out there", or were the developments considered to be of equal importance to those in Europe? What kind of subtle undertones or hidden images might have been conveyed through these articles? I intend to examine potential references to the Indigenous population's perspective, if indeed it was covered at all. If and to what extent there were traces for an exchange of planning ideas between colonial cities and the metropoles that were not a one-sided relation but mirrored the adaptation of European trends back to their places of origin. In order to make the analysis and comparison of both journals tangible, I will identify examples of direct exchange and where planners crossed borders for conferences and work. They acted as intermediaries in Saunier's sense[12], who initiated a circulation of ideas between metropoles and periphery as well as among both categories.

Analytical procedures

My approach to answer these various questions is based on a qualitative and quantitative analysis of both planning journals. As a first approximation, I listed all available contributions for every single edition from 1910 to 1939 (*Der Städtebau*, with the exceptions of 1923/4 and 1937) or 1943 (*The Town Planning Review*), creating a catalogue with all headlines and the authors' names which can later be searched by particular keywords. All articles were examined to judge their contents and categorise them according to their focus. Initially I created four categories to sort the articles:

Category

a) **Particular country:** if they were addressing a specific case study city, competition, or explaining a new law that is clearly based on respective national circumstances, or if it resembled a kind of travel report on that very country.

b) **International matters:** if their content was explicitly contrasting at least two case studies in two different countries, or reporting on international conferences, excursions and the like, as well as historical descriptions on urban development if they were clearly referring to several countries beyond mere name-dropping.

---

[12] Saunier 2013: 42.

c) **General matters:** if they report on or compare historic urban challenges without direct reference to a particular nation, or if these challenges were of an unspecific nature. Aesthetic debates are one example for this category, as there were several series on the question of how to design streets, open spaces and where to place street furniture. But this category does also comprise of historical summaries on urban development without clear national references, or of socio-economic debates. Similarly, new technologies like aerial photography[13] and photogrammetry, which had been introduced during the interwar decades, and which showed subsequent impacts on the planning profession at large, are subsumed here.

d) Originally, **editorial news and forewords** were collected as a separate category. In quantitative terms they turned out to be negligible and were merged with the general matters. They will be considered if they indicate a new editorial policy for one of the journals.

For the category of *particular countries*, there is a question as to how to draw national territorial borders. This problem becomes more delicate considering the extent of the analysis, spanning roughly 30 years; a phase that saw several turning points redrawing and adjusting the borders by political contract or military force throughout these decades. Since the original premise for the analysis was the period between 1914 and 1945, whereas the pre-First World War editions are only considered as part of the journal analysis to trace potential references to German colonies, I decided to rely on a year close to the mean at the turn of 1929/1930. This decision was then supported by the Statute of Westminster, defining the sovereignty of British Commonwealth nations and Dominions in 1931. Therefore, all articles referring to a particular city are sorted according to the country's national borders as internationally recognised on 1st December 1931. Articles already published before, will be considered from the point of view of this date as will be all articles published thereafter. This approach to define borders intends to maintain comparability of the analytical results over the full period, without the need to divide the analysis into several chronological subchapters which do not generate substantial additional benefits or insights for this work.

For example, even though reports on the city of Merano in 1910 were actually written under the auspices of the Austro-Hungarian monarchy, they are considered as an Italian contribution to which the city belonged in 1931. Specific rules apply to colonial entities such as Algeria or Malta. In order to identify articles on them as

---

[13] DS (1919) 3/4: Abendroth: 28-32; (1920) 5/6: Abendroth: 46-50; (1926) 12: no author: 186.

contributions about colonial matters, these territories are considered as separate countries, and not as part of the French or British Empire. The latter recognition of Algeria as French *département* would have, at least, distorted – if not destroyed – one of the key objectives of this analysis, which is to investigate colonial contributions to both planning journals. Where I refer to these cases in my description of the results and conclusions, the ruling imperial power or specific context is mentioned.

In order to adequately visualise the quantitative extent of international coverage in both planning journals, particular efforts have been devoted to review the articles and count their respective pages.[14] I have set the absolute quantitative minimum for every article to be considered in the statistical assessment at half a page, although not just the mere text counted but illustrations, even if these were not published immediately within or close to the article but as plates in separate sections of the journals. Due to printing procedures, the latter form was very common for the earlier volumes. Short contributions of less than half a page were not counted for the statistical analysis. They do not show up in the final results but these neglected contributions remain at marginal levels. Such brief news represented slightly more than ten percent of all pages in exceptional years, and – on average – around seven percent for *The Town Planning Review* and less than six percent, on average, for *Der Städtebau*. Examples of how the counting procedures were managed are demonstrated in the following illustrations.

Figure 2: Journal Analysis: a) Contribution not considered; b) Example of half-page contribution; c) Example of one-page contribution

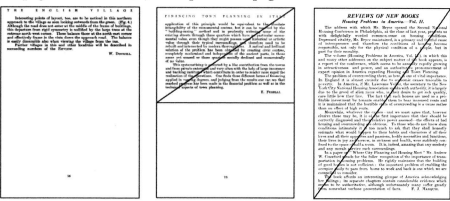

[14] This task turned out to be a time consuming and demanding issue, hovering between the need to keep it at a manageable workload and to reflect the articles and their contents as precise as possible.

89

Figure 2 a) shows a short article which was not counted for the statistical journal analysis, whereas the next text in **figure 2 b)** ideally qualifies to be considered as the minimum half-page contribution. Another easy to judge on example is the full one-page contribution in **figure 2 c)**.

Of course not all articles fitted exactly with these examples, particularly if they were spanning over several pages. In this case I rounded off the counts. **Figure 3** demonstrates an example that counted as two-page contribution.

All results of these page-counting activities were accumulated, sorted and displayed based on the three major categories already described above. They represented an annual basis for the *particular countries* as well as for *general* and *international matters*. Through this approach I was able to calculate the percentages for all countries in

Figure 3: Journal analysis: Example of two-page contribution

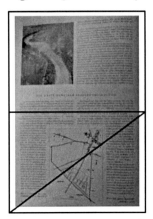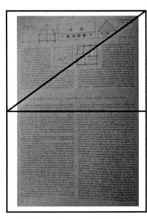

order to visualise their distribution in both journals. In addition I could differentiate accordingly between the share of reports on domestic and foreign cases in relation to overall coverage. Articles that did not fall under one of these categories, like single reports on small countries, are represented under the category "not shown." **Figures 4 and 5** illustrate the results for *The Town Planning Review* and *Der Städtebau* respectively.

Figure 4: Journal Analysis: International coverage - The Town Planning Review

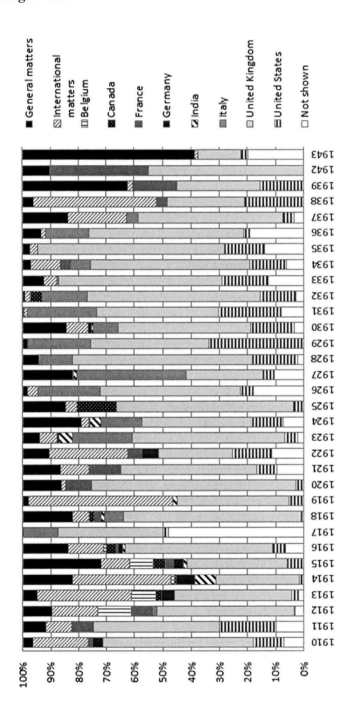

Figure 5: Journal Analysis: International coverage - Der Städtebau

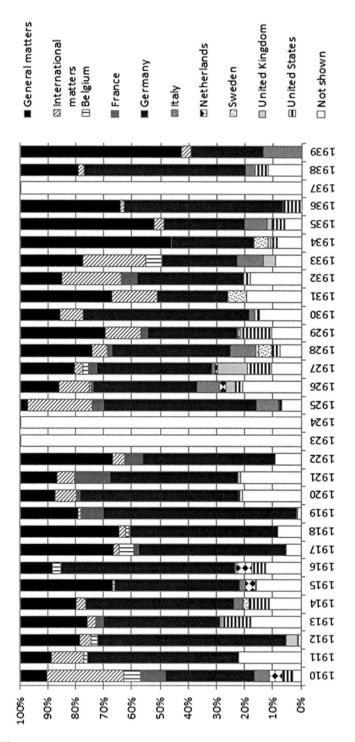

3.3 Findings of the journals' evaluation

The above stated methods produced a set of results which are shedding some light on the various questions and goals, as laid out in the previous section. As a starting point, the analysis of both planning journals does help to realise the key challenges in urban development from a historic standpoint. Based on the collection of headlines, there appear certain topics that were the focus of attention in many articles, and, hence, seemed to have dominated those days' agenda. Debates related to planning the realms of the tangible built environment such as housing, public health concerns and transportation infrastructure can be separated from debates on the legal realms and potential impacts of then introduced new laws. These two realms dominated the debates in both language areas, and they were linked at several levels. Nevertheless, there were various other topics and national specificities, which will be addressed in the following sections.

Topics covered in the journals

The number of contributions devoted to each topic already gives a rough indication of its perceived significance among the planning community. **Figures 6 and 7** visualise a collection of the most frequently addressed topics from 1910 to 1943 for *The Town Planning Review* and until 1939 for *Der Städtebau* respectively. For each year it is indicated if at all and how many articles were devoted to one of the listed subjects whilst grey dots mark certain peaks (light grey: >3, dark grey: >6, black: >10). All topics considered here were classified as either related to developments in the colonies, to the built environment, or to legal frameworks.[15] My results of the journal analysis are corroborated by a summary written by then editor-in-chief of *Der Städtebau* Friedrich Paulsen in 1935. In his review of "La città moderna", a book originally written by Cesare Chiodi to summarise challenges in Italian urban development, Paulsen admitted that those challenges were of similar significance in the German context. He listed traffic, means of transportation, housing, green spaces, renovation of city centres and city extension, as well as spatial planning as core subjects.[16] This collection mirrors my general analysis findings with some additions, for example regarding the question of legal frameworks, which Paulsen did not refer despite many on-going discussions in Germany and abroad. The significance of hygiene and social welfare considerations are prominent. Though it was a major concern of planners in those years to improve urban living conditions, many articles dealing with these issues were entitled unspecifically with the 'renova-

---

[15] Although several keywords were used, these collections may still be a bit distorted, since some potentially relevant articles referring to the same topic were published under non-related headlines.

[16] DS (1935) 7: Paulsen: 84.

tion of city centres', or they simply described the layout of 'green spaces.' Therefore, every contribution was skim read in order to reflect its actual contents, irrespective of the article's headline.

Contextualisation into the colonial environment

The journal analysis helps identify a collection of important challenges to urban development. It is my intention to further contextualise these findings within relevant planning debates as presented in secondary literature of the time. Whereas some European topics were merely echoed, two challenges require a more detailed assessment of their context as they shed light on the planning community's social thinking and habits at large. In this respect housing was not just a matter of quantity and how to accommodate the people. Instead, it touched social concerns such as public health, and many interwar housing schemes were intended to transform the way of living in fundamental terms. Hence, a total of four excursuses will summarise the social backgrounds and aspirations affiliated with some of the schemes and try to illustrate how those schemes were used to carry out a domestic civilising mission towards the urban poor. This mission intended to create the 'New Man' before similar ideas were applied to the colonial environment (see 3.3.2 and 3.3.5). Infrastructures were equally charged with an idealised image as being carriers of 'modernisation', and therefore their impact on the metropole and the colonial entities will be investigated further in three excursuses (see 3.3.2 and 3.3.4).

Basically, infrastructures have impacted urban development in the colonial context at three levels: first the rise of motor traffic and its consequences for the city's lifestyle and structures. Secondly, new technologies like aviation opened new perspectives on the cityscape and offered additional options for surveillance. The final level represents a mix of the previous two and links them with the provision of electricity. Although electric power had a tremendous impact on cities in industrialised countries and helped to transform society towards mass consumption and culture, and linked to the diffusion of electrical household appliances meant as symbols of 'progress' at home. On this basis I will investigate the case study of Windhoek and to what extent similar images have played a role in that colonial context.

Figure 6: Journal Analysis: Frequently discussed topics - Der Städtebau

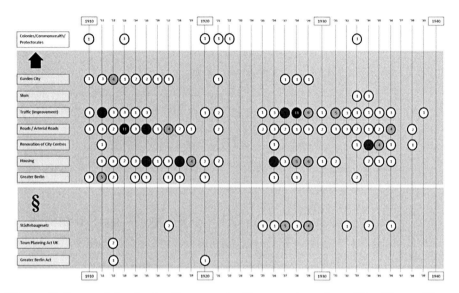

Figure 7: Journal Analysis: Frequently discussed topics - The Town Planning Review

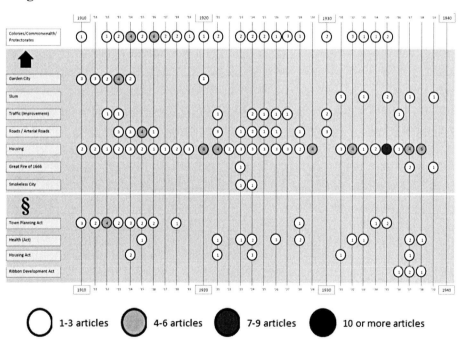

3.3.1 Housing challenges

For both journals housing remained a pressing issue in virtually every volume. The initial challenge was housing shortage. This turned out to be very urgent during and after the First World War in both countries, though for different reasons. A first extensive contribution as to the lack of supply on Germany appeared in 1915. Berlin-based architect Steinbrücker pointed to the financial constraints leading to insufficient resources being allocated to housing construction, whilst the limited building materials available during wartimes remained unmentioned.[17] References were made to illustrate miserable living conditions and the need to develop proper schemes for small houses. This latter challenge dominated the housing debate in Germany during the years preceding the Great War and to a certain extent anticipated later attempts such as Ernst May's concepts for 'minimum housing' ('Wohnen für das Existenzminimum', see 3.3.2 and 3.3.5). Housing construction was suspended during the war and despite various efforts to encourage housing construction, the problem still remained urgent as late as 1926 when one article reported on creative ways to deal with the shortage through the reuse of former railway carriages.[18] Some stereotypical correlations between bad housing conditions through overcrowding and social or sexual offences persisted. They were brought back to the planning community's attention by Werner Hegemann in his 1926 review of Victor Noack's book "Die Wohnungsnot als Sexualproblem" (Housing Shortage as Sex Problem).[19] This book, published by Berlin's then-mayor, was based on official statistical reports for the capital city about the spread of venereal diseases with a focus on children, linking housing questions with public health considerations. Although Hegemann admitted that overcrowding had decreased slightly in comparison to previous decades due to lower birth rates and smaller families, the issue of subletting to non-relatives remained a pressing one. Thus social problems attached to these trends in housing seemed to regain momentum by the mid-1920s, as the figures in Noack's book suggest. Noack and his publications were banned by the National Socialists as part of their 'Action Against the un-German Spirit'.[20]

The journal articles reported that housing shortages remained a problem in Germany despite all efforts to register the existing housing stock and potentially identify vacant dwellings[21]and governmental policies to fight the housing shortage.[22]

---

[17] DS (1915) 12: Steinbrücker: 114-6.
[18] DS (1926) 7: Elkart: 105.
[19] DS (1926) 1: Hegemann: 16.
[20] Website Berlin: http://www.berlin.de/geschichte/verbannte-buecher/ (retrieved on 24.04.2015).
[21] DS (1926) 11: no author: 176; (1928) 3: no author: 76.

Some articles underscore attempts to improve the scientific basis for planning decisions based on demographic statistics, in order to make best use of the available resources. Housing construction was considered as part the compromise between demography and economy. Interestingly, the discussed demographic trends of the late 1920s sound familiar to those faced today, with population growth based on migration for certain urban areas, an ageing society, and the creation of new households due to structural changes regarding family backgrounds. In his article based on official statistical data by the *Statistische Reichsamt* (Reich's Statistical Office) published in 1931, Martin Pfannschmidt calculated this with two figures: the existing housing shortage estimated at 600,000 to 1,000,000 units in 1925; and the additional demand due to on-going demographic trends, calculated at an annual 284,400 for the peak years 1930 to 1935, thus 50,000 more than during the period between 1925 and 1930.[23] The only comprehensive official census of dwelling units carried out in interwar years, the 1927 *Reichswohnungszählung*, estimated a deficit of 750,000 flats across Germany and revealed the country's overcrowded housing situation that directly affected 3.2 million dwellers of small-size apartments.[24] Another report published in 1936, conceded a more or less similar situation, though the figures might have been whitewashed for propaganda purposes. The structural housing shortage was estimated at minimum 1,000,000 units and an additional demand of at least 700,000 needed to be constructed by 1945 in order to accommodate people already living in the cities under poor conditions.[25] This goal was put out of reach with the outbreak of the Second World War. Another indication of the persisting housing shortage canbe found in the extremely low vacancy rates across Germany. A comprehensive statistical evaluation published in *Der Städtebau* in 1928 came to the conclusion that only 0.4% of all flats were registered as vacant, and this number was slightly lower for cities with 0.3%. These percentages were significantly lower than the 2 to 3% on record for pre-Great War years.[26] Those 2 to 3% can be considered as marginal and are still today referred to as structural vacancy rate due to residents' change of domicile.[27] It can be concluded that German authorities failed to keep their constitutional obligations as laid down in § 119 of Weimar Constitution (Weimarer Reichsverfassung) related to the pro-

---

[22] DS (1928) 1: Adler: 24.

[23] DS (1931) 10: Pfannschmidt: 479.

[24] Rodenstein, Marianne; Böhm-Ott, Stefan: *Gesunde Wohnungen und Wohnungen für gesunde Deutsche*. In: Kähler, Gert [Ed.]: Geschichte des Wohnens – Band 4. Stuttgart: Deutsche Verlagsanstalt 1996: 466-71.

[25] DS (1936) 5: Neumann: 50.

[26] DS (1928) 3: no author: 76.

[27] E.g. Stadt Frankfurt 2013: 3.

tection of marriages[28] and § 155 related to the distribution of land and the aimed for provision of a flat to every German.

The British situation

For the British the housing question was mostly affiliated with poorer parts of the population, and articles focused on living qualities rather than quantities. In 1913 Mr Marquis's review in "Warburton Lectures on Housing" published by Rowntree and Pigou referred to inadequate living conditions for the poor, which in turn allegedly provided the ideal environment for "crime and debauchery." The authors argued that this problem could only be eradicated through an attempt to completely restructure housing the poor in new neighbourhoods at new sites. This approach would serve to create "a better race" in the long run, which indicates again the close interrelations with public health considerations and a rather holistic interest in social reform.[29]Such ideas were not completely new to the British context, as the Boer War and the national efficiency debate illustrate[30] (see the excursus in 3.3.5). Similar motives lead governmental policies drafted during the First World War and called for the construction of better housing schemes for returning soldiers in order to compensate for their sacrifices in the trenches. One editorial summarised a 1916 parliamentary debate intended to secure funding for Prime Minister Lloyd George's "Homes fit for Heroes" programme.[31] Mr. Shawcross, chairman of the parliamentary deputation, emphasised the close link to public health when he stated,

> "that the provision of housing was the most important of all efforts for social improvement, that it lies at the root of all social reform, and that it is the most pressing."[32]

The close of the Great War brought reports of a more demanding character referring to quantitative deficiencies. Estimations in 1918 ranged between 500,000 and 1,000,000 units as backlog across the UK, and these figures were complemented by an estimated additional annual demand of 100,000 dwellings to cater for the population growth, plus an indefinite number for the replacement of existing slums.[33]

---

[28] Rodenstein, Böhm-Ott 1996: 474.
[29] TPR (1913) July: Marquis: 160-1.
[30] During the Boer War in 1899-1902 one third of all potential recruits were refused by the military for health reasons and insufficient physical condition (Hopkins 1990: 145).
[31] Hopkins 1990: 225.
[32] TPR (1916) October: no author: 2.
[33] TPR (1918) April: no author: 219-20.

The full extent of this situation is illustrated by John Clarke in his 1926 review of three international retrospective publications on housing.

"The numerical shortage of houses and the urgency of the need have surpassed anything known before."[34]

Similar to Germany, sub-let houses were described as a challenge, as exemplified in 1920 in Liverpool where 16,600 houses were reported to have been used under these conditionshousing approximately 150,000 people.[35] In the general planning debate such congested neighbourhoods were affiliated with the spread of diseases such as tuberculosis – with more than 1,600 registered cases treated at Liverpool's medical institutions in 1918.[36] These figures formed the ammunition for authors to argue in favour of a concerted action, not just against the structural shortage, but against still existing and tolerated miserable living conditions in slum-like areas too. The British Government tried to keep faith to her wartime promises of "homes fit for heroes" and used many means at her disposal to fight the housing shortage at the legal and financial front. Ward refers to the instrument of 'council houses' as one such remedy[37], although its quantitative extent remained limited compared to private housing construction before the Great War. As of late August 1920 many projects were on their way, and a meticulously organised questionnaire addressed to all local authorities was meant to help provide for a comprehensive overview of the current housing sector's status. The questionnaire was part of the obligations introduced through the *Housing, Town Planning, etc., Act, 1919* and Longstreth Thompson devoted an elaborate review on its results.[38] Based on the replies received from across the country, it became apparent that just a tiny fraction of the projected housing units were finished (5,231), whilst another 140,000 had been approved, although these figures were still not sufficient to balance the immediate demand projected at 800,000 units.[39] In addition, the results generated based on those questionnaires were not per se considered as truly reflecting the housing situation for the whole country, and were put into question.[40] Articles on housing in Great Britain, again, turned their attention to the question of quality over the following years, while quantitative deficiencies remained relevant to rehousing the population of existing slum-like areas. Hall produced a description of the extraor-

---

[34] TPR (1926) November: Clarke: 139.
[35] TPR (1920) April: Kyffin-Taylor: 110-1, 114.
[36] TPR (1920) April: Kyffin-Taylor: 110-1, 114.
[37] Ward 2004: 16.
[38] TPR (1920) December: Thompson: 145-62.
[39] TPR (1920) December: Thompson: 162.
[40] TPR (1921) March: no author: 58.

dinarily bad living conditions in such neighbourhoods that developed in late 19th century London.[41]

The post-Great War housing markets on the continent as well as the UK were transformed by a shift towards state intervention as some early figures in *The Town Planning Review* indicate: for 1922 it was assumed that out of the 800,000 dwellings needed to ease the most urgent demand, 88% were constructed as part of municipal activities; whilst Public Utility Societies responsible for 6%; and private activities for the remaining 6%. These turned pre-war statistics upside down, since private enterprise used to provide for 95% before the Great War.[42] Coincidentally, Berlin replicated the British statistics almost exactly. By the mid-1920s 6.3% of all loans for subsidised dwellings were given out to low-income families (*Einzelsiedler*) willing but otherwise unable to become owner occupiers, whereas the overwhelming majority was constructed by large societies.[43] This picture persisted during the following years, although private persons were eligible to apply for loans granted out of the German housing-tax revenues.

Explanations for the interwar housing shortage

The housing shortage was easy to identify in the cessation of the building construction during the Great War, which subsequently worsened the backlog post war. This backlog became tangible in the number of sub-let houses situated in overcrowded neighbourhoods. The shortage was affected by financial calculations made by those private investors, who used to fund the overwhelming parts of housing construction. As one contribution to *The Town Planning Review* in 1918 explains from the private investors' point of view, investments in housing, with its protective measures for tenants introduced during war times, did not promise profits at such attractive levels as were attainable in other post-war or overseas businesses.[44] In consequence, the available private financial resources remained insufficient to fight the shortage in face of post-war inflation[45] which kept interest rates at high levels. Such a negative financial environment added to the complexity of the housing question in the aftermath of the First World War. While private investments were at a low, public bodies were forced to take the initiative but they were faced with another monetary challenge. Both planning journals similarly reported about problems created by rising construction costs in Germany and the

---

[41] Hall, Peter, *Cities of Tomorrow - An Intellectual History of Urban Planning and Design Since 1880*, Chichester: Wiley Blackwell 2014: 12-48.
[42] TPR (1920) December: Thompson: 145-6.
[43] DS (1926) 11: no author: 176.
[44] TPR (1918) April: no author: 221.
[45] Ward 2004: 37.

UK as well as other countries like Denmark, where costs for governmental building contracts were reported to have more than doubled between 1913 and 1919.[46]

These increases represented a severe obstacle to swiftly respond to the housing demand. In 1920 Longstreth Thompson gave a brief exemplary summary of the reasons and identified two major challenges. Firstly, the construction business was hit hard by a shortage of skilled labourers by the war effect. Besides young men not having the opportunity to pursue their apprenticeship in construction, the industry suffered from losses on the battlefields as well as from former tradesmen, who took up a new profession upon their return from the trenches. Secondly, Thompson considered the output to be low due to a perceived, but in his opinion unjustified, psychologically motivated fear of becoming unemployed if the constructions had been completed too fast.[47] For the German context, the limited output was excacebated by the coal shortage as well as a bad food situation after the end of war.In one article published in *Der Städtebau* in 1922, complaints were still reported about the struggle to find new apprentices in building trades.[48] As a result, wages rose significantly over the following years and remained for long-term periods at a higher level than the average incomes in many other industries, as one comparison of prices for 1914 and 1932 in the UK and US indicates.[49] The extent of inflationreached its peak in the UK in 1920, when Thompson delivered his elaborate contribution to *The Town Planning Review* quoted before, soaring inflation has hit Germany until 1923. The situation was hampered by monopolies in the construction business trying to keep prices for materials at high levels, as was exemplified for light castings following an investigation by the 'Committee on Light Castings' for the Lloyd George Coalition Government in 1919.[50] Aside from general inflation Germany was hit hard by soaring prices for building materials like construction timber, where post-Great War prices in 1919 were reported to have risen by 2,264% in comparison to 1914 prices; similar trends applied to cement (+1,915%) or bricks (+800%), increasing the price for one cubic metre of masonry including wages from 14 marks to between 180 and 200 marks.[51] A substantial part of those price increases in Germany can be attributed to the prevailing shortage in coal supply which had, in consequence, curtailed the output in other industries.

---

[46] DS (1919) 1/2: no author: 24.
[47] TPR (1920) December: Thompson: 157-8.
[48] DS (1922) 3/4: no author: 40.
[49] DS (1935) 4: no author: 44.
[50] TPR (1923) September: Clarke: 216-7.
[51] DS (1920) 3/4: no author: 39.

Excursus: The Extent of the Housing Shortage

As already carved out in the previous analysis of contributions to *The Town Planning Review* and *Der Städtebau*, housing was one of the key topics in industrialised countries throughout the interwar period. As Hall summarises,

> "[…] that twentieth-century city planning, as an intellectual and professional movement, essentially represents a reaction to the evils of the nineteenth-century city."[52]

In order to reflect some of these evils, I will go beyond what was reported in the journals' mainstream agenda, and this excursus will combine some additional interwar years' opinions with the prevalent reform ideas which permeated the housing debate. These reformist concepts form an essential key to understanding why housing was perceived as an important social challenge that went far beyond the mere quantitative aspects. Aspirations to create a new society need to be borne in mind as the comprehensive reference framework when it comes to certain planning habits and concepts that directly impacted the colonial context.

The architect Frederick Ackerman, editor-in-chief Charles Whitaker, and two more colleagues tried to illustrate the complexity of the housing question in a joint publication they prepared on behalf of *The Journal of the American Institute of Architects* in 1918, and in which they drew on European examples from architectural, administrative and legal perspectives.[53] Referring British housing policies, which were considered as a potential blueprint for interventions in the domestic housing market in the US-American planning debate – similar to Rodgers's transatlantic findings in social politics – Ackerman then stated,

> "[i]t is not enough to understand the elaborate legislative technique surrounding the British operation, nor will mere graphic descriptions of the schemes suffice. We must understand fully the forces which brought about this new condition in England in order that we may determine what phases of English methods are applicable in America."[54]

The quantitative limitations in housing supply did play a role for many commentators. In 1920 Morris Knowles estimated the "house famine" at two million missing residential units in the US alone[55], when the author – trained and registered as civil

---

[52] Hall [1988] 2014: 7.

[53] Whitaker, Charles Harris/Ackerman, Frederick L./Childs, Richard S./Wood, Edith Elmer, *The Housing Problem in War and in Peace*, Washington D.C.: The Journal of the American Institute of Architects 1918.

[54] Whitaker, *et al.* 1918: 17.

[55] Knowles 1920: 9-10.

engineer and town planner on both sides the Atlantic –the levels necessary to produce housing at industrial scales. Virtually all industrialising countries around the world were facing similar problems, as Charles Whitaker emphasised in his book chapter "The House and the Home – A World Problem" stating that,

"[t]oday the attention of a large part of the world is directed to the housing problem. […] The housing question will not down, nor will it be content with the palliatives of the past."[56]

When talking about those "palliatives", Whitaker referred to various attempts that were made in the late 19th century to remedy the severe housing shortage due to the first major industrialisation and its subsequent unprecedented urbanisation, which had been grounded in Britain's first planning legislation such as the *Public Health Act* of 1875[57] with its bye-laws and the complementing *Housing of the Working Classes Act* of 1890.[58] Knowles differentiated three phases for early industrial housing improvements which he labelled as periods of *criticism, study* and *construction*.[59] According to his framework, *criticism* referred to 'early humanitarians' like Robert Owen, owner of a Scottish textile mill at New Lanark, who experimented with 'model' tenements for his employees based on cooperative ideas at the beginning of the 19th century. Following the period of *study*, that was characterised by an investigation of different reasons and theories behind possible housing improvements, the last period of *construction* represented the time at which Knowles's book had been published.

"The present stage of the movement for better housing may be described as one of preventive, constructive and economic activity."[60]

At this stage he assumed that the newly enacted planning tools made available through the British *Housing, Town Planning, Etc., Act* 1909 effectively helped to replace the outdated and by then unlawful monotonous neighbourhoods with their seemingly endless rows of back-to-back houses. These originated from the first planning laws before the turn of the century and came under sharp criticism for their poor living qualities. In addition, George Cadbury, Jr. – who was a member

---

[56] Whitaker, Charles Harris, *The Joke about Housing*, Boston: Marshall Jones Company 1920: 26-7.
[57] Although other laws such as the *Public Health Act* 1848, the *Common Lodging Houses Acts* 1851 and 1853 or the *Sanitation Act*, 1866 had been passed prior to this Act, they proved to be ineffective with regards to the construction of sanitary housing and were therefore neglected by authors like Ackerman, Cadbury and Whitaker.
[58] Whitaker, *et al.* 1918: 24.
[59] Knowles 1920: 4-6.
[60] Knowles 1920: 5.

of Birmingham City Council's Town Planning Committee – underscored those neighbourhoods' lack of green spaces, complementing their architectural monotony and creating an environment that deprived its inhabitants from the basic need to experience nature. Surprisingly, Cadbury, in contradiction of his critique, explicitly affirmed the settlements' general healthy conditions despite their lack of air and light.[61] Considered as part of the "preventive activity" quoted above, the new planning legislation was grounded in experiences made with model settlements like Port Sunlight or Bourneville, and it was inspired by reform ideas like those for Garden Cities formulated by Ebenezer Howard (see 3.3.2).[62] Further steps were taken in the amended *Housing, Town Planning, Etc., Act* to which some sources referred to as *Addison's Town and Country Planning Act* – named after then President of the Local Government Board and Minister of Reconstruction and Health Dr Christopher Addison – and which had been passed in 1919, subsequently initiated new construction activities.

Beyond the Germany and the UK, the cessation of building activities during the First World War added to the already existing shortages prior to its outbreak. The consequences were felt in large and smaller countries alike, regardless of whether or not they were located in one of the combatting nations. Zurich's vacancy rate dropped to a record low of 0.05 percent in 1919 and in retrospect Hans-Rudolf Galliker marked this situation as typical for all across Switzerland's cities at that time.[63] Therefore, Edith Elmer Wood concluded her 1918 analysis of industrialised countries' housing situation with reference to their difference in degree but not in kind.[64] As an attempt to maintain social peace and to avoid riots over insufficient housing supply, many governments introduced measures to control rents. The British Government tried to fight excessive price increases and therefore passed the *Increase of Rent and Mortgage Interest (War Restrictions) Act, 1916* through which rents were frozen at 1914 levels.[65] Such measures seemed to be reasonable under the given circumstances but considering higher costs for borrowing capital they did not, and were not intended to, stimulate housing construction. Given the lack of labour and financial resources, it does not come as a surprise that housing construction virtually ceased. Severe overcrowding was one of the results which Galliker described as housing misery in neutral Zurich during the immediate years to

---

[61] Cadbury, George Junior, *Town Planning: With Special Reference to the Birmingham Schemes*, London *et al.*: Longmans, Green and Co. 1915: 113.

[62] Whitaker, *et al.* 1918: 24.

[63] Galliker, Hans-Rudolf, *Tramstadt: Öffentlicher Nahverkehr und Stadtentwicklung am Beispiel Zürichs*, Zürich: Chronos 1997: 130.

[64] Whitaker, *et al.* 1918: 76.

[65] Hopkins 1990: 215.

follow the war.[66] The situation was equally difficult in the UK as noted by Unwin in *Nothing Gained by Overcrowding* in 1912.[67] Surprisingly, despite his work's significance it drew very little attention in contributions to *The Town Planning Review.*

Reactions to the shortage

Goverments were determined to cope with housing shortages and rising prices as *The Town Planning Review* reported by centralised purchasing, as was the case in the UK. In the first years following the Great War the formally responsible Ministry of Health was assisted by a new specialised bureau but the attempts were at the same time accompanied by moves towards greater rationalisation.[68] Based on the ideas of Taylorism and Fordism, mass production was to become part of the housing construction business, as the first application of techniques to work with standardised concrete and steel reinforcement in-situ illustrate.[69] Already during the First World War, calls for standardisation in architecture were formulated in the planning journals in order to cut costs through new norms and standards for doors, windows or larger bricks, to mention few examples.[70] Such attempts to use economies of scale became popular among architects and the broader planning community, and permeated public housing schemes of many industrialised countries. Ward mentions some of the first moves towards standardisation in British housing schemes created under Raymond Unwin's influence on the Tudor Walters Report in 1918[71], before they were broadly adopted in modernist schemes such as Ernst May's settlements for *Das Neue Frankfurt* (The New Frankfurt)[72] or propagated by Ernst Neufert under National Socialist rule[73], as Hartmut Hofrichter and Werner Durth described respectively. Despite their positive effects on a cheaper production of dwellings, those efforts were later criticised for their negative side-effects on aesthetic qualities. British council housing was criticised for its uniformity.[74] In contrast to the other side of the Atlantic, the dominant social ideas and concepts were primarily based on private initiative.[75] European governments tended to mix

---

[66] Galliker 1997: 15.

[67] Ward 2004: 34.

[68] TPR (1921) March: no author: 57.

[69] Ibid.: 58.

[70] DS (1918) 2/3:Wehl: 35.

[71] Ward 2004: 38.

[72] Hofrichter 1995: 122-6.

[73] Durth, Werner, *Deutsche Architekten: Biographische Verflechtungen 1900 – 1970*, Stuttgart/Zürich: Karl Krämer 2001: 150-6.

[74] E.g. TPR (1935) December: no author: 332.

[75] Rodgers 1998. Daniel Rodgers's work is not just telling in terms of the housing market's character on both sides of the Atlantic, he also focuses on the transnational circulation of social politics between Europe and North America and reveals their reciprocal influences.

several measures to improve the housing situation, including direct interventions on the housing markets. They used the legal tools at their disposal in order to shield tenants from the immediate effects of excessive rents or subsequent eviction. Wartime measures to freeze rents at certain maximum levels were legally extended across many European countries. Despite similar problems, rent control exercised by governmental institutions did not play a significant role in the US according to reports published in *The Town Planning Review*. Such tools remained very limited in spatial terms to hard-hit cities, notably New York and Washington and usually restricted to the immediate aftermath of the First World War with the only exception until 1929 in parts of New York.[76]

Under those circumstances it was not enough to maintain the status quo for those who had a place to stay, as the descriptions above suggest. Many new homes were needed to ease the situation, and considering the financial environment this turned out to be a costly business. Therefore, as mentioned by Klaus Novy, the protection of tenants went hand in hand with a reorganisation of the taxation system in several European countries in order to balance the side-effects of the high inflation levels in particular.[77] Germany and Austria introduced a new tax on existing apartment buildings (*Hauszinssteuer*), which helped skim parts of the beneficial increments for many property owners caused by the devaluation of their mortgages due to the influence of inflation. Peter-Christian Witt has analysed the circumstances and frameworks of the German *Hauszinssteuer*[78], which was meant to make owners pay at least 75% of the pre-war mortgage values as tax. The money levied from 1924 was pooled to encourage new housing construction. It was handed out as loans at favourable conditions to interested and eligible stakeholders. Subsequent regular instalments made as repayments for these loans would, again, be used for housing purposes as stipulated by law (*Lex Lipinski*).

Revenues from *Hauszinssteuer* were not exclusively earmarked for housing in governmental budgets and the tax's impact on social housing therefore diminished in the course of the Great Depression. Since the tax nonetheless formed an essential instrument to stimulate housing construction from 1924 to 1931, Rolf Kornemann

---

[76] TPR (1929) December: Veiller: 239.

[77] Novy, Klaus, *Genossenschafts-Bewegung: zur Geschichte und Zukunft der Wohnreform*, Berlin: Transit 1983: 111-2.

[78] Witt, Peter-Christian, *Inflation, Wohnungszwangswirtschaft und Hauszinssteuer: Zur Regelung von Wohnungsbau und Wohnungsmarkt in der Weimarer Republik*. In: Niethammer, Lutz [Ed.]: Wohnen im Wandel: Beiträge zur Geschichte des Alltags in der bürgerlichen Gesellschaft. Wuppertal: Hammer 1979.

labelled this period as "Era of Hauszinssteuer" to underscore its significance.[79] Similar to Kornemann, Klaus Novy and Michael Prinz argue that the tax's revenues were first deviated in order to subsidise middle class housing, and eventually used for general purposes at the municipal level. New loans based on revenues from *Hauszinssteuer* for housing construction ceased in 1932.[80] Articles in *Der Städtebau* subsequently reflect this general trend and reported, the tax had originally been projected as a tool for several decades but that it was partially waived off in Germany since 1932 as a concession to the consequences of the global economic depression. Under National Socialist rule it was intended to further reduce the housing tax in several steps until its final, projected abolition in 1940, while making use of the repayments for loans as kind of perpetual bond. Nonetheless, until 1935 all tax revenues based on this system accrued to loans worth a total amount of almost six billion marks.[81] Much of this money was used by local building associations, either directly run by municipalities or in favour of cooperative societies. Berlin's 'Wohnungsfürsorgegesellschaft' housing company was one of the eligible beneficiaries and constructed more than 19,000 dwellings based on housing-tax loans.[82] It can be concluded that the interwar years were characterised by a significant shift from private investments to direct state interventions.

Excursus: Movements to fight the housing problems – the example of Vienna and cooperative societies

Under post-Great War circumstances, when private capital avoided the housing sector and governments were, for various reasons, unable to step in, traces of local inhabitants' own initiatives can be found. In this context, economist and social scientist Klaus Novy highlighted efforts made in those years by allotment holders and settlers to create 7,000 smallholdings at Vienna's urban fringes. Those smallholdings were constructed on illegally squatted public land which had been subdivided in more or less regular parcels and provided their dwellers with space to grow their own food. Due to their informal nature Novy labelled them as an exceptional and true "poor people's movement"[83] which marked one of the kind's first bottom-up initiatives. He underscored that, these self-help activities were not recognised as adequate substitution for proper state intervention or 'official' hous-

---

[79] Kornemann, Rolf, *Gesetze, Gesetze… – Die amtliche Wohnungspolitik in der Zeit von 1918 bis 1945 in Gesetzen, Verordnungen und Erlassen*. In: Kähler, Gert [Ed.]: Geschichte des Wohnens – Band 4. Stuttgart: Deutsche Verlagsanstalt 1996: 707-8.
[80] Novy, Klaus/Prinz, Michael, *Illustrierte Geschichte der Gemeinwirtschaft: wirtschaftliche Selbsthilfe in der Arbeiterbewegung von den Anfängen bis 1945*, Berlin/Bonn: Dietz 1985: 134-42.
[81] DS (1935) 12: Wölz: 139-40.
[82] DS (1926) 11: no author: 176.
[83] Novy 1983: 22.

ing schemes. Nonetheless, this grassroots movement formed one of the nuclei in Vienna's interwar reformist housing policies, after it had been incorporated into formal municipal activities which later generated the well-known housing schemes for "Red Vienna."[84] Further key elements were rent control, which was exercised until 1934 with politically defined caps on rents ('reasonable rent')[85], extended protective measures for tenants de facto reducing the threat of evictions[86], and a restructured taxation system. The legal framework applicable to this context was a close collaboration between taxation system and land rights which did grant two essential powers to local authorities. Firstly, new expropriation rights provided the public hand with the legal basis to purchase land at prices 20% below pre-war levels, and in turn to hand it out to eligible cooperative societies on leasehold terms only.[87] Secondly, since Austria – just like Germany – was faced with hyperinflation after the First World War which privileged property owners, they were levied a housing tax (Hauszinssteuer) to compensate for what was described by Novy as their gains at the expense of the common welfare.[88] Lessees, on the other hand, were made to pay a different kind of housing tax (Wohnbausteuer) on top of their rents, which was graded based on their flat's size and varied between 2% and 37%. All revenues accrued to the municipality from these taxes were invested in the construction of new affordable housing schemes across Vienna.[89] Soon after Vienna became a regional government within Austria's First Republic in 1922, the Municipality embarked on a path inspired by its new Socialist government.[90] In September 1923 the Municipality decided to construct 25,000 dwellings within five years to be let almost for free, and in total the "Red City" was able to complete more than 65,000 residential units in accordance with reformist principles during the First Republic's existence.[91] In this was Vienna emblematic of the transformation of housing from a privately dominated business towards a service provided for by public bodies.

In the immediate aftermath of the First World War, Germany initiated the replication of unconventional solutions like in Vienna. All across the country cooperative societies sprung up and experienced a boom period. Builders and other craftsmen tried to organise themselves in building societies in an attempt to counter prevail-

---

[84] Novy 1983: 23.
[85] Novy 1983: 117.
[86] Novy 1983: 33.
[87] Novy 1983: 34.
[88] Novy 1983: 122.
[89] Novy 1983: 111-3.
[90] Blom, Philipp, *Die zerrissenen Jahre: 1918-1938*, München: Hanser 2014: 248.
[91] Novy 1983: 47-8.

ing shortages in supply as well as those monopolies which tried to keep prices at unreasonably high levels, as both planning journals have reported. Novy confirms this trend and describes the establishment of 'housing construction cooperatives' ('Bauhütten') as the construction workers' answer to cope with the situation. Workers started their own construction activities in order to circumvent local trusts which tried to control the market supply with new homes. In Novy's opinion, these new housing cooperatives were intended to undermine private opportunities of enrichment at the expense of workman's households and to limit the impact of private investment capitalism on the housing sector. Throughout Germany, almost 200 Bauhütten have been established within three years after the war and they were able to cut costs by up to 30%.[92] Architect Kähler explains the significance of squatter settlements in interwar years which complemented such Bauhütten initiatives.[93] For Berlin and its environs an estimation dating from 1930 gives the number of makeshift dwelling units at 170,000 to 180,000. Most of these dwellings existed in allotment gardens, wild settlements or as part of subsidised *Erwerbslosensiedlungen* (settlements for the unemployed) at the urban fringe.

The cooperative approach idea remained popular during the interwar period including on British society. Whilst Cooperative Wholesale Societies in the UK manufactured and traded virtually everything from biscuits to soap, they extended their services and covered loans or insurance schemes. By 1914 retail societies open to individual membership had three million members and their retail sales reached £88 million.By 1945 those numbers had tripled to nine million members and retail sales quadrupled to £361 million.[94] Their success was based on reliable and good quality products as well as equally shared gains. Social historian Eric Hopkins emphasises how the cooperative movement tried to impact on the people's lifestyle such as; attempts to convert their members to fully incorporate the virtues of temperance. Novy confirms this comprehensive approach among cooperative societies, although he focuses on the grassroots democracy element they contained.[95] Nevertheless, all these reform elements were indicative of the cooperative movement's intention to transform society in the long run and in some cases aiming to abolish the capitalist system. They mirrored Howard's comprehensive ideas behind his Garden City concept with its "path to real reform."

---

[92] Novy 1983: 12.
[93] Kähler, Gert, *Nicht nur Neues Bauen! Stadtbau, Wohnung, Architektur*, Stuttgart: Deutsche Verlags-Anstalt 1996: 394-401.
[94] Hopkins 1990: 167-9.
[95] Novy 1983: 51.

Excursus: "Better workers better housed"

After the First World War garden cities were not as much *en vogue*. Its reformist element had been absorbed by many architects, planners and designers who were then inspired to come up with new ideas for urban development. The need for a change was not only justified by quantitative demands. It also lacked adequate qualities in living standards. Hence, George Cadbury, Jr. summarised them in his 1915 publication on "Town Planning" as follows.

> "The housing conditions in most of our large cities and towns, and indeed in rural areas too, are a scandal to our civilisation."[96]

Although Cadbury wrote his book with special reference to Birmingham and the proposed new planning schemes, his judgement on housing conditions could be transferred from the British to the European context at large. The existing housing stock did not fulfil minimum requirements in many respects – at least in certain neighbourhoods, so that Cadbury and many of his colleagues back then used frank language to appeal to a broader audience.

Bearing the severe quantitative demand in mind, housing construction in many cases created a supply with the simplest possible structures.[97] For Brinckmann, quality in housing construction still revolved around the question of aesthetics above anything else in 1921. He argued in favour of an up-to-date definition of what post-Great War architecture should be. He was convinced that his contemporaries were able to set new standards beyond the simplest solution based on the technologies at hand, and to come up with a distinctive new form resembling more than just a random and unreflecting collection of good looking but 'old' patterns. He criticised colleagues and demanded a focus concentrate on the overall goal of healthy living conditions which respect the tenants' social and economic requirements.[98] In this quest he was not the only voice making such demands and interrelations between architecture and society heard, as Whitaker asked one year earlier.

> "The great question is this: In what manner can we so house all our workers, no matter whether they are clerks or masons or teamsters, as to develop men and women able to play their full part with the greatest advantage to world-progress and human betterment. This is not a question of sentimental value – it is an economic

---

[96] Cadbury 1915: 3.
[97] Brinckmann, Albert Erich, *Deutsche Stadtbaukunst in der Vergangenheit*, Frankfurt: Frankfurter Verlags-Anstalt 1921: V.
[98] Brinckmann 1921: 1-2.

question which must be solved, because the national economic structures of the future will have to depend upon better workers better housed."[99]

Brinckmannsaw society at large in search for a new spirit since, in his opinion, traditional architectural patterns and interdependencies between the individual building and its surrounding urban context did not work out anymore. He concluded that each period would have to reassess its interpretation between the individual building and urban forms based on the progress made in the living standards.[100] Therefore it was necessary to keep pace with improved amenities for buildings to offer all available interior qualities andreconsider their outer structures. For Brinckmann it was not necessary to make every façade an architectural expression of new-found individuality like in 18th century cities.[101] Instead, a consistent urban context should evolve to respond to rapidly changing urban perception and experience through new means of transportation. This echoes an earlier statement by Behrens on the observer's inability to identify details and urban patterns due to cars' and trains' higher speeds. Similarly in 1929, Le Corbusier states, "Town Planning demands uniformity in detail and a sense of movement in the general layout."[102]

The city as organism – a depiction that became widespread among the planning community during the following decades – Brinckmann attributed each building with a particular function within the whole urban organism. He formulated this as an explicit critique against Camillo Sitte's historicising aesthetic interpretation of the city, which supported the idea of individualism and the insistence on singularity in architectural design. The new spirit Brinckmann alluded to instead, could be interpreted as a forerunner of Modern or International Style.

> "Das vornehme Gefühl für Maß- und Zurückhaltung ist vielleicht unserer Zeit nicht recht verständlich, die Effekt neben Effekt an den Straßenzeilen und Plätzen losbrennt und Reichtum von Motiven für Schönheit hält."[103]

This search for a new spirit contested the existing housing patterns in Germany's tenement barracks or British back-to-back houses and the accompanying urban

---

[99] Whitakcr 1920: 13.
[100] Brinckmann 1921: 4, 26-7.
[101] Brinckmann 1921: 188-90.
[102] Le Corbusier, *The City of To-morrow and its Planning*, New York: Dover Publications [1929] 1987: 76.
[103] Brinckmann 1921: 181. "The elegant sense for moderation and self-effacement is perhaps not that intelligible to our times, which tend to collate one effect next to the other along street fronts and squares, and which consider abundance of motives to be beauty." (author's translation).

structures at large. It comprised of an aesthetic *and* a social dimension, although both overlapped with functional considerations on how to make best use of modern amenities in housing. The latter functional elements were a necessity to alleviate historic miserable living conditions in many parts of the cities. Such attempts to improve the living conditions coincided with Patrick Geddes' publication of *Cities in Evolution* which appeared in 1915 after its previous rejection. It had been written three years earlier. Geddes not only described the cities' extension into the wider regional context for which he coined the term "conurbation."[104] He further outlined their transition from what he called the "palaeotechnic" era in urbanism based on steam and coal to the "neotechnic" one based on electricity and motor vehicles.[105]

An example of living conditions which provoked Cadbury's "scandal to our civilisation" directed at Birmingham. The city and her surroundings was an exceptional area in negative terms, as historian Hopkins commented in his description of the English working classes. Planners in those days tried to fight the existing shortcomings, creating a vicious circle of redevelopment where rehabilitation efforts towards slum clearance were under way. These interventions to reduce population densities in the worst affected areas improved the living conditions for some households but left others without shelter. They in turn had to move into the next already decaying and affordable houses, hence perpetuating the downgrading process. In 1913 some 200,000 people were forced to live in 43,366 back-to-back houses and more than 42,000 homes did not possess a separate water supply or sink.[106] It must be kept in mind that circumstances varied markedly between cities and, of course, amongst their districts. Birmingham reflected the strong division between England's decaying industrial northern parts and the prosperous southern sections especially in London throughout the interwar period. It was in and around the capital city that new well-paid jobs were created, whilst regional labour divisions impacted on the whole country as historian Lees has pointed out.[107] Lees attributes Liverpool with a strong negative historic image, and equals this city to Manchester as the new 'shock city' due to Liverpool's staggering unemployment rates during the 1930s.[108] The amended legal frameworks tried to tackle the situation. In a piecemeal process new bye-laws demanded better qualities in all newly constructed houses. They did so although some private investors struggled to pro-

---

[104] Ward 2002: 51.
[105] Hall, Peter: *The Centenary of Modern Planning.* In: Freestone, Robert [Ed.]: Urban Planning in a Changing World: The Twentieth Century Experience. London: E&FN Spon 2000: 21.
[106] Hopkins 1990: 113.
[107] Lees 2000: 79-80.
[108] Lees 2000: 63.

vide these amenities and standards due to rent control exercised by governmental institutions and subsequent low returns on the private investments.

Both planning journals reported on new housing schemes experimenting with small houses, which provided for decent accommodation that but utilised new modes of production. One early attempt was made by German architect Metzendorf for Margarethenhöhe settlement in Essen and Hüttenau worker's housing estate in Hattingen. Both settlements were laid out according to Garden City principles but in order to treat the available budgets with care he plotted a limited number of modular floor plan designs and reiterated them in variation over the whole project. Furthermore, Metzendorf used economies of scale through prefabricated construction elements for windows, heating and plumbing.[109] In his research on the settlement, architect Andreas Helfrich highlights the wholehearted support of Essen's city representatives and how Margarethenhöhe was exempted from usual building codes and bye-laws to support it as a 'model case study.'[110] Knowles interpreted governmental efforts made by the UK and US to provide decent shelter at war factories and shipyards during the First World War as similarly experimental in characterthat led the way for future housing projects in the urban context.[111]

How Zurich confronted its housing shortage is in an article published in *Der Städtebau*[112]. Its city government decided to embark on a comprehensive spatial planning scheme which did not just cover housing but transportation and green spaces too. With regards to housing, it was guided by a combination of decent living conditions with sufficient light and air for each dwelling, embedded into urban patterns inspired by a 'condensed' Garden City idea that was oriented at a bourgeois-industrial society. Besides flats the scheme provided for green belts and efficient tramway lines.[113] In this respect, Zurich was a forerunner of comprehensive ways to approach the housing shortage through large scale production, which Knowles considered as the only way to provide sufficient housing at adequate qualities.[114] As the broader impacts of industrialisation made their way into daily life habits and architecture, this development was not welcomed by all as reflected in the different planning schools of thought (see 3.3.5). Helfrich describes the con-

---

[109] Helfrich, Andreas, *Die Margarethenhöhe Essen: Architekt und Auftraggeber vor dem Hintergrund der Kommunalpolitik Essen und der Firmenpolitik Krupp zwischen 1886 und 1914*, Weimar: Verlag und Datenbank für Geisteswissenschaften 2000: 154-6.
[110] Helfrich 2000: 167.
[111] Knowles 1920: 9.
[112] DS (1916) 6/7: Brockmann: 62-5.
[113] Galliker 1997: 15.
[114] Knowles 1920: vii.

troversy within the German Werkbund where two opposing positions in architecture and design were fighting each other. One faction, led by Hermann Muthesius, advocated the mass production of articles of daily use in order to use economies of scale and stimulate exports. The other faction was led by Henry van de Velde and supported by Bruno Taut, Walter Gropius and Peter Behrens who tried to defend handcraft and the artist's position as individualist in their attempts to create new designs.[115] Since this dispute was largely fought by key architects and urban designers, the issue affected urban planning for the years to come.

3.3.2   Public health concerns

The second half of the interwar years was dominated by attempts to improve the living conditions in congested and rundown neighbourhoods. As a consequence, several articles in *The Town Planning Review* explicitly focussed on slums or slum-like conditions as a major urban challenge during the 1930s. *Der Städtebau*, in contrast, was referring to slums as a particularly British phenomenon in one contribution in 1933 and 1934 respectively, although similarly bad living conditions were admitted in the context of the renovation of city centres (Altstadtgesundung) in Germany as well. Kampffmeyer emphasised the quantitative similarities between British and German housing developments, refering to projected demographic trends based on the society's age structure, with many new families, and which would in turn lead to higher demand.[116] Based on 1931 census results for the UK, it was hence estimated in his article for *Der Städtebau* that one million flats in slum-like areas needed to be replaced out of a total four million flats to be constructed within the next 20 years. Considering Kampffmeyer's remark about quantitative similarities between both countries, these figures can be interpreted as correction of sugar-coated Nazi figures.

For the US-American housing market Lawrence Veiller tried to summarise the major deficiencies and his extensive description published in 1929 underscored similar problems as in European cities where the lack of light and adequate ventilation went hand in hand with a lack of fire safety.[117] The latter problem was mainly due to American preferences for houses entirely built of wood though. Veiller criticised the bad preparation of housing and architectural schemes as well as about the poor quality of the buildings, which were constructed at unreasonably high prices and as speculative objects for private enterprises. Many voices made themselves heard in the journals in order to propose a potential solution to these deficiencies. In F. Herman Flesche's 1934 contribution to *Der Städtebau*, commenting

---

[115] Helfrich 2000: 161-2.
[116] DS (1934) 6: Kampffmeyer: 298.
[117] TPR (1929) December: Veiller: 243-7.

on German old city centres, similar criticisms to Veiller in highlighting.[118] These older parts of the city had been readjusted in a piecemeal process over previous generations in order to cater for changing needs. Unfortunately those readjustments were carried out to the detriment of their inhabitants, with low ceilings, insufficient sanitary facilities, no open inner courtyards and poor ventilation. In order to alleviate the situation, it was made permissible to use housing-tax loans for the renovation of these buildings, despite the loans' original goal to create additional housing. One report on such improvements made in Brunswick highlighted the benefits for tenants of the revitalised structures.

Standard of living in private households

Particular debates ensued in both journals concerning the provision of certain amenities in private households. Clarke in 1932 attempted to promote the definition of, "the absolute minimum standard for the English working man's family" as follows: "a living room; three bedrooms; scullery, bath, larder, coal-store and w.c."[119] Such standards, however, required developments from scratch, carried out on greenfields at the urban fringe in most cases. A few years later, reports in *The Town Planning Review* served to illustrate how the US tried to push for the limits, as some authors insisted on the need and opportunity to prepare a widespread use of modern amenities in social housing. Their list included a bathroom with tub, WC and lavatory as well as a kitchen equipped with a sink, refrigerator and stove fuelled by electricity or gas. Straus and Wegg, whose book on housing schemes built for working class people in the US was reviewed in 1938[120], anticipated the disbelief or astonishment of their planning companions to send former slum dwellers to such an 'advanced' place. Their countering argument was to point to the affordability due to economies of scale and a deliberate demonstration of what was possible at new sites. To Straus and Wegg the purchase of those devices seemed realistic, such as for electric refrigerators bought at half the retail price in quantities of more than 16,000., Former slum dwellers would be able to afford them based on cheap wholesale electricity rates in large housing schemes.

The latter argument turned out to be essential, if one takes the experiences made at many of the Bauhaus-style settlements in Germany into consideration. Novy and Prinz describe their standards as luxurious and unaffordable to the targeted low-income working class households in face of the global economic depression in the

---

[118] DS (1934) 4: Herman Flesche: 197-201.
[119] TPR (1932) June: Clarke: 47.
[120] TPR (1938) December: A.P.: 147-8.

early 1930s.[121] Martina Heßler comes to a similar conclusion in her reference to Ernst May's settlements for Frankfurt. At the *Römerstadt* project monthly rents for fully equipped flats ranged between 52 and 90 marks, depending on their respective size. These numbers illustrate a severe mismatch, since according to Heßler's calculations, unskilled labourers were only able to spend between 36 and 45 marks per month on their accommodation.[122] Furthermore Heßler mentions several complaints brought to the public attention by 8,000 residents of the settlement about the additional charges for electricity. For 95.5% of all residents at Römerstadt additional charges turned out to be higher than those of their previous flat and according to their statements prices had risen by 80% on average. Such extra costs were prohibitive for the intended low-income households met byarrogant reactions by the settlement's architects who claimed to know the tenants' needs better.[123] Social debates on the side-effects of electrical appliances and technical infrastructures will be discussed in more detail in the following excursuses.

These far-reaching US-American ideas and the amenities provided for in modernist reform housing schemes were an extreme contrast to what many people then experienced in their neighbourhoods, particularly if they were housed in rundown areas. But housing policies in NS-Germany were oscillating between the need to cater to propaganda purposes illustrating improvements and progress on one side, and mathematical calculations of what was actually affordable and efficient at larger scales on the other. There are reports in *Der Städtebau* on the provision of WCs and sewerage systems in city extensions, particularly when it came to small houses in peripheral areas. On one hand, new, reliable and cheap technologies made water provision, even in remote rural areas, an affordable amenity as Fritz Förster reported in 1928.[124] The question of wastewater disposal and sewerage systems, on the other hand, then initiated a fierce debate among German urban planners that was committed to party ideology. Hitler's NSDAP showed a lot of ambivalence and inconsistencies when it came to housing policies but for propaganda purposes the 'blood and soil' myth was fostered by many leading representatives. From their point of view, the congested city with tenants squeezed into apartment blocks seemed to be the complete opposite of what their idea of the future city should look like with small plots and detached houses at the cities' fringes. This idea can be described as a continuation of the small holdings constructed under the umbrel-

---

[121] Novy, Prinz 1985: 138.
[122] Heßler, Martina, *Mrs Modern Woman: Zur Sozial- und Kulturgeschichte der Haushaltstechnisierung*, Frankfurt: Campus 2001: 272, 295.
[123] Heßler 2001: 296-7, 301.
[124] DS (1928) 1: Förster: 8-11.

116

la of a job creation scheme initiated by Chancellor Brüning in 1931/32.[125] Unemployed persons were provided with small state loans to construct their own homes based on the self-help principle and with extremely limited amenities. The scheme as well as similar projects sparked fierce debates about minimum qualities in housing construction and the following three statements in *Der Städtebau* on waste water illustrate the ambivalence of NS ideology on this matter. Defending the idea of detached small houses in 1934, Waldemar Nöldechen, then Head of the Planning Department for the city of Saarbrücken, argued in favour of limits to certain amenities that "modern civilisation" was able to provide for urban citizens. In his opinion, small houses attached to larger garden plots represented the new role model in housing. They combine different opportunities for private pleasures with the joy and liberty of an urban life. At the same time small houses were closer to nature and offered the opportunity to grow some fruits and vegetables. Nöldechen hence explained, the only price to be paid for this scheme would be the omission of certain piped infrastructures like the sewerage system in such low-density neighbourhoods, where they proved to be too expensive.[126] This suggested self-imposed limitation for sewerage systems was rejected in an article by Hans Kölzow published in 1935, who called for an investigation of waste waters' potential use as fertiliser. As it fitted with his concept, he agreed with Nöldechen to do without wastewater treatment plants which required imported spare parts with this eschewal complying with autarky policies.[127] Betge pursued the idea of autarky too but in order to achieve high crop yield on their own plots, settlers in his argumentation needed a WC draining into piped infrastructure instead of individual cesspools. In Betge's opinion such cesspools proved insufficient as source for what he called "liquid fertiliser." He argued supported by other results that a cesspool would generate results too dry to be used as fertiliser.[128] In Betge's opinion the toilet did not necessarily need to be connected to a fully operational sewerage system but could be laid out as autonomous cycle for each smallholding.[129]

Excursus: Towards the networked and electrified city

Many journal articles addressed the planning profession's evolution towards a mature and self-contained discipline. Additionally authors tended to stress their profession's interdisciplinary nature and the many different concerns they had to

---

[125] Rodenstein, Böhm-Ott 1996: 530-1.
[126] DS (1934) 3: Nöldechen: 143-4.
[127] DS (1935) 3: Kölzow: 34-5.
[128] For hygienic reasons Betge's assumptions are wrong, although similar solutions have been suggested for Klein Windhoek Location (see 4.2.3).
[129] DS (1936) 11: Betge: 129-30.

take into consideration during the planning procedure. By the end of the analysed period, Conzen's paper in *The Town Planning Review* entitled "Towards a Systematic Approach in Planning Science: Geoproscopy"[130] summarised state-of-the-art efforts to integrate the various conflicting topics (Figure 8). Geoproscopy was an attempt to coin a new term word encompassing the various layers addressed by planning inspired by new theories like Christaller's central place theory. It did underscore the aspiration to transform planning into a science as precise as physics or chemistry.

Figure 8: Historic illustration of planning as interdisciplinary profession

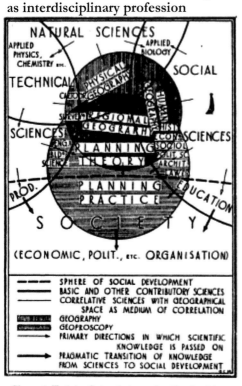

Diagram to illustrate a Systematic Approach to Planning Science.

Aside from such theoretical considerations, this self-perception among the planning profession reflects its broader context and the determination with which it tried to achieve social reforms. Similar to architectural design schools, planners wanted to contribute to the evolution of the 'New Man' and technological 'advances' helped them to achieve their goals. These goals applied to the metropole as well as the colonies, though technical appliances were less relevant due to their frequent substitution with manual labour. This difference marks a clear contrast between European colonisers and the developments in the colonies. Therefore the case of Windhoek will be investigated in more detail in the following section (see 4.2.3). Several amenities made their way into housing during the interwar period, complementing the already mentioned water provision and sewerage systems. Historian Friedrich Lenger confirms those journal articles which reported these two amenities as being almost ubiquitous in countries like Germany or the UK, whilst Europe's south and east lagged behind during the late 1920s, with a pronounced difference in service

---

[130] TPR (1938) July: Conzen.

provisions between central areas and the urban periphery.[131] Furthermore, gas became more widespread and Knowles emphasised its conveniences for daily life in his publication on "Industrial Housing", where he alluded to the declining need to carry loads of coal and ashes. Furthermore, he attributed it abating smoke as a health hazard.

> "While gas can probably not be classed as a necessity in the same sense as a water supply or sewerage system, and is no longer the usual means of lighting, it is by no means a luxury."[132]

For domestic purposes gas constituted a significant share of heating and cooking but was superseded by electricity for lighting which was safer and more efficient.[133] The journal analysis highlights electricity became more widespread in interwar years although there were a lot of complaints about its high costs. It moved from the wealthier neighbourhoods of a city[134] and formed the basis for many industrial activities from lighting to electrical engineering. Early figures indicate that electricity remained a predominantly urban amenity though. In 1920 most domestic electric power was used for lighting purposes, with an estimated 10 to 20 kilowatt hours usage per month on average for six to eight room dwellings in the US. Knowles lists some usage with washing, ironing, cleaning, cooking, and heating appliances.[135] British households remained reluctant with respect to these modern amenities for cooking and preserved the domestic hearth as central place of family life in those days[136], a system without central heat that Whitaker deemed unimaginable for the US context.[137] In a later publication, he demanded for the provision of central heating and hot water as well as other piped utilities such as, vacuum pipes to hoover away 'dust-carrying disease germs' in every household. This should serve as a step forward towards healthier living conditions and the elimina-

---

[131] Lenger 2013: 326-7.
[132] Knowles 1920: 256.
[133] Knowles 1920: 259-60.
[134] Kühl, Uwe, *Anfänge städtischer Elektrifizierung in Deutschland und Frankreich*. In: Schott, Dieter [Ed.]: Energy and the City in Europe: From Preindustrial Wood-Shortage to the Oil Crisis of the 1970s. Stuttgart: Franz Steiner 1997, 134. Similar in Fisch, Stefan, *Die Anfänge der elektrischen Straßenbahn im Spannungsfeld von Elektroindustrie und Städtebaureform*. In: Schott, Dieter; Klein, Stefan [Eds.]: Mit der Tram ins nächste Jahrtausend: Geschichte, Gegenwart und Zukunft der elektrischen Straßenbahn. Essen: Klartext 1998, 34.
[135] Knowles 1920: 285-6.
[136] Mosley 2001: 54.
[137] Whitaker, et.al. 1918: 4.

tion of germs.[138] He demonstrated a strong belief in engineering and technical solutions.

> "Again I am constrained to believe our nineteenth century sociology and not our twentieth century engineering is at fault"[139]

Although the use of electrical household appliances remained very limited in interwar Germany, Lenger has pointed out how electricity was associated with the notion of modernity which in turn was associated with the US.[140] In contrast to major European countries, use of electricity in North America was already relatively widespread as Karl Ditt demonstrated with an average annual per capita consumption in 1925 for Canada (900 kWh), the US (500 kWh) and the UK (200 kWh).[141] Despite higher annual consumption in Canada, Martina Heßler describes the US as the country with the world's highest prevalence in electrical appliances in the 1920s and 1930s. Distribution statistics of most devices available in the US had doubled between 1922 and 1928, although she highlights a clear disparity along class divisions.[142] In contrast to those American numbers, use of electrical appliances was of very limited extent in Germany, as Heßler has further illustrated for Berlin in 1928. The only devices that have reached substantial distribution in private households were the flatiron, available in 56% of all households, and the vacuum cleaner with 27.5% respectively.[143] Electrical washing machines or refrigerators, by contrast, remained rare despite explicit attempts by manufacturers and electricity suppliers.

In this context, Ditt mentions the example of revised marketing strategies by regional electricity suppliers in Great Britain which, in fact, followed similar paths as already used by gasworks. In order to encourage gas use for purposes other than lighting, gasworks offered private customers the opportunity to buy cookers based on a hire-purchase system.[144] Those monthly instalments paid as surcharge on the usual gas rate made cookers available to larger numbers of households. British electricity suppliers copied this model and introduced it on a large scale in the 1930s in an attempt to compete with gasworks. However, Ditt points to the initial technical and financial disadvantages of electrical cookers in comparison to their gas fuelled counterparts. Electrical cookers were less durable, required specific

---

[138] Whitaker 1920: 189-91.
[139] Whitaker 1920: 191.
[140] Lenger 2013: 353.
[141] Ditt 2011: 135-6.
[142] Heßler, Martina, *Kulturgeschichte der Technik*, Frankfurt: Campus 2012: 75-7.
[143] Heßler 2001: 60-1.
[144] Ditt 2011: 358-72.

cookware, took longer to prepare the meals, and were more expensive in their acquisition and maintenance costs. It was only by the early 1930s that electric cookers were able to compete with traditional coal and gas cookers. Backed by the hire-purchase system, distribution of electrical cookers boomed from only 120,000 in 1930 to 1,480,000 by 1939 in the UK. This surpassed the increase in electrical connections (3.5 million in 1930 and 10.1 million in 1939).[145] These statistics demonstrate that electrical cookers still only reached a minority of potential customers.

In the German context Heßler refers to an increase for the use of electrical household appliances towards the end of interwar years with flatirons and vacuum cleaners being in the lead position. She emphasised the role certain pressure groups, associations such as the "Reichsverband Deutscher Hausfrauenvereine" (Reich's association of German housewives' clubs) and politically motivated interventions played. These groups and associations served as "mediators" to encourage the dissemination of electrical devices in order to 'rationalise' private households parallel to industrial production.[146] The only device primarily used for leisure activities was the radio, which reached significant numbers of households in industrialised countries within a relatively short period of time.[147]

These developments contain different layers of symbolism beyond their significance in household routines.[148] They impacted on the social realms with the introduction of electrical cookers transforming traditional habits with regards to the choice and preparation of food. Heßler illustrates a triangle consisting of the three components 'electricity' which was used synonymously for 'progress' in historic debates and they both represented metaphors for 'modernity. The use of powered light overcome where there was darkness before. This allowed people to make use of the evening hours for leisure activities but it extended working hours previously limited by natural light. Electric tramways transformed urban mobility for growing sections of the population. Electricity inspired artists and authors to come up with their visions of a less arduous future allowing it to enhance social harmony.[149] All these advances amounted for many authors the creation of a 'New Man.' Heßler

---

[145] Ditt 2011: 369.
[146] Heßler 2012: 82-5.
[147] Ditt 2011: 775-6.
[148] Heßler 2001: 64-88.
[149] Zionist Theodor Herzl has written a remarkable example of a social utopia that encompasses all these elements as well as detailed descriptions for the electrified urban environment of a future Jewish state in Palestine (Herzl, Theodor, *AltNeuLand*, Norderstedt: Books on Demand GmbH/haGalil.com [1902] 2004).

distinguishes two levels of symbolic 'modernity' with a first focusing on the individual person.

> "*Allen* Gruppen ging es genau darum: einen neuen Menschentypen zu schaffen, ihn an eine Zeit anzupassen, die als unüberwindbar geprägt von Technik verstanden wurde."[150]

Adelheid von Saldern illustrated these modernist housing schemes across Germany like May's settlements in Frankfurt or Taut's designs for Berlin.[151] Despite criticisms then expressed by tenants or other architects and planners, the tenants were willing to accept and embraced these modern elements to a limited extent.

The second level in Heßler's discussion of symbolic 'modernity' is focused on the national perspective and chauvinist competition in the 1930s.

> "Diese "Umgestaltung" hatte allerdings auch eine *symbolische* Dimension, indem die Geräte als Katalysatoren eines modernen Lebensstils betrachtet wurden, der zum nationalen Prestige Deutschlands beitragen würde."[152]

At the level of national prestige that economic considerations play a significant role. Ditt has analysed how all electrical appliances in the work environment as well as in domestic households transformed industrialised countries into mass consumer societies. The devices themselves were produced and sold to the masses. At the same time they conveyed a new culture specifically produced for consumption by the masses like on radio and in the movies screened at cinemas around the globe. Lenger gives the examples of London and Vienna, where bars and pubs suffered from both new mediums and were less frequented in interwar years. At the same time, major broadcasting networks were controlled and dominated by the state and helped to fulfil governmental intentions to instruct and educate their people – another instrument to achieve the 'New Man.'[153] National prestige was based on comparative statistics showing the distribution of certain electrical appliances, which hence represented an indicator for a respective country's 'progress' as

---

[150] Heßler 2001: 87 "*All* groups attempted to create a new man, to adapt him to a time that was interpreted as being insurmountable dominated by technology." (author's translation, emphasis in original).
[151] Von Saldern, Adelheid, *Neues Wohnen: Wohnverhältnisse und Wohnverhalten in Großwohnanlagen der 20er Jahre.* In: Schildt, Axel; Sywottek, Arnold [Eds.]: Massenwohnung und Eigenheim: Wohnungsbau und Wohnen in der Großstadt seit dem Ersten Weltkrieg. Frankfurt/New York: Campus 1988: 211-2.
[152] Heßler 2001: 86. "This 'transformation' however also carried a *symbolic* dimension as those appliances were regarded as catalysts of a modern lifestyle that would contribute to Germany's national prestige." (author's translation, emphasis in original).
[153] Lenger 2013: 379-80.

Heßler has demonstrated.[154] In addition, developments on the labour market saw electrical appliances promoted as a means to substitute tasks previously carried out by housemaids. Domestic jobs were too expensive for middle class families under the economic instabilities many were faced in interwar Germany. Instead of domestic servants, electrical appliances were considered as the new status symbols reflecting a family's wealth. Heßler argues it was rather the anticipation of what technology and the 'modernisation' of domestic life could be than its factual transformation on a large scale.[155] In this respect, Ditt supports Heßler's point when he underscores the quick dissemination of the radio as leisure appliance, whilst comparably expensive but supposedly 'productive' and durable household appliances needed more time before they entered the majority of private households.[156]

Smoke nuisance

Despite the attempts to disseminate new 'clean' electrical technologies as mentioned above, air pollution made its impact on interwar urban development. Stephen Mosley summarised the complex links between the prevalence of many polluting sources in industry, traffic and domestic economy, and how they impacted on daily life in Victorian and Edwardian times.[157] In retrospect I would argue their impact was underestimated at the the time. The smoke nuisance as challenge in urban health was an issue in interwar years that both journals did not address it at an extensive level. For the German perspective contributions to *Der Städtebau* rather suggested smoke was more an aesthetic problem. The two articles dealing with soot and other pollutants published 1910 and 1913 with their tenor focused at the aesthetically deplorable consequences. Rather, Nussbaum, author of the first article, declares algae to be an underestimated problem in Hanover, surpassing street dust and soot in significance for their negative effects on building façades.[158] The second German article briefly comments on dust and soot as harmful pollutants, which can nevertheless be eliminated with appropriate technical solutions.[159] Mikael Hård and Marcus Stippak came to similar conclusions about historic air quality in most German cities and the admiration these cities received by British authors.[160] Taking the different heating systems and climatic conditions into consid-

---

[154] Heßler 2001: 77-80.
[155] Heßler 2001: 71-5.
[156] Ditt 2011: 776.
[157] Mosley, Stephen, *The Chimney of the World: A History of Smoke Pollution in Victorian and Edwardian Manchester*, Cambridge: The White Horse Press 2001.
[158] DS (1910) 12: Nussbaum: 141.
[159] DS (1913) 11: no author: 130.
[160] Hård, Mikael/Stippak, Marcus, *Progressive Dreams: The German City in Britain and the United States*, Cambridge: MIT Press 2010: 134.

eration, smoke proved to be a heavier burden to public health in the UK, where according to Bill Luckin the domestic hearth traditionally provided for private comforts.[161] Nonetheless the journal analysis did only reveal two articles in *The Town Planning Review* explicitly dealing with potential ways on how to achieve the 'smokeless city.' In his 1923 book review, Harold Shawcross argues in favour of an appropriate balance when weighing between the impacts of industrial smoke pollution and those from domestic hearths on urban health. He pointed to solutions at hand and already used in other countries, where industrial smoke did not play as much of a role as in the UK, demanded vigorous efforts to reduce the emission of industrial smoke, and the pointlessness of just relying on zoning according to prevailing winds as a solution, if nothing was done about the root causes. For him a comprehensive path to the smokeless city included measures to reduce both kinds of smoke, private pollution from domestic hearths *and* pollution from industrial production.[162] Through the second explicit contribution to the journal – an editorial published just a couple of months later in 1924 – the debate received a different spin, despite a general concession to the need to reduce air pollution.[163] It presented the production of smokeless fuel based on the "low temperature carbonisation" principle as potential solution to the problem, without having to change the general setup. This fuel should ideally be produced at municipal enterprises, and due to its lower emissions avoid the immediate need to reduce domestic and/or industrial smoke pollution. Aside from the search for completely new technological solutions to the problem, the substitution of coal for gas played a role in those days' efforts to reduce the smoke nuisance in the UK. This substitution proved to be successful as Ditt notes its abundant distribution in British private households on the eve of the Second World War.[164] In addition *The Town Planning Review* articles were written on related questions such as housing, open spaces or zoning, and where additional arguments on the smoke nuisance and its consequences were expressed.

Though attention in both journals was limited, its impacts on the living qualities in interwar industrialised regions became tangible during interruptions of production. Strikes like the ones in Germany's Ruhr district in 1923 or Great Britain's General Strike in 1926 made those side-effects literally visible. Franz-Josef Brüggemeier and Thomas Rommelspacher have exemplified those effects for the Ruhr, where

---

[161] Luckin, Bill, *Town, Country and Metropolis: The Formation of an Air Pollution Problem in London, 1800-1870*. In: Schott, Dieter [Ed.]: Energy and the City in Europe: From Preindustrial Wood-Shortage to the Oil Crisis of the 1970s. Stuttgart: Franz Steiner 1997: 81.
[162] TPR (1923) May: Shawcross: 127-30.
[163] TPR (1924) February: no author: 1-2.
[164] Ditt 2011: 103.

French occupation caused passive resistance by local inhabitants.[165] The strike affected all heavy industries and led to a collapse in production from spring to autumn in 1923. Subsequently, it became apparent the beneficial side-effects these circumstances had on people's health and vegetation due to the virtual disappearance of air pollution with its usual dust and soot emissions. Instead, vegetables, shrubs and trees flourished in 1923. In some cases local farmers were able to harvest crops three times throughout that season as compared to the usual two. In the strike's aftermath, these experiences supported new efforts to introduce additional measures and legislation aimed at the reduction of industrial emissions for the Ruhr area as well as the creation of a first conservationist movement aimed to protect forests. However, as Brüggemeier and Rommelspacher report, their impact was extremely limited and during the Great Depression smoke was, again, seen as a positive but rare sign of prosperity and wealth in the Ruhr.

The role of Howard's Garden City

One completely different and more comprehensive solution than the use of different fuels or the reduction of emissions reverberated during interwar years, despite its original inception already at the previous turn of the century was Ebenezer Howard's Garden City concept. Both planning journals contained several contributions arguing for and against the this idea but it received more attention in *Der Städtebau*, though the real outcomes in Germany remained limited to garden suburbs rather than new and independent cities, as stipulated in the original drafts. From a retrospective perspective, Ward comes to similar conclusions[166] and Ekke Feldmann backs this position with regards to inadequacies in German regulations concerning the right to construct a building on land owned by another person.[167] In the *The Town Planning Review* interest in the Garden City movement was abruptly stopped with the start of the First World War, except for one article in 1920 presenting the achievements at Welwyn. The prevailing view of Howard's concept can be illustrated by the following statement, made in the journal's first editorial in 1914.

"The term Garden City or Garden Suburb was very happily chosen at the time of its inception, and since, much actual practical work has been carried out under its tutelage; accordingly, what was at first merely a theoretic idea needing stimulus, is now an actual and accomplished fact. In its more real aspect as we see it to-day, the

---

[165] Brüggemeier, Franz-Josef/Rommelspacher, Thomas, *Blauer Himmel über der Ruhr: Geschichte der Umwelt im Ruhrgebiet 1840 – 1990*, Essen: Klartext 1992: 50-7.
[166] Ward 2002: 52-5.
[167] Feldmann, Ekke, *Bauordnungen und Baupolizei: zur Entwicklungsgeschichte zwischen 1850 und 1950*, Frankfurt: Lang 2011: 313-5.

original term Garden City and Suburb is perhaps too restricted. In point of fact as an issue it has been absorbed in others of wider significance."[168]

Even though the term itself did not show up again in the journals' headlines, the concept was still borrowed and adapted by several authors to inform new trends, especially in their contributions on the transformation of urban development into a regional matter. In this respect Raymond Unwin has played an important role during his work as Town Planning Inspector at the Local Government Board.[169] Hall explains how Unwin skilfully managed to introduce his ideas as laid down in his 1912 pamphlet *Nothing Gained by Overcrowding* into the Tudor Walters report published in 1918. This report as well as those published over the following years led to new legislation which effectively initiated new suburban housing construction along railway and underground infrastructure. Between 1919, when the *Housing and Town Planning Act* under Christopher Addison came into force, and 1933-4, local authorities completed 763,000 new houses, many of them at new satellites around London. Hall declares Becontree as the largest planned residential suburb in the world, where 116,000 homes were constructed. It was through this large-scale housing programme and its successors under various British governments that Howard's Garden City concept was supplanted. Howard's original cooperative element dissipated over time although it touched an important question - the ownership of land and its subsequent increases in value due to planning interventions.

3.3.3   The land question

Due to its rather liberal organisation across most industrialised countries under democratic conditions, land ownership sparked fierce debates among the planning community during interwar years. Whilst Howard's reform idea, which tried to reallocate the tenure rights from individual owners to the municipality's benefit, making her the land owner on which all building and other economic activities would take place, mostly remained an utopian dream. The years before the Great War broke out witnessed a massive increase in land prices to the benefit of private holders. In 1914, W. Davidge reported in *The Town Planning Review* property prices on the north side of London's Oxford Street had risen more than 90% within ten years thanks to the construction of large business buildings.[170] This example was not an exceptional case reflecting London's expensive metropolitan core, instead it expressed rather general concerns about the question of urban planning's impact on the determination of land values and who should benefit thereof. Anton Hoenig cites Rudolf Eberstadt in his 1928 *Der Städtebau* article on land values with the

---

[168] TPR (1914) January: no author: 275.
[169] Hall [1988] (2014): 70-83.
[170] TPR (1914) January: Davidge: 290.

following statement. "Der neuere Städtebau ist in allen seinen Teilen ein Problem der Wertbildung geworden."[171] Planners faced complex interdependencies between planning interventions, (potentially allowed) land use and real estate prices. In Adolf Damaschke's opinion, the housing question is about land rights which could only be resolved fairly based on building codes that would help to limit land speculation.[172] Hans Jürgen Teuteberg and Clemens Wischermann have summarised the main debates revolving housing construction, as discussed at the turn of century, by two of their key proponents Carl Johannes Fuchs and Andreas Voigt.[173] Aside from the dichotomy between small houses and tenement barracks, land speculation and structures of land ownership in the hands of few larger owners fuelled the discussions around the valuation of land (Bodenpreisbildung) and the idea of economic rent (Grundrente).

Debates on the unearned increment of land

The extension of existing transportation infrastructures into suburban areas created additional values for those areas and led to higher prices at the urban core whose catchment area had thus been increased as well. This effect on property values did not just affect already built up parcels but unused plots too. One means to skim the 'unearned increment', or 'betterment' as Ward calls it[174], was an appropriate tax called *Wertzuwachssteuer* in the German context. Its experimental preparations will later be analysed in the Windhoek case study and refers back to planning debates before the First World War (see 4.2.1). In the journals however this topic appeared for the first time immediately after the First World War in 1919. In his contribution to *Der Städtebau* Surveyor Dieck pointed out how speculation was keeping prices of already developed plots in many German cities at high levels. Municipalities were forced to acquire new cheaper land in remote areas for housing purposes that required additional resources to be spent on the necessary infrastructure provision. Dieck produced pessimistic projections on the ability to fulfil long-term estimates of demand until 1950 and 2010.[175] He complained that the public

---

[171] DS (1928) 10: Hoenig: 231. "Recent urban design has become a problem of accumulation of value in all its elements."(author's translation).
[172] Feldmann 2011: 316.
[173] Teuteberg, Hans-Jürgen/Wischermann Clemens, *Wohnalltag in Deutschland 1850-1914: Bilder – Daten – Dokumente*, Münster: Coppenrath 1985: 366-72. Similar in Teuteberg, Hans-Jürgen, *Die Debatten der deutschen Nationalökonomie im* Verein für Socialpolitik *über die Ursachen der „Wohnungsfrage" und die Steuerungsmittel einer Wohnungsreform im späten 19. Jahrhundert*, Berlin: Duncker und Humblot 1986.
[174] Ward 2004: 29-30.
[175] DS (1919) 5/6: Dieck: 57-9.

had to bear the expenses for the provision of infrastructures in suburban areas whilst created land values were windfall profits to the private property owners.

The situation was further complicated by speculative investments in new houses at as yet undeveloped plots or by the extension of existing buildings as deliberate disregard of alignment plans. According to reports in *Der Städtebau*, both actions were popular in Germany where expropriation rules clearly favoured the property owners and asked for public compensations to be paid not just for the demolition and reconstruction of the already existing buildings but for all potentially attainable revenues as well. These compensation rules were amended by new upper limits introduced in 1917. Bewig suggested in his article that those new powers should be linked to the option of using building bans.[176] In his alternative concept, compensation would only have to be paid based on those property values valid on the date of the building ban's issuance. For Bewig this comprehensive approach would mark a turning point towards sufficient options, not only 'to regulate but to organise' urban development.

Despite the 1917 amendments it remained difficult to determine compensation payments in case of expropriation. Anton Hoenig gave a detailed explanation of those rules applicable in 1928.[177] *Der Städtebau* praised its clear and exact description of the mechanisms linking developments at the property market and urban planning interventions. Hoenigpointed out how private owners benefitted from speculation through extortionate rentssupported by legal rules in place. There remained discord in the journal articles on how the unearned increment could be transferred from private owners to the benefit of the commonwealth. Except for the renovation of old city centres, this particular question remained a challenging one to urban planning in Germany as the legal section (see 3.3.8) will describe. Instead, necessary legal powers remained split into almost 400 different building codes applicable across the various states, regions and cities in the country.[178] A comprehensive town planning act had not been introduced in the interwar years, although numerous drafts were discussed as Feldmann has demonstrated.[179]

Germany was not the only country faced with this challenge. In 1912 *The Town Planning Review* included a book review of a US-American publication by Benjamin Clarke Marsh who assessed several options of future land taxation.[180] The anony-

---

[176] DS (1917) 10/11: Bewig: 123-4.
[177] DS (1928) 10: Hoenig: 231-5.
[178] Feldmann 2011: 7.
[179] Feldmann 2011: 317-68.
[180] TPR (1912) January: no author: 331-2.

128

mous author of this review saw the value of Marsh's book based on its suggestions for reform in taxation systems, which would be of relevance to virtually any country in the world. Among those suggestions were calls to reduce taxation on buildings but to increase those on land values. Specific taxes on the increment of land values, similar to German *Wertzuwachssteuer*, as well as widespread municipal land ownership were considered. In face of the dominance of private investments, and within the context of liberal rules in the US, such statements can be considered to be exceptional.

In the UK, the issue of municipal ownership initiated several debates in *The Town Planning Review* immediately before the First World War broke out. It was a rare exception that the Corporation of Birkenhead acquired vast portions of land from industrialist William Lever.[181] As another article in 1913 describes, British legal frameworks then prohibited municipal land purchase without clear indication of each plots' purpose in the context of future land-use plans. These frameworks therefore complicated the situation on the property market.[182] In 1904 Thomas Horsfall, then member of the British National Housing Reform Council, had advocated for German type legislation with its ownership rights granted to municipalities making it possible for them to acquire a pool of land rights as potential solution to such questions, and he published his recommendations in the book *The Improvement of the Dwellings and Surroundings of the People: The Example of Germany*.[183]

Similar to Anton Hoenig's meticulous work for *Der Städtebau* on the relations between urban planning and property market in Germany, Stanley Adshead visualised those interrelations for the British context in *The Town Planning Review*, though without the former author's mathematical underpinning.[184] Although he acknowledged the underlying but concealed considerations of speculative investors, Adshead explained why they must not benefit exclusively from increasing land values, if the increase is due to other stakeholders' interventions and without any contribution of their own.

"It is preposterous that a landowner should obtain £1,000 an acre for sites, which due to no effort of his own were worth but £50 twenty years ago."[185]

Such tremendous increases were detected in some journal articles as one global cause for the on-going housing shortage. In the late 1930s special attention was

---

[181] TPR (1913) January: no author: 223-4.
[182] TPR (1914) January: no author: 271.
[183] Ward 2004: 25.
[184] TPR (1913) April: Adshead: 47-8.
[185] TPR (1913) April: Adshead: 48.

then paid in *The Town Planning Review* to the impact that improvements in traffic infrastructures had on land values. Some authors referred to the US as the example of what the British future might look. R. H. Mattocks reviewed a publication on the US parkway system written by John Nolen and H. V. Hubbard.[186] This book specifically investigated the economic effects of the different kinds of highways on the property market. Nolen and Hubbard analysed three road networks, then called "regional parkway systems"[187] across the country and came to the conclusion that,

> "'[f]rom all our study we have come to a firm conviction that parkways, properly designed in their relation to all needs of a considerable population, will be worth their expense and that their value will be reflected in the taxable values of property so that, in truth, the community as a business will be better off financially on account of the parkway because it will ultimately be receiving annually in added taxes more than the annual charges to the community for creating and maintaining the parkway.'"[188]

Despite some perceived weaknesses in the wording of a new Section, which formed part of the British *Town and Country Planning Act, 1932* in 1942 John Clarke reported on greater municipal powers to regulate the use of land hereby granted to British planners at local authorities by the end of the analysed interwar period.[189] These new rules can be interpreted as an expression of a new self-perception in British planning under the circumstances of the Second World War. Ward has underscored the significance of those transformations when he concludes: "The 1940s thus became the most critical decade in the development of British planning policy."[190] In comparison to its previous hesitant nature, planning in the UK was then vested with far more authoritative powers, for example in the acquisition of war-affected property by municipalities under the *Town and Country Planning Act 1944*, commonly labelled as 'Blitz and Blight' Act.[191] In comparison to NS-Germany, it left a relatively liberal environment with strong individual rights. What the situation in Germany looked like under Nazi ideology will be investigated in more detail below (see 3.3.6).

---

[186] TPR (1938) December: Mattocks: 132-4.
[187] Jeffry Diefendorf gives a brief explanation to the context of such parkway plans as part of his comparative analysis for Cologne, Basel and Boston. Diefendorf, Jeffry M., *Motor Vehicles and the Inner City*. In: Freestone, Robert [Ed.]: Urban Planning in a Changing World: The Twentieth Century Experience. London: E&FN Spon 2000: 175-8.
[188] TPR (1938) December: Mattocks: 133.
[189] TPR (1942) October: Clarke: 246-56.
[190] Ward 2004: 74.
[191] Ward 2004: 74-106, here 86.

3.3.4 Provision of transportation infrastructures

The close interrelations between the increases of land values and the construction of new transportation infrastructure have been referred to in journal articles. At a more general level, traffic and various modes of transportation played a significant role in the interwar years as a vast number of specific articles in both journals suggest, which were complemented by additional remarks in other non-related contributions. The analysis revealed two types of reports: articles dealing with traffic and the improvement of its infrastructures; and articles focusing on road construction and the need for new arterial and ring roads. Both topics were perceived as more important in Germany than in the UK. *Der Städtebau* covered the issue of traffic in 70 specific articles during the analysed period with a remarkable boom in the late 1920s, when in 1927 alone nine articles were published and this number further increased to 11 the following year (see figure 7). This is a reflection of the good economic situation during those years as well as a fascination for modernising efforts in Berlin. Road construction and the question of new arterial roads were covered in a total of 66 separate articles, although there were antecedents preceding the First World War with 11 reports in 1913 and eight in 1915. *The Town Planning Review* by contrast reported but at comparatively lower frequency and with a rather limited thematic scope. Traffic improvements were specifically addressed in just 11 articles without any significant peaks. The construction of arterial roads received most of its attention in the years immediately before the Great War, when out of a total 23 articles on this subject, four were published in 1915 and three in 1913 and 1914 respectively (see figures 6 and 7).

The impact of motor traffic

In Britain motor traffic impacted urban planning earlier. In a 1913 editorial to *The Town Planning Review* there was a call for action with regards to motor traffic in face of the rising numbers of fatal accidents on British streets. This call was additionally linked to administrative demands for one competent authority in charge of traffic planning for the whole of Greater London. The editorial appeared after the parliamentary Select Committee presented its first report on the challenges posed by fatal accidents as a consequence of increased traffic volumes.[192] These reported fatalities marked increased public concern with the issue of traffic speed. Furthermore, Christoph Merki illustrated how the distances urban inhabitants travelled increased based on the available means of transportation.[193] They were not limited

---

[192] TPR (1913) October: no author: 188-91.
[193] Merki, Christoph Maria, *Verkehrsgeschichte und Mobilität*, Stuttgart: UTB/Eugen Ulmer 2008: 27, 80. Merki estimates the daily distances an average French citizen covered in 1800 at three to four kilometres as opposed to roughly 40 kilometres today.

to those ranges they could manage as pedestrians anymore but they had the opportunity to use horse-drawn and then electric trams and eventually motor vehicles. As a consequence, these new means impacted the built environment such as new and extended street layouts. In Germany people predominantly depended on bicycles for financial reasons as their means of transportation[194] and the country therefore lagged behind other major industrialised countries such as France, the UK or US, where motorised vehicles played an increasing role. German planners nonetheless had to latter adapt to these new circumstances as interwar years progressed.[195]

Since the number of motor vehicles was not yet large enough to cause traffic congestion in the very early years analysed, *Der Städtebau* focused to a large extent on design and aesthetic questions when it came to street planning, as was the case with the position of monuments[196] or the preservation of streetscapes for their artistic qualities.[197] As traffic increased articles raised the question of how to make street intersections suitable for larger traffic volumes.[198] The discussion in both journals revolved around examples of the demolition of buildings in order to widen existing streets as well as the construction of completely new arterial or ring roads. In Werner Hegemann's opinion London symbolised a pacemaker in this respect, for which reason a larger delegation of renowned German planners took part in an excursion to the city in 1925 and visited road construction projects. Hegemann has summarised their impressions in a short travel report for *Der Städtebau*[199]. Similar experiences had not yet been associated with German cities in the journal. With growing domestic traffic volumes the journal's attention was soon diverted from London to Berlin though.

Brian Ladd has recounted the automobile's story of dissemination from its early days as a toy available to a tiny affluent elite at the turn of the century to mass motorisation starting in the US during interwar years.[200] Ladd refers to the sense of individuality and, "the drug of speed"[201] provided by the car and offers an account of the ambivalent reactions urban drivers provoked when they were driving their noisy and polluting vehicles in the countryside. Here it was not just a clash with preservationists trying to defend their romanticised images of nature but how it

---

[194] Merki 2008: 50.
[195] Merki 2008: 56.
[196] DS (1913) 1: Klaiber: 9-10.
[197] DS (1913) 4: Landwehr: 44-7; (1913) 5: Landwehr: 51-2.
[198] DS (1913) 6: Schachenmeier: 67-71; (1913) 7: Schachenmeier: 77-82.
[199] DS (1925) 7/8: Hegemann: 116.
[200] Ladd, Brian, Autophobia – Love and Hate in the Automotive Age, Chicago/London, University of Chicago Press 2008: 13-42, 69-96.
[201] Ibid.: 16.

created new problems such as dust emissions and road accidents injuring or killing people and fowl. Whilst those accidents created a hostile environment in the countryside in the beginning of mass motorisation, automobiles had their implications for urban planning too as was the case with speed limits and suburbanisation.

The journal analysis is equally telling in this respect. According to a report published in *Der Städtebau* in 1930[202], the global number of motor vehicles rose by 15.1% in just two years, from 27.7 million in early 1927 to 31.88 million in early 1929. The clear majority were (private) cars which accounted for 27.15 million. Germany in 1929 had a total of 567,000 vehicles excluding motorcycles officially registered across the country as compared to 1,088,000 in France and 1,309,000 in the UK. The author emphasised increased problems created by road traffic during the second half of the 1920s, when registration almost quadrupled until 1929 from an initial 152,000 in 1924. The number of 608,000 motorcycles, as given by Merki, outpaced all other registered motor vehicles in Germany.[203] The second traffic census carried out between 1st October 1928 and 30th September 1929 on all major streets at state, provincial and district level recorded a doubling in traffic volumes compared to the preceding first census four years earlier. Although the number of registered vehicles for my case study of Windhoek remained limited, I will explore the debates caused by the anticipation of rising motor traffic (see 4.2.4).

Authors discussed the layout of new street surfaces that were able to withstand those higher levels of abrasion.[204] Due to their different speeds, a demarcation of separate street sections for the various kinds of transportation modes entered the debate and they started to compete for the available space. Dieter Schott and Stefan Klein refer to early signs of the tramways' decline in German cities since 1928 where buses represented their prime competitor, before cars started to dominate traffic planning.[205] This competition can be traced back to the 1920s, when first complaints were made about trams as perceived obstacles to motor vehicles as formulated in 1927 by Walter Ewoldt in his contribution to *Der Städtebau* on the case study of Hamburg. Based on Fritz Schumacher's comprehensive plans, Ewoldt deemed a complete reorganisation of traffic infrastructures in the city centre necessary whichmeant the exclusion of trams from central areas and their sub-

---

[202] DS (1930) 6: F. H.: 296.

[203] Merki mentions the still growing number of registered motorcycles throughout the 1930s, making Germany's the world's largest stock with one motorbike per 45 inhabitants in 1938 (Merki 2008: 56).

[204] TPR (1923) September: G. E. H. R.: 214.

[205] Schott, Dieter/Klein, Stefan, *Mit der Tram ins 21. Jahrhundert: Geschichte, Gegenwart und Zukunft der Straßenbahn*, Essen: Klartext 1998: 14-5.

stitution through either elevated or underground rapid transit systems detached from the street level.[206] Ideas for unconventional solutions were discussed, either based on existing foreign patterns like the autonomous road system consisting of one-way streets in the Cuban capital of Havana[207], or theoretical concepts like that one of honeycomb-like city structures described by Mr Hartmann which avoided street intersections at right angles.[208] According to their authors, such concepts make it easier to see other motor vehicles approaching an intersection and the concepts offer more convenient urban structures. Hartmann describes the hexagons' inner courtyards created by the honeycomb-like structure to be advantageous to shield sensitive infrastructures like schools from traffic noise. In 1929 Georg Fest contributed an article[209], in which he discussed several schematic alternatives of how to distribute the available space among all road users and to reduce the number of potential peril points for motor traffic at street intersections. In his drafted street sections he saw the necessity to separate through traffic from slower, internal city traffic. Trams still formed an integral part of his concepts but their lines were designed on partly separate tracks that reduced the required intersections with motor vehicles. Additionally, pedestrians and cyclists would receive separate lanes, and the sketches Fest produced resemble some of the recommendations still used today.[210]

Excursus: Ascension of the "motor age"

Motor vehicles initially catered to the luxurious leisure time interests of a wealthy and therefore limited elite. They could not only afford to buy the automobile but to cover its maintenance costs. It was not before they made their way into daily routines, and motor traffic at large becoming the symbol for a new era. The sheer number of motor vehicles that made their way onto the streets of more and more cities generated a new problem for the organisation of urban routines. Le Corbusier alluded to this problem in the late 1920s, when he referred to the more than 250,000 motor vehicles in those days' Paris which had completely replaced the previously common horses.[211] In contrast to those horses, motor cars were driving at a speed ten times faster, inevitably leading to many dangerous situations for pedestrians who were not yet used to these new circumstances.

---

[206] DS (1927) 9: Ewoldt: 133.
[207] DS (1929) 4: Malcher: 97-108.
[208] DS (1926) 5: Hartmann: 70-1.
[209] DS (1929) 5: Fest: 129-32.
[210] As laid down for Germany in *Richtlinie zur Anlage von Stadtstraßen*. FGSV [Ed.] 2007.
[211] Le Corbusier [1929] 1987: 266.

By the end of the analysed interwar period, Ludwig Hilberseimer was convinced of three major problems in urban development and ranked them by priority: air pollutionin part caused by traffic; slums; and traffic.[212] In his assessment, he emphasised the problems in virtually all central areas caused by traffic congestion in major cities at the metropole that were unable to cope with continuously growing traffic quantities in their existing structures at that time. He pointed to the problem of mixed spaces for pedestrians and automobiles which have led to many traffic accidents. Their figures skyrocketed over time such as in the US, where 23,300 people were killed in car crashes in 1943 alone and more than 800,000 were injured. He calculated the estimated accumulated losses to the US economy due to wage losses, costs for medical treatment or repairs induced for that yearwhich reached a staggering US$1.2 billion. And 1943 was not the worst year, for 1941 recorded an all-time high of 39,969 reported fatal accidents compared to 'only' 21,900 in 1925.

These depressing figures must have been shocking due to the speed and weight of the new vehicles involved. One suggested solution to remedy this urgent problem was described in the separation of transportation modes, which included the enforced construction of motorways exclusively devoted to motor vehicle traffic as the many articles published in both journals. One of those significant and admired early plans had been introduced by the Committee on the Regional Plan for New York in the 1920s, where an elevated highway along the Hudson River whould help establish a safer environment for other road users.[213] Blueprints for the separation of tramways from motor traffic were drafted as another means to ensure order under those seemingly chaotic circumstances.[214] In this respect, Hilberseimer's position blended perfectly into demands formulated by the Athens Charter and closely followed Le Corbusier's modernist ideas. Modern traffic produced further, though less fatal, problems besides accidents. Instead of horse droppings urban dwellers were confronted with new nuisances in terms of air pollution[215] and noise. The latter problem was discussed in Windhoek too (see 4.2.4). In 1929 Le Corbusier complained about the modern noise and almost nostalgically remembered a not too distant past.

---

[212] Hilberseimer, Ludwig, *The New City : Principles of Planning*, Chicago : Paul Theobald 1944: 49-52.
[213] Le Corbusier [1929] 1987: xii.
[214] Cadbury 1915: 62-8.
[215] As documented in aerial photos taken by Marcel Lods across interwar Paris (Haffner, Jeanne, *The View from Above: The Science of Social Space*, Cambridge: MIT Press 2013: 42).

"I think back twenty years, when I was a student; the road belonged to us then; we sang in it and argued in it, while the horse-'bus swept calmly along."[216]

The remarkable presence and increased share of motor vehicles in transportation inspired authors such as Matheson, who in 1910 – as one of the first – saw the widespread arrival of the motor vehicle as "an epoch-making event"[217], to the association of the 20th century with the "motor age" that was taking over the predominant role in transportation from its predecessor, for which he called the 19th century the "railway age." Based on similar impressions, Morris Knowles a decade later pointed out that railway links were not a first priority to industrial companies anymore since trucks had taken over their functions.[218] This major shift in means of transportation in the US as early as 1920 was about to reach Europe. Further, Matheson was confident that the 21st century's would be dominated by aeroplanes.[219] By the end of the interwar period Hilberseimer confirmed this projection in 1944.

"Soon we will see new shifts conditioned by the airplane. Many a seaport will decline, while those cities at junction points of airlines will gain importance as they become traffic centers for passengers and freight."[220]

Motorways

During the second half of the 1920s both planning journals reported on plans for the construction of nationwide road networks exclusively dedicated to fast motorised through traffic and based on the principle of fly-over crossings, hence separating traffic flows in accordance with their travel directions at different street levels. New York's Regional Plan and the motorways it contained were recommended by Wesley Dougill in his 1926 review for *The Town Planning Review* as part of a blueprint solution to many British planners. Based on the quoted US-American ratio between its population and motor vehicles, which was 45:1 in 1916, 16:1 in 1923 and estimated to be at 6:1 in 1935, he substantiated his belief in the necessity of a specific motorway system to cope with future traffic growth.[221] Initially, their suitability for Germany was rejected in some articles in *Der Städtebau*, since motorways were considered an unnecessary but expensive competitor to the existing railway

---

[216] Le Corbusier [1929] 1987: xxiii.
[217] Matheson, A. Scott, *The City of Man*, London/Leipzig: Fisher Unwin 1910: 160.
[218] Knowles 1920: 50.
[219] Matheson 1910: 161.
[220] Hilberseimer 1944: 41.
[221] TPR (1926) November: Dougill: 145-7.

lines, as Robert Schmidt argued in a contribution published in 1926.[222] Despite Schmidt's negative view on motorways it was in the same year, that the so-called "HAFRABA"Association was founded in Frankfurt am Main with its goal to prepare the construction of a motorway linking the cities of Hamburg, Frankfurt and Basel contained in the original acronym.[223] Karl-Heinz Friedrich has described how the association intended to construct and maintain the motorway as a private undertaking following the example of Italian autostrada. However the project did not materialise during Weimar Republic, as was the case for similar projects across Germany except for a short section in Cologne. Autobahns as a German version of motorways came emerged under Hitler's regime for propaganda purposes, as Roland May illustrates in his design analysis of bridges.[224] Irrespective of the attention autobahns received, due to general economic constraints even with the meticulous supervision of Fritz Todt in his function as Inspector for German Roads Construction (*Generalinspektor für das deutsche Straßenwesen*), their construction was limited to routes opening up the country's major regions. Friedrich mentions 3,300 km as completed at the outbreak of the Second World War.[225] The network did not include those systemic featuressuch as ring roads projected and described in a 1935 contribution to *Der Städtebau*.[226]

Railways

Although much attention was drawn to road traffic, other modes of transportation featured in the articles published, especially in *Der Städtebau*. Railways still accounted for the majority of transported passengers and goods. Despite all the debates about competition with cars, buses and lorries many suggestions dealt with potential improvements in their networks. In 1921 Ewald Genzmer and Cornelius Gurlitt presented their ideas for a rapid transit system in Greater Dresden based on lower than usual construction and maintenance costs, ideas which they considered to be transferable to other cities of similar size.[227] Genzmer envisaged a network of detached tramlines that did not demand for the construction of expensive elevated or underground tracks but which were more or less at street level, though in specific sections without street intersections. Their platforms and tramcars should be

---

[222] DS (1926) 8: Schmidt: 128.
[223] Friedrich, Karl-Heinz, „*Tunlich geradlinig*". *Die Gründung des Vereins „HAFRABA" 1926 und der Bau der deutschen Autobahnen*. In: Mitteilungen aus dem Bundesarchiv 2/2006.
[224] May, Roland, *Von der Ingenieurästhetik zur Monumentalarchitektur: Der Brückenbau der Reichsautobahnen und der Architekt Paul Bonatz*. In: Harlander, Tilman; Pyta, Wolfram [Eds.]: NS-Architektur: Macht und Symbolpolitik. Berlin: LIT Verlag 2010.
[225] Friedrich 2006: 76.
[226] DS (1935) 3: G.: 28-31.
[227] DS (1921) 1/2: Genzmer: 3-8.

prepared to match at almost the same height for the passengers' comfort when entering or leaving the trains. Genzmer referred to the already existing types of trains running between Bonn and Godesbergcomparable to modern days light rail systems, although the latter are based on low-floor vehicles.

Besides those rather general ideas which could be replicated in many cities, at least eight reports published in *Der Städtebau* between 1927 and 1929 covered the continuous efforts intended to tackle Greater Berlin's deficits in rail infrastructure with its many terminus stations. Several authors delved into the topic, and presented or discussed options to build a new and so far missing North-South link that would enable direct connections into the city centre for regional and long distance trains of all major national routes.Out of the 13 lines just four had such direct access in 1928, when Mr Von Ritgen summarised the situation and potential solutions at a comprehensive level.[228] Michael Braun had recently illustrated the conceptual considerations behind the link's construction.[229] The extent of such new ideas discussed does become apparent in the reorganisation of Berlin's public transportation under the umbrella of one competent authority, the Berliner Verkehrsgesellschaft (BVG) in 1928.[230] The new authority laid the foundation for the central coordination of all fares and schedules around Germany's capital city.

Canals

Merki has pointed out how, in contrast to the UK, Germany's waterways did not create a dense network in early interwar years and that some regions were not linked at all.[231] A few projects were under construction or consideration in interwar years to canalize the rivers Danube, Main and Neckar, and to further use them, at least partially, for electricity generation. For river Neckar completion of works up to the town of Plochingen was mentioned in a contribution to *Der Städtebau* in 1936 whilst the original plans for the Danube canalization on its section from Ulm to Regensburg already submitted in 1928 reportedly needed further revision.[232] Anyhow besides topographical reasons the required heavy investments in completely new canals made their extension less likely. During the analysed period some voices made themselves heard in *Der Städtebau* arguing that canals could have a larger share in the transportation of various kinds of freight, if they were prepared for inland water vessels able to carry up to 1,000 tons of cargo. Otto Blum

---

[228] DS (1928) 7: Von Ritgen: 170-3.
[229] Braun, Michael, *Nordsüd-S-Bahn Berlin: 75 Jahre Eisenbahn im Untergrund*, Berlin: Gesellschaft für Verkehrspolitik und Eisenbahnwesen/Berliner S-Bahn-Museum 2008: 10-5.
[230] Schützler, Heiko, *Die BVG wird gegründet*, 2000.
[231] Merki 2008: 38-42.
[232] DS (1936) 6: Schwab: 70.

tried to counter this idea in 1931 since, in his opinion, it did not offer convincing advantages when compared to freight trains. Instead the retrofit programme for waterways would prove to be a heavy financial burden to the state. Blum insisted that the railway network's full potential had not been made use of so far. He questioned whether Berlin's freight traffic, to which waterways contributed an estimated share of 35 to 40%, necessarily had to be transported by vessel or if they could be replaced by trains.[233]

These debates were particularly fierce in face of the projected modernisation of existing canals with vessels able to carry 1,000 tons of cargo. Many articles dealt with the consequences on Berlin's inner city where massive interventions were needed to adapt the existing locks, including the subsequent demolition of historic buildings like 'Palais Ephraim' adjacent to Mühlendamm locks. Similar to Blum's tone, and published in the same issue of *Der Städtebau*, Werner Hegemann used a different argument when he referred to the specific historic circumstances that once supported the canals' construction as part of attempts to demonstrate Prussia's royal prestige. For those interwar projects he pointed out that waterways could not be expected to be financially sustainable means of transportation at larger scale if compared to railways.[234] This position was only challenged under National Socialist rule, when plans were revealed which aimed at the construction of new canals extending the network of waterways into some parts of Southern Germany. Those plans presented in an article by Mr Schwab contained, amongst many other projects, the extension and canalisation efforts along the river Danube and a new canal that was supposed to link Danube and Neckar. According to Schwab's description this connection was intended to form a new central axis, and was therefore called "southern Midland Canal" in the style of the already existing Midland Canal linking central Germany.[235] Nonetheless, the "southern Midland Canal" remained a paper tiger as was the case with those plans for a canal linking the rivers Rhine, Main and Danube. Despite the contract already signed in 1921 between Reich's Government and the State of Bavaria, the canal's construction was only carried out in post-war times and completed in 1992.[236]

---

[233] DS (1931) 2: Blum: 96.
[234] DS (1931) 2: Hegemann: 95.
[235] DS (1936) 6: Schwab: 70-1.
[236] Website RMD Wasserstraßen:
https://web.archive.org/web/20071008084609if_/http://www.rmd-wasserstrassen.de/
(retrieved on 05.11.2017).

Unconventional systems and air traffic

Technological progress was reflected in the journals, although thoughts to replicate the system of a suspension railway beyond its unique implementation in the city of Wuppertal, as suggested in two contributions to *Der Städtebau* in 1928, remained at the theoretical level.[237] Aviation was covered as part of modern developments but played a very limited role in both journals from the viewpoint of urban planning. In 1927 Jürgen Brandt reported about the first German seadrome whose construction at Travemünde close to Lübeck had been started. This combined airport with onshore facilities as well as potential landing places for seaplanes servinge as hub for connections to the Baltic countries and, according to Brandt's description, as test ground for a future transatlantic airport.[238] Another article generally confirms the marginal significance that aviation and airports then had in terms of urban development. In 1931 Wilhelm Luthardt summarised recently introduced planning and building codes for the state of Thuringia, and how they matched with already existing laws at the national level. He emphasised building codes' advances since they, for the first time, provided the basis for comprehensive planning of airports and their surroundings, vesting local authorities with powers to limit building activities that could render the operation of an airport impossible.[239] The law did stipulate rules for participation processes of relevant stakeholders to ensure that the interests of neighbouring owners and businesses were considered. A similar book analysing the situation of 85 existing airports in the US was published by Henry V. Hubbard was reviewed in *The Town Planning Review* in 1931.[240] Despite its admiring undertone, the review nonetheless underscores the different situation on the American continent, where aviation played a role to establish links on long distance routes comparatively early. Although civil aviation did not matter that much in terms of urban planning, it was an important means of transportation for Windhoek in interwar years for travels to South Africa. Therefore SWA Legislative Assembly discussed a motion to take over the authority for civil aviation from the Union in 1938 but the motion was eventually dropped.[241] In addition, there was another factor that contributed to the general difficulties in planning the necessary infrastructures for civil aviation. Until the tragic accident at Lakehurst in 1937 it was undecided whether airplanes or airships would represent the preferred means of air transportation give both had different environmental effects in terms of

---

[237] DS (1928) 7: L.A.: 174-5; (1928) 12: Petersen: 309.
[238] DS (1927) 4: Brandt: 49-50.
[239] DS (1931) 1: Luthardt: 48.
[240] TPR (1931) May: Kelly: 211.
[241] VPLA Fourth Session, Third Assembly 1938: 5, 36.

140

space and buildings.[242] Nonetheless, Friedrich Lenger emphasises the prestige attached to the construction of an airport for interwar cities.[243]

Excursus: New perspectives from above

Although Hilberseimer's prediction made in 1944 concerning a shift towards the air transport only materialised in the second half of the 20th century, has contributed a transformation in the perception of the earth's surface and cityscapes in particular during interwar years. Civil aviation has benefitted throughout the analysed period from several advances in the construction of airplanes and Christoph Merki quotes a tremendous increase. Scheduled flights operated in 1925 covered a distance of 0.1 billion passenger-kilometres and these numbers multiplied to 8 billion in 1945. However, they are miniscule compared to 3,300 billion passenger-kilometres recorded in 2000.[244]

Aviation's limited relevance in civil terms reflects its birth as a large-scale application for military purposes during the First World War. Jeanne Haffner has submitted a compilation of the airplane's impact on the perception of space from the viewpoint of social sciences. Her findings reveal valuable insights on the side-effects for urban development. She emphasised the airplane's original role as a medium to monitor the enemy's activities as part of trench warfare. Members of the French air force were full of appreciation for what they called the "vue d'ensemble"[245], a comprehensive picture of the landscape that was generated by the joint efforts of interdisciplinary teams who were at the same time able to interpret those aerial photos. Hence, Haffner underscores how the First World War has helped to disseminate the technical skills in reading aerial photography, not only in military realms but in several other disciplines ranging from the arts to social sciences too.

Ethnography was one of the key disciplines which benefitted from these developments during the interwar period.[246] Ethnographers and anthropologists used this means to analyse social patterns as part of their research methodologies during fieldwork. Haffner mentions French Africanist Marcel Griaule as one of the first to take advantage of this tool. Parts of those scholarly research activities by ethnographers were carried out in collaboration with the colonial administrations, as was the case for Paul-Henry Chombart during his research trip to northern Came-

---

[242] Merki 2008: 61-3, 70-2.
[243] Lenger 2013: 326.
[244] Merki 2008: 66.
[245] Haffner 2013: 8.
[246] Haffner 2013: 32.

roon in 1937.[247] Haffner argues that some of the research efforts also represented a reaction to previous war experiences.

> "As was true of many other scholars and artists working in the 1920s and the 1930s, the war had undermined Gourou's [a French human geographer] faith in the European ideals of modernization and rationality, and he had turned to the study of non-Western societies in search of alternatives to Western values, ways of life, and modes of production."[248]

Hence, not all research activities were carried out with the aim to repeat and support the Eurocentric notion of 'progress' and the colonial 'civilising mission.'

Aside from the few articles on photogrammetry already mentioned in the journal analysis (see 3.2), aerial photography did influence the realms of architecture and urban design. Le Corbusier had revised his design philosophies of the straight line. Based on the analysis of those images he saw during a trip to Brazil's Amazon, he developed the "Law of the Meander" which complemented his later publications.[249] His aerial photography was used as an instrument to display and promote new housing schemes as something particularly modern and to underscore the planner's emminence. For the early 1930s Marcel Lods is mentioned as one example who, according to Haffner, took his own aerial photos of the housing scheme in the Parisian outskirt of the "Cité de la Muette", which he had drafted in collaboration with architect Eugène Beaudoin and in accordance with Le Corbusier's modernist ideas.[250] Beyond aviation's symbol of 'modernity', anthropologist James Scott argues that aerial photography was of particular relevance in the colonial environment.[251] Here, it served the colonisers' interests to effectively take control over their subjugated territories and to monitor the Indigenous population, as was done through the application of similar scientific instruments like cartography and statistics. Two of those results produced by the South African Air Force on Windhoek are reproduced in the appendix (see A4 and A5).

3.3.5 Planning schools of thought

Traffic remained a prominent challenge throughout the analysed time period but the different means of transportation it produced offered new options to rethink urban structures. This was first tested as part of the comprehensive urban design competition for Greater Berlin in 1910/11 which encompassed housing, traffic

---

[247] Haffner 2013: 38.
[248] Haffner 2013: 26.
[249] Haffner 2013: 45.
[250] Haffner 2013: 43.
[251] Haffner 2013: 16.

142

and legal aspects in one regional plan.[252] City development was not confined to walkable areas. The aesthetic ideas behind the Garden City concept remained appealing as part of potential blueprint solutions for city extensions. The Garden City was discussed, then criticised and – not formally but de facto – abandoned soon after the First World War though, as was the case with other planning concepts in interwar years too. Howard's disciples formed just one of the many voices among the planners' concert, and although the ideal of a life in lower density environments seemed to be appealing to larger sections of society in many countries, garden cities as a comprehensive concept lost more and more ground. The original design ideas behind this concept, instead, permeated into the planning community at large. They were adopted and translated into new urban and regional strategies like satellite cities. Peter Hall has summarised those transitions for the interwar period which do represent a guideline for this subchapter.[253]

During the first half of the interwar period, both journals were able to serve as arenas to present different ideas and to argue about their respective assumed advantages and disadvantages for urban development. Later Germany's transformation from democratic structures towards Hitler's dictatorship narrowed down the available options for 'real' debates. Instead, the political agenda played an ever-increasing role and hence diminished opportunities to use *Der Städtebau* to present different opinions, as the journal analysis has confirmed. This trend occurred before the National Socialists came into power, because the journal's language began to change from in the early 1930s towards nationalistic sentiments. This self-censorship intensified with the substitution of Werner Hegemann as the journal's editor-in-chief with Friedrich Paulsen with the April-issue in 1933. Hegemann's dismissal served the Nazi's 'Action Against the un-German Spirit', intended to eliminate all opposing voices that did not comply with NS core beliefs.[254] These developments did affect the international exchange of ideas and the dissemination of schools of thought although not completely.

The skyscraper controversy

A defining divide mirrored in both planning journals was their respective opinions on several subjects which tended to separate traditionalists (e.g. attached to arts and crafts) from modernists (e.g. affiliated with Bauhaus ideas). A key example

---

[252] Hofrichter 1995: 117-9.
[253] Hall, Peter, *Cities of Tomorrow: An Intellectual History of Urban Planning and Design in the Twentieth Century*, Malden: Blackwell [1988] 2014: 90-148.
[254] Website Berlin: http://www.berlin.de/geschichte/verbannte-buecher/ (retrieved on 24.04.2015).

where their contradicting ideas of the future built environment collided in the German context were skyscrapers. In 1919 a short article appeared in *Der Städtebau*, which discussed the idea of constructing what was then called 'Turmhaus' ('tower house' in literal translation but meaning skyscraper) in Düsseldorf and potentially in Berlin. The article was a reprint of a newspaper report from *Deutsche Allgemeine Zeitung* and based on its style it can clearly be interpreted as one of the conservative traditionalist voices. Most of its critique was based on economic considerations and the contributor doubted a profitable maintenance of skyscrapers due to their high construction costs. In addition, it was argued that these buildings would, exacerbate the existing traffic congestions in the cities' central areas, particularly during rush hours and a densification of workplaces would counter the supposedly consensual decentralisation efforts for the housing sector into small houses.[255] In following editions the skyscraper project, again, came under attack and in 1920 its potential construction was directly affiliated with Bruno Taut's 'City Crown' concept by the article's anonymous author. Plans were heavily criticised for their perceived architectural megalomania that did not demonstrate 'real' goals except for an arbitrary accumulation of functions. In an attempt to discredit the skyscraper plans for Düsseldorf, the author accused works as representations of what he called the 'pre-First World War loudmouth era' (Großmaulära). He insinuated its construction could easily be supported by American investments, thus underscoring the project's unacceptability for historic and nationalistic reasons.[256]

Confronted with severe housing shortages, later reports remained reserved but hesitantly took a different position towards skyscrapers and explicitly condemned their disregard or denigration. Their construction still seemed unrealistic to Wolf, who submitted the next article on this subject in 1922, looking at economic considerations and suitable sites. The author argued that under the framework of controlled housing economy, no effort should be focused on one single point at the urban periphery where costly new infrastructures needed to be installed first, whilst voids between buildings in the inner city with their existing infrastructures would have been ignored.[257] In 1925 Werner Hegemann collated several opinions on plans drafted by Fritz Schumacher for the construction of a skyscraper at Cologne's centrally located Heumarkt square. This article was one of the first that did not reject skyscrapers per se but emphasised their effects on the cityscape as well as on traffic. This serves as an example of *Der Städtebau's* liberal era when differing

---

[255] DS (1919) 7/8: no author: 87-8.
[256] DS (1920) 5/6: no author: 58.
[257] DS (1922): 9/10: Wolf: 92-4.

144

opinions were welcomed.[258] Though a meticulous evaluation of the potential advantages of skyscrapers with regards to traffic and time served to prove their inappropriateness under German and European circumstances[259], there remained a fascination for their potential construction. This fascination became tangible for the last time in *Der Städtebau's* coverage on the competition for a redevelopment of the Reichstag's neighbourhood as well as its extension in 1930. In the vicinity of Paul Wallot's old Reichstag building commentators were in those days not just willing to accept but expressed their appreciation for Hans Poelzig's entry for a skyscraper.

> "Eine weniger gemeinschädliche Lage für ein Hochhaus könnte kaum gefunden werden. Nur für einen öffentlichen Zweck und nur in solcher Lage ist ein Hochhaus überhaupt zu rechtfertigen."[260]

Other German examples for competitions working with skyscrapers or tall buildings as part of their solutions, like famous Chile-House in Hamburg, were not covered in the planning journals. For *The Town Planning Review* skyscrapers played a comparatively limited role, and their perception among the British planning community followed the same lines as in Germany though without the chauvinistic sentiment of a war-defeated nation. In a total of four specific articles the construction of high-rise buildings was addressed and the first three of them focussed on the developments in New York.

The first contribution written by Thomas Adams in 1911 openly plays with the dichotomy of modernist and traditionalist views on such buildings and mirrors later German debate. Though expressing his fascination for skyscrapers from the technical viewpoint and as a suitable means to alleviate America's housing shortage through this new type of edifice, Adams regarded the skyscraper as rather unsuitable to the European context. Furthermore he argued in favour of a stronger and more consistent town planning regime in the US in order to deal with the situation of overcrowding in prosperous regions and to provide adequate infrastructure as well as healthy living environments.[261] Only one and a half decades later, in 1926, Thomas Adams again portrayed skyscrapers as an underestimated building type of peculiar beauty. Based on statistics from 1925 indicating the increasing number and height of high-rise buildings in New York, he tried to illustrate their growing

---

[258] DS (1925) 11/12: Hegemann: 153-5.
[259] DS (1928) 3: Leo: 60-4.
[260] DS (1930) 2: Hegemann: 102. "A less harmful site for a skyscraper can barely be found. Just for public purposes and just at such a location is a skyscraper to be justified at all". (author's translation).
[261] TPR (1911) July: Adams: 139-46.

significance for urban planning. In 1902 the city counted for 181 buildings with 10 to 19 storeys and just three buildings with 20 storeys or more on Manhattan Island below 65th Street. These numbers grew to 838 and 97 respectively in 1925 and Adams felt obliged once again to underscore their benefits to a city's development if high rise buildings were part of a proper urban layout plan. In that case he did not see a specific limit to their height and was of the opinion that skyscrapers could eventually be applied to the European context.[262] A few years later Wesley Dougill attributed the US with the label "nation of builders" due to their contributions to the construction of skyscrapers in his 1931 review of Colonel Starrett's book "Skyscrapers, and the Men who build them."[263] Although Dougill still referred to high-rise buildings as a genuinely American type, he also mentioned debates in some British cities where the construction of skyscrapers were discussed. Taking each city's peculiarities into consideration he saw no basis for a nationwide statement on higher buildings but supported solutions at their individual discretion. Furthermore most of the book review focussed on the history of this building type and its technical and socio-economic background that transformed many US-cityscapes of those days. Whilst those three articles primarily presented the matter of skyscrapers as a particular curiosity of urban development in the US, the last article explicitly dealt with the situation in London and other major cities in the UK. It was a reprint of the fifth Report of the Royal Fine Art Commission published in 1934 addressing the side-effects of high buildings on the British cityscape. The Commission regarded such buildings as intrusive which represented a, "[…] new and growing menace to the beauties of the Metropolis […]"[264] that had the potential to destroy the previously harmonious city development characterised by sufficient light and air for neighbouring edifices as well as respect for existing city prospects like the one on St. Paul's Cathedral. The Report reflects the reluctance for the skyscraper to cross the Atlantic and reach European soil.

Modernist versus traditionalist viewpoints

From an international perspective the controversy surroundings skyscrapers was addressed as well and opinions were equally divided. Besides their widespread construction across the US, skyscrapers were of course linked to many modernistic plans drafted by Le Corbusier. He was a strong advocate of skyscrapers and proposed to replace the old city centres like in Paris with such skyscrapers embedded into large green spaces as exemplified in his outstanding 1925 'Plan Voisin.' On the other hand, Willy Fuchs-Röll reported in *Der Städtebau* that such monumental

---

[262] TPR (1926) May: Adams: 79-83.
[263] TPR (1931) December: Dougill: 286.
[264] TPR (1934) December: Royal Fine Art Commission: 128.

buildings were temporarily prohibited for London's development based on a council decision in 1929.[265] Despite London's reserved position on skyscrapers, Le Corbusier's *Vers une Architecture*, which has been reviewed in its English translation *Towards a New Architecture* by F. X. Velarde in 1929[266], was welcomed in *The Town Planning Review* for its logical and clear-sited vision offering convincing arguments about architecture and urban planning. Although Le Corbusier's interwar impact on Europe remained limited as Françoise Choay has analysed[267], the 1938 'Town Planning Exhibition and Congress' held at Johannesburg testifies to his impact on the colonial environment as Mabin and Oranje have analysed.[268]

Some debates among the different planning schools were sparked by differing opinions on such supposedly simple architectural and urban questions like the layout of straight or curved streets, or the controversies on the style of roofs. To some commentators in those days, these disputes reflected a low in architecture and Stanley Adshead considered it as anachronistic, when he explains in 1930,

> "[n]ever in the history of the world has there been a period so embarrassing as the present in the varied display of its architectural character and style."[269]

It depicts the diametrically opposed positions as represented by Le Corbusier's and Camillo Sitte's planning principles as well as their respective limitations. But it is a gentle reminder of the challenges in urban development planners faced. When referring to Le Corbusier's city of 3 million as laid out in his *The City of To-morrow and its Planning*, Adshead remarks,

> "[h]e [Le Corbusier] shows us that the application of modern inventions in transport and building, if taken advantage of to the extent that they might be, will bring about the building of an entirely new kind of city, and though M. Le Corbusier's city is never likely to be built, we are convinced that the 'Pack Donkey' methods of the mediaeval builders, even when led by Camillo Sitte, will have to give way to the measured motor tracks of Le Corbusier, if populations of millions instead of populations of thousands, are to be accommodated in the city of to-morrow which certainly are a misfit in the city of to-day."[270]

---

[265] DS (1930) 3: Fuchs-Röll: 150.
[266] TPR (1929) May: Velarde: 201.
[267] Choay, Françoise, *L'urbanisme, utopies et réalités : Une anthologie*, Paris : Points [1965] 2014: 233-49.
[268] Mabin, Oranje 2014.
[269] TPR (1930) November: Adshead: 85.
[270] TPR (1930) November: Adshead: 93.

Regardless of whether or not Adshead fully agreed with Le Corbusier's propositions in aesthetical terms, he made clear that most of Sitte's principles were unsuitable for the urban challenges of interwar years. Across the English Channel, the NS regime's statements and concepts remained ambiguous in their architectural and urban planning goals as will be further explained in the following section. The regime preferred an architectural style expressing conservative values and regional elements in housing projects whilst industrial buildings or transportation infrastructure represented symbols of modernity. As Durth has summarised with regards to Ernst Neufert's works[271], those regional patterns in housing were mixed with efforts for standardisation. NSofficially rejected those aesthetic modernist experiments as carried out under Bauhaus supervision. This attitude became obvious in Stuttgart where an opposition to Bauhaus formed its own school of thoughts relatively early. The Stuttgart School's proponents antedated aesthetic values similar to those under the Nazi regime. Already in 1925 did a report apparently submitted to *Der Städtebau* by the school's disciples commented positively on their developments in line with this "new spirit"[272], as the subsequent rejection of an office skyscraper in Stuttgart's city centre mentioned in this report illustrates. The school was linked to names like Paul Bonatz, Adolf Muesmann or Theodor Fischer and under these proponents the design of roofs was made a core element for localised building typologies. As Muesmann already explained in a 1922 article for *Der Städtebau*, a flat roof was not considered as suitable for a city at mountain slopes.[273]

The example of Stuttgart

It was in the city of Stuttgart that a new settlement, the "Weißenhofsiedlung" project, initiated planning debates. Here on the city's mountain slope, the design element of the flat roof played a pivotal role in its modern style houses drafted by international architects. The settlement project was associated with Werkbund and, as a short remark in *Der Städtebau* proves, the contributions from those 16 leading architects drew growing public attention and resulted in an extension of the official exhibition.[274] Weißenhof however provoked fierce rejection from Stuttgart School's disciples and they organised the construction of "Kochenhof" settlement. Weißenhof was intended to serve as an experimental test ground to prove the applicability of a traditionalist design agenda. It comprised of 10 commands for building orders drafted by Stuttgart's then Mayor Karl Strölin, who belonged to

---

[271] Durth 2001: 150-6.
[272] DS (1925) 11/12: no author: 179.
[273] DS (1922) 7/8: Muesmann: 63-4.
[274] DS (1927) 10: no author: 160.

148

NSDAP, after he came into office. Erich Hengerer in *Der Städtebau* in 1935 high-lights the journal's then status as a propaganda medium, as the journal extensively covered those commands and praised them for their reflection of party goals. According to the commands building efforts should serve the commonwealth instead of self-interest and asked for "simple and calm roofs."[275] Hengerer described how the 10 commands helped to prepare an official municipal bye-law. Hence Kochenhof was used to test the commands' architectural requests. During its construction in 1933 the settlement was well received among the planning community according to Hengerer's description.[276] This reported appreciation for Kochenhof as well as for the one similar in style settlement called "Im Vogelsang" started in 1934, were part of NS propaganda as an ideological answer to "Weißenhofsied-lung." These traditionalist approaches were incorporated by Strölin and municipal design principles were subsequently formulated and enacted as a local bye-law for the city of Stuttgart along those ideas. The bye-law was meant as a clear statement in line with NS ideology and can be interpreted to conclude the debates on a possible national planning law (*Städtebaugesetz*, see below).

Utopian ideas

Throughout the interwar years space in both journals was devoted forlonged for utopian visions of the urban future. There was no consistent utopian school. The First World War prompted several architects and planners to create a space to commemorate the war's human tragedy as well as to initiate hope through new construction activities. In 1917 J. Häuselmann and Theodor Goecke summarised some of those plans in *Der Städtebau*.[277] Among those plans presented in his article was Hans Kampffmeyer's draft for a "Friedensstadt" (City of Peace) accommodating 100,000 inhabitants, and his draft was supposed to reflect German virtues in architectural terms and to incorporate Howard's Garden City concept. Whilst the idea of reconciliation between previous warring parties played a limited role in Kampffmeyer's plan, another anonymous Austrian writer came up with a comprehensive plan. He was referred to by Häuselmann who describes the idea of another Friedensstadt that should be located right on the border between Austria and Germany as former allies to symbolise and remember their armies 'joint sacrifices' during the Great War. Goecke made the connection to another plan for the so-called 'World Centre of Communication' close to the Dutch city of The Hague but this vision never materialised.[278] Across the English Channel, Patrick Abercrombie

---

[275] DS (1935) 5: Hengerer: 50-1.
[276] DS (1935) 5: Hengerer: 52.
[277] DS (1917) 12: Häuselmann, Goecke: 138-9.
[278] The book cover for Ward 2002 comprises of an illustration for this World Centre.

initiated a mini-series on ideal cities for *The Town Planning Review* after the war had ended. As part of this series, he highlighted one concept called "Christianopolis" based on Christian and pietist values drafted in 1619 by Johann Valentin Andrae[279] and the 19th century concept of "Victoria" by James Silk Buckingham that emphasised civic society.[280] The search for the 'ideal city' was further represented in the journals and generated several contributions, with a peak during the second half of the analysed interwar period. In a series of contributions published in 1929, Georg Münter reflected on the historic roots of ideal city plans such as Vitruvius or renaissance foundations.[281] His list included various designs by Albrecht Dürer, Francesco de' Marche, Daniel Speckle or Sebastien Leprestre de Vauban.[282] This historic view was contrasted by an article submitted to *Der Städtebau* in 1929 by Alfred Maul[283], who described Paul Wolf's model of an interwar ideal city which had been displayed at the 1928 Dresden exhibition "Die technische Stadt" (The technical City). However, in his description of the model, Maul noted an inscription, stating that cities were not the aspired living environment for human beings but a necessary evil before more decentralised structures would make them superfluous. Under NS-rule, and in the face of threats caused by potential air raids during war times, the question of ideal cities came up anew and was linked to a resilient city structure based on air-raid protection principles.[284]

Excursus: Standardisation and Modern Style – towards the 'New Man'

All those concerted efforts to produce many new homes did not only react to a quantitative deficiency. Instead, they blended in debates that already impacted the social realms for several years and applied in several ways to the metropoles as well as the colonial entities. Though, there was a clear focus on the White settler community and with a rather paternalist stance for the Black community there (see 4.2.3, 4.3.4 and 4.3.5 for a description of facilities made available in Windhoek). Many actors involved agreed on ideas, which were grounded on the will to eventually achieve a higher standard of living for the majority of the people that would have ended previous miserable conditions and were supposed to stimulate better performances among the workforce. In this respect, several investigations had shocked the British public at the turn of the century and shaken the fundaments of the Empire. One such indication was drawn from the 1899-1902 Boer War in

---

[279] TPR (1920) April: Abercrombie: 99-104.
[280] TPR (1921) March: Abercrombie: 15-20.
[281] DS (1929) 9: Münter: 249-56.
[282] DS (1929) 12: Münter: 317-40.
[283] DS (1929) 11: Maul: 313-4.
[284] DS (1933) 10: Schoßberger: 476-9.

South Africa, when one in three recruits were eventually rejected based on their height, weight and eyesight.[285] These figures were a particular problem of the urban poor and as a confirmation Benjamin Rowntree published his survey *Poverty: A Study of Town Life* on the situation in York in 1901. In his findings he made it clear that poverty was not the result of drunkenness or laziness. Instead, Rowntree revealed the impact of low wages as the root cause to more than half of all persons affected by what he distinguished as "primary" poverty, where their income was unable to afford a living, even though these people had a regular employment. Further significant reasons were the size of families with more than four children in 22% of "primary" poverty cases and the death of the chief wage-earner for almost 16% of the cases. According to Rowntree's survey, more than 7,200 persons were affected by "primary" poverty in York whereas "secondary" poverty concerned more than 13,000 persons. In the latter category income would actually have been sufficient but was reported as misspent.[286] Rowntree's proportion of York's population living in poverty was 27.84% and thus almost matched the results produced as part of Charles Booth's extensive research on *Life and Labour of the People in London* published between 1889 and 1903 which he recorded at 30.7%.[287] In contrast to Rowntree, he attributed the worst excesses of poverty to the one percent of the population who allegedly was prone to drunkenness, and Hopkins cites his summary.

> "Their life is the life of savages, with vicissitudes of extreme hardship and occasional excess. Their food is of the coarsest description, and their only luxury is drink…They render no useful service, they create no wealth; more often they destroy it. They degrade whatever they touch, and as individuals are perhaps incapable of improvement…"[288]

This representation of the poor represents the pejorative view of upper class depriving them of basic human dignity. These results were used to defend their concerns about the imperial future if the population at the Empire's core was not healthy anymore. To underscore the point, Hopkins cited Sidney Webb's provocative question.

> "What is the use of talking about the Empire if here, at its very centre, there is always to be found a mass of people, stunted in education, a prey of intemperance,

---

[285] Hopkins 1990: 145. As Hall has quoted, this situation did not improve until the First World War. He then does refer to similar figures for the German context with only 42% of Berliners fit for army service (Hall [1988] 2014: 35).

[286] Hopkins 1990: 144-5.

[287] Hopkins 1990: 143-4.

[288] Hopkins 1990: 144.

huddled and congested beyond the possibility of realizing in any true sense either social or domestic life?"[289]

At this point, social hierarchies in Europe can be seen against the background of the world's classical imperial centre-periphery division (see 2.1 and 2.3). Furthermore, the statement demonstrates an ingrained notion of fatalism that these members of the population at the perceived very bottom would be hopelessly destined to perpetuate their useless life from the common welfare's viewpoint. It was explicitly against this background that reform movements came up with their ideas on how to improve social life and to create a new and better man. The interwar period was characterised by many attempts trying to initiate modernisation processes which directly affected the living qualities in housing.

Standardisation and rational production to use economies of scale as part of Fordism and Taylorism were no invention of post-Great War years. They had made their way into architecture and housing as part of improving the average standard of living. The creation of technical and industrial norms was fuelled by experiences during the First World War and attempts to avoid wasting resources which subsequently hampered efficiency.[290] These ideas were hailed by authors as the logical consequence of industrialisation and technological progress in civilian terms. Whitaker commented,

> "[w]e accept similarity in automobiles because of economies, and there is no reason why we should not accept it in houses."[291]

Examples that applied this industrialised approach were created by members of Bauhaus Academy in Dessau. Showcase housing schemes were implemented under the supervision of Martin Wagner in Berlin (e.g. Horseshoe and Siemensstadt settlements) or under Ernst May in Frankfurt am Main (e.g. Römerstadt or Westhausen neighbourhoods), amongst others. These settlements explicitly carried the label of 'modernity', and hence those housing schemes in Berlin have deliberately been marketed as something special. Historian Adelheid von Saldern lists up a vast collection of motives behind those 1920s neighbourhoods which underscore their significance in the demonstration of several layers of progress in Weimar Republic. The new democratic state not only attempted to prove its ability to construct these large housing estates all of a piece but to herald a future in which market rules could be overcome through cooperative actions. A new architectural language was

---

[289] Hopkins 1990: 183.
[290] Van Laak 2004: 174.
[291] Whitaker 1920: 188.

152

designed to change daily habits.[292] If the existing social and built context sketched above is taken into consideration, it becomes understandable whyflats in these modern settlements were judged as major progress when compared to tenement barracks or back-to-back houses. They were usually equipped with their own toilets, either bathtub or shower, running cold and warm water, balconies or loggias, and in most cases central heating.

The transformative rationale was also applied to articles of daily use or furniture. One well-known example is the meticulously planned 'Frankfurt kitchen' designed in 1926 by Margarete Schütte-Lihotzky, which perfectly fitted floor plans in Frankfurt's newly constructed large housing estates and catered to the usual tasks and course of motions by its (female) users.[293] Historian Martina Heßler points out how Frankfurt's Römerstadt settlement represented those days' interpretations of "progress." Here Ernst May's planning ideas for 'minimum housing' (Wohnen für das Existenzminimum) went beyond architectural expression but aimed at the widespread introduction of electrical household appliances. Therefore, the settlement has been labelled as "pioneer of electrification"[294], and I have already carved out the far-reaching impact of technical appliances over the interwar years (see 3.3.2).

The many new amenities offered inside each flat were in many cases complemented by joint facilities such as rooftop terraces, washhouses, and kindergartens.The buildings were embedded in large open green spaces which served two general functions at the same time: firstly, they ensured a healthy environment with sufficient light and air for its inhabitants; secondly, they provided for children's playgrounds, allotment gardens and communication spaces.[295] In this respect, they were comparable to the developments in "Red Vienna", where the inclusion of the many new settlements within the existing urban fabric as well as their tenants' mix can be characterised as a deliberate attempt to avoid social segregation. In his description of the 'Karl-Marx-Hof' housing scheme, Blom comes to the conclusion that,

---

[292] Von Saldern 1988: 201.

[293] Lenger offers another explanation for the origin of this structure when he refers to kitchens in dining cars as those operated by German "Mitropa" (Lenger 2013: 352-3). According to Lenger, almost 10,000 kitchens were manufactured for tenants in Frankfurt's settlements. Heßler offers similar explanations (Heßler 2012: 78-82).

[294] Heßler 2001: 268.

[295] Von Saldern 1988: 204-7.

"[…] – dieser Komplex war für eine neue Welt gebaut, er war Ausdruck der Macht und der Würde der 'kleinen Leute', die auch die Hauptwählerschaft der Regierung waren."[296]

This political element proved to be an important motive in interwar years, not just in Vienna as Blom has summarised[297], but for many industrialised countries. Politicised decisions and actions permeated into private life. In a way architects and planners tried to impose their notions of modern amenities on the new housing schemes, irrespective of their inhabitants' desires, needs or social habits. Considering the collection of new amenities the buildings offered, building societies provided their residents with 'user manuals' instructing them on how to ventilate correctly or how to best decorate the flat in a tasteful and appropriately modern style. Not all of these rules were obeyed but assigned caretakers and counsellors tried to enforce them, in some cases following house inspections.[298] In this context, Le Corbusier introduced his concept of the 'house-machine' in which modern style standardised flats would offer all necessary amenities to highly mobile and flexible residents, and where the individual home would not be tailored to the taste of one single family and for a pre-defined time period anymore.[299]

Restrictions of individual freedoms entered the democratic environment and became far stricter under authoritarian rule. At this point NS ideological inconsistency becomes tangible. They were promoting the idea of different vernacular architectural patterns for exterior façades to reflect regional styles but at the same time these patterns did only mask the standardised interior design behind. This interior design would have made most inhabitants live the same style all across Germany as historian and sociologist Dieter Münk explains.[300] The idea of standardisation did, in this case, explicitly include fitted furniture as introduced by Schütte-Lihotzky's Frankfurt kitchen, though their production under the NS regime remained very limited and did not exceed some samples for show rooms.[301] Additional, and more durable attempts, were prepared by Ernst Neufert who was assigned by Hitler and Speer to formulate norms for prefabricated housing and industrial construction in order to make this industry ready to cope with war-related shortages. He was conferred the position as "commissary for standard specification" (*Normenbeauftragter*

---

[296] Blom 2014: 249. "[…] – this complex was built for a new world, it was an expression of power and dignity to the 'man in the street' who also represented the government's main electorate." (author's translation).
[297] Blom 2014: 251.
[298] Von Saldern 1988: 208.
[299] Le Corbusier [1929] 1987: 231.
[300] Münk 1993: 217.
[301] Münk 1993: 219-20.

154

Speers).[302] Neufert designed a construction machine which facilitated the simple, fast and efficient construction of large housing structures in the course of Berlin's projected north-south axis.[303] Such ideas blended into Le Corbusier's modernist vision, in which he saw the machine age looming and implicitly confirmed Geddes's earlier statement on the transition in urbanism.

> "We come at a moment between two epochs – the pre-machine age and the machine age. The machine age is not yet fully conscious of itself; it has not yet gathered its forces, nor begun to construct; [...]"[304]

Both, 'machines' and the rather unspecific term of 'modernity' proved to be a double-edged sword that was frequently addressed in interwar debates, not just in the planning community but in society at large as Kristiana Hartmann has summarised.[305] They promised new opportunities and improvements and therefore aroused a particular fascination. Many Bauhaus representatives or Le Corbusier were in this respect followed by artists like Otto Umbehr whose collage depicting the 'roving reporter Kisch'[306] made this fascination popular. His collage can be counted as one of those days' positive connotations of an amalgamation between man and machine.[307] Rather reluctant and sceptical statements surfaced when the emphasis was laid on the potential threats that this development might cause. One notable example for such sceptical expressions can be found on UNESCO's *Memory of the World Register* with the movie "Metropolis" directed by Fritz Lang.[308] Those two pieces of art served to illustrate the scope of reactions expressed to a broader audience and the debates have reverberated in urban contexts too. Historian Philipp Blom refers to Soviet Russia where the idea of a 'New Man' based on rational principles affected work and living environments at the same time. For the former environment, engineer and poet Aleksei Gastev was eye-witness to how Taylorism made its way into car manufacturing at a Renault plant in Paris during

---

[302] Durth, Werner, *Städtebau und Macht im nationalsozialistischen Staat.* In: Harlander, Tilman; Pyta, Wolfram [Eds.]: NS-Architektur: Macht und Symbolpolitik. Berlin: LIT Verlag 2010: 56-7.

[303] For illustration see: Durth 2001: 155.

[304] Le Corbusier [1929] 1987: 244.

[305] Hartmann, Kristiana, *Alltagskultur, Alltagsleben, Wohnkultur.* In: Kähler, Gert [Ed.]: Geschichte des Wohnens – Band 4. Stuttgart: Deutsche Verlagsanstalt 1996: 241-51.

[306] For illustration see: SPIEGEL GESCHICHTE 5/2014: 94.

[307] In her recent publication, Heßler has devoted a full chapter on the historic reception of 'cyborgs' (Heßler 2012: 142-74).

[308] Website UNESCO: http://www.unesco.org/new/en/communication-and-information/flagship-project-activities/memory-of-the-world/register/full-list-of-registered-heritage/registered-heritage-page-5/metropolis-sicherungsstueck-nr-1-negative-of-the-restored-and-reconstructed-version-2001/ (retrieved on 25.05.2015).

his forced emigration in the years preceding the First World War. After his return to Russia in 1917, he took with him the inspiration he gained in France and continued to elaborate on his careful analysis of Henry Ford's works. At his Central Institute of Labour, founded in 1920, he accompanied the preparation of what was called "cyclogram;" a detailed instruction for the supposedly most efficient way to perform certain jobs such as cutting metal, intended to be internalised by employees as the right 'mechanical rhythms.' For the living environment Blom refers to drafts prepared by the "Society of Contemporary Architects" established in 1928. Their concepts went far beyond architectural patterns and did address the individual way of life, which should have been confined to a very strict regime where a uniform timeframe would have defined the life of all Soviet city dwellers in an identical structure.[309] Similar ideas were nonetheless produced under capitalist environments too, as Heßler argues with reference to Le Corbusier.[310]

3.3.6 The impact of National Socialist ideology

One extreme school of thought was defined within the foundations of National Socialist ideology and propaganda, which exercised a tremendous impact on Germany's planning concepts after 1933. *Der Städtebau* not just reflected these trends but served as medium to disseminate them due to the country's Nazification (Gleichschaltung). Hence, the editor-in-chief Friedrich Paulsen took great care to ensure the journal complied with the ruling party's intentions. It is nonetheless necessary to characterise the NS planning school as a diverse and incoherent one, and which appeared to have been very ambiguous as the above stated positions on the question of toilets and sewage systems already indicate. In their attempts to secure power, the NSDAP-representatives needed to appeal to many different interest groups and their planning concepts therefore had to cater to sometimes contradicting positions. There were some basic ideas that guided all activities regardless of their final shape or aesthetic qualities.

First and foremost, Germany's economy and society needed to be geared up for war, and the regime therefore embarked on its self-sufficiency policy which was intended to ensure the country's viability under its expected isolation during wartimes. From an urban planning perspective, this policy left some direct imprints on the existing urban fabric as well as it generated new cities from scratch. The question of air raids received particular attention and several articles published in *Der Städtebau* in NS-rule's early months explicitly addressed the challenge as a quest for

---

[309] Blom 2014: 230-7.
[310] Heßler 2012: 77-82.

156

"eine 'luftsichere' Idealstadt"[311], a new ideal city concept designed to withstand air raids, as Hans Schoßberger has formulated it in one article in October 1933. He elaborated similar concepts as Gottfried Feder whose ideas will be presented below. Schoßberger presented his concept of decentralised urban structures and tried to contextualise it as part of broader international debates among the planning community on the same question. He skilfully summarised foreign ideas along with economic reasons for their implementation, although his focus was on the military components those foreign concepts contained. Hence, Schoßberger made references to the military advances and he referred to Vauthier in France or Milyutin in Russia. He described the resulting threats caused by other countries' advances if Germany would not react and improve her ability to protect her own cities. Schoßberger presented the Linear City concept, originally developed by Spaniard Arturo Soria[312], as potential solution to the problem created by congested city centres with their allocation of relevant institutions and high population densities, which in turn made them vulnerable to potential air raids. Despite the presented ideal city plans, he concluded his article with the call for piecemeal improvements since, according to his argumentation, the ideal city should serve as long-term objective but could not be the blueprint to reconstruct the existing patterns soon.

This relatively level-headed recommendation was already replaced in early 1935 by an article written in alarming words, when Paul Wolf presented his "10 guiding principles" for air raid protection at the occasion of a specific planning seminar, and which were first summarised by Ludorf. He does not question the potential outbreak of a new war but considers it as an inevitable future event. As a reaction to this danger, Wolf drafted his guiding principles which demanded strict decentralisation and a complete reorganisation of the existing urban structures. However, it turned out that Ludorf's published reaction to Wolf's original principles was based on a printing error[313], for Ludorf read the call for *centralisation* of industrial compounds at the urban periphery as one demand – instead of the correct term *decentralisation*. In his reply he therefore depicted this centralisation as nonsense, whilst he also underscored the large economic efforts that would have to be invested in order to make the existing urban structures comply with Wolf's guiding principles. Besides, Ludorf did not see the long-term effectiveness of such costly interventions into the existing urban structures because the threat posed by air raids might be eliminated through new means of defence within a limited period of time. He compared it to the historic example of fortification walls which became

---

[311] DS (1933) 10: Schoßberger: 476.
[312] Hall [1988] 2014: 8.
[313] DS (1935) 6: Wolf: 70.

obsolete through the introduction of new weaponry and he therefore argued that air raids might become less menacing too.[314]

"Die Stadt der 22000" and other developments from scratch

Gottfried Feder was an influential figure behind NS planning philosophies. In this context Albers tends to rather emphasise his methodological approach to urban design as laid down in the 1939 publication *Die neue Stadt* (The New City).[315] As the synopsis compiled by Albers proves[316], urban planning was intended to reflect NS ideologies with a focus on its idealised 'Volksgemeinschaft' (people's community) and which, in its application to town planning, reminded Dieter Münk of a medieval image of urban life as the regime's long-term goal.[317] Aside from these roots, Feder did encourage a relatively large flexibility to draft plans for completely new cities or extensions as long as they complied with his interpretation of a city as organism. Following this idea, all essential components like roads, parks, public facilities or industrial and residential areas were to be determined based on a site's specific topography and the city's envisaged functions. In many cases he used the idea of neighbourhood units to describe his aimed for urban pattern, through which he intended to limit the distances inhabitants had to cross between their homes and their respective work places or shopping facilities.[318] In resemblance to Howard's Garden City design, he suggested the creation of settlements planned for a maximum population of 20,000 people that were able to combine the advantages of the rural countryside with the amenities of a city. At such size all relevant facilities could still be reached within walking distances but demand a sufficient level of economic and cultural activities.

The architects Paul Köhler and Rudolf Winkler incorporated Feder's recommendations and translated them into a blueprint for future cities which they called "The

---

[314] DS (1935) 5: Ludorf: 59-60.

[315] Albers 1975: 18. Dieter Münk attributes the empirical part of the analysis with Feder's assistant Fritz Rechenberg and is of the opinion that Feder has only written the book's chapter on its ideological background as well as the conclusions (Münk, Dieter, *Die Organisation des Raumes im Nationalsozialismus: Eine soziologische Untersuchung ideologisch fundierter Leitbilder in Architektur, Städtebau und Raumplanung des Dritten Reiches*, Bonn: Pahl-Rugenstein 1993: 280).

[316] Albers 1975: 226-63.

[317] Münk 1993: 282.

[318] The concept of *neighbourhood units* was introduced by sociologist Clarence Perry as part of the preparatory works on the Regional Plan for New York during the late 1920s. According to the concept, a new residential area should create a community which was grouped around basic social facilities like schools and shops at walking distances (Ward 2004: 50-2).

City of 22,000" (Die Stadt der 22000).[319] Their design, presented in the May issue 1939 of *Der Städtebau*, just a couple of months before the Second World War broke out, envisaged the construction of a new self-sustaining settlement in the vicinity of the town of Finsterwalde near Cottbus. It was drafted to alleviate an immediate housing shortage prevalent around the existing factory complex but did equally bear in mind the factory's projected extension. The scheme comprised of several neighbourhood units fully equipped with basic social infrastructures to ensure their functionality despite piecemeal construction. For reasons of air raid protection, the residential parts of the settlement were grouped at a certain distance from the industrial compound, although the latter was described as mere assembly plant which would not have hazardous impacts on the population since, according to the descriptions, it did not produce noxious fumes. Nonetheless their pragmatic drafts revealed two inconsistencies in NS planning philosophy in regards implementation. Firstly all public institutions were still clustered at the central square of "The City of 22,000" despite propagated decentralisation efforts for air raid protection, and secondly all detached houses were to receive garden plots limited to between 400 and 600 square metres in size. These gardens were explicitly intended as flower gardens and therefore contradicted the usual goal of self-supply with vegetables.[320]

Rimpl's "Stadt der Hermann-Göring-Werke"

Köhler and Winkler's concept shows similarities to Herbert Rimpl's comprehensive plans for "Stadt der Hermann-Göring-Werke," the city later renamed as Salzgitter. Rimpl presented his plans in an extended special contribution to *Der Städtebau* in 1939.[321] The project for this completely new city exceeded those plans for the "City of 22,000" in scale and reflected NS autarky ambitions. As part of war preparations as projected in the four-year-plan, for strategic reasons the new city was a top priority for the Nazis. Here, at Germany's geographical centre, a full-fledged heavy industrial complex comprising of mines, coking and steel plants ensured the armaments industry's supplies. The location was also chosen for strategic reasons mainly based on local ore deposits to avoid additional transportation costs for raw materials. In comparison to other industrial sites like Ruhr or Saar it seemed less exposed to air strikes or foreign seizure due to its remote position but could still draw on existing transportation infrastructures. The residential zones of the new city were projected to accommodate 130,000 inhabitants in its core areas and, upon completion of all industrial extensions, for a population of 300,000 in-

---

[319] DS (1939) 5: Köhler: 37-52.
[320] DS (1939) 5: Köhler: 40.
[321] DS (1939) 9: Rimpl: 77-92.

habitants – including all projected satellite settlements.[322] Beyond functional considerations, this new city and the adjacent industrial compounds were used for propaganda purposes and marked a symbolic spatial expression of the NS regime.

Redevelopment plans for existing cities

Whereas previous sections focussed on the construction of completely new or additional urban structures, the following two sections address NS redevelopment plans for existing cities. Through such interventions the Nazis wanted to openly demonstrate their power in the built environment. It was intended as part of their symbolic cut with the previous political establishment, denigrated as "system", democratic Weimar Republic. This regime was to be overturn both at the legal and the built front. The urban planner Hans Reichow considered the NS period to be, "fundamentally revolutionary times."[323] In some cases the redevelopment plans were mainly guided by aesthetic considerations to generate a public stage that visualised the party's ideology, and which emphasised the mythical relevance of certain places for its historic connotations. This was particularly true for Munich's Königsplatz and Karolinenplatz where the already existing obelisk commemorated those 30,000 soldiers who died during Napoleon's Russian campaign, and to which two small temples at the edge of Königsplatz took up a relation of spiritual commemoration for those 'party soldiers' who died in the failed 1923 Hitler-Ludendorff-Coup. Their mortal remains were relocated and buried in one of the temples in order to epitomise the propaganda myth of blood sacrificed for the Nazi regime. Friedrich Paulsen explained the symbolic representation of the "new" aesthetic values as designed by Paul Ludwig Troost in a keynote description published in *Der Städtebau* in 1934.[324] The development around both squares in Munich represented the regime's attempts to underscore its architectural links with the past, although the design of the public spaces and the new buildings served to accent the latter rather than the old ones. Besides the intended magnificent vistas evoked between the buildings, the square was paved in order to make it suitable for demonstrations of between 60,000 to maximum 100,000 participants as Paulsen estimated.[325] Those rallies should publicly demonstrate the image of a strong leader/system and his reception by a deferential national community (in German labelled as 'Volksgemeinschaft'). Munich belonged to a group of five preferred cities (complemented by Berlin, Hamburg, Linz, and Nuremberg) called *Führerstädte*, which received the regime's particular attention and were attributed

---

[322] DS (1939) 9: Rimpl: 84.
[323] DS (1934) 4: Reichow: 193.
[324] DS (1934) 5: Paulsen: 245-8.
[325] DS (1934) 5: Paulsen: 246.

160

with specific functions or historic connotations such as Hamburg as 'City of Foreign Trade' or Nuremberg as 'City of Reich's Party Conventions.'[326]

Similar redevelopment plans were prepared for many cities across the country, and they all served the goal to create parade streets and squares for mass demonstrations combined with buildings of intimidating sizes. These structures were labelled as "Gauforum", although the only fully completed and instructive example can be found in Weimar on which *Der Städtebau* did not report. Through their size and architectural shape the spatial environment was to incorporate ideological elements and conveyed the message that the individual counts nothing but as part of the national community. Surprisingly, there were not that many articles published on those Gauforum developments in *Der Städtebau*. Wuppertal was selected as the only comprehensive and instructive example to demonstrate what such redevelopment plans would look like.[327] The city itself was the result of a recent amalgamation of previously independent municipalities, with Barmen and Elberfeld being their largest. The city's topography along a valley caused a lot of traffic congestion and the necessity to rethink its settlement patterns and transportation infrastructure at regional scale led to a competition. Walther Bangert's submission proposed a clear and representative axis connecting Barmen and Elberfeld along the bottom of the valley as well as a new iconic building on top of one of the northern hills. It set a limit to the city's future growth along the valley and wanted to redirect further extensions to collective settlements based on the NS principles of neighbourhood units ('nationalsozialistische Gemeinschaftssiedlungen'). For its appealing clarity, Bangert's submission was awarded the jury's first prize despite some requested amendments. An essential part of the plans was the widening of an already existing avenue in the district of Barmen and its transformation into the main axis for representation purposes. In order to define a centre for the new amalgamated city, Bangert suggested the construction of an oversized square at which a variety of public buildings and institutions were to be grouped, including a new town hall, office buildings for municipal and party bodies. The square itself would have served for demonstrations and party rallies and therefore represented the archetype of a Gauforum. Although other examples were virtually absent in *Der Städtebau*, similar redevelopment plans were underway for many German cities.[328]

---

[326] Durth 2001: 157; Münk 1993: 306-7.
[327] DS (1939) 10: P.aulsen: 93-6.
[328] Durth 2010: 48.

Renovation of city centres as German slum clearance

Further interventions in the existing urban fabric were carried out under public health considerations and they often focused on the renovation of old city centres ('Altstadtgesundung'). The measures were intended to improve the quality of life for inhabitants in many neglected streets and adjacent courts. In some of the reported cases, like Frankfurt am Main, these efforts were presented as a continuation of attempts to renovate the old city, which dated as far back as to Mayor Adickes in 1902 and then once more under Ernst May in the 1920s, highlighting the tremendous extent of this work and its piecemeal realisation due to limited financial resources.[329] The Nazis well aware these areas served as homes to (political) opponents, their living space was reduced through these interventions. *Der Städtebau* frequently reported on the developments in the realm of legislation and based them on case studies. Several articles captured state-of-the-art 'progress reports' from several cities such as Brunswick, Frankfurt am Main, or Kassel. They mirrored the NS rejection of big cities, which were usually criticised by party spokespersons and their disciples as overcrowded, unhealthy areas[330] that formed an obstacle to modern motorised vehicles. With more and more resources tied up in war preparations according to the Four-Year Plan decreed in 1936, the Nazis realised the housing question could not be solved based on the detached house scheme.[331] Flats had to remain an essential part of the solution. In one of his contributions Hans Reichow argued in favour of the improvement of the existing housing stock in old city centres, as long as they would – upon completion of renovation works – offer similar living qualities like those in new housing schemes at the periphery.[332] He came to the conclusion that Hitler's motto of "blood and soil" partially needed to be abandoned, since it did not match the reality in city centres where tenants of small flats barely had immediate contacts or relations to the soil. Reichow therefore geared to an adjusted interpretation of the motto as "sense of belonging" (Heimatgefühl) that renovated apartments should evoke in the tenant's mind.

> "Nur so viel muss gesagt werden, dass es nicht angeht, auf der einen Seite ideale Heimstätten mit der vollkommenen Erfüllung des Wortes von „Blut und Boden" und zugleich für die übrige Hälfte des Volkes durch verschärfte Gesetzgebung und eine dürftige Gesundung nur Geringstes an Licht, Luft und Sonne als höchstes Ziel

---

[329] DS (1935) 1: Rodenbach: 2.
[330] DS (1936) 6: Labes: 62.
[331] Münk 1993: 235-7.
[332] DS (1934) 4: Reichow: 194.

zu erstreben. Damit allein lässt sich das einmal verlorengegangene Heimatgefühl nicht wieder erwecken und lebendig erhalten."[333]

The impact of politics and propaganda on planning

Der Städtebau contained a lot of articles that clearly reflected NS propaganda positions although they varied in intensity. Many authors like Reichow adapted themselves to the regime's expectations and preferences at rather opportunistic levels. The rejection of large cities was in 1939 a subject matter for Swiss architect and town planner Martin Mächler, whose anti-urban contribution was accepted for publication, where he complained about the unsystematic growth of large cities.[334] He argued large cities represented an almost uncontrollable evil that denied its citizens acceptable living conditions. In the tradition of Social Darwinism, Mächler regarded cities with fatalism since they historically represented the highest level of a civilisation's development but at the same time they heralded its inevitable decay.

Although Germany's new motorways, the autobahns, were a success in official propaganda they played a minor role in *Der Städtebau*. Except for brief references in some of the articles on transportation planning and road construction, there was just one report specifically addressing the construction of motorways around Cologne. In this report, Max-Erich Feuchtinger highlighted the extraordinary opportunity to ease the city's as well as the region's traffic situation at large but also to conveniently integrate those new streets into the existing green spaces at Cologne's city fringes.[335]

Other contributions overtly embraced the Nazi's political achievements, like the one article published soon after Austria's annexation by Germany in 1938 indicates. This article had one purpose: to praise Hitler as the genius 'Führer'; and to repeat the blessings as promised in propaganda messages that would now become tangible to the Austrian population (i.e. thorough geological survey of its mineral wealth and the construction of autobahns). Although the article was entitled "Der Anschluss, auch des Städtebaues" ('Annexation, also in urban development'), its content superficially mentioned some planning tasks relevant in those days such as

---

[333] DS (1934) 4: Reichow: 194. "It is at least necessary to say that it is unacceptable to aim for, on one side, ideal homesteads fully accomplishing the motto of "blood and soil" whilst tightened legislation and rudimentary renovation efforts, at the same time, provide the remaining half of the people only with a minimum of light, air and sun as their highest achievements. This is by far not sufficient to revive and maintain a once lost sense of belonging." (author's translation).
[334] DS (1939) 7: Mächler: 63.
[335] DS (1938) 7: Feuchtinger: 16-9.

urban planning's self-definition as integral part of spatial planning and the renovation of city centres, before the anonymous author went on with his account of the 'German miracle' that the world was able to witness a few weeks earlier.[336]

Besides these contributions that clearly demonstrate the journal as propaganda, some articles did respond the racial ideology, although those references remained carefully chosen owing to the planning profession's traditional international links. Such a hesitant tone was used when the draft for an urban planning law with its sections on land ownership was assessed. Alfred Karger tried to emphasise that foreigners were still eligible to own property in Germany as long as their rights were sanctioned by internationally recognised bilateral contracts with their home countries. For security reasons he insisted on exemptions for plots in direct vicinity to the German border.[337] From today's interpretation of political correctness, some reports were written in typical language with terms like 'Negro' which would not be used anymore but the wording would be similar in the US at that time and hence is not a distinctive of Nazi-Germany. It is illustrative of the regime's awareness of foreign developments and their subsequent interpretation according to the NS ideology. One example are those few reports which reflected the situation of Afro-Americans and where a pejorative view on ethnic groups was expressed that attributed them with inferior human characteristics. The reports addressed housing developments in the US and with a focus on Chicago and described them as a potential menace to Germany. The city's image as immigrant city by the end of the 19th century has Hall refering to investigations carried out by the Chicago School of sociologists started in the 1920s under Park, Burgess, McKenzie and Worth as well as their later disciples.[338] They emphasised the perceived instabilities caused by migration to the city, and which arguably did not provide for the immigrants' sufficient social integration. To the contrary, many members of the Chicago School were investigating social disintegration and the reactions labelled as the "white flight" due to perceived invasions of Black people into White neighbourhoods and work places. This development had sparked the 1919 "community riot" causing 38 peoples' death and leaving 537 injured.[339] From the German perspective, mobility and migration were therefore regarded with suspicion. One anonymous author criticised the US-American mobility as expressed in the will to move between various cities across the country, and linked these developments to his interpretation of the "white flight" as a social trading-down process that might happen in Europe too.

---

[336] DS (1938) 4: no author: 25.
[337] DS (1934) 8: Karger: 404.
[338] Hall [1988] 2014: 487-520.
[339] Hall [1988] 2014: 495-6.

164

"In dem Augenblick beispielsweise, in dem die erste Negerfamilie in eine Straße zieht, verlassen die Weißen die Gegend. Schnell sind die Häuser von Negern in einer unsagbaren Weise überfüllt und bald völlig heruntergewirtschaftet. Ähnliches gilt von Vierteln mit Bewohnern südosteuropäischer Herkunft."[340]

It is important to note that contributions to *Der Städtebau* in the NS period reflected current ideas and developments in other countries. However the statements they contained tended to be restricted to the NS position and mirrored Nazi-Germany's limited openness to international exchange. One instructive example was published in summer 1939. At the occasion of the 17th International Town Planning and Housing Congress held at Stockholm in July 1939, at which more than 900 representatives from 40 countries convened, an anonymous German commentator identified almost insurmountable discrepancies between the European peoples based on their political orientation as either democratic or authoritarian, although the author tried to denigrate the UK in particular.[341] Meant as a reply to accusations against Nazi-German suppression and exploitation in Europe's east, the author referred to 'dreamers' (Schwärmer) in Great Britain.

"Auch die Befürworter so paradiesischer Gartenstädte, wie sie Ebenezar [sic] Howard schilderte, sind Schwärmer mit 500 000 000 Kolonialen hinter sich."[342]

Hence, this contribution outlined a rift that was to become fatal reality with the outbreak of the Second World War. The war itself offered the opportunity to apply ideas for the colonisation of Europe's east that were derived from theories and models originally developed to understand mechanisms behind regional settlement patterns, and which will be described in the following subchapter.

3.3.7 Regionalisation of urban planning

Many of the problems planners were faced with turned out to be difficult to deal with at only the local level. Plannerswere best served to look beyond to the regional approaches of urban planning. This trend was nonetheless a piecemeal process within set legal confines that started with rather small and focused forms of coop-

---

[340] DS (1935) 4: no author: 43. "In that instant when, for example, the first Negro family moves into a street, Whites leave the area. Soon the Negro's houses are overcrowded at unutterable scales and shortly after completely run-down. Similar applies to districts with inhabitants of Southeast European origin." (author's translation). At the same time, Howard Odum has formulated equally pejorative views on Afro-Americans as part of his social studies on southern parts of the US (Hall [1988] 2007: 440-1).
[341] DS (1939) 8: no author: 74-6.
[342] DS (1939) 8: no author: 76. "Even supporters of such heaven on earth like Garden Cities as drafted by Ebenezar [sic] Howard are dreamers with 500,000,000 colonial subjects behind them." (author's translation).

eration, and which in some cases led to the forced amalgamation of neighbouring municipalities at the administrative level, although it remained a spectre to many stakeholders involved. Representatives of smaller municipalities tried to defend their local autonomy and this parochialism affected local administrations in the colonies as I will explore for the case of Windhoek where the agricultural village of Klein Windhoek tried to resist its ordered amalgamation with Windhoek proper (see 4.1).

Examples of voluntary cooperation and forced amalgamation are represented in *The Town Planning Review* as well as in *Der Städtebau*. In 1912 the British journal published a report by Patrick Abercrombie about the administrative divisions of planning authorities into more than 82 local authorities for London's Metropolitan Police area. He argued in favour of cooperation for the benefit of Greater London. In his opinion, these moves were very much needed to overcome the problems in housing and road construction, namely of radial roads.[343] To underscore the urgency with which a new planning authority for the whole of London needed to be established, Abercrombie drew the following picture.

> "London is, in a true sense, a monster, which it needs every effort to protect oneself from – not to keep out altogether – that is impossible – but to curb and control in some sort of way."[344]

How long it actually took to install a new planning system in London, and who was involved in this process was analysed by Richard Dennis.[345] Some figures given by John Burns in his function as President of the Local Government Board at the conference for all Greater London authorities in November 1913 might serve to illustrate the extent of those "monster" developments for the last years preceding the First World War.

> "Greater London was filling up with tremendous rapidity. In six years only, 1,100 streets had been constructed and 75,000 houses erected, while over 300,000 acres had become absorbed in the urban area. In other words, during six years a city of nearly 400,000 people had sprung up."[346]

In the same article written by W. R. Davidge, another comment made by Raymond Unwin underscored the limited focus that those early interventions had, when he demanded that similar conferences should in future not be addressed as, "*Road*

---

[343] TPR (1912) January: Abercrombie: 261-4.
[344] TPR (1912) January: Abercrombie: 262.
[345] Dennis 2000.
[346] TPR (1914) January: Davidge: 287.

conferences, but *Town Planning* conferences."[347] An early example for such conferences was the 1910/11 Exhibition (Städtebau-Ausstellung) in Berlin which formed an important cornerstone to the regional planning efforts around the German capital. Harald Bodenschatz edited a comprehensive collection on the exhibition's circumstances and impulses.[348] Planning left its more narrow urban confines and became responsible for a comprehensive view on a "wide area" as Abercrombie has put it in 1923.[349] Another term to describe these trends was coined in 1915 by Patrick Geddes in his publication *Cities in Evolution* where he calls the coalescence of Manchester and Liverpool a *conurbation*. Given his influence it is surprising that *The Town Planning Review* paid little attention to Geddes's work. The journal did publish a review of *Cities in Evolution* written by Lascelles Abercrombie, in which the book was praised with the following words,

> "[w]hatever else may be said of the book, this must first be said: that it is an earnest and most invigorating invitation to take Town Planning seriously. Prof. Geddes was plainly the man to be spokesman for Town Planning to the world at large."[350]

But at the same time the author tried to limit the book's significance by commenting,

> "'Cities in Evolution' is not a perfect book by any means; it will scarcely be a classic treatise on its subject."[351]

Only two personal contributions from Patrick Geddes were accepted for publication in *The Town Planning Review*: the first appeared in 1912, dealing with his differentiation between the "paleotechnic" and "neotechnic" age in urban development[352] (see 3.3.1) and thus gave a preview of one core theme eventually contained in his *Cities in Evolution*; his second article was a summary on the International Exhibition held at Ghent in 1913 and the main plans and items on display.[353] Over the following years the journal published one more review on a report by Geddes dealing with town planning in the Indian city of Balrampur, though the review's anonymous author emphasised that the report is,

---

[347] TPR (1914) January: Davidge: 290, emphasis in original.
[348] Bodenschatz, Harald [Ed.], *Stadtvisionen 1910/2010*, Berlin: DOM 2010.
[349] TPR (1923b) May: Abercrombie: 111.
[350] TPR (1915) October: Abercrombie: 137.
[351] Ibid.
[352] TPR (1912) October: Geddes: 176-87.
[353] TPR (1913) July: Geddes: 78-94.

"[…] giving us an admirable example of Professor Geddes' philosophical teaching in its practical application […]."[354]

Regardless of Geddes's work being at the intersection of new urban conceptualisations and practice, his publications left an imprint on planning community and opened new perspectives towards a transition from urban to regional development. Besides road construction and housing, regional planning efforts started to absorb further layers of intervention, such as the organisation of green spaces. The Regional Park Systems as laid out in the US, with Boston a prime example, as an article in *The Town Planning Review* from 1925 illustrated.[355] Similar developments can be reported from the German perspective, where the congestion around Greater Berlin called for coordinated reactions although they were not welcomed by everyone. Another example for regional developments inspired by Boston was the careful consideration on how to preserve the existing open green spaces in the Ruhr industrial district, given under the supervision of Robert Schmidt who was the responsible local planner in Essen. Ursula von Petz has summarised his ideas and explicitly describes them as part of the first concerted planning efforts at regional and state level.[356] In a memorandum published in *Der Städtebau* in 1912 he deemed the acquisition of forests for regional green spaces and the designation of future regional traffic routes a prime necessity.[357] As Von Petz explains, these green spaces were not intended to serve aesthetic purposes but counterbalanced industrialisation's negative side-effects on the inhabitants and ecology and therefore serve as recreational areas. In a 1919 journal contribution, Schmidt argued in favour of a law that granted the permission to establish a municipalities' association (Zweckverband) for the whole industrial region eventually called 'Siedlungsverband Ruhrkohlenbezirk' and which was vested with regional planning powers.[358] He based his argumentation on previous successful experiences in self-organised regional attempts to restructure the drinking water and waste water systems as well as failed attempts for an improved rapid transit system for this very region. It was therefore an exceptional move that the government approved the first regional planning law in 1920, which transformed those improvised moves for cooperation into a sustainable and formal planning body at the Ruhr's regional level and Schmidt became the association's first director in 1920. In his function he

---

[354] TPR (1918) April: no author: 274-5.
[355] TPR (1923b) May: Abercrombie: 109-18.
[356] Von Petz, Ursula, *Robert Schmidt und die Grünflächenpolitik im Ruhrgebiet*. In: Kastorff-Viehmann [Ed.]: Die grüne Stadt: Siedlungen, Parks, Wälder, Grünflächen 1860-1960. Essen: Klartext 1998: 25.
[357] DS (1914) 4: no author: 50.
[358] DS (1919) 9/12: Schmidt: 91-3.

highlighted the uniqueness of this legal framework in 1927 including its global scale.[359] Considering his international relevance, also for the planning profession's evolution at large, Ursula von Petz has published her research on Robert Schmidt's biography and his impact on the Ruhr district's development in *Planning Perspectives*.[360] In her latest book on Schmidt she describes his extensive contributions to regional planning beyond the Ruhr and emphasises his international contacts to Raymond Unwin and George Pepler as well as his membership in renowned organisations like the British Town Planning Institution.[361]

The developments in Hamburg's neighbouring cities as reported in *Der Städtebau*, by contrast, illustrate the legally ordered amalgamation of municipalities during those years. After fierce fights between the Free Hanseatic City and Prussia about options to extend Hamburg's seaport and to create new settlement areas at the urban fringe for this major city, the Prussian Parliament passed a law to redraw the municipal borders of Altona to the west and Harburg to the south on 29th June 1927. Those amalgamations were meant as an explicit attempt to curtail Hamburg's intentions to grow and to undermine her economic viability as an independent city. Jürgen Brandt depicted these mergers as political power games and criticised them in his article for their total ignorance of urban planning considerations.[362] This stalemate was eventually settled a decade later with the *Greater Hamburg Act* (see below).

Theoretical frameworks in interwar years

While planning practice experimented with new forms of collaboration with or without legal powers incorporating additional competences, so did scholarly work. After Schmidt had summarised his complaints in 1926 that there was still no definition of what regional planning at the state level actually comprised of[363], he offered a solution that differentiated between a general form of spatial planning ('allgemeine Landesplanung') and a specific form ('besondere Landesplanung'). The general one would have to be prepared by the Ministry of Economics at Reich's level, outlining Germany's overall planning goals and guiding principles as well as drafts for the construction of roads, railways and waterways of national relevance. Dirk van Laak illustrated the impact of infrastructures on the develop-

---

[359] DS (1927) 1: Schmidt: 12.
[360] Von Petz, Ursula, *Robert Schmidt and the public park policy in the Ruhr district, 1900-1930*, 1999.
[361] Von Petz, Ursula, *Robert Schmidt 1869-1934, Stadtbaumeister in Essen und Landesplaner im Ruhrgebiet*, Tübingen, Berlin: Wasmuth 2016, here 147-52.
[362] DS (1927) 9: Brandt: 144-5.
[363] DS (1926) 8: Schmidt: 127.

ment of spaces focussing on the colonial context. He analysed infrastructures regarding their function to connect or 'open up' spaces and the extent imperial policies impacted on the preparation of such plans.[364]

According to Schmidt, the specific form of spatial planning in Germany functions as a kind of magnifying glass, through which regional sections can further be specified. These plans should display all relevant measures to be implemented by regional bodies along those goals already outlined in the national, general plans.[365] Schmidt's defined rules of 'subsumption' in 1926 which are still applicable in planning today, where things that can be decided at the regional level will not be taken to the higher national level. Based on those ideas it was possible to initiate various concepts of 'social engineering' as described in a book edited by Thomas Etzemüller.[366]

During the following years, further contributions were devoted to the evolution of spatial planning as the highest level of planning authority. Urban planning by contrast formed a lower level planning authority. A couple of years after Schmidt had published his definition based on practical experiences, Walter Christaller's scholarly research offered a theoretical model. His geographical analysis of Southern German settlement patterns formed the basis for his central place theory published in 1933, a theory that for planners was to become the key to make their profession as exact and predictable as physics or chemistry, thus adding new prestige. Despite its significance, appreciated in hindsigh, *Der Städtebau* covered Christaller's theory only in one specific contribution, and this review by Friedrich Paulsen was emphasised Christaller's roots in geography, though remaining very reserved in terms of the theory's potential impact on urban planning. Paulsen made a direct reference to the similarity of Christaller's findings with the results produced during the historic colonisation of Germany's east. In addition, Paulsen, for political reasons, appreciated the mechanisms which invisibly led to the development of those central places as formulated by Christaller, since they seemed to justify state intervention.[367] The relevance of this concept for a colonisation of Europe's east will be briefly explained below.

---

[364] Van Laak 2004.
[365] DS (1926) 8: Schmidt: 127-31.
[366] Etzemüller, Thomas [Ed.], *Die Ordnung der Moderne: Social Engineering im 20. Jahrhundert,* Bielefeld: Transcript-Verlag 2009.
[367] DS (1933) 11: Paulsen: 526.

Examples for regional planning practice

Although *The Town Planning Review* did not mention Christaller's work in a specific contribution, regionalisation of planning did play an important role. After Patrick Abercrombie's early warnings on London's dominant role as mentioned above, he demanded for a thorough investigation of the national resources through a 'Regional Survey' in an article published during the last months of the First World War.[368] This demand was fulfilled, as at least 27 articles published in the British journal linked to regional planning over the following decades demonstrate, though under various headings. The first report on South Wales represented early subchapters of the Regional Survey and was subsequently considered a test run for similar activities across the UK.[369] Soon after the first planning schemes appeared, like the one for Doncaster region. The latter's relevance was underscored in a 1923 book review by Longstreth Thompson, for the scheme,

> "[...] marks the opening of a very important phase of urban planning. It has long been recognised that in many of our industrial districts the tendency towards the coalescence of groups of towns into what Professor Geddes has called vast 'conurbations' has rendered imperative the adoption of a larger planning unit than that of a single town."[370]

Many British regions like East Kent[371], and Haifa Bay in the mandated territory of Palestine[372], were to follow Doncaster's example as further contributions to *The Town Planning Review* illustrated. Aside from the implementation through such new schemes, the issue of regional planning received attention due to new impulses from the USA. Here, the comprehensive *Regional Plan of New York and its Environs* (RPNY) published between 1927 and 1931[373] set new standards considering its meticulous antecedent survey which covered the region's economic structure, population growth and land values as George Pepler has highlighted in his 1932 article for *The Town Planning Review*.[374] Following his description, the survey and plan contained a comparison of different planning ideas like the neighbourhood unit concept and Garden Cities, before it presented its planning recommendations grouped according to different categories such as 'zoning', 'transportation', 'communication' or 'building guidance.' It can therefore be concluded that this plan

---

[368] TPR (1918) April: Abercrombie: 203-10.
[369] TPR (1922) May: no author: 259.
[370] TPR (1923) May: Thompson: 134.
[371] TPR (1926) February: Lanchester: 292-6.
[372] TPR (1927) June: Kauffmann: 206-11.
[373] Ward 2002: 116-7.
[374] TPR (1932) November: G.L.P.: 123-36.

reflected the challenges attached to urban growth which ignored the original core cities' boundaries and led to first indications of urban sprawl.

Beyond the already mentioned ordered amalgamation of municipalities, *Der Städtebau* reported on how Hamburg tried to cope with this phenomenon and became another example for collaboration at regional level. Parallel to the amalgamation of Hamburg's neighbouring municipalities in Prussia, which deliberately curtailed the core city's development opportunities, measures to protect the port's viability as well as to improve the traffic and housing situation were to be rethought based on comprehensive plans drafted by Fritz Schumacher in 1927.[375] A NS biased article published in 1936 by Mr Knutzen in his function as administrative advisor points to a voluntary and supposedly uncontrolled migration of families during the last years of Weimar Republic, who moved from the core city to suburban areas within a radius of 30 km where land was considerably cheaper.[376] This trend was intensified under the NS regime by politically encouraged resettlements to newly constructed housing schemes at the urban periphery, as Knutzen reported on the new planning philosophy. According to then up-to-date statistics quoted in the article, this migration accelerated from1931 and by the end of 1934 almost 39,000 people had already left Hamburg for the surrounding municipalities. The consequences caused by these resettlements were addressed by new laws which reorganised administrative competencies and transferred financial allocations towards the urban periphery for new housing and (social) infrastructures. Laws related to these developments were tied to the umbrella law, the *Greater Hamburg Act* (Gesetz über Groß-Hamburg und andere Gebietsbereinigungen). It was passed in 1937 and defined the territorial borders of Hamburg that are still in force today, as the municipality explains on her website.[377]

The Second World War offered an exceptional environment to apply Christaller's central place theories and to use them as pretext for brutal governmental interventions at large scale in Europe's east pursued by the Nazi regime. On one hand, those attempts were focused on areas that once belonged to the German Reich before the Treaty of Versailles had redrawn Germany's borders, and where a significant German-speaking minority lived as was the case for several regions in Poland. On the other hand, plans covered areas where such a pseudo-justification did not exist. All those efforts can be subsumed under master plan called "Generalplan Ost", and Bruno Wasser submitted a detailed analysis of this plan's im-

---

[375] DS (1927) 9: Ewoldt: 129-36.
[376] DS (1936) 5: Knutzen: 54-6.
[377] Website Hamburg: http://www.hamburg.de/geschichte/2207758/gross-hamburg-gesetz/ (retrieved on 06.08.2015).

pacts on Poland as carried out under the supervision of Heinrich Himmler.[378] He emphasised how regions without particular ties to German history suffered the most from what he calls "neo-colonisation and spatial planning in the east".[379] Here the non-German population was rigidly classified based on its employability[380] and potential (forced) integration into German society, before they were deported either to 'their' designated new home regions further in the east, to labour camps, or extermination camps like Auschwitz. In this context, Wasser uses the image of 'pacifying activities' (Pazifizierungsaktionen) that the Nazis applied, a term commonly used as a reference to the violent subjugation of imperial overseas domains.

Though disputed, "Generalplan Ost" presented two sides of the same coin. On one hand, it epitomised regional planning practice in the very late interwar period where none of the usual legal restrictions applied and the Europe's east appeared to the planners involved as 'terra nullius' available for a complete make over. On the other hand, the plan depicted key features of imperial conquest and the struggle to exploit the local population that were applied in colonial possessions overseas in the decades before. Hence, aside from pacifying activities, Wasser's descriptions resembled many elements typical for colonial interventions in the African context, including the focus on the exploitation of the local labour force, limited forms of indirect rule based on the collaboration with local people and the racial component with regards to the settler community[381], as will be discussed for my case study in Windhoek (see 4.3). Dietrich Eichholtz underscores that the elements of genocide and imperialistic expansion differed significantly between the colonial contexts of 18th and 19th century Africa and those developments in Europe's east during the Second World War.[382] According to his argument "Generalplan Ost" expressed certain continuities, for example in its racist views and exploitative nature towards the subjugated population. However, the plan did include characteris-

---

[378] Wasser, Bruno, *Himmlers Raumplanung im Osten: Der Generalplan Ost in Polen 1940 - 1944*, Basel *et al.*: Birkhäuser 1993.

[379] „[.] Neokolonisation und Raumplanung im Osten […]" Wasser 1993: 8.

[380] Such classifications in terms of African peoples' employability had already been applied under German rule in SWA (Zimmerer 2001: 181-2).

[381] Wasser 1993: 9-10.

[382] Eichholtz, Dietrich, *Der „Generalplan Ost" als genozidale Variante der imperialistischen Ostexpansion*. In: Rössler, Mechthild; Schleiermacher, Sabine [Eds.]: Der „Generalplan Ost": Hauptlinien der nationalsozialistischen Planungs- und Vernichtungspolitik. Berlin: Akademie Verlag 1993: 118.

tics that made it historically unique, considering the genocidal preparation for the deportation and extermination of millions of Europeans in the east.[383]

3.3.8 The question of legal frameworks

Throughout the interwar period several laws were enacted in the UK and in Germany, which were analysed regarding their overarching goals or the new practical tools they provided. First of all, there were rather general laws, such as the several versions of *Town Planning Acts* which had been passed in the UK during the interwar years. Within these Acts rules concerning formal procedures and the stakeholders to be involved were defined. They addressed the question of how to tax land values fairly and to include compensation to be paid by private owners for planning-induced increments. Aside from similar controversies in Germany related to land pooling[384], *Der Städtebau* frequently reported on new draft versions of a comprehensive planning law, which would have ended the fractious status in the preparation of building bye-laws and granted similar powers to all local authorities. However, this never came into force before the Second World War (and still after it took some years to realise). Ekke Feldmann analysed the German planning framework's evolution and the several draft versions prepared in interwar years.[385] Withthe changing political environment, the journal continued to argue about the reasons as to why those new drafts failed and had not been enacted. Interestingly the first two articles presenting drafts for a *Town Planning Act* in Germany were written by the Austrian author Siegfried Sitte in 1917 and therefore followed Austrian lines.[386] The drafts comprised a request for each municipality to prepare a land-use plan for its whole territory and a collection of all major information on land use and existing infrastructures. But Sitte went further, and even demanded specific references to houses with sanitary deficiencies that subsequently were earmarked for demolition. The plans covered areas for the extension of residential zones in order to keep up with the projected population growth. He advocated the plans have regular updates and revisions at intervals of five years. He demanded their preparation by skilled experts, which for him meant architects and surveyors.[387] Sitte advocated of regional planning, if certain tasks were beyond the limits and resources of a single municipality.[388]

---

[383] Eichholtz 1993: 122.
[384] Feldmann 2011: 345.
[385] Feldmann 2011: 317-68.
[386] DS (1917) 1: Sitte: 7.
[387] DS (1917) 1: Sitte: 7-9.
[388] DS (1917) 2/3: Sitte: 17.

174

In several respects Siegfried Sitte's draft anticipated many of the rules established later in interwar years, such as in Greater Berlin and the Ruhr district, as well as after the Second World War. Robert Schmidt from the Ruhr district was responsible for another attempt to prepare a holistic town planning law in 1925 that would have ended the split competences so far scattered to several, very limited and technical laws.[389] Despite the intensive debates this draft version initiated in the late 1920s, when 10 contributions to *Der Städtebau* dealt with it, the *Town Planning Act* did not materialise. In 1932 Werner Hegemann offered reasons for this failure, and for that matter agreed with Friedrich Paulsen on the point that the question of 'land rights and liberty to build' (Bodenrecht und Baufreiheit) needed to be reorganised first, before a comprehensive planning law could provide the appropriate basis for future urban development. As further improvement, Paulsen demanded limitations for individual (land) rights in preference for common welfare which was closely linked to the question of increments in land values.[390]

Besides these general laws, both journals included coverage on specific legal frameworks that tried to tackle the challenges in public health and housing as well as the trend towards regional planning. In this respect, the *Greater Berlin Act* provided the legal basis for a comprehensive planning system in Berlin and its previously autonomous neighbouring cities, both in spatial terms and with regards to several infrastructural, social and economic layers.

Comparing both journals, *The Town Planning Review* devoted more specific articles to legal questions. The British *Town Planning Act* received much attention after its first version was passed in 1909. By the first years of the Great War a total of 18 articles were published on this subject, demonstrating the opportunities attached to these new rules introduced by the Act. Most of the contributions were entitled with "Progress of the Town Planning Act", underscoring incremental advances made for the planning profession and its procedures, despite some contradicting opinions on specific sections.[391] In *Der Städtebau* the law was welcomed in two articles published in 1912, and their Budapest-based author Emerich Forbáth highlighted the multi-directional exchange of ideas which evolved around the Act. This exchange belonged to a learning process between German and British planners as well as beyond, and was described by Schott as part of the "Urban Internationale"

---

[389] DS (1925) 11/12: Koeppen: 161-2.
[390] DS (1932) 6: Hegemann: 301-2.
[391] For example: TPR (1912) October: no author: 168; (1914) October: P.A.: 232-5; (1915) July: Adams: 64-5.

in the years preceding the First World War.[392] It was allegedly inspired by German municipal experiences that a delegation from Birmingham encountered during an excursion in 1906.[393] Forbáth explicitly encouraged its adoption in other European "civilised countries"[394] and helped to intensify transnational links. During the following decades, *The Town Planning Review's* interest was limited to the appearance of the Act's amended versions enacted in 1925 and 1932. The articles and book reviews published on the legal framework were intended as an opportunity to bridge academic debates and tools to disseminate practical experience and to help planning officials with the laws' appropriate application.[395]

Special laws related to planning

In the *1909 Town Planning Act* represented a conglomerate of various goals which were reflected in separate legal sections for public health and housing construction. Due to planning's multifaceted nature, the British journal paid attention to new laws enacted throughout the interwar years that were not directly linked to urban planning but impacted on these matters. References were made to the *Housing Act*, the *Health Act* and, in the late 1930s, to the *Ribbon Development Act*. The *Housing Act* was frequently covered, since it was subject to many amendments over the course of the years. Those amendments were meant as an immediate remedy to war effects on housing construction when in 1914 a £4,000,000 governmental grant was promised.[396] Another trigger was the projected continuation of governmental interventions on housing construction aiming for 2.5 million new dwellings over the next 15 years was announced in 1924. These included measures to keep construction outputs up through specific agreements with the industry addressing the pressing issue of young unemployed adults who could be offered positions as apprentices in the building trades.[397] During the second half of the analysed interwar period, the *Housing Act's* focus shifted towards the eradication of slum-like areas, as the following introduction to one extensive contribution by John Clarke in 1931 indicates.

---

[392] Schott, Dieter, *Die Stadt als Thema und Medium europäischer Kommunikation – Stadtplanung als Resultat europäischer Lernprozesse.* In Roth, Ralf [Ed.]: Städte im europäischen Raum: Verkehr, Kommunikation und Urbanität im 19. und 20. Jahrhundert. Stuttgart: Franz Steiner 2009: 218-9.
[393] DS (1912) 4: Forbáth: 44.
[394] DS (1912) 5: Forbáth: 52.
[395] TPR (1933) May: Hill: 222-3.
[396] TPR (1914) October: no author: 180-2.
[397] TPR (1924) December: Clarke: 119-27.

"It is a cause of deep disappointment to all those who are concerned with the removal of the appalling slums which still exist in our great cities that the remarkable national achievement of erecting some 1,200,000 houses since the Great War has done very little to alleviate the slum problem. The difficulties of procedure have been mainly responsible for the fact that the number of houses pulled down in the course of carrying out slum clearance schemes between 1st April, 1924 and December, 1928, amounts to only the total of 6,000."[398]

Relevant changes with regard to the *Health Act* were presented in reviews on the *Glen's Law of Public Health and Local Government* textbook which had been updated regularly to reflect recent changes in the Act itself as well as all related legal frameworks.[399] Towards the end of the analysed interwar period, the subject of public health had grown in complexity to such an extent that the British Parliament was unable to pass one single law covering all relevant issues, as John Clarke remarked in 1937.

"It was explained in this Report, which deals with most of the substantial amendments of the law which are contained in the Act, that a Bill covering all the provisions of the Public Health Acts and their associated statutes would include not less than 1,000 clauses. Instead of producing a Bill of this size, which would have more clauses and be longer than the Government of India Act, 1935, the Committee decided that it would be expedient to produce several Bills of what they call 'moderate length.'"[400]

The construction of building frontages along existing and new arterial or bypass roads dedicated to through traffic was labelled 'ribbon development' in the UK. Peter Hall has summarised how these new roads, originally designed to ease traffic congestion, were misused for bungalow constructions at massive scale instead.[401] Since the late 1920s, architects expressed a fierce criticism mainly directed at the bungalows' aesthetics. These dwellings on their respective building plots were a spatial manifestation of social segregation as well as expressing a lack of building control. Eventually, the *Ribbon Development Act, 1935* was intended to reduce the risks attached to this, as yet, uncontrolled development. In one article for *The Town Planning Review* in 1936, John Clarke identified the access to frontages at these roads for service connections, parking places or their deficit in the provision of social infrastructures due to remote and/or isolated locations as severe problems for traffic safety and the inhabitants' living qualities.[402] Nevertheless, the *Ribbon Devel-*

---

[398] TPR (1931) May: Clarke: 163.
[399] For example TPR (1923) January: Clarke: 57-9.
[400] TPR (1937) July: Clarke: 184.
[401] Hall [1988] 2014: 78-83.
[402] TPR (1936) June: Clarke: 11.

opment Act imposed restrictions on these spontaneous buildings at the expense of comprehensive town planning, as T. F. Thomson argued in his review on S. Pascoe Hayward's legal commentary "Restriction of Ribbon Development Act, 1935."[403]

3.3.9   National specificities reflected in the journals

Based on my international comparison and the thematic fields covered in the previous sections, it shows how general trends in urban development applied beyond national borders. Still both planning journals did focus on certain national specificities, be they of an historic or prompted current issues. Figures 6 and 7 do illustrate examples of local reports too. From time to time *The Town Planning Review* referred to the historic event of the Great Fire in 1666 which destroyed large sections of inner city London and the subsequent reconstruction plans initiated by Christopher Wren. Besides their local flavour and the fascination for the redevelopment opportunities caused by the Fire's disastrous effects, contributions like the one by Patrick Abercrombie in 1923 can be interpreted in two ways: first as attempts to highlight national ingenuity in urban planning[404]; and second to prove the planning community's long-standing historic roots as a distinctive profession.[405] Other reconstruction plans such as those by John Evelyn or Dutchman Marcus Doornick were also mentioned, though noting their inferiority in comparison to Wren's concept.[406] Wren's work was used as warning to planners in those days that yet the best plans with advantages supposedly obvious to many people will not be carried out without the consistent explanation and supervision of skilled planners.[407]

It exemplified tendencies of inertia in town planning when it comes to land rights, since the following reconstruction was mostly carried out alongside existing foundations and plots. Fascination for the Fire was fuelled by articles drawing on newly discovered historic documents in the 1930s.[408] Found in the registers of the Privy Council, they demonstrated the historic principles for London's reconstruction through governing public bodies in terms of street widening, improvements for wheeled traffic based on reduced gradients as well as the introduction of pavements and drains.[409] Another reconstruction plan originally drafted by Richard Newcourt, the elder, in Somerset was uncovered, and both – plan and planner -

---

[403] TPR (1937) February: Thomson: 144-7.
[404] TPR (1923a) May: Abercrombie: 73.
[405] TPR (1937) December: Reddaway: 277.
[406] TPR (1923) May: Abercrombie: 75.
[407] TPR (1923) May: Abercrombie: 71, 76-7.
[408] TPR (1937) July: Reddaway: 205.
[409] TPR (1937) December: Reddaway: 274-5.

were then claimed to be cornerstones for the planning profession by T. F. Reddaway.[410]

On the continent, *Der Städtebau* was focused developments around Berlin and the related question of Greater Berlin. This topic was much debated in the German planning community and its affect in the political arena on public administration, to a certain extent hurting sentiments of local patriotism in municipalities that were incorporated by a larger Berlin. Two articles argued about the legal basis for the creation of a public body that would eventually be able to represent Berlin as a metropolis. In 1920 the *Greater Berlin Act* (Groß-Berlin Gesetz) came into force and created a joint city administration that covered the many previously autonomous local authorities. This forced amalgamation can be interpreted as a proof of Peter Hall's description of interwar years as being the planning community's period of regional extension. Besides its legal framework, Greater Berlin served as a foil for several interwar topics which were then discussed for the larger region. Reports were thematically mixed including articles on the creation of green spaces for gymnastic exercise and public health[411], as well as the ideal location for public buildings within the urban fabric[412], or the potential limits to metropolitan growth. In this context, an early statement for the rejection of large cities as desirable place to live in was made in 1920 by Martin Mächler as kind of a prelude to the ensuing planning debate described above in, "Das Problem der gegenwärtigen Epoche der abendländischen Kultur ist die Weltstadt."[413]

3.4 Quantitative results

Now that the most important challenges and trends in urban development have been summarised in conjunction with some of their schools of thought, it is necessary to turn the analysis's attention from qualitative to some quantitative aspects. This move will help to investigate the degree of international coverage in both planning journals. A detailed overview of how the coverage was distributed among the most relevant countries is illustrated based on the results of my page counting activities in **figure 4** for *The Town Planning Review* and in **figure 5** for *Der Städtebau*. All detailed statistics are collated as part of the appendix (see A1 and A2).

---

[410] TPR (1939) July: Reddaway: 155-61.
[411] DS (1910) 2: Pudor: 21-2; (1910) 4: no author: 45-6.
[412] DS (1917) 6/7: Goecke: 70-1.
[413] DS (1920) 5/6: Mächler: 54. "The problem of the current era in occidental culture is the cosmopolitan city" (author's translation).

It does not come as a surprise that a significant part of all articles was devoted to domestic topics in the respective journals. Their shares varied significantly over the years. A specific British perspective on urban topics can be detected for an average of roughly 46.7% of all contributions[414] in *The Town Planning Review*, although they reached an all-time low of 15.3% in 1943, whereas the highest share was recorded at 72.5% in 1920. Those figures were, on average, slightly lower for specifically German contributions in *Der Städtebau* where they reached 45.4%, with a record low of 25.4% in 1931 and its all-time high of 68.6% in 1919. It is interesting to note that both journals reached their peak in publications on domestic topics in the immediate aftermath of the First World War. Although one could then assume that the German planning journal would focus its main attention on domestic topics after the Nazis took control of the country. This assumption is not verified based on statistical evidence. For most editions, the domestic share remained relatively stable between 25 and 30% of all articles published in *Der Städtebau*, with the exceptions of 1936 and 1938, when German coverage rose to more than 50%. Still they remained significantly lower in comparison to those for domestic coverage in the British journal during the same time period, which usually ranged around 55%. There is another similarity concerning domestic coverage during wartimes where both journals published more contributions on domestic topics to compensate for a lack of foreign news. The statistical results suggest that the latter point represented a stronger difficulty for *Der Städtebau* during the First World War when the journal was virtually cut off from many developments abroad. As a consequence between 50 and 60% of all contributions during those years dealt with domestic topics, whereas reports falling under the category of explicitly international matters plummeted to shares between 2 and 3%, or less, in war time volumes. Some foreign contributions did still appear, but they remained almost exclusively limited to immediate neighbouring countries like France, Poland or Switzerland and their share declined from 26.1% in 1916 to 10.2% in 1918.

On average, 'international matters' (see categories as defined in 3.2) made up for 10.9% of all articles in *The Town Planning Review* whilst those numbers remained lower, at just 7.6%, for the German journal. *Der Städtebau* covered international reports and comparisons often in some of the years before the Great War, with an all-time high of 27.4% in 1910, and once more for over one decade in 1925. Although *The Town Planning Review* contained many international articles in the years preceding the First World War, it recorded its highest coverage immediately after

---

[414] All percentages given in the following description are based on the page counting activities as laid down in 3.2. Hence, 100% means that all articles published over the course of one volume (i.e. one year) in DS or TPR dealt with this particular topic or country.

the fighting had ceased with 51.6% in the 1919 volume. Another brief period of strong international interest can be detected for the years 1937 and 1938.

A remarkable difference becomes apparent with regards to the category of 'general matters', whose average share was more than twice as much in *Der Städtebau* where they accounted for 25% in contrast to just 11.9% in *The Town Planning Review*. This divergence reflects a stylistic difference in the reports considered for publication in both journals too. For the British one the authors tried to contextualise their contributions to selected case study cities or countries, even when it came to street decoration or other aesthetic as well as economic questions, whereas the German journal tried to report on similar challenges through the lens of a rather neutral and distant observer. Hence it was sometimes easier to associate articles in *The Town Planning Review* with a particular country than it was the case for *Der Städtebau*.

A closer look at the respective countries that were covered in both planning journalsreveals a remarkable result. In terms of their national counterpart, *The Town Planning Review* only dedicated a negligible 0.9% on average per year to reports from Germany, and the country seemed to have virtually disappeared after the First World War in contrast to its regular inclusion before the war. *Der Städtebau* devoted equally limited attention to British developments which made up for an average 1.1% of all contributions per year, although most of them were published after the First World War. Both editorial boards remained open to other foreign contributions but language played of course a role. Therefore, the British journal had easier access to news from the US and included the country at an average of 9.3% per year, whilst *Der Städtebau* specifically referred to that nation in 2.8% of all articles. Both shares are, in comparison to other countries, of certain relevance and can be interpreted as an indication for the US's higher significance in those years' urban development trends. Existing linguistic advantages did not play a role per se, as German contributions on Austria or Switzerland indicate which were covered at an average of 0.9% per year for both countries respectively, owing to their perceived limited relevance. This is the probable reason why Switzerland was not at all covered in *The Town Planning Review* whilst the Austrian figures matched it likewise reaching 0.9%. Another country that attracted substantial attention in both journals was France with 3.3% per year from the British perspective and 2.1% from the German one, significantly less than the US. One remarkable result relates to Italian authors contributing to both planning journals. Although one would assume that Germany as closer ally during the country's Fascist period would pay more attention, it was in the UK that it allocated significantly more space with an annual share of 7.2% *The Town Planning Review* contained almost three times as much coverage on Mussolini's nation than *Der Städtebau* with its 2.7%.

These statistics are telling in two respects. In first instance they are indicative of the editorial staffs' agenda, intentions and preferences; a fact that impacted on the very selection of countries and developments covered as well as the tone and style in which those articles have been published. *Der Städtebau* offers a foil to such developments, bearing its transformation into a propaganda organ for the NS regime's ideology in mind. But *The Town Planning Review* took the deliberate decision to focus on developments in Italy, although the journal's authors were explicitly admitting the dominance of US-American and German contributions to the planning profession's development at large. The decision in favour of Italy was taken by its editor-in-chief Stanley Adshead as early as in 1912[415], and it remained part of the journal's philosophy over the following decades.[416] In addition, all these national percentages do not represent the full extent to which each country might have been referred to, since further links are contained in the international matters and in many of the domestic articles. For the latter, these references formed part of apparently less relevant clauses and were therefore not considered as international in character.

At some points reports were running in parallel, soon after, or inspired by the other journal's articles. Reconstruction plans for the war-devastated French city of Reims were dealt with in both journals at more or less exactly the same time. Whilst the extensive British report on the American ideas for the reconstruction prepared by George B. Ford was published in March 1921[417], the German reports predated the British one but remained rather superficial and nationalistic in tone. They were printed in *Der Städtebau's* double features 11/12 at the end of 1920 and in feature 1/2 at the beginning of 1921.[418] Similar in timing, but less so in attention, did they address the question of reconstruction in Belgium, to which the British journal referred in an editorial in January 1915[419] and on which German news appeared in 1915 and 1917.[420] Yet Belgium's reconstruction after the First World War was not addressed in both journals.

---

415 TPR (1912) April: Adshead: 52.
416 It is nonetheless surprising that TPR maintained its focus on Italian developments despite the Fascist regime's general scepticism towards large cities and its preferential treatment of rural areas. In this context Lenger refers to Italy's slow growth of urban dwellers in large cities among the country's overall population from 12.9% in 1921 to 17.8% in 1936 (Lenger 2013: 323).
417 TPR (1921) March: Holliday: 5-11.
418 DS (1920) 11/12: no author: 119; (1921) 1/2: De Fries: 21.
419 TPR (1915) January: no author: 257-9.
420 DS (1915) 7/8: no author: 84; (1917) 2/3: no author: 34.

In very exceptional cases both journals contained contributions written by the same author. Examples were the many articles on Italian developments handed in by Luigi Lenzi. He was a frequent commentator for *The Town Planning Review*, where a total of eight contributions had been accepted for publication between 1928 and 1937. Each of them described recent urban planning in one single city from Arezzo and Brescia to Padua or Pavia. Most of these descriptions were based on national competitions for the cities' redevelopment rooted in Fascist ideas. For *Der Städtebau* two articles by Lenzi were accepted and published in 1935 and 1939, again describing Fascist urban ideas but exclusively focusing on Rome. Besides Lenzi there were many more authors reporting on Italy and they tailored their articles to the readers' tastes. In this respect, a similar trend can be detected for both journals according to which Italy was assessed as experimental environment for new urban design patterns developed under, at least from a British standpoint, different political circumstances. But reports on Italy were not limited to a collection of the Fascist movement's impacts as the articles' subjects suggest. They were fuelled by a rediscovered impetus to explore remnants of the ancient Roman Empire and by a general appreciation of Italian beauty when it comes to the design qualities of public squares (piazzas). From the German perspective special interest was laid on the reclamation of land under Fascist rule.

3.4.1 The journals' internationality

As a summary with regards to internationality the statistical results reveal a continuous circulation of international ideas and both journals offered space for direct comparison and reflection on foreign developments. If the above stated shares for domestic coverage are reversed, it can be argued that at least half of the contributions were impacted by foreign ideas. These impacts were conveyed in journal articles either on case studies on foreign cities or on events where other influences became tangible. One major opportunity to get first-hand encounters were international excursions, and for *Der Städtebau* there can be counted no less than 18 reports that referred to such chances for the exchange of ideas. This flow of ideas fits with Schott's results, who has equally dealt with the international exchange among the planning community for pre-Great War years analysing the reception of Howard's Garden City and the British *Housing and Town Planning Act, 1909*.[421] These (self-) organised excursions covered different destinations as well as thematic fields. In 1925 a German delegation comprising of 16 members travelled to London in order to make themselves familiar with latest trends in road construction, and upon return they summarised their experiences and disseminated them among the wider planning community, thus multiplying the effects of such trav-

---

[421] Schott 2009: 214-9.

els.[422] Similar trips focused on housing or recent achievements in garden cities and therefore offered the chance for certain pressure groups to promote their ideas, as did the German Garden City Association with their annual trips such as in 1927 to England and the Netherlands.[423] The Association therefore revived a pre-war tradition in the German planning community.

In addition to excursions, international conferences offered another broadly used opportunity to mingle with other planners and get inspired by the experiences made in other contexts. International congresses on town planning or housing formed an important meeting point from early days on like the 1910 exhibitions at Berlin and London or at Ghent in 1913, and the invitations occasionally made a special remark about their welcoming nature to female participants as advertised in *Der Städtebau*.[424] These exhibitions were popular among contemporaries and attracted many attendees. Robert Freestone and Marco Amati have edited a book on a collection of relevant conferences that contributed to the planning profession's evolution.[425] In the aftermath of the First World War and under the then unfavourable economic situation, German representatives were unable to attend such conferences during the first half of the 1920s. As Von Petz suggests, the town planning exhibition at Amsterdam attracted many German attendees[426] but it was not covered in *Der Städtebau* due to its cessation of publication in 1923/4. According to the journal's coverage it was only at the occasion of the international urban congress held at Vienna in 1926 that Germans were anew able to participate in larger numbers. Among the congress's reported 1,100 delegates from all over the world, a clear majority of speakers came from Germany.[427] Topics addressed in Vienna were land ownership and expropriation tools as well as housing and future prospects for detached houses and apartment buildings. As the 1926 congress already indicates, such congresses were in many cases mixed businesses taking their published agendas and summary reports in *Der Städtebau* into account. Topics subsequently ranged from housing and land rights to traffic, public health or waste management. Besides their international character, they served to review academic questions regarding their practical relevance in planning policy, and planning au-

---

[422] DS (1925) 7/8: Hegemann: 116.

[423] DS (1927) 3: no author: 43.

[424] DS (1910) 4: no author: 48.

[425] Freestone, Robert/Amati, Marco [Eds.], *Exhibitions and the Development of Modern Planning Culture*, Farnham/Burlington: Ashgate 2014.

[426] In this context Von Petz highlights those high-ranking positions within the *International Federation for Town and Country Planning* assumed by prominent German planners Gustav Langen, Robert Schmidt and Fritz Schumacher after elections held during the Amsterdam exhibition (Von Petz 2016: 148).

[427] DS (1926) 11: no author: 175.

thorities used them as an opportunity to share their latest experiences in the applicability of certain laws or tools with other experts.[428] In rare cases these planning events were even explicitly combined with colonial exhibitions as reported about the City Exhibition held at Lyon in 1914.[429]

Interwar impact of international scholarships and travel grants

Just like today, participation in these conferences would require every attendee to pay the admission fee and related travel costs as advertised in the respective invitations. Nonetheless, in exceptional cases German urban planners have directly been invited to attend a particular conference, or to work as kind of freelance consultant to US-American public authorities at the local level, as had happened to Dr Otto March in his function as *Geheimrat* at the Greater Berlin administration in 1911.[430] In 1929 *Der Städtebau* published an extensive contribution by Alphons Siebers comparing the two US-American cities of Butte in Montana and Longview in Colorado. Both cities are described as 'boom towns' due to economic prosperity based on copper mining in Butte and timber industries in Longview which subsequently induced rapid population growth. In his contribution Siebers tried to contrast the effects of comprehensive planning carried out by the main industrial company in Longview with the rather spontaneous and uncontrolled sprawl in Butte, which he flagellated as waste of resources. Siebers drew the city's image as important move towards new planning standards which complied with a report similar in tone published in the *The Town Planning Review* in 1935.[431] His report was not just a first-hand account of those days' urban challenges in two remote US cities, brought to the attention of the German planning community. It also served to disseminate his results as part of a two-year scholarship offered to him by the Rockefeller Foundation, with the explicit task to study international urban design as Siebers mentioned himself.[432] Those invitations were, of course, rare opportunities but they were nonetheless offered during the interwar years and therefore represent a remarkable proof for transnational networks for intermediaries in Saunier's sense.[433] If plan-

---

[428] DS (1914) 6: Goecke: 70-3.

[429] DS (1914) 5: no author: 64.

[430] DS (1911) 5: no author: 60. Berlin-based March was not just architect and professor but also uncle of Werner Hegemann (Von Petz 1998: 30).

[431] TPR (1935) December: Hare: 279-86.

[432] DS (1929) 1: Siebers: 32.

[433] Travels to the other direction were also limited but nevertheless underscore the existing links: estimations for American students visiting German universities from 1815 to 1914 range between a total of 9,000 and 10,000 (Watson, Peter, *The German Genius: Europe's Third Renaissance, the Second Scientific Revolution and the Twentieth Century*, London *et al.* Simon & Schuster 2010: 323).

ners were not fortunate enough to receive such generous funding, or if they were unable to attend one of the events in person, the planning journals provided them with a great variety of articles on foreign developments and trends.

Range of countries and contributors in the journals

News coverage in *Der Städtebau* was not limited to particular countries. The journal tried to consider reports from many regions of the world and it did reach a remarkable breadth in its efforts. With as many as 34 countries in Europe, Asia, Africa, Australia and the Americas covered in the German journal throughout the decades, it surpassed *The Town Planning Review* with 26 countries covered, equally representing all continents. Nevertheless, as the statistics in the appendix indicate, for some of the countries there were just very brief contributions which are of course considered for reasons of statistical completeness but they are not displayed individually in figures 4 and 5. All these various contributions from around the globe basically served two functions. Firstly, they catered to the reader's interest of getting to know something about exotic places. Secondly, in terms of the planning profession's evolution the more relevant reason, they were intended to track down latest trends in particular topics such as housing. *Der Städtebau* covered several case study reports from Nordic countries such as Sweden with five articles referred between 1928 and 1934, focusing on Stockholm's concepts for small houses. Both journals looked at developments in the Netherlands in late 1920s and throughout the 1930s when, amongst other topics, extension plans for Amsterdam were prepared. From a retrospective viewpoint, Sweden and the Netherlands represented interesting cases of progressive smaller planning traditions as Ward has summarised for the interwar period.[434]

The journal analysis has revealed that the two magazines relied on contributions submitted by both, UK or German-born and foreign correspondents whose texts were either written in the respective journal's language, or translated by an associated expert familiar with that country due to own work or travel experience. The latter kind of familiarity was drawn on for one of the many reviews that were published in virtually every issue. It is remarkable how many international publications, be it books, other journals, or exhibition catalogues have been received, merely listed as new publication or reviewed in detail. In this respect, *The Town Planning Review* and *Der Städtebau* were comparable since both considered a large number of foreign publications, although the British journal devoted more pages to those reviews. Such reviews did reveal a high level of internationality when in his 1935 article for *The Town Planning Review*, Patrick Abercrombie appreciated the catalogue

---

[434] Ward 2002: 129-39.

produced in the aftermath of the 1931 Berlin City Exhibition for its references to small and less often covered countries, although he, at the same time, explicitly missed sections on British India or more well-balanced information on Palestine. In addition, Abercrombie openly admitted the lack of a comparison at international scale regarding the professional advances made in town planning and housing.[435]

Above all, many contributions which were counted as part of domestic debates in either of the journals for the matter of my analysis, contained references to foreign developments, laws or tools. There are numerous examples of such minor references, which underscore an underlying international touch. Planners in interwar years were very well aware of trends and laws in other countries and used those case studies to illustrate and discuss problems in their respective home countries. This supports Saunier's concept of transnational history and highlights the mutual familiarity with those foreign developments among large sections of the planning community, since otherwise those remarks and references in domestic journal articles would have been pointless. Over the past years, several authors have come up with similar results like already mentioned David Rodgers in terms of networks on social politics across the Atlantic[436], Renzo Riboldazzi on housing debates at IFHTP congresses[437], or Liora Bigon and Yossi Katz as editors of a book on the reception of garden city ideas in colonial contexts.[438] Familiarity with various schools of thought and international ideas was enhanced through specific series such as the one published on planners in *The Town Planning Review*. From 1927 to 1930 four articles were dedicated to one specific planner who contributed to the planning profession's evolution at large. The series included the works of Haussmann, Sitte, L'Enfant and the reconstruction plans drafted after London's Fire in 1666. It is indicative that no woman appeared on this list, despite the fact that female positions were reflected in both planning journals during interwar years – though at varying degrees. For *Der Städtebau* they formed just a minor detail, with a total of four contributions over the full period of the journal's publication either submitted by female authors or as review written on a book published by a female planner. The journal referred to Stefanie Frischauer, Marie Luise Gothein, Theodora Kimball and Renate Mönckeberg. Surprisingly nothing was reported on Margarete Schütte-Lihotzky and her contributions to modern style housing with the often-quoted Frankfurt fitted kitchen.[439] This was contrasted by *The Town Planning Review* and its 21 specific articles related to female contributions; among them were

---

[435] TPR (1935) June: Abercrombie: 228.
[436] Rodgers 1998.
[437] Riboldazzi 2015.
[438] Bigon, Katz 2014.
[439] Von Saldern 1988: 205.

several submissions on town planning in the US, again handed in by Theodora Kimball. Nonetheless, with the exception of one article by the Assistant Director of the British School at Rome, Eugenie Strong, all female contributions appeared after the First World War. More than half of them were published during the 1930s and in two cases they were apparently a co-production between spouses, Mary and Russell Black as well as Nora and Manning Robertson. From a thematic standpoint they mostly covered housing, which could have echoed Octavia Hill's early housing reform ideas in urban planning she already contributed in the 1880s[440] or Catherine Bauer, who in 1937 helped to pass Federal housing legislation through the US Congress.[441] Other topics such as urban aesthetics, refuse collection or public health were included as well. The other publications were written by Carol Aronovici, Ethel Bright Ashford, Sybilla Branford, Ella Carter, Isobel Chambers, Yvonne Cloud, Elizabeth Denby, Kathleen England, Edith MacIver, Esther Meynell, Elva Miller, Marjorie Pentland, and Edith Elmer Wood. In addition to these articles by female authors, few articles mentioned the works of female planners.

It is useful to have a look at the authors' professional backgrounds as far as they are indicated as academic titles or professional abbreviations. With regards to *Der Städtebau* that information can be retrieved for the vast majority of contributions, and it is remarkable to state that during the full analysed period a total of almost 120 articles came from persons who held the position of university professor. A larger number was submitted by authors who had received their doctorate; 327 articles fall under this category. In some cases, those authors bore an academic degree such as a PhD and were currently employed as 'Baurat' (government building officer) or had already retired from such a position. Although there are no definite figures for persons with such an overlapping background, at least 173 contributions were submitted by authors in a position at Baurat. Furthermore, over the period in question, the number of contributions written by architects decreased and, instead, more specific professionals such as from Baurat, or other positions closely related to urban planners took the lead. Short news and advertisements promoted specialised trainings to fit these new job positions. This development helps to illustrate the contrast with previous generations of planners. Schott mentions the case of James Hobrecht who was assigned with the task to draft new layout plans for Berlin in 1859 under the professional title as a 'Baumeister für den

---

[440] Ward 2004: 18. As Nightingale has shown how it transpired into the South African context, Hill's ideas influenced SWA indirectly through transnational personal exchange with South African planners too (Nightingale 2012: 242-3).
[441] Hall [1988] 2014: 181-2.

Wasser-, Wege- und Eisenbahnbau' (Master Builder for Waterways, Roads and Railway constructions) but not as a town planner.[442]

Unfortunately, such a detailed overview about the authors' background cannot be given for *The Town Planning Review* as the required relevant credentials are only provided for a minority of articles. Hence it is impossible to draw a similarly comprehensive image as for the German journal but according to editorials and hints in some of the articles the general situation seemed to be comparable. This impression is further substantiated as *The Town Planning Review* was by its very origin part of the efforts of Liverpool University. Many contributions therefore came either from professors or other university staff members, as Masters Degrees mentioned for some authors suggest. In a few cases, the authors held a governmental position or worked as representative of local building administrations as indicated by their professional title or explained within their reports. For some authors their professional background is traceable due to their high reputation, like for Patrick Abercrombie, Wesley Dougill, Barry Parker or Raymond Unwin.

3.4.2 Reports on colonial developments

Planners in interwar years seemed well aware of developments in their neighbouring countries and beyond, or at least the journals had a closer look upon those cases. Last it needs to be assessed how much attention was paid to the colonies.

Comparing the coverage of developments in colonial entities unearths significant deviations between *The Town Planning Review* and *Der Städtebau*. Whereas the former journal continuously contained contributions about the colonies, with at least one or more articles in almost every volume until the mid-1930s, the latter contained just sporadic articles. Surprisingly from the German perspective, her own colonial overseas possessions were not addressed in any form, neither in the years preceding the Great War nor from a revisionist viewpoint after their loss according to the Treaty of Versailles. The only exception to this finding is one brief but biased report from Samoa published in 1921, when the former German colony had already been formally handed over to New Zealand as mandated territory under the League of Nations' supervision. This report formed part of a book intended as a kind of critique (Kulturkritik), which recorded 11 speeches allegedly given by a 'Samoan Chief' reflecting on European and German lifestyles from the Indigenous perspective.[443] Anyhow there is no indication given about the article's fictional

---

[442] Schott 2014a: 310.
[443] DS (1921) 1/2: no author: 16-7. Jürgen Reulecke mentions a similar example from the "East African perspective" written by Hans Paasche under his alias Lukanga Mukara in 1912 and whose letters remained popular over the following century (Reulecke, Jürgen, *Das*

nature, since the book itself neither reflects a Samoan point of view nor does it contain relevant hints on the Indigenous community, as Horst Cain has summarised.[444] The reproduced "speech" was in fact written by Erich Scheurmann as a critique at German urban life. Firstly, it plays with the stereotypical and romanticising contrast between cities and rural countryside in Europe. Secondly, it is plotted on an assumed viewpoint of the Indigenous Samoan which attributes them with a primitive but idealised lifestyle. Despite its different character as *kulturkritik*, it is emblematic for German interpretations of colonial philosophies. On one side, the report conveys stereotypical images of the admired 'Noble Savage', linked to subtle criticism directed at urban lifestyles in those days and where this admiration contrasted with the idea of a 'civilising mission.' On the other side, the report's imprudent reprint without any hint about its fictional nature does blend with a certain naïve attitude when it comes to German colonialism which contrasted with some its self-defined goals.

Focus on British Empire

Most of the remaining colonial articles in *Der Städtebau* were devoted to urban developments within the British Empire's domain, and the colonies received their maximum attention in the 1913 volume when three reports were accepted for publication. Among the colonial articles, attention was paid to the exploration and the following competition for Australia's new federal capital at Canberra. One of the articles covering the competition was not just calling for German participation but pointed to the exemplary organisation of land rights, which were held by the public and only handed out based on leasehold contracts[445] – once again taking up the question of land ownership and who should eventually benefit from the increment in land values as already discussed (see 3.3.3). Individual ownership, by contrast, should be prevented in this scheme. In addition, British endeavours to transfer the capital of its Indian colony to Delhi and to construct new governmental quarters were addressed, although the report by Albert Bencke remained to a certain extent vague about the final decisions in terms of their exact location as well as the size of all building measures.[446] Both cities were of course covered in *The Town Planning Review* although several months earlier, with more explicit aesthetic critique[447], just

---

Pathos der Jugend: Die Entdeckung des jugendlichen "Selbst" und der "Hohe Meißner" 1913. In: Mares, Detlev; Schott, Dieter [Eds.]: Das Jahr 1913: Aufbrüche und Krisenwahrnehmungen am Vorabend des Ersten Weltkriegs. Bielefeld: Transcript 2014: 25-7).

[444] Cain, Horst, *Tuiavi'is Papalagi.* In: Duerr, Hans Peter [Ed.]: Authentizität und Betrug in der Ethnologie. Frankfurt am Main: Suhrkamp 1987, 252-70.

[445] DS (1911) 10: no author: 119.

[446] DS (1913) 9: Bencke: 106.

[447] TPR (1912) October: no author: 165-168.

in editorials whereas the German journal devoted specific reports on them. Both journals agreed in their disappointment concerning the small and domestic jury composition assessing all submissions for the Australian competition. The British reaction was more pronounced and explicitly deplored the missed opportunity to ask the 'mother country' for advice.[448] It is here, that a fine distinction or hierarchy becomes apparent when dealing with colonial entities from the Eurocentric perspective. Whilst, with regards to Australia, the close relations between colony and 'mother country' were emphasised, authors made a clear difference between colonised and colonisers in other colonies. The British comments on the plans for Delhi can be taken as an example, for they included an allusion to two distinct realms, and conveyed the idea of a dual city.

> "In the first place, it must be remembered that the so-called new capital City of Delhi cannot, after all, be anything more than a European section of an Eastern town of the same name."[449]

This clear separation was used as background canvas for other descriptions as well. W. H. McLean focused in his 1913 contribution entitled "Town Planning in the Tropics" on the natural physical characteristics of the "native population" as being accustomed to the local climate as opposed to,

> "a portion of the population [which] are not in their natural zone, and are, therefore, not in adjustment with their environment."[450]

When McLean went on to explain his principles of town planning in the colonial context, he justified his preferential treatment of (mostly) European men based on the advantages the Indigenous population would already enjoy from its natural adjustment to the climatic conditions. Instead, he emphasised that "white men"[451] deserved particular protection from sunshine as "one of their greatest enemies", and in order to prevent the spread of epidemics, spatial separation was deemed necessary from a public health standpoint. Whilst McLean separated White and Indigenous people in a strict way, he did not consider the European community as one homogenous group. Europeans should be registered in more detail by means of civic surveys.

> "The civic survey in the tropics should therefore include statistics of the nationality of the population, so that zones may be arranged as far as possible suited to the re-

---

[448] TPR (1912) October: no author: 165.
[449] TPR (1912) October: no author: 167-8.
[450] TPR (1913) January: McLean: 225.
[451] All quotes in this paragraph are taken from TPR (1913) January: McLean: 225.

quirements of the various sections of the population. As a general rule, it is well, if possible, to segregate the native population, as the epidemics to which all tropical cities are liable can be so much more easily dealt with."[452]

Based on the example of Sudan's capital city Khartoum – then under British imperial influence – in 1913, McLean mixed ethnic criteria with social ones to further substantiate the concept of residential segregation within the city limits, as well as with regards to the neighbouring villages of Khartoum North and Omdurman which mostly served to accommodate the Indigenous population. For these villages, no plans were drafted at all and for Khartoum itself extension plans were based on zoning regulations that were linked to social classes. Three classes were distinguished for the construction of the city's quarters and each of them was attributed with particular building requirements. The first two classes requested permanent structures made of brick, concrete or stone and subsequently excluded the Indigenous population based on higher costs as McLean admitted himself.[453] It was just within the confines of the least attractive and remote areas of third-class quarters that mud buildings were permitted, thereby limiting the available residential areas for the Indigenous population if taking their economic resources into account. Hewas unable to estimate future Indigenous migration from surrounding areas towards third-class quarters in the city but he was, at the same time, convinced that houses in good condition might be taken over by lower income Europeans. In contrast to the "native population" in his descriptions, which was considered as one homogenous block, McLean refers to different social classes within the European community to which Khartoum's town planning catered with first- and second-class quarters. Except for minor changes in architectural patterns intended to prevent the spread of tuberculosis, he did not see any need for direct planning interventions or regulations to the benefit of the autochthonous inhabitants.[454] McLean rather considered it positive and with certain satisfaction that,

"[t]he natives, however, can live comfortably in much more crowded circumstances; so that owing to this and to the cost of land in the city, the houses in the native quarter are often built abutting and with courtyards (hooshes) in the centre of them."[455]

---

[452] TPR (1913) January: McLean: 225.
[453] TPR (1913) January: McLean: 227.
[454] TPR (1913) January: McLean: 226-31.
[455] TPR (1913) January: McLean: 226-7.

Examples of transnational exchange

The Town Planning Review did reflect on examples for direct transnational exchange of ideas resembling a *circuit* in accordance with Saunier's concept[456], when – with a certain delay – the 1909 British *Town Planning Act* served as blueprint for similar legal frameworks in Canada and India. In 1916 Stanley Adshead summarised the drafted planning laws as stipulated in the *Bombay Town Planning Act, 1915* and the Canadian *Draft Act with respect to Planning and Regulating the Use and Development of Land for Building Purposes in Cities, Towns, and Rural Municipalities* prepared in 1914.[457] Within this context he pointed out where the commonalities with the British original were, and what kind of amendments had been made in the colonial environment. His report can therefore be considered as an account that exemplified how colonial experiences were received in the UK and were considered as a progress for the urban planning profession at large. Adshead expressed his curiosity and introduced his readers with reference to the Indian act that,

> "[t]his Act is of great interest to us in Great Britain as showing not merely variations from our Act of 1909 due to altered conditions of location and administration, but also as showing variations undoubtedly due to what have been considered improvements in its general construction."[458]

Colonial laws were treated with equal respect, and the Indian framework was praised for its clear definition of the increment to land values induced by planning and rules on how to skim half of it to the benefit of the commonwealth. However, this relative equality remained an exception, as a book review on Mr Lanchester's *Town Planning in Madras* just few years later in 1919 illustrated again.[459] His publication is another example for direct exchange of ideas between Europe and India based on first-hand encounters, although from the Eurocentric perspective, as it insisted on the division between urban planning in its "European sense" and what it could contribute to the Indian context. Lanchester in a way functioned as link trying to interpret the British concepts to what he considered to be Indian lifestyle.[460] The summary highlighted the specific chapter that contained a comparison of Indian and European cities, yet it lacked the Indigenous perspective on the sub-

---

[456] Saunier 2013: 43-6.
[457] TPR (1916) April: Adshead: 250-3.
[458] TPR (1916) April: Adshead: 250.
[459] TPR (1919) April: L. P. A.: 56-7.
[460] William Bissell refers to an example of Lanchester's contributions to colonial planning in Africa: in 1922 he was involved in the preparation of a new master plan for Zanzibar. Bissell 2011: 223.

ject matter. The implicitly construed differences become apparent in the following summary.

"[…] [T]he special quality which might be expected from a series of lectures delivered in India by an English town planner remains distinctly marked. By this we mean that the author has felt it necessary firstly to establish clearly what is meant in the European sense by town planning in general, and then to apply these principles to the special conditions of Indian life, before directly approaching the particular town which is the subject of his suggested improvements."[461]

The last clause of this quote conveyed the message that it needed external expertise in order to solve Indian problems. It was made clear that *The Town Planning Review* would be willing to delve deeper into the topic and the country of India.

"We could wish that all the principal cities in this country would see the force of preparing a Development Plan on such lines, and would not hesitate at the publicity, which is so desirable for the purpose of general enlightenment."[462]

Other articles, such as the one by Charles Reade published in 1921[463], revealed the interwar work division in colonial domains like British Malaya where most high-rank planning positions remained in European hands, whilst it was just for the lower-rank draftsmen and tracers that local employees were hired. And although Reade's report proved that borders were still permeable enough to allow for direct exchange among the various colonial entities, it further demonstrated that high-ranking positions remained a White domain as was the case with many Australian surveyors who worked in British Malaya. Similarly, German regulations concerning the reorganisation of land holdings founded, "on a system of debit and credit based on compensation and betterment"[464] easily crossed the borders, and were used for the *Bombay Town Planning Act* which, in turn, inspired Reade for future application in Malaysia. During the following years, urban development and planning in India drew some attention from authors of *The Town Planning Review*, and this interest was justified by the cities' rapid growth and the problems migration from the countryside caused in terms of living conditions, housing or public health.[465] Aside from planning laws there are traces of bidirectional exchange in India, where systems of land registration merged and resembled British elements

[461] TPR (1919) April: L. P. A.: 56.
[462] TPR (1919) April: L. P. A.: 57.
[463] TPR (1921) December: Reade: 162-5.
[464] TPR (1921) December: Reade: 165.
[465] TPR (1930) May: W.D.: 71-2.

based on Indian traditions.[466] Wesley Dougill in his 1930 book review of *Town Planning in India* written by J. M. Linton Bogle appreciated it for,

> "[t]his book makes a timely appearance when, to-day, so very much attention both from a political and a social point of view, is being focussed on India."[467]

Bogle was credited with the adoption of various foreign methods for the Indian context. This repeated the narrative of the colonies as being incapable of developing appropriate solutions to their urban challenges without European support. It becomes understandable, why Patrick Abercrombie critically remarked on the abovementioned neglect of British India in the catalogue on the 1931 International Exhibition in Berlin, and which was produced with some delay by Bruno Schwan in 1935.[468] Nonetheless, British attention was not exclusively focused on India but did extend to other colonies and protectorates too. Kenya was another example, and the legal transformations made in the planning ordinances of this country did have an impact back in the UK, as John Clarke pointed out in his review of *The Town Planning and Development Ordinances and (Procedure) Regulations 1931 of the Colony and Protectorate of Kenya*. In contrast to the British version, the colonial law provided for the legal basis to skim the full unearned increment due to planning interventions.

> "Altogether, this constitutes a marked advance on the legislation of the Mother Country and the authors are to be heartily congratulated."[469]

His statement underscores that the exchange with the colonies was not unidirectional, though he started his review full of admiration for the British impact on legal procedures within her global Empire.

> "It is always refreshing to observe in what manner the legislation of the Mother Country has influenced that of the Colonies and Protectorates as well as of the Dominions, [...]"[470]

Towards the end of the analysed interwar period, the British perspective on urban planning in its imperial domains was guided by the idea of a custodian with the mother country still taking care of and overseeing the colonial progress. As C. R. Knight summarised in 1935, this was true for the Dominion of New Zealand.

---

[466] Nightingale 2012: 98.
[467] TPR (1930) May: W.D.: 71.
[468] TPR (1935) June: Abercrombie: 228.
[469] TPR (1932) June: Clarke: 74.
[470] TPR (1932) June: Clarke: 73.

"Town Planning in New Zealand is not yet out of the preliminary educative phase but signs are not lacking that the goal of real achievement is not far distant."[471]

In contrast to these reports in *The Town Planning Review*, *Der Städtebau*, although including articles from colonial countries like India or Indonesia, did in many cases focus on representative historic buildings like Taj Mahal[472] or traditional patterns of what was interpreted as "Hindu-Malayan" urban design. The latter was used to reflect on then ongoing and, to a certain extent, nationalistic debates, and led Gerhard Jobst to three questions.

"Warum konnte man damals Millionenstädte in weiträumigem Flachbau errichten, ohne Verkehrsschwierigkeiten zu empfinden? Warum konnte man damals Stadt und Land als Einheit betrachten? Und warum bringen wir es nicht fertig, in gleich hoher Planmäßigkeit und sauberer Ordnung unseren Boden zu bewirtschaften?"[473]

Eventually, with the formulation of these questions Jobst skilfully blended some of the general challenges of interwar urban planning with the colonial context.

3.5 Intermediary conclusions

For the general picture of interwar urban challenges, the analysis and comparison of *The Town Planning Review* and *Der Städtebau* was able to identify a strong focus on housing, (perceived) traffic congestion, and land rights which were later overlapped by trends towards regionalisation. These four topics were addressed in hundreds of specific articles, and, additionally, formed the background to many other debates at the legal level as well as with respect to public health considerations. They can be further attributed with global importance regardless of national borders, as reports from correspondents and related book reviews suggest. The analysis revealed that during interwar years a profound shift transformed urban development at large. Building activities on the housing sector were more and more dominated by direct state intervention, trying to fill the gap that private investors had left who turned their attention to other businesses in the aftermath of the First World War. In an environment temporarily characterised by a lack of adequate financial resources, skilled labourers and – due to land speculation – available building sites, the plan-

---

[471] TPR (1935) June: Knight: 220.
[472] DS (1920) 3/4: Keyserling, Von Tschirner-Tschirne: 33-8.
[473] DS (1933) 4: Jobst: 190. "Why was one then able to build megacities in spaciously scattered low-rise buildings without the perception of traffic problems? Why was one then able to regard town and countryside as one entity? And why are we unable to cultivate our land with equally high orderliness and neat order?" (author's translation).

ning profession matured to yet unprecedented levels. Governmental bills granted planners new powers and their self-esteem grew as well, making them determined to think of urban development at rather comprehensive levels. Inspired by the works of Patrick Geddes, they left their merely aesthetic and architectural stage behind, and started to see cities as a complex entity or organism whose vital functions needed to be placed well among each other, in order to make the functions work to the best benefit of all inhabitants. To achieve this goal, urban planning progressed and developed itself into an interdisciplinary profession. This transformation can best be exemplified by the activities and efforts at Bauhaus Academy. On parallel, planning left its local confines and took a more comprehensive position at the regional level where coerced or voluntary cooperation gained ground. Of course, these transformative processes were not welcomed by all but it turned out to be almost impossible to stop them.

Apart from utopian theorists, two mainstream of planning schools tried to adapt to these challenges. Traditionalist approaches aspired to preserve, not just in aesthetic terms, a romanticised image of cities which, in their opinion, should resemble manageable 'organic' towns and rejected megacities. New developments like motor vehicles were in this case integrated into their plans, as long as they complied with this image and served to maintain a pleasant environment. Modernist approaches, by contrast, were characterised by their strong fascination for modern technologies, minimalist architectural designs and their determination to define a completely new urban environment that would impact the inhabitant's way of living and hence help to create a 'New Man.' Standardisation played an increasing role in modern schemes but behind vernacular façades it also made its way into traditionalist concepts; it was firstly aimed at construction techniques before it later impacted on interior designs. Heßler has demonstrated how those standardisation efforts did affect hygiene and gender roles in private households, keeping homework a female domain.[474]

For an appreciation of the developments it is important to bear the political and economic context with its instabilities in mind. Sooner or later they affected every country and determined the possibilities at hands to intervene in urban planning. In Germany these instabilities became tangible several times when, first, the economic downturn in the aftermath of the Great War caused the interruption of *Der Städtebau's* publishing activities in 1923-4, whilst political turmoil occurred in face of the rise of nationalistic sentiments and the country's subsequent transition from democratic structures to Hitler's dictatorship. Individual opinions were then force-

---

[474] Heßler 2012: 72-89.

fully silenced as demonstrated by Werner Hegemann's dismissal as *Der Städtebau's* editor-in-chief, and the ruling NSDAP took possession of urban spaces for political power demonstrations: the public space should be converted into 'their' visual urban imprints as representative meeting places surrounded by intimidating building structures forming the new arena for political mass demonstrations. *Der Städtebau* only covered a limited collection of cases like Munich's Königsplatz or the redevelopment plans for the city of Wuppertal. Other examples which were expected to cause far more significant impacts on the existing urban fabric, such as Albert Speer's plans for Berlin as future capital 'Germania' or the construction of 'Gauforums' in preselected regional capitals all across Germany, with Weimar eventually being the only built example, were not covered at all. The question of land rights was, for ideological reasons, charged with the 'blood-and-soil' motto, although possibilities for its implementation remained limited and this fact was obvious to at least some commentators. Whilst these ideological debates were less relevant for the developments in democratic Great Britain, the country was predominantly trying to cope with the large extent of slum-like housing conditions, growing traffic demands and questions of land ownership.

The interwar years were characterised by massive transformations that have left an imprint on cities and urban theories. In agreement with Lenger the urban environment at large served as background canvas for the trope of the city as a place where man and machine merged, and where the 'machine age' reigned as exemplified in Fritz Lang's movie 'Metropolis.'[475] This environment has created positive aspirations as well as clear rejections by authors at that time. Ditt has summarised the full extent of electrification in conjunction with the rise of automobiles and chemical industries as the second industrial revolution. One of the revolution's consequences was the transformation of Western societies into mass consumer societies and mass culture.[476] This transformation was made possible through the provision of several new infrastructures as well as technical devices which, in subsequence, had a severe impact on urban planning. Their effects on the urban fabric were nonetheless subject to various critiques such as the one formulated by Le Corbusier: Haffner has revealed, how the view from above has turned Le Corbusier into a critic of the capitalist "chaos" as made visible in the urban fabric, and similar concerns had been expressed by Lewis Mumford.[477] Under those circumstances the colonial environment could be interpreted as an experimental environment to avoid similar trends but the colonial development remained ambiva-

---

[475] Lenger 2013: 375.
[476] Ditt 2011: 9.
[477] Haffner 2013: 48.

198

lent. It is important to note how these developments at the metropole were used as a kind of revered role model for the colonial context, though they did not necessarily materialise there to the same extent. In terms of motor vehicles, their significance rather lay in the anticipation of such transformations as will be explained for the colonial context of Windhoek (see 4.2.4). But these trends and the scale of their impact on European cities have nonetheless inspired planners in the colonial environment. Metropolitan efforts towards the creation of a 'New Man' among the European working classes were transplanted to the colonies and, as an adjustment of the 'White Man's burden', aimed to uplift the Indigenous population as part of the classical narrative of imperial civilising missions. It is nevertheless necessary to analyse, whether or not stakeholders in the colonial cities were willing to accept Eurocentric attempts to avoid the same 'mistakes' that had been made at the metropole, or if they actually considered those developments as blueprints for their own future.

In addition, interwar years saw the rise of regionalisation as part of the planning discipline and thus did London receive a new planning system with the Greater London Regional Planning Committee (GLRPC), which started its operations for the metropolitan region in 1927 and published its first report in 1931 under the supervision of Raymond Unwin.[478] The GLRPC pursued a strategy for London's decentralisation as well as the protection of a greenbelt and proposed the layout of new satellite towns. All these suggested measures were intended to address the capital city's growth, which also symbolised the economic North-South divide in the UK as recognised in the Barlow Report. Officially published in January 1940, the report revealed the country's uneven distribution of population and employment, and Ward considers it to be, "the single most important document in British planning history."[479] This significance became tangible in face of the Second World War, when various institutions called for a reduction of such high population concentrations.

Internationality

Throughout the entire interwar period both journals remained open to foreign ideas and they sometimes applied these ideas as a background canvas to discussions within the context of domestic challenges. It seems that the planning community at large was not just susceptible to international ideas but planners actively incorporated them in their current activities. Although, on average, roughly half the reports were related to domestic urban affairs these figures are to a certain

---

[478] Ward 2004: 49.
[479] Ward 2004: 80.

extent misleading, because they do not fully reflect the international atmosphere of those days. Contrasting juxtapositions between several countries were frequently made when it came to latest housing schemes or the question of land ownership. These articles were complemented by summaries of relevant international conferences which were organised for a broad range of topics, and which provided for opportunities of first-hand encounters. Besides, excursions were offered and associated travel reports brought reflections from some of the remotest cities in the Americas or Australasia to the readers' desks in Europe. These travel reports were a mixed business in terms of topics and covered many different countries; they were neither limited to immediate neighbours nor to countries where the respective journal's language is spoken. Instead, the contributions published in both journals covered case studies from all continents, and in exceptional cases submissions to both journals were written by the same author. Some examples are Italian Luigi Lenzi, Harvard librarian Theodora Kimball or George Pepler who was, aside from his function as adviser to the British Ministry of Health, President of IFHTP.[480] The analysis of *Der Städtebau* confirms Stephen Ward's statement that German planners still remained well informed on the developments of the international planning community at large after the National Socialists usurped power.[481]

Nonetheless, it is necessary to acknowledge a distinction that characterised virtually all articles - the difference between "civilised countries" and the remaining "Others." This division was not per se meant as a kind of racial or social division but these connotations played a role with respect to colonial developments. At least for *The Town Planning Review* reports on colonial cities were an integral and perpetual element covered in the journal. Predominantly White settlement colonies such as Australia or New Zealand were included as was the case with India or Protectorates like Kenya or Sudan. All contributions were written from the Eurocentric perspective and the same applied to the few colonial articles in *Der Städtebau*, where surprisingly none of them was devoted to former German colonies. Neither the British nor the German journal included any article that was actually submitted to reflect on the Indigenous perspective. On the contrary, *The Town Planning Review's* contributions made it clear that all colonial entities, including the Dominions, should keep close contacts with their "mother country" in order to benefit from the UK's perceived expertise and advances. Authors such as H.V. Lanchester represented direct links between metropole and colonial periphery; Lanchester served as *intermediary* in Saunier's transnational terms, and helped to disseminate planning

---

[480] DS (1929) 1: Pepler: 6; Riboldazzi 2015: 50.
[481] Ward 2002: 89.

ideas through his works in Zanzibar or India.[482] Countries like New Zealand were considered to be in a state of infancy where a helping and guiding hand was needed. It was in this context that a clear division between European and Indigenous populations was made in descriptions of colonial cities. Racist undertones were common for both journals and in several cases there was a clear demand for residential segregation formulated. The division was partially justified by their authors with public health considerations in order to prevent the feared spread of epidemics but it was also intended as the manifestation of social prestige and status. In this context, the assumed colonial stratification needs to be kept in mind, where Indigenous communities were usually considered as one more or less homogenous block – except for racial characteristics like Chinese, Indian or Malayan origins. The European communities, by contrast, were subdivided based on ethnic *and* social characteristics. For them, social hierarchies played an important role and should hence be reflected in the built environment. Anyhow members of the European lower social classes were usually not expected to live next doors to Indigenous families.

Beyond those tendencies for strict rules of separation, the colonies were not only considered as subjects of exotic curiosity. On the contrary, when it comes to urban planning they actually demonstrated how permeable national borders were during interwar years in two respects: the physical exchange of planners and in terms of planning ideas. Both journals each represented one major planning tradition in Ward's sense – the British and the German one – but they remained open to foreign contributions and devoted some attention to smaller countries. In addition, The *Town Planning Review* welcomed reports on colonial cities and their planning laws for the advances they mirrored back to the metropole. In this respect planning was by far no one-way street and remained open to new ideas from other smaller planning traditions as well as the emerging planning communities in colonial entities; though the latter were admittedly dominated by respective European compatriots.

The voids

It is nevertheless necessary to point out some gaps where the results of the journal analysis leave, at least from a retrospective point of view, a potentially incomplete image of interwar urban developments. First and foremost both journals mirrored the developments in Germany and the UK which showed striking similarities in the topics covered. Despite the summarised international openness they did only include some hints on the French circumstances, although this country represented

---

[482] Bissell 2011: 223-5.

the only other major European planning tradition in Ward's concept. Furthermore, there remain few voids in relation to some of the described urban challenges. It is necessary to recognise the different connotation the land question had in the European context as compared to the colonial setup. Hence, the issue of land acquisition and ownership rights in colonial cities with their peculiarities were not addressed. Further relevant examples are related to those ideas behind certain reform movements that impacted the housing sector. They were not only focusing on means to produce sufficient quantities but their ambitions went further and eventually aimed at a 'New Man.' These aims and consequences are touched on in some articles but journal coverage remained superficial in this respect; therefore it seems advisable to complement those articles, and to have a closer look at the reform movements in order to trace their potential similarities with the self-proclaimed "civilising mission" in colonial entities. Similarly, the debates centred on infrastructures will be taken up in more detail, especially in face of their interpretation as symbols for 'modernity' as well as of their significance as relief works in interwar SWA.

Some additions on urban challenges relevant in the colonial cities will complement my results of the journal analysis. The analysis also formed the basis to select some other publications intended to complement additional positions beyond the mainstream agenda.

Based on the results generated through this journal analysis of two major planning traditions, it lastly induces the question of what the potential results may be, if repeated for one smaller country like the Netherlands or Sweden. Such an extension on a smaller country could on one hand help to judge on their role as intermediaries between the major planning traditions. On the other hand it could exemplify potential similarities in terms of the urban challenges addressed or the coverage on international matters and colonial developments.

4. The case of Windhoek

The previous chapter with its analysis and comparison of *Der Städtebau* and *The Town Planning Review* laid the foundations to understand the general challenges and debates in interwar urban planning. These impacted on and inspired the developments in Windhoek too. As I will try to illustrate, these debates either served as a direct reference point or they were adopted indirectly as part of the underlying ideas and ways of thinking. This chapter is intended to demonstrate how the general debates were translated into the colonial context of SWA and how they were used to establish a complex system of residential segregation for my selected case study city between 1914 and 1945.

The descriptions will start with a subchapter on the overall historic context of Windhoek's earlier periods (see 4.1) and include references to SWA at large, if deemed necessary. Those explanations are helpful to understand the continuities and ruptures in the transition from German to South African rule over the 'Territory', as SWA was also referred to. Wherever possible and relevant, emphasis is laid on links to segregationist policies. The second subchapter is devoted to urban challenges with which the town was faced in the interwar years. As a reflection of the results derived from the comparison and analysis of the planning journals in the previous chapter they are grouped according to thematic fields, such as technical infrastructures (4.2.3), public health (4.2.5) and housing (4.2.6). This will help realise the similarity of problems (and potential answers) in urban development that colonial and metropolitan cities had to address. Furthermore, it highlights how long it took the Municipality to implement certain technological amenities when faced with its limited financial, human capacities and its remote geopolitical location. Particular attention is, again, paid to the consulted opportunities for international exchange (4.2.2), as well as measures and tools that complemented the efforts for residential segregation. The various instruments that were used to enforce segregation in virtually all spheres of daily life convey an image of the systematic and holistic exclusion of the autochthonous population in Windhoek.

The last subchapter (4.3) is dedicated to the explicit elements of the policies which helped to implement residential segregation. African access to the European sections of the city was restricted and Black people were confined to "their" neighbourhood usually called *Location*. Furthermore this subchapter will illustrate how these policies extended beyond residential areas for the Indigenous alive, and cover the debates about the layout of cemeteries too.

4.1 Historic context

Officially, Windhoek was founded on 18th October 1890 by German military officer Curt von François.[1] His decision was supported by favourable climatic conditions due to the site's altitude at 1,600 metres above sea level and the almost complete absence of potentially threatening tropical diseases, such as malaria or yellow fever. Besides, there were some hot springs which provided for ample supply with potable water. Windhoek firstly served as a site for barracks and was complemented by few ramshackle bars and hotels. Still the town's development was soon based on proper plans that were drafted by Von François as part of the military administration which ruled the city during the early years. Figure 9 is a reprint of his 1892 plan and as the area marked by (1) illustrates, he envisaged the town to be orderly structured based on a grid pattern with some administrative buildings interspersed into the urban fabric. The prospective built-up area was located on relatively plain grounds whilst military buildings formed the only exception to the grid pattern for topographical considerations. The fort, now called "Alte Feste", was planned at a hilltop position overlooking the town and its environment (2). The same applied to the adjacent stables (3). These military buildings were constructed on a mountain slope that separated the administrative and commercial town from its agricultural neighbour Klein Windhoek (4), which initially sprung up as a separate municipality under German rule. Besides the urban layout-plan, Von François has drafted all plans for major public buildings, the fort being the most prominent, and he supervised their construction.

---

[1] Earlier ideas already came up in August but his first plan drawn for a fort at Windhoek dates back to 3rd October; his troops only arrived on the 17th instant though, and construction was eventually started on the 18th (Bravenboer 2004: 15-6).

Figure 9: Layout plan for Windhoek by Curt von François (1892)

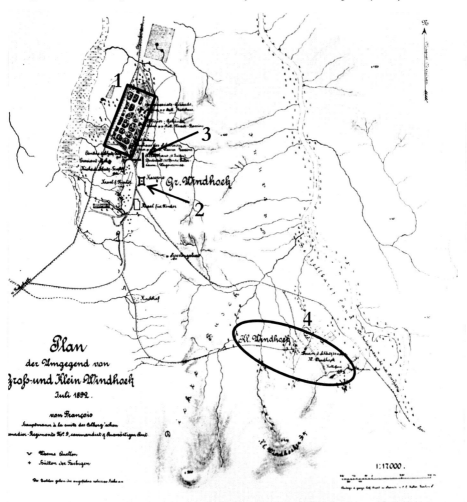

Windhoek's pre-colonial past

Aside from this official narrative there are traces of a much older past. Despite Windhoek's short record as a 'modern' city, its history as a place of human interaction and settlement can be traced back into Stone Age times. Archaeological excavations, that were conducted in the city centre's so-called Zoo Park during the 1960s, uncovered findings such as stone tools made of quartz and several remainders of a killed pre-historic elephant. Based on radio-carbon analysis these bones can be dated back to c. 5,200 BC.[2] During those days, Windhoek served as promising hunting spot for hunter-gatherers due to its hot springs. It was these hot springs that later on generated the first name of the ancient settlement in local Nama language: /Ae//Gams[3] or /Ai//gams[4], which both mean "Place of Hot Water" in literal translation. Another denomination is *Otjomuise* or "Place of Steam" in Herero language, though this designation rather refers to nearby former Klein Windhoek.[5] Regarding the place's European inscription as Windhoek there are many explanations for the etymological origin of the name. The most obvious is its direct translation from Dutch or Afrikaans as 'windy corner.' Despite German attempts to change the city's official spelling to *Stadt Windhuk* as of 1913[6], this was the case for a short interlude until it was repealed by South African mandate law on 16th January 1923.[7]

Further archaeological and geological finds point to the changing climatic conditions in the area, which were markedly wetter in Stone Age times than they are in modern days as the appearance of peat has proven. Although the springs will most probably have provided for human encounters in this area during the ensuing millennia, a permanent settlement only came into being in late 1840, despite a settlement encountered and recorded by German missionary Schmelen at the same site as early as 1823.[8] It was Jonker Afrikaner, a leading local Nama tribesman, who decided to establish his residency here. His decision was mainly based on two factors: a) the grazing lands extending eastward offered sufficient supply for the cattle, with many of them having been seized in previous skirmishes with nearby Herero; b) the opportunity to control the crucial trading routes between the coastal areas at

---

[2] Bravenboer 2004: 203.

[3] Bravenboer 2004: 203.

[4] Lau, Brigitte, *Two Square Miles of History.* In: Heywood, Annemarie; LAU, Brigitte [Eds.]: Three Views into the Past of Windhoek. Windhoek: John Meinert 1993: 4.

[5] Bravenboer 2004: 6.

[6] NAN SVW S.3.b, municipal bye-law published on 23rd October 1913, sheet 16. Since 1909 it was simply called Gemeinde Windhuk.

[7] Bravenboer 2004: 219.

[8] Barth 1926: 15.

Walvis Bay, the remote hinterland as well as towards the interior of the Western Cape. According to Bravenboer, the latter formed the destination for up to 12,000 head of cattle per year.[9] From the settlement's very beginning, Jonker Afrikaner kept ties with missionaries – in this case with Carl Hugo Hahn and Franz Heinrich Kleinschmidt from the Rhenish Missionary Society who had arrived in October 1842 upon his explicit request and invitation – who were able to broker a peace accord with the Herero on Christmas Eve 1842. In the following years the settlement started to blossom in its literal sense and several gardens were established in its vicinity. Bravenboer quotes an estimation by the missionaries, according to which the population was considered to be between five and seven thousand inhabitants. In addition to the Rhenish missionaries based in their new station "Elberfeld" in Klein Windhoek valley, there were two British missionaries from the Wesleyan denomination arriving in 1844, creating some dissent and competition between the clerics. The Britons actually followed other branches of the Afrikaner 'tribes' who had been invited to settle close to Jonker Afrikaner in Windhoek. Eventually, the Germans left Afrikaner's settlement for the Herero village of Otjikango.

Despite their peace agreement, there were several armed battles with the Herero taking place over the following years. On a visit to Windhoek in 1852, missionary Hahn counted approximately 5,200 people but the situation became destabilised, and the town started to decline with Jonker Afrikaner's decision to move to his former outpost at Okahandja which he turned into his new headquarter. Jonker died in 1861, as soon did his succeeding son Christian Afrikaner who was killed in 1863. His younger brother Jan Jonker Afrikaner became the new leader but he was reportedly not as charismatic and successful. Eventually, he lost the armed battles against the unified Herero troops under 'Chief' Maharero and was subsequently forced to leave Windhoek. It was up to the "Peace of Okahandja" signed on 23rd September 1870 to end seven years of bloodshed and to grant Jan Jonker Afrikaner the land tenure and right to settle back in Windhoek again. Notwithstanding these agreements, the town fell into disrepair as missionary Hahn observed on a journey in 1873, during which he wanted to visit his fellow Christian Johann Georg Schröder who had settled at Klein Windhoek in 1871. Not just did the Nama now have to compete with the powerful Herero for pasture land for their diminishing cattle, their economic situation depended on their livestock and worsened over time. In 1876 the population declined to just 400. On 20th August 1880, as an act of desperation, Jan Jonker raided Maharero's ox which was destined for the latter's funeral feast. Considering the already tense situation between Herero and Nama,

---

[9] Bravenboer 2004: 7.

this event was the straw that broke the camel's back and led to a brutal revenge. Maharero ordered the killing of all Nama in the vicinity of his headquarters in Okahandja and decided to destroy Windhoek. In addition to the destruction of the remaining gardens, all inhabitants were forced to leave including the foreign missionary. As a consequence, Windhoek turned into a "no man's land"[10] that was perceived as such in historic sources and counted for no permanent inhabitants by 1880.[11]

Windhoek under German rule

It was under these circumstances that the German colonial troops decided to reclaim the site as their new headquarters. As unclaimed territory and they were not drawn into any on-going local conflicts, in which the German forces with 42 men were unable to make a difference anyways. As has already been mentioned (see 1.1), nowadays Namibia was made the German 'protectorate' of SWA in 1884. Yet this formal status did by no means imply the ability to exercise control over the whole of its territory or all judiciary matters. Instead, the Germans were eager to negotiate protection treaties with local leaders and 'Chiefs' to acquire their influence on paper. Even then were they unable to enforce their own laws beyond the borders of a demarcated police zone, and they had to rely on a collaborative spirit with local leaders who were still fighting for supremacy amongst each other.[12] Zollmann used the terms of 'herrschaftsnahe' (close to the authorities) and 'herrschaftsferne' (in distance to the authorities) spaces to describe the effective ability of German police forces to impose their rules on DSWA.[13] In his description, those spaces under colonial control merely represented an "Insel der Herrschaft" (island of authority) within the Indigenous colonial fabric.[14] Areas along the northern border region with Angola, where German presence and authority in so-called 'Ovambo land' remained extremely limited, did not qualify as such island in Zollmann's categorisation.

The decision to make Windhoek the capital was a forced and coincidental one based on external factors than the result of thorough plans, prepared at an administrative desk and intended as clear demonstration of the coloniser's power. Perhaps the plans would have had to be cancelled, if only Samuel Maharero had known about the construction earlier. In a letter dated 23rd October 1890, Samuel

---

[10] Bravenboer 2004: 10.
[11] Lau 1993: 10.
[12] Nevertheless, the reliability of such accounts of violence remains limited, since the establishment of 'pacified territories' belongs to the narrative of European colonial successes.
[13] Zollmann 2010: 213-15.
[14] Zollmann 2010: 215.

Maharero – son of the previously deceased Maharero – strongly objected the construction of a new fort in Windhoek, but due to the progress already made with the construction works he gave in at last.[15] Therefore, the city started with weaknesses and the overall situation did not improve significantly over the following decades.

Windhoek's development under German colonial administration was characterised by slow growth and extension. Despite its relatively favourable natural environment the town had to cope with its remote location and the weak overall interest of German settlers willing to migrate to DSWA. First settlers came from South Africa, whilst the first farmers from the heartland only arrived in the second half of 1892. As already mentioned above, two separate neighbourhoods were distinguished at the early stage of Windhoek's development both divided by a mountain slope. Klein Windhoek was the preferred destination for farmers and later received the temporary status of an autonomous municipality. Groß Windhoek, or simply Windhoek, was the administrative and business oriented centre and served as capital of then DSWA. The latter function was officially conferred upon Windhoek on 7th December 1891 through the relocation of the *Reichskommissariat* from Otjimbingwe, which served as the seat of government before.[16] Throughout the initial years, the city's supply of all imported products from the sea harbours relied on oxen carts. The vulnerability that this dependency on draught animals created became obvious with the spread of rinderpest disease[17] (cattle-plague) in 1897. To varying degrees all parts of the Territory were affected, although the Indigenous population's livestock suffered the most compared to those herds owned by Europeans. The latter could afford to vaccinate their animals and did so as part of their routine. The problem was exacerbated by an unpredictable reliability of the locally generated vaccine.[18] As a consequence of this disease, the construction of a railway line linking Windhoek with the port of Swakopmund was commissioned in October 1897 and it became fully operational in 1902. The first town plan was drawn in 1898 to reflect the up-to-date status of the development.

---

[15] Bravenboer 2004: 16.

[16] Bravenboer 2004: 25.

[17] Aside from smallpox, rinderpest is the only disease that today has officially been recognised as exterminated at global scale since 2011 (Website Spiegel Online).

[18] Gewald, Jan-Bart, *Kolonisierung, Völkermord und Wiederkehr: Die Herero von Namibia 1890-1923*. In: Zimmerer, Jürgen; Zeller, Joachim [Eds.]: Völkermord in Deutsch-Südwestafrika: Der Kolonialkrieg (1904-1908) in Namibia und seine Folgen. Augsburg: Weltbild 2011: 108-11.

Architecture and urban planning under Gottlieb Redecker

Aside from some private investments, Windhoek's extension was driven by public projects, a trend that was prevailing during German rule as well as in South Africa's mandated period throughout the interwar years in face of (global) economic downturns. In order to supervise most of these public projects, the position of a Government Architect (Regierungsbaumeister) was created in 1896. First incumbent was Carl Ludwig, whose three-year contract had not been extended because of the excessive costs created by his plans for the construction of the Governor's residence. He was succeeded by Gottlieb Redecker, who then held this position beyond the formal end of German rule in 1915 until he resigned municipal office in Windhoek's Building Committee in November 1917.[19] Joined by his assistant Heinrich Finke, Redecker exercised a significant impact on the urban image of Windhoek and its architecture. Both were responsible for the preparation and implementation of the Municipality's first *Building Regulations* too.[20] Construction figures reached a first peak in 1907 which saw the completion of 99 buildings in total, with the vast majority of 77 buildings as private investment whereas the remaining 22 were public.[21] The list of government buildings constructed under the supervision of Gottlieb Redecker is long and covers virtually all relevant realms of public life. Redecker supervised the final facelift of the Alte Feste (Old Fort) in 1901, commissioned the construction of Tintenpalast as seat of the colonial administration (nowadays used as Parliament's building) in 1913, the extension of Kaiserliche Realschule (Imperial secondary school) in 1913, and Christuskirche (Christ Church) as main Protestant church with a seating capacity for 400 people. The latter's construction took more than three years until it was officially consecrated in October 1910.[22] His architectural style was a mixture of typical German elements then used like Art Nouveau with regional adaptations.

Redecker's biography demonstrates the dominance of European planning and building education for the colonial context. Though Redecker's personnel records are not preserved at the National Archives[23], his career path was collated by Walter

---

[19] NAN SVW B.2.b, letter by the Mayor dated 28th November 1917, sheet 36.
[20] Bravenboer 2004: 33.
[21] Bravenboer 2004: 40.
[22] Bravenboer 2004: 92, Moritz, Walter, *Vier Generationen Redecker in Namibia seit 1866: Aus Westfälischer Vergangenheit in die Namibische Zukunft*, Windhoek: John Meinert 2010: 77-80.
[23] Moritz refers to a copy of Redecker's personnel records which is supposed to be preserved at Stadtmuseum Gütersloh, the city where the builder and his wife died in an air raid during the Second World War (Moritz 2010: 86, 117). In contradiction to this information, the museum itself does not own such a copy and, again, provided me with Moritz's text instead, which does contain some parts of the records as a reproduction. The information

210

Moritz.[24] According to Moritz's collection of documents, Redecker grew up on his parents' farm where he learnt to speak local languages fluently, a skill that made him valuable as being the only German interpreter for all important hearings at DSWA's High Court. Following his mother's death at the boy's age of 11, he was sent to relatives in Germany but back then, in 1882, he had to travel via Walvis Bay, Cape Town and Southampton, where he temporarily stayed with one of his uncles and practiced his English skills. He then moved on to Germany in order to attend secondary school before he studied architecture and building trades, and took on some first jobs as construction engineer in the Ruhr district. Redecker stayed for almost 15 years in Germany but travelled back to DSWA for some commissioned assignments in 1896. In 1899 he was offered the position as Government Architect (Regierungsbaumeister) in DSWA. During several holiday trips which he spent in Germany and South Africa, he explored new architectural elements that he merged to his interpretation of veranda architecture.[25] Bravenboer points to his borrowing from South African veranda architecture which he encountered during a trip through the neighbouring country in 1906.[26] Moritz found some earlier traces for such impacts, when he refers to one of Redecker's works that was already constructed in 1902.[27] Furthermore, the Government Architect was eager to integrate other elements he considered to be suitable, such as German style plaster, which it is assumed he had brought back from a trip to Germany in 1904. According to Moritz's brief description, Redecker created, at least in parts, a new architectural style, which is argued to be exemplified in the unique style of Christ Church in Karibib where Art Nouveau elements are mixed with brickworks typical for Northern Germany deviating from then typical forms as used for Kaiser Wilhelm Memorial Church in Berlin.[28]

Developments under local self-administration since 1909

An intermediate position between public bodies and private engagement in SWA was represented by the churches through their missionary activities. In his 1926

---

therein does also match with one identical fragmentary electronic file preserved at the National Archives of Namibia's internal database.

[24] Moritz 2010: 70-85.

[25] Walter Peters has come up with a brief description of veranda architecture in the context of SWA and its later dissolution due to modernist ideas in the 1930s (Peters, Walter, *Das Verandenhaus – Beispiel einer klimatisch wohltemperierten Bauweise*. In: Hess, Klaus A.; Becker, Klaus J. [Eds.]: Vom Schutzgebiet bis Namibia 2000. Göttingen/Windhoek: Klaus Hess Verlag [1984] 2002).

[26] Bravenboer 2004: 83.

[27] Moritz 2010: 80.

[28] Moritz 2010: 87.

publication *Südwest-Afrika*, Paul Barth underscores their far-reaching influence, even in economic fields, by calling the missions to be, "possibly the only wholesale firm" in SWA's early days.[29] This position was, of course, based on their social activities covering pastoral care for the faithful, the provision of (basic) health services to all parts of the population, support for the elderly with first retirement homes, and education. In comparison with governmental schools, confessional schools hosted the majority of all pupils in SWA under German rule, providing basic education to the Indigenous population. The missionary societies were owners of vast portions of land, making them the second largest owner of real estate property in the Territory after the State and exceeding private mining and development companies. Their activities went beyond the social sphere and included relevant daily businesses such as agriculture and trade.[30]

A significant change to the city's development occurred with the formal restructuring of the administrative framework in 1909. This year generated several legal provisions which altered the distribution of powers. On 28th January, the foundations for autonomous self-governance at the local level was laid by Governor Bruno von Schuckmann through the creation of town councils, whose members were half appointed by the Governor whereas the other half was elected. This institution was to become responsible for all decisions made related to the municipalities' future. Through this alteration of the legal status, local town councils received almost as much power as the Governor within their individual territorial confines. On 5th February, Windhoek and Klein Windhoek were granted the status of a municipality, and as of 1st November 1909 a municipal bye-law introduced the official functions of Mayor and Deputy-Mayor for Windhoek's highest-ranking representatives.[31] In order to allow for all municipalities' financial independence, major real estate assets were transferred to them by the Treasury, a transaction that came into effect as of 3rd May 1911, and for the transitional period financial assistance at the State's expense was made available to the local authorities. In addition to all streets, squares and springs both municipalities received a total of 115,000 acres of land.[32] The Municipality was allowed to levy its own taxes which were supposed to become a significant source of revenues. Taking all these changes as a whole, the military administration passed its functions onto an autonomous civil administration. This transition resembled the typical turnover as has happened in other colo-

---

[29] Barth 1926: 16.

[30] Missionary activities were of more relevance in German East Africa, where Conrad mentions that almost one quarter of all privately owned plantations were in the churches' hands (Conrad 2008: 72; Knopp 2010: 208; C. Marx 2008: 75-6).

[31] NAN SVW S.3.b, sheet 2.

[32] Bravenboer 2004: 99.

212

nial domains like Algeria too.[33] One of the few strings attached to local self-administration was the required approval by the Reichskolonialamt (Reich's Colonial Office) for all transactions dealing with land rights as of May 1912.

Based on its demographic and economic development, Windhoek was granted the legal status of a town and carried the official German title "Stadt Windhuk" since 23rd October 1913.[34] Regarding population statistics, several difficulties have caused a lot of inaccuracies which persisted during German and South African rule. The administrative procedures for the registration of White inhabitants turned out to be very ineffective, as explained in a letter by the District Office responsible dated 13th June 1911.[35] Delays in the respective registrations as well as a high staff turnover allegedly prevented a thorough keeping of the records. In addition, registration of Government staff members and members of the Armed Forces were regularly omitted and Indigenous inhabitants were not managed at all under this system. The District Office suggested replacing the existing procedure by regular annual censuses based on similar standards like in Germany, with the first census envisaged for autumn 1911. As a preliminary result for 1911, a total of 1,697 White persons were identified as residing at Windhoek (including Klein Windhoek). 1005 thereof were men, 363 women and 329 children under the age of 15 years. The overwhelming majority of them were German nationals (1593) and the only demographically mixed groups (with women and children) of any relevance came from the so-called 'colonial entities of the British Empire' (45) as well as Russia (14).[36] For the Indigenous population, the census gave the total number at 8,147 with 3,403 men, 2,390 women and 2,354 children. Similar to the nationalities for White inhabitants they have been subdivided according to their 'tribal' origin. According to this categorisation, another significant share of foreigners becomes apparent with those 1,394 'Cape Boys' who, in strict application of those days' legislation, would have to fall under the category of 'British subjects from colonial entities' and constituted the largest group of foreign nationals. In total, Windhoek counted almost 10,000 inhabitants in 1911. Based on refined census instructions and their stricter application, the number for the White population rose to 2,162 persons by 1st January 1913 whilst the remaining population was not recorded.[37] In a letter sent on 11th November 1919 to the Central News Agency at Cape Town, the total population of Windhoek was reported to be 8,215 as per 30th October 1919. Though one might assume that the lower recorded number of White inhabitants of

---

[33] Çelik1997: 65.
[34] NAN SVW S.3.b, municipal bye-law published on 23rd October 1913, sheet 16.
[35] NAN SVW S.9.c, sheet 2.
[36] NAN SVW S.9.c, sheet 2-3.
[37] NAN SVW S.9.c, sheet 27.

just 1,465 was due to the repatriation of German citizens, there was no similar explanation for the equally reduced number of Indigenous inhabitants which stood at 5,750. Much of this decrease was caused by a statistical distortion. Members of the Armed Forces and the administration were not considered in this census.[38] Still the statistics recovered soon and marked Windhoek as a growing town again.

In his exaggeration of the German edificial achievements referring to the *Tintenpalast* and church hill, Barth described mid-1920s' Windhoek as having the shape fitting a more populous town than it actually was at that time.[39] Some quarters of the town reminded him of the characteristics typical for a civil servant's city (Beamtenstadt) which contributed to the special image Windhoek created beyond colonial days, and which stood in stark contrast to the interpretation as little Gomorrah during its early decades (see 4.2.5). Although the colonial Germans wanted to create something distinct and more attached to rural life, they were, on the other hand, mimicking traditional elements of a typical German town of comparable hierarchical level at the metropole.[40] This included shops displaying the latest Berlin fashion trends, lawyers to take care of legal affairs such as getting divorced, or parks and a zoo to stroll along on the weekends.[41] At a rather general level, Windhoek tried to present itself as a conservative town that tried to get rid of its premature image. Some of those attempts smack of provincialism though, as the recurrent debates about shopping hours under German as well as later on under South African rule demonstrate.

In a letter dated 4th July 1914, the District Office approached the Municipality to pass rules concerning shopping hours and the options to open businesses on Sundays in particular.[42] Windhoek's Town Council prepared a draft version of such regulations, and ordered all shops to close between eight o'clock in the evening and five o'clock in the morning. On Sunday mornings, barber shops, bakeries, pastry shops, and butchers were allowed to open from five to eleven o'clock whilst it was usually limited to nine o'clock for all others. Bars, restaurants, cafés, and pharmacies were completely exempted from these rules.[43] In a letter dated 7th Oc-

---

[38] NAN SVW S.9.c, no sheet number.

[39] Barth 1926: 83.

[40] It is here that those typical deficiencies attached to the category of colonial cities used as framework for analysis, as discussed by Katrina Gulliver, become tangible. This self-perception in historic Windhoek supports her idea, "[…] that the colonial city was the site of an emergence of a third culture" beyond the centre-periphery dichotomy (Gulliver 2015: 7).

[41] Bravenboer 2004: 72, 100-1.

[42] NAN SVW O.1.b, sheet 8.

[43] NAN SVW O.1.b, sheets 10-11.

tober 1916 on behalf of the Administrator, then under South African rule, it was made clear that he considered those regulations as too lax, and hence required the Mayor of Windhoek to further narrow down those hours as much as possible to respect Sabbath.[44] Based on a draft regulation issued by the Military Magistrate, the previous German rules were reformulated stricter in tone and therefore curtailed most of the exceptions. As advertised in the Official Gazette on 12th December 1916, bars and restaurants for example had to close from 10 to 12 in the morning so as to allow for church going.[45] These restrictive rules reflected the difference between German and British customs. In addition the rules helped Windhoek on its way to improve its reputation from a remote provincial town towards a well-organised administration within the Commonwealth. Those strict rules were anew changed in face of the city's growth, when the idea of a new formulation for restrictions on "shop hours" was dropped completely by the Legislative Assembly in 1930.[46]

Windhoek's and SWA's conservative position did, nonetheless, leave a heavy impact on White female residents who remained disadvantaged over the full interwar period. As the advertisement for a public land auction in the German Official Gazette (ADSWA) issued on 15th December 1910 illustrates, women were not allowed to bid for the Government farm then on sale.[47] Women's discrimination later remained an issue with regards to female suffrage; although the matter had been debated favourably several times at the Legislative Assembly's sessions in 1930 and 1938, it was usually adjourned despite other legal frameworks within the Commonwealth. Only at the occasion of the 1939 session, the Assembly's members agreed on an amendment of the Territory's Constitution, effectively granting European women the right to vote.[48] Here, Windhoek and SWA clearly lagged behind respective developments at the metropole and even in neighbouring South Africa White women were allowed to vote since 1930.[49] The town nevertheless offered a social life that was characteristic for colonial cities with choirs, sports clubs (which could convene at a gymnasium) and bars. Bravenboer refers to Windhoek's unique charm and atmosphere which is, according to her descriptions, under threat through recent development projects.[50]

---

[44] NAN SVW O.1.b, sheet 15.
[45] NAN SVW O.1.b, sheet 16.
[46] VPLA Second Session, Second Assembly 1930: 32.
[47] ADSWA 1910: 244.
[48] VPLA Second Session, Second Assembly 1930: 10, 31, 34-5, 67-8; Fourth Session, Third Assembly 1938: 9, 21, 30; Fifth Session, Third Assembly 1939: 2, 6-7.
[49] Nightingale 2012: 261.
[50] Bravenboer 2004: 152.

Transition to South African rule after the First World War

This supposedly cosy atmosphere was disrupted by the events of the First World War. Specific pre-arrangements were made to prevent unnecessary bloodshed, as a public notice issued by Mayor Peter Müller on 8th May 1915 proves.[51] It requested all White inhabitants to stay at home during the expected invasion by English occupation troops and to urge their Indigenous employees and servants to do the same. Müller's order turned out to be a success, as Windhoek was handed over peacefully to the South African forces under General Louis Botha on 12th May 1915.[52] Over the course of the following months, several public notices were issued in order to introduce new legal regulations which first fell under Martial Law. The administration of the city, by then, lay in the hands of a Military Magistrate, although German institutions such as the Town Council were temporarily preserved – in contradiction to formal electoral regulations[53] – and granted executive powers, before the Council was dissolved as of 1st January 1919. The Council was then transformed into a kind of advisory board to which only two members of the German community were admitted.[54] Just a couple of weeks later, another reorganisation at the local level came into effect when Klein Windhoek was amalgamated with Windhoek. In 1913 a first attempt towards such amalgamation had been discussed upon petition by Windhoek's Mayor Houtermanns but it was rejected by Klein Windhoek's Town Council.[55] It turned out to be a temporary victory for the smaller authority only, for both municipalities were merged into Windhoek proper under the South African Military Magistrate's rule who ordered this step in a letter dated 23rd January 1919.[56] It was decided to dismiss all staff members of the smaller authority and to distribute their tasks among Windhoek's officers, whereas the financial accounts still had to be kept separately.

This decision at the local level, 1919 represented a general turning point in SWA's history, for many Germans were forcefully repatriated at the specific orders issued by Acting Military Magistrate Harry Drew from 21st May 1919.[57] In addition to the administrative level, relevant legal frameworks were affected too. With the transi-

---

[51] NAN SVW S.4.b, sheet 1.
[52] Bravenboer 2004: 105.
[53] NAN SVW S.3.d.2, Public Notice dated 20th November 1916, sheet 132. The term in office was extended despite the legal requirement to hold new elections.
[54] NAN SVW S.3.a, letter dated 28th December 1918, no sheet number.
[55] NAN SVW S.3.p, sheet 3.
[56] NAN SVW S.3.p, no sheet number.
[57] NAN SVW S.4.ab, Instructions re. Repatriation of Enemy Subjects dated 21st May 1919, no sheet number.

tion to Military Magistrate's rule, Roman Dutch laws[58] became applicable while previous imperial laws remained valid unless they were in conflict with the new legislation; in this case, the old ones were explicitly repealed. Under these circumstances, an unconventional and complex legal environment evolved where different legal understandings applied simultaneously. The specific set of rules concerning the taxation or restriction of movements of the Indigenous communities did in fact contribute another level. As late as 1942, in one of its decisions to settle unresolved land issues in Windhoek, SWA's Township Board was still directly referring to imperial German legislation and contracts.[59] There remained uncertainty about the future status of Windhoek and DSWA which were only eliminated by the Treaty of Versailles. Under the latter's terms, the future of Germany's previous colonial possessions was decided: SWA was thereafter labelled a Class C mandate[60] and officially handed over into the trusteeship of the Union of South Africa. From then on, it formed part of the British Commonwealth and Martial Law was repealed. The decision to transfer SWA as mandated territory was partially based on the Blue Book prepared under supervision of the British Government and which reviewed the Indigenous population's treatment under German colonial rule.[61] This document compiled all available information from DSWA and paid particular attention to the Namibian War between 1904 and 1908. From the historic German standpoint, the Blue Book's results were considered a humiliation.

The European communities' perspective on interwar years

In accordance with this general decision, SWA was formally governed by an Administrator to be appointed by and responsible to South Africa. The Territory's interests could still be addressed to him by petition and, as of 1926, through the Legislative Assembly, which helped in the preparation of SWA's legislation along South African lines. Indirectly, Indigenous matters were in many cases covered by this Assembly but usually their issues remained subject to a distinct subordinated administration and judiciary system. Non-White persons were regularly not admit-

---

[58] Roman Dutch laws were and still are a dominant part of the applicable legal framework in South Africa and Namibia, which have their origin in traditional Dutch laws brought to the Cape Colony by Dutch colonists (Website Britannica: https://www.britannica.com/topic/Roman-Dutch-law retrieved on 15.11.2017).

[59] NAN MWI 101/3/40, Resolution No. 24/1942 in Minutes of the Townships Board's meeting held on 16th July 1942, no sheet number.

[60] Formal supervision remained with the League of Nation's Permanent Mandates Commission, although it did not have specific authority to enforce its recommendations. Mandated territories in former German and Ottoman domains were no colonies or independent states but fully entrusted to allies or their dominions.

[61] Blue Book, *Report on the Natives of South-West Africa and their Treatment by Germany*, London: His Majesty's Stationery Office 1918.

ted to the Assembly's sessions. However, this is not to say that the European community can be considered as a homogenous bloc. To a certain extent such an argument can be made with regards to the collective attitude to exploit Indigenous people as inferior labourers. Among the European community itself there were nevertheless many fractures traceable that worked along language lines as well as social distinctions. Within the first category, Germans were a constant cause for suspicion from the Afrikaans and English speaking communities' perspective. Already in Government Notices No. 1 and 2 published on 19th July 1915, the Military Magistrate had imposed tough restrictions on the mobility of all persons.[62] Except for members of the Union Defence Forces and governmental staff members on active duty, no one was allowed to enter or leave the Territory, or to move vehicles and/or livestock without official permit. Despite those restrictions, all Germans were offered the opportunity to be voluntarily repatriated, either at their own expenses or to a port in the Netherlands at someone else's expense. This rule did generally not apply to interned members of the German Troops nor to males of military age. Statistics on how many persons actually made use of this offer were not attached to the file. At the occasion of its meeting on 27th November 1918, Windhoek's Town Council formulated its expressed hope for a return of SWA under German colonial rule. Nevertheless this explicit part of the minutes had been censored by the Germans and was not officially published in the newspapers, as a handwritten remark explains.[63] At the very same meeting, an official resolution was prepared and addressed to the Military Government, in which the German community was quick to officially and unanimously confirm its intention to remain part of the German Reich. Its content was specifically referring to US President Woodrow Wilson and his programmatic speech from 27th September 1918. The resolution can be interpreted as a rejection of the accusations that came up in preparation of the Blue Book, and pointed to the improvements made in SWA under German rule from which all its residents benefitted, irrespective of their nationality. The Germans felt obliged to underscore their honesty in the accompanying letter.

"If there should be any scepticism as to whether the whole of the german [sic] population of this town is supporting this resolution, the Municipal Council beg you to allow that either the resolution would be laid out at public places for being signed

---

[62] NAN SVW S.4.o, no sheet number.
[63] NAN SVW S.3.b, minutes of the Council meeting from 27th November dated 4th December 1918, no sheet number.

by the citizens or that the resolution would be brought to the knowledge of the citizens in any other way for being generally approved of."[64]

The 1920s were characterised by a general spirit of reconciliation among the European community's factions, although requests by the German community to make their language one of the official languages in SWA was regularly rejected. Their first attempt in the Legislative Assembly's 1927 meetings was denied by the Administrator based on the argument that it would actually fall under the jurisdiction of the Union Government to decide but the Government had no intentions to consider this matter at those days.[65] In this case, it did not make any difference that the German community confirmed its loyalty to South Africa without any intention for repatriation of the Territory to Germany at the same meeting.[66] Christo Botha has nonetheless pointed to the differentiated opinions between Germans living in Windhoek, who in their majority refused to accept the South African citizenship offered under the conditions of the *1923 London Agreement* and farmers at the countryside who were more open to this alternative.[67] Despite an Assembly's vote in favour of their demand one year later[68], which was subsequently overturned by the Union Government, all later motions related to the official recognition of German in 1932 and 1938, were declined.[69] Afrikaans and English remained the official languages which were used alternatingly in some administrative files, whilst German had a privileged but second class status. This was done despite their respective statistical significance, as a table on registrations at Government school hostels in 1929 demonstrated: it counted for 68 English-speaking, 728 Afrikaans-speaking and 233 German-speaking students.[70]

Open resentments arose when the mutual balance was disturbed by the rise of Nazism. It made its impact on SWA felt after Hitler came into office, when, for example at one occasion in April 1933, unidentified persons pulled down the Union flag at Government buildings in Windhoek and hoisted the German national flag instead. Police investigations ensued but the Legislative Assembly did not

---

[64] NAN SVW S.3.b, letter to the Military Magistrate dated 27th November 1918, no sheet number.

[65] VPLA Second Session, First Assembly 1927: 32, 37.

[66] VPLA Second Session, First Assembly 1927: 55-6.

[67] Botha, Christo, *The Politics of Land Settlement in Namibia, 1890-1960*, 2008: 238-9. The *1923 London Agreement* was negotiated between the Union of South Africa and the German Government in order to settle and clarify the legal status of the German-speaking community in SWA.

[68] VPLA Third Session, First Assembly 1928: 29, 38.

[69] VPLA Fourth Session, Second Assembly 1932: 10 and Fourth Session, Third Assembly 1938: 46.

[70] VPLA Fourth Session, First Assembly 1929: 15.

require a special investigation of this incident nor did it feel obliged to introduce new legislation.[71] The Afrikaans-speaking community, on the other hand, was eager to make SWA a proper and integral part of the Union of South Africa as its fifth official Province. They prepared a motion in this direction during the Assembly's meetings in November 1934, after the power balance had shifted in their favour during the previous Assembly's last meeting, when virtually all German members declared their resignation.[72] This now approved motion eventually led to first negotiations with the Union Government on the matter, which were presented as being in accordance with the League of Nations rules and the people of SWA's will.[73] For formal reasons, this annexation nonetheless failed and harmony among the European community remained very fragile, if it existed at all.

The Indigenous perspective on interwar years

For the Indigenous population the colonial period was characterised by continuous socio-economic decline but not exclusively due to administrative interventions. The local societies of Nama and Herero were heavily dependent on their livestock – cattle in particular. Aside from the livestock's crucial role as being a source of food, the people drew much of their social and religious prestige from the wellbeing of their cattle.[74] In this respect, the occurrence of rinderpest disease in 1897 severely diminished the cattle herds, which in turn hit the peoples' social cohesion and caused an almost complete collapse of the meat market. Vaccination campaigns were partly successful but remained limited to suitable sites which provided good opportunities to control the cattle. Here, up to 80% of all animals could have been preserved whilst almost 95% of unvaccinated animals died. Most of Herero animals had not been vaccinated though. Gründer has pointed to the coincidence with a parallel severe outbreak of malaria among vast parts of the Herero population, and both events were followed by a plague of locusts and severe droughts.[75] In summary, rinderpest and all other natural disasters had a tremendous effect on the Indigenous population who, in their majority, had to indebt themselves to compensate for the losses.

Under those unstable conditions, the Namibian War (1904-8) broke out and turned out to be an effective genocide of the Herero and Nama population carried out by the German colonisers. All these events have laid the foundation for the

---

[71] VPLA Fifth Session, Second Assembly 1933: 19.
[72] VPLA Seventh Session, Second Assembly 1934: 2, 7, 14.
[73] VPLA First Session, Third Assembly 1934: 11, 16-7, 19-20, 23-4.
[74] Krüger 2011.
[75] Gründer 2012: 126; Zimmerer, Jürgen, *Krieg, KZ und Völkermord in Südwestafrika: Der erste deutsche Genozid*, Augsburg: Weltbild [2003] 2011: 46.

220

systematic subjugation and exploitation of the Indigenous population by the White community as 'their' cheap labour force. After the Namibian War, Indigenous people were barred from the legal option to own land or cattle. This decision expressed the administration's goal to eliminate all potential alternative forms to make a living and was intended to formally force the African population into wage labour. One example for such provisions is documented for the period under the South African Military Magistrate's rule in 1916, when Captain Venter made a proposal to the German Town Council in Windhoek regarding the 'Taxation of Native livestock' dated 24th May.[76] His suggestion was meant as a reaction to the move of Indigenous farmers to let their animals graze at Windhoek's pastures where no grazing fees were charged.

> "Cpt. Venter schlägt daher vor, auch in Windhuk und im städtischen Weidegebiet eine Viehsteuer zu erheben, hauptsächlich aus dem Grunde, um die Leute zur Arbeit zu zwingen."[77]

Handwritten comments on that particular sheet prove the Council's general consent, whilst the exact amount remained unspecified.

Grazing fees or taxes on livestock were just part of a meticulously planned taxation system which formed another step towards the attempted Indigenous population's total subjugation. They were further subject to 'Native taxes', as Zimmerer has laid down in detail for the context of SWA.[78] German authorities introduced those taxes towards the end of their colonial rule around 1909 but the idea had already been developed before the Namibian War. Zimmerer has in this context analysed to what extent the administration in DSWA under Deputy Governor Hintrager adopted ideas from British colonies.[79] The question of whether the tax would be levied per capita or per 'hut' initiated many debates but it was argued early on that a hut tax appeared to be impossible to implement. The administration expected the population to simply abandon their 'ramshackle huts' as soon as they were required to pay taxes on them. But there were some concerns about the justification for such a hut tax which would have, for formal reasons, rendered its introduction illegal. Administrative divisions were eager to underscore the hut tax's arbitrary and sweeping nature and therefore rejected its implementation. Instead, the taxation system was based on personalised payments and it became operational with the

---

[76] NAN SVW S.10.x, sheet 6.
[77] NAN SVW S.10.x, sheet 6. "Cpt. Venter therefore suggests levying a tax on livestock grazing in Windhuk and its municipal pastures, mainly for the reason to force the people into labour." (author's translation).
[78] Zimmerer 2001: 250-81.
[79] Zimmerer 2001: 252-4.

introduction of local self-administration. Despite original intentions to introduce same rules for the whole Territory[80], the exact definition relied on municipal bye-laws and varied slightly among the cities across DSWA. In cross-comparison, Windhoek lagged behind and introduced its Native Tax on 9th February 1912.[81] It followed the usual pattern and required every Indigenous person over the age of 14 years to pay a kind of income tax, which was scaled according to the monthly wage, ranging from a minimum of 0.25 marks to 2 marks if the wage exceeded 60 marks per month. Those persons without a job had to pay at least 1 mark to be performed in labour to the Municipality. Since 1st April 1913 married women were exempted by a new bye-law published on 1st March the same year, if they were not contractually employed.[82] Tax payments were immediately deducted by their employers but the administration was still not satisfied with the solution found, since – in their eyes – neither the Natives nor the White settlers could be trusted and were suspected to evade taxes. Regardless of these suspicions, at least from the Municipality's viewpoint the tax turned out to be a success and provided it with a substantial and stable source of revenues, which was maintained under South African rule. In a public notice published on 29th May 1915, the Military Magistrate ordered all employers to report their servants in order to keep the official register of Indigenous labourers up-to-date.[83] The meticulous registration procedures made it necessary for the employer to show up in person. Furthermore, the Notice required him to bring with him his Indigenous employee(s) as well as their respective pass token and labour book – as if all three were mere possessions. During a meeting of the Location Committee in July 1921, Windhoek's Mayor explicitly recommended the on-going application of former German Native tax rules and did only suggest that some alterations were made to them.[84]

Zimmerer noted the forceful nature behind this taxation system, which primarily pursued the goal to impose wage labour on the Indigenous population, and to prevent them from pursuing a self-determined life in economic terms.[85] Though it was clearly expressed and widely accepted that the revenues of this tax had to be used for Indigenous purposes, the introduction of the tax as such can be interpreted as deliberate move towards DSWA's self-sufficiency from its mother country in financial terms. Back in those days the administration tried to fulfil the Colonial

---

[80] Zimmerer 2001: 275-7.
[81] NAN SVW E.1.n, sheet 5.
[82] NAN SVW E.1.n, sheet 6.
[83] NAN SVW E.1.b, sheet 5.
[84] NAN MWI 37/5/37, minutes no. 4 of Location Committee held on 16th July 1921, no sheet number.
[85] Zimmerer 2001: 269.

Office's expectations. The motive remained the same during the interwar years under South African rule when the Union Government had to cover the deficit accrued by its mandated Territory, as Administrator Werth explained in his opening address to the Second Session of the Legislative Assembly in 1927.[86] Nevertheless, Windhoek's Native Commissioner Todt had to fight for the appropriate use of Native Taxes, as a letter dated 5th July 1913 regarding the tax's revenues in its first fiscal year proves.[87] More than 10,000 marks were yielded but the Municipality wanted to cover her expenses for Indigenous public latrines as well as for the construction of a pedestrian bridge across the Gamams River which linked the Native Location with the White town out of this budget. The commissioner argued that both facilities were actually exclusively in the sanitary interests and for the convenience of the Europeans, and therefore refused to accept any deduction from the Indigenous accounts. As a result of the following dispute, the commissioner agreed in a letter dated 29th November 1913 that the costs for the bridge were covered by the Native Tax and that the costs for the latrines should be shared equally between the Municipality and Indigenous accounts.[88] It was at this occasion that he pointed to the Indigenous population's limited wages; in his opinion they were too low and should hence be exempted from taxes. Todt took his duties as Native Commissioner seriously, who was expected to serve as the custodian of the Indigenous population's interests, although this interpretation changed under his successors in South African mandated times. They would rather argue that Native Taxes represented a means to create fairness between Indigenous people and Whites, and where the latter already had to pay several taxes.[89]

Over the course of the analysed time period the attitude towards the African population lost its last considerate and humane elements and was replaced by growing exploitative tendencies. The taxation system went hand in hand with other instruments aimed to manifest Indigeneous subjugation. Restrictions on the freedom of movement had already been imposed under German colonial rule and were maintained in interwar years. Except for their daily walks from the Location to work and journeys they made at the explicit order of their employers, Blacks had to request a specific travel permit before they were allowed to buy a train ticket.[90] These regulations were intended to control their movements and to eventually direct them according to prevailing demands on the different regional labour markets. The travel restrictions were directly linked to the pass tokens that every Indigenous

---

[86] VPLA Second Session, First Assembly 1927: 2.
[87] NAN SVW E.1.n, sheet 7-8.
[88] NAN SVW E.1.n, sheet 19.
[89] Zimmerer 2001: 270.
[90] ADSWA 1911: 113.

person was requested to carry clearly visible with him or her. Police rights to control compliance with this rule were conferred upon White civilians.[91] Those pass tokens were issued at regional levels and carried a specific number to identify every Black person. In search for a job, they officially had to mention their number as well as to submit their labour book, where all employments needed to be registered and confirmed with the local authorities. Zimmerer has described how the system, at least on paper, should have provided for the Africans' a minimum of social security through the ability to select their employer; de facto this option was nevertheless extremely limited. Zimmerer uses the term "halbfreier Arbeitsmarkt" (semi-open labour market) to describe this environment.[92] The level of administrative interference extended beyond the public realms and mattered for private life. Africans were put under a special curfew. During nights they were not allowed to leave their homes at the Location, except for those cases where they were issued a specific work permit.[93] The consumption of alcoholic beverages was basically narrowed to the availability of (diluted) beer[94], and some municipalities like Swakopmund set strict boundaries for the use of pavements: here, Black people generally had to give preference to Whites, and if they were carrying heavy loads they were prohibited from using the pavements and had to walk on the streets instead.[95] Furthermore, Indigenous people were not allowed to hunt unless they had obtained the required official – but expensive – licence as decreed by the German Governor on 1st October 1910.[96] In combination, all those and many other decrees made it almost impossible for them to earn a living by means other than wage labour, and those decrees remained valid during the interwar years.

Economic situation in the 1930s

Aside from those legal restrictions, the economic development of SWA between the World Wars had tremendous impacts on the Indigenous population's life. The Territory's remote geographic location and its limited economic significance under the mandated supervision by the Union of South Africa did not attract many foreign investments. Instead, the country's wellbeing largely depended on the Union Government's good will and resources. Despite SWA's mineral wealth, it was under fierce competition by the Union itself where alluvial deposits of diamonds

---

[91] ADSWA 1911: 85-6, Zimmerer 2001: 88.
[92] Zimmerer 2001: 182-99.
[93] ADSWA 1910: 260.
[94] ADSWA 1910: Special edition dated 18th March 1911, no page.
[95] ADSWA 1910: 272.
[96] ADSWA 1910: 178.

were cheaper to exploit.[97] Over the following years, the Legislative Assembly lamented about the South African dominance in the diamond's market where the mandate power turned a deaf ear to Windhoek's interests and the suggested quotas. In consequence, SWA accumulated reserves of more than 300,000 carats which proved to be unsaleable at profitable rates for the time being.[98] Similarly, the discovery of gold deposits at Rehoboth did not alter this situation significantly in favour of SWA, despite the royalty and taxes yielded thereof.[99] Despite its remoteness, the Territory was hit hard by the economic downturn as a consequence of the Great Depression.

The Depression lowered the potential global sales prices on domestically exploited commodities like tin or copper, whilst diminishing demand for certain agricultural produces following the downturn hit the second economic backbone of SWA. Furthermore, farmers remained prone to the extremely volatile climatic conditions which turned out to be very discouraging in interwar years. An enduring and severe drought kept a close grip on the country from 1929 to 1934; over those years, the Government tried to assist farmers and handed out financial as well as material support which effectively cost her more than £50,000.[100] Despite those generous subsidies, many farmers were forced to close down their businesses with some of them defaulting on debt loans or returning their Government farms. Immediately after the drought had ceased, heavy rainfalls devastated parts of the country, its farms, and the infrastructure.[101] Soon after, the agricultural businesses were confronted with the spread of foot and mouth disease which had brought the meat market to a temporary standstill in 1934-5. First accusations by the settler community were directed towards the Indigenous population who were immediately made responsible of allegedly having introduced the disease to SWA; an opinion that was soon falsified by the Government.[102] It is nonetheless indicative for the predominant stereotypes, where the Indigenous population served as an assumed root cause for all diseases and hazards.

In conjunction with the side-effects of the Great Depression, SWA's Government initiated a comprehensive system of direct subsidies, cheap loans – handed out by the publicly owned Land Bank – and commissioned relief works. With regard to the latter the Europeans, and the Afrikaans-speaking community in particular, were

---

[97] VPLA Second Session, First Assembly 1927: 2.
[98] VPLA Fifth Session, Second Assembly 1933: 17, 40.
[99] VPLA Fifth Session, Second Assembly 1933: 16.
[100] VPLA Sixth Session, Second Assembly 1933: 35.
[101] VPLA First Session, Third Assembly 1934/1935: 1-2.
[102] VPLA First Session, Third Assembly 1934/1935: 14-5.

extremely observant to make sure that governmental aids primarily reached needy Whites. During one of the peak periods of crisis in 1932, SWA officially registered 736 unemployed (White) persons and 375 thereof were temporarily employed at relief works. Windhoek played a pivotal role, for many people from neighbouring districts migrated to the city in hope for better prospects here. According to administrative calculations, a total of 1,903 persons were directly and indirectly depending on Government aid.[103] The Government was prepared to spend a maximum of £100,000 on relief works which had been provisionally approved as part of the budget loan votes.[104] Much of these aids were spent on infrastructure projects, and though some of them were of a rather general nature, like the improvement of roads or (later) irrigation works[105], Windhoek benefitted in particular. Its water provision was stabilised through the construction of a new reservoir (Avis Dam)[106], whilst parts of the funds were invested in sanitary facilities such as the extension of the capital's waterborne sewerage system. The latter project tied up significant parts of the public investments throughout the interwar period (see 4.2.3).[107] Priority at those construction sites was given to Whites, and at several sessions of the Legislative Assembly questions were addressed to the Administrator concerning the number of White and Indigenous persons employed at relief works or governmental positions and their respective salary.[108] Most of these assessments intended to make sure that no Black or Coloured person earned more money or received a position higher in rank than the least qualified European. This evaluation complied with the goal to prevent the evolution of a White *lumpenproletariat* in SWA. The strategy did include protective measures to prevent the immigration of unemployed foreigners who would exacerbate the problem.[109] Based on similar intentions, many members of the Assembly carefully assessed the formulation of legal texts to be enacted by the House.[110] From their perspective it had to be avoided by all means, that accidental loopholes might be used to improve the legal status of the Indigenous population in comparison to the White community.

In summary, the context of the political and administrative developments in interwar SWA and Windhoek can be interpreted in line with Zimmerer's opinion, that

---

[103] VPLA Fourth Session, Second Assembly 1932: 28-9, 31-2.
[104] VPLA Third Session, Second Assembly 1931: 75.
[105] VPLA Fifth Session, Second Assembly 1933: 35, 40.
[106] Bravenboer 2004: 118.
[107] E.g. VPLA Third Session, Third Assembly 1937: Annex Financial report: 50. The report states the costs at £1,956 for 1937 or almost one quarter of the annual SWA budget for public buildings.
[108] E.g. VPLA First Session, Second Assembly 1929: 34, 42-3.
[109] VPLA Fifth Session, Second Assembly 1933: 33.
[110] E.g. VPLA First Session, Third Assembly 1934/1935: 20.

all legal tools and implemented measures served to prepare a privileged society that was based on the racial divide.[111] The White community did everything in its power to use the prevailing circumstances to bolster its superior socio-economic position and to further subjugate the Indigenous African population. The social order it created, reminded Zimmerer of feudal Prussia as insinuated by Ernst Rudolf Huber for the time period between 1820 and 1840.[112]

4.2   Urban development in interwar years

Windhoek experienced several transformations and improvements between the First and Second World War, and the most relevant ones will be presented in this subchapter. The selection is based on their significance towards an understanding of the general environment, under which the system of residential segregation has been implemented. Further it tries to illustrate the social atmosphere and prevailing attitudes. Following a short description of the city's historic status in terms of urban planning and the administrative structures (see 4.2.1), attention is paid to the transnational links that were established at public and private realms in order to enhance the flow of planning ideas (see 4.2.2). It will be demonstrated, how Windhoek was integrated into international debates which impacted on the town despite its remote hinterland location. Technical infrastructures were consistently considered as 'mirror of progress' or 'modernity' and did therefore receive particular attention in the city's development (see 4.2.3). Although many of them had already been proposed under German rule, they remained ideas on paper whilst their actual construction needed to be postponed until after the cessation of the First World War. How far expectations and reality differed, becomes apparent if traffic planning is concerned (see 4.2.4). The last two sections on public health (see 4.2.5) and housing (see 4.2.6) then make the connections to residential segregation more explicit.

4.2.1   Urban planning

During its first administrative years the city's development remained under the firm control of the military. Curt von François's early layout, which he had drawn in 1892 as starting point for Windhoek's 'modern' development was, as already mentioned above, based on a grid iron pattern. This simple urban fabric was usually easy to apply and provided for adequate options for extension at later stages[113]

---

[111] Zimmerer 2001: 93.
[112] Zimmerer 2001: 285.
[113] Eric Ross has undertaken thorough investigations of the grid iron pattern in African cities including its pre-colonial origins. For one of his latest publications on this subject: Ross, Eric, *The Grid Plan in the History of Senegalese Urban Design*. In: Silva, Carlos Nunes

Besides, this pattern fitted well with the need for orderliness and surveillance that a military strategist like Von François wanted to achieve. Despite these preparations for later city extension, the first plan was actually unable to envisage a proper layout for Windhoek's future growth. Several reasons may be listed to explain those deficiencies: first of all, the grid pattern was primarily oriented towards military considerations and needs, as the location of relevant infrastructures like stables, magazines and ammunition depots indicate. The site selection seems to have been rather random and without much consideration for topography. The Old Fort and some related infrastructures represented an exception to this rule, for they were located at a hilltop. The plan did not anticipate the town's growth into an administrative and civil centre. Specific building plots for a town hall or railway station were not set aside. The situation exacerbated due to the almost complete absence of an administration that was indeed able to monitor a proper implementation of the first plan. As a consequence, Windhoek's growth turned into urban sprawl and was of a rather spontaneous nature, in which Von François's plan did not play much of a role due to questions of land ownership. Therefore, the built urban structures did not resemble the aimed for grid iron pattern in its very strict sense and, instead, grew rather organically in some of its sections.

A reflection on the situation in 1917

Exactly a quarter century later, his plan came under fierce criticism by Joseph Eppeler, engineer (*Techniker des Hochbaureferats*) and staff member of the former German building administration, who was – maybe intentionally – unable to remember Von François's name as the plan's author.[114] Eppeler's petition, submitted on 20th October 1917, can be considered as intermediary conclusions about Windhoek's German planning period in aesthetical and functional terms that questioned the municipality's departmental planning structures. His document is therefore of some value as historic criticism and was intended by its author to initiate some new impulses for the city's future urban design.

Eppeler handed in a short pamphlet about Windhoek's current state of affairs in urbanism[115], which was accompanied by recommendations for its future building administration in structural terms as well as regarding its responsibilities.[116] He considered the events of the First World War, which brought many public projects

---

[Ed.]: Urban Planning in Sub-Saharan Africa: Colonial and Post-Colonial Planning Cultures. New York/London: Routledge 2015: 110-28.

[114] NAN SVW B.2.a, sheet 14. For the full German transliteration of Eppeler's petition to the Mayor see Appendix A3.

[115] NAN SVW B.2.a, sheets 14-7.

[116] NAN SVW B.2.a, sheets 18-20.

228

to a complete standstill, as favourable occasion to reorganise the administration and to use wartimes for the preparation of comprehensive plans.

> "Die Kunst des Städtebaus besteht darin, die Technik des Geometers mit der Kunst des Architekten und der Wissenschaft des Ingenieurs so zu vereinen, dass der entstehende Bebauungsplan technisch und künstlerisch vollkommen ist, das heißt nicht nur das Verkehrsbedürfnis berücksichtigt, sondern auch den zahlreichen Forderungen gerecht wird, die sich ergeben z.B. aus der geschichtlichen Entwicklung des Ortes, aus dem bestehenden Besitzstand, aus den mannigfachen Terrainverhältnissen, aus den geographischen und klimatischen Lagen, aus den meteorologischen und hydrologischen Verhältnissen, aus der bodenständigen Bauweise, und so fort."[117]

Although he aimed for such a comprehensive approach, and despite the city's below-mentioned apparent functional deficiencies, much of his criticism was focused on aesthetic design qualities. He explicitly criticised the grid iron pattern with its straight streets as inappropriate for Windhoek's climatic conditions. Through his preference for medieval urban patterns with their bended streets he outed himself as disciple of Camillo Sitte's works, which was further exemplified by his calls for urban vistas as well as a city's compactness. Eppeler expressed his particular problems with previous attempts to create a distinguishable architectural style for DSWA. This attempted style has attracted many followers, although it was mainly based on an eclectic but random *style* that tried to emphasise German elements. This kind of interpretation must not be confused with those attempts supported by the German Colonial Society (Deutsche Kolonialgesellschaft), which called for submissions to show some advances in the field of architecture *adapted* to meet specific regional and climatic conditions ahead of the 1914 Werkbund Exhibition at Cologne.

> "Das Reichskolonialamt wird gebeten, darauf hinzuwirken, dass die in den deutschen Kolonien entstehenden Neubauten, sowohl öffentliche wie private, mehr als bisher in ihrer äußeren Erscheinung dem Charakter des Landes angepasst und sowohl hinsichtlich des Materials wie der Bauformen mehr im Sinne einer bodenständigen Architektur ausgeführt werden."[118]

---

[117] NAN SVW B.2.a, sheet 14. "The art of urban design comprises the skills to merge the geometer's techniques with the architect's arts and the engineer's sciences, and to thus ensure that the evolving layout plan is perfect in technical and artistic terms. This means, the plan does not just consider traffic needs but also the various other demands, which are derived from the place's historic development, the existing land tenure, its prevailing topographical, geographical and climatic conditions, as well as meteorological and hydrological circumstances or the vernacular architecture, and so forth." (author's translation).
[118] NAN SVW A.6.b, cited in invitation letter dated 25th October 1913, sheet 5. "The Colonial Office is kindly asked to work towards a stylistic readjustment in the German colo-

In his petition, Eppeler referred to developments at the metropole and he found comments of appreciation for some pre-war German settlements' layout. Despite this appreciation he generally distasted those days' aesthetic preferences for what he considered to be useless ornamentation. Through this position he detached himself from Art Nouveau and similar styles. His minimalist design becomes apparent in the draft sketches he attached to his petition, and which are reproduced in figure 10 below. They contrasted with those criticised eclectic interpretations of a vernacular architecture in DSWA, which in Eppeler's opinion tended to make clear and simple structures look German without any additional benefit. It eventually only fitted a trend that has been labelled as 'Deutschtümelei' (excessive display of Germanness).

nies which encourages new buildings, both public and private, to be adapted to the specificities of local conditions. They should be more vernacular in their selected materials as well as their architectural design." (author's translation).

Figure 10: Mock sketches by Joseph Eppeler about envisaged (top) and realised projects (bottom), 1917

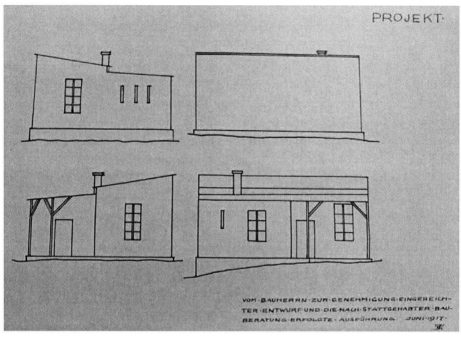

Writing under the prevailing chauvinist tendencies of war, Eppeler felt obliged to emphasise German architectural superiority in comparison with those British-style constructions built over the past years of the war, when they were in fact competing in SWA.[119] Despite such remarks, he tried to add weight to his arguments by some international references to recent developments he encountered himself, and which underscore the existing transnational networks for the accumulation of planning knowledge aside from the colonial mother country. Turning his attention to the existing functional structure, he used Pretoria instead of a German town as suitable example to explain some structural deficits in Windhoek's urban patterns. Although both cities are described as having similar historic origins, Pretoria's construction followed a more organically structured and compact urban design in Eppeler's view than SWA's capital did – a confession that did not come easy in face of his rather pejorative views on the Boers. Whilst Pretoria reportedly had one single square where most central functions were concentrated, he deplored the scattered distribution of urban functions in Windhoek which had, in turn, caused a waste of resources on transportation, and allegedly prevented the creation of specific functional areas within the township. In his opinion, it was due to this difference that Windhoek by 1917 did still not have a proper CBD on one side, or calm and pleasant residential areas on the other. Instead, he argued that delivery carts commuting between outspan square in the south and the railway station in the north caused an unnecessary nuisance to the main commercial street and many adjacent residential streets. Aside from these structural deficits revealed in his international comparison, he once more complained about negative trends in the town's architectural aesthetics and propagated administrative advice (Bauberatung) as a remedy to this problem, which are described to be in line with ubiquitous rules and habits in metropolitan Germany.

In his conclusion, all these deficiencies served to justify a reorganisation of the departmental structures. It was clear to Eppeler that Windhoek's building administration needed to lie in the hands of experts in order to avoid a repetition of such perceived previous mistakes, though he tried to make clear that this move did not need to be an expensive one. To him, the most convenient and financially manageable solution was to hire one single but competent person, who had been educated and trained in Germany.[120] This person would then have to prepare the post-war development plans for Windhoek. In addition to his demand for an up-to-date version of the town plan which would have to reflect the topographic situation, he

---

[119] NAN SVW B.2.a, sheet 15. All explanations and arguments in this paragraph are based on this document.
[120] NAN SVW B 2.a, sheet 20.

submitted a list of urgent improvements that needed to be made over the following years. Amongst them werethe complete renovation of the existing but chaotically laid out public water supply and the construction of a waterborne sewerage system in order to put an end to the use of cesspits, which were argued to pollute the soil.[121]

Even though it can be assumed that Eppeler submitted his petition driven by self-interest and as kind of recommendation and 'application' for a future administrative position, it nevertheless sheds some light on Windhoek's urgent urban challenges. The reactions it caused on the local administration's side can be described as reserved but extremely telling at the same time. In a more than three-page long statement[122], Mr Koch, the Councillor responsible, generally agreed with Eppeler's conclusions. He recommended them as suitable introductory reading to laypersons among the Town Council but strongly rejected the accusations made towards the Municipality.[123] Instead, Koch attributed the Colonial Office's administration (*Gouvernement*) with the full responsibility for those 'grievances', since all relevant decisions fell under the powers of the District Office or the Imperial public works service. The Municipality only 'inherited' those remnants and was hardly able to make her voice heard in those institutions' preparatory procedures. The exact sites for the mentioned railway station and other public buildings had been determined by the *Gouvernement*. Particular consent is expressed in relation to Eppeler's statement on the inconvenient location of several governmental buildings, though the Councillor tries to emphasise the efforts made by the Municipality to concentrate public functions at the city's centre, as was in his view done with regards to the school and town hall.[124] At this point, the Councillor contradicted an earlier statement made by the Mayor in 1910, who asked the Post Office to install a second public notice board at their premises in central Kaiser Street.[125] The Mayor justified his request with the town hall's remote site and the identified subsequent impossibility to receive sufficient attention to public notices at the notice board there. For the municipal school and town hall Koch nevertheless points to the competitions held to achieve good quality architectural results. He further replied that a new town plan with contour lines was already commissioned in 1916 and partially car-

---

[121] NAN SVW B.2.a, sheet 19.
[122] NAN SVW B.2.a, statement by Councillor Koch dated 3rd January 1918, sheets 6-9.
[123] NAN SVW B.2.a, sheet 6.
[124] NAN SVW B.2.a, sheets 7-8.
[125] NAN SVW P.4.b, letter by Mayor dated 8th February 1910, sheet 6.

ried out[126] but it was postponed by the war.[127] He could not anticipate that it would actually take another 15 years to prepare a new comprehensive version of the plan. At this occasion, Koch admitted that a demand for proper municipal police powers to enforce building regulations existed which, so far, had proved difficult to implement, as his reference to legal disputes with residents that effectively delayed the construction of proper streets revealed. In summary, and reversing those statements made by Eppeler and Koch, governmental buildings did not serve as the expected functional and aesthetic role models to private developers before the First World War, but the Government seemed not inclined to take such a lead position in interwar years either. As late as in 1929 the Administrator's Office made clear, that it did not feel obliged to erect all its buildings within the inner town area as massive constructions in accordance with applicable building regulations; instead, it intended to rely on cheaper materials such as wood and corrugated iron, if deemed appropriate.[128]

The experiment with a betterment tax under German rule

Aside from such aesthetic and functional debates, Councillor Koch's reply referred to legal disputes about the construction of new streets in Windhoek and reflects one out of two debates that was similarly going on at the metropole. On one hand the matter of recoupment charges for local public infrastructures was relatively well organised and required property owners to contribute their share to such investments in public improvements. On the other hand, there is a second and more general question attached to this matter, which relates to the options at hand of public administration to skim parts of the increasing land values induced by planning. Such concerns about betterment formed part of the planning profession's cornerstones, and initiated far-reaching reform ideas like Howard's Garden City Movement as has already been analysed (see 3.3.2). Although the efforts practically went unnoticed in those days' planning arena, DSWA was made an experimental test ground to apply a *betterment tax* (Wertzuwachssteuer). Many property owners around Windhoek benefitted from such windfall profits created by the construction or improvement of railway lines during the very last years of German colonial rule. The administration developed a taxation system that was intended to skim parts of these profits. One archival file contains all relevant instructions on its

---

[126] NAN SVW V.1.c, public notice requesting owner's permission for Surveyor to enter private property for levelling works published in *Reuter-Telegramme* dated 19th January 1916, sheet 10.

[127] NAN SVW B.2.a, sheet 9.

[128] NAN MWI 102/2/40, letter by the Administrator's Office dated 22nd February 1929, no sheet number.

introduction and explains the meticulously formulated regulations behind.[129] According to a circular letter by Governor Hintrager sent to all District Offices on 29th August 1913, he expected these offices to start the betterment tax's implementation by the first half of November the same year.[130]

In his letter, the Governor explained the general rules on how the tax would have to be levied, and what represented its calculation basis. The District Offices were ordered to prepare the assessment orders in collaboration with the Surveyor's Offices which had already been instructed accordingly. For all property owners along the new or improved railway lines terminating at Windhoek, a thereby induced betterment should be partially skimmed. Therefore, the Surveyor's Offices were asked to assess the land values along the lines before and after the construction of those railways based on available deeds of sale. Subsequent differences in prices formed the basis for the tax to be collected, and the Governor used an example to explain the calculations: if a property was sold for 2.00 marks per square metre before the construction whilst, for a similar plot, 2.50 marks were paid after, then one third of these extra 0.50 marks would be charged as betterment tax. Further differentiations applied, for example based on the individual plot's distance to the railway station. The full regulations were laid down in the Provisions[131] and further explanatory Conventions.[132]

All in all, the regulations proved to be extremely complicated and as a first step the actual beneficiary of the improvements needed to be identified, as the Provisions ordered in section 1. This might have been obvious if the owner had not changed, but the authorities were asked to figure out the individual shares in case land had been sold in the meantime. Whoever actually benefitted from the new railway lines would then have to pay the most for the induced unearned increment. For both new railway lines reference dates for the ensuing assessments were fixed, and it was ruled that owners of parcels in the vicinity of both would be considered liable to pay for the older railway line only. The Indigenous population was exempted from the tax as long as their land was used as commons. Yet since members of the community of Rehoboth Bastards[133] were entitled to individual ownership, they by

---

[129] NAN SVW S.10.ab.

[130] NAN SVW S.10.ab, sheets 3, 16.

[131] NAN SVW S.10.ab, Provisions by the Governor's Office dated 26th August 1913, sheets 7-9.

[132] NAN SVW S.10.ab, copy of Conventions 18414/13, sheets 10-3.

[133] Rehoboth Bastards form a regional population community concentrated around the town of Rehoboth to Windhoek's south. They themselves used the term bastard to highlight their mixed ancestry and already migrated to Namibian territory with Afrikaner settlers in 19th century. Socially, they have been considered as in-betweens of Europeans and

contrast were subject to the general rules as stated in section 2. Section 4 increased the betterment tax from 33 to 50 percent, if the land title did include licences based on mining law. According to section 5, the betterment itself was calculated based on the "mean average prices" among private sellers before and after the railway constructions, although discounts or supplements based on the distance to the railways had to be considered too. Usually the tax was levied in cash, to be paid either in the full amount instantly or as annual instalments over a period of five years; in the latter case, no extra fees or interest payments would be charged as section 6 defined. Furthermore, property owners were in exceptional cases allowed to balance their tax through compensation in land. This exception was explicitly justified with the Government's interest in the acquisition of fiscal property along the railways, which could later be handed out to new settlers and to, "prevent unhealthy land speculation."[134]

In contrast to the usual property tax which had to be paid annually on all estates, the betterment tax was a one-time charge. As the explanatory conventions further laid down, this charge was justified by the railways' beneficial effects on the overall economy; al-though their share was assumed to be lower in the remote agricultural areas in DSWA's southern districts.[135] Furthermore, it was determined that the tax were to be levied on the land only but not on buildings or other components thereon.[136] Through its detailed regulations, DSWA's administration wanted to comply with similar legislation applicable in Prussia, though one statement alluded to mistakes made in Togo during the construction of the railways there and which should be prevented in Windhoek.[137] First reports on the revenues were due by 1st January 1914, but the implementation of those complicated rules was apparently delayed and due to the outbreak of the First World War no documentation on the actual results can be retrieved.

As the reference to experiences in Togo already illustrates, the debates around the betterment tax were embedded into a larger transnational context. Reichstag discussed the tax's introduction for DSWA as early as in 1906[138] but despite the parliament's favourable position the tax was then postponed due to the Namibian

---

Africans and benefitted from some legal exemptions (ADSWA 1910: Verordnung des Gouverneurs von Deutsch-Südwestafrika, betreffend die Einfuhr und den Vertrieb geistiger Getränke in dem südwestafrikanischen Schutzgebiet, no page number; Wallace 2015: 168; Zimmerer 2001: 63).
[134] NAN SVW S.10.ab, sheet 13.
[135] NAN SVW S.10.ab, sheet 10.
[136] NAN SVW S.10.ab, sheet 11.
[137] NAN SVW S.10.ab, sheet 12-3.
[138] RT Protokolle, Bd. V, 129. Sitz.: 4001-2; Bd. V, 130. Sitz.: 4045.

War. At the metropole by contrast the tax was introduced in Germany as of January 1911 after the Reichstag's approval as reported in DSWA's Official Gazette.[139] More than another year later, members of the German parliament in Berlin already demanded its abolition, because the revenues were far less than originally projected, and did not compensate for the bureaucratic expenses of tax collection.[140] Those discouraging experiences at the metropole seemed to have contradicted the results made by German colonial authorities in the Chinese possessions at Qingdao. For this case study Sebastian Conrad mentions the positive financial results of tax regulations developed by the colonial officer responsible, Wilhelm Schrameier.[141] The taxation's complex regulations and the human resources it required for their implementation can be considered as one of the main reasons, why no final results about the betterment tax are documented for DSWA. The idea of perfectionism behind the betterment tax's mechanisms does blend with the tendency in Germany's colonial administration to be prepared for all eventualities, as described by Zimmerer for the context of Native Pass Laws.[142]

Planning administration under South African rule

For the general context of SWA, the transition from German legislation and bureaucratic procedures to the Roman Dutch system under South African rule has already been mentioned (see 4.1). These changes were echoed in the administrative domain of Windhoek's urban planning, where former imperial building regulations still remained applicable after Martial Law was abolished in 1920 and SWA was put under the control of a civil administration. The only amendments made through the introduction of *Municipal Proclamation No. 22 of 1920* and other related regulations effectively reflected the new departmental structures.[143] For a better overview on the new structure, all key stakeholders are visualised in figure 11.

---

[139] ADSWA 1910: 273.
[140] RT Protokolle, Bd. 285, 67. Sitz.: 2199.
[141] Conrad 2008: 93.
[142] Zimmerer 2001: 89.
[143] Indicated in a letter by Town Clerk Kerby addressed to the Town Police and dated 30th November 1923. NAN MWI 102/2/40, no sheet number.

Figure 11: Stakeholders in building administration

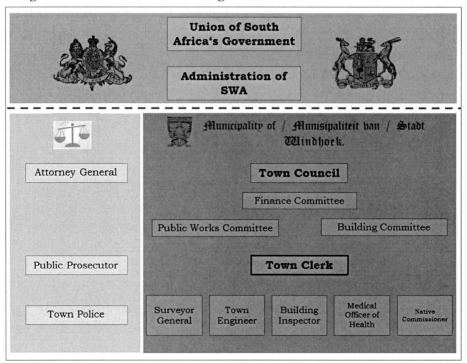

As the illustration indicates, there existed three main administrative and judiciary levels that eventually impacted on the Municipality's developments. Whilst most decisions lay at the discretion of local authorities and hence preserved important elements of local self-administration according to the German system, the Administration of SWA did play a significant role: following the applicable municipal laws, the Administrator was in the legal position to create new municipalities from scratch or to redraw their boundaries. He would decide on a Municipality's subdivision into wards, the size of her Town Council and give advice on many legal matters such as land questions.[144] Anyhow the Administrator was not permitted to interfere with the daily routines of a Municipality, unless he had been requested to do so by the very Municipality's petition. In a way, the Administration of SWA provided for the checks and balances of local authorities' actions and complemented their services through administrative departments at the national level. Although SWA was not integrated as part of the Union of South Africa in formal terms, Windhoek's fortunes were decided on by the Union Government. This does

---

[144] NAN MWI 5/9, *Municipal Proclamation No. 1 of 1922*, Chapter 1, Sections 4-12. In: Official Gazette published on 1st February 1922: 584-6.

particularly affect financial matters such as public subsidies; for this reason the Municipality kept close ties to Pretoria.

As already mentioned, legal questions posed a tricky domain in face of the simultaneous application of Roman Dutch laws and remnants of previous German rules. Therefore, the judiciary played another significant role in Windhoek's development, where a lot of consultancy was done by the Attorney General in order to translate South African laws into rules applicable at the local level. In this case, the Public Prosecutor took on the role as intermediary and helped the Town Clerk with a correct implementation of legislation. The Town Police carried out functions at two levels, first acting on behalf of the (national) judiciary system to enforce legal rulings and second acting on behalf of the local authorities to implement municipal orders.

Lastly it is indicative that figure 11 does not refer to the public community as a stakeholder. It rather shows the community's extremely limited impact on urban planning decisions in interwar years. In *Municipal Proclamation No. 1 of 1922* it was laid down that local residents were only allowed to vote for their Town Council and in order to be eligible for the passive right to vote, a person had to be White and own or occupy, "[…] immovable property within the Municipality to the assessed value of three hundred pounds […]."[145] Female suffrage was only granted under the same preconditions of proprietorship and the Indigenous population was excluded from these procedures anyways. In addition, the *Municipal Proclamation No. 1 of 1922* contained a provision in section 5 according to which half of the Council members were appointed by the Administrator, which in turn limited the opportunities for public interventions further. In face of those formal restrictions, Windhoek's situation fits well with Brenda Yeoh's conclusions drawn from the example of colonial Singapore.

> "Institutional inequality in which only a minority of the city's residents were legally and socially incorporated into the urban power structure was basic to the hierarchical nature of colonial society."[146]

In accordance with the rule of local self-administration as introduced in 1909 (see 4.1), Windhoek's future was in many respects framed by municipal agents, although a predominant role was conferred upon the local Town Council. Just like under German administration before, all relevant decisions needed to be taken or at least backed by the Town Council, who was supported in its duties by several

---

[145] NAN MWI 5/9, *Municipal Proclamation No. 1 of 1922*, Chapter 1, Sections 13-8, here section 13. In: Official Gazette published on 1st February 1922: 586-8.
[146] Yeoh 1996: 30.

expert committees. The latter had to address specific questions which were delegated to them by the Council, like in building matters; usually the Council later based its decisions on those preparations and followed the committees' recommendations. Final execution of all such decisions lay in the hands of Windhoek's various municipal administrative authorities.

Under the new organisation in accordance with South African rule, the Town Clerk would play a pivotal role in pulling the different strings of Windhoek's development together.[147] South African George Kerby was appointed as the municipality's Town Clerk and served this position over the full analysed period, with the exception of several months during the Second World War when he temporarily had to exercise his duties for the South African Armed Forces. During his term in office, Kerby accumulated such a wealth of experience and administrative knowledge that he had been approached by other colleagues to give advice on legal questions. The Town Clerk demonstrated the difference a single person could make within the system, if this person would be well versed in administrative regulations as well as the relevant legislation, skilled in negotiations and knew about all relevant matters going on in the Municipality. One letter illustrated Kerby's skills to 'play the game' by using existing loopholes to push for certain decisions – in this case to the benefit of public health considerations.[148]

In contrast to the debates at the metropole as summarised in the journal analysis (see 3.3), there did not exist a specific office for town planning in Windhoek, neither under previous German administration nor under South African rule described here. Instead, the responsibilities were shared and distributed among several departments: everything that had to do with the actual measurement and surveying of land was assigned to the Surveyor General. In addition, he was responsible for the inspection of submitted building plans as to whether or not they were in line with the applicable building regulations. Sanitation projects or the construction of the sewerage system, by contrast, belonged to the realms of the Town Engineer. He was supposed to be consulted for all preparatory plans and to monitor the execution of works for new constructions; the latter did extend to private construction activities which needed his approval. It was here that the Town Engineer's duties partially overlapped with those of the Building Inspector, who was

---

[147] The introduction of the Town Clerk's paid position in Windhoek marked a fundamental turn to the British administrative system, where a Clerk represents the senior administrative officer by appointment and who is responsible to take care of the administration and minutes of council meetings.

[148] NAN MWI 102/2/40, letter by Town Clerk Kerby, dated 15th March 1930, no sheet number.

240

supposed to monitor existing buildings and to detect buildings being in a dilapidated condition too. Windhoek's Medical Officer of Health was equally assigned with duties in sanitation, though he held no direct responsibilities for building activities and focused on the organisation of vaccination campaigns or medical examinations. In the context of the housing question he was nonetheless consulted and gave his expertise on the preparation of new housing typologies supposedly suitable to Indigenous needs for the projected African quarter called *Location* (see 4.3.3 for details). The Native Commissioner did also contribute to Windhoek's urban development although, for formal reasons, his office was not part of the European administration proper. I have included him as one of the key stakeholders due to his responsibility regarding the African population's accommodation and Location. Assigned with the duties to defend their interests as kind of trusteeship, he came into conflict with governmental institutions and the Superintendent of Locations. Among all these various offices and interests, Town Clerk Kerby had to coordinate the administrative efforts, an interdisciplinary work at the intersection of those institutions similar to figure 8 which supposedly matched with a Town Planner's job description.

One important and recurrent task comprised of the protection of sanitary conditions in accordance with Windhoek's building regulations applicable to all edifices within the township's limits. Their disregards were immediately pursued by the Town Police upon Kerby's request. Many examples for such regulatory interventions are well documented in the archival sources, and range from orders to improve the ventilation of hotel rooms[149], or the repairs of building parts which posed a, "great danger to the public"[150], to those requesting the full demolition of dilapidated buildings. The latter cases were of specific urgency, if they supposedly 'invited' the Indigenous population to forms of misconduct such as the alleged abuse of those buildings as public toilets.[151] Supervision of the demolitions was then conferred upon local police officers.

Execution of Building Regulations

A reformulation of the municipal *Building Regulations* was initiated by the Attorney General and the Public Prosecutor in 1924, when parts of the former German version became inoperative due to some repealed sections, of which the Admin-

---

[149] NAN MWI 102/2/40, as suggested by the acting Medical Officer of Health in Resolution No. 263 of Public Works Committee dated 5th July 1934, no sheet number.
[150] NAN MWI 102/2/40, letter by Town Clerk Kerby dated 14th January 1925, no sheet number.
[151] NAN MWI 102/2/40, letter by Town Clerk Kerby dated 8th November 1935, no sheet number.

istration and the Town Council were apparently unaware of.[152] The new *Building Regulations* were promulgated by *Government Notice No. 3* of 11th January 1927 and corresponded to South African legislation as laid out in the Union's *Public Health Act No. 36* of 1919. Those new regulations were explicitly sent to all building contractors in town, so as to make them familiar with the most significant amendments and future requirements such as the need to submit plans for all projected new buildings or alterations before their construction was started.[153] Through Resolution No. 39, passed at the Council's Ordinary Meeting on 20th January 1927, extensive powers and many responsibilities had been delegated to the Building Committee and the Town Clerk as well as the Assistant Town Engineer for Buildings, who were then empowered to take care of the stipulated inspections and permits.[154]

The British impact on her Commonwealth domains became apparent in a legal statement by the law firm Lorentz and Bones on the question, as to whether or not the Administration of SWA would be subject to municipal statutes and therefore bound in their building activities by Windhoek's *Building Regulations*.[155] Referring to similar legal cases in South Africa, the law firm explained that local legislation cannot limit the Crown in her activities, unless such limitations are explicitly formulated in those statutes. All other general formulations would usually be interpreted as being too wide to encompass Government projects which would constitute a category of their own. Aside from rather clear issues, the Council was confronted with cases of very specific nature, when the implementation of *Building Regulations* stipulated the compliance with defined Building Lines along which new edifices had to be erected. Nevertheless, there existed the legal option to apply for an exemption from this rule and in such cases, for matter of competence, the Council regularly asked the Surveyor General to consider the respective case and to take an appropriate decision at his discretion.[156]

As a consequence of the new *Building Regulations* with their requirements about the exact location of future construction sites, the urgent demand for a new up-to-date town plan displaying the subdivision of *erven* (parcels of land) became eventually

---

[152] NAN MWI 102/2/40, Resolution No. 74 in Council Minutes No. 73 dated 21st February 1924, no sheet number.
[153] NAN MWI 102A/2/40, circular letter dated 24th March 1927, no sheet number.
[154] NAN MWI 102A/2/40, Resolution No. 39 in Council Minutes No. 131 dated 20th January 1927, no sheet number.
[155] NAN MWI 102/2/40, letter by law firm Lorentz and Bones dated 15th March 1929, no sheet number.
[156] E.g. NAN MWI 102/2/40, letter by Town Clerk Kerby dated 11th August 1926, no sheet number.

apparent. Although it had already been discussed over the preceding decade, in September 1927 the Town Clerk received a Council's directive to ask the Surveyor General for assistance in the preparation of such a new town plan for the whole territory of Windhoek and Klein Windhoek. The plan was expected to be produced on tracing paper to allow for a subsequent production of sufficient copies.[157] 500 copies were ordered in any case, and an additional 100 were to be produced and given out for administrative purposes free of charge.[158] Due to various reasons, such as limited capacities at the only technically capable printer in Southern Africa (located at Cape Town)[159], the production was delayed and the final version of the map was ready for sale by 1931 only.[160] The Council passed an exceptional resolution, in which the Building Committee expressed its appreciation of the work delivered[161], and free copies were sent to newspapers, municipal departments, local schools and to universities in Germany.[162] In 1944 a new version of the town plan was envisaged but due to the outstanding decision about the future site for the Location, its production had been postponed.[163]

All maps of interwar Windhoek would depict a relatively quiet and small-size town that was characterised by a limited number of administrative or industrial sites accompanied by urban sprawl in its residential areas. Its highest population density was given at 30 inhabitants per hectare within the European sections in 1914[164] and did only alter slightly during the following decades. Whilst several commercial and office premises were constructed along central parts of Kaiser Street, villas mushroomed at the urban fringes at the city's northern extent.

---

[157] NAN MWI 102/1/40, letter by Town Clerk Kerby dated 29th September 1927, no sheet number.

[158] NAN MWI 102/1/40, letter by Surveyor General's office dated 20th April 1928, no sheet number. Except for the 1928 specimen section of a few central streets, unfortunately none of those copies is preserved at NAN.

[159] NAN MWI 102/1/40, invoice letter by Surveyor General dated 5th September 1930, no sheet number.

[160] NAN MWI 102/1/40, Resolution No. 193 in Council Minutes No. 217 dated 24th March 1931, no sheet number.

[161] NAN MWI 102/1/40, Resolution No. 217 in Building Committee's Minutes dated 28th March 1931, no sheet number.

[162] NAN MWI 102/1/40, list prepared by Town Clerk dated 11th July 1933, no sheet number.

[163] NAN MWI 102/1/40, letter by Surveyor General dated 8th July 1944 and Resolution (without number) in Finance Committee Minutes dated 14th September 1944, no sheet numbers.

[164] NAN SVW A.4, Erläuterungsbericht über eine Kanalisationsanlage nach dem Trennungssystem in der Stadt Windhuk, dated 30th January 1914, sheet 9.

4.2.2 Transnational exchange of ideas

In many respects SWA and Windhoek were integrated with and attached to urban debates that penetrated territorial borders and crossed the continents as well. This awareness of developments around the world was typical since the German period, when the Municipality had subscribed to journals and series like – naturally – the Official Gazette for DSWA (ADSWA) as well as the *Reichsgesetzblatt* (Reich's Law Gazette), *Preußisches Verwaltungsblatt* (Prussian Administrative Gazette), *Kommunale Rundschau* (Municipal Review), or *Das Deutsche Kolonialblatt* (The German Colonial Gazette), as a list from 1913 indicates.[165] At the turn of the year 1914 the municipal library expanded its collection of publications on civil engineering and urban planning such as *Die Wasserversorgung von Deutsch-Südwestafrika* (Water Supply in German SWA) by König (1907), *Die künstliche Verwendung des Wassers im Städtebau* (The Artificial Use of Water in Urban Design) by Volkmann (1911), or *Die Wasserversorgung der Ortschaften besonders für Feuerlöschzwecke* (Water Supply of Towns especially for Purposes of Fire Extinguishing) by R. Fried (1903), as two orders dated 28th November 1913 and 2nd January 1914 respectively indicate.[166] Whilst the engineering focus was on water provision and sewerage disposal as well as the layout of streets, the ordered books on planning complemented these topics but did cover municipal undertakings. The acquisition of these books correlated with negotiations with external experts and draft plans for the introduction of a proper sewerage system in Windhoek to improve the municipal amenities and to end the collection of night soil through a bucket system as will be presented in more detail later (see 4.2.3 and 4.2.4). Besides, the administration received direct offers for subscriptions in the architectural and urban arena, like from the Saxon State Association for the Protection of Arts and Crafts (Landesverein Sächsischer Heimatschutz) trying to promote small houses in 1913.[167] Earlier attempts to spread these ideas were already made since 1909 by several interested parties like the journal *Der Kleinwohnungsbau*

---

[165] NAN SVW Z.1.b, sheet 7.

[166] NAN SVW B.9.d, sheets 5, 8. The list contained the following additional titles: Liebmann: *Der Land-Straßenbau* (1912), Mareus: *Etat und Bilanz für stattliche [sic] und kommunale Wirtschaftsbetriebe* (1912), König: *Taschenbuch der Hydrotekten für Wasserversorgung und Städte-Entwässerung* (1905), König: *Die Wasserversorgung innerhalb der Gebäude und ihrer Grundstücke* (1905), *Mitteilungen aus der kgl. Prüfungsanstalt für Wasserversorgung und Abwässerbeseitigung zu Berlin* (1902), Fried: *Der Straßenbau* (1911), Knauer: *Der städtische Straßenbau* (1910), Liebmann: *Der Landstraßenbau* (1912), Rappaport: *Steigende Straßen – Eine Studie z. deutschen Städtebau* (1911), Schmidt: *Die Kosten städtischer Straßen und deren Einfluss auf d. Anbau* (1911), Weyl: *Die Betriebsführung städtischer Werke* (1910), Lindemann-Südekum: *Jahrbuch d. kommunalen Technik* (1912), Riese: *Kommunale Wirtschaftspflege* (1911), Wippermann: *Die Zukunft kommunaler Betriebe* (1912), Friedrich: *Kulturtechnischer Wasserbau* (1. Bd. 1912, 2. Bd. 1908), Weyrauch: *Der Wasserbau* (1908).

[167] NAN SVW B.2.d, sheets 1-4.

(Small house construction).[168] Such promotional material filed i.a. under 'Municipal Building Affairs, Homes for civil servants and employees' made an impact on the administration and led to controversial aesthetic debates as discussed for Mr Eppeler's petition (see 4.2.1). In this respect, DSWA followed those general trends in Germany where small houses dominated the debate as the journal analysis has already revealed (see 1).

Links to external sources

In some cases such information was sent at random to the Municipality of Windhoek by spokespersons and agents trying to draw administrative attention. In many cases the administration ordered those materials to prepare its decision making process. Further Windhoek did not want to be confined to receiving end and hence sent out its own promotional material to the metropole as exemplified at the 1914 *Werkbund* exhibition at Cologne. This bidirectional link was substantiated by the city's administrative experience with experimental tools like the betterment tax which was partially triggered debates in political Berlin.

Despite intense links to Germany, the country was not the only source of information that was tapped. Authorities in SWA paid particular attention to the developments in neighbouring colonial entities, though the Union of South Africa's role was pre-eminent. One example for the years preceding the First World War might illustrate the matter. As a response to the severe impacts on agricultural businesses posed by locusts swarms, the Governor's office disseminated the annual reports published by the South African Central Locust Bureau addressing state-of-the-art ways to fight one of the recurrent natural threats in Southern Africa. Copies of those reports were bought in South Africa and then sent to all Municipalities in DSWA.[169]

The municipalities of DSWA tried to make their voices heard in the metropole and at Reichstag with a letter dated 22nd February 1910 proves.[170] They initiated a co-ordinated lobbying campaign to promote the interests of DSWA, which was supposed to balance some of the difficulties that Windhoek and the other towns were faced with in legal terms. They approached colonial expert Paul Rohrbach[171], who

---

[168] NAN BAU 125 0000.
[169] NAN SVW P.3.a.
[170] NAN SVW S.3.b, sheet 5.
[171] Rohrbach (1869-1956) was theologian by profession but he played a significant role as advocate of German colonial interests. He published on and travelled extensively to the colonies, where he served as Settlement Commissioner (*Ansiedlungskommissar*) in DSWA. In his publications Rohrbach supported the ideas of racist and segregationist colonialism as

was expected to pay the Territory a visit, and who should be convinced of the necessity to promote DSWA's plea for a seat in the German parliament Reichstag.[172] In his letter addressed to the Mayor of Omaruru, Windhoek's Mayor expressed his hopes for Rohrbach as mouthpiece for the campaign, which could have multiplied its reach based on Rohrbach's extensive publicising activities. Nevertheless, the Mayor had no false illusions and admitted the constitutional obstacle their plea was facing – and which actually made it a long-term goal. From his viewpoint it would already have been a satisfactory short- or medium-term goal, if they were admitted a place in the Reichstag's Budgetary Committee. Within the same letter, the Mayor promoted the idea of an annual meeting of DSWA's larger towns and municipal authorities to share and discuss their recent challenges and experiences. Their first meeting was already scheduled by him for September 1910 in commemoration of one year of local self-administration. In preparation of this meeting the Municipality of Windhoek started a collection of annual reports issued by other local authorities across the Territory, which was complemented by municipal bye-laws from DSWA and beyond.[173] Those reports and bye-laws were used as a source of reference to identify similar challenges as well as to learn from the examples and experiences other cities had already made therewith. The archival files do not contain specific links to the German Association of Municipalities at the metropole (*Deutscher Städtetag*).

As soon as the political circumstances were settled in the aftermath of the First World War and SWA's final status was sorted out in the Treaty of Versailles, Windhoek had been incorporated into new formal and informal networks for the dissemination of planning ideas. The effects eventually became tangible in the 1930s, when the Municipality received circular letters that were addressed, "to each Urban Local Authority in the Union"[174], thereby clearly indicating where the city now belonged to in administrative terms. Copies of South Africa's *Municipal Magazine* equally belonged to Windhoek's readings, and were used to keep the city's staff members updated on latest challenges in urban development and some of the an-

---

well as a civilising mission in order to underscore German cultural achievements to the world (Gründer 2012: 116, 137, 251; Olusoga, Erichsen 2010: 113-5; Walgenbach, Katharina, *Rassenpolitik und Geschlecht in Deutsch-Südwestafrika (1907-1914)*. In: Becker, Frank [Ed.]: Rassenmischehen – Mischlinge – Rassentrennung. Zur Politik der Rasse im deutschen Kolonialreich. Stuttgart: Franz Steiner Verlag 2004: 172-4).

[172] NAN SVW S.3.b, letter dated 8th April 1910, sheet 8.

[173] NAN SVW S.3.n.

[174] E.g. NAN MWI 36/32/37, Circular No. 4 of 1936 dated 23rd March 1936 and issued by the Department of Public Health, no sheet number.

swers other authorities had found to address them.[175] With regards to Indigenous housing schemes developed for Windhoek's future Location at a new site the various templates and examples of good practice from across the Union were deliberately compiled by municipal authorities, as they, "will have to be sorted out now and a suitable local type evolved from them."[176] The ideas for a "Native Model Housing", which derived from these efforts, did in turn appeal to top-rank authorities at the Union administration, and Windhoek was considered to be a good example to other cities (see 4.3.3). The Central Housing Board at Pretoria[177] invited a representative over to discuss the project in detail. In 1933 SWA's capital was considered to be at eye level with other South African cities, when its Town Council were invited to send delegates to attend a conference on Native Affairs held at Johannesburg.[178]

Aside from these formal relations, many direct personal contacts were established over the interwar years between representatives of Windhoek's administration and their counterparts at various Municipalities in South Africa. Those relations intensified through several visits and as part of these networks a kind of work division based on specific fields of expertise evolved at the various local authorities. One example refers to the question of Native housing and the future layout of Locations, an issue that became urgent towards the end of the 1930s, and which eventually had to be postponed until after the Second World War. Windhoek's Town Clerk George Kerby corresponded with the Secretary of Pretoria's Central Housing Board, who provided SWA's administration with recent reports about development trends in the Union as well as some informal information.[179] That flow of planning ideas was highly significant, though its impacts only became tangible in the post-Second World War goals and designs for Windhoek's Locations. Private investors and businessmen were equally drawn into networks which crossed the borders of SWA. One example in the context of building regulations refers to the construction of a new cinema in Windhoek. Regarding its interior design and the exact site of the technical appliances, state-of-the-art regulations in South Africa

---

[175] NAN MWI 5/11, Copy of *Municipal Magazine* Vol. 20, No. 237 May 1937, no sheet numbers.

[176] NAN MWI 36/32/37, Extract from the Report of the Town Clerk, Capt. G. Kerby, on Proceedings whilst in the Union, dated 28th June 1944, no sheet numbers.

[177] The South African Central Housing Board was installed under the 1920 Housing Act and it fell under the Board's jurisdiction to approve grant applications for housing schemes across the country and the Mandated Territory. As Maylam has underlined the Board pursued a clear policy of racial segregation (Maylam 1995: 27).

[178] NAN MWI 36/26/37, invitation letter by Native Affairs Department of Johannesburg dated 6th August 1933, no sheet number.

[179] NAN MWI 36/32/37.

and Europe were used by both, private developer and administration, as role models.[180]

Interrelations between SWA and the Union of South Africa became ever closer during the interwar period. At the same time the mandated Territory did consider itself as somewhat integral part of the Commonwealth, although centrifugal forces remained active among the European community every now and then, and the Indigenous community did not have a say in this respect. The 1925 Wembley Exhibition represented one exceptional opportunity to demonstrate SWA's and Windhoek's place as part of the extended British Empire. At the same time, the exhibition was used for marketing purposes, and the Administrator therefore reserved an exhibition stand in London to promote SWA and its capital city.[181] In a letter dated 7th February 1925[182] he specifically invited the Municipality to contribute to a brochure, which was under preparation as part of these marketing efforts by SWA's preparatory committee. The Municipality seized the opportunity and did not just financially subsidise the brochure with £10, but submitted several photos for the brochure and exhibition stand as well as a two-and-a-half page long description of the city. This description contains many emblematic examples where Windhoek tried to define herself as a 'modern' city, encompassing all state-of-the-art technical infrastructures, and where explicit references were made to developments, "on European lines."[183] The authors of this description felt obliged to point out that some of the facilities, such as abattoirs and cold storages, "compare favourably with many larger towns" and, "with any town of similar size." Written in the style of those days' marketing brochures, the text highlighted Windhoek's health facilities and explicitly confirmed the, "entire absence of tropical diseases." It conveyed the image of a small but modern and expanding town as centre of SWA, which represented European lifestyle and its amenities at a rather remote place. In the aftermath of the rainy season it could, at least based on this description, be considered a garden city. The only reference to the Indigenous population was made regarding demographic statistics, according to which 3,400 out of a total population of 9,000 were Europeans.

---

[180] NAN MWI 102/2/40, Report by Building Committee dated 7th November 1928, p 4, no sheet number.
[181] According to Richard Dennis the British Empire Exhibition attracted more than 27 million visitors (Dennis 2000: 127).
[182] NAN MWI 37/9/37: Included as part of the Council meeting minutes from 20th February 1925, no sheet number.
[183] All following quotes: NAN MWI 37/9/37: "Windhoek," no sheet numbers.

The SWA's Commonwealth identity was not just based on public or administrative efforts. The same file contains an extended correspondence between some farmers and Windhoek's municipal administration about a box of butter. This butter manufactured at the colony was supposed to form part of the exhibits at the Wembley Exhibition. Due to a mistake – the exact reason was not disclosed in the official letters exchanged over several months – it had only been sent back and forth between Windhoek and its place of origin at Aukam, without ever leaving the Territory.[184] Other occasions at which this Commonwealth identity still reverberated, were almost exclusively attached to the British royal family, like at the Silver Jubilee celebrations on 6th May 1935 in honour of King George V which were equally made a public holiday in SWA. Still a certain reservation can be identified, since the Legislative Assembly did not envisage any official celebrations except for church services the day before and,

> "[…] a Royal Salute [that] will be fired from the Government Buildings at the time their Majesties enter Westminster Abbey."[185]

In this respect SWA considered itself to be in good company with other colonial entities, "This procedure is, it is understood, being followed in other overseas Dominions."[186] Christo Botha has nonetheless described the struggles during interwar years between proponents like South Africa's Prime Minister Jan Smuts who saw SWA's future as extended bridgehead for the British Commonwealth, as opposed to a rather nationalistic integration within an autonomous Union of South Africa based on Afrikaner identity as proposed by Smut's predecessor General Louis Botha.[187]

All documented accounts of Windhoek's direct administrative correspondence with, as well as the archival references made to other cities and institutions around the globe, are collated in the maps displayed in figures 12 and 13. In accordance with one of Pierre-Yves Saunier's recommendations on the means at hands to actually convey the results of transnational history, all three maps help to visualise the city's extended network of interaction. They consider the various sources of information, that were tapped by the administrative departments dealing with Windhoek's urban development at large over the full analysed interwar period from 1914 to 1945. On the other, they further illustrate those cities from which SWA's capital drew its inspiration for new legislation, housing schemes, or the like.

---

[184] NAN MWI 37/9/37: e.g. first delivery slip dated 30th March 1925, letters dated 2nd, 5th and 15th July 1925, no sheet number.
[185] VPLA First Session, Third Assembly 1934/1935: 41.
[186] VPLA First Session, Third Assembly 1934/1935: 41.
[187] Botha 2008: 237-8.

The network actually reached its most comprehensive extent at the beginning of the analysed period, when the First World War and the accompanying political uncertainties created a relatively open environment to rethink administrative rules. Neither the city nor SWA were exclusively focused or dependent on input from the former colonial mother country, although of course many examples were compiled from German sources. By contrast, German sources were explicitly counterbalanced by input from other colonial entities. Here SWA's administration could count on similar experiences in terms of climatic conditions or natural threats, which differed significantly from the German environment and where metropolitan templates and instructions hence proved to be useless. It was at these occasions that direct exchange with neighbouring colonies was maintained, in order to draw on results produced under relatively similar circumstances. Over the following decades this range of potential sources practically melted down, and at last centred on a one-sided relationship between SWA and the Union of South Africa, except for occasional references (mostly) to the British Empire and Germany.

This development can be contextualised in the geopolitical environment, where the Territory's status as a League of Nations' mandate did not bear too many liabilities or checks-and-balances, and where South Africa was able to develop its own political agenda as a consequence of the Statutes of Westminster, as defined in 1931. The stronger South Africa's impact on SWA grew, the fewer were the opportunities for Windhoek's administration to work on its own agenda. SWA's options to choose between various reference points diminished over time. This development trend was not predetermined from the very beginning, a result of different factors that have left their imprints at several levels. The *political frameworks* gave South Africa a dominant role in SWA's future after the First World War, although the League of Nations rather envisaged it to be the relationship of a custodian towards his obligations for a trusteeship and not an administrative integration. Christo Botha has summarised the reluctant position of US President Woodrow Wilson behind, although leading South African politicians pursued their strategic agenda to expand the Union's regional influence.[188] Yet the Treaty of Versailles provided the legal basis for SWA's official annexation and integration as the Union's fifth province.[189] As a consequence, Union and, to a lesser extent, British law permeated into the Territory which partially replaced previous German legislation. In the long run, it formed an essential pre-requirement for a less formal but still significant *integration* of Windhoek into South African debates, which was further complemented by the administrative amalgamation of infrastructures with regards to railways, har-

---

[188] Botha 2008: 237-9.
[189] Treaty of Versailles: Articles 22 and 119.

bours and civil aviation. Under this umbrella a constant *exchange of staff* members was organised, which helped to secure South Africa's direct influence on decisions taken at Windhoek's and SWA's authorities, or at least in their preparations. These civil servants, who represented intermediaries according to Saunier's concept of transnational history, can be interpreted as a kind of "Fifth Column" for the issues of South Africa. Though they are not considered on such drastic terms here, they nonetheless helped to further disseminate Union ideas. This limited quantitative flow of public employees was complemented by the significant immigration of settlers from the Union. In this context Botha has summarised the South African strategy.

> "To effectively neutralise the German section, it was necessary to subdue them through sheer weight of numbers."[190]

All these direct encounters helped to impact the *social habits* and *ways of thinking* along South African lines.[191] SWA developed a mind-set different from mainstream German ideas in imperial times. Decisions then taken 'on the ground' contrasted with the expectations at the metropole.[192] Another important dimension was formed by SWA's *economic dependency* on South Africa; examples have been mentioned in terms of the public accounts which were balanced by the Union, as well as the competition and limitations caused in important export markets like diamonds or meat (see 4.1). Subsequent attempts to make the Territory less dependent on such unilateral sources and to establish economic diversity through new trade relations, for example to countries at the African West Coast, remained unsuccessful. Furthermore, Botha has mentioned how the South African Government tried to keep meat from SWA out of the market and to prevent the economy to become autonomous.[193]

It can therefore be concluded that Windhoek's opportunities to actively decide on its future urban development based on different foreign concepts and ideas to choose from, were curtailed towards the second half of the interwar period when the South African influence became a relatively dominating one. The examples

---

[190] Botha 2008: 238.

[191] Dubow has nonetheless demonstrated how first-hand encounters with segregationists from the US American south have inspired key representatives of the South African administration, underscoring the extent of transnational exchange of ideas (Dubow 1995: 151).

[192] E.g. Becker illustrates such opposing ideas with regards to the ban of interracial marriages as proposed by Wilhelm Solf in his function as State Secretary at the Colonial Office in 1912. Reichstag passed a draft law in reply, condemning Solf's ban but the law was openly rejected in DSWA (Becker 2004: 210-1).

[193] Botha 2008: 236.

then referred to remained limited to cities in the Union but virtually did not go beyond. These basic trends need to be borne in mind when consulting the maps in figures 12 and 13.

If these results are reviewed through the lens of Ward's conceptual framework for the diffusion of planning ideas, two different categories can then actually be applied in order to describe Windhoek's transnational links. Its early stages until the First World War represented the setup of *undiluted borrowing*; similar to Ward's example of the dominions and their close ties to British developments DSWA's capital was attached to German input.[194] Still local planners were, for various reasons, willing and able to include other sources into their concepts, as the exchange with colonial entities across Africa illustrates. It was later under South African mandate rule that SWA lost its broader international links and was increasingly focused on the neighbouring country's solutions. In face of this limited setup, Windhoek descended on Ward's classification and merely qualified as *negotiated imposition*.[195] The South African influence became overwhelming and local authorities were only able to negotiate and select the examples, legal tools or urban patterns they would like to apply to SWA, whilst other foreign sources remained virtually out of reach.

Figure 12: Windhoek's context in transnational networks during inter-war years (left) with zoom into Southern Africa (right)

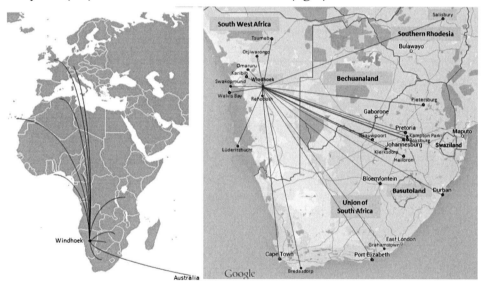

---

[194] Ward 2000: 49-51.
[195] Ward 2000: 51-2.

Figure 13: Windhoek's transnational links to Europe during the first half of interwar years

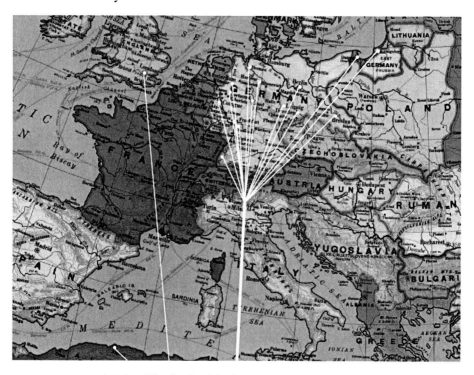

4.2.3   Technical infrastructures

Over the interwar period many public planning efforts were focused on the 'modernisation' of Windhoek's technical infrastructures. In the debates any 'advance' made in this direction could immediately be exploited as a symbol for the city's progress, and it was the Municipality's intention to end some of the backlogs that existed since the days of German rule.

Water provision and sewerage system

Although the different stakeholders at Windhoek's various administrative departments each favoured their own specific infrastructure project, the improvement of the city's water supply and the introduction of a waterborne sewerage system can be considered a common interest and as *the* most symbolic move for the aspired 'modernisation.' The system's construction mirrored Hård's and Misa's conclusion that, "[e]ven such unlikely structures as water and sewage systems were icons of modernity a century ago."[196] It served to resolve two problems at the same time:

---

[196] Hård, Misa 2010: 15.

on one hand the existing bucket system to discard the night soil could be replaced; on the other hand, it heralded the capital city's image of progress towards similar standards of convenience which were ubiquitous in most industrialised cities (see 3.3.2 and 3.3.6). Under German administration Windhoek tried to catch up with developments in the metropole and worked on the improvement of its water supply. Aside from the existing natural springs that had made this spot a favourable grazing place in pre-colonial times, local authorities as well as private persons tried to increase the available daily water quantitythrough new or deeper boreholes. In the face of the prevailing climatic conditions with its preponderance of droughts, the city had to constantly fight with water scarcity. Under these circumstances this problem had heavy impacts on the Indigenous population whilst the White community's demands were served with priority. Therefore, the administrative file on the Location's water supply is full of reports about shortages and their consequences on the Black people's health.[197]

The situation was partially to be blamed on an insufficient management and maintenance of all piped infrastructures. Its full extent has been documented in the Municipality's Annual Report for 1918.[198] The report explains the transition made in the city's service provision from efforts to secure a sufficient level of available water quantities to improvements towards a steady and rational supply in all neighbourhoods. New machines were purchased to modernise the (pumping) equipment, and parts of the previously privately maintained machineries were taken over by the Municipality in a form of municipal socialism. These efforts were complemented by the construction of new pipes in the city's central streets to stabilise the water provision, as well as the introduction of hot water from a hot spring as a new convenience, for which a separate pipe was laid across several parts in Windhoek's northern districts where the Europeans' villas were located. For this reason, it took until the end of German rule before sufficient water quantities allowed the Municipality to start planning its own waterborne sewerage system. Parallel to the water works, Windhoek's administration had already collected relevant information about the elements required for a proper sewerage system and started to draft first plans for its construction in 1913. In one of the marketing brochures for waste water treatment plants, obtained from the specialised German developer *Gesellschaft für Abwässerklärung m.b.H.* based in Berlin, the idea of modernity was emphasised in its very first sentence.

---

[197] NAN SVW E.1.f.
[198] NAN SVW S.3.o, Jahresbericht 1918, sheets 2-3.

"Neben einer einwandfreien Wasserversorgung nimmt unter den größeren modernen Kulturaufgaben der Gemeindewesen zweifellos die Beseitigung der Abfallwässer eine besonders hervorragende Stelle ein."[199]

Windhoek's people in power did not just read those marketing materials carefully, as marks written with a pencil suggest, they also aimed for the implementation. German examples and most notably Danzig represented their role models, since the file on the planned sewerage system contains a collection of schedules of fees from the metropole.[200] In 1914 the Government Architect (*Regierungsbaumeister*) Gottlieb Redecker compiled a memorandum, in which he strongly advised the construction of a waterborne sewerage system in Windhoek.[201] Although he acknowledged that there still existed some towns without such amenity in the mother country, he emphasised its advisability for DSWA's capital where the existing bucket system proved to be a disadvantage in financial but most of all in hygienic terms with reference to the fly pests it regularly created.[202] This first comprehensive memo on a waterborne sewerage system was intended to serve the European town sections only, and instead of (separate) WCs for Indigenous and White employees at every public building it recommended the construction of central public conveniences for the exclusive use of Indigenous people.[203] They represented a preservation of the existing ten separate lavatories for Africans constructed across Windhoek's central areas in 1912.[204] As part of the ensuing public debates in the Building Committee and Town Council, the plans were amended and did eventually cover the Location.

This amendment formed part of the official promotional documents submitted to take out a loan with a German bank willing to finance the tender, and which had been submitted in support of the application for a financial subsidy from the Imperial Governor and the Colonial Office at Berlin too.[205] As the relevant file proves[206], Windhoek's attempts to issue a loan worth 1.5 million marks in order to cover the costs for the sewerage system as well as a gasworks for lighting purposes

---

[199] NAN SVW G.5.ar, marketing brochure "Das Kremersche Klärverfahren und seine Bedeutung in der Klärtechnik," undated, sheet 14. "Aside from an immaculate water provision, the disposal of waste waters belongs, without a doubt, among the greatest modern cultural missions in municipal systems." (author's translation).
[200] NAN SVW G.5.ar, sheets 1-10.
[201] NAN SVW G.5.ar, Transcript of memo "Äußerung des Baumeisters Redecker über die Ausführung einer Kanalisationsanlage in Windhuk" dated 5th January 1914, sheets 73-84.
[202] NAN SVW G.5.ar, idem, sheets 80-1.
[203] NAN SVW G.5.ar, idem, sheet 83.
[204] NAN SVW G.5.w, decision by Town Council dated 4th March 1912, no sheet number.
[205] NAN SVW G.5.ar, letter by Mayor dated 6th February 1914, sheets 118-9.
[206] NAN SVW A.4.

and an abattoir was not well-received by financial institutions at the metropole, such as Berlin-based Disconto-Gesellschaft or Darmstädter Bank. All attempts were refused by the banks based on the Municipality's insufficient collaterals[207], and even a joint loan for the cities of Windhoek, Swakopmund and Keetmanshoop was ruled out during the preceding negotiations. This example helps to illustrate how careful Germany's financial institutions were in their selection of overseas investments. Profitability and security apparently played a more important role than national prestige, and Windhoek's experience in this respect fits well with Francesca Schinzinger's general findings. Neither Government and Reichstag were excessively inclined to support the colonial dependencies, as their limited loan votes prove[208], nor did these domains play a significant role in terms of metropolitan private investments.[209]

It was under these circumstances that the Municipality applied for financial assistance from the Governor. Windhoek explicitly aimed for support from the Colonial Office on similar lines as had already been granted to Dar es Salaam, and according to which the East African city was offered a loan issued by private banks but guaranteed by the German Empire. The Municipality hoped for a favourable decision and further substantiated the application as being a significant improvement in terms of public health. Specific reference was made to the Location's inclusion in the drafted sewerage system, the place where it was argued that many cases of typhus and malaria had broken out. The investment could help to effectively reduce threats to the health of African and European populations alike. From Windhoek's perspective her arguments were further substantiated by the dominant share of Government employees, since, firstly, 1,500 out of 5,000 inhabitants at the Location and approximately half the European population were presented to be directly or indirectly dependent on jobs with DSWA's administration, as well as, secondly, its fiscal real property which covered more than 40 percent of the whole township.[210] Hence without a substantial contribution from the Governor, in whose interest the sewerage system supposedly was, the project could not be carried out. Whilst the total expenditures for the sewerage system were estimated at 830,000 marks, the Municipality asked for a public grant at 270,000 marks basically to cover the investments at public buildings and to the Indigenous population's benefit.[211] Although the latter investments were officially highlighted as the most

---

[207] NAN SVW G.5.ar, copy of letter by Mayor dated 29th July 1914, sheet 156.
[208] Schinzinger 1984: 149-53.
[209] Schinzinger 1984: 117-28.
[210] NAN SVW G.5.ar, letter by Mayor dated 6th February 1914, sheets 118-9.
[211] NAN SVW A.4, Erläuterungsbericht über eine Kanalisationsanlage nach dem Trennungssystem in der Stadt Windhuk dated 30th January 1914, sheet 62.

significant part, their share was internally estimated to contribute merely 115,000 marks. These arguments formed part of the municipal strategy to convince the Government, and Windhoek was in this case assisted by the private developer – in modern language a 'consultancy firm' – "Gesellschaft für Wasserversorgung & Abwässerbeseitigung m.b.H. Berlin" that had been contracted with the construction of the sewerage system on 30th January 1914.[212] Engineer Erich Merten was appointed to act as the developer's authorised person and led parts of the negotiations on behalf of the Municipality. According to the archival file there was no further contender for this project.

Global politics impacted those negotiations and with the outbreak of the First World War, all attempts to secure the financial means for such a heavy investment were instantly nullified. Under those uncertain circumstances, where local authorities were unable to initiate the construction of the sewerage system on a comprehensive scale, the installation of first segments fell into the hands of private initiatives. A letter from the bookstore branch of 'Swakopmunder Buchhandlung' sent to the Municipality in early 1921 informed the local authorities about its taking into operations of their own water closets, which were linked to another private facility for waste water treatment draining into a small and mostly dry riverbed, and the bookstore therefore asked the authorities not to charge for the bucket system anymore.[213] Except for such private initiatives that benefitted from their favourable site close to those small-scale treatment facilities and the adjacent river as outlet, the vast majority of Windhoek's built-up areas had to rely on the bucket system for at least another decade. It was in the early 1930s that administrative records reported on, "the inauguration of the Municipal water-borne sewerage scheme".[214] This inauguration proved to be a piecemeal process. During those years parts of the construction works were carried out under the umbrella of relief works, intended to alleviate the sometimes precarious economic situation caused by the Great Depression. In its attempt to convince the Administrator of Windhoek's plans for the construction of a new dam, municipal documents reported the completion of all works on the sewerage system in early 1932, at least as far as local resources were concerned.

---

[212] NAN SVW A.4, idem, sheet 43.

[213] NAN MWI S.W.M.13, letter by Swakopmunder Buchhandlung dated 12th January 1921, no sheet number.

[214] NAN MWI 5/8, Extract from Town Clerk's Report re Improvements in Location attached to Minutes of Conference on Native Location Affairs held on 19th March 1931, no sheet number.

"[…] [A]nd through the construction of the Water Borne Sewerage System it has also considerably assisted in relieving the situation caused through the depression even at the expense of incurring considerable liabilities. All these works, however, have now come to an end and the Council finds that it is impossible to impose any further financial burdens on its rate payers in this connection."[215]

Even though the sewerage system itself was not yet completed, the Municipality's attempt to tap external sources for its construction proved to be successful. Substantial shares of those public expenditures administered by SWA's Legislative Assembly were still allocated to the extension of Windhoek's sewerage system in the late 1930s. In 1937 it received a loan of £1,956 which constituted almost one quarter of all expenditures for public buildings covered by this particular vote[216], and in 1938 it was granted another £1,619 out of a, by then, significantly increased budget under which Windhoek's sewerage system merely represented circa seven percent of the investments.[217] Despite these costs the amenities described above were not available to both parts of Windhoek's population, European and African, at equal shares.

Segregationist tendencies with regards to the sewerage system

Whilst the introduction of private WCs was debated and (later) executed for the European areas, improvements were discussed for the Location too but at far less sophisticated levels. Already the first drafts for the waterborne sewerage system – as discussed and finalised in the 1914 contract with the Berlin-based private developer – provided for private and convenient WCs in the European sections, whilst the African population would only be serviced by public conveniences at every ethnic quarter within the Location, each equipped with squat toilets.[218] Despite the officially attested positive impacts of a waterborne sewerage system at the Location, mostly from the European community's perspective[219], such ideas were soon put aside internally after the First World War, and in 1921 the Town Engineer officially presented his scheme to replace the then still existing trench system through the erection of closets and the collection of excrement in form of the

---

[215] NAN MWI 5/8, Memorandum Unemployment Relief and Location Improvement Scheme dated 15th April 1932, no sheet number.
[216] VPLA Third Session, Third Assembly 1937: Annex Financial report: 50.
[217] VPLA Fourth Session, Third Assembly 1938: Public Accounts: 52.
[218] NAN SVW A.4, Erläuterungsbericht dated 30th January 1914, sheet 26.
[219] NAN SVW G.5.ar, transcript of "Gutachterliche Äußerung des Medizinalreferenten zu dem Erläuterungsbericht über das Kanalisationsprojekt von Windhuk dated 26th December 1913, sheets 165-7. Here sheet 167.

258

widely-used bucket system.[220] His scheme's cost estimation at £650 was supplemented by the Town Council with another loan of £350 to erect separate closets for Indigenous workers in the European areas.[221] This differentiation is just one more symbolic example for the subconscious perception of the Indigenous population as dirty and the subsequent efforts to conceal both domains, where direct interactions could not be avoided. In addition, the simple numbers reflect on the real distribution of available public resources between the African and European communities. Although the introduction of a waterborne sewerage system at the existing Location had been discussed several times during interwar years, no waterborne sewerage but the bucket system was envisaged for the future new Location's site.[222]

This idea matched with South African sanitary standards recommended for similar Indigenous settlements in the Union which favoured the construction of pit privies. Instructions for their construction required a minimum depth of eight feet (c. 2.4 metres) with a diameter of less than three feet. It was assumed that such facilities, complemented by a 'foul-proof pedestal' and accommodated in a green brick building, would serve its purpose for approximately 12 years, if used by five to six adults and regularly inspected with regards to its cleanliness.[223] Total costs accrued over the full 12-year-period were estimated at £6, before a new pit would have to be dug. As a letter by Windhoek's Superintendent of Locations addressed to his colleague at Johannesburg's municipal administration points out[224], the Location at Klein Windhoek with its 500 inhabitants created an exceptional problem that required unconventional solutions to its sanitary system. A final decision about Klein Windhoek Location's closure and its subsequent amalgamation with the Location at Windhoek proper had been postponed for several times in the late 1930s, and therefore the sanitary conditions became a matter of urgency. In 1943 the problem was still unresolved, as the Manager of Windhoek's Native Affairs Department had to admit.

---

[220] Nightingale refers to Johannesburg and many cities around the world including Europe and North America (Nightingale 2012: 257).
[221] NAN MWI 37/5/37, Minutes No. 4 of the Location Committee meeting held on 16th July 1921, no sheet number.
[222] NAN MWI 36/27/37, Minutes of Meeting of Commission appointed to enquire into Location Affairs held on 20th January 1926, no sheet number.
[223] NAN MWI 36/20/37, Notes on a Privy Pit Service as adopted in schemes approved and subsidised by the Central Housing Board, undated, no sheet number.
[224] NAN MWI 36/20/37, letter by Superintendent of Locations dated 19th February 1942, no sheet number.

"As you know the old trench system has been condemned by our Health Officers and cannot be retained indefinitely."[225]

It was argued that a different system would be needed here, as all solutions typically applied were out of question. Neither a waterborne sewerage system was deemed feasible, officially due to the necessary but costly four-mile-long pipes, nor the bucket system could be applied due to its equally necessary transportation over to Windhoek proper to discharge the contents, and pit privies fell through because they were considered to endanger local ground water sources. Johannesburg's Non-European and Native Affairs Department furnished Windhoek with some blueprints of an alternative solution[226], and put the Superintendent in contact with a private mining company where this alternative was already in use. It comprised of a drain system for urine whilst faecal excrements were collected with carts and burnt at a new sludge incinerator close to Klein Windhoek Location, where the ashes could be used as fertiliser. As a handwritten remark indicates, the Superintendent forwarded the documents to Windhoek's Town Council since he was convinced that, "you will find this interesting."[227]

Waste removal, electricity and postal services

A system for waste collection was developed under German administration, and the so-called trolley (see 4.2.4) served to transport the refuse towards Windhoek's deposit site at the town's southwestern fringe close to the road to Rehoboth. Despite the use of such rail infrastructure and specific groups of Indigenous and European staff members assigned with the collection and removal of domestic waste, occasional complaints were addressed about unclean conditions on the streets. In 1920 Town Clerk Kerby sent a letter to the Sanitary Inspector to state that in the Municipality's opinion, "[t]he cleaning up of Streets leaves much to be desired"[228], and requested him to take all necessary actions, "irrespective of costs" in order to alleviate the situation. The request was in turn forwarded to the Road Overseer for matter of responsibility.[229] Those minor deficiencies in the European section do

---

[225] NAN MWI 36/31/37, letter by Manager of Native Affairs Department dated 15th November 1943, no sheet number.
[226] NAN MWI 36/20/37, letter by Manager of Non-European and Native Affairs Department at City of Johannesburg dated 17th March 1942 as well as attached blueprints and marketing brochures, no sheet numbers.
[227] NAN MWI 36/20/37, letter by Superintendent of Locations dated 19th February 1942, no sheet number.
[228] NAN MWI S.W.M.13, letter by Town Clerk dated 17th February 1920, no sheet number. Same source for the following quote.
[229] NAN MWI S.W.M.13, letter by Sanitary Inspector dated 17th February 1920, no sheet number.

not compare to those conditions prevailing at Windhoek's Location, where those services were equally part of municipal duties and charged to the Indigenous inhabitants as part of their rents (see 4.3.3). At first, Indigenous waste was collected and buried at garbage pits dug within the Location's confines at every 'tribal' section[230] but this system proved to be insufficient. The quantities collected increased and in February 1917 the Sanitary Inspector and the municipal Advisory Board responsible realised the limitations of the present deposit site, where the remaining capacities were estimated to last for a maximum of 12 more months.[231] Both, Town Council and Military Magistrate had already explored alternative solutions beyond the selection of a new deposit site and, based on the experiences made with the self-designed incinerator at the city of Karibib, they agreed on the construction of a similar but slightly improved incinerator at the existing deposit site.[232] Quotations for a tender had been solicited on parallel in December 1916[233], and the Municipality was prepared to provide some of the necessary building materials in order to bypass potential shortages in metal supply.[234]

Just like cities in the metropole, Windhoek debated the improvement of its street lighting, which had been identified as urgent matter during the last months before the First World War broke out as the relevant committee meeting minutes illustrate.[235] According to these minutes, the Council compared all options but the committee members expressed their hesitation in terms of granting a concession to run the lighting system as a private business. Technical experiences of other towns in DSWA were taken into consideration as well and the debate focused on the question to either install a municipal gas works or an electric power station. In this respect Windhoek mirrors classic debates that equally evolved in cities at the metropole as I have already summarised (see 3.3.2). Interestingly, the already mentioned engineer Erich Merten, who was commissioned to construct the municipal sewage system, likewise offered to prepare the quotation and tender procedures for the lighting system. Due to this personal coincidence, his company was among those directly asked to make a bid. Other firms were either based in DSWA or leading companies from Germany such as *Siemens-Schuckert* or, at a later stage in

---

[230] NAN SVW E.1.e, transcript of letter by Police Sergeant Kröber submitted on 5th May 1914, sheet 18.
[231] NAN SVW G.5.at, letter by Military Magistrate dated 17th February 1917, no sheet number.
[232] NAN SVW G.5.at, copy of letter by Public Works Department dated 7th March 1917, no sheet number.
[233] NAN SVW G.5.at, public notice dated 23rd December 1916, no sheet number.
[234] NAN SVW G.5.at, undated template quotation form, no sheet number.
[235] NAN SVW S.3.f, Volume 1, minutes of commission meeting dated 15th January 1914, no sheet number.

June 1914, *Allgemeine Elektrizitäts-Gesellschaft* (AEG).[236] As a consequence of war, the projected street lighting and the construction of a power station had to be postponed. The construction of a proper electric power plant was further delayed over the following decades. This can be proved based on a collection of relevant regulations published in Official Gazettes during the 1920s and 1930s[237] as well as a letter debating the advances on the matter in negotiations with the Administration from 1944.[238]

Aside from such basic amenities, Windhoek's European inhabitants embraced technological advances in certain domains and made frequent use of all the various offered postal services. In order to meet demand, the telephone network had been continuously extended throughout the analysed interwar period. In central parts of the town the necessary wires and poles were increasingly considered as blights and that they posed an obstacle to traffic. In 1912 the German Imperial Post Office started to replace the poles and overhead wires with underground cables along Windhoek's main street, then called Kaiser-Wilhelm-Street.[239] New, stronger cables with 50 fibres were expected to serve the growing demand, and two years later the Post Office continued to extend its underground networks in the adjacent streets of the city centre. These improvements formed a core part in the preparations for further projected extensions.[240] Archival sources indicate that most of the telephone system's users were businessmen and public institutions, as a request by the Post Office to reduce service hours on Sundays and Public Holidays suggests which was eventually approved of by the Town Council.[241] It does match with the relatively expensive annual rates for a landline which, in 1916, were just slightly lower for private households (£ 7/10) than those for commercial businesses (£ 10/-).[242] A wireless station was commissioned and constructed in 1913/14 and provided for Windhoek's fast link to other nodes in Africa and Europe, helping to bypass submarine cables dominated by foreign powers.[243]

---

[236] NAN SVW S.3.f, Volume 1, letter by Carl Bödiker & Co. dated 8th June 1914, no sheet number.
[237] NAN MWI 5/11, e.g. The Province of the Cape of Good Hope Official Gazette dated 11th April 1930, 540-61.
[238] NAN MWI 36/32/37, copy of letter by Town Clerk dated 14th June 1944, no sheet number.
[239] NAN SVW P.4.d, letter by Imperial Post Office dated 27th April 1912, sheet 8.
[240] NAN SVW P.4.d, letter by Post Office dated 18th February 1914, sheet 17.
[241] NAN SVW P.4.d, letter by Post Office dated 18th November 1912, sheet 9.
[242] NAN SVW P.4.d, public notice published in *Reuter-Telegramme* on 1st May 1916, sheet 24-5.
[243] NAN SVW P.4.f.

Whilst telecommunication and the exchange of information traditionally played an important role in SWA's lifestyle, the White community was not interested in a large scale availability of electrical mains. Petitions or administrative notes on this subject cannot be traced in the available archival files and demand for (private) power generation remained limited to few businesses such as the cinema at city centre or manufacturers and craftsmen at the urban fringe. As part of Windhoek's preparations for a municipal electric power station, the administration nonetheless projected the provision of private supplies and calculated with the installation of 3,000 electric lamps for domestic purposes.[244] Although it was not expressed in this file, it can be assumed based on the relevant building files that the African quarters at the Location was not to be linked to the electricity network. Generally the findings suggest a very selective implementation of new technologies where electrical household appliances played an insignificant role. It supports the assumption of SWA as a society, where conservative values were maintained and where the availability of cheap Indigenous labour as domestic servants reduced the need to substitute certain tasks by machines, as was the case at the metropole.

The 1914 regional exhibition (Landesausstellung), which was organised as a four-day event, mirrors SWA's habits, preferences and demands at those days. First of all, access for African visitors was strictly limited to three and a half hours on the very last day and it cost one mark admission fee.[245] Besides state-of-the-art exhibits in agriculture and technical equipment like heavy machinery, which were linked to an all-encompassing competition for prizes and awards in terms of their respective innovation, one of those categories listed "Native education" just like "architecture and construction engineering."[246] In this respect the exhibition itself revealed the intention behind such "education", which was aimed at the preservation of an African labour force just sufficiently trained to take care of the hard manual labours, in turn ensuring the European community's convenience.

4.2.4   Traffic

Despite some local specificities, debates related to traffic in Windhoek did in many respects mirror those general developments in the metropole I have summarised in the planning journals' evaluation (see 3.3.4). Similar to European cities the different modes of transportation were competing for space in SWA's cities and motor vehicles slowly made their way into daily life routines. Their quantity remained

---

[244] NAN SVW S.3.f, Volume 1, drafted letter by Municipality dated 7th February 1914, no sheet number.
[245] NAN SVW A.6.a, Mitteilungen des Arbeitsausschusses der Deutsch-Südwestafrikanischen Landesausstellung 1914, undated, sheets 1-2.
[246] NAN SVW A.6.a, idem, sheet 4.

fairly limited throughout the full interwar period analysed here, which in turn did not create many of those days' debates concerning the construction of arterial or bypass roads that typically dominated the debates in Europe. In conclusion, the topic effectively only entered the political arena and legislative efforts by the late 1920s/early 1930s.

Motor traffic

Aside from demography, the limited traffic quantities can at least partially be attributed to the taxation system introduced in the interwar years, as well as they were a result of SWA's remote geographical position which in turn made the import of all related products from vehicles and spare parts to petrol an expensive issue. In 1929 the Legislative Assembly agreed on the introduction of a new tax on imported motor spirits and made it compulsory to obtain a licence for the sales of petrol at same occasion.[247] This tax complemented those fees and taxes already imposed on owners of motor vehicles for several years. They had to pay an annual licence fee under the conditions of the *Licences, Wheel Tax and Motor Vehicle Licence Instalments Draft Ordinance*[248], where the tax correlated with the vehicle's weight. The latter two taxes formed part of the local authorities' main revenues which they received from the Administrator of SWA.[249] These frameworks were amended in 1937 and, by then, still allocated 50 percent of the wheel tax to that local authority where it had been collected. The petrol tax, by contrast, was linked to a vehicle's weight.[250]

Despite these levies, motor traffic was on the rise anddebates about potential traffic regulations can be traced among the archival sources which help to distinguish between 'real' and 'anticipated' traffic problems. The Legislative Assembly was forced to address a different kind of bypass in 1931, when it passed an ordinance in order, "to provide for the construction of motor by-passes in fences across public roads"[251] which presented obstacles to many roads outside the actual urban areas. These motor by-passes were constructed to link Windhoek with other towns and were usually fenced in at both sides to cross private pastoral land and intersecting public roads, which were used by horse-drawn carriages and for driving cattle and other animals. The discussed *Roads (Motor By-Passes) Draft Ordinance* was aimed to organise the maintenance of such bypasses. Windhoek's collection of

---

[247] VPLA First Session, Second Assembly 1929: 69, 84-5.
[248] VPLA Fourth Session, Second Assembly 1932, 18, 22-4.
[249] VPLA First Session, Third Assembly 1934/1935: 25.
[250] VPLA Third Session, Third Assembly 1937: 31, 50-1, 58-9.
[251] VPLA Third Session, Second Assembly 1931: 12.

264

traffic regulations issued by other cities across the Union of South Africa was equally telling.[252] These regulations represented a wholesale mix between typical elements of a road traffic act and traffic planning, ranging from the designation of parking areas to the much debated question of stop streets. Stop streets monitored by one or two traffic officers, if necessary, were considered a sufficient alternative to control motor traffic at street intersections, where traffic lights – then called "robots" – appeared to be unnecessary.[253] These stop streets seemed to have been of particular relevance to Windhoek's administration, as those sections are under-lined in several copies of Provincial Gazettes and other documents imported from South Africa.[254] In terms of legal powers it was disputed among the city's admin-istration whether or not local authorities had the statutory powers to order their establishment. Windhoek's Town Clerk had eventually been instructed by the At-torney General that these streets formed just one small part of the powers at the Municipality's discretion. From the legal documents he forwarded to the Town Clerk, the Attorney General concluded,

> "[t]his fortifies the opinion already conveyed to you that under sub-section 17 of section 158 of Ordinance 24 of 1935 your Municipality has the powers necessary to esatblish [sic] stop streets, and to do a great many other things which fall under the general term control of traffic."[255]

Other options used to effectively control the perceived traffic problem were speed limits[256] and the closure of defined roads, or sections thereof, as was applied to Windhoek's central areas. Firstly, bans on driving cattle and through traffic with carts were imposed under German rule on Park Street in 1905[257] and along Kaiser-Wilhelm-Street in 1911, from which deliveries were exempted only[258] but it was later followed by restrictions on vehicular traffic at large. From 1933 such regula-tions were applied to parts of François Street under the provision that this ban would be retained just as long as it were deemed necessary, and the minutes reveal opposing opinions put forward by two Board members too. Suggestions were made to expropriate the owners of adjacent parcels under these circumstances in

---

[252] Contained in NAN MWI 5/11.

[253] NAN MWI 5/11, *Municipal Magazine* Vol. 20, No. 237 May 1937: 3.

[254] E.g. NAN MWI 5/11, The Province of the Cape of Good Hope Official Gazette dated 11th July 1942: 539; Copy of *Municipal Magazine* Vol. 20, No. 237 May 1937: 3.

[255] NAN MWI 5/11, letter by Attorney General's Office dated 27th March 1942, no sheet number.

[256] E.g. NAN SVW S.4.i, copy of Police Order dated 26th June 1914, sheet 57.

[257] NAN SVW S.4.i, letter by Imperial District Officer dated 17th May 1905, sheet 3.

[258] ADSWA 1911: 151.

order to widen the street to both sides[259] but the idea was not followed up within the interwar years. In fact, official complaints about traffic congestion as public nuisance are virtually absent in the administrative files. Two exceptions can be traced to 1913 and 1919 respectively when, in the former case, a local citizen submitted a petition to the Municipality about the continuous dust nuisance caused by heavy traffic in front of his house in Stübel Street. According to his description, the traffic furthermore posed a danger to children, due to what he summarised as 'irresponsible' Indigenous carriage drivers.[260] The second complaint made by the Director of Posts and Telegraphs, referred to the nuisance of noise caused by the removal of silencers from all sorts of motor vehicles,

> "with the result that Telegraph and Telephone work at times is impossible when these vehicles start, stop or pass the Post Office."[261]

Both nuisances reflected a problem equally reported by Merki for the early European context, before streets were paved and society grew accustomed to the new noises.[262] Aside from such complaints, the overall situation does fit with statements made in newspapers and journals. The South African *Municipal Magazine* commented in 1937.

> "A word of warning was given recently in the Zoutspansberg Review against minor municipalities magnifying their traffic difficulties, and by the provision of unnecessary by-laws creating traffic difficulties where, for the moment, none exist." And the article finally concluded that, "[s]ome control of traffic is necessary, even in the smallest town, but there is little to be gained by anticipating problems which may never arise."[263]

The commentator called upon the authorities responsible to calm down and wait for the actual results, before they indulge themselves in hypothetical preparations. Instead of the phenomenon's exaggeration, the author referred to the opportunity to benefit from experiences made at other municipalities once the problem really occurs. Growing densities in towns or the persistence of slow (agricultural) vehicles in villages created individual challenges that rendered the formulation of blueprint solutions impossible and asked for tailor-made solutions instead. This article can be considered as another reflection of circulating planning ideas and tools.

---

[259] NAN RTO UA3, Resolution 16 in Minutes of the Townships Board's meeting held on 10th November 1933, no sheet number.
[260] NAN SVW S.4.i, letter by Jacob Frantzen dated 20th January 1913, sheets 51-2.
[261] NAN SVW V.2.c, letter by Office of the Director of Posts and Telegraphs dated 30th October 1919, no sheet number.
[262] Merki 2008: 58.
[263] NAN MWI 5/11, *Municipal Magazine* Vol. 20, No. 237 May 1937: 3.

Windhoek's "Trolley Line"

As has already been mentioned, Windhoek's early development was pushed after the completion of a first railway line connecting the capital with the port at Swakopmund in 1902. All railways were constructed as narrow gauge lines and later extended into the southern parts of SWA. Whilst those interregional lines were later retrofitted to comply with cape gauge – the prevailing track gauge in southern Africa – the existing extensions within the township were preserved. Although some sources call it tram[264], the official records usually referred to it as "Trolley Line."[265] The archival documents highlight its significance for public health purposes[266], in particular for the removal of night soil and refuse. In addition it was used to transport building materials on a network measuring approximately ten kilometres in length at its heydays.[267] Although the Official Gazette as well as the Legislative Assembly later permitted owners of appropriate private vehicles to use the rails for passenger transportation, this use remained of marginal significance once the railways eventually shut down their services on these inner-city sections. Therefore, a passenger coach is mentioned in one administrative record only.[268] In contrast to developments at the metropole, Windhoek's trolley had not been electrified, and its initial ownership was subdivided between a majority of governmental sections and minor municipal additions, before all sections were fully transferred to the Municipality based on a hire-purchase system in 1923.[269] Operations were carried out by the Municipality as a letter by SWA's Director of Works from 1922 states.

---

[264] E.g. Bravenboer 2004: 37.

[265] E.g. NAN MWI 117/1/44. For Pretoria it was ruled that, "[t]he word 'trolly' [sic] shall mean any vehicle plying for hire and used for any other purpose than the conveyance of passengers" whereas, "[t]he word 'Tramcar' shall mean any vehicle drawn or propelled by mechanical power running on rails in the streets and used for the conveyance of passengers." (NAN MWI 5/11, Municipality of Pretoria – Traffic By-Laws. Section 2 (j) and (k), as promulgated by Administrator's Notice No. 330 dated 3rd July 1935, no sheet number).

[266] NAN MWI 117/1/44, letter by Town Clerk dated 1st March 1922, no sheet number.

[267] NAN MWI 117/1/44, summary of inventory dated 10th October 1921 in conjunction with Resolution No. 626 in Minutes No. 146 of Ordinary Council meeting dated 27th October 1927, where it explains that 50 sections equal 250 metres; no sheet numbers.

[268] NAN MWI 117/1/44, letter by headman of Rehoboth railway station dated 15th January 1922, no sheet number. Despite Georg Bräuer's offer to sell all local surplus stock to Windhoek, the Municipality did only negotiate about the purchase of locomotives but not the passenger coach (written reply by Town Clerk dated 19th January 1922, no sheet number).

[269] NAN MWI 117/1/44, Resolution No. 337 in Minutes No. 60 of Adjourned Council meeting dated 20th August 1923, no sheet number.

"I would further point out that it is the rails, points, etc. which are leased to you but the system as laid down is left to you to control, […]."[270]

From late 1923 use of the trolley system was strictly limited to sanitation purposes and road repairs as part of the contractual agreements signed between Administration and Municipality.[271] The removal of night soil was usually carried out by small teams of changing Indigenous subworkers and one permanent White staff member who supervised those procedures, and in whose responsibility laid the punctual removal as well as the safety of all employees. Particular precautions and responsibilities were vested in the White foreman at the trolley section around the artillery depots, whilst the Indigenous staff members were completely demoted to second-class subworkers.[272] The work with those heavy trolleys during night-time and on still unpaved streets made this job dangerous, as several reports about accidents suggest.

First recorded cases date back to 1919[273], when the White overseer was instructed to report on the cause for the accident in order to prevent similar incidents in future. These reports were regularly complemented by statements of the persons involved to collect eye-witness accounts from both, Indigenous labourers and their supervisor. Due to the administrative procedures on how to record the African workers' accounts, their reports were in many cases made to fit with their supervisor's statements and lack credibility. Since the Indigenous witnesses were usually illiterate, the reports were prepared and written down by their direct superior administrative staff member. Moreover, such statements were often translated and regularly blamed the wrong-doing on the African person's side. The African workers mentioned did not bear full names and just signed the minutes with "X."[274] As a consequence, official statements about injuries among the Indigenous workers tended to play down their full extend. For the first case in 1919 the official record summarises that, "[t]he native Ezack (2) reported sick next morning […]," but,

---

[270] NAN MWI 117/1/44, letter by Director of Works dated 21st March 1922, no sheet number.
[271] NAN MWI 117/1/44, letter by Director of Works dated 8th November [1923], no sheet number.
[272] NAN SVW S.4.i, Anweisung für die Betriebsleiter dated 27th April 1917, sheet 94.
[273] NAN MWI S.W.M.13, letter by Sanitary Inspector dated 8th August 1919, no sheet number.
[274] NAN MWI S.W.M.13, accident report dated 8th August 1919, no sheet number.

"[a]s this boy has not as yet resumed duty I have made enquiries but can get nothing to prove that the injuries are serious."[275]

Although this record was produced on 11th August and refers to statements made by the supervisor Mr Kriebel, it ignored the latter's earlier written account in which Kriebel states that he saw that, "[…] Isaak 2 am Kopf verwundet war."[276] The same file contains other similar cases and biased reports which subconsciously conveyed the message of Black workers' unsuitability to drive vehicles like trolley locomotives. Africans who fell victim to such accidents could count themselves lucky, if they were not dismissed afterwards and still received their full payment and food rations while being hospitalised[277] but they did not receive any kind of specific compensation for their injuries. In late 1920s the Council eventually decided to substitute Windhoek's trolley system for a motor vehicle, and in 1927 the Town Clerk approached the railway authorities in order to sell off the municipal rail stocks in view of this projected transition.[278] Except for a small strategic reserve to be used for potential construction works, all remaining stocks were sold or leased until 1942.[279]

Throughout the interwar period many efforts were made to formally integrate SWA's transportation infrastructure into South African administrative structures. The Territory's railways and harbours were subsequently amalgamated with their counterparts in the Union, and similar steps were taken once civil aviation started to play a role. A motion by the Legislative Assembly drafted in 1938 to request the Union Government to transfer legislative powers over civil aviation to SWA was dropped after its first discussion among the Assembly members.[280]

If the above urban challenges in traffic and the regulations they induced are considered, it can be concluded that the vast majority addressed issues of the European community. The Indigenous population by contrast was subjected to discriminative rules and habits, as already exemplified by those accidents with trolleys, or

---

[275] NAN MWI S.W.M.13, letter by foreman at Municipal Compound Mr Knight dated 11th August 1919, no sheet number.
[276] NAN MWI S.W.M.13, undated accident report by Heinrich Kriebel but attached to the accident report dated 8th August 1919, no sheet number. "Isaak 2 was wounded at his head" (author's translation).
[277] NAN MWI S.W.M.13, Statement made by William Jaarsaack dated 5th June 1920, no sheet number.
[278] NAN MWI 117/1/44, letter by Town Clerk dated 1st September 1927, no sheet number.
[279] NAN MWI 117/1/44, letter/rental contract by Town Clerk's Office dated 19th November 1942, no sheet number.
[280] VPLA Fourth Session, Third Assembly 1938: 5, 36.

by further interventions that aimed at their exclusion from most modern means of transportation. First regulations in that direction were introduced under German rule as a consequence of repeated complaints, such as those expressed by Windhoek's Mayor about the misconduct of Indigenous carriage drivers.[281] They were blamed for their arbitrary use of street space which posed a danger to other road user but their most severe offence apparently was their 'talkativeness' while having a seat on the carriage with some of their companions instead of walking at the front of the draught animal. The Mayor complained about their impudence to sit while working and implicitly draws the image of laziness when referring to their 'talkativeness.' He came up with a solution and recommended thorough inspections by traffic police officers one or two times a week as a potential 'cure' to this perceived offence. Just three months later an Imperial Decree was issued that ruled, besides other matters like the rule of the road, that Natives were not allowed to take a seat on the carriage unless it was absolutely necessary.[282] Contraventions to those rules were subject to hard fines.[283] By public notice promulgated on 1st February 1916 the rule of the road was switched from German (right-hand traffic) to English (left-hand traffic) provisions.[284]

4.2.5 Public health

In contrast to many colonial cities, Windhoek was usually not affected by tropical (infectious) diseases due to its climatic and geographic conditions. This fact was generally confirmed by the German public health officer Dr Seibert in his expertise on the Government's fight against malaria, he had prepared by December 1911.[285] He, nevertheless, felt obliged to point to man-made threats which favoured the spread of transmitting mosquitoes in town. Carelessness regarding wastes such as tins scattered in gardens and a lack of maintenance for drain pipes and storage basins represented ideal breeding grounds for mosquitoes. He recommended to keep these facilities in good and functioning conditions, and to remove the garbage in order to limit the risks for malaria. Apparently his recommendations were not

---

[281] NAN SVW S.4.i, letter by Mayor dated 5th August 1910, sheet 1.

[282] NAN SVW S.4.i, Section 4 of "Verordnung des Kaiserlichen Bezirksamtmannes von Windhuk betreffend das Ausspannen und den Straßenverkehr im Bezirk Windhuk" as promulgated on 18th November 1910, sheets 13-5.

[283] The first regulations date back to German rule: ADSWA 1910: 223.

[284] NAN SVW S.4.i, public notice dated 26th January 1916 published in *Reuter-Telegramme* on 1st February 1916, sheet 67.

[285] NAN SVW G.5.u, sheet 2.

implemented thoroughly as 12 recorded cases of malaria in 1912 prove.[286] Occasionally, the Municipality had to fight against fly pests as was the case in 1920.[287]

Recorded infectious diseases

The advantageous natural environment did not prevent the emergence of other diseases, and on 25th May 1915 the Medical Office published a list with all diseases which had to be reported within 24 hours after diagnosis. Among them were cholera, dysentery, plague, smallpox and typhus.[288] During the First World War and in its immediate aftermath, the administration paid particular attention to the spread of infectious diseases. Although the fear of such incidents was deep-seated and recurring in many statements on Windhoek's urban development, actual cases remained limited and mostly resembled problems that occurred frequently in industrialised cities at the metropole too.[289] All preserved documents extending over the period from 1918 to 1920 suggest sporadic but intense peaks for measles and scarlet fever.[290] Measles hit Windhoek particularly hard in September and October 1918 but it was described as a predominantly Native problem, and its spread to the European community had to be prevented by all means. Indigenous schools were temporarily forced to close down as of 9th September, and, by Military Magistrate's order issued on the same day, rigid regulations were imposed on the Indigenous population, effectively curtailing their freedom of movement to a minimum.[291] In order to prevent the spread of measles, Natives were neither allowed to leave the city without written permission nor were they allowed to leave the confines of their Locations. Africans working for the Municipality were officially exempted from these restrictions and received permits for their walk back and forth to the city, as long as there was no reported case of measles among their family members. All other employed Indigenous persons had to remain at their employer's premises so as to make sure the usual amenities of their services were still available to the Europeans. Employers were requested to report any potential infection. All those one-sided measures were unable to prevent the disease from spreading, and cases of measles eventually were reported among the Indigenous and White population, indicating the uselessness of segregationist efforts. Due to insufficient statistical

---

[286] NAN SVW G.5.u, sheet 7.

[287] NAN MWI S.W.M.13, letter by Town Clerk dated 19th July 1920, no sheet number.

[288] NAN SVW G.5.u, sheet 13.

[289] TPR (1926) February: Clarke: 249-51. In his article, Clarke refers to measles, whooping cough and scarlet fever as the most significant infectious diseases registered in the City of Liverpool for the time period 1915 to 1923.

[290] NAN MWI S.W.M. 2, no sheet numbers.

[291] NAN SVW E.1.g, sheets 8, 10-11b.

data it is difficult to judge on the proportions of infected persons among African and European communities.

In consequence, precautions for White children were taken almost three weeks later when 'their' kindergartens were closed down, and clear instructions on who might still attend school had been handed out on 28th September.[292] The municipal librarian Mr Schuh was convinced about the contagious effects of Indigenous servants returning the books with their bare hands, and he already complained about the spread of scarlet fever in June 1917. He then asked for a disinfection of the books and his premises since his child had, according to his opinion, contracted the disease due to contact with infected books.[293] In case of confirmed cases of scarlet fever, the respective family was put under quarantine and all its contacts under considerate observation.

Another major threat was posed by Spanish Influenza which eventually hit the town twice. A first peak can be detected in late 1918, when the Town Council sent its sympathies to those who had lost beloved ones and wished all others affected a speedy recovery.[294] Despite one officially recorded contraction in June 1919, another second and relatively mild wave was recorded in 1920. This limited extent was credited to the health officers' preparations whilst their preparatory documents did point to the severity of waves in Durban as well as Great Britain and Australia hitting these places at the same time. Maynard Swanson gives an estimation of 130,000 deceased Africans during the 1918 peak.[295] For Windhoek, the only significant peak of this second wave can be identified for November 1920 with 13 confirmed cases but no deceased.[296] Nonetheless, the administration was, from time to time, faced with exceptional incidents such as one recorded case of anthrax that had been identified in a specimen from a dead municipal ox. Dysentery and typhus remained singular and rare incidents with a maximum of one case per year. Further, typhus caused a lot of fear among the German Inspector for the Location as a letter from 1913 proves.[297] In his attempt to convince the District Office about the necessity to construct a new Inspector's Office at Windhoek Location, he ex-

---

[292] NAN SVW G.5.u, sheet 45.

[293] NAN SVW B.9.c, sheets 125-6.

[294] NAN SVW S.3.b, minutes of the Council meeting from 27th November dated 4th December 1918, no sheet number.

[295] Swanson [1977](1995): 39.

[296] Coquery-Vidrovitch equally refers to two waves for the Spanish Influenza in Africa and dates them for 1918-19 and 1921-22, with a total of several million deceased across the continent (Coquery-Vidrovitch 2011: 52).

[297] NAN BAU B.78, letter by Imperial Natives Commissioner dated 10th December 1913, sheets 2-3.

plicitly referred to the potential spread of this disease, if he would be prevented from carrying out his duties on the ground due to sick leave. Keeping the Location clean was argued to be of prime relevance to the wellbeing of Indigenous and European inhabitants and could only be entrusted to a White civil servant. He tried to substantiate his argument with the occurrence of eight typhus cases, which had to be treated at hospital within the two months of November and December. According to his description, two infected patients deceased and both were inhabitants of the Location.

Several (circular) letters, with some of them issued by the Union of South Africa, requested immediate reports on every new case of a contracted infectious disease, and gave instructions about recommended time periods for quarantine or appropriate disinfection of beddings.[298] In contrast to those formal lists used to record cases for the Indigenous population, which remained very limited in terms of the information covered, those statistical forms for the White community were elaborated ones asking about every detail of the patient's living environment and potential contacts who might have been infected. The registration of cases among the European community was handled with negligence and great delay in contrast to the African inhabitants. At the occasion of an outbreak of diphtheria in 1920, the Medical Officer of Health urged for the establishment of a separate station at the hospital to put patients with contagious or infectious diseases under quarantine.[299] The need to rush in 1920 comes as a surprise considering the Town Council's foreward-looking approval of a separate ward in 1916. Back then the Municipality soon withdrew her application to construct a public ward and trusted in the ward to be constructed at the expense of the Catholic hospital instead, which never materialised.[300]

Provision of health care to the African population

Besides the provision of hospitals for the European community, it did fall under the Municipality's responsibilities to take care of the Indigenous hospitals. This matter caused a long dispute between Windhoek's local administration and Government representatives at the District Office, which ensued between 1910 and 1914 and eventually remained unresolved due to the First World War.[301] The Municipality considered herself to be overwhelmed by all the duties she had to per-

---

[298] NAN MWI S.W.M. 2, e.g. letters dated 19th/ 21st February, 7th August, and 25th October 1919, no sheet numbers.
[299] NAN MWI S.W.M. 2, letter dated 24th September 1920, no sheet number.
[300] NAN SVW G.5.u, sheets 18-9, 22.
[301] NAN SVW E.1.h.

form since self-administration was granted to her the year before.[302] Instead, she asked the District Office to step in since the Municipality was of the opinion that welfare for the Indigenous population belonged to the Government's responsibilities. The Municipality expressed its willingness to reimburse parts of the running costs as grant from the Native Tax revenues. Aside from the financial obligations, further bureaucratic obstacles were faced in relation to the hospital's selected site at the city's fringe, once the District Office had submitted its plans to replace the existing corrugated iron sheds through permanent structures. On this occasion, the Government made it clear that applicable legislation prohibited the construction of permanent buildings on land that did not belong to government bodies. The Municipality was in turn asked to sell the Indigenous hospital's plot to the Government.[303] In 1911 it had been agreed that the Native hospital's current compound should not be reduced by municipal interventions to less than three hectares, and that Windhoek would lease the plot to the Government free of charge.[304]

As a reaction to some of the infectious diseases, the German Government of SWA drafted a Vaccination Order regarding smallpox for the whole population. Since the files do not contain hints about an outbreak of this disease, the order has not been officially enacted.[305] Its content is telling, considering the discriminatory distinctions made in the treatment between White and African subjects. The authors of the draft order seemed subconsciously convinced of the Africans' contagious nature, for it required all Coloured[306] people to take part in booster injections every five years. White residents had to be vaccinated against smallpox just twice in their whole life. Of course, one can argue the Indigenous population would thus be better protected but the required quality standards for their vaccinations were significantly lower than those for White persons. The regulations did not require the vaccination to be carried out by an approved German physician, as was the case for Whites, but could have been done by anyone licenced to do so. Besides, the vaccine was subject to lower quality standards, and it was put under the discretion of the responsible District Office whether or not the routine check-up five to ten days after the vaccination was carried out without formulating clear criteria for this decision. In contrast to Whites, African patients were not entitled to receive a personalised certificate of vaccination. They were supposed to be centrally administered by the Native's Registry. Disobedience against the vaccination orders could

---

[302] NAN SVW E.1.h, letter by Acting Mayor dated 28th December 1910, sheet 6.
[303] NAN SVW E.1.h, letter by District Office dated 30th June 1914, sheet 15.
[304] NAN SVW E.1.h, letter by District Office dated 3rd October 1911, sheet 8.
[305] NAN SVW G.5.af, sheets 1-3.
[306] Coloured was in this case used in opposition to White people, and not in its later sense under South African rule (see 4.3.2).

274

be punished with the rules permitting up to 14 days of imprisonment and hard labour for any Coloured person who tried to contravene the order.

The German draft vaccination order was symbolic for the attempted dualism in SWA's society which de facto extended beyond the realms of residential segregation. Even marketing campaigns by chemical companies trying to sell insecticides played the game of dualism and clichés, when they emphasised the adequacy of their product,

> "[…] zur Vertilgung von Moskitos und anderen Krankheitsträgern in Eingeborenenhütten, Ställen, Lagerräumen, aber auch in den Behausungen der Europäer [...]."[307]

Africans' discrimination: The matter of venereal diseases

The Indigenous population was subject to further discrimination in terms of public health which remained a persisting motive throughout the interwar years: Regardless of what the causes for such accusations might have been, they were constantly associated with the occurrence and spread of venereal diseases. In 1917 the Native Affairs Office carried out a medical examination of all Natives within the borders of Windhoek Municipality. In his request for support from the local authority dated 31st March, the Officer in Charge Bowker stressed the least possible interference with their work duties as the examination of 500 persons could be done in one hour. The examination was in full accordance with governmental intentions, "[a]s it is the wish of the Secretary for the Protectorate that no natives escape this examination [...]."[308] More than two decades later the Legislative Assembly of SWA was anew made to discuss the issue, after venereal diseases broke out at *three* government school hostels in the district of Otjiwarongo. The Assembly used these incidents as a pretext and agreed on a motion that focused on the examination and treatment of *all* Indigenous servants employed at schools and hostels, as there seemed no doubt about who caused the spread of the disease. The final motion stated, amongst other things,

> "that the House recommends that the Administration should cause all coloured and native servants in all government schools and hostels to undergo a thorough medical examination, and if there should be the slightest doubt or suspicion as to their state of health that they be immediately dismissed, and subjected to medical treat-

---

[307] NAN SVW G.5.u, sheet 3. "[…] to exterminate mosquitoes and other causative organisms in Native huts, stables, storerooms but also in dwellings of the Europeans [...]." (author's translation).
[308] NAN SVW G.5.v, sheet 2.

ment and that great care should be taken that their successors are clean and healthy, and that in future periodical medical examinations be conducted in order to establish satisfaction as to their state of health."[309]

The accusations and the repressive focus against the Indigenous population are all the more irritating considering Windhoek's notoriously bad reputation concerning the European community's moral behaviour since its re-establishment in 1890. Zollmann has described the early impressions and experiences made by the first missionaries who took seat in the young town since 1895. They complained about the marginal interest in the Gospel and the little willingness to participate in Church services among both, the European and Indigenous communities. The second missionary Wandres, who arrived at Windhoek in 1899, particularly bemoaned immoral tendencies like singing 'dirty songs' in front his home which he attributed to the White community: "natürlich ist dies von Weißen geschehen, denn die Farbigen sind noch nicht so weit in der Cultur."[310] In face of his complaints it remains questionable and inconsistent, why he equalled the singing of such songs with 'culture' but he, of course, had to justify 'his' personal civilising mission which was one of the reasons for those songs as Zollmann argues. Missionary Wandres had explicitly condemned the intercourse between his German fellows and "Kaffir" women.[311] Some of those relations were based on long-term relationships but many can clearly be counted as prostitution, which represented one of the ever-present nuisances in Windhoek and formed a cornerstone of the town's bad reputation. The municipal files recorded a first official order issued by the Mayor in 1910, when he urged the Town Police to take action against offensive prostitution around public buildings in the city centre.[312] Apparently their interventions were of limited impact only, for new complaints were again recorded at central premises in 1917. This time, one property owner wrote a drastic letter dated 18th August, in which he referred to the impossibility to rent out his new apartments due to the 'nuisance' over the road.

> "I beg to request the Municipality to take steps in this matter and to cause that remedy would be obtained, as it seems not to bewell-timed [sic] to carry on such a business in a much frequented street and I cannot be expected to build houses and

---

[309] VPLA Fourth Session, Third Assembly 1938: 7, 19, 30.

[310] Cited in Zollmann 2010: 217-8. "of course this was done by Whites, for Coloureds are, as yet, not that far advanced in culture" (author's translation).

[311] It is nonetheless interesting to note how this critique about conditions in Windhoek, then still a relatively small village, resembles those days' upper class criticism about immoral behaviour and physical degeneration in large cities as mentioned by Schott (Schott, Dieter, *Die Großstadt als Lebensraum des modernen Menschen*, Bielefeld: Transcript 2014: 74).

[312] NAN SVW O.1.e, sheets 1-2.

make expensive improvements and that after this the rooms stand empty merely because a whore has chance to earn more in this section of the town than outside the town."[313]

Even though the last clause was earmarked for deletion, it pointed to the owner's frustration in face of his actions to fight the prevailing housing shortage (see 4.2.6). Less than two months later, on 9th October, the Office of the Military Magistrate was able to report progress in the matter of prostitution as the lady had indeed moved to the outskirts. In this respect it might have helped that Windhoek was one of the best staffed police stations in the German Empire with a ratio of one police officer on 175 inhabitants, which in fact surpassed that of Berlin in those years with one on 350.[314]

The perceived problem of interracial intercourse persisted more or less obvious over the following decades, and was one way to undermine the interventions in support of segregation. Mixed concubinage was practiced relatively frequently and actually in the city centre too, despite the legal and social sanctions imposed on them.[315] One of the frameworks providing for those sanctions can be cited as another proof for the direct circulation of ideas: in 1934 the Legislative Assembly approved of a motion on the prohibition of, "illicit carnal intercourse between Europeans and Natives"[316], which was based on similar rules already applicable in South Africa.

Africans' discrimination: The matter of alcoholic beverages

Indigenous private life was subjected to many additional legal restrictions later referred to as the "Durban system", where it first applied since 1916 as a rather comprehensive system before it was copied by many South African cities.[317] One of the legal restrictions affected Indigenous peoples' consumption of alcoholic beverages. The idea to restrict the access to 'intoxicating' drinks has a long tradition, which can be traced back way into the German period. Already in 1910 the Official Gazette published a public notice, laying down the customs regulation for the import and distribution of alcoholic drinks in DSWA that explicitly prohibited

---

[313] NAN SVW O.1.e, no sheet number.
[314] Zollmann 2010: 218. Zollmann in this context refers to the average ratio of one on 2,500 at the turn of the century.
[315] Zimmerer 2001: 94-109; Zollmann 2010: 238-42.
[316] VPLA Seventh Session, Second Assembly 1934: 8.
[317] Maylam 1995: 30. Aside from restrictions on the consumption of alcohol, Maylam lists night curfews and pass inspectors as some of the measures interpreted by contemporaries as 'model.'

the sales of all such drinks to Africans.[318] The only exception was made for the community of mixed ancestry called Rehoboth Bastards, who were allowed to buy a very limited quantity based on special permits to be obtained from the Administration. In general terms this legislative framework can be interpreted as (late) administrative reaction to the experiences of the Namibian War. Although the war turned out to be genocide against the Indigenous population, the European community was caught off guard at the beginning and it created a situation where some remote farmers were left vulnerable to assaults, which has created a deep-seated fear among the Whites of a repetition that must be prevented by all means. Aside from such negative stigmatisation further rules included well-meaning precautions to protect the Indigenous population from bad-intending employers. Section 10 stipulated,

> "Dienstherrschaften können indes den in ihren Diensten stehenden Eingeborenen geistige Getränke, aber höchstens glasweise, verabfolgen, jedoch dürfen die Getränke nicht die Stelle des Lohnes oder eines Teiles des Lohnes vertreten."

In the face of the dissatisfaction among the African population, those strict rules had been marginally relaxed over the following years through the introduction of so-called "Kaffir beer", a kind of light beer with a limited maximum alcoholic content of usually three percent specifically brewed for Natives.[319] This alleviation only granted the right of alcohol consumption to male Africans, whilst women and all minors under the age of 18 years were still not allowed to drink. Furthermore, this decision initiated intense debates among the White community which basically covered two dimensions: an economic one and a social one. Within the economic arena the production of such Kaffir beer was an additional market, first welcomed by local White breweries and run as a private business but later, de facto, dominated by the Municipalities themselves.[320] In 1932 a new legal framework was prepared including municipal rights to produce Kaffir beer and to fully control the sales of such beverages which led to strategic alliances with the breweries.[321] The

---

[318] ADSWA 1910: Verordnung des Gouverneurs von Deutsch-Südwestafrika, betreffend die Einfuhr und den Vertrieb geistiger Getränke in dem südwestafrikanischen Schutzgebiet, no page number. Also for the quote: "Masters may nevertheless dispense alcoholic beverages to Natives under their employment, but no more than one glass at a time, and as long as those beverages do not serve to compensate for their wage, or parts thereof." (author's translation).
[319] NAN MWI 36/26/37, Resolution No. 385 in Minutes of Finance Committee meeting dated 29th March 1932, no sheet number.
[320] Maylam has illustrated how these municipal beer monopolies, first introduced in Durban in 1909, formed a common practice in South African cities too and curtailed informal sources for the economic independence of Black women (Maylam 1995: 32).
[321] NAN MWI 36/26/37, ibid.

municipalities then urged other public authorities responsible to prevent Indigenous inhabitants from 'illegal' beer brewing, allegedly as part of public health considerations. As a side-effect, this prohibition of illegal brewing did mean the prevention of another economic basis for the African community and echoed similarly repressive developments in Johannesburg.[322] This part of the economic dimension was linked to the usual tax levied on such beer and where illegal brewing did mean tax evasion; a thorough supervision of those illicit activities was in the public authorities' interest. Such an offence could, upon conviction for three cases, be used as official pretext to expel an Indigenous person from the eligibility to reside at an urban area, which in turn led to its deportation to one of the rural Native Reserves.[323] The quantities produced and distributed had to be controlled for another economic argument. The excessive abuse of such beer needed to be prevented, since contraventions would have harmed the Indigenous population in its 'function' as a labour force. Their availability for the Europeans' convenience had to be maintained at highest possible levels, and excessive consumption was therefore considered undesirable. At this point the coloniser's views on beer brewing did mirror the prevalent power relations in the colonial context as Cooper has argued.

> "Harassing squatters, beer brewers, and prostitutes underlined the hegemony of the dominant class, whose orderly ways were made to appear legitimate, while the illegitimacy of lower-class life was rubbed in by the humiliation of police raids."[324]

The social dimension focused on the prevention of riots and civil unrest or disobedience which might be caused by excessive beer consumption. In this direction legal provisions were introduced or renewed in *Proclamation No. 4 of 1932*[325], which restricted the sales of alcoholic beverages to specific eating houses and beer halls, clarified on police powers to confiscate illegal beer and made larger meetings among the African community subject to official permits. Section 8 requested under paragraph (i),

> "(o) the conduct, control, supervision and restriction of meetings or assemblies of natives within the urban area: Provided that no such meeting or assembly may by virtue of any such regulation be prohibited except with the special approval of the magistrate after reference to the local police officer and an officer of the urban local

---

[322] Nightingale 2012: 273.
[323] NAN MWI 5/8, Minutes of Conference on Native Location Affairs dated 19th March 1931, no sheet number.
[324] Cooper 1983: 8.
[325] NAN MWI 36/26/37, *Proclamation No. 4 of 1932*. In: Official Gazette published on 1st February 1932: 7706-12.

authority appointed under sub-section (1) of section *ten* and then only if there be reasonable ground for believing that the holding of such meeting may provoke or tend to a breach of the peace."[326]

Social considerations remained exclusively focused on the European community's concerns and did not cover the potential risks attached to alcohol addiction and their consequences for an African family.

Air pollution and other administrative concerns

Aside from debates about transmissible diseases and a focus on Indigenous impacts, the topic of public health did cover other nuisances as well. At the times of the First World War Windhoek's economy did not include any significant heavy industries and, by 1918, much of the economic revenues were in fact still generated by small and medium size craftsmen, as the Municipality's Annual Report explained.[327] Nonetheless, the town was affected by its own kind of smoke nuisance: in late 1913 several residents submitted complaints about local bakeries, which reportedly produced a lot of smoke while baking bread but where no proper chimneys were attached to the ovens. Since the Town Council considered itself not to be in charge of this matter, it asked the District Office for intervention and to request the bakeries to install chimneys of at least six metres in height.[328] The successful implementation of this request was reported by the District Office on 10th March 1914, by when all bakeries possessed such a chimney, except for one where negotiations were still pending.[329] Specific details on the heating system used here are not contained in the files. That is equally the case for other building projects, although the warm and dry climatic conditions significantly reduce the demand for such systems. Based on restrictions on imported goods wood was used as the main fuel, at least during the first half of interwar years.[330]

In addition, the Municipality held the responsibility for various seemingly unrelated matters. For example her Public Health Department did check the functionality of fire extinguishers[331] whilst in 1912 the Mayor's Office dealt with a petition demanding for the introduction of a voluntary municipal health insurance scheme. The petition was rejected based on draft calculations according to which an insuf-

---

[326] NAN MWI 36/26/37, *Proclamation No. 4 of 1932*. In: Official Gazette published on 1st February 1932: 7709-10.
[327] NAN SVW S.3.o, Annual Report for 1918, sheet 10.
[328] NAN SVW B.1.e, letter by Town Council dated 1st December 1913, sheet 3.
[329] NAN SVW B.1.e, letter by District Office dated 10th March 1914, sheet 4.
[330] E.g.: NAN SVW S.3.o, Annual Report for 1918, sheet 10.
[331] NAN SVW S.4.h.

ficient number of premium-paying members and an anticipated free-rider problem would render its introduction impossible, and the idea was postponed until a compulsory scheme would be introduced.[332]

4.2.6 Housing

During the analysed time period Windhoek faced two, to a certain extent opposing, trends in housing. They do match with those tendencies prevalent in the metropole as condensed from the analysis of the planning journals (see 3.3.1), and do focus on quantitative and qualitative aspects. The Municipality had to deal with a constant shortage in accommodations for governmental staff members. In order to deal with all staff members who applied for governmental housing, but were put on the official waiting list, the Housing Board was established as institution responsible. The file containing all minutes of the Board's meetings since 1926 helps to show, how tense the situation remained throughout interwar years up until the end of the Second World War.[333] The urgency and attention paid to this topic can further be illustrated by the frequency of meetings, which in peak periods took place almost on a weekly basis. In preparation of its meeting on 8th May 1926 the Chairman admitted that the number of applicants by far exceeded the number of available homes.[334] At this meeting several rules were formulated in order to cope with this structural imbalance. First of all, 18 governmental premises were strictly reserved to accommodate those staff members holding the highest offices, such as the Secretary for SWA, Attorney General, Medical Officer, Native Commissioner or Master of the High Court.[335] The minutes then clearly instructed on the selection criteria to be considered for future occupants of governmental housing. It was stated that,

"[...] the following order of precedence shall be observed, in so far as 'Rank of Applicant' is concerned, subject however to the principles laid down by the Administrator:

1.) Administrative and Higher Professional & Technical,
2.) Clerical and Lower Professional & Technical,
3.) Non-prescribed posts in General Division, Police and Prison Warders,
4.) Temporary Officials."

---

[332] NAN SVW V.3.d, letter by Mayor of Windhoek dated 11th June 1912, sheets 9-10.
[333] NAN RHO UA1.
[334] NAN RHO UA1, letter by Chairman of Housing Board dated 29th April 1926, no sheet number.
[335] NAN RHO UA1, Minutes of Board meeting held on 8th May 1926, no sheet number. Equally for the following quote.

The minutes were concluded with a remark about the scarcity of quarters for married officials.

Windhoek's Housing Board

Throughout its existence, the Housing Board had to manage the governmental housing stock and its job resembled a switchyard in its attempt to deal with the administration of shortages. The Board had the power to order a current tenant to vacate a premise in order to give space to another staff member, and therefore the minutes are full of applications and decisions indicating the subsequent high turnover. The Board took the responsibility as custodian of governmental housing and decided on necessary maintenance works and repairs. Aside from those routine tasks it ruled at its meeting on 18th June 1926, that subletting of governmental premises by employed officials was prohibited[336], so as to secure its own prerogative position. Subletting was only permitted, if the Board expressed its explicit consent. Over time the Board had to deal with changing demand as well, and ordered the alteration of single quarters into married quarters as happened with the so-called "Six Men House" in 1926, when costs for renovation works for the building's preservation in its current function were considered too high.[337] There remained a specific housing shortage for single females in governmental employment as a letter by the Director of Education indicates in late 1926, and this shortage was exacerbated by the Board's decision to apply a strict separation of sexes at its hostels.[338]

Despite the difficult overall situation, the Board did not have the power to order the construction of new dwellings as a remedy to improve those circumstances in the long run. The Board itself admitted in 1943 that it,

> "[..] has in the past, and will continue, to do everything in its power to promote the building of additional houses for the servants of the Administration."[339]

The only option was to launch a petition to the Legislative Assembly as happened in August 1929, when attention was paid to the supposedly "serious overcrowding" at SWA's sleeping accommodation for police officers as well as to the general shortage of Government houses. In this case the Housing Board had to admit that

---

[336] NAN RHO UA1, Minutes of Board meeting held on 18th June 1926, no sheet number.
[337] NAN RHO UA1, letter by Mr Borchert dated 9th September 1926, no sheet number.
[338] NAN RHO UA1, letter by Director of Education dated 8th December 1926, no sheet number.
[339] NAN RHO UA1, Minutes of Board meeting held on 20th August 1943, no sheet number.

22 applications for dwellings could not be satisfied immediately whilst there was, at least then, no official shortage in single quarters.[340] Towards the end of the analysed period the Board changed its opinion and saw its main responsibility in the allocation of existing dwellings. Therefore, it refused to further take care of any alterations and conferred those tasks to the Works Department.[341] During the Second World War the situation worsened again and the Board's decisions were driven by social considerations, when the prohibition of subletting was relaxed so as to leave no wife alone in case her husband was on military service.[342] One remarkable exception to such social concerns was stipulated at the meeting on 7th August 1940 when, upon instruction by the Administrator, the Board was asked to give priority to, "[…] applications for houses by Civil Servants with salaries exceeding £700 per annum […]."[343] The increasing urgency of the developments becomes apparent, if some of the Board's following relevant decisions are compiled. Since 27th January 1941 the rules had been amended one more time, now giving access to three reserved houses if the applicants were married and had dependants living with them, a regulation that was upheld during the remaining wartime.[344] At the occasion of the meeting held on 15th March 1943, the Board noted the Administrator's ruling that governmental housing was only available to staff members on active duty, whilst this right ceased upon their retirement.[345] An urgent shortage of single quarters for female employees had, again, to be conceded at the meeting on 28th April 1943.[346] Since 12th May 1943 applications for governmental housing by Union staff members were directly put on waiting lists only, as it was already impossible for the Board to accommodate domestic staff members from SWA.[347] This procedure blends with a general policy change introduced by SWA's administration in early 1930s, in order to give preference to local applicants trying to acquire farm land.[348] Faced with the persistent shortage, the Administration, in late 1943, allocated the necessary resources to construct at least 14 new

---

[340] NAN RHO UA1, Notices of Questions dated 13th October 1929, no sheet number.

[341] NAN RHO UA1, handwritten note signed by several Board members dated 6th May 1938, no sheet number.

[342] NAN RHO UA1, Minutes of Board meeting held on 6th March 1940, no sheet number.

[343] NAN RHO UA1, Minutes of Board meeting held on 7th August 1940, no sheet number.

[344] NAN RHO UA1, Minutes of Board meeting held on 27th January 1941, no sheet number. The file lists the following houses for the Master of the High Court, the Accountant and the Additional Native Commissioner.

[345] NAN RHO UA1, Minutes of Board meeting held on 15th March 1943, no sheet number.

[346] NAN RHO UA1, Minutes of Board meeting held on 28th April 1943, no sheet number.

[347] NAN RHO UA1, Minutes of Board meeting held on 12th May 1943, no sheet number.

[348] Botha 2008: 241.

houses within one year.[349] As of 24th October 1944 the Board managed a total of 111 houses in Windhoek, and 16 thereof were still reserved for specific governmental job functions.[350] 36 employees were then on the general waiting list whereas another 12 were registered on the list for so-called "artisans houses."[351]

Housing shortages during wartimes

This structural deficit was exacerbated during periods of political uncertainty or economic downturns, when construction activities were in particular unable to meet the demand. Similar to some, but not all, of the trends summarised in the planning journals' accounts (see 3.3.1), both World Wars had severe impacts on the housing situation in SWA. They both contributed to a construction deficit, and therefore the Municipality tried to assist needy persons in their search for a home during the First World War. In July 1916 several advertisements were published in local newspapers or at the public notice board and serve to illustrate the range of requests. Quarters for single persons were always appreciated, although those for men tended to be available at farms outside the city itself[352] whereas women preferred a place in central areas.[353] This demand was complemented by a family in need of a large and well equipped house, as another public notice demonstrates.[354] In contrast to the metropole SWA experienced a significant difference in its construction activities. Though the shortage itself was, of course, exceedingly felt in 1918, construction activities were reported as 'lively' by the Municipality in her official Annual Report. The erection of new buildings was primarily hampered by high prices for imported building materials, and the shortage was exacerbated due to the specific geopolitical circumstances in SWA where the administrative future, at that time, remained unclear. The report refers to the simultaneous physical presence of two administrative teams.

---

[349] NAN RHO UA1, Minutes of Board meeting held on 10th November 1943, no sheet number.
[350] Unfortunately the file does not contain another overview to compare these numbers with previous years. The other documents usually refer to the applications for governmental housing dealt with at the meetings and to alterations proposed to be carried out in existing buildings.
[351] NAN RHO UA1, Minutes of Board meeting held on 24th October 1944, no sheet number.
[352] NAN SVW W.9.b, public notice dated 14th July 1916, sheet 3.
[353] NAN SVW W.9.b, advertisement published in *Reuter-Telegramme* on 11th July 1916, sheet 4.
[354] NAN SVW W.9.b, public notice dated 15th July 1916, sheet 6.

284

"Die Bautätigkeit war verhältnismäßig rege; sie war veranlasst durch die noch immer nicht völlig behobene Wohnungsknappheit, nicht zuletzt infolge der gleichzeitigen Anwesenheit der englischen und deutschen Beamtenschaft."[355]

According to the 1918 Annual Report, Windhoek was able to manage her financial obligations based on tax revenues, with 70,000 marks accrued from income tax and without the need to take out additional loans.[356] In the building trades however, high prices for materials formed a similarity to the trends summarised for the metropole. Many owners of building companies tried to counterbalance them by curtailing their own as well as their employees' wages to the lowest possible level.

"Immerhin lähmten die hohen Preise das Geschäftsleben erheblich. Dies gilt namentlich vom Handwerk. Für Hölzer, Farbe, Glas, Zement u.a. mussten Preise bezahlt werden, die nur unaufschiebbare Arbeiten erlaubten, und jedes Arbeiten auf Vorrat ausschlossen. Um überhaupt Arbeit zu bekommen, begnügten sich die Handwerker fast durchweg mit erhebliche [sic] geringerem Verdienst."[357]

An inflation driven by both, soaring prices for building materials and rising labour costs due to a lack in labour supply, as can be concluded as a war effect for the metropole, was not the case in SWA. To the contrary, craftsmen were heavily competing for the scarce contracts in order to keep their businesses up and running. A similar trend can be summarised during the Second World War, although SWA was by then more tied up in the geopolitical considerations and had to subordinate itself under the full control exercised by South Africa. Legal uncertainties and loopholes to bypass those restrictions, which still existed to a limited extent during the First World War, had by then been closed. Available stocks for housing construction were centrally managed by the Controller of Buildings and the Controller of Building Materials, both based in the Union, as Town Clerk Kerby explained in a report he produced about one of his travels to South Africa in 1944.[358] At the occasion of this trip he visited a concrete work from where he originally

---

[355] NAN SVW S.3.o, Annual Report for 1918, sheet 10. "Construction activities were relatively lively; much of them were caused by the still not yet remedied housing shortage in consequence of the parallel presence of English and German civil servants." (author's translation).

[356] NAN SVW S.3.o, Annual Report for 1918, sheet 9.

[357] NAN SVW S.3.o, Annual Report for 1918, sheet 10. "After all, high prices have significantly paralysed business life. This is particularly true for craftsmen. Prices due on wood, paint, glass, cement, etc. did only allow for those works which could not be delayed any further, whilst they prohibited all works to build up stocks. In order to obtain work in the first place, craftsmen had to content themselves with significantly lower earnings." (author's translation).

[358] NAN MWI 36/32/37, Extract from the Report of the Town Clerk, Capt. G. Kerby, on Proceedings whilst in the Union dated 28th June 1944, no sheet number.

expected a reply on the feasibility of the scheme for Klein Windhoek Location he had submitted before. His focus of attention changed during the stay and he acquainted himself with some housing schemes for Europeans and all other activities were concentrated on housing for this part of the population thereafter. This decision was based on the scarcity of available supplies which Kerby summarised.

"The position of material is very serious and it is clear that supplies of cement cannot be obtained until the end of the year, as the military authorities have requisitioned the whole output of S.[outh] A.[frica]. As a consequence even Government programmes in the Union are brought to a standstill and substitutes are being used whenever possible. The Controller certainly will not give any permits for making cement bricks and in future we will have to provide for lime bricks."[359]

The restrictions imposed, which diverted most available materials to military projects, subsequently curtailed all other construction activities except for the mentioned governmental schemes. Kerby's visit to the Union does not only help to illustrate the intensity of links between SWA and South Africa, which exemplify his importance as agent to 'push' certain projects based on the personal networks he had established during all those travels. He used them to convince the South African authorities in charge of housing projects about Windhoek's unique situation in terms of regional development, for he,

"[…] endeavoured to impress with the particular situation in which Windhoek is placed being isolated far away from any neighbouring town where a surplus population could be accommodated."[360]

Due to the accruing urgency of the city's housing shortage and based on individual agreements with the Controllers, he therefore suggested to the Town Council that Windhoek should embark on her own municipal housing scheme to be submitted for governmental approval. An application for building materials to construct 25 houses was, in turn, expected to be considered favourably by the authorities. Just one week later the Council adopted a resolution that backed such an undertaking, since all other projects' prospects for implementation were rendered dire.[361] Housing construction was temporarily made a governmental domain, and it fits into this context that in the same resolution it was noted that the Railway Administration

---

[359] NAN MWI 36/32/37, Extract from the Report of the Town Clerk, Capt. G. Kerby, on Proceedings whilst in the Union dated 28th June 1944, no sheet number.
[360] NAN MWI 36/32/37, Extract from the Report of the Town Clerk, Capt. G. Kerby, on Proceedings whilst in the Union dated 28th June 1944, no sheet number.
[361] NAN MWI 36/32/37, Resolution No. 39/516 in Minutes No. 516 of Ordinary Council Meeting dated 5th July 1944, no sheet number.

were able to obtain six prefabricated houses which could, upon their completion, be inspected by the Council for future replication in municipal projects.

The Great Depression's impact on housing

Quantitative shortages remained an issue throughout the full interwar period and, aside from wartimes, the problem became evident during the Great Depression. Official statistics point to the economic downturn's side-effects on the housing market, for many unemployed persons and families were apparently unable to rent a flat or house, and had to move out. As a consequence, in November 1932 the Municipality registered a total of 115 vacant flats with a dominant share of two-room[362] (42) and three-room[363] (40) apartments as well as additional 108 available single rooms.[364] The following two statistics, which were compiled in June 1933 and April 1934 respectively, recorded a decrease for almost all categories, and in September 1934 virtually all reserves within the existing housing stock were exhausted and residential vacancy rates dropped to the structural minima for fluctuation. Only 40 flats remained available, 12 thereof with two rooms and 16 with three, whilst 47 single rooms were vacant at the same time. Over the period of those two years, the calculated monthly loss of rent for all vacant premises, including offices and shops, was reduced from £850 to £280, whilst the number of buildings affected by vacancies was cut by more than half, from 128 to 60. Similarly, economic improvements became visible in the available offices whose numbers dropped from 30 in 1932 to just nine in 1934.

Qualitative aspects

The topic of quality can be separated into two categories, where the first focuses on actual dangers to public health, such as overcrowding, whilst the second deals with the living qualities available to tenants due to their socio-economic status.

In order to address the first category each municipality kept record of housing conditions prevalent in her township, and these statistics were regularly complemented by specific reports from the Medical Officer of Health and the Building Inspector responsible. Based on the results of such assessments local authorities took action as part of their social welfare interventions. When the economy started to consolidate after the Great Depression, SWA was integrated into South African efforts to fight overcrowding and slum-like housing conditions. These efforts,

---

[362] Equivalent to the British one bedroom flat.
[363] Equivalent to the British two bedroom flat.
[364] All figures: NAN MWI 5/6, Report "Leerstehende Wohnungen nach dem Stande vom 10. September 1934", no sheet number.

287

which gained specific momentum in the second half of the 1930s, in fact resembled similar interventions taken by the British Government (see 3.3.1). Therefore, local authorities were eligible to apply for several financial schemes issued by the South African Government in Pretoria to subsidise housing projects. Windhoek was at least aware of such financial assistances, as a collection of filed circulars dispatched by the Department of Public Health, "to each Urban Local Authority in the Union" proves.[365] *Circular No. 4 of 1936* instructed the authorities that the framework of such schemes basically provided two options to initiate the construction of projects in the style of council housing, which was here labelled as "subeconomic housing" and catered to classified groups of needy persons. As part of the first option, Government and the respective local authority constituted a financial co-partnership, according to which both parties would bear losses at equal terms. This co-partnership should explicitly cover losses due to interest rates and redemptions charged at lower-than-market levels as well as reduced typical charges, such as for depreciation, loss of rentals or fees. As part of the second option the Government would enter into a contract with a company or society that would be backed by a local authority to form a municipal undertaking. Though the circular does not refer to this term and only mentions the prohibition of profits, this organisational structure represents the second alternative. Both schemes, financial co-partnership and municipal undertaking, should serve the goal to provide,

"[…] for the reduction and prevention of overcrowding, the repair or the closure and demolition of dilapidated, insanitary and unfit dwellings and removal of slum and unhealthy areas."[366]

The Government in this exceptional case extended her aid beyond the realms of Europeans, as the circular goes on to explain.

"Originally subeconomic [sic] loans were only granted for assisting local authorities to provide housing for the very poor among the European and coloured population, but the scheme has since been extended to cover the provision in locations of additional housing for natives consequent upon the enforcement of measures for ridding the local authority's areas of slum conditions which are a menace to the public health."[367]

---

[365] NAN MWI 36/32/37, Circulars No. 4 of 1936 dated 23rd March 1936; No. 12 of 1936 dated 7th August 1936; No. 14 of 1936 dated 4th November 1936; No. 8 of 1937 dated 31st March 1937, no sheet numbers.
[366] NAN MWI 36/32/37, Circular No. 4 of 1936 dated 23rd March 1936, no sheet numbers.
[367] NAN MWI 36/32/37, Circular No. 4 of 1936 dated 23rd March 1936, no sheet numbers.

What makes this circular particularly interesting, is its final definition of the minimum qualities that should be aimed for in terms of housing the different communities.

> "It is generally agreed that the minimum accommodation for Europeans and better class non-Europeans should consist of dwellings each comprising at least two bedrooms, a living room with kitchenette, a bathroom, closet and small outhouse, but that the minimum accommodation to be provided for non-Europeans generally should be left to the discretion of the local authority."[368]

The above formulation is another clear symbol for the discrimination of the African population, who was not made subject to strict regulations but was left subjected to arbitrary decisions taken differently at every municipality. Furthermore, it explicitly supports the assumption of social hierarchies among the Non-European communities whilst the Europeans are in this case considered as one homogenous entity. All dwellings constructed under the provisions of such schemes were intended for letting purposes only, although exceptional conditions applied to individual owners as applicants who were also eligible to apply for the subsidies. These provisions resemble a mix of parallel British planning legislation and its attached financial frameworks, to encourage the construction of council housing as Stephen Ward has summarised.[369] Generally adapted to the South African conditions with its segregated society, those circulars, on one hand, operated with standards and regulations similar to those first applied under the *Housing, Town Planning Etc. Act 1919* based on the Tudor Walters recommendations. But they on the other hand echo later amendments like the ones initiated by the *Housing Act 1930* which covered slum clearance and redevelopment as a new element. *Circular No. 4* has been complemented by *Circular No. 14 of 1936* in order to clarify on those cities that were already eligible to grants for "slum elimination", though Windhoek was not among the 20 Municipalities listed – in fact, none of them was in SWA.[370]

Soon after the dissemination of relevant information on those housing schemes for the general poor, a more specific version was started concerning "Housing the Aged Poor"[371], for which a first instalment of £50,000 (out of a total £100,000) was made payable with the 1936-37 governmental budget. Accommodations con-

---

[368] NAN MWI 36/32/37, Circular No. 4 of 1936 dated 23rd March 1936, no sheet numbers.

[369] Ward 2004: 38-40.

[370] NAN MWI 36/32/37, Circular No. 14 of 1936 dated 4th November 1936, no sheet number.

[371] NAN MWI 36/32/37, Circular No. 12 of 1936 dated 7th August 1936, no sheet numbers.

structed under the provisions were to be let out to eligible occupants by charitable organisations, whilst construction and maintenance belonged to the local authority's duties. Eligibility criteria for future occupants were kept relatively open but prescribed that such dwellings,

> "[…] should not be made available for persons who are still capable of doing an ordinary full day's work on an economic basis."[372]

Similarly, it was not pre-defined what kind of accommodation should be constructed, neither in terms of "class" which referred to its construction as separate cottages or hostels nor in its costs; those decisions were left to the local authority's discretion. Although it was originally ruled out that persons with physical disabilities may be accommodated at those schemes, a new regulation as promulgated in *Circular No. 8 of 1937* reported about the amendments made by the Treasury so as to extend the scheme to, "needy persons who are totally unfit physically."[373] The local authorities were urged to make sure that only needy people rented those dwellings, and in order to keep it this way, the Department of Public Health recommended to revise the building standards accordingly.

> "Local authorities will thus have to display caution in not building in excess of the likely requirements of the class of accommodation under consideration."[374]

Whereas the standards described above primarily aimed at the reduction of potential threats to public health posed by overcrowding or unacceptable sanitary conditions, the second category of quality addressed the factual range of buildings that has been constructed to accommodate governmental staff members in particular. Already under German rule the Imperial Building Department (Kaiserliche Bauverwaltung) drafted and constructed houses of different standards for various public institutions. As will be demonstrated for the example of Indigenous railway workers (see 4.3.6), the African population formed the bottom of the social hierarchy where cheapest possible standards were applied. Similarly, European employees were subjected to differentiations according to their ranks – although not at such drastic levels. One German case gives a particularly instructive example for the top-ranking personnel and their expectations about residential amenities, which eventually filled one complete individual file and whose correspondence between

---

[372] NAN MWI 36/32/37, Circular No. 12 of 1936 dated 7th August 1936, no sheet numbers.
[373] NAN MWI 36/32/37, Circular No. 8 of 1937 dated 31st March 1937, no sheet number.
[374] NAN MWI 36/32/37, Circular No. 8 of 1937 dated 31st March 1937, no sheet number.

290

the Imperial Post Office as client and the building administration extended over almost two years.[375]

In a letter dated 30th December 1908 the Post Office asked the Building Department to draft plans for the construction of a new residential building ready to accommodate two high-rank civil servants of the postal service with the 'usual' amenities, and specifically enquired for a quotation based on the following minimum requirements that,

> "[…] für jeden der beiden Postbeamten zwei Zimmer nebst Badezimmer und Veranda und unter Umständen ein Vorratsraum vorzusehen wäre."[376]

Gottlieb Redecker's plans for such a building measuring more than 265 square metres in size were estimated at construction costs of 35,000 marks. Although this budget was later cut down to 30,000 marks[377], the Post Office still insisted on a completion close to the original plans and requested several changes and improvements, like a warm water tap[378] or to repaint the living rooms with red oil paint.[379] None of the other documented administrative housing projects in German times proved to be equally difficult. Such prices roughly indicate the average building standards of those years, since dwellings constructed for members of the same institution, but at a slightly lower rank, cost 36,500 marks[380] whilst employees of the railways at the lowest rank were accommodated for 32,000 marks[381]. The last quotation covered the costs for three married staff members instead of two unmarried in the previous examples, though. All these buildings were made subject to the supervision by health officers who had to ensure the maintenance of habitable qualities. Such inspections did not apply to Indigenous accommodations and, except for the abovementioned financial schemes and some minimum requirements for domestic servants, etc., Indigenous housing needs were primarily addressed within the confines of the Location (see 4.3.3).

---

[375] NAN BAU B.49.

[376] NAN BAU B.49, letter by Kaiserliches Postamt dated 30th December 1908, sheet 2. "[…] it should be arranged for both post office clerks to have, each of them, two living rooms along with a bathroom and veranda as well as, potentially, a store room" (author's translation).

[377] NAN BAU B.49, letter by Kaiserliches Postamt dated 9th April 1910, sheet 22.

[378] NAN BAU B.49, letter by Kaiserliches Postamt dated 13th October 1910, sheet 149.

[379] NAN BAU B.49, letter by Kaiserliches Postamt dated 6th October 1910, sheet 152.

[380] NAN BAU B.47, final calculations, sheet 220.

[381] NAN BAU B.51, letter by Kaiserliches Eisenbahnkommissariat des Nordens dated 27th June 1911, sheet 165.

Preliminary conclusions

Based on all evaluated archival sources and plans, it can firstly be conceded that qualitative housing debates in Windhoek had a different focus from what was discussed in the metropole. This difference does not just originate in the city's distinction between Indigenous and European housing schemes; it has rather to do with a lacking inclination to follow such reformist movements which inspired and initiated many projects in industrialised countries (see 3.3.2 and 3.3.5). Comprehensive modernist development schemes such as those produced under Ernst May in Frankfurt were – regardless of their actual results and the comments they then received – neither replicated nor thought of in Windhoek. Instead, qualitative debates were on one side interpreted as means to visually demonstrate European superiority in comparison to the Non-European communities. On the other side since this was then considered to be 'common knowledge' anyways and done at a rather impalpable level, the question of quality eventually revolved around social distinctions among Europeans. This range can be illustrated based on some of the governmental building projects for employees at various ranks.

In contrast to the metropole, a distribution of certain amenities such as electrical appliances or other technical equipment in private households did not play such a significant symbolic role. As already described in the subchapter on technical infrastructures (see 4.2.3), this difference can be attributed to the availability of comparatively cheap domestic servants which limited the demand for 'modern' appliances. At the same time, it did not make this backlog appear as a 'disadvantage' or 'setback' for SWA's White community in comparison to urban lifestyles in the metropole. In Windhoek such amenities were not interpreted as similarly important status symbols, because much of the manual labour which had to be substituted by machines in Europe could here still be delegated to Indigenous labourers. Housing projects in SWA's capital furthermore remained fragmentary and limited in their extent, barely exceeding a handful of buildings constructed at the same time. Despite a constant shortage, no concerted efforts towards the construction of a new neighbourhood were made and all activities followed a rather piecemeal process. One of the process's essential components was the attempted implementation of residential segregation as described in the following subchapter.

4.3 Residential segregation

The dichotomous spatial separation of the European colonisers from the Black and, in SWA later on, from the Coloured population has been mentioned as a common characteristic of colonial cities by many authors (see 2.3). Yet this phenomenon cannot be described as genuine structural feature in Windhoek's development that was strictly enforced at every potential opportunity. Like in other colonial cities too, there developed spaces of encounter and hybridity. As the previous subchapters have already demonstrated, residential segregation formed just one out of many measures to discriminate the Indigenous population, serving the overall goal to create an environment of exploitation in which they were made a mere 'tool' for the White colonisers' convenience.

What follows is an analysis of the different instruments and spheres, at which segregation applied and how the mechanisms behind them worked. Similar to the debates on land speculation for the general development of cities at the metropole (see 3.3.3), land and the access to this resource played a vital role for the implementation of segregation (see 4.3.1). In contrast to reformist movements in the industrialised countries, the application of their new ideas was not intended to serve the wellbeing of all inhabitants in the colonial city but they had been interpreted to benefit almost exclusively of the ruling White minority. After a brief description of the administrative and legal frameworks involved (see 4.3.2), the Black population's largest neighbourhood at Windhoek's Location will be analysed in detail (see 4.3.3). Since it was the colonisers' intention to conceal the racialized living environments as much as possible, a limited amount of social facilities had to be maintained at the Location too (see 4.3.4). Historically, the term Coloured was used with a different connotation in DSWA, where it rather singled out the non-White population at large, in contrast to its more specific meaning in SWA where the Asian component entered the debate at a later stage. Nevertheless, this population should be accommodated at a separate Location and the plans illustrate their somewhat higher social rank among Windhoek's colonial hierarchy in comparison to the Black population (see 4.3.5). Despite all attempts at segregation, this structure was undermined at various stages and a collection of such examples is presented in a separate subchapter to emphasise the city's actual hybridity (see 4.3.6).

4.3.1 Resolution of the land question

German as well as succeeding South African legal frameworks and bureaucratic mechanisms were intended to make the acquisition of land by Whites a legitmate procedure, at least from their formal standpoint. This has already been the case under German rules which remained valid during the First World War, and in some relevant cases beyond. The acquisition of land and its administrative registration based on the land register was usually advertised in the Official Gazette (AD-SWA), and became valid in case of formal non-complaints by other interested parties.

Land registration under German rule

These procedures did at their very core exclude the Indigenous population by various means, as I will explain below based on the system's three core components. Figure 14 reproduces a typical advertisement published in the Gazette on 1st April 1911.

Making sense of this notice requires several skills and a particular knowledge about the binding legal consequences of the procedure attached, at least from the coloniser's viewpoint. The three explicit bureaucratic bars to get one's own claims recognised are indicated with numbers.

Figure 14: Example for notice on private land registration in ADSWA (April 1911)

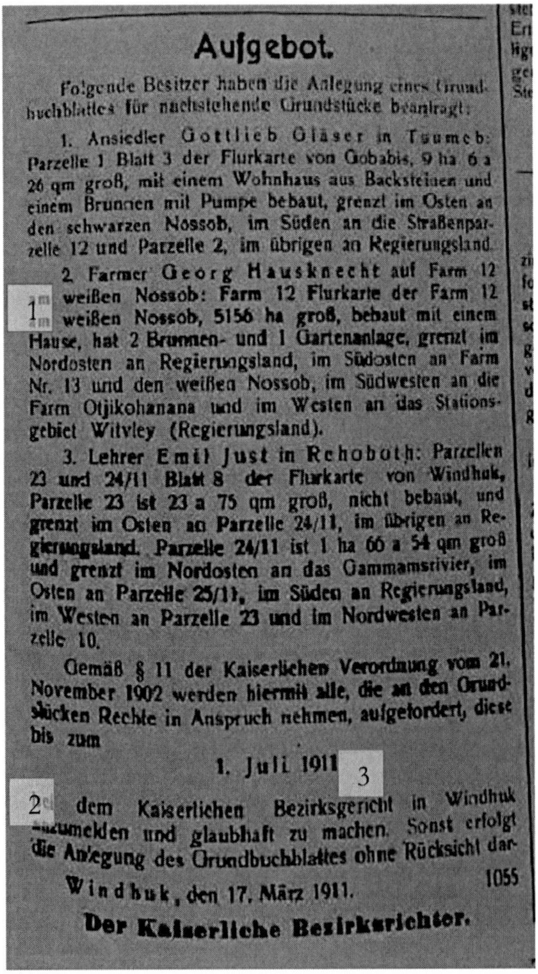

Aufgebot.

Folgende Besitzer haben die Anlegung eines Grundbuchblattes für nachstehende Grundstücke beantragt:

1. Ansiedler Gottlieb Gläser in Tsumeb: Parzelle 1 Blatt 3 der Flurkarte von Gobabis, 9 ha 6 a 26 qm groß, mit einem Wohnhaus aus Backsteinen und einem Brunnen mit Pumpe bebaut, grenzt im Osten an den schwarzen Nossob, im Süden an die Straßenparzelle 12 und Parzelle 2, im übrigen an Regierungsland.

2. Farmer Georg Hausknecht auf Farm 12 am weißen Nossob: Farm 12 Flurkarte der Farm 12 am weißen Nossob, 5156 ha groß, bebaut mit einem Hause, hat 2 Brunnen- und 1 Gartenanlage, grenzt im Nordosten an Regierungsland, im Südosten an Farm Nr. 13 und den weißen Nossob, im Südwesten an die Farm Otjikohanana und im Westen an das Stationsgebiet Witvley (Regierungsland).

3. Lehrer Emil Just in Rehoboth: Parzellen 23 und 24/11 Blatt 8 der Flurkarte von Windhuk, Parzelle 23 ist 23 a 75 qm groß, nicht bebaut, und grenzt im Osten an Parzelle 24/11, im übrigen an Regierungsland. Parzelle 24/11 ist 1 ha 66 a 54 qm groß und grenzt im Nordosten an das Gammamsrivier, im Osten an Parzelle 25/11, im Süden an Regierungsland, im Westen an Parzelle 23 und im Nordwesten an Parzelle 10.

Gemäß § 11 der Kaiserlichen Verordnung vom 21. November 1902 werden hiermit alle, die an den Grundstücken Rechte in Anspruch nehmen, aufgefordert, diese bis zum

1. Juli 1911

bei dem Kaiserlichen Bezirksgericht in Windhuk anzumelden und glaubhaft zu machen. Sonst erfolgt die Anlegung des Grundbuchblattes ohne Rücksicht darauf.

Windhuk, den 17. März 1911. 1055

Der Kaiserliche Bezirksrichter.

First of all, one needs to have access to the Gazette, in order to get an overview of such advertisements and other news which were disseminated through this medium. The ability to digest the information then needs the ability to read and adequate German skills to understand those formal notices; such sophisticated language skills were, however, regularly not provided for at schools instructing the Indigenous population. In order to verify if one's own interests were effectively concerned, it then needed familiarity with the land register to identify the individual plot's site (1). Based on the assumption that someone was indeed affected by this advertisement, he or she then needed to go to the district court at Windhoek in order to make an official complaint at the registrar's office (2). Of course, this complaint has to comply with the set deadline (3) and the person must have been able to substantiate his or her rights and claims based on some kind of official documents. In face of traditional customary rights in African societies where land was often used collectively, for example as grazing grounds by the whole community, chances were extremely limited to get the Indigenous case accepted. And, after all, this procedure takes a lot of time and money, for example for the Gazette, related travels and court fees, which most Indigenous community members were unable to spend on this matter.

Indigenous exclusion under South African rule

This bureaucratic exclusion was accompanied by direct and explicit limitations on property ownership as shown by Jürgen Zimmerer.[382] He describes the legal rules and policies according to which priority was given to Whites and, on a far less secure basis, to Rehoboth Bastards.[383] The question of non-White land ownership remained potent during interwar years, and in the administrative or legal replies it becomes apparent to what extent SWA had already been integrated into mainstream South African debates and opinions. Regarding the Black population, diverging opinions cannot be traced; existing frameworks did not arrange for Black peoples' legal eligibility to own real property, and by the mid-1920s it was already a commonly accepted practice that building plots within both demarcated Locations in Windhoek would remain in the hands of the Municipality or Government, as a letter by the Administrator's Office pointed out.[384] Similar to the Union's interpretation of enacted legislation, the Administrator made it clear that since,

> "[n]o title to the ground is being given and for the purpose of Proclamation No. 34 of 1924 [i.e. *Natives (Urban Areas) Proclamation*, see below] absolute accuracy of measurement is surely not required."[385]

The survey of plots at Locations was subsequently limited to 'rough' ones, which stood in strong contrast to the sophisticated efforts taken to demarcate European parcels or public property. During surveying activities for a new railway station and streets, several landmarks (*Grenzmarken*) to demarcate the plots were deliberately

---

[382] Zimmerer summarises, how the Indigenous Herero population has already been disenfranchised and partially deported to small and remote reserves before the turn of the century as a consequence of unequal treaties with the German colonisers (Zimmerer 2001: 25). After the Namibian War stricter rules were prepared, virtually prohibiting Indigenous land ownership in order to force them into wage labour (Zimmerer 2001: 63).

[383] Zimmerer 2001: 63.

[384] NAN MWI 36/27/37, letter by Office of the Administrator for SWA dated 27th April 1926, no sheet number.

[385] NAN MWI 36/27/37, letter by Office of the Administrator for SWA dated 27th April 1926, no sheet number.

removed, some of them by Indigenous people who supposedly used them for the erection of tents. One can argue, such disturbance of land survey procedures was an attempt to contest the colonial authorities but the official reactions by the Mayor were equally revealing in their discriminative nature. Whilst subsequent instructions were issued to White employees involved in street construction,

> "[…] that the removing of landmarks when carrying out labour which requires the lifting out of ground is not allowed"[386],

those formulations, which addressed the African population, used a harsher tone as the Director of Railways was asked,

> "[…] to point out to the foremen of the Natives there, that they will be severely punished for such offences."[387]

African individual ownership (on leasehold terms) beyond the Locations' confines was prohibited and Indigenous communal ownership remained limited to so-called 'Native Reserves.' Africans were under all these frameworks only eligible to build and own their houses, for which compensation payments applied under certain preconditions. Such payments had been discussed as part of redevelopment efforts concerning Windhoek's Location, when the existing houses should either be translocated to the proposed new site, or their demolition would be required in order to enable the construction of officially approved housing types at the existing site.[388] Regardless of the actual decision, and despite those regulations, it becomes apparent how vulnerable the African population remained. Their houses were considered fit for translocation in one to five percent of all cases but their individual compensation values had only been estimated at roughly £1 by the Administration. Hence compensation remained far less than the estimated costs for a new house ranging from £18 to £25 as documented in official minutes.

In contrast to the Black community, the situation turned out to be of a different quality for the Coloured community. In a letter dated 4th July 1933[389] the acting Attorney General Rosenow has sent his legal comments on the question, whether or not the Administrator had the power to restrict the acquisition or leasehold of

---

[386] NAN SVW V.1.g, letter by Mayor dated 11th December 1916, sheet 4.
[387] NAN SVW V.1.g, letter by Mayor dated 11th December 1916, sheet 3.
[388] NAN MWI 36/27/37, Notes of Interview by Deputation from the Town Council with the Secretary in regard to Native Location Matters, attached to a letter dated 8th December 1925, no sheet number.
[389] NAN MWI 101/4/40, no sheet number.

296

"Asiatics, Natives and Coloured people" regarding any erven[390] in a declared township[391] based on the 1928 *Town Planning Ordinance* then still in place. Drawing on previous South African court rulings in similar cases and the far too general formulations of the Administrator's powers, he had to negate this option, though not without regret.

> "Unfortunately all these provisions are too wide and general in their terms to justify any discrimination against a class or section of the community."[392]

Furthermore, the court rulings did interpret racial discrimination as class discrimination, as becomes apparent in the following paragraphs and examples of Rosenow's letter. His negative reply was nevertheless primarily based on the missing consent by the legislature. As long as such discrimination had not been legalised at this end, any municipal attempt towards the exercise of discrimination would automatically be doomed to failure – a logic consequence of a municipality's lacking power to issue statutory instruments. He did refer to the debate on public health considerations which might have been used as a reason in favour of residential segregation. Still Rosenow's statement offers an account that different opinions on segregation were still present in early 1930s.

> "It may be difficult to have a clean and sanitary township, if the native and Asiatic quarter is not separated from the Europeans, but I do not know that it is impossible. In many villages in the Union Europeans, coloured, native and coolie still live quite happily cheek by jowl."[393]

By pointing to the argument of public health and sanitary conditions Rosenow nevertheless offered a main reason to justify any legal amendments towards segregation. This statement is all the more interesting, since Dubow has emphasised how widespread the notion of racial segregation was internalised by interwar South African society, even among more liberal thinkers.[394] The road to apartheid was opened, but deviations and alternative ways still remained available.

4.3.2 Administrative frameworks

The general move towards the pure exploitation of the Indigenous population was foreseeable by other previous, and seemingly less significant, decisions as well. One example is constituted around the Location Committee, which had been estab-

---

[390] Erven or the singular erf is the Afrikaans term used in Namibia and South Africa to describe a parcel of land.

[391] Demarcated area of a local authority, vested with all powers of a Municipality.

[392] NAN MWI 101/4/40, no sheet number.

[393] NAN MWI 101/4/40, no sheet number.

[394] Dubow 1995: 157.

lished as the first official platform to debate African issues and the specific living conditions prevailing at the Location among members of the Town Council and the administration responsible. Aside from the Mayor, at least two Councillors had to be appointed as the Committee's elected members and they usually met once a year. In preparation of these meetings, they would visit the Location themselves and discuss with the Superintendent of Locations or similar persons in charge of the Location about urgent issues that needed to be resolved, though all these representatives were Whites. Those meetings represented one of the rare occasions, where the Indigenous inhabitants actually got to see a municipal representative other than the Superintendent of Locations or the Officer for Native Affairs on the ground.

Despite such relevant assignments the Committee was dissolved in 1924, without prior notice to the Superintendent of Locations. As he explains in a confidential letter addressed to the Town Clerk dated 7th November, he only found out about the dissolution by the Town Council's minutes, which did not contain any specific remark about the reasons. The Superintendent, nevertheless, stressed the significance and necessity for the Committee's work as a platform to discuss the occurring matters. Although he had sent this letter for personal reasons – since he primarily wanted to improve his own position in a competition over power and prestige with the Native Affairs office – he tried to further substantiate his argument through his hint that the Town Council's reputation might be at risk.

"As I have remarked before I believe the chief trouble lies in the fact that the council is inaccessible as a rule to the natives, and this 'OUT OF TOUCHNESS' could be remedied by the appointment of a special LOCATION COMMITTEE."[395]

Unintentionally, he had revealed another dimension of segregation which encompassed the political arena. The Town Council dealt with the Superintendent's request and came to the following resolution.

"After discussion Council resolves unanimously, on the motion of the Mayor, seconded by Councillor Menmuir, that a location Committee be not appointed, as in their opinion the Council has no power whatsoever to remedy the state of affairs in the Location."[396]

[395] NAN MWI 37/5/37, confidential letter by Superintendent of Locations dated 7th November 1924, no sheet number, emphases in original.
[396] NAN MWI 37/5/37, Resolution No. 638 taken at the Council meeting on 8th December 1924, no sheet number.

The matter was simply referred to the police and the Administrator to be dealt with. Through this decision, the Council, nonetheless, made the Location a blank spot on their imaginative map, which apparently made it a non-integral part of the official township that should, hence, be preserved as exclusively European area. Through this position Windhoek shows a striking similarity with South African cities for which Maylam has mentioned a full set of legal instruments to close down Black access to municipal political space.[397] This move to redraw one's imaginative map contrasts with the usual appropriation of the colonial territory as it had been carried out by the renaming of farms, amongst other means. Examples for this domination of space in Foucault's sense are to be found plentiful in the Official Gazette.[398]

The role of the *Natives (Urban Areas) Proclamation, 1924*

The Location Committee's dissolution in 1924 was not an act of arbitrariness but went hand in hand with the introduction of a new regulatory framework, the so-called *Natives (Urban Areas) Proclamation, 1924* as promulgated in the Official Gazette on 2nd January 1925, and which came into effect on 1st February 1925.[399] Its goals are defined in the first paragraph, where the Administrator usually announced the motives for a new legislation enacted by him. In this case he called for the improvement of Indigenous living conditions in terms of housing but he equally made clear that the influx of Indigenous residents close to the cities should be restricted. It followed the general outlines of its South African archetype introduced there one year earlier. Carl H. Nightingale has summarised *The Natives (Urban Areas) Act, 1923*.

> "[It] certainly represented in its time world history's most extensive, explicit, and complex legal plan for segregating the cities of an entire country, far more elaborate than such colony-encompassing schemes as the Raj's cantonment codes, the Colonial Office's recommendations for segregation in West Africa, or Lyautey's Moroccan urban-planning laws."[400]

SWA followed an extreme position on the division of the Territory's cities. As already described above, the Municipalities were, according to Section 1 (1) (a), allowed to demarcate specific sites for the accommodation of Indigenous people

---

[397] Maylam 1995: 29.
[398] E.g. ADSWA 1910: 129, 199, 211, 227, 301, 313; and ADSWA 1911: 5, 34, 60, 74, 91, 115, 128, 141, 153, 186, 201, 214, 226, 245, 256.
[399] NAN MWI 36/26/37, Official Gazette of SWA published on 2nd January 1925, no sheet number.
[400] Nightingale 2012: 293.

which were officially called Locations. In this section it was further stipulated that land would only be offered to the African occupants on leasehold terms and, through the formulation, "[…] for the erection thereon of houses or huts for their own occupation", any kind of Indigenous lodging business or subletting was prohibited from the very beginning. Access to Locations should fully remain under the control of the White Administration. Section 1 (1) (d) granted exceptions from the rule that Indigenous people usually had to be accommodated at those municipal Locations to all, "employers of more than twenty-five natives", if they could absolutely not agree on their employees being housed centrally. Those employers then had to maintain their own Location as approved of by the Municipality. Further exemptions are formulated in Section 6 and were basically granted to domestic servants staying at their employer's home and to Indigenous people residing at mission houses whilst all others had to reside at the Location. It remained at the discretion of the Administrator to confirm the suitability of a Location's site, and he had to give his consent to any demolition or relocation as Section 1 (2) and Section 2 explain. Section 3 made it clear that the Administrator was allowed to carry out any works he deemed necessary on behalf of a Municipality and at her expense, if she consistently did not comply with his instructions. Any kind of transaction within the Location was basically limited to contractual agreements between Natives and the authorities in accordance with Section 5 (1). Coloured people, however, fell under the specific provisions of sub-section (3), which granted them the right to occupy a plot on rental basis within the Location, until suitable accommodation would be made available to them elsewhere in the urban area as Section 9 (1) clarifies. From a formal standpoint, they were not considered to be legally of the same status like Black people – at least for some more years.

As prescribed in Section 7, the Municipalities were required to keep a separate account for all revenues and expenses related to the Location and Indigenous sources. This comprised of service fees and rental payments, though the latter needed the Administrator's approval and had, "[…] to be fair and reasonable" in accordance with Section 8 (1). Official registration of all employed Natives and their permission to reside at the Location was supposed to be done under the Provisions of Section 11. Such registrations were beneficial to the public authorities in two respects: they required the Africans to pay the so-called 'Pass Fee', and they should help to monitor the people's mobility. Only employees of the Administration and Missions were exempted from these fees. The Location's character as a temporary compound[401] for a labour force maintained for the European communi-

---

[401] In addition to the term "Location" there existed so-called "compounds" as specific form of labour shelter amid industrial sites such as the Ovambo Compound in Windhoek

ty's convenience becomes apparent in Sections 16 and 17, which both clarify on the legal right to expel and deport any "idle" or "habitually unemployed" person to their (rural) place where they belong to, or to any other Native Reserve. The clause on 'habitually unemployed' people was the pretext to be used in many cases, and, therefore, this clause was underscored with a pen in the administrative file. Municipalities were allowed to impose further restrictions in accordance with Section 20, where sub-section (2) introduces specific rules in paragraph (h) on the keeping of animals and grazing fees for stocks, and where paragraph (i) forms the legal basis for restrictions to any non-resident of a Location to enter it at certain hours. This regulation was accompanied by the curfew for Black people and the Locations were usually fenced in with a central entrance monitored by White administrative staff members. The abovementioned regulation related to the grazing fee is of particular relevance, since it helped to achieve the Administration's goal to limit the Indigenous population's sources of income other than wage labour.

Africans were regarded with universal suspicion yet without a specific evidence, since Section 21 (2) authorised the administrative staff in charge with the right to, "warrant any native reasonably suspected of having contravened any provision of this Proclamation" to further investigations. It is symbolic for the historic existing separated legal spheres, which granted African people only second-class legal status in comparison to Europeans. This was further substantiated through the application of customary law and a specific Indigenous jurisdiction as Zimmerer has meticulously described.[402] Under Section 24, the *Natives (Urban Areas) Proclamation, 1924*, also defined a "Coloured Person", which in administrative terms,

> "[..] means any person of mixed European and native descent and shall include any person belonging to the class called Cape Malays,"

whereas "Native,"

> "means any person who is a member of an aboriginal race or tribe of Africa. Where there is any reasonable doubt as to whether any person falls within this definition the burden of proof shall be upon such person."

Here, again, the modern legal principle concerning the onus proof had been reversed in order to make it fit with the colonisers' intentions.

(see 4.3.6). With regards to Johannesburg's mines Nightingale defines the compounds as "[…] severe living places for the tens of thousands of migrant all-male black workers […]" (Nightingale 2012: 230).
[402] Zimmerer 2001: 127-33.

Conclusions on African people's legal status in SWA

Within the context of the described Proclamation, Attorney General Rosenow's statements about the legal applicability of restrictions for "Asiatics, Natives and Coloured people" were, in their full scope, intended to support the idea of racial separation, and the mechanisms of land acquisition already described above were of particular relevance to the urban context. Here, Indigenous people had a crucial role to play for the economic prosperity of the towns as well as for the convenience of their White inhabitants. Therefore, they had to be excluded from the usual social and economic opportunities that cities typically offer. Indeed, this repellent environment does match with Lord Lugard's concept for the development of colonial cities with a clear separation of communities like in Nigeria, and under which the African population was actually not granted a status as urban residents.[403] Instead, they merely formed a pool of labour force that needed to be accommodated at convenient but secure distance to the European premises, without – for paternalist reasons – threatening the African rural way of living. The so-called Locations were a result of SWA's interpretation of this idea. These distinct and, at the beginnings less clearly, demarcated compounds were intended to accommodate the predominantly male African labourers working at the towns. They were actually expected to keep close contacts with their rural relatives and to move towards the urban centres for a limited time period only, before they would return home and be replaced by new arriving labour migrants. The term Location as a description for enclosed segregated residential areas was borrowed from late 19th century British Cape Colony and Johannesburg. Nightingale already underscored that this separation between social classes among the White community as well as along racial colour lines was based on "purposes of sanitation"[404]; a concept controversially debated in interwar years.[405] At first sight, one might consider this concept of temporary accommodation for labour migrants to be a success, when having a look at the reports in the Official Gazette updating on the latest monthly migration figures of Ovambo labourers, coming in to central districts from the Territory's northern border regions.[406] In fact the Locations developed into a far more complex neighbourhood than originally expected.

---

[403] Home 2015: 59-60. Home nonetheless points to the complex social stratification of urban spaces in colonial cities that have developed over time.
[404] Nightingale 2012: 241-2.
[405] Nightingale 2012: 251-55. Nightingale refers to the earliest examples of Locations established in the cities of Port Elizabeth in 1834 and East London in 1849.
[406] E.g. ADSWA 1910: 143, 182, 226, 252, 275, 301.

The Locations represented the African urban component of SWA's segregationist system whilst Native Reserves provided for their rural and remote counterparts. Zimmerer has summarised that the White minority did only represent 10 to 15 percent of the total population but they owned 80 percent of the Territory's land. This share was not just unfair in quantitative terms, it was also distributed unfair in its quality as can be exemplified based on the Native Reserves. Their sites were intended to provide the rural Indigenous community with an own agricultural basis, but – in accordance with the general goal to force the African population into wage labour – without sufficient perspectives for economic subsistence. Therefore, the Africans received barely suitable plots of inadequate size at remote places, which were rather unattractive to the White community's farming purposes[407]; some of those reserves have already been established under German colonial rule and are indicated with a "G" in the map in figure 15. The map does also display the often referred to territory of the Rehoboth Bastard community south of Windhoek and 'Ovamboland' to the north at the border with Angola. The latter area was not included in the so-called police zone.

---

[407] Werner 2002: 217.

Figure 15: Map of SWA's Native Reserves, 1924

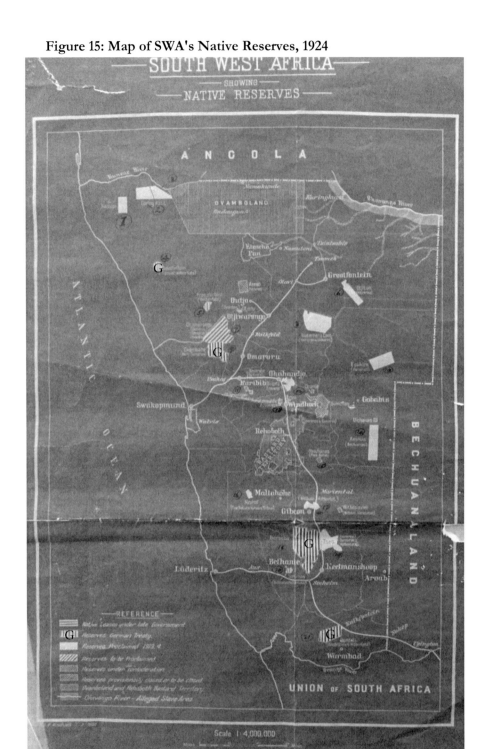

4.3.3 Windhoek's (Old) Location

Spontaneous urban Indigenous settlements, which formed the first Location in Windhoek, were noted in 1898 and were officially indicated on a map in 1903 for the first time[408], although they were unfenced, less organised and barely controlled by the German authorities back then. This relaxed attitude towards Indigenous settlements was completely reversed through the experience of the Namibian War, despite some similar calls that were made before. The atrocities between 1904 and 1908 poisoned the relation between colonisers and colonised, although the vast majority of victims were Africans. Despite this fact, the German community considered itself to be endangered by the Indigenous 'threat' and created the most extreme form of residential segregation through the establishment of concentration camps across DSWA.[409] In Windhoek, the camp's construction started in early 1904 underneath the Old Fort and combined the idea of an enclosed compound for the captured and interned enemies with their best-possible surveillance. Several pictures of the camp were taken throughout its existence and they illustrate its speedy transformation from disorganised and ramshackle huts to the neatly organised camp shown in figure 16, which represents its final outline circa in late 1904.

In the background the Old Fort and the adjacent stables marked the colonisers' impact at the hilltop position overlooking the fenced in tents for the imprisoned Herero people. Their nutshell-like tents were erected each at the same small distance in several rows along the slope and they roughly covered two thirds of the available space. One third was left as open space with one single traditional-style hut set aside as well as one larger tent that resembles a mobile army surgical hospital, although it did not bear any clear indication such as a red cross. In the picture four African children were sitting outside the camp where shrubs formed a low fence. This structure made it easy for the German troops to monitor every move of the interned Herero.

---

[408] Zollmann 2010: 224.

[409] The instrument of concentration camps has an earlier track record and was already applied by the Spanish in Cuba, later in the Philippines and during the Boer War. Zimmerer, nevertheless, highlights their structural difference from later Nazi concentration and extermination camps (Olusoga, Erichsen 2010: 194; Zimmerer 2001: 42, idem 2011: 55-6).

Figure 16: Concentration camp in Windhoek (c. 1904)

Deutsch-Südwest-Afrika - Wohnungen der gefangenen Hereros

The camp's inmates were exploited as slave labourers, either for governmental building projects like railways or rented to private businesses.[410] Food rations and general living conditions at the camps were extremely bad, which resulted in a high mortality rate. Many of the administrative experiences made at the concentration camp's organisation have been applied to the management of the Location after the end of the Namibian War.

A cordon sanitaire for Windhoek's Location?

Aside from the perceived fear of immediate violent attacks carried out by their African neighbours, the equally imagined potential spread of infectious diseases posed a veritable and recurrent motive for the spatial separation of the Indigenous population at some distance from European premises. The Administration specified this distance at one mile[411] and Zollmann has cited an estimation of those days, according to which it took almost half an hour to walk from Windhoek's Location to the town's European parts.[412] Nevertheless, this distance did not represent a cordon sanitaire in its classical sense; instead, the Location was more and more under pressure by the growing European section, and railway tracks repre-

---

[410] Olusoga, Erichsen 2010: 203-5; Zimmerer 2001: 45.
[411] NAN MWI 36/27/37, Notes of Interview by Deputation from the Town Council with the Secretary in regard to Native Location Matters, attached to a letter dated 8th December 1925, no sheet number.
[412] Zollmann 2010: 230.

sented the only permanent physical barrier between both elements. The municipal Commission enquiring Location Affairs concluded at its meeting on 4th June 1926,

"[t]hat in order to establish a Buffer Zone at the present Location, it would be necessary to remove natives from practically half of it."[413]

Hence, it was concluded that this perceived problem could only be remedied through the Location's transfer to a conveniently situated new site, which complied with the demand,

"[t]hat any permanent Location should be separated from the European occupied portion of the town by the Buffer Zone."[414]

The opinion that the demolition of half the existing Location would be necessary was not shared unanimously, since the Native Commissioner insisted to have his opinion recorded,

"[…] that he dessents [sic] from the views from the rest of the Commission in regard to the necessity for removing natives from approximately half of the present Location in order that that half should form a Bufferzone [sic] between the Native and European Community. He feels that having regard to the fact that servants except under very exceptional circumstances are not allowed to sleep in town, no good case has been made out for their being required at the present stage to live so much further from their work that both they and their employers are bound to suffer very great inconvenience."[415]

Although Windhoek's public health officer had, as already stated, confirmed the town's advantageous position in his 1911 report, according to which tropical diseases were actually not endemic, this narrative was constantly used for the discriminative treatment of non-White people. Forced medical examinations and comprehensive vaccination campaigns were carried out frequently, not only for venereal diseases or measles but for other diseases too.[416] Many of the campaigns were dispensed on the ground, which means within the confines of the Location itself. This kind of spatial separation was combined with restrictions on the access for members of the respective other group. Whilst Africans were put under curfew and officially unable to leave the Location from nine o'clock in the evening to four

---

[413] NAN MWI 36/27/37, Minutes of the Meeting held at the Town Hall on the 4th of June 1926, no sheet number.
[414] NAN MWI 36/27/37, Minutes of the Meeting held at the Town Hall on the 4th of June 1926, no sheet number.
[415] NAN MWI 36/27/37, Minutes of the Meeting held at the Town Hall on the 4th of June 1926, no sheet number.
[416] NAN MWI 37/5/37, Bekanntmachung No. 28 von 1921, no sheet number.

o'clock in the morning[417], unless they received a special permit, Europeans were equally restricted in their access to the Location. Already under German rule specific regulations ordered anyone who wanted to enter the Location to ask for a permit from the Superintendent of Locations (Büro des Werftinspektors[418]).

All these limitations pursued the goal to strictly control the mobility of the Indigenous population and to keep contacts between them and the White community at a minimum. These rules left and created spaces for privacy, the evolution of African urban cultures and forms of contestation, as limited as they nonetheless were in face of occasional inspections or the constant presence of Indigenous police staff. In mid-1920s there were complaints recorded among bureaucrats about the existing many loopholes for Africans to absent themselves from their contractual job employment by simply making false statements about their names and hut number at the Location, as the Superintendent for Locations emphasised in a letter.[419] This letter demonstrated contradicting opinions between the Superintendent of Locations and the Officer-in-Charge of Native Affairs, where the latter wanted to avoid superfluous red tape. The monitoring of African labourers remained incomplete throughout the interwar period, despite all efforts put into the matter by White administrative staff members. It belongs to one of the continuities that the permits to enter the Indigenous settlements remained in place under South African rule and they were still necessary under official Apartheid policies, if White persons wanted to enter the new Black settlement of Katutura.[420] This new neighbourhood served to replace what is today called Old Location (i.e. Windhoek Location) after its forced demolition in 1958. Due to the removal's forced nature, the name Katutura translates as, "the place where we do not want to stay."[421]

Demography and social hierarchies

The Locations can be described as microcosms of their own that represented interwar African urban lifestyle as far as administrative instructions allowed. Their primary function was to serve as a separate residential area for the Indigenous working population, and in contrast to SWA's German period the artificially created categorisation became a bit more complex under South African rule, when it

---

[417] NAN SVW E.1.a, transcript of public notice dated 21st August 1914, sheet 20.
[418] The German term *Werft* was used synonymously to describe the African premises later called Location.
[419] NAN MWI 36/27/37, letter by Superintendent of Locations dated 24th September 1925, no sheet number.
[420] Bravenboer's book contains a picture of an instruction plate with almost the same instructions as applicable under German rule (Bravenboer 2004: 306).
[421] Bravenboer 2004: 185.

eventually comprised of at least three racial classes: Europeans, Coloured and Blacks, and among Blacks seven 'tribes' were identified.[422] For each of those alleged tribal groups, an individual section within the Location had been demarcated by the Administration in order to avoid potential social conflicts among the Indigenous population. This move carried the idea of ethnic segregation into the African community's context. To a certain extent social distinctions provided further options for differentiation through the eyes of bureaucracy, though this mainly applied to the European community.

Demographic structures within the Location have changed over the analysed period: at the beginning the compounds were a spatial expression of European intentions, which neglected the development of an African urbanity and tried to develop the Location into a simple temporary accommodation for 'their' labour reserve. Therefore, migration to the Location was restricted and monitored by public authorities who, from time to time, expelled what they considered to be 'idle' or 'vagrant' persons. This interpretation is supported by a continuously dominant share of male inhabitants throughout the Location's existence. Exact population figures are hardly mentioned in the official files but were given at 5,316 people in 1944, among them 2,316 male and 1,222 female tax payers, 117 persons of both sexes who did not pay taxes, 488 married women and 1173 children.[423] The gender balance still favoured men of workable age by the end of the analysed interwar period. In 1926 a group of unmarried men felt obliged to express their complaints about the insufficient provision of services, in particular the lack of opportunities to buy cooked food at an 'eating house', as they had no wife who could take care of them.[424] This deficiency did not really bother the authorities and on one occasion the Administration's Chief Clerk, Mr Clark, summarised the matter very openly.

> "[…] [T]he natives are here for the need of the public […]. If they were not in town for the convenience of the Europeans they would be in one of the Native Reserves."[425]

---

[422] NAN MWI 36/27/37, Notes of Interview by Deputation from the Town Council with the Secretary in regard to Native Location Matters, attached to a letter dated 8th December 1925, no sheet number.

[423] NAN MWI 36/32/37, handwritten letter by Superintendent of Locations dated 18th August 1944, no sheet number.

[424] NAN MWI 36/27/37, Minutes of meeting of commission appointed to enquire into Location Affairs, pp 5-6, no sheet numbers.

[425] NAN MWI 36/27/37, Notes of Interview by Deputation from the Town Council with the Secretary in regard to Native Location Matters, attached to a letter dated 8th December 1925, no sheet number.

Living conditions at the Location and debates about its relocation

The demographic composition was reflected in the housing schemes provided by the governmental authorities: aside from few plots typically prepared to accommodate families, many plans were drawn for quarters for single men and women. Estimations for the new Location based on 1944 population figures proposed the construction of 150 cottages, each with six living rooms and two communal kitchens to house the 900 male singles and another 50 similar cottages for the 300 female singles.[426] But these improvements did not materialise during interwar years, and many administrative reports consistently described the living conditions at Windhoek's Location as bad. They specifically stressed its situation as being impacted by heavy overcrowding. In 1931 it was estimated that 1,100 persons were not accommodated properly due to the prevalent congestion.[427] Housing shortage can therefore be concluded as a characteristic of both, Windhoek's Location and the European area (see 4.2.6). The number of houses – or officially called by their pejorative term 'huts' – is given at 3,000 in 1925 and, despite a constant growth numbered with at least 15 new homes officially built in the same year, the number of houses was still estimated at 3,000 in 1939.[428] Furthermore, these figures do not reflect frequent unreported cases of new homes. Most of them were squatted by a large number of people and due to this congestion as well as poor building materials used for their construction, they soon presented themselves to be in dilapidated conditions upon the Administration's inspection, who in turn considered less than one percent of the existing houses to be "worth shifting."[429] This existing congestion impacted on the projected construction schemes for new approved residential buildings, roughly 5x3 metres in size, which were expected to house six persons.[430] The 1927 Annual Report by the Superintendent of Location drastically summarised the consequences of those conditions and linked them to the White man's obligation or burden to take care of 'his' entrusted Indigenous people, who were primarily regarded as an important source of economic wellbeing.

---

[426] NAN MWI 36/32/37, handwritten letter by Superintendent of Locations dated 18th August 1944, no sheet number.

[427] NAN MWI 5/8, Extract from Town Clerk's Report re Improvements in Location dated 2nd April 1931, no sheet number.

[428] NAN MWI 36/32/37, letter dated 13th April 1944, no sheet number.

[429] NAN MWI 36/27/37, Notes of Interview by Deputation from the Town Council with the Secretary in regard to Native Location Matters, attached to a letter dated 8th December 1925, no sheet number.

[430] NAN MWI 36/27/37, letter by Officer-in-Charge of Native Affairs in Tsumeb Municipality dated 2nd June 1926, no sheet number.

"There is still a large number of cases of pulminary [sic] tuberculosis and other chest complaints owing chiefly to the poor type of hut used by natives. In a country where thatched roofs cannot be made it is a matter of urgency for the Council to seriously consider the question of an improved housing system. Apart from what we, as the ruling race, owe the native the economic future of the country must suffer if the health of the native population is neglected."[431]

It were those recorded complaints about the consequences of overcrowding as well as sanitary deficiencies, amongst other Eurocentric motives, that initiated a debate about the potential search for a new site for the Location since the mid-1920s. At a meeting of high-ranking representatives from the Municipality and Administration in December 1925, the municipal proposal to relocate the Location was officially discussed for the first time.[432] This debate coincided with the Location's prior legal transfer from governmental into municipal ownership. The White community wanted to seize this opportunity in their own interests: in fact, the projected relocation to a new site close to the Native hospital was based on the reason to provide cheap and easy to develop space for the extension of European residential areas. The Indigenous settlement was in this context interpreted as obstacle that needed to be removed at estimated costs of £30,000, before the White settlements could be extended in this direction. Similar to the negotiations about the town's new sewerage system (see 4.2.3), this number was to a certain extent exaggerated, for Windhoek's Town Council tried to convince the Administrator of the Municipality's inability to shoulder the necessary expenses for the Location. Instead, they appealed to the Government to have the Location retransferred to the Administration's management[433], a move commonly attempted by other municipalities in South Africa too.[434] But the Administrator's Office was not at all convinced of the necessity to relocate the Location and favoured improvements at its existing site. Maylam has illustrated how this motive of material interests has perpetuated itself in neighbouring South African urban history.[435]

In an attempt to fight overcrowding at Windhoek's Location, the municipal delegation discussed with the Administrator's Secretary the idea to lay out proper parcels

---

[431] NAN MWI 36/27/37, Annual Report 1927 furnished by Office of the Location Superintendent on 31st December 1927, no sheet number.
[432] NAN MWI 36/27/37, Notes of Interview by Deputation from the Town Council with the Secretary in regard to Native Location Matters, attached to a letter dated 8th December 1925, no sheet number.
[433] NAN MWI 36/27/37, Resolution No. 592 in Minutes No. 128 of Special Council Meeting dated 2nd December 1926, no sheet number.
[434] Maylam 1995: 38.
[435] Ibid.: 25-6.

at the existing site.[436] From municipal perspective this intervention was intended as temporary remedy until all residents would be moved into a new Location. For the time being, a standard plot of approximately 15x15 metres should be demarcated per house, and still under the application of such relatively small parcels it was estimated that the Location would extend three-fold.

Water provision would be limited to taps in the streets[437] which, in conjunction with scarce rainfalls, render it virtually impossible to use the attached land for growing some flowers or vegetables. Private bathrooms for every house were not deemed necessary and substituted by public bath houses and latrines based on the commonly applied bucket system. A simple refuse collection service was offered and charged in conjunction with the other sanitary services but according to reports it did not work well: large piles of rubbish evolved at the Location's outskirts and were, "[…] becoming an eye-sore a public nuisance and a danger to health."[438] The houses themselves were made out of cheapest possible building materials, which may not cost more than a maximum amount of £10.[439] The stigma of residential segregation should furthermore become visual through the use of green colour bricks for any new and officially approved housing construction at the Location[440], whereas same bricks were amongst the classified sorts of bricks explicitly prohibited for the European sections, according to the Building Regulations.[441] Although the use of wood and (corrugated) iron was not expressly prohibited in the Location, in contrast to Windhoek's European sections[442], they had only been officially accepted as a makeshift. With regards to the Coloured community, who could legally not be fully prevented from squatting in the European sections during interwar years, regulations concerning prescribed building materials[443] served, to a certain extent, the purposes of their economic exclusion, similar to other colonial

---

[436] NAN MWI 36/27/37, Notes of Interview by Deputation from the Town Council with the Secretary in regard to Native Location Matters, attached to a letter dated 8th December 1925, no sheet number.

[437] NAN MWI 36/27/37, letter by Officer-in-Charge of Native Affairs in Tsumeb Municipality dated 2nd June 1926, no sheet number.

[438] NAN MWI 36/27/37, Annual Report 1927 furnished by Office of the Location Superintendent on 31st December 1927, no sheet number.

[439] NAN MWI 36/27/37, Minutes of the meeting held at the Town Hall on the 4th of June 1926, no sheet number.

[440] NAN MWI 36/27/37, letter by Officer-in-Charge of Native Affairs in Tsumeb Municipality dated 2nd June 1926, no sheet number.

[441] NAN MWI 102A/2/40, Building Regulations, Chapter II: No. 26, no sheet number.

[442] NAN MWI 102A/2/40, Building Regulations, Chapter II: No. 20, no sheet number.

[443] Further requirements were for example laid down for the thickness of party walls in NAN MWI 102A/2/40, Building Regulations, Chapter II: No. 42, no sheet number.

312

entities like German East Africa and its rules for Dar es Salaam or Tanga.[444] Whilst the allocation of plots measuring 225 square metres was discussed and presented as key progress in the authorities' attempts to improve housing conditions at the Location, they further exemplified the existing discrepancies between Indigenous and European schemes. For the latter, Windhoek's Building Regulations stipulated a minimum lot size of 600 square metres[445], although most parcels actually measured around 1,000 square metres. What kind of different results those varying circumstances, requirements and conditions created, can be compared in figure 17 with two photographs from late German times, one taken of residential areas at the Location and the other in the European section to the town's north.

---

[444] Speitkamp 2005: 110-1.
[445] NAN MWI 102A/2/40, Building Regulations, Chapter I: No. 3, no sheet number.

Figure 17: Residential areas in Windhoek - Location (top), European villas (bottom)

Reform tendencies in layout and design requirements

Based on those minimalist experiences at Windhoek's as well as other Locations, the administrative authorities realised the insufficiency of those early schemes and started to discuss (comparatively slight) improvements and alleviations for implementation at the new Location, to be constructed after the Second World War. Such new ideas contrasted with those requirements defined in the 1920s but they

314

can be considered as an updated reflection of positions taken in the Union of South Africa by late 1930s/early 1940s. George Kerby has documented then ongoing trends in his correspondence with various colleagues across the Union. Furthermore, it is interesting to note that Windhoek wanted to embark on a kind of experimental programme, intended to make the Municipality's Native housing schemes a role model for SWA and beyond. Input on good examples for improved housing construction based on rational schemes was gathered during visits to the Union as well as to then Southern Rhodesia, as exemplified by the Assistant Secretary for SWA John Neser and his trip to Salisbury in November 1942. Upon his return, he directed Town Clerk Kerby to collect the relevant information from the neighbouring country's offices, since Neser,

> "[…] had seen the housing of native police constables at your centre, which struck him as being eminently suitable for a native housing scheme."[446]

The city's moves can be interpreted as limited efforts for reformism, although the primary focus was on the construction of easy to assemble and replicate low-cost houses for the African population, as the following remark in a letter by G. J. Opperman, Naauwpoort's Secretary of the Village Management Board[447], addressed to Kerby confirms.

> "Mr. E. Sander of your town spent some time at Naauwpoort on his way to the Wilderness, on which occasion, he inspected our subeconomic housing scheme, and he expressed the opinion that it may be helpful in your efforts on similar lines if I should write you on the subject."[448]

Reform ideas encompassed the design and building materials selected for future housing projects accommodating the Black population. For the first time, reformism was partially inspired by sociocultural considerations as an informal handwritten note by Zwalton Jameson indicates, asking the Municipality to take, "[…] available materials, climate, people's customs […]"[449] into account. Yet two things remain important: first, reform ideas in this case did not resemble modernist attempts to create a "Model Native Township" as displayed at the 1938 Johannesburg "Town Planning Exhibition and Congress."[450] Secondly, all calculations were

---

[446] NAN MWI 36/32/37, letter by Town Clerk dated 5th December 1942, no sheet number.
[447] In its function this institution equalled the Town Council at small and rural local authorities.
[448] NAN MWI 36/32/37, letter by Secretary of Village Management Board of Naauwpoort dated 14th December 1942, no sheet number.
[449] NAN MWI 36/32/37, informal note by Zwalton Jameson, undated, no sheet number.
[450] Mabin, Oranje 2014.

primarily made on the respective affordability of those houses to their future residents and subsequent expected returns on the public expenditures. For the Naauwpoort example it was estimated that the Municipality had to cover annual losses of approximately £485, if no further options to minimise costs were applied.[451] Such options could be secured by various means, like standardisation of the buildings' frames with steel reinforcements as well as the production of bricks by local labourers on site to avoid the purchase and transport of industrial products.

The consideration of Naauwpoort's case by Windhoek's Municipality, since the former's building requirements explicitly asked in their second 'instruction rule' that, "[a]ll material and workmanship shall be the best of their respective kinds."[452] The full document is written based on this principal instruction for all components, although the cost estimate of £110 for a two-room Indigenous house as opposed to £750 for the Superintendent's house still help to get the dimensions of those intentions right.[453] Still Naauwpoort was far more generous than Windhoek would ever have been, if the latter Municipality's usual maximum of £25 per house is considered. It can furthermore be taken as indication for Windhoek's economic environment and lower average Indigenous wages paid here. From the administrative perspective in those days this gap was, by contrast, not interpreted as economic difference but justified by a severe 'evolutionary' difference that existed between the autochthonous peoples in SWA and those in the Union, as one statement by George Kerby in the context of housing demands proves. In his opinion,

> "[…] it must be considered in this connection that the local class of natives is not as advanced as the Union domestic type of native and, therefore, a simple system of housing is all that is required."[454]

In aesthetic terms attempts were made to construct those houses with durable materials such as steel and cement bricks whilst typically used wood and corrugated iron became less popular for Windhoek's model housing. Instead, innovative products such as asbestos partition doors were assessed regarding their potential applicability to new housing schemes.[455] One private construction company be-

---

[451] NAN MWI 36/32/37, letter by Secretary of Village Management Board of Naauwpoort dated 14th December 1942, no sheet number.
[452] NAN MWI 36/32/37, Village Management Board of Naauwpoort: Sub-Economic Housing Scheme for Natives, no sheet number.
[453] NAN MWI 36/32/37, letter by Secretary of Village Management Board of Naauwpoort dated 14th December 1942, no sheet number.
[454] NAN MWI 36/32/37, letter by Town Clerk Kerby dated 13th April 1944, no sheet number.
[455] NAN MWI 36/32/37, Extract from the Report of the Town Clerk, Capt. G. Kerby, on Proceedings whilst in the Union dated 28th June 1944, no sheet number.

came aware of those municipal intentions, and submitted its patented design for the so-called "Wonder Hut" which was almost exclusively composed of concrete, though the marketing material stated it to still weigh less than five tons. This prototype house, with its air space of almost 34 cubic metres[456], is illustrated in figure 18 with dimensions given in imperial scale. In its promotion the developer did not shy at using similar descriptions, as if he were selling a kennel.

> "Hotel owners, farmers and plot holders at seaside resorts will see Wonder Hut a boon. It's just the thing for the garden, […]."[457]

Figure 18: Sketches for "Wonder Hut" as opposed to conventional building

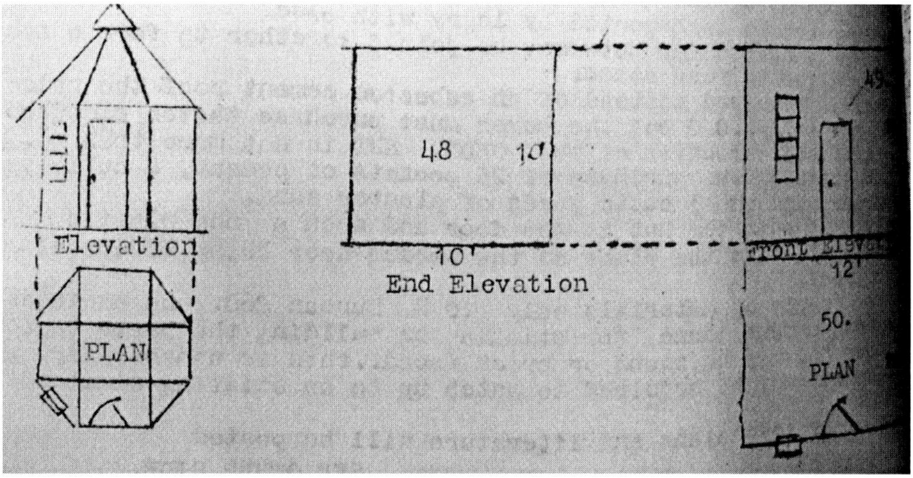

Elevation

PLAN

48   10'

10'

End Elevation

Front Elevation

12'

50.

PLAN

Aside from aesthetics and materials, the authorities concerned then discussed the sanitary amenities that would have to be provided to those housing schemes. Despite the summarised debates about Windhoek's waterborne sewerage system and its potential coverage of the Location (see 4.2.3), the implementation of such idea was completely uncommon as Opperman indicates with regard to Naauwpoort's sanitary system.

---

[456] This number was barely over the minimum requirements for European rooms with 31.5 cubic metres and a height of three metres for all new habitable rooms, as stipulated in the *Building Regulations*. NAN MWI 102A/2/40, Building Regulations, Chapter II: No. 44, no sheet number.

[457] NAN MWI 36/32/37, letter by Brenner & Gamsu about The Wonder Hut, undated, no sheet number.

"You will notice that each family will have its separate plot, its separate house and its separate closet and store room. We will have a pail removal system, but our Union Health Department I believe are strongly in favour of pit privies."[458]

In order to answer, "[o]ne of the burning questions at present"[459], in 1944 Windhoek's Town Clerk, on behalf of the Council, enquired directly from the South African Central Housing Board about the advisability of pit privies if a waterborne sewerage system is out of reach. This request helps to underscore once more the integration of SWA into South African structures, both in terms of administration and policies. In addition, the South African Department of Public Health considered Windhoek's "Model Native Location" to be of such importance, that the city's Town Engineer had been invited to come to Pretoria for thorough consultations with the Central Housing Board about the project.[460] Within this letter the Central Housing Board gave some provisional recommendations on the plans Windhoek had already submitted. It was emphasised that those plans contained too many streets which, in combination with the projected plots of 100 feet by 100 feet (~31m x 31m) in size, rendered the plan too expensive. All previous plans in Windhoek were based on plots of 50 feet by 50 feet (~15m x 15m), but the Central Housing Board suggested 60 feet by 80 feet (~18.5m x 25m) as 'ample' compromise instead. A final decision on this matter, however, had not been taken before the end of the Second World War.

4.3.4   Social facilities at Windhoek Location

Aside from its residential function there were, indeed, just very few public facilities available at Windhoek Location. Shops are in this context of particular relevance, since they were in the focus of Indigenous population's attention in several petitions submitted to the authorities.

The matter of trading licences

Although Section 19 of the *Natives (Urban Areas) Proclamation, 1924* stipulated that trading was to remain in Native hands, required sites or permits were only granted upon application to the Municipality. Hence, provision (ii) represented the legal basis to keep trading businesses in White hands, if the Administrator would be of the opinion that the applying Indigenous traders demonstrated themselves to be

---

[458] NAN MWI 36/32/37, letter by Secretary of Village Management Board of Naauwpoort dated 14th December 1942, no sheet number.
[459] NAN MWI 36/32/37, letter by Town Clerk Kerby dated 13th April 1944, no sheet number.
[460] NAN MWI 36/32/37, letter by Secretary of Central Housing Board dated 11th May 1944, no sheet number.

incapable of fulfilling the official expectations. This loophole was used in Wind-hoek, and one of the earliest examples for petitions against this practice is documented for 1926, when the Native Commissioner urged the Town Council to state its reason for the general rejection of applications for trading licences made by residents of the Location. Commissioner Harry Drew, in this context, pointed out that the Proclamation entitled the inhabitants to trade within the Location, and that, "[…] this principle cannot be regarded or treated as a dead letter."[461] Without a substantiated reply, he was not inclined to accept this general refusal any longer. Half a year later it was, at least, agreed that specific sites within the Location need-ed to be set aside for trading purposes as legally requested, and that 'Coloured races' were granted the right to carry out the trades.[462] This move, in turn, under-mined African prospects of being granted a licence and their aspirations for an alternative way to earn a living. The decision fitted with the overall ideological frameworks and where prevailing attitudes towards segregation changed among the European community over the analysed interwar period. Similar to the abovemen-tioned developments around housing functions, a tendency in favour of a more firm implementation of separating frameworks is traceable, whilst options for in-terracial encounters diminished.

This did include the sphere of trading business, where tensions eventually became tangible in the 1930s when inhabitants of the Location again applied for trading licences. Those attempts challenged the White community in whose hands Native trading was, which further supports the idea of the Africans' deliberate exploitation irrespective of legal requirements to keep separate accounts for Indigenous reve-nues. In 1932 the *Natives (Urban Areas) Proclamation* had been amended in two re-spects: first, it procured the legal basis for the Municipality, under the direction of the Administrator, to let certain plots within Locations for trading or business purposes to African applicants. Although this right was still a rather hypothetical option and ruled out in practice, the second amendment at the same time vested the Municipality with stricter powers to prohibit the Indigenous population from hawking and peddling[463], effectively eliminating potential competition. Despite the fact that further provisions among the amended sections instructed that all reve-nues accrued by the Municipality in her function as a general dealer, would have to be carried out "fully and fairly" to Native accounts, the Administration did not

---

[461] NAN MWI 36/27/37, letter by Native Commissioner dated 16th January 1926, no sheet number.
[462] NAN MWI 36/27/37, Minutes of the Meeting held at the Town Hall on the 4th of June 1926, no sheet number.
[463] NAN MWI 36/26/37, Section 19 of *Native (Urban Areas) Proclamation* as promulgated in Official Gazette on 1st February 1932, no sheet number.

make efforts to conceal their intentions since the second half of the 1930s, as a 'Note regarding Native Trading Licences' dated 21st October 1936 proves.

> "The Assistant Native Commissioner emphasized the point that it is the Administration's declared policy of segregating European life from that of native life."[464]

In order to achieve this goal, which asked for the exclusion of Africans from trading businesses where otherwise contacts between European wholesale dealers and Indigenous retailers were unavoidable, the request by inhabitants of the Location to grant them such licences was rejected throughout the following years. Europeans tried to preserve their dominant position in two ways: either discreetly behind the scenes, like those activities by owners of Native stores in the Location who, "have had a meeting and resolved to take combined action in the matter".[465] Or they did it openly by entering into "sleeping partnerships" as the files recorded for milk vendors.

> "Similar circumstances have arisen in the past in as much as milk vendors etc., who have no admission to the location, have engaged natives to supply and distribute milk."[466]

Effects of the Great Depression on the Black population

Debates about such trading licences for the Black population were stimulated by the bad economic situation many of its members were living in. It has already been described that, despite the opportunity to absent themselves from their respective employer, the African community was forced into wage labour with its limited options to choose a suitable and fair employer. Instead, the consequences of the Great Depression in late 1920s and early 1930s have hit the community particularly hard: recorded unemployment among the Location's inhabitants was at more than 300 persons in early 1931, although representatives from the Administration and Municipality at their 'Conference on Native Affairs' were of the opinion,

> "[...] that the position is at present not alarming but will become so if the number of unemployed natives increase."[467]

---

[464] NAN MWI 36/27/37, Notes re Native Trading Licences dated 21st October 1936, no sheet number.
[465] NAN MWI 36/27/37, Resolution No. 287 in Minutes No. 382 of Ordinary Council meeting dated 20th October 1936, no sheet number.
[466] NAN MWI 36/27/37, Notes re Native Trading Licences dated 21st October 1936, no sheet number.
[467] NAN MWI 5/8, Minutes of Conference on Native Location Affairs dated 19th March 1931, no sheet number.

320

They agreed on precautions to prevent unemployed Indigenous people from surrounding districts to migrate to Windhoek's Location as,

> "[…] a circular has recently been issued by the Administration instructing officials not to issue passes to natives to proceed to Windhoek in search of employment."[468]

This move broke with previous legislation that granted the African population the option to apply for a residence permit at any town they wanted, as long as they were not contractually bound to another employer. The economic situation did not improve over the following year and Blacks' unemployment doubled to more than 600 persons in 1932, as a memo by Town Clerk Kerby to the Administrator states. He subsequently summarised, "the location population is in a very precarious situation."[469] Although the memo – just like the conference one year before – tried to convince the Administrator about the necessity and urgency of relief works to alleviate the Indigenous population's dire situation, their problems were used as a pretext to receive support for improvements that actually benefitted the White community in the first instance. This does refer to the two suggested projects compared in the memo and it concludes,

> "[t]he construction of the water borne [sewerage] system in the location in any case will give work for about 100 to 150 natives only and then merely for a period of a few months."[470]

These effects were contrasted with the projected so-called Location Dam, which was estimated to generate employment for Europeans and Natives over one to two years and which should help to stabilise the water supply.[471] Of course, it cannot be ruled out that the Municipality held down the sewerage system's effects on purpose, to make the dam project more appealing. These attempts did not work out, for the Administration eventually granted the available subsidies to another barrage at Omatjenne. This decision, in turn, pushed the Municipality to underscore once more the advantageous nature of the Location Dam, addressing the European unemployed.[472] Focus of attention was on projects that physically improved the White community's amenities as well as their economic basis. Indigenous interests

---

[468] NAN MWI 5/8, Minutes of Conference on Native Location Affairs dated 19th March 1931, no sheet number.
[469] NAN MWI 5/8, Memorandum re Unemployment Relief and Location Improvement Scheme dated 15th April 1932, emphasis in original, no sheet number.
[470] NAN MWI 5/8, Memorandum re Unemployment Relief and Location Improvement Scheme dated 15th April 1932, emphasis in original, no sheet number.
[471] NAN MWI 5/8, Memorandum re Unemployment Relief and Location Improvement Scheme dated 15th April 1932, emphasis in original, no sheet number.
[472] NAN MWI 5/8, letter by Town Clerk dated 20th April 1932, no sheet number.

mattered to a far lesser extent, if at all, and help to further illustrate the levels of segregation beyond the spatial and housing realms. Such economic circumstances were of course not inclined to improve the situation at the Location, but contributed to the level of desperation with which the Indigenous community would fight for their trading licences.

Cultural facilities

As a site for social gatherings, the so-called beerhall played an important role in daily life at Windhoek's Location. Besides its literal function as bar, it was the central place for the dissemination of news and gossips or social events such as improvised music and dance performances or wedding celebrations. In the absence of a proper cinema open to Indigenous viewers[473], the beerhall did serve to screen movies too but administrative censorship applied to their actual selection. The selection was made based on criteria to supposedly improve and uplift the African population's cultural and moral behaviour, and was directly linked to public health considerations and the recurrent motive of a White Man's burden to take care of the Natives who were entrusted in 'his' care. This attitude is summarised in one statement on the matter made by Louis Taljaard, member of the Legislative Assembly, in 1931.

> "Was Kinovorführungen und den Verkauf von leichten Getränken an Eingeborene anbetrifft, muss der Stadtrat dafür sorgen, dass diese unter strengster Kontrolle des Stadtrates bleiben. [...] Die Kinovorführungen müssen irgendwie lehrreich sein, und jeder Versuch, eine schlechte Art Film vorzuführen, oder der Missbrauch im Verkauf von Getränken muss strengstens bekämpft und nicht zugelassen werden. Hier muss der Stadtrat dafür sorgen, dass die Eingeborenen, die so leicht beeinflusst sind, nicht durch Vorführungen von Filmen erregt werden."[474]

---

[473] A first proposal for the construction of such an institution was already rejected by the German municipal administration in 1911, despite the option to put it under her censorship (NAN SVW O.1.d, copy of correspondence dated 20/21 July 1911 and handwritten remark about Council decision taken accordingly on 31st July 1911, sheet 1).

[474] NAN MWI 5/8, letter "Verlegung der alten Werft" by L. Taljaard dated 8th June 1931, no sheet number. "In relation to movie screening and the sale of intoxicating beverages to Natives, the Town Council has to take precautions so as to keep them under strictest control of the Town Council. [...] Movie screenings have to be of a somehow instructive nature and any attempt to show a kind of bad film or the abuse in terms of the sales of beverages must be fought and prevented at the strictest. It is at the discretion of the Town Council to take care so as to prevent the Natives' arousal through such movie screenings, for it is a matter of common knowledge how easy to influence they are." (author's translation).

Further considerations about the perceived problem of 'Kaffir beer' have already been discussed in the subchapter on public health (see 4.2.5).

Besides the beerhall there were only very few recreational facilities available at the Locations. In several plans for the Coloured Location, as well as in descriptions for a relocated Native Location to be implemented after the Second World War, play-grounds and sportsgrounds were demarcated. Anyhow they were usually considered as potential improvements at some distant future, as the letter by Mr Worms, then Chairman of Windhoek's Finance Committee, exemplifies; he urged that the question of a final site for the Location had to be decided on and the sanitary conditions needed to be improved.[475] In 1939 the *Natives (Urban Areas) Proclamation, 1924* was again amended, in order to provide municipalities with the right to confer land to religious denominations and school bodies to be occupied for school purposes, other similar educational institutions or churches within the Location. At this occasion, the detailed provisions still made clear that those bodies would not own the plot which remained municipal property. They were granted a certificate of occupation detailing the leasehold rights to the ground therein specified.[476]

4.3.5 The Coloured Location

As mentioned in the section on the administrative frameworks above, authorities in SWA copied the South African idea of a tripartite society, where aside from European areas and Locations for Black people, another separate section for the Coloured community was established. Within those days' social hierarchies members of the Coloured community were eager to challenge White supremacy. In several cases they had the financial means and access to legal support to fight for their rights, most notably for the one to squat in European neighbourhoods, at courts in the Union. Attempts by Johannesburg's town council to assign members of the Indian community to specific sites at a planned "Asiatic bazaar" were impeded by the Transvaal Supreme Court.[477] Busani Mpofu reports about similar regulations in colonial Zimbabwe, where laws introduced in 1930 prohibited Indians from residing at the African Location in the city of Bulawayo. They were nonetheless not admitted to the European sections either and remained confined to a legal in-between-status that should be terminated by the construction of a specific

---

[475] E.g. NAN MWI 5/8, letter by Chairman of Finance Committee dated 19th May 1931, no sheet number.
[476] NAN MWI 36/26/37, Amendment of *Natives (Urban Areas) Proclamation, 1924* published 15th August 1939, no sheet number.
[477] Nightingale 2012: 284.

Indian Location.[478] Despite an originally existing legislation that ruled in favour of those equal rights to the city, the Administration prepared the implementation of stricter frameworks and therefore ignored those objections submitted by Coloured persons. First official proposals for a Coloured Location in Windhoek are mentioned in 1937[479], and one year later the administration envisaged situating it close to the existing Native Location, at a site nearby the former wireless station. Final drafts were prepared in 1944 for a plot adjacent to the Native hospital and a bit closer to Windhoek's central areas.[480] Although these later drafts can be interpreted as a concession to the Coloured community not to select a site close to the Native Location, and to reflect their perceived comparatively higher social status, they actually blended perfectly with the Administration's long-term goal to transfer Windhoek's Location to a site north of the Native hospital which had already been defined in mid-1920s.[481] There, both Locations would in fact be merged in the long run.

From a legal standpoint, the Coloured community's comparatively higher social status was later withdrawn through the *Natives (Urban Areas) Proclamation's* amendment as promulgated on 1st October 1938, when it was defined that,

> "[a]ny coloured person residing in a location as provided for in terms of the foregoing paragraphs shall during such residence be considered as a native for purposes of this proclamation and any regulations issued thereunder."[482]

The 1944 drafts are reproduced in figure 19, and at first sight it seems they were inspired by garden city elements, though in Howard's schematic and concentric layout. Of course, the Coloured Location was far from Howard's social ideals, but its centre was supposed to be a tree lined semi-circle with the White Administration's building dominating at its central point, where the main entrances to the fenced in compound were projected. The square was surrounded by four plots which all served public purposes as playground, beerhall, administrative block and store. One radial axis should serve as main link between the central square and an external sportsground. Most streets were planned at 15 metres in width, except for

---

[478] Mpofu, Busani, *'Undesirable' Indians, Residential Segregation and the Ill-Fated Rise of the White 'Housing Covenants' in Bulawayo, Colonial Zimbabwe, 1930-1973*, 2011: 554, 563.

[479] NAN MWI 5/8, Resolution no. 611 in Minutes of Finance Committee Meeting dated 16th February 1937, no sheet number.

[480] NAN MWI 5/4.

[481] NAN MWI 36/27/37, Minutes of Meeting of Commission appointed to enquire into Location Affairs held on 20th January 1926, no sheet number.

[482] NAN MWI 36/26/37, Official Gazette of SWA published on 1st October 1938, no sheet number.

those smaller ones in the inner ring; this design can be interpreted as deliberate attempt to make it spatially difficult for the Location's inhabitants to meet spontaneously and in larger groups at the Administration's building, for example during a riot. This interpretation is substantiated, if the Building Regulations are taken as reference point: they require "principal thoroughfares" to be at least 20 metres in width and no other street to be less than 15 metres.[483] Besides, in formal terms, meetings and assemblies among members of the Non-European communities were already made subject to the expressed consent by the Municipality in 1932.[484]

Figure 19: Draft plan for Coloured Location, 1944

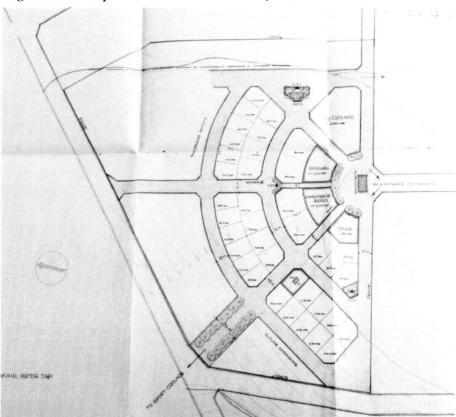

Aside from the drafted site map there are no specific explanations about the planning concept preserved. It does therefore remain subject to assumptions, what the

---

[483] NAN MWI 102A/2/40, Building Regulations, Chapter I: No. 4, no sheet number.
[484] NAN MWI 36/26/37, Resolution No. 385 in Minutes of Finance Committee dated 29th March 1932, no sheet number.

White administration's guiding principles were and how the Coloured Location should be erected. Similar to the Native Location, further amenities are very scarce: a sanitary system serving individual homes was not part of the plans. Instead, the Administration envisaged one bathhouse at the eastern corner and WCs at the western, whilst three water taps in the streets provided for the inhabitants' water supply. In comparison to the Native Location the individual lots were significantly larger and varied between 385 square metres for the smallest ones and 800 as their largest, a clear indication of the community's relative wealth as well as social distinctions within.[485] The majority of lots measured around 450 to 500 square metres. Compared to its first plans the Coloured Location was eventually designed on more generous outlines. Besides, the fenced in site provided for space to accommodate future extensions. Plans for single quarters are in this case not contained in the administrative files, which did only refer to typologies tailored to family homes. All drafted house plans for the three different projected designs are based on concrete construction types[486] and reproduced in figure 20. In aesthetic terms they partially follow those patterns for the Native Location but are mixed with European housing elements too. Joseph Eppeler's drawings, which he produced for his aesthetic criticism of German architectural styles in SWA 20 years earlier (for a reprint see 4.2.1), did not look very dissimilar from those for 'modern' Coloured housing. Despite the efforts already put into the project, the Coloured Location remained a plan on paper and was not realised in interwar years.

---

[485] Mpofu mentions similar distinctions for the case of colonial Bulawayo (Mpofu 2011: 563-4).
[486] NAN MWI 5/4, Coloured Township: Type C of houses; Haustype E; Plan of House F, all ndated, no sheet numbers.

Figure 20: House types C, E and F drafted for Coloured Location

Type C

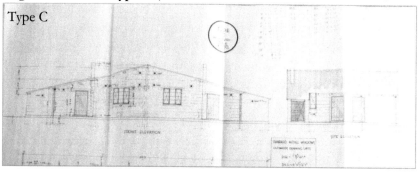

Type E

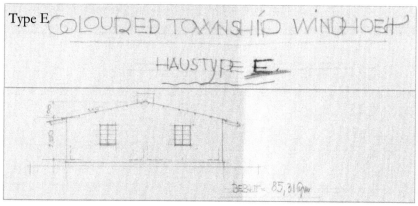

Type F

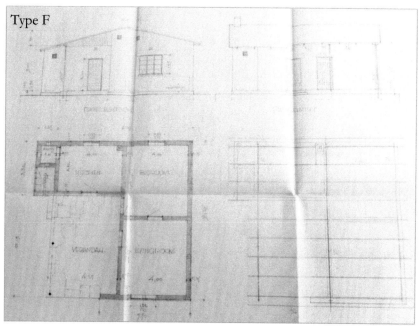

4.3.6 Traces of a contemporary hybrid city

For various reasons the concept of segregation was not implemented at the strictest possible level which, in fact, would have meant the construction of a dual city with two completely separate sections for the White and non-White communities respectively, divided by a cordon sanitaire. Interethnic contacts can in this case be kept at a very minimum. Instead, there existed several Indigenous enclaves that were distributed across the township, as a closer look at Windhoek's city map in figure 21 tries to visualise (the numbers in brackets refer to the respective sites on the map). Its contents represent an approximation of the prevailing conditions in 1921, which were compiled based on specific or indirect hints and remarks contained in various archival files. The base map used for this purpose is symbolic for the dilapidated condition in which many historic maps are, if they are preserved at all.

Figure 21: Traces of hybridity in Windhoek, 1921

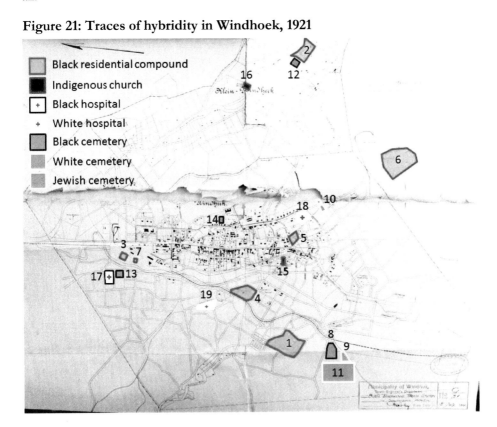

Of course, the two Locations far at the top (east) at Klein Windhoek (2) and at the bottom, towards the western fringe of Windhoek proper (1) accommodated the majority of the Indigenous population. Both complied very well with the predomi-

328

nant considerations of public health as they were located at some distance from the Municipality's central parts where the Europeans lived. The Locations accommodated those people whose contractual obligations did not require them to stay at their employers' premises. Their start of work apparently provided them with sufficient time to walk there, although complaints by Whites about the 'unreliability' and 'tardiness' of Indigenous employees are nothing uncommon and formed part of the bossy tone used in many related historic descriptions.

Other institutions depended on the immediate 'availability' of their Indigenous employees, as was the case with public authorities such as railways, postal services or the police. Since their rota system usually did not fit well with the imposed curfew, and red tape attached to the issuance of special permits in order to bypass the curfew made things too laborious, it seemed more convenient for those institutions to maintain separate small compounds for their Native workers. The map indicates the compound for railway workers (3) close to the station. Its construction was initiated as one of the last German projects in 1914 at estimated costs of 45,000 marks, and it was designed to accommodate a total of 40 male workers in four wings, each comprising of 10 apartments in simplest quality. The building application justified the construction with two arguments: the demand for workers on the evening and morning shifts; as well as legal obligations to provide Indigenous workers kept aloof from the Location with permanent accommodations as stipulated in the public health bye-laws. Additional attention was paid to the site selection in order to avoid any kind of "disadvantages" to European homes.[487] By the mid-1920s the administrative viewpoint on this compound began to change, and some officials demanded to close it down and to relocate its inhabitants to Windhoek Location.[488] This new assessment was partly based on the prevailing bad sanitary conditions at the site, where by then more than 400 people instead of the projected 40 crowded the limited space. On the other hand, it symbolised the intention to enforce a stricter system of segregation without that many exceptions. The two separate Locations maintained by the Government (4) as well as the one for the Police Forces (5) were regarded with growing suspicion.

Such scattered distribution of Indigenous people was not only done for the colonisers' convenience but it represented administrative attempts to reflect what they perceived as 'insurmountable' ethnic divisions. They became tangible in the erection of the so-called "Ovambo Compound" (6) at Windhoek's south-eastern

---

[487] NAN BAU G.Wi.4, sheets 1-2.
[488] NAN MWI 36/27/37, Minutes of Meeting of Commission appointed to enquire into Location Affairs held on 20th January 1926, no sheet number.

fringe, on a plot almost 160,000 square metres in size[489], exclusively dedicated to migrant labourers from SWA's northern border region. This kind of predominantly male labour migration has a long tradition that dates back to German colonial rule and it had then, as mentioned above, been well documented in the Official Gazette where the official migration statistics were published on a monthly basis.[490] Migrating workers were much appreciated by the European community, for they fitted well with their intentions to allegedly preserve the African rural traditions and to limit urban residency to the White community. For the Ovambo community, the administration did not just maintain a separate Compound but their travels were organised detached from other ethnic groups. Therefore, in 1913 the Government of DSWA constructed a smaller 'copy' of the Compound comprising of a sleepover shed, latrines and a storage shed to accommodate arriving or departing migrant workers at the railway station (7).[491] Furthermore, the migrating Ovambos help to make two things clear. Firstly, there existed the opportunity for the Indigenous population to decide on their general willingness to accept wage labour and to select their employer, at least if they lived outside SWA's 'police zone' in the country's north. This fact becomes obvious in the on-going complaints that were articulated by administrative representatives during summer months in 1914, when no Ovambo was willing to come to Windhoek, as a file about governmental recruitment activities illustrates.[492] Secondly, this file proved the Administration's view on the Indigenous population as mere 'trading goods.' The Acting Native Commissioner, then under South African rule, dared to sell child labourers aged fourteen years or younger as,

> "[i]t is thought that these Natives could be usefully employed in various households in this town, or as herd boys on the adjoining farms, and that you may wish to draw the attention of your fellow townsmen to this labour supply."[493]

In case those boys – called "piccanins" in the letter – really found an employer willing to hire them for the requested period of nine months, the employer had to pay them a fixed wage of five shillings a month. It was further stipulated that the

---

[489] NAN SVW P.4.f, letter by Town Clerk's Office dated 11th December 1923, no sheet number. In this case the compound's origins as part of slave-era laws becomes extremely obvious, as Nightingale refers to slave owners' requirement, "to provide shelter in their own households for their human property" (Nightingale 2012: 251).
[490] E.g. ADSWA 1910: 143, 182, 226, 252, 275, 301.
[491] NAN BAU B.67. The budget was limited to 6,500 marks and actual construction costs almost met with 6,551 marks (official bill of cost, no sheet number).
[492] NAN SVW E.2.f.
[493] NAN SVW E.2.f, letter by Acting Native Commissioner dated 6th December 1915, sheet 77.

330

employer then had to pay a "recruiting fee" of £ 1:15:0 per child to the Administration for her performed procurement efforts. Those regulations were published in a Public Notice on 6th December 1915, signed by Captain Harland Bell in his function as Officer in Charge of Native Affairs.[494] Hence the Administration of SWA was officially an accomplice in the promotion of child labour and earning profits with such activities as late as 1915.

Indigenous accommodation at European premises

Aside from these larger premises for Indigenous labourers, it is extremely difficult to properly reflect the vast number of employees who were accommodated at their employer's homes. As late as 1940 preliminary notes concerning the reconstruction of Klein Windhoek's Location mentioned an almost equal distribution: 157 African people were registered at the Location whilst 147 stayed at their employer's premise.[495] Although it needs to be taken into consideration that Klein Windhoek was traditionally a community dominated by farmers and had more options to accommodate people in decentralised ways, it can be assumed that similar trends were applicable to Windhoek too. Therefore, the map in figure 21 would actually have to be dotted with a multitude of indications for Indigenous 'enclaves' across the whole township. Employers were nonetheless not free to decide whether or not they would let Indigenous workers stay at their plots. Instead, they had to officially apply for a permit from the Municipality in accordance with the *Natives (Urban Areas) Proclamation, 1924* and its subsequent amendments. Since March 1932 Windhoek was not only granted the right to decide on those applications within the township's confines. The new legislation vested it with the option to levy a fee as well as to define certain minimum requirements for Indigenous accommodations at European premises.[496] One month earlier the Finance Committee debated the potential amount to be levied as such fee, which should explicitly compensate for the losses in hut tax, and it was already recommended to the Council that,

> "[…] the permits for natives to reside on employers [sic] properties should be restricted as much as possible as it is undesirable to have too many natives residing in town."[497]

---

[494] NAN SVW E.2.f, Public Notice dated 6th December 1915, sheet 78.
[495] NAN MWI 36/31/37, Klein Windhoek Location: Proposals for Re-Construction dated 10th April 1940, no sheet number.
[496] NAN MWI 36/26/37, Resolution No. 385 in Minutes of Finance Committee Meeting dated 29th March 1932, no sheet number.
[497] NAN MWI 36/26/37, Resolution No. 332 in Minutes of Finance Committee Meeting dated 22nd February 1932, no sheet number.

In conclusion, the work environment established by the White community for 'their' Black employees with all its restrictions resembles those rules applied to the menial staff in 18th and 19th century rural and urban Germany as laid down by Rainer Schröder.[498]

Segregation at cemeteries

Residential segregation did not end with a person's death, as administrative files on the maintenance of cemeteries and their future relocation illustrate. A a severe imbalance has to be conceded in terms of the expenditures spent on cemeteries for Europeans of Christian denomination as opposed to those for all other groups – and the Indigenous population in particular. Already under German rule the Native Commissioner was forced to intervene, due to the Native cemetery's (8) poor condition and its vulnerability to grazing animals and unrestricted human access. In his letter to the Municipality of Windhoek dated 14th May 1913 he complained about delays of, by then, almost a year in the projected works to fence the graveyard in. This delay occurred despite the approved of budget to carry out those works[499] and a confirmation by the Railway Authorities to lease their parcel of the cemetery for a period of 20 years, which was actually part of the projected second (southern) railway station.[500] The second public tender was started on 4th September 1913, and it was organised in order to obtain the cheapest possible fence.[501] One decade later a competition broke out over the construction of new cemeteries for the Indigenous as well as for the European community which were both competing for similar sites.

Already in 1920 the Town Council realised that the old European cemetery at the south eastern city limits at Friedensstraße (10) soon needed to be closed down for capacity reasons, and it decided to open a new cemetery (11) at the road to former wireless station close to the Location, which was a stone's throw away from the old Native cemetery (8).[502] Despite those timely decisions, the actual relocation was procrastinated for several years and eventually had to be carried out in a rush. These urgent interventions were then attributed with some heavy extra expenditure, such as those for a petrol engine as water pump since electrical mains could

---

[498] Schröder 1992.
[499] NAN SVW E.1.l, letter by Native Commissioner dated 14th May 1913, sheet 14.
[500] NAN SVW E.1.l, letter by Native Commissioner dated 29th August 1913, sheet 17.
[501] NAN SVW E.1.l, public notice about tender dated 4th September 1913, sheet 20.
[502] NAN MWI 120/3/44, letter by the Director of Works dated 20th April 1920, no sheet number.

not be laid on time.[503] More or less on parallel it was foreseeable in 1923 that the old Native cemetery was unable to provide sufficient space for future graves[504] but the Town Council made it clear, "that it is undesirable to extend the old cemetery in direction of the new European cemetery."[505] For both new cemeteries it was clearly expressed who was to be buried where: in case of the Native cemetery, *Regulations for the Control and Management of Cemeteries for Non Europeans* instructed the administrative staff members to follow a biological determination of those people.

> "<Non Europeans> shall mean all persons whose parents or one whose of [sic] parents is a member of any Non European race."[506]

For the other case, Administrator Johannes Werth pointed out in his inaugural address at the consecration ceremony for the new cemetery at which, amongst others, representatives from all Christian denominations attended, that those 3,840 square metres were intended, "for the exclusive use for the burial of human bodies of Europeans."[507] At this occasion it did explicitly include the Jewish community who received a demarcated section within the new cemetery, although they were subjected to similar discriminations like the Indigenous population before. There existed a separate Jewish cemetery (9) vis-à-vis the old Native one[508], and a later application to fence it of was rejected by the Town Council based on the argument not to create a precedent.[509]

In contrast to their European counterparts, the Indigenous population was subject to discriminative rules under the above mentioned Regulations. According to section 6 they were not allowed to erect any kind of tomb, monument, inscription or the like without the Town Council's consent.[510] In addition, access to the cemetery could arbitrarily be limited or restricted in application of section 8, whilst hearses

---

[503] NAN MWI 120/3/44, Resolution No. 451 in Minutes No. 122 of Ordinary Council Meeting dated 23rd September 1926, no sheet number.

[504] NAN MWI 36/24/37, Resolution No. 64 in Minutes No. 50 of Ordinary Council Meeting dated 30th January 1923, no sheet number.

[505] NAN MWI 36/24/37, Resolution No. 262 in Minutes No. 58 of Adjourned Council Meeting dated 13th July 1923, no sheet number.

[506] NAN MWI 36/24/37, Regulations for the Control and Management of Cemeteries for Non Europeans, undated, no sheet number.

[507] NAN MWI 102/3/44, Inaugural address by the Administrator dated 28th October 1926, no sheet number.

[508] NAN MWI 117/1/44, shown in blue print of trolley line deviation along Lazarett Street, no sheet number.

[509] NAN MWI 120/1/44, Resolution No. 340 in Minutes No. 140 of Ordinary Council Meeting dated 23rd June 1927, no sheet number.

[510] NAN MWI 36/24/37, Regulations for the Control and Management of Cemeteries for Non Europeans, undated, no sheet number.

and other carriages were generally prohibited from entering the Indigenous cemetery, following section 9. Europeans by contrast were not subjected to similar instructions at 'their' cemetery; the road leading to the new European cemetery was improved to withstand future traffic by visitors and hearses as three resolutions since 1921 instructed, the last urgent one submitted in 1926.[511] But the differences also became visually apparent: Lush gardens were laid out for the European cemetery to be tended by the Assistant Gardener of Windhoek's zoological garden.[512] In order to ensure a stable water provision for the cemetery, improvements at the Location's water supply through new boreholes were suggested by Committee member Mr Arnold. In an attempt to avoid additional expenses for the Municipality, Councillor Kemp linked this proposal with his idea for a new wash and bath house for the Indigenous population. In his letter to the Town Clerk he expected monthly revenues from £15 to £20 for tickets to use those facilities, which would in turn cover the on-going expenditures on the cemetery's water supply once the boring and installation costs were repaid.[513] A seemingly positive investment in the Location would have been exploited to the White community's benefits.

Whereas the old Native cemetery had to wait long for its simple fence, the one for the new European cemetery was finished before its actual inauguration and, at the occasion of an early inspection, the Town Council still demanded further improvements, "so as to prevent small stock from encroaching on the New Cemetery and damaging the plantations."[514] The contrast between the well-tended European cemetery and the adjacent Indigenous areas of both, the Location and the Native cemetery can be observed in the aerial photos in the appendix (see A4 and A5). Potential ethnic divisions, which could be linked to different religious denominations, were considered in section 3 of the Regulations, where it stipulated that, "[c]ertain portions of the public cemetery shall be set aside for certain religious denominations [...]."[515] These separate portions blended with the distinctions made among the inhabitants living at the Location. Furthermore, a request for burials of deceased members of the Cape Coloured community at the European

---

[511] NAN MWI 102/3/44, Resolution No. 223 in Minutes No. 115 of Ordinary Council Meeting dated 6th May 1926, no sheet number.

[512] NAN MWI 102/3/44, Town Engineer's Report to the Public Works Committee, undated, no sheet number. Such work division was commonly accepted, as Saxony's royal *Gartenbaudirektor* explained in his conference contribution to the 1903 Dresden City Exhibition (Von Petz 1998: 27-8).

[513] NAN MWI 102/3/44, letter by Mr Kemp dated 26th April 1922, no sheet number.

[514] NAN MWI 102/3/44, Resolution No. 230 in Minutes No. 99 of Adjourned Council Meeting dated 5th June 1925, no sheet number.

[515] NAN MWI 36/24/37, Regulations for the Control and Management of Cemeteries for Non Europeans, undated, no sheet number.

cemetery was rejected by the Town Council in 1927 but the demarcation of a specific section for them close to the Native cemetery was ordered instead.[516] After the closure of the Native cemetery at Klein Windhoek Location (12) in the early 1930s[517], the new Native cemetery at Windhoek Location remained the only one in operations and it was extended two more times in 1937[518] and 1944[519] respectively, though always at cheapest costs. The proximity of the new European cemetery to the Location caused several complaints from the White community about what was considered as 'disrespectful behaviour' towards visitors and disturbances at funeral services, as a letter by Assembly Member Taljaard reported in very pejorative descriptions, attributing the African population with beastlike characteristics.[520] In retrospect, it cannot be verified to what extent Taljaard's descriptions reflected real circumstances or if they were, at least partially, the result of individual hypersensitivity or imagination. But to a certain extent it can be assumed that those incidents represented deliberate attempts for Indigenous contestations, which reflected prevailing different cultural attitudes.

Historically, there were two more confirmed burial sites for members of the Herero community. The first one is directly linked to the Namibian War and represented a mass grave for victims of the concentration camp. During an inspection in late 1919, at least 190 tombs were identified by municipal authorities though it was estimated that at least 300 must have existed on a site 80x100 metres in size.[521] The Administration's archival files remain relatively vague on this matter, as it seems that the whole cemetery (deliberately) fell into oblivion from the bureaucratic point of view. Neither an exact site nor the deceased were recorded but the cemetery is still traced on the map (13). It can still be assumed that a multiple number of people were interred at this cemetery, as cited personal accounts in a letter by the Office for Native Affairs suggest. "It is said as many as 10 persons are buried in one grave, so heavy and rapid was the death roll [sic]."[522] In contrast to the official

---

[516] NAN MWI 36/24/37, Resolution No. 381 in Minutes No. 141 of Ordinary Council Meeting dated 28th April 1927, no sheet number.

[517] NAN MWI 36/24/37, Resolution No. 688 in Minutes of Public Works Committee Meeting dated 8th July 1932, no sheet number.

[518] NAN MWI 36/24/37, unnumbered Resolution in Minutes of Public Works Committee Meeting dated 29th January 1937, no sheet number.

[519] NAN MWI 36/24/37, unnumbered Resolution in Minutes of Public Works Committee Meeting dated 26th July 1944, no sheet number.

[520] NAN MWI 5/8, letter "Verlegung der alten Werft" by L. Taljaard dated 8th June 1931, no sheet number.

[521] NAN MWI 120/1/44, memo concerning Old Herero cemetery dated 28th November 1919, no sheet number.

[522] NAN MWI 120/1/44, letter by the Office for Native Affairs dated 20th February 1920, no sheet number.

records the Indigenous community remembered the circumstances very well, which can be interpreted as another form of resistance to the colonisers' narratives. The letter goes on,

> "[t]he natives hold that the mortality was due to insufficient food, overcrowding, bad weather conditions, scanty clothing and blankets and excessive application of the lash."[523]

Nevertheless, the Administration was unwilling to approve of the Indigenous application for a proper demarcation of the Old Herero Cemetery, based on the cynical argument that the Hereros themselves would have to provide the administrative staff members with all relevant information on the deceased, such as,

> "[…] names of persons buried, ages, dates of decease, and whether there are any relatives who may undertake the maintenance of the plots in this cemetery."[524]

Over the course of this correspondence the Town Clerk became aware of another Herero cemetery which further undermined the idea of segregation. Apparently, several Indigenous people were buried in the vicinity of the Government Buildings at Windhoek's centre (14, as approximation only) and George Kerby asked for their move to another grave at the Native cemetery.[525] The execution of this translocation is not documented in the archival files.

Native churches

The Native cemeteries were complemented by spiritual succour and church services on Sunday, although Windhoek's track record was initially not that good in this respect as already pointed out. Nevertheless, religious institutions played an increasing role in Indigenous urban culture, and therefore two churches were specifically devoted to Native parishes – one in Windhoek (15) and the other in Klein Windhoek (16). Due to its site at Talstraße in city centre, the church in Windhoek caused direct social encounters between the different social communities, which extended beyond work-related contacts and made the Indigenous community, at least, visible on weekends and holidays too. Those interactions on the street were further extended by loopholes within the regulatory framework of the curfew. Despite the maintenance of Locations and specific compounds with their curfew as well as the restrictions imposed on domestic servants, the files do report on,

---

[523] NAN MWI 120/1/44, letter by the Office for Native Affairs dated 20th February 1920, no sheet number.
[524] NAN MWI 120/1/44, letter by Town Clerk dated 9th December 1919, no sheet number.
[525] NAN MWI 120/1/44, letter by Town Clerk dated 25th March 1920, no sheet number.

336

"loitering of native youths in Township areas"[526] in 1931. Such incidents happened at daytime in central areas of Windhoek and tended to openly contest White supremacy. Therefore, it did not take long for the administrative institutions to come to the following conclusions.

> "The point was fully discussed and it was unanimously agreed that the Administration be asked to make the necessary legislation by which the movements of native youths outside the location can be checked. It has been ascertained that at present the Council does not possess any statutory powers to intervene."[527]

Municipal representatives, in this case, considered compulsory education for those youths one potential solution but left the decision and responsibility with the Administration. On the other side, this situation once again underscores how limited the social services at the Location during interwar years actually were, though the Wesleyan Mission had erected some buildings within it at an estimated value of £550.[528] The other religious denominations relied on their premises at Windhoek's central areas. It shows where the idea of a dual city de facto reached its limits. Further social services were only offered by the Municipality in form of one hospital (17) at the northern fringe that was run at Windhoek's expenses as part of the obligatory Native social welfare. Within the city's urban fabric it was situated diametrically opposed to the general military hospital (Lazarett) for the White population (18) in the south. The sites for both hospitals did reflect those days' attempts to separate sick people at sanatoria, although additional smaller hospitals existed at least temporarily.[529] Somewhat in between both of them laid the maternity ward called *Elisabethheim* (19).

Fears of a European *lumpenproletariat* in SWA

Of course, most restrictions were imposed on the African population but as already indicated in the first subchapter on the historic context (see 4.1), some regulations did directly and exclusively affect the European community. It is here that social distinctions and the perceived fear of a White *lumpenproletariat* came into question. Social considerations did always impact administrative policies and subsequent actions. One continuous idea was the preservation of the White communi-

---

[526] NAN MWI 5/8, Minutes of Conference on Native Location Affairs dated 19th March 1931, no sheet number.
[527] NAN MWI 5/8, Minutes of Conference on Native Location Affairs dated 19th March 1931, no sheet number.
[528] NAN MWI 5/8, Minutes of Conference on Native Location Affairs dated 19th March 1931, no sheet number.
[529] Bravenboer mentions a total number of five hospitals erected during German rule (Bravenboer 2004: 85).

ty's image as the superior element of Windhoek's society. All relevant stakeholders therefore had a very critical eye on the potential evolution of a European proletariat in SWA that might have undermined the established hierarchical order. The appearance of White vagrants or other destitute persons in the town would have damaged their self-esteem and the perpetuated image towards the African population. In 1926 SWA's Advisory Council explicitly prohibited entrance to poor Whites from neighbouring South Africa as a general rule in order to restrict vagrancy.[530]

Under German colonial rule strict regulations applied to people, who were either financially unable to sustain their stay in DSWA and Windhoek any longer or who were classified as being a 'lunatic.' Prospective immigrants arriving at one of the Territory's ports were requested to prove their financial means before receiving official admission to enter the colony. These controls remained in place and had been intensified under South African rule between the two World Wars.[531] Christo Botha refers to the official advice stated in a letter to the assistant German Consul in Pretoria from 1924 that prospective German settlers should bring at least £1,000 with them to make a start, whilst the official requirement for South Africans was only at £250.[532] Such controls were complemented by specific administrative reports about single persons, or families, who were depending on public welfare or charitable organisations for an extended period. In this case it did not matter if their precarious situation was due to accidents, sickness or unemployment. The municipal administration collected information on potential cases and monitored the mobility of these persons very carefully. If the prospects for speedy recovery could not be confirmed by a public health officer, or the administration was convinced of a person's inability to find a new employment in due time, bureaucratic procedures for their respective deportation were set in motion.

For the German period there are four reported cases in Windhoek between 1912 and 1914, although the correspondence to settle the costs extended until 1921.[533] For every person almost cynical calculations were made, comparing the costs of their medical treatment in DSWA as opposed to their deportation. If the result was, like in the case of a man suffering from "incurable heart disease", a negative one and the deportation turned out to be the cheaper alternative, then this person

---

[530] Botha 2008: 241.
[531] VPLA Fifth Session, Second Assembly 1933: 33. Immigrants from overseas were required to make a cash deposit payment of £40.
[532] Botha 2008: 239.
[533] NAN SVW A.4.f.

338

was sent home as soon as his or her health condition allowed for the journey.[534] Some documents suggest that public authorities dared to make relevant documents fitting in order to justify the person's deportation.[535] The cited man died soon after in consequence of his heart disease, and his widow as well as their three children and the coffin were sent back to Germany less than two months later.[536] In addition, the Municipality tried all in their means to get those costs reimbursed: the deported person either had to sign a formal obligation to repay the debt, or a relative was identified and then served as bailsman. Such cases could therefore extend well into the South African period.

The aforementioned rules applied to all White persons regardless of their nationality, and the European community was in this respect interpreted as homogenous entity. A specific law was drafted that should eventually rule all cases of poor relief, which transferred first stage duties for help to the municipal or district level, whilst the Territory was responsible for cases exceeding municipal support, or for persons who did not qualify for such local support in first instance.[537] This draft did not include specific regulations for the repatriation of the poor. Since the draft itself is undated and the file does contain two starting dates (1st January 1911 and 1st August 1916) it remains speculative, whether the missing option for repatriation or the outbreak of the First World War prevented the enactment of this draft version under German rule. In addition to those persons covered by poor relief, similar rules were applied to 'lunatics' who needed to be sent home to Germany or Cape Town under the pretext of better treatment at insane asylums there. Correspondence for the years 1911 to 1916 confirms five cases where mental illnesses had been diagnosed and those patients were then repatriated.[538] Many documents were specifically double checking the person's ability and willingness to work[539], as well as their potential to be a public danger[540], and during the war the British Military Government covered the travel expense in case of repatriation to Germany.[541]

Through these regulations and selection procedures, the administration followed the Social Darwinian model and tried to make sure that just the fittest parts of the European society were admitted to the Territory. The correspondence does con-

---

[534] NAN SVW A.4.f, sheets 2-3.
[535] NAN SVW A.4.f, sheets 31-2, 37-8, 42.
[536] NAN SVW A.4.f, sheets 6-12.
[537] NAN SVW A.4.e.
[538] NAN SVW G.5.ae.
[539] E.g. NAN SVW G.5.ae, sheet 26.
[540] NAN SVW G.5.ae, sheets 40-1.
[541] NAN SVW G.5.ae, sheet 28.

firm that these checks were not repealed under British/South African military rule, though no further cases are documented in the Municipality's files.

5. Conclusions

In order to summarise the range of results generated as part of this research project, I will reflect on them at two levels.

1. My work has presented different strands of the *transnational planning background* that played a role in the debates at both, the metropole as well as the context of SWA. Hence it is necessary to reflect on how and why these different strands mattered and what their coherent elements were.

2. To a certain extent these debates and the transnational networks created the necessary context to understand the policies implemented in my Windhoek case study and how *residential segregation* could be enforced in this specific environment.

Transnational circulation of planning ideas

The analysed time period from 1914 to 1945 is characterised by a rapid succession of various development trends. These trends render it impossible to describe interwar urban development in connection with colonial history as one coherent narrative. One key result of my work instead is the dissection of three domains in the transnational circulation of planning ideas that reflect the plurality of those years' debates and schools of thoughts. The first domain concentrates on the challenges at the metropole as reported in the planning journals. My thorough analysis and comparison of *Der Städtebau* and *The Town Planning Review* has revealed a level of international exchange that was – at least to me – surprising in its extent. Readers of both journals were supplied with a mix of domestic topics, which usually represented roughly one half of all contributions, as well as a wide range of international matters from all around the world. Those international articles went beyond what could be characterised as kind of superfluous travel or conference reports but did in many cases demonstrate a thorough level of understanding for the legal frameworks in other countries. Furthermore, some authors tried to make sense of those regulations and explicitly searched for opportunities of selective borrowing and adaptation to their domestic contexts to use Ward's theoretical framework.[1]

In terms of contents both journals paid attention to similar topics. The omnipresent housing question in quantitative and qualitative terms is just one example of

---

[1] Ward 2000: 40-60.

urban challenges, which were covered extensively on both sides of the North Sea. Other frequently addressed topics ranged from traffic and its impacts due to the prevalence of motor vehicles and their speed, to planning legislation and urban aesthetics. National specificities played a role, both in planning terms e.g. the regionalisation around Greater Berlin and in the political arena. Interwar changes under the given political circumstances posed a severe rupture to (the willingness to accept) the transnational circulation of planning ideas. International reports were an important asset to *The Town Planning Review's* reputation, though the journal's editors decided to focus on countries like Italy early in interwar years. Through this decision they explicitly wanted to counterbalance what they interpreted as the pre-eminent role of the US and German planning traditions. *Der Städtebau* had an equally international stance but suffered from the rise of Nazism. Although the international planning community regarded the German tradition as a pariah, *Der Städtebau* was able to keep some of its international links. Nevertheless, both planning journals kept an eye on each other and there were still some forms of exchange, either through reviews on the respective other's recent issues or through contributions from the same author to both journals, as has happened on some occasions during the analysed time period from 1910 to 1945.

The expertise of authors did in several cases establish direct comment on the colonial context, where they carried out early forms of what is nowadays called 'consultancy work', or were involved in the preparation of urban planning schemes. It is here that the second domain of transnational circulation can be identified which extended between the metropole and the colonies. This domain worked as a bidirectional exchange and developments at colonial cities were covered in both journals. Anyhow plans for large scale projects like the new capital cities of Canberra and New Delhi drew specific attention. Despite the effort to analyse at least a few pre-First World War years in order to trace potential coverage on them, German colonies did not play a role in the planning journals; instead *Der Städtebau* devoted most of its colonial attention to the British Empire. From the Eurocentric viewpoint the reception of colonial developments was characterised by a certain ambiguity, which ranged from a fascination for the exotic 'Other' just like in Edward Said's terms for Orientalism, to a clearly defined belief in European superiority. Indeed some of the results produced in colonial environments, such as planning schemes or legal tools, were well received in the metropole and considered as 'progress' that could be adapted to the benefit of the mother country too. This view fits with the colonial cities' perception as tabula rasa and experimental ground, which was also the reason for a subtle – but constant – level of reservation towards planning ideas created at colonial entities. From the metropole's view they were interesting but needed translation into the domestic context. The European planning community was absolutely clear that a colonial city should be based on the dual city concept. Further all substantial planning efforts would only be carried out by European planners and not by Indigenous people.

The latter statement was commonly agreed upon among colonial planners, who were virtually all White. Despite their ancestry, colonial planners had a reserved view on the metropole. The archival sources suggest that European cities represented an important source of inspiration and an admired role model to be taken as the colonial city's yardstick for comparison. At the same time, colonial planners drew a subtle but distinct line to demarcate their own domains, where they expressed scepticism about a mere 'copy-and-paste' of European solutions or rejected them as inappropriate for the colonial context. Both planning communities regarded their respective counterpart as somewhat quirky and detached from the 'real' circumstances 'on the ground.' The results demonstrate that the idea of a dichotomy between the metropoles in Europe as one secluded sphere as opposed to colonial entities at the imagined periphery becomes in fact obsolete in the face of the existing transnational networks. Instead my findings support Katrina Gulliver's recently formulated argumentation towards an interpretation of colonial cities as a distinct category in historical analysis, representing an emerging new culture.[2]

The third domain represents the circulation of ideas among and between colonial cities themselves. Among them exchange was less formalised since there virtually did not exist a specific journal or other medium similar to the planning journals at the metropole. One minor exception to this rule can be identified for the context of Windhoek and SWA in form of the *Municipal Magazine* originally published in the Union of South Africa but read elsewhere in the region too. Nonetheless, much of the circulation was based on personal contacts and travels, which highlights the impact individual persons could make on the development of a single town. For Windhoek, Town Clerk George Kerby or Government Architect (*Regierungsbaumeister*) Gottlieb Redecker, as part of the former German administration before Kerby, represented important intermediaries in the context of Saunier's concept of transnational history. Despite its remote location the town was extremely well connected with other colonial entities in Africa as well as with Germany and, to a lesser degree, Great Britain. Many of those links in the planning discipline were based on personal contacts usually established among administrative staff members, but in exceptional cases they belonged to the realm of private businesses. One extreme example occurred towards the end of German rule in

---

[2] Gulliver 2015.

1914, when the Municipality entrusted the local representative of a private developer with the preparation of tender documents. The Town Council had delegated the negotiations about pertaining financial schemes with banks at the metropole to him. It could not be verified to what extent the local authorities in fact exploited his free services to their benefits or were actually made a pawn in his hands. This incident nonetheless illustrates a level of naivety or nonchalance among the German administration.

For the case of Windhoek it has to be conceded that the scope of international sources reached its greatest variety during the First World War, before the mandated Territory was successively drawn into South African domains, which then became its prime source of inspiration. Despite few traces of a Commonwealth identity in SWA, its close interrelations with South Africa structurally resemble forms of sub-imperialism.[3] Those forms are traceable in the Territory's economic dependency on the neighbour, which could not be loosened despite some attempts to establish alternative ties across the African continent. Instead, similar to previous German imperial rule, SWA remained glued to a position of pauper where the colony had to somehow justify the external expenses made for it. From Windhoek's perspective the only change was that the donor did not represent the imperial mother country anymore but the custodian of a League of Nations' mandate, whilst the donor's policies remained driven by an impetus of economic imperialism.

Translated into the planning realms the results can be classified based on Stephen Ward's concept for the diffusion of planning ideas. During the First World War SWA's administration was still able to tap several sources and to select appropriate ideas for subsequent implementation in Windhoek's urban development. The Municipality would therefore qualify as *undiluted borrowing* according to Ward where external impacts prevailed but local planners were able to play a marginal role in their implementation. This situation changed under the dominant role South Africa played in interwar years; Windhoek's planning regime then drifted one step down in Ward's classification and did only qualify as *negotiated imposition*. SWA heavily depended on input from the Union and local authorities were barely able to select those tools deemed appropriate to the city's context. The Territory's transition in terms of applicable legislation created a mixture of German and Roman Dutch with English laws that would justify an up-to-date research project on its own.[4]

---

[3] Mommsen 1987: 84-5.
[4] A first contribution for the case of Strasbourg was made by Stefan Fisch on the continuities in architecture and urban design under German and French administration between 1907 and 1957 (Fisch, Stefan, *Der Straßburger "Große Durchbruch" (1907-1957). Kontinuität und*

344

Windhoek mirrors the experiences made in the French border region of Alsace-Lorraine to which Saunier already referred in his explanations of transnational history and its concept as, "[…] places in-between different countries"[5], and where the mix of legal systems prevailed and created a basis for mutual understanding as well as problems in their execution.

Those three domains of transnational circulation do help me to approach my first research question.

How did the European urban planning debate impact on the development of colonial cities between 1914 and 1945?

As the analysis of the planning journals and the archival sources has revealed, there existed many direct relations between European planning debates and colonial cities. In some cases they tended to be obvious through the physical presence of European planners on the ground, but in many cases they were conveyed at a rather indirect level through the translation and application of European-style ideas. The routines and knowledge of administrative institutions as well as higher education have made an impact on expectations, habits and moral values in the colonial context. This can be exemplified with reference to European debates on the working classes and their neighbourhoods, which were dominated by bourgeois moral and ethical values. From a middle-class viewpoint inhabitants of such socially deprived areas were automatically associated with negative attributes such as laziness, drunkenness or debauchery.

Residential segregation and the case study of Windhoek

It is in this respect necessary to remember how the term 'slum' actually entered urban debates as artificial outsider's view on working class neighbourhoods as Alan Mayne and Tim Murray have exemplified.[6] Similar mechanisms applied to the colonial context where the outsider's view clashed with Indigenous cultural habits, and where the social stratification of the metropole was made the future yardstick. Although living conditions in those European working class neighbourhoods were admittedly low from current perspective, their historic pejorative descriptions were equally biased based on bourgeois or upper class values. To them, those shock-like

---

Brüche in Architektur, Städtebau und Verwaltungspraxis zwischen deutscher und französischer Zeit, In: Cornelissen, Christoph; Fisch, Stefan; Maas, Anne [Eds.]: Grenzstadt Straßburg. Stadtplanung, kommunale Wohnungspolitik und Öffentlichkeit 1870-1940. St. Ingbert: Röhrig 1997: 103-204).
[5] Saunier 2013: 113.
[6] Mayne, Murray 2001.

conditions at their doorstep initiated two reactions. In the first place, as Ellen Ross has summarised[7], women started a domestic 'civilising mission' with the long-term goal to uplift those poor 'sub-human creatures' to bourgeois interpretations of a 'New Man.' Early British planning legislation was aimed at the betterment of minimum living qualities, which went hand in hand with the improvement of hygiene and public health. Particularly the latter motive represented the reason for the second bourgeois reaction, which comprised of a tendency towards social segregation in European cities. In order to physically leave the supposedly 'immoral', overcrowded and potentially infectious working class neighbourhoods in central areas behind, they moved to new, geographically privileged areas at the urban fringe.[8]

Interwar colonial cities were a complex reflection of these developments at the metropole. As I have tried to demonstrate, this bourgeois mind-set has permeated into the colonial context in various ways and adaptations but it blended perfectly with the imperial policies of a civilising mission. What used to be a hierarchy of social distinctions within Europe was then translated into a concept of racial divide for the colonial context. Interestingly at least some South African legal documents labelled the hierarchy as a matter of 'social classes.' Although social ranks did still make a difference among the European community and, less often mentioned, among the Indigenous community, the roles were distributed differently in African colonial societies. The Black population suffered the most and was attributed with the working class status as defined in the European context. Their 'education' and moral uplift did not just represent part of a long-term goal under the umbrella of the so-called 'White man's burden', thus replicating the image to create a 'New Man'. At the same time it formed a perfect justification and pretext for Black discrimination and exploitation. In this direction residential segregation was one of the tools to provide for the 'right' environment, which had to be maintained at both ends: patronising the Black population; as well as preventing the evolution of a feared *lumpenproletariat* among the European community itself. The latter would have undermined the inherent assumption of White supremacy.

Colonial policies did change their attitudes towards the Indigenous population and SWA serves as an example. At the beginning, the concept was based on a paternislist-style civilising mission and aimed for a cultural uplift of the Black population. In the long run, at least some of them were considered capable of assimilating European values. This concept was then abandoned with the rise of Social Darwinism and racist ideologies which determined the populations' status on assumed

---

7 El. Ross 2001.
8 See Galliker 1997, Hopkins 1990 and Ward 2004.

biological reasons as part of eugenics. Under these circumstance Blacks were confined to a function as mere labour reserve for the Europeans and hence among Whites electrical household appliances did play a less significant role as status symbol than was the case in the metropole. Despite some severe difficulties in the aftermath of the Namibian War to hire Indigenous labourers from both, the Territory's northern border regions and within the police zone as Zimmerer has demonstrated[9], the need to replace manual labour by technical devices was still not considered to be urgent. Yet this does not mean that technological progress was rejected as such, but the archival sources suggest a rather selective distribution in SWA.

Those interrelations between local and imperial population actually help to address my second research question.

What kind of similarities and differences did the European planning debate produce in the colonial context with regards to residential segregation?

The previous paragraphs already pointed to some of the general similarities and differences between the European debate and the production of urban lifestyles in colonial cities. For a detailed look at residential segregation it is firstly necessary to underscore the plurality of colonial cities and policies, which make it difficult to formulate a comprehensive answer. I will therefore focus on the results for Windhoek as presented in the archival sources. Even in this remote town European social distinctions impacted the colonial setup and were further complicated by overlapping strong racial divisions.

The classical image is the dual city concept that consisted of two clearly detached spatial and legal realms for the Black and White communities respectively. Abu-Lughod's early concept of dual dichotomy reached its limit in face of the exceptional developments in Southern Africa, for Windhoek's colonial society presented itself to be more complex. Apart from those lines drawn between European and Indigenous communities in official policies, the European community was by far no homogenous bloc. It is here that a clear difference to circumstances at the metropole becomes tangible. Those typical socio-economic distinctions based on rank did play a role for Whites, as the varying levels of sophistication in terms of accommodation for governmental employees have demonstrated. The higher a person's rank, the better were her prospects to first have access to such dwellings at all, and second to receive a house more generous in space and equipment. Considering Windhoek's relatively small size, those hierarchies remained less pro-

---

[9] Zimmerer 2001: 176-7.

nounced than in industrialised cities though. Furthermore, though there was a general consensus among members of all three language groups (Afrikaans, English, and German) about the subaltern status of the Black population, each group jealously competed for its own share in the available resources and this competition dominated the political arena at varying degrees throughout the interwar period. A last element that contributed to the complexity of Windhoek's specific environment on the European side was religion. Similar to many cities in the metropole Jewish citizens were subjected to discrimination. Although there was no specific residential section assigned to them, the Jewish community originally received a separate cemetery close to the Black one and therefore far away from the White one.

Windhoek under South African mandated rule did constitute a tripartite racial society, where it was understood that the Europeans represented the pyramid's top. The Black population by contrast was attributed with a position at the inferior bottom level, hence resembling the working classes in Europe, and both residential areas were intended to be strictly separated from each other. No Black would be allowed to live in the European sections of Windhoek and vice versa White access to the Black Locations was equally restricted and monitored, at least on paper. Despite a curfew imposed on the Indigenous population, many exceptions were actually granted to domestic servants, in consequence undermining the dual city concept. This dichotomy was further disturbed by the Coloured community who filled a gap between the White and Indigenous community. The Coloured community was attributed with a legal and socio-economic position which officially classified them to be superior to Blacks, and even access to European residential areas was not completely ruled out. Following some successful legal contestations by Coloured inhabitants in the Union of South Africa to receive permission to reside at European sections of the cities, the legislator was determined to close such loopholes.

Windhoek's tripartite social stratification was characterised by a severe imbalance in civil rights, which did neither grant equal rights among the Europeans themselves nor with respect to the Coloured and Black community. In most spheres of life SWA was dominated by conservative ideas since the German period. With the remarkable exception of communication technologies, the country's society showed a reluctant attitude towards innovations and technological advances. Under these circumstances, debates about universal suffrage remained unresolved for most of interwar years. Instead, electoral rights were limited to affluent White citizens at the local level, and to White men for the Territory's Legislative Assembly. In order to defend its supreme position, SWA's administration followed the ideas of Social Darwinism among the European community and expelled those members deemed to be physically, mentally or financially unfit to stay in Windhoek, as some archival files have shown. It falls under this conservative framework, which was heavily inspired by the racial divide, that Africans did not receive a kind of burgher status. Instead, they were explicitly classified as migrant labourers hired for the Europeans' convenience, and who had to be temporarily accommodated in the vicinity of the city. This image blended with paternalist concepts to preserve Indigenous traditions and links to their rural relatives. Of course, similar to the European community there did not exist one single and homogenous Black population bloc. Despite the classification's artificial and Eurocentric nature, regional origins and kinships constituted an element to organise the internal structure of Windhoek's Location. It would hence be interesting to shed more light on the matter of residential segregation from the African perspective but here the archival sources have set a clear limit of what can be depicted or not. As a consequence of the available sources my work tends to replicate a Eurocentric narrative on Windhoek's interwar past despite my initial comprehensive intentions.

In retrospect my second research question suffers from a shortcoming as it is of a Eurocentric nature. Despite the significance of European cities as potential role models, the question's formulation is too focused to cover other sources of inspiration for colonial urban development. Residential segregation cannot be properly addressed or explained based on European references. Colonial cities with their complex social stratification are a distinct creation based on experiences made 'on the spot' instead. As soon as I detected this shortcoming, I have opened my research to include external sources to the colonial planning debate as well.

Nevertheless, my third research question helped me in this respect, as it was explicitly inquiring the international exchange.

To what extent has there been international exchange of ideas for the case study of Windhoek, and how did it impact on planning residential segregation?

Windhoek was, as already summarised, part of an extensive transnational network among which planning ideas circulated from the metropole and from other colonial entities, with a focus on South Africa. But whilst the industrialised countries did only set the stage through an adopted set-up of social distinctions, residential segregation was heavily impacted by other colonial examples. This was in fact true for previous German rule as well as for the mandated period under Union law. Some external frameworks did reach SWA through a kind of relay adaptation, as has been illustrated with regards to the financial and legal schemes for social housing in the 1930s. Here, South Africa apparently used British schemes for council housing and slum eradication as its role model for domestic legislation. It is therefore interesting to see how such templates can be interpreted and modified to fit with the precondition of racial segregation.

The general outline of urban developments follows similar lines at the metropole and the colonies, whilst their differences come with the details. The housing shortage can for this purpose be considered an excellent example. At the micro level, Windhoek was faced with an insufficient housing supply over the full interwar period. In this respect it de facto did not matter what skin colour a person had, since the Housing Board was unable to provide all governmental staff members with a dwelling and official reports on the Location's housing conditions were worse, drawing the image of insanitary overcrowding. During wartimes this problem was exacerbated due to the almost complete cessation of construction activities; Windhoek blended with similar trends at the macro level, where the European nations were unable to achieve sufficient completion figures. Nevertheless, the reasons serve to illustrate the differences between metropole and perceived periphery. The former inflation had a tremendous impact on the construction activities and was fed by high prices for materials as well as a scarcity of skilled labourers. Windhoek by contrast really was impacted by its peripheral geographical location and saw a cessation of construction activities which was mainly due to skyrocketing prices for imported materials. In order to compensate for this problem, and to keep their businesses up and running, owners of construction firms tried to cut down their employees' wages as much as possible.

Windhoek's development did draw on international examples as reference points in its general evolution, which became particularly obvious in some criticism of the city's urban patterns. Despite its smaller size and remote location, SWA's capital was equally affected by urban sprawl, and it was this sprawl that fuelled the implementation of residential segregation. Although Windhoek's earliest layout plan in 1892 envisaged a grid iron pattern, the town grew rather organically and spontaneously over the following decades with several significant public functions scattered almost randomly over the evolving urban structure. In face of an insufficient administrative ability to effectively control the application of colonial (planning) regulations, separate Black residential areas sprung up spontaneously at the beginning. Following the Namibian War in 1904-8, the German colonisers started to 'protect' themselves and implemented stricter rules for residential segregation. Some of these rules contradicted the mother country's will and they reversed the war's actual outcomes: in fact, not the Germans would have needed further protection but the African population who fell victim to the colonisers' atrocities. Whilst parts of

350

those rules can be attributed to local ingenuity, many of them were based on other colonial examples and before the First World War South Africa was a frequently used role model.

Residential segregation was not limited to the built environment. For my work I have contextualised them within the scope of relevant regulations, which covered the economic, legal and social spheres and did not spare the deceased. The urban African population was systematically denied all options other than entering into wage labour for White employers to earn their living. Similar restrictions applied to all relevant legal issues, extending from individual land rights to building regulations which implicitly excluded the local population based on the required building materials. As part of the social interventions Africans' mobility and alcohol consumption was officially curtailed, whilst interracial relationships were stigmatised too.

In order to return to the matter of urban sprawl, in face of typical plot sizes measuring 1,000 square metres, Windhoek's European sections were growing and slowly encroached the Black Location, where plots merely reached 225 square metres on average. Due to the city's rather spontaneous development, this area came under review and was identified as suitable place for future European extensions. Several plans for the Location's transfer to a new site were discussed during interwar years, although the actual implementation only took place under apartheid in 1958.

Furthermore, the sources emphasise that interwar debates revolving around residential segregation did not provide a linear path to those post-Second World War apartheid policies. Admittedly, segregationist ideas and the belief in White supremacy belonged to a widespread attitude among the European community and its self-conception. But despite those strict policies already in place to preserve the tripartite colonial social hierarchy, the debate could still have taken a different direction. This interpretation can further be substantiated by the circumstances as laid down in the archival sources. Of course, there were strong elements, like the curfew imposed on the African population, which support the classical notion of a dual city, as did the stereotypical associations of Indigenous people with various kinds of infectious diseases. There existed many legal and informal loopholes, and at formal levels did the administration grant several exceptions effectively undermining the implementation of a dual society in its strictest sense.

Osterhammel and Jansen are right in their characterisation of colonial cities as important spaces of encounter and conflict.[10] In fact, Africans and Europeans alike can be attributed with the impetus for such disintegrating activities. To the former, Windhoek represented an opportunity to participate and benefit from the city in social and, to a lesser extent, in economic terms. The frequent administrative reports about Black labourers absenting themselves from work without the local authorities' ability to trace them in the Location's anonymity illustrate those existing informal loopholes. Europeans, on the other side, were not inclined to accept those legal restrictions like the Indigenous curfew as soon as they affected their own level of convenience. The many special permits for Black domestic servants, or other African labourers, accommodated at White premises give another indication for the factual limitations of the dual city concept in Windhoek. Maybe it helps to attribute this finding to the 'real life' situation, where the dual structure represented the imagined and aspired long-term goal in the eyes of the White community. At the same time everyone was adapted to ignore and tacitly accept its limitations in application. Those limitations clearly indicated the extent of the colonial grip, which might have been prepared to deal with all eventualities on paper but lacked the capacities to actually enforce those rules in the interwar years. It is here, that I am fully in line with Zimmerer's findings on the colonial administration's options and limitations for intervention.[11]It leads me to see my results as an indication to reconsider the dual narratives as they suggest the recognition of hybridity in Windhoek's history. Although the administrative files do not label every form of civil disobedience or similar actions as African contestation of White rule – if they did record them at all – it is at least important to recognise those attempts. My results for Windhoek's urban developments with regards to residential segregation in many respects confirm Libby Porter's judgement on colonialism as being violent, messy, incomplete, and contradictory.[12] My study has at least tried to shed some light on the often neglected African perspective within this scientific work.

I would like to finish on prospective related options that might build on this research. In order to follow up with Beeckmans's and Saunier's recommendations to further cross Africa's regional and linguistic confines, the results for Windhoek have stimulated a keen interest to investigate and compare the situation for a settler colony in the French context. This would have to follow similar lines like in this PhD dissertation and firstly requires the analysis of a leading French planning journal, to identify the planning tradition's openness to transnational circulation at

---

[10] Osterhammel, Jansen 2012: 96.
[11] Zimmerer 2001: 285.
[12] L. Porter 2010: 65.

352

the metropole and the extent of colonial coverage. In a second step an appropriate case study needs to be selected and it seems advisable to focus on an Algerian city. This would reflect its relevance as settler colony, but it could also help to shed some light on potential differences in face of its background as colonial entity being formally integrated into France proper. Considering the attention paid to Algiers in previous research, not just from the French perspective, the city might serve well as case study despite its location and function as seaport, since Saunier has criticised the focus on such cities in transnational research.[13] Under these circumstances the research would have to clarify on the applicability of the European's narrative of a '*mission civilisatrice*' considering the city's long pre-colonial urban history. Furthermore, it could explicitly address the differences between the racial divide inherent to British, German and South African policies as opposed to French ideas of assimilation. Another level of the work could investigate the colonial grip on Algeria in face of the preparations for the Centennial celebrations of French rule in 1930. The results could be rounded off by an analysis of modernist impacts on Algiers, considering the many plans drafted by Le Corbusier and the specific Algerian delegations at panels like CIAM or IFHTP in those years. But taking the workload attached to such an undertaking into account, this must form a scientific work of its own.

A journal analysis for one of the smaller planning traditions in Europe, such as the Netherlands, does constitute another separate field of research. As mentioned in the intermediary conclusions for the journal analysis, their role in the dissemination and exchange of planning ideas could thus be investigated, and it would reveal their potential perception of colonial cities.

In retrospect of my results for Windhoek's colonial past in interwar years and the attempts made to enforce policies of residential segregation, I would like to conclude with a quotation by William Bissell.

> "If duality often characterized the forms of appearance of colonial urbanism, its actualization was marked by incompleteness and inconsistency."[14]

---

[13] Saunier 2013: 112-5.
[14] Bissell 2011: 225.

References

Primary Sources

National Archives of Namibia

    Section BAU – Kaiserliche Bauverwaltung

BAU 98 0000	Baumeister Röhrig
BAU 98 0000	Dienstreise Finke 1907
BAU 102-103 0000	Akten Skizzen Bauten
BAU 125 0000	Kleinwohnungsbau
BAU B.47	Postbeamtenhaus mittlere Beamte
BAU B.49	Post-Beamtenhaus
BAU B.51	Wohnhaus Eisenbahn Unterbeamte
BAU B.67	Unterkunftsschuppen Ovambos
BAU B.75	Wohnhaus Eisenbahn
BAU B.78	Aufseher-Wohnhaus
BAU E.3	Eingeborene Arbeiter
BAU G.Wi.4	Eisenbahner-Werft

    Section LVE – Kaiserliche Landesvermessung

LVE B.12	Akte Betr. Eingeborene Arbeiter

    Section MWI – Municipality Windhoek

MWI 5/4	Coloured Township: Betonhäuser
MWI 5/6	Housing: Empty Houses (Leerstehende Wohnungen)
MWI 5/8	Native Affairs
MWI 5/9	Regulations, etc. Municipal Law: Municipal Proclamations
MWI 5/11	Regulations re Townships
MWI 36/20/37	Location Sanitation
MWI 36/24/37	Native Cemetery
MWI 36/26/37	Natives Urban Area Proclamation 1924
MWI 36/27/37	Native Affairs Joint Commission
MWI 36/30/37	Enquiry re Native Beer
MWI 36/31/37	Klein Windhoek Location
MWI 36/32/37	Native Housing
MWI 37/5/37	Location Committee
MWI 37/9/37	Wembley Exhibition 1925
MWI 101/3/40	Township Board
MWI 101/4/40	Town Planning Ordinances
MWI 102/1/40	Town Plans
MWI 102/2/40	Building Regulations
MWI 102A/2/40	Building Regulations

MWI 117/1/44	Trolley Line
MWI 120/1/44	Cemeteries
MWI 120/3/44	New Cemetery
MWI S.W.M.2	Infectious Diseases
MWI S.W.M.13	Sanitary Services

Section RHO – Housing Board

RHO HB 17/126	Single Quarters for Men 126
RHO UA1	Housing Board Minutes

Section RTO – Township Board

RTO TB73	Correspondence Windhoek
RTO UA1	Minutes Township Board
RTO UA2	Minutes Township Board
RTO UA3	Minutes Township Board
RTO UA4	Minutes Township Board

Section SVW – Stadtverwaltung Windhoek

SVW A.4	Aufnahme einer Anleihe
SVW A.4.e	Armenaufgaben: Fürsorge für Arbeits- und Obdachlose
SVW A.4.f	Heimsendung Mitteloser
SVW A.6.a	Ausstellungen Allgemeines
SVW A.6.b	Ausstellungen Besonderes
SVW B.1.a	Baupolizei: Baurecht und Bauordnung
SVW B.1.b	Baupolizei: Genehmigung von Neu- und Umbauten
SVW B.1.c	Baupolizei: Bebauungspläne und Baufluchten
SVW B.1.d	Baupolizei: Überwachung der Bauausführung und Bauabnahmen
SVW B.1.e	Baupolizei: Anordnungen hinsichtlich vorhandener Bauten
SVW B.1.f	Baupolizei: Städtischer Baubeamter
SVW B.2.a	Baupolizei: Allgemeines
SVW B.2.b	Bausachen der Stadt: Bauausschuss
SVW B.2.d	Bausachen der Stadt: Wohnhäuser für Beamte und Angestellte
SVW B.9.c	Bibliothek und Karten: Städtische öffentliche Bücherei
SVW B.9.d	Bibliothek und Karten: Anschaffung von Büchern
SVW D.1.b	Denkmäler
SVW E.1.a	Eingeborenenangelegenheiten: Allgemeines, Verordnungen
SVW E.1.b	Eingeborenenangelegenheiten: Registrierung, Passmarken
SVW E.1.c	Eingeborenenangelegenheiten: Viehhaltung
SVW E.1.d	Eingeborenenangelegenheiten: Werften, Anlage, Verlegung
SVW E.1.e	Eingeborenenangelegenheiten: Werften, Reinigung
SVW E.1.f	Eingeborenenangelegenheiten: Werften, Wasserversorgung
SVW E.1.g	Eingeborenenangelegenheiten: Gesundheitswesen der Eingeborenen
SVW E.1.h	Eingeborenenangelegenheiten: Eingeborenen-Krankenhaus
SVW E.1.l	Eingeborenenangelegenheiten: Friedhöfe für Eingeborene, Anlage und Unterhaltung

SVW E.1.n	Eingeborenenangelegenheiten: Eingeborenenbesteuerung und Verwendung der Steuer
SVW E.1.o	Eingeborenenangelegenheiten: Bedürfnisanstalten für Eingeborene
SVW E.2.a	Eingeborene Arbeiter: Allgemeines
SVW E.2.c	Eingeborene Arbeiter: Gemeindearbeiter, Annahme, Entlohnung pp
SVW E.2.f	Eingeborene Arbeiter: Ovamboanwerbung
SVW E.3.a	Eingeborenen Strafgerichtsbarkeit: Allgemeines
SVW E.3.b	Eingeborenen Strafgerichtsbarkeit: Besonderes
SVW E.4.a	Eingeborenen Zivilgerichtsbarkeit: Allgemeines
SVW G.5.ac	Gesundheitspolizei: Badeanstalten
SVW G.5.ae	Gesundheitspolizei: Geisteskranke, Unterbringung und Heimsendung
SVW G.5.af	Gesundheitspolizei: Schutzpockenimpfung, Allgemeines
SVW G.5.ag	Gesundheitspolizei: Schutzpockenimpfung, Besonderes
SVW G.5.ar	Gesundheitspolizei: Kanalisation
SVW G.5.at	Verbrennungsofen
SVW G.5.u	Gesundheitspolizei: Bekämpfung ansteckender Krankheiten
SVW G.5.v	Gesundheitspolizei: Bekämpfung von Geschlechtskrankheiten
SVW G.5.w	Gesundheitspolizei: Öffentliche Bedürfnisanstalten
SVW G.6.a	Gesundheitswesen Allgemeines
SVW O.1.b	Ordnungs- und Sittenpolizei: Sonntagsruhe, religiöse Ordnung
SVW O.1.c	Ordnungs- und Sittenpolizei: Polizeistunde, Aufsicht über den Wirtschaftsbetrieb
SVW O.1.d	Ordnungs- und Sittenpolizei: Verbotene Spiele, Sammlungen und Lotterien
SVW O.1.e	Ordnungs- und Sittenpolizei: Prostitution, Bordelle
SVW O.1.g	Ordnungs- und Sittenpolizei: Gesinde- und Wohnungssachen
SVW O.1.i	Ordnungs- und Sittenpolizei: Tragen von Uniformen durch Eingeborene
SVW P.3.a	Pflanzenschädlinge und schädliche Pflanzen: Heuschreckenbekämpfung
SVW P.4.b	Post-, Telegraphie- und Fernsprechwesen: Besonderes
SVW P.4.d	Post-, Telegraphie- und Fernsprechwesen: Fernsprechwesen
SVW P.4.f	Post-, Telegraphie- und Fernsprechwesen: Funkenstation Windhuk
SVW R.1.e	Rechtsangelegenheiten: Notariats- und Urkundensachen
SVW R.2.b	Revisionen und Geschäftsübergaben: Geschäftsübergaben
SVW S.3.a	Selbstverwaltung: Allgemeines. Selbstverwaltungsordnung und andere Bestimmungen
SVW S.3.b	Selbstverwaltung: Gemeindeverband Windhoek. Verfassungen
SVW S.3.d.1	Selbstverwaltung: Wahlrecht, Wahlordnung
SVW S.3.d.2	Selbstverwaltung: Stadtratswahlen
SVW S.3.f	Selbstverwaltung: Stadtratssitzungen und Protokolle
SVW S.3.g	Selbstverwaltung: Ortssatzungen Windhuk
SVW S.3.n	Selbstverwaltung: Ortssatzungen anderer Kommunen
SVW S.3.o	Selbstverwaltung: Jahresberichte, Verwaltungsberichte anderer Kommunen
SVW S.3.p	Selbstverwaltung: Gemeinde Klein-Windhuk

SVW S.3.r	Selbstverwaltung: Lastenverteilung im Bezirk Windhuk
SVW S.4.ab	Heimsendungen
SVW S.4.b	Sicherheitspolizei: Auflauf, Aufruhr, Belagerungszustand
SVW S.4.c	Sicherheitspolizei: Meldewesen für Weiße, Allgemeines
SVW S.4.d	Sicherheitspolizei: Meldewesen für Weiße, Besonderes
SVW S.4.h	Sicherheitspolizei: Feuerlöschwesen, Besonderes und Geräte pp
SVW S.4.i	Sicherheitspolizei: Straßenpolizeiliche Anordnungen
SVW S.4.o	Sicherheitspolizei: Einwanderungs- und Passwesen
SVW S.7.a	Naturalisation Allgemeines
SVW S.7.b	Naturalisation Besonderes
SVW S.9.b	Statistik: Besonderes
SVW S.9.c	Statistik: Volkszählungen
SVW S.10.a	Steuersachen: Allgemeines
SVW S.10.ab	Steuersachen: Wertzuwachssteuer
SVW S.10.b	Steuersachen: Besonderes
SVW S.10.e	Steuersachen: Grundsteuer
SVW S.10.n	Steuersachen: Eingeborenensteuer, Veranlagung
SVW S.10.o	Steuersachen: Eingeborenensteuer, Hebung und Niederschlagungen
SVW S.10.q	Steuersachen: Anliegerbeiträge Allgemeines
SVW S.10.x	Steuersachen: Viehsteuer
SVW UA2	Beleuchtungsanlage
SVW UA4	Einwohnerliste 1915
SVW V.1.a	Vermessungssachen: Allgemeines
SVW V.1.c	Vermessungssachen: Ortsvermessungen, Weichbild
SVW V.1.d	Vermessungssachen: Grundstücksvermessungen
SVW V.1.g	Vermessungssachen: Signale, Grenzbolzen und -steine
SVW V.2.a	Kolonialgesetzgebung
SVW V.2.c	Verordnungen: Verordnungen des Bezirksamts (Aufsichtsbehörde)
SVW V.3.a	Versicherungssachen: Allgemeines
SVW V.3.d	Versicherungssachen: Krankenversicherung
SVW W.5.a	Wegesachen: Allgemeines
SVW W.9.b	Wohnungsnot: Besonderes
SVW Z.1.b	Zeitungen, Zeitschriften: Besonderes
SVW Z.2.a	Zollsachen: Allgemeines

Section VWI – Vermessungsamt Windhoek

VWI 14	Gerichtliche Benachrichtigungen in Landregister- und Grundbuch-Sachen
VWI G	Jahresberichte
VWI S.4	Schriftwechsel Bezirksamt Windhuk

Amtsblatt für das Schutzgebiet Deutsch-Südwestafrika

ADSWA 1910: Amtsblatt für das Schutzgebiet Deutsch-Südwestafrika. 1. Jahrgang. 1910
ADSWA 1911: Amtsblatt für das Schutzgebiet Deutsch-Südwestafrika. 2. Jahrgang. 1911
ADSWA 1912: Amtsblatt für das Schutzgebiet Deutsch-Südwest-Afrika. 3. Jahrgang. 1912

ADSWA 1913: Amtsblatt für das Schutzgebiet Deutsch-Südwestafrika. 4. Jahrgang. 1913
ADSWA 1914: Amtsblatt für das Schutzgebiet Deutsch-Südwestafrika. 5. Jahrgang. 1914-15

Reichstagsprotokolle

RT Protokolle, Bd. V, 129. Sitz.: 4001-2;
RT Protokolle, Bd. V, 130. Sitz.: 4045
RT Protokolle, Bd. 285, 67. Sitz.: 2199

South West Africa Votes and Proceedings of the Legislative Assembly

VPLA Second Session, First Assembly 1927: 1st April to 4th May
VPLA Third Session, First Assembly 1928: 13th April to 11th May
VPLA Fourth Session, First Assembly 1929: 4th to 7th February
VPLA First Session, Second Assembly 1929: 19th July to 16th August
VPLA Second Session, Second Assembly 1930: 25th April to 16th May
VPLA Third Session, Second Assembly 1931: 17th April to 12th May
VPLA Fourth Session, Second Assembly 1932: 25th April to 16th May
VPLA Fifth Session, Second Assembly 1933: 12th to 20th May
VPLA Sixth Session, Second Assembly 1933: 21st July to 3rd August
VPLA Seventh Session, Second Assembly 1934: 18th to 25th May
VPLA First Session, Third Assembly 1934/1935: 23rd to 29th November and 22nd March to 12th April
VPLA Second Session, Third Assembly 1935/1936: 25th October to 14th November and 23rd March to 3rd April
VPLA Third Session, Third Assembly 1937: 22nd to 25th March and 12th to 27th April
VPLA Fourth Session, Third Assembly 1938: 28th March to 8th April
VPLA Fifth Session, Third Assembly 1939: 27th March to 28th April

Treaty of Versailles: The Treaty of Peace between the Allied and Associated Powers and Germany, the Protocol annexed thereto, the Agreement respecting the military occupation of the territories of the Rhine, and the Treaty between France and Great Britain respecting Assistance to France in the event of unprovoked aggression by Germany. Signed at Versailles, June 28th, 1919. Retrieved at: http://net.lib.byu.edu/~rdh7/wwi/versailles.html (retrieved on 28.11.2015)

Journals

Der Städtebau

DS (1910) 2: PUDOR, Heinrich: Der Volkspark von Groß-Berlin: pp 21-2;
DS (1910) 4: NO AUTHOR: Hauptausschuss zur Förderung von Leibesübungen in Groß-Berlin : pp 45-6
DS (1910) 4: NO AUTHOR: Royal Institute of British Architects: p 48
DS (1910) 12: NUSSBAUM, H. Chr.: Das rasche Schwarzwerden der Gebäudeflächen und seine Ursachen: pp 140-1

DS (1911) 5: NO AUTHOR: Zur Wertschätzung deutscher Städtebaukunst in Nordamerika: p 60

DS (1911) 10: NO AUTHOR: Ein internationaler Wettbewerb: p 119

DS (1912) 4: FORBÁTH, Emerich: Das englische Städtebaugesetz vom 3. Dezember 1909: p 44

DS (1912) 5: FORBÁTH, Emerich: Das englische Städtebaugesetz vom 3. Dezember 1909 – Schluss: pp 51-2

DS (1913) 1: KLAIBER, Chr.: Französische Monumente in ihrer Beziehung zu Straße und Platz: pp 9-10

DS (1913) 4: LANDWEHR, F.: Der Schutz künstlerisch (und geschichtlich) bedeutsamer Straßen und Plätze in Alt- und Neustadt auf Grund der Verunstaltungsgesetze: pp 44-7

DS (1913) 5: LANDWEHR, F.: Der Schutz künstlerisch (und geschichtlich) bedeutsamer Straßen und Plätze in Alt- und Neustadt auf Grund der Verunstaltungsgesetze: pp 51-2

DS (1913) 6: SCHACHENMEIER, E.: Über Straßenkreuzungen – Mathematische Festlegung der Fahrlinien: pp 67-71

DS (1913) 7: SCHACHENMEIER, E.: Über Straßenkreuzungen – Mathematische Festlegung der Fahrlinien: pp 77-82

DS (1913) 9: BENCKE, Albert: Vom Bau der neuen indischen Reichshauptstadt: p 106

DS (1913) 11: NO AUTHOR: Wanderausstellung: pp 130-1

DS (1914) 4: NO AUTHOR: Denkschrift, betreffend Grundsätze zur Aufstellung eines General-Siedelungsplanes für den Regierungsbezirk Düsseldorf: pp 50-1

DS (1914) 5: NO AUTHOR: Internationale Städte-Ausstellung: p 64

DS (1914) 6: GOECKE, Theodor: Ein Nachwort zum ersten Internationalen Städtekongress in Gent 1913: pp 70-3

DS (1915) 7/8: NO AUTHOR: Die Frage des Wiederaufbaues der durch den Krieg beschädigten Orte Belgiens: p 84

DS (1915) 12: STEINBRÜCKER, Franz: Wohnungsmangel und Wohnungselend: pp 114-6

DS (1916) 6/7: BROCKMANN, Oskar: Wettbewerb für einen Bebauungsplan der Stadt Zürich und ihrer Vororte: pp 62-5

DS (1917) 1: SITTE, Siegfried: Entwurf für ein Städtebau-Gesetz: pp 7-9

DS (1917) 2/3: NO AUTHOR: Belgisches Bauwesen: p 34

DS (1917) 2/3: NO AUTHOR: Städtebauliches aus Löwen: p 34

DS (1917) 2/3: SITTE, Siegfried: Entwurf für ein Städtebau-Gesetz – Schluss: pp 14-8

DS (1917) 6/7: GOECKE, Theodor: Zur Denkschrift, betreffen die Stellung öffentlicher Bauwerke und die Wahl ihrer Bauplätze in Groß-Berlin: pp 70-1

DS (1917) 10/11: BEWIG: Enteignungsrecht und Städtebau: pp 122-4

DS (1917) 12: HÄUSELMANN, J.F.; GOECKE, Theodor: Eine Friedensstadt - Nachschrift: pp 138-9

DS (1918) 2/3: WEHL, Bernhard: Alte und neue Gedanken zur Wohnungsfürsorge: pp 35-7

DS (1919) 1/2: NO AUTHOR: Die Baukosten in Dänemark: p 24

DS (1919) 3/4: ABENDROTH, Alfred: Die Förderung der räumlichen Auffassung im Städtebau durch das Luftbild: pp 28-32

DS (1919) 5/6: DIECK: Über zeitgemäße Bodenpolitik: pp 57-60

DS (1919) 7/8: NO AUTHOR: Turmhäuser: pp 87-8

DS (1919) 9/12: SCHMIDT, Robert: Siedlungsverband Ruhrkohlenbezirk: pp 91-3

DS (1920) 3/4: KEYSERLING, Hermann; VON TSCHIRNER-TSCHIRNE, Hans Erich: Taj Mahal – Ein monumentales Grabdenkmal in Indien: pp 33-8

DS (1920) 3/4: NO AUTHOR: Niedersächsische Tagung für neuzeitliches Bauen in Hildesheim: pp 39-40

DS (1920) 5/6: ABENDROTH, Alfred: Die Bedeutung des Luftbildes für die Erschließung der Landschaft: pp 46-50

DS (1920) 5/6: MÄCHLER, Martin: Ein Detail aus dem Bebauungsplan Groß-Berlin: pp 54-7

DS (1920) 5/6: NO AUTHOR: Letzte Zuckungen des Vorgestrigen: p 58

DS (1920) 11/12: NO AUTHOR: Der Wiederaufbau von Reims und Arras: p 119

DS (1921) 1/2: DE FRIES, Heinrich: Das amerikanische Projekt für Reims: p 21

DS (1921) 1/2: GENZMER, Ewald: Zur Frage der großstädtischen Schnellbahnen: pp 3-8

DS (1921) 1/2: NO AUTHOR: Der Papalagi: pp 16-7

DS (1922) 3/4: NO AUTHOR: Mangel an Bauarbeitern: p 40

DS (1922) 7/8: MUESMANN, Adolf: Stuttgarter Städtebau: pp 61-5

DS (1922): 9/10: WOLF: Das Turmhaus in der Wohnsiedlung: pp 92-4

DS (1925) 7/8: HEGEMANN, Werner: Studiengesellschaft für Automobilstraßenbau: p 116

DS (1925) 9/10: NO AUTHOR: no page

DS (1925) 11/12: HEGEMANN, Werner: Berg-Breslau und Cremers-Essen über den Streit ums Kölner Hochhaus: pp 153-5

DS (1925) 11/12: KOEPPEN, W.alter: Ein preußisches Städtebaugesetz: pp 161-2

DS (1925) 11/12: NO AUTHOR: Eine städtebauliche Rettung in der Stuttgarter Innenstadt: p 179

DS (1926) 1: HEGEMANN, Werner: Bücherschau – Die Wohnungsnot als Sexualproblem: pp 15-6

DS (1926) 5: HARTMANN: Die „Bienenwabenstadt" – Ein Vorschlag zur Lösung des Verkehrsproblems: pp 70-1

DS (1926) 7: ELKART, Karl: Eisenbahnwagen als Notwohnungen in Hannover: p 105

DS (1926) 8: SCHMIDT, Robert: Landesplanung: pp 127-31

DS (1926) 11: NO AUTHOR: Internationaler Städtebaukongress in Wien 1926: p 175

DS (1926) 11: NO AUTHOR: Leerstehende Wohnungen in Berlin: p 176

DS (1926) 12: NO AUTHOR: Internationale Gesellschaft für Photogrammetrie: p 186

DS (1927) 1: SCHMIDT, Robert: Fehlerquellen deutschen Städtebaus – Die richtige Stadtbildung ist nur im Rahmen der Landesplanung möglich: pp 11-2

DS (1927) 3: NO AUTHOR: Studienreise nach Holland und England: p 43

DS (1927) 4: BRANDT, Jürgen: Der erste deutsche Seeflughafen: pp 49-50

DS (1927) 9: BRANDT, Jürgen: Die Eingemeindungen an der Unterelbe: pp 144-5

DS (1927) 9: EWOLDT, Walter: Auf dem Wege zur Lösung der Groß-Hamburg-Frage: pp 129-36

DS (1927) 10: NO AUTHOR: Verlängerung der Werkbundausstellung „Die Wohnung" Stuttgart 1927: p 164

DS (1928) 1: ADLER, Leo: Zur Denkschrift des Reichsarbeitsministeriums über die Wohnungsnot und ihre Bekämpfung: p 24

DS (1928) 1: FÖRSTER, Fritz: Die neuzeitliche Hauswasserbeschaffung auf dem Lande: pp 8-11

DS (1928) 3: LEO, Gustav H.: Vertikal- und Horizontalverkehr – Ein Beitrag zur Frage „Hochhaus und Citybildung": pp 60-4

DS (1928) 3: NO AUTHOR: Endgültige Ergebnisse der Reichs-Wohnungszählung: pp 74-6

DS (1928) 7: L.A. (Leo Adler): Die Schwebebahn Elberfeld-Barmen: pp 174-5

DS (1928) 7: VON RITGEN: Eine Nordsüd-Verbindung für das Berliner Bahnnetz der Reichsbahn: pp 170-3

DS (1928) 10: HOENIG, Anton: Gesetze der Bodenwertbildung: pp 231-5

DS (1928) 12: PETERSEN, Richard: Die Schwebebahn als Stadtschnellbahn: p 309

DS (1929) 1: PEPLER, G. L.: Landesplanung in England und Wales: pp 4-6

DS (1929) 1: SIEBERS, Alphons: Butte und Longview – Planlosigkeit und Höchstleistung: pp 26-32

DS (1929) 4: MALCHER, Fritz: Verkehrs-Reform – Das System „Straßenkreuzung ohne Fahrkreuzung" als Grundlage des neuen Verkehrsprojektes für Havana, die Hauptstadt von Cuba: pp 97-108

DS (1929) 5: FEST, Georg: Betrachtungen über die Querprofil-Gestaltung der Haupt-Verkehrs-Straßen: pp 129-32

DS (1929) 9: MÜNTER, Georg: Die Geschichte der Idealstadt: pp 249-56

DS (1929) 11: MAUL, Alfred: Die „Idealstadt": pp 313-4

DS (1929) 12: MÜNTER, Georg: Die Geschichte der Idealstadt - Fortsetzung: pp 317-40

DS (1930) 2: HEGEMANN, Werner: Turmhaus am Reichstag?!: pp 97-104

DS (1930) 3: FUCHS-RÖLL, Willy P.: Die Hochhausfrage in Stuttgart: pp 150-2

DS (1930) 6: F. H.: Die Entwicklung des deutschen Kraftfahrzeugverkehrs: p 296

DS (1931) 1: LUTHARDT, Wilhelm: Der Flugverkehr in der Baugesetzgebung: p 48

DS (1931) 2: BLUM, Otto: Der Umbau der Mühlendammschleuse in Berlin und die Leistungsfähigkeit der Eisenbahn: p 96

DS (1931) 2: HEGEMANN, Werner: Palais Ephraim, Berlins Städtebau und die Reichs-Planung: p 95

DS (1931) 10: PFANNSCHMIDT, Martin: Die Deckung des zukünftigen Wohnungsbedarfs: pp 478-80

DS (1932) 6: HEGEMANN, Werner: Woran scheitern die Entwürfe zu einem Städtebaugesetz?: pp 301-2

DS (1933) 4: JOBST, Gerhard: : pp 1-90

DS (1933) 10: SCHOSSBERGER, Hans: Luftschutz und Städtebau – Vorschläge für eine „luftsichere" Idealstadt: pp 476-9

DS (1933) 11: PAULSEN, Friedrich: Christaller: p 526

DS (1934) 3: NÖLDECHEN, Waldemar: Die Abfallbewirtschaftung im Aufbau des städtischen Siedlungskörpers: pp 143-7

DS (1934) 4: HERMAN FLESCHE, F.: Die Gesundung der Altstadt Braunschweig: pp 197-201

DS (1934) 4: REICHOW, Hans: Altstadtgesundung – Zielsetzung, Finanzierung und Rechtsordnung für Altstadt- und Wohnungsgesundungen: pp 193-6

DS (1934) 5: PAULSEN, Friedrich: Städtebau! Wie sich das neue Reich städtebaulich darstellt: pp 245-8

DS (1934) 6: KAMPFFMEYER, Bernhard: Der Feldzug gegen die Slums in England: pp 298-9

DS (1934) 8: KARGER, Alfred: Städtebaugesetz und Ausländer: p 404

DS (1935) 1: RODENBACH, Ph.: Altstadtgesundung in Frankfurt a.M. – Erste Vorbereitung / Ergebnisse eines Wettbewerbs: pp 2-5

DS (1935) 3: G.: Kraftverkehr und Städtebau: pp 28-31

DS (1935) 3: KÖLZOW, Hans: Neue Gesichtspunkte zur Abwasser-Verwertung: pp 34-5

DS (1935) 4: NO AUTHOR: Amerika auf europäischen Spuren: pp 42-5

DS (1935) 5: HENGERER, Erich K.: Die neue Ortsbausatzung der Stadt Stuttgart: pp 49-56

DS (1935) 5: LUDORF: Luftschutz durch Städtebau?: pp 59-60

DS (1935) 6: WOLF, Paul: Luftschutz und Städtebau – Eine Berichtigung und Erwiderung: p 70

DS (1935) 7: PAULSEN, Friedrich: Bücherschau – La città moderna: p 84

DS (1935) 12: WÖLZ: Verwendung der Hauszinssteuer für Zwecke des Wohnungsbaus und der Altstadterneuerung pp 139-40, following page(s) missing

DS (1936) 5: KNUTZEN: Städtebauliche und siedlungspolitische Gemeinschaftsarbeit im hamburgisch-preußischen Unterelbegebiet: pp 54-6

DS (1936) 5: NEUMANN, F.: Die Zukunftsaufgaben der Großstädte auf dem Gebiete der Wohnungsbeschaffung: pp 49-51

DS (1936) 6: LABES: Grundsätzliches zur Altstadtsanierung und Altstadterhaltung: pp 61-9

DS (1936) 6: SCHWAB, A.: Wasser- und Siedlungspolitik in Schwaben: pp 70-1

DS (1936) 11: BETGE, Paul: Abwasser- und Abfallstoffverwertung: pp 129-30

DS (1938) 4: NO AUTHOR: Der Anschluss, auch des Städtebaues: p 25

DS (1938) 7: FEUCHTINGER, Max-Erich: Eine Studie über die Reichsautobahnen um Köln: pp 16-9

DS (1939) 5: KÖHLER, Paul: Die Stadt der 22000: pp 37-52

DS (1939) 7: MÄCHLER, Martin: Die Großstadt als Kultur- und Raumproblem und die Grenzen ihrer Größe: p 63

DS (1939) 8: NO AUTHOR: Das Ergebnis in Stockholm – „Trabantenstadt" oder „Lebensraum": pp 74-6

DS (1939) 9: RIMPL, Herbert: Die Stadt der Hermann-Göring-Werke: pp 77-92

DS (1939) 10: P.AULSEN, Friedrich: Der Wettbewerb um die Pläne für Wuppertal: p 93-6

Journal of Namibian Studies. Otjivanda Presse: Essen

Mitteilungen aus dem Bundesarchiv 2/2006. Retrieved at: http://www.bundesarchiv.de/imperia/md/content/bundesarchiv_de/oeffentlichkeitsarbeit/fach-publikationen/mitteilungenausdembundesarchiv/heft_2-2006__14._jahrgang.pdf

SPIEGEL GESCHICHTE 5/2014: Die Weimarer Republik. Spiegel-Verlag Rudolf Augstein: Hamburg

Town Planning Review

TPR (1910) April: NO AUTHOR: Editorial Foreword: pp 1-2

TPR (1911) July: ADAMS, Thomas: Some American Impressions – I. The "Art Atmosphere" of New York and the Relation of the Skyscraper to Town Planning: pp 139-46

TPR (1912) January: ABERCROMBIE, Patrick: Town Planning in Greater London – The Necessity for Co-operation: pp 261-80

TPR (1912) January: NO AUTHOR: Review – Taxation of Land Values in American Cities: pp 331-2

TPR (1912) April: ADSHEAD, S. D.: An Introduction to the Planning of Modern Italian Towns: pp 52-4

TPR (1912) October: GEDDES, Patrick: The Twofold Aspect of the Industrial Age - Paleotechnic and Neotechnic: pp 176-87

TPR (1912) October: NO AUTHOR: Editorials – The Federal Capital for the Common-wealth of Australia: pp 165-7

TPR (1912) October: NO AUTHOR: Editorials – Delhi: pp 167-8

TPR (1912) October: NO AUTHOR: Editorials – The Progress of the Town Planning Act: p 168

TPR (1913) January: MC LEAN, W. H.: Town Planning in the Tropics – With Special Reference to the Khartoum City Development Plan: pp 225-31

TPR (1913) January: NO AUTHOR: Editorials – Municipal Ownership of Land: pp 223-4

TPR (1913) April: ADSHEAD, S. D.: Land: pp 47-8

TPR (1913) July: GEDDES, Patrick: Two Steps in Civics – "Cities and Town Planning Exhibition" and the "International Congress of Cities," Ghent International Exhibi-tion, 1913: pp 78-94

TPR (1913) July: MARQUIS, F. J.: Review – Warburton Lectures on Housing, 1913: pp 160-1

TPR (1913) October: NO AUTHOR: Editorials – The Motor Traffic Report: pp 188-91

TPR (1914) January: DAVIDGE, W. R.: Conference of the Greater London Authorities: pp 287-91

TPR (1914) January: NO AUTHOR: Editorials – Land and Municipal Purchase: pp 271-2

TPR (1914) January: NO AUTHOR: Editorials – A Controversy: p 275

TPR (1914) October: NO AUTHOR: Editorials – Housing Act No. 2 (1914): pp 180-2

TPR (1914) October: P.A.: The Progress of the Town Planning Act: pp 232-5

TPR (1915) January: NO AUTHOR: Editorials – Replanning Belgium/Ypres: pp 257-9

TPR (1915) July: ADAMS, Thomas: Progress of the Town Planning Act: pp 64-5

TPR (1915) October: ABERCROMBIE, Lascelles: Prolegomena – On Professor Geddes' Book-Cities in Evolution: pp 137-42

TPR (1916) April: ADSHEAD, S. D.: New Town Planning Legislation for India and Can-ada: pp 250-3

TPR (1916) October: NO AUTHOR: Editorials – Housing after the War: pp 2-3

TPR (1918) 4:

TPR (1918) April: ABERCROMBIE: The Basis of Reconstruction – The Need for a Re-gional Survey of National Resources: pp 203-10

TPR (1918) April: NO AUTHOR: Housing After the War – Some Current Notes on Sali-ent Aspects: pp 219-42

TPR (1918) April: NO AUTHOR: Town Planning in Balrampur: pp 274-5

TPR (1919) April: L. P. A.: Review – Town Planning in Madras: pp 56-7

TPR (1920) April: ABERCROMBIE, Patrick: Ideal Cities No. 1 - Christianopolis: pp 99-104

TPR (1920) April: KYFFIN-TAYLOR, G.: Review – The Housing Problem: pp 105-16

TPR (1920) December: THOMPSON, Longstreth: State Housing: pp 145-62

TPR (1921) March: ABERCROMBIE, Patrick: Ideal Cities No. 2 - Victoria: pp 15-20

TPR (1921) March: HOLLIDAY, A. C.: The Rebuilding of Rheims: pp 5-11

TPR (1921) March: NO AUTHOR: Review – How England is Meeting the Housing Shortage: pp 56-8

TPR (1921) December: READE, Charles C.: Town Planning in British Malaya: pp 162-5

TPR (1922) May: NO AUTHOR: Review – South Wales Regional Survey: p 259

TPR (1923a) May: ABERCROMBIE, Patrick: Wren's Plan for London after the Great Fire: pp 71-8

TPR (1923b) May: ABERCROMBIE, Patrick: Regional Planning: pp 109-18

TPR (1923) May: SHAWCROSS, Harold: Review – The Smokeless City: pp 127-30

TPR (1923) May: THOMPSON, Longstreth: Review – The Doncaster Regional Planning Scheme: pp 134-8

TPR (1923) September: CLARKE, John J.: Review – The Housing Question: pp 216-7

TPR (1923) September: G. E. H. R.: Review – Streets, Roads and Pavements: p 214

TPR (1924) February: NO AUTHOR: Editorial: pp 1-2

TPR (1924) December: CLARKE, John J.: The New Housing Act, 1924: pp 119-27

TPR (1926) February: CLARKE, John J.: Housing in Relation to Public Health and Social Welfare: pp 243-78

TPR (1926) February: LANCHESTER, H. V.: Review – East Kent Regional Planning Scheme Preliminary Survey: pp 292-6

TPR (1926) May: ADAMS, Thomas: The Skyscrapers of New York: pp 79-83

TPR (1926) November: CLARKE, John J.: Review – European Housing Problems since the War: pp 139-40

TPR (1926) November: DOUGILL, Wesley: Review – Regional plan of New York and its Environs – Highway Traffic: pp 145-7

TPR (1927) June: KAUFFMANN, Richard: Preliminary Regional Planning Scheme for Opening up the Territory of Haifa Bay, Palestine: pp 206-11

TPR (1929) May: VELARDE, F. X.: Review – Le Corbusier. Towards a New Architecture: pp 201-2

TPR (1929) December: VEILLER, Lawrence: The Housing Problem in the United States: pp 228-56

TPR (1930) May: W.D.: Review – Town Planning in India: pp 71-2

TPR (1930) November: ADSHEAD, S.D.: Camillo Sitte and Le Corbusier: pp 85-94

TPR (1931) May: CLARKE, John J.: Slums and the Housing Act, 1930: pp 163-93

TPR (1931) May: KELLY, Sydney A.: Review – Airports: their Location, Administration, and Legal Basis: p 211

TPR (1931) December: DOUGILL, Wesley: Review – Skyscrapers, and the Men who build them: pp 286-9

TPR (1932) June: CLARKE, John J.: Housing and Public Health: pp 44-8

TPR (1932) June: CLARKE, John J.: Review – The Town Planning and Development Ordinances and (Procedure) Regulations 1931 of the Colony and Protectorate of Kenya: pp 73-4

TPR (1932) November: G.L.P.: Regional Plan of New York and its Environs: pp 123-36

TPR (1933) May: HILL, S.: Review – The Law Relating to Town and Country Planning: pp 222-3

TPR (1934) December: ROYAL FINE ART COMMISSION: High Buildings: pp 126-8

TPR (1935) June: ABERCROMBIE, Patrick: Review – Town Planning and Housing throughout the World: pp 227-8

TPR (1935) June: KNIGHT, C. R.: Town Planning in New Zealand: pp 216-20

TPR (1935) December: NO AUTHOR: Review – Housing England: pp 331-3

TPR (1936) June: CLARKE, John J.: Restriction of Ribbon Development Act, 1935: pp 11-32

TPR (1937) February: THOMSON, T. F.: Review – Restriction of Ribbon Development Act, 1935: pp 144-7

TPR (1937) July: CLARKE, John J.: The Public Health Acts, 1936: pp 184-96

TPR (1937) July: REDDAWAY, T. F.: The Rebuilding of London after the Great Fire: pp 205-11

TPR (1937) December: REDDAWAY, T. F.: The Rebuilding of London after the Great Fire: pp 271-9

TPR (1938) July: CONZEN, G.: Towards a Systematic Approach in Planning Science: Geoproscopy: pp 1-26

TPR (1938) December: A.P.: Review – Housing Comes of Age: pp 146-9

TPR (1938) December: MATTOCKS, R. H.: Review – Parkways and Land Values: pp 132-4

TPR (1939) July: REDDAWAY, T. F.: The Rebuilding of London after the Great Fire: pp 155-61

TPR (1942) October: CLARKE, John J.: Town and Country Planning – Powers of Authorities and Owners to Enter into Agreements Restricting the Use of Land: pp 246-56

Secondary Sources

ABU-LUGHOD, Janet L. (1965): Tale of Two Cities: The Origins of Modern Cairo. In: Comparative Studies in Society and History 7, 4: pp 429-57. Cambridge

ABU-LUGHOD, Janet L. (1981): Rabat: Urban Apartheid in Morocco. Princeton University Press

ALBERS, Gerd (1975): Entwicklungslinien im Städtebau: Ideen, Thesen, Aussagen 1875-1945: Texte und Interpretationen. Bertelsmann Fachverlag: Düsseldorf

ANDERSON, Warwick (2002): Introduction: Postcolonial Technoscience. In: Social Studies of Sciences 32/5-6 (October-December 2002): pp 643-658. London, Thousand Oaks, New Delhi.

BARTH, Paul (1926): Südwest-Afrika. John Meinert: Windhoek.

BÄHR, Jürgen; JÜRGENS, Ulrich (2005): Stadtgeographie II: Regionale Stadtgeographie. Westermann: Braunschweig

BECHER, Jürgen (1997): Dar es Salaam, Tanga und Tabora: Stadtentwicklung in Tansania unter deutscher Kolonialherrschaft 1885-1914. Franz Steiner Verlag: Stuttgart

BECKER, Frank [Ed.] (2004): Rassenmischehen – Mischlinge – Rassentrennung. Zur Politik der Rasse im deutschen Kolonialismus. Franz Steiner Verlag: Stuttgart

BEECKMANS, Luce (2013): Editing the African city: reading colonial planning in Africa from a comparative perspective, pp 1-13. In: Planning Perspectives. London

BEECKMANS, Luce; LAGAE, Johan (2015): Kinshasa's Syndrome-Planning in Historical Perspective: From Belgian Colonial Capital to Self-Constructed Megalopolis, pp 201-24. In: SILVA, Carlos Nunes [Ed.] (2015): Urban Planning in Sub-Saharan Africa: Colonial and Post-Colonial Planning Cultures. Routledge: New York, London

BELFORD, Paul (2001): Work, space and power in an English industrial slum: 'the Crofts', Sheffield, 1750 – 1850, pp 106-17. In: MAYNE, Alan; MURRAY, Tim [Eds.] (2001):

The Archaeology of Urban Landscapes: Explorations in Slumland. Cambridge University Press: Cambridge

BETTS, Raymond F. (1985): Dakar: Ville Impériale (1857-1960), pp 193-206. In: ROSS, Robert; TELKAMP, Gerard J. [Eds.] (1985): Colonial Cities: Essays on Urbanism in a Colonial Context. Martinus Nijhoff Publishers: Dordrecht, Boston, Lancaster

BIGON, Liora (2009): A History of Urban Planning in two West African Colonial Capitals: Residential Segregation in British Lagos and French Dakar (1850-1930). Edwin Mellen: Lewiston

BIGON, Liora (2013): Transnational Networks of Administrating Disease and Urban Planning in West Africa: the Inter-Colonial Conference on Yellow Fever, Dakar, 1928, pp 103-11. In: GeoJournal, published online 4 April 2013. Springer Science+Business Media: Dordrecht

BIGON, Liora; KATZ, Yossi [Eds.] (2014): Garden Cities and Colonial Planning: Transnationality and Urban Ideas in Africa and Palestine. Manchester University Press

BISSELL, William Cunningham (2011): Between Fixity and Fantasy: Assessing the Spatial Impact of Colonial Urban Dualism, pp 208-29. In: Journal of Urban History 37 (2). Sage: London

BITTERLI, Urs (1991): Die "Wilden" und die "Zivilisierten": Grundzüge einer Geistes- und Kulturgeschichte der europäisch-überseeischen Begegnung. Zweite, durchgesehene und um einen bibliographischen Nachtrag erweiterte Auflage. C.H. Beck: München

BLEY, Helmut (1968): Kolonialherrschaft und Sozialstruktur in Deutsch-Südwestafrika 1894-1914. Leibniz-Verlag: Hamburg

BLOM, Philipp (2014): Die zerrissenen Jahre: 1918-1938. Hanser: München

BLOTEVOGEL, Hans Heinrich [Ed.] (2002): Fortentwicklung des Zentrale-Orte-Konzepts. Akademie für Raumforschung und Landesplanung: Hannover

BLUE BOOK [Edited by Administrator's Office] (1918): Report on the Natives of South-West Africa and their Treatment by Germany. His Majesty's Stationery Office: London

BODENSCHATZ, Harald (1988): Die Berliner „Mietskaserne" in der wohnungspolitischen Diskussion seit 1918, pp 127-149. In: SCHILDT, Axel; SYWOTTEK, Arnold [Eds.] (1988): Massenwohnung und Eigenheim: Wohnungsbau und Wohnen in der Großstadt seit dem Ersten Weltkrieg. Campus: Frankfurt, New York

BODENSCHATZ, Harald [Ed.] (2010): Stadtvisionen 1910/2010: Berlin, Paris, London, Chicago: 100 Jahre Allgemeine Städtebau-Ausstellung in Berlin. DOM: Berlin

BOTHA, Christo (2008): The Politics of Land Settlement in Namibia, 1890-1960, pp 232-76. In: South African Historical Journal, 42:1

BRAUN, Michael (2008): Nordsüd-S-Bahn Berlin: 75 Jahre Eisenbahn im Untergrund. Gesellschaft für Verkehrspolitik und Eisenbahnwesen/Berliner S-Bahn-Museum: Berlin

BRAVENBOER, Brenda (2004): Windhoek: Capital of Namibia. Gamsberg Macmillan: Windhoek

BREITWIESER, Lukas (2012): "We are going to put South West Africa on the map this time." The homogenisation and differentiation of Namibian tourist spaces, pp 7-27. In: Journal of Namibian Studies, 11/2012

BRINCKMANN, Albert Erich (1921, second extended edition): Deutsche Stadtbaukunst in der Vergangenheit. Frankfurter Verlags-Anstalt: Frankfurt

BRÜGGEMEIER, Franz-Josef; ROMMELSPACHER, Thomas (1992): Blauer Himmel über der Ruhr: Geschichte der Umwelt im Ruhrgebiet 1840 – 1990. Klartext: Essen

BUDER, Stanley (1990): Visionaries and Planners: The Garden City Movement and the Modern Community. Oxford University Press: New York, Oxford

BURROUGHS, Peter (1999): Imperial Institutions and the Government of Empire, pp 170-97. In: PORTER, Andrew [Ed.] (1999): The Oxford History of the British Empire: Volume III The Nineteenth Century. Oxford University Press: Oxford, New York

CADBURY, George Junior (1915): Town Planning: With Special Reference to the Birmingham Schemes. Longmans, Green and Co.: London, New York, Bombay, Calcutta, Madras

CAIN, Horst (1987): Tuiavi'is Papalagi, pp 252-70. In: DUERR, Hans Peter [Ed.] (1987): Authentizität und Betrug in der Ethnologie. Suhrkamp: Frankfurt am Main

ÇELIK, Zeynep (1992): Le Corbusier, Orientalism, Colonialism. In: Assemblage 17, April 1992: 58-77.

ÇELIK, Zeynep (1997): Urban Forms and Colonial Confrontations: Algiers Under French Rule. University of California Press: Berkeley (http://ark.cdlib.org/ark:/13030/ft8c6009jk/)

CHOAY, Françoise [1965] (2014): L'urbanisme, utopies et réalités : Une anthologie. Points : Paris

COMMEY, Pusch (2014): Landless blacks: Why the impasse continues. In: New African 542 (August/September 2014): pp 8-11. London, Paris

CONRAD, Sebastian (2008): Deutsche Kolonialgeschichte. C.H. Beck: München

COOPER, Frederick [Ed.] (1983): Struggle for the City: Migrant Labor, Capital, and the State in Urban Africa. Sage: Beverly Hills, London, New Delhi

COOPER, Frederick (2012): Kolonialismus denken: Konzepte und Theorien in kritischer Perspektive. Campus: Frankfurt, New York

COQUERY-VIDROVITCH, Catherine (2005): Introduction: African Urban Spaces: History and Culture, pp xv-xl. In : SALM, Steven J.; FALOLA, Toyin [Eds.] (2005): African Urban Spaces in Historical Perspective. University of Rochester Press: Rochester, NY

COQUERY-VIDROVITCH, Catherine (2011): Petite histoire de l'Afrique: L'Afrique au sud du Sahara de la préhistoire à nos jours. La Découverte: Paris

CROSSLEY, Nick; ROBERTS, John Michael [Eds.] (2004): After Habermas: new perspectives on the public sphere. Blackwell: Oxford

DARWIN, John (2008): After Tamerlane: The Rise and Fall of Global Empires, 1400 – 2000. Penguin: London

DAUNTON, Martin [Ed.] (2000): The Cambridge Urban History of Britain – Volume III 1840-1950. Cambridge University Press: Cambridge

DE BRUIJNE, G. A. (1985): The Colonial City and the Post-Colonial World, pp 231-243. In: ROSS, Robert; TELKAMP, Gerard J. [Eds.] (1985): Colonial Cities: Essays on Urbanism in a Colonial Context. Martinus Nijhoff Publishers: Dordrecht, Boston, Lancaster

DE VRIES, Johannes Lucas (1980): Namibia: Mission und Politik: 1880-1918. Neukirchener Verlag: Neukirchen-Vluyn

DENNIS, Richard (2000): Modern London, pp 95-132. In: DAUNTON, Martin [Ed.] (2000): The Cambridge Urban History of Britain – Volume III 1840-1950. Cambridge University Press: Cambridge

DIEFENDORF, Jeffry M. (2000): Motor Vehicles and the Inner City, pp 175-193. In: FREESTONE, Robert [Ed.] (2000): Urban Planning in a Changing World: The Twentieth Century Experience. E&FN Spon: London

DITT, Karl (2011): Zweite Industrialisierung und Konsum: Energieversorgung, Haushaltstechnik und Massenkultur am Beispiel nordenglischer und westfälischer Städte 1880-1939. Schöningh: Paderborn

369

DUBOW, Saul (1995): The Elaboration of Segregationist Ideology, pp 145-75. In: BEINART, William; DUBOW, Saul [Eds.] (1995): Segregation and Apartheid in Twentieth Century South Africa. Routledge: New York

DURTH, Werner; GUTSCHOW, Niels (1988): Vom Architekturtraum zur Stadtlandschaft: Wandlungen städtebaulicher Leitbilder unter dem Eindruck des Luftkrieges 1942-1945, pp 326-359. In: SCHILDT, Axel; SYWOTTEK, Arnold [Eds.] (1988): Massenwohnung und Eigenheim: Wohnungsbau und Wohnen in der Großstadt seit dem Ersten Weltkrieg. Campus: Frankfurt, New York

DURTH, Werner (2001): Deutsche Architekten: Biographische Verflechtungen 1900 – 1970. Karl Krämer: Stuttgart, Zürich

DURTH, Werner (2010): Städtebau und Macht im nationalsozialistischen Staat, pp 37-59. In: HARLANDER, Tilman; PYTA, Wolfram [Eds.] (2010): NS-Architektur: Macht und Symbolpolitik. LIT Verlag: Berlin

EICHHOLTZ, Dietrich: Der „Generalplan Ost" als genozidale Variante der imperialistischen Ostexpansion, pp 118-24. In: RÖSSLER, Mechthild; SCHLEIERMACHER, Sabine [Eds.] (1993): Der „Generalplan Ost": Hauptlinien der nationalsozialistischen Planungs- und Vernichtungspolitik. Akademie Verlag: Berlin

ENGELS, Friedrich [1887] (1995): The Housing Question. Reprint by Co-operative Publishing Society of Foreign Workers. Online version retrieved at http://www.marxists.org/archive/marx/works/1872/housing-question/ (retrieved on 02.05.2014)

ETZEMÜLLER, Thomas [Ed.] (2009): Die Ordnung der Moderne: Social Engineering im 20. Jahrhundert. Transcript-Verlag: Bielefeld

FAUVELLE-AYMAR, François-Xavier (2013, édition mise à jour): Histoire de l'Afrique du Sud. Points: Paris

FELDMANN, Ekke (2011): Bauordnungen und Baupolizei: zur Entwicklungsgeschichte zwischen 1850 und 1950. Lang: Frankfurt

FERGUSON, Niall (2004): Empire: How Britain Made the Modern World. Penguin: London

FERRO, Marc (1994): Histoire des colonisations: Des conquêtes aux indépendances XIIIe-XXe siècle. Points : Paris

FGSV [Ed.] (2007): Richtlinie zur Anlage von Stadtstraßen: RASt 06. Forschungsgesellschaft für Straßen- und Verkehrswesen/Arbeitsgruppe Straßenentwurf: Köln

FISCH, Stefan (1997): Der Straßburger „Große Durchbruch" (1907-1957). Kontinuität und Brüche in Architektur, Städtebau und Verwaltungspraxis zwischen deutscher und französischer Zeit. In: CORNELISSEN, Christoph; FISCH, Stefan; MAAS, Anne [Eds.] (1997): Grenzstadt Straßburg. Stadtplanung, kommunale Wohnungspolitik und Öffentlichkeit 1870-1940. Röhrig: St.Ingbert

FISCH, Stefan (1998): Die Anfänge der elektrischen Straßenbahn im Spannungsfeld von Elektroindustrie und Städtebaureform, pp 31-9. In: SCHOTT, Dieter; KLEIN, Stefan [Eds.] (1998): Mit der Tram ins nächste Jahrtausend: Geschichte, Gegenwart und Zukunft der elektrischen Straßenbahn. Klartext: Essen

FISCHLER, Raphaël (2000): Planning for Social Betterment: From Standard of Living to Quality of Life, pp 139-157. In: FREESTONE, Robert [Ed.] (2000): Urban Planning in a Changing World: The Twentieth Century Experience. E&FN Spon: London

FOUCAULT, Michel (2009): Security, Territory, Population: Lectures at the College De France, 1977-78. Palgrave Macmillan: Basingstoke

FREESTONE, Robert (2000): Learning from Planning's Histories, pp 1-19. In: FREESTONE, Robert [Ed.] (2000): Urban Planning in a Changing World: The Twentieth Century Experience. E&FN Spon: London

FREESTONE, Robert; AMATI, Marco [Eds.] (2014): Exhibitions and the Development of Modern Planning Culture. Ashgate: Farnham, Burlington

FREUND, Bill (2007): The African City: A History. Cambridge University Press: Cambridge, New York, Melbourne, Madrid, Cape Town, Singapore, São Paulo

FRIEDRICH, Karl-Heinz (2006): „Tunlich geradlinig". Die Gründung des Vereins „HAFRABA" 1926 und der Bau der deutschen Autobahnen, pp 71-8. In: Mitteilungen aus dem Bundesarchiv 2/2006

GALLIKER, Hans-Rudolf (1997): Tramstadt: Öffentlicher Nahverkehr und Stadtentwicklung am Beispiel Zürichs. Chronos: Zürich

GEWALD, Jan-Bart (2011): Kolonisierung, Völkermord und Wiederkehr: Die Herero von Namibia 1890-1923, pp 105-20. In: ZIMMERER, Jürgen; ZELLER, Joachim [Eds.] (2011): Völkermord in Deutsch-Südwestafrika: Der Kolonialkrieg (1904-1908) in Namibia und seine Folgen. Weltbild: Augsburg

GRÜNDER, Horst (2012): Geschichte der deutschen Kolonien. 6. überarbeitete und erweiterte Auflage. Schöningh/UTB: Paderborn, München, Wien, Zürich

GULLIVER, Katrina (2015): The Colonial City as a frame of historical analysis. Retrieved at: https://unsw.academia.edu/KatrinaGulliver

HABERMAS, Jürgen [1962] (reprint 2006): Strukturwandel der Öffentlichkeit: Untersuchungen zu einer Kategorie der bürgerlichen Gesellschaft. Suhrkamp: Frankfurt am Main

HABERMAS, Jürgen [1989] (paperback reprint 1991): The Structural Transformation of the Public Sphere: An Inquiry into a Category of Bourgeois Society. Translated by Thomas Burger with the assistance of Frederick Lawrence. MIT Press: Cambridge/Massachusetts

HAFFNER, Jeanne (2013): The View from Above: The Science of Social Space. MIT Press: Cambridge/Massachusetts

HALL, Peter [1988] (2014, fourth edition): Cities of Tomorrow: An Intellectual History of Urban Planning and Design Since 1880. Blackwell: Chichester.

HALL, Peter (2000): The Centenary of Modern Planning, pp 20-39. In: FREESTONE, Robert [Ed.] (2000): Urban Planning in a Changing World: The Twentieth Century Experience. E&FN Spon: London

HAMER, David (2000): Planning and Heritage: Towards Integration, pp 194-211. In: FREESTONE, Robert [Ed.] (2000): Urban Planning in a Changing World: The Twentieth Century Experience. E&FN Spon: London

HÅRD, Mikael; JAMISON, Andrew (2005): Hubris and Hybrids: A Cultural History of Technology and Science. Routledge: New York, London

HÅRD, Mikael; MISA, Thomas (2010): Modernizing European Cities: Technological Uniformity and Cultural Distinction, pp 1-20. In: HÅRD, Mikael; MISA, Thomas [Eds.] (2010): Urban Machinery: Inside Modern European Cities. MIT Press: Cambridge/Massachusetts

HÅRD, Mikael; STIPPAK, Marcus (2010): Progressive Dreams: The German City in Britain and the United States, pp 121-140. In: HÅRD, Mikael; MISA, Thomas [Eds.] (2010): Urban Machinery: Inside Modern European Cities. MIT Press: Cambridge/Massachusetts

HARDY, Dennis (2000): Quasi Utopias: Perfect Cities in an Imperfect World, pp 61-77. In: FREESTONE, Robert [Ed.] (2000): Urban Planning in a Changing World: The Twentieth Century Experience. E&FN Spon: London

HARLANDER, Tilman; PYTA, Wolfram (2010): NS-Architektur: Macht und Symbolpolitik: Eine Einführung, pp 7-19. In: HARLANDER, Tilman; PYTA, Wolfram [Eds.] (2010): NS-Architektur: Macht und Symbolpolitik. LIT Verlag: Berlin

HARTMANN, Kristiana (1996): Alltagskultur, Alltagsleben, Wohnkultur, pp 183-301. In: KÄHLER, Gert [Ed.] (1996): Geschichte des Wohnens – Band 4. Deutsche Verlags-Anstalt: Stuttgart

HEGE, Patrick C. (2015): The German Variation: A Sketch of Colonial *Städtebau* in Africa, 1884-1919, pp 165-79. In: SILVA, Carlos Nunes [Ed.] (2015): Urban Planning in Sub-Saharan Africa: Colonial and Post-Colonial Planning Cultures. Routledge: New York, London

HELFRICH, Andreas (2000): Die Margarethenhöhe Essen: Architekt und Auftraggeber vor dem Hintergrund der Kommunalpolitik Essen und der Firmenpolitik Krupp zwischen 1886 und 1914. Verlag und Datenbank für Geisteswissenschaften: Weimar

HERZL, Theodor [1902] (2004): AltNeuLand. Books on Demand GmbH/haGalil.com: Norderstedt

HESSLER, Martina (2001): Mrs Modern Woman: Zur Sozial- und Kulturgeschichte der Haushaltstechnisierung. Campus: Frankfurt

HESSLER, Martina (2012): Kulturgeschichte der Technik. Campus: Frankfurt

HEYWOOD, Annemarie; LAU, Brigitte [Eds.] (second printing, 1993): Three Views into the Past of Windhoek. John Meinert: Windhoek

HILBERSEIMER, Ludwig (1944): The New City: Principles of Planning. Paul Theobald: Chicago

HILBERSEIMER, Ludwig (1955): The Nature of Cities. Paul Theobald & Co.: Chicago

HILLEBRECHT, Werner (1985): Namibia in Hochschulschriften: A Bibliography on all Aspects of Namibian concern including German Colonial Policy and International Law 1851-1984. Basler Afrika-Bibliographien: Basel

HILLEBRECHT, Werner (1992): Central Register of Theses on Namibia: 1992 Edition. National Archives of Namibia: Windhoek

HOFRICHTER, Hartmut [Ed.] (third edition, 1995): Stadtbaugeschichte von der Antike bis zur Neuzeit. Vieweg: Braunschweig

HOME, Robert (2015): Colonial Urban Planning in Anglophone Africa, pp 53-66. In: SILVA, Carlos Nunes [Ed.] (2015): Urban Planning in Sub-Saharan Africa: Colonial and Post-Colonial Planning Cultures. Routledge: New York, London

HOPKINS, Eric (1990, sixth impression): A Social History of the English Working Classes: 1815-1945. Hodder and Stoughton: London, Sydney, Auckland, Toronto

KÄHLER, Gert (1996): Nicht nur Neues Bauen! Stadtbau, Wohnung, Architektur, pp 303-452. In: KÄHLER, Gert [Ed.] (1996): Geschichte des Wohnens – Band 4. Deutsche Verlags-Anstalt: Stuttgart

KAULICH, Udo (2001): Die Geschichte der ehemaligen Kolonie Deutsch-Südwestafrika: 1884-1914: Eine Gesamtdarstellung. Peter Lang: Frankfurt am Main

KAUPEN-HAAS, Heidrun (1988): Eugenik, Volk und Raum: Städtehygiene und Bevölkerungspolitik, dargestellt an einer Karriere seit 1926, pp 288-305. In: SCHILDT, Axel; SYWOTTEK, Arnold [Eds.] (1988): Massenwohnung und Eigenheim: Wohnungsbau und Wohnen in der Großstadt seit dem Ersten Weltkrieg. Campus: Frankfurt, New York

KING, Anthony D. (1985): Colonial Cities: Global Pivots of Change, pp 7-32. In: ROSS, Robert; TELKAMP, Gerard J. [Eds.] (1985): Colonial Cities: Essays on Urbanism in a Colonial Context. Martinus Nijhoff Publishers: Dordrecht, Boston, Lancaster

KING, Anthony D. (1989): Colonialism, Urbanism and the Capitalist World Economy. In: International Journal of Urban and Regional Research, 13: pp. 1-18

KING, Anthony D. (1990): Global Cities: Post-Imperialism and the Internationalization of London. Routledge: London

KING, Anthony D. (2005): Spaces of Global Cultures: Architecture Urbanism Identity. Routledge: London

KING, Leslie J. (1984, second printing 1985): Central Place Theory. Sage: Beverly Hills, London, New Delhi

KNOPP, Guido [Ed.] (2010): Das Weltreich der Deutschen: Von kolonialen Träumen, Kriegen und Abenteuern. Pendo: München, Zürich

KNOWLES, Morris (1920): Industrial Housing. McGraw-Hill Book Company: New York, London

KORN, Wolfgang (2012): Schienen für den Sultan: Die Bagdadbahn: Wilhelm II., Abenteurer und Spione. Komet: Köln

KORNEMANN, Rolf (1996): Gesetze, Gesetze… – Die amtliche Wohnungspolitik in der Zeit von 1918 bis 1945 in Gesetzen, Verordnungen und Erlassen, pp 599-723. In: KÄHLER, Gert [Ed.] (1996): Geschichte des Wohnens – Band 4. Deutsche Verlags-Anstalt: Stuttgart

KRÜGER, Gesine (2011): Das Goldene Zeitalter der Viehzüchter: Namibia im 19. Jahrhundert, pp 13-25. In: ZIMMERER, Jürgen; ZELLER, Joachim [Eds.] (2011): Völkermord in Deutsch-Südwestafrika: Der Kolonialkrieg (1904-1908) in Namibia und seine Folgen. Weltbild: Augsburg

KÜHL, Uwe (1997): Anfänge städtischer Elektrifizierung in Deutschland und Frankreich, pp 129-140. In: SCHOTT, Dieter [Ed.] (1997): Energy and the City in Europe: From Preindustrial Wood-Shortage to the Oil Crisis of the 1970s. Franz Steiner: Stuttgart

KUNDRUS, Birthe (2003): Moderne Imperialisten: Das Kaiserreich im Spiegel seiner Kolonien. Böhlau: Köln, Weimar, Wien

LADD, Brian (2008): Autophobia – Love and Hate in the Automotive Age. University of Chicago Press: Chicago, London

LAU, Brigitte (1993): Two Square Miles of History, pp 4-17. In: HEYWOOD, Annemarie; LAU, Brigitte [Eds.] (second printing, 1993): Three Views into the Past of Windhoek. John Meinert: Windhoek

LAUBER, Wolfgang [Ed.] (1988): Deutsche Architektur in Kamerun 1884-1914: Deutsche Architekten und Kameruner Wissenschaftler dokumentieren die Bauten der deutschen Epoche in Kamerun/Afrika. Krämer: Stuttgart

LAUBER, Wolfgang [Ed.] (1993): Deutsche Architektur in Togo 1884-1914: Ein Vorbild für ökologisches Bauen in den Tropen. Krämer: Stuttgart

LAUKÖTTER, Anja (2013): Das Völkerkundemuseum, pp 231-43. In: ZIMMERER, Jürgen [Ed.] (2013): Kein Platz an der Sonne: Erinnerungsorte der deutschen Kolonialgeschichte. Campus: Frankfurt

LE CORBUSIER [1929] (1987): The City of To-morrow and its Planning. Dover Publications: New York

LE CORBUSIER [1943] (1973): The Athens Charter. Grossman Publishers: New York

LEES, Lynn Hollen (2000): Urban Networks, pp 59-94. In: DAUNTON, Martin [Ed.] (2000): The Cambridge Urban History of Britain – Volume III: 1840-1950. Cambridge University Press: Cambridge

LEES, Andrew; LEES, Lynn Hollen (2007): Cities and the making of modern Europe: 1750-1914. Cambridge University Press: Cambridge

LEGASSICK, Martin (1995): British Hegemony and the Origins of Segregation in South Africa, 1901-14, pp 43-59. In: BEINART, William; DUBOW, Saul [Eds.] (1995): Segregation and Apartheid in Twentieth Century South Africa. Routledge: New York

LENGER, Friedrich (2013): Metropolen der Moderne: Eine europäische Stadtgeschichte seit 1850. Beck: München

LEWERENZ, Susann (2006): Die Deutsche Afrika-Schau (1935-1940): Rassismus, Kolonialrevisionismus und postkoloniale Auseinandersetzungen im nationalsozialistischen Deutschland. Peter Lang: Frankfurt am Main, Berlin, Bern, Bruxelles, New York, Oxford, Wien

LUCKIN, Bill (1997): Town, Country and Metropolis: The Formation of an Air Pollution Problem in London, 1800-1870, pp 77-92. In: SCHOTT, Dieter [Ed.] (1997): Energy and the City in Europe: From Preindustrial Wood-Shortage to the Oil Crisis of the 1970s. Franz Steiner: Stuttgart

MCGREGOR, Gordon D. L. (2013, second edition): The Native Pass Tokens of German South West Africa. Namibia Scientific Society: Windhoek

MABIN, Alan; ORANJE, Mark (2014): The 1938 Johannesburg 'Town Planning Exhibition and Congress': Testament, Monument and Indictment, pp 97-110. In: FREESTONE, Robert; AMATI, Marco [Eds.] (2014): Exhibitions and the Development of Modern Planning Culture. Ashgate: Farnham, Burlington

MARES, Detlev; SCHOTT, Dieter [Eds.] (2014): Das Jahr 1913: Aufbrüche und Krisenwahrnehmungen am Vorabend des Ersten Weltkriegs. Transcript: Bielefeld

MARX, Christoph (2008): Pelze, Gold und Weihwasser. Handel und Mission in Afrika und Amerika. Primus: Darmstadt

MARX, Karl; ENGELS, Friedrich [1872] (2010): Manifest der Kommunistischen Partei. Reclam: Stuttgart

MASSAQUOI, Hans Jürgen (1999): "Neger, Neger, Schornsteinfeger!:" meine Kindheit in Deutschland. Fretz und Wasmuth: Bern, München, Wien

MATHESON, A. Scott (1910): The City of Man. Fisher Unwin: London, Leipzig

MAY, Roland (2010): Von der Ingenieurästhetik zur Monumentalarchitektur: Der Brückenbau der Reichsautobahnen und der Architekt Paul Bonatz, pp 193-209. In: HARLANDER, Tilman; PYTA, Wolfram [Eds.] (2010): NS-Architektur: Macht und Symbolpolitik. LIT Verlag: Berlin

MAYLAM, Paul (1995): Explaining the Apartheid City: 20 Years of South African Urban Historiography, pp 19-38. In: Journal of Southern African Studies, Vol. 21, No.1, Special Issue: Urban Studies and Urban Change in Southern Africa (Mar., 1995)

MAYNE, Alan; MURRAY, Tim [Eds.] (2001): The Archaeology of Urban Landscapes: Explorations in Slumland. Cambridge University Press: Cambridge

376

MERKI, Christoph Maria (2008): Verkehrsgeschichte und Mobilität. UTB/Eugen Ulmer: Stuttgart

MICHAEL, Theodor (2015): Deutsch sein und schwarz dazu: Erinnerungen eines Afro-Deutschen. Dtv: München

MIÈGE, J. L., (1985): Algiers: Colonial Metropolis (1830-1961), pp 171-179. In: ROSS, Robert; TELKAMP, Gerard J. [Eds.] (1985): Colonial Cities: Essays on Urbanism in a Colonial Context. Martinus Nijhoff Publishers: Dordrecht, Boston, Lancaster

MOMMSEN, Wolfgang J. (1987): Imperialismustheorien: Ein Überblick über die neueren Imperialismusinterpretationen. 3. Auflage. Vandenhoeck & Ruprecht: Göttingen

MORITZ, Walter (2010): Vier Generationen Redecker in Namibia seit 1866: Aus Westfälischer Vergangenheit in die Namibische Zukunft. John Meinert: Windhoek

MOSLEY, Stephen (2001): The Chimney of the World: A History of Smoke Pollution in Victorian and Edwardian Manchester. The White Horse Press: Cambridge

MPOFU, Busani (2011): 'Undesirable' Indians, Residential Segregation and the Ill-Fated Rise of the White 'Housing Covenants' in Bulawayo, Colonial Zimbabwe, 1930-1973, pp 553-80. In: South African Historical Journal, Vol. 63, No. 4, December 2011

MÜNK, Dieter (1993): Die Organisation des Raumes im Nationalsozialismus: Eine soziologische Untersuchung ideologisch fundierter Leitbilder in Architektur, Städtebau und Raumplanung des Dritten Reiches. Pahl-Rugenstein: Bonn

MÜNKLER, Herfried (2007): Imperien: Die Logik der Weltherrschaft – vom Alten Rom bis zu den Vereinigten Staaten. Rowohlt: Berlin

MURUNGA, Godwin R. (2005): "Inherently Unhygienic Races": Plague and the Origins of Settler Dominance in Nairobi: 1899-1907, pp 98-130. In: SALM, Steven J.; FALOLA, Toyin [Eds.] (2005): African Urban Spaces in Historical Perspective. University of Rochester Press: Rochester, NY

NIETHAMMER, Lutz [Ed.] (1979): Wohnen im Wandel: Beiträge zur Geschichte des Alltags in der bürgerlichen Gesellschaft. Hammer: Wuppertal

NIGHTINGALE, Carl H. (2012): Segregation: A Global History of Divided Cities. University of Chicago Press: Chicago, London

NJOH, Ambe J. (2015): French Colonial Urbanism in Africa. In: SILVA, Carlos Nunes [Ed.] (2015): Urban Planning in Sub-Saharan Africa: Colonial and Post-Colonial Planning Cultures. Routledge: New York, London

NOVY, Klaus (1983): Genossenschafts-Bewegung: zur Geschichte und Zukunft der Wohnreform. Transit: Berlin

NOVY, Klaus; PRINZ, Michael (1985): Illustrierte Geschichte der Gemeinwirtschaft: wirtschaftliche Selbsthilfe in der Arbeiterbewegung von den Anfängen bis 1945. Dietz: Berlin, Bonn

OLUSOGA, David; ERICHSEN, Caspar W. (2010): The Kaiser's Holocaust: Germany's Forgotten Genocide. Faber and Faber: London

OSTERHAMMEL, Jürgen; JANSEN, Jan C. (2012): Kolonialismus. Geschichte, Formen, Folgen. C.H. Beck: München

PARKER, Simon (2004): Urban Theory and the Urban Experience: Encountering the City. Routledge: London, New York

PETERS, Walter (1981): Baukunst in Südwestafrika 1884-1914: Die Rezeption deutscher Architektur in der Zeit von 1884 bis 1914 im ehemaligen Deutsch-Südwestafrika (Namibia). SWA Wissenschaftliche Gesellschaft: Windhoek

PETERS, Walter [1984] (2002): Das Verandenhaus – Beispiel einer klimatisch wohltemperierten Bauweise, pp 240-7. In: HESS, Klaus A.; BECKER, Klaus J. [Eds.] (2002): Vom Schutzgebiet bis Namibia 2000. Klaus Hess Verlag: Göttingen/Windhoek

PEYROUX, Elisabeth (2004): Windhoek, capitale de la Namibie: changement politique et recomposition des périphéries. Karthala: Paris, Johannesburg

PORTER, Andrew [Ed.] (1999): The Oxford History of the British Empire: Volume III The Nineteenth Century. Oxford University Press: Oxford, New York

PORTER, Libby (2010): Unlearning the Colonial Cultures of Planning. Ashgate: Farnham, Burlington

REULECKE, Jürgen [Ed.] (1997): Geschichte des Wohnens: Band 3: 1800-1918: das bürgerliche Zeitalter. Wüstenrot Stiftung/Deutsche Verlagsanstalt: Stuttgart

REULECKE, Jürgen (2014): Das Pathos der Jugend: Die Entdeckung des jugendlichen „Selbst" und der „Hohe Meißner" 1913, pp 25-46. In: MARES, Detlev; SCHOTT, Dieter [Eds.] (2014): Das Jahr 1913: Aufbrüche und Krisenwahrnehmungen am Vorabend des Ersten Weltkriegs. Transcript: Bielefeld

RIBOLDAZZI, Renzo (2015): The IFHTP Discourse on Urbanism in Colonial Africa between the Wars, pp 41-52. In: SILVA, Carlos Nunes [Ed.] (2015): Urban Planning in Sub-Saharan Africa: Colonial and Post-Colonial Planning Cultures. Routledge: New York, London

RIEHL, Axel T. G. (1993): Der "Tanz um den Äquator": Bismarcks antienglische Kolonialpolitik und die Erwartung des Thronwechsels in Deutschland 1883 bis 1885. Duncker und Humblot: Berlin

RODENSTEIN, Marianne; BÖHM-OTT, Stefan (1996): Gesunde Wohnungen und Wohnungen für gesunde Deutsche, pp 453-555. In: KÄHLER, Gert [Ed.] (1996): Geschichte des Wohnens – Band 4. Deutsche Verlags-Anstalt: Stuttgart

RODGERS, Daniel (1998): Atlantic Crossings: Social Politics in a Progressive Age. Harvard University Press: Cambridge, Mass.

RÖSSLER, Mechthild; SCHLEIERMACHER, Sabine [Eds.] (1993): Der „Generalplan Ost": Hauptlinien der nationalsozialistischen Planungs- und Vernichtungspolitik. Akademie Verlag: Berlin

ROSS, Ellen (2001): Slum journeys: ladies and London poverty 1860 – 1940, pp 11-21. In: MAYNE, Alan; MURRAY, Tim [Eds.] (2001): The Archaeology of Urban Landscapes: Explorations in Slumland. Cambridge University Press: Cambridge

ROSS, Eric (2015): The Grid Plan in the History of Senegalese Urban Design, pp 110-28. In: SILVA, Carlos Nunes [Ed.] (2015): Urban Planning in Sub-Saharan Africa: Colonial and Post-Colonial Planning Cultures. Routledge: New York, London

SAHLIN, Kerstin; WEDLIN, Linda (2013): Circulating Ideas: Imitation, Translation and Editing, pp 218-42. In: GREENWOOD, Royston, et al. [Eds.] (2013): The SAGE Handbook of Organizational Institutionalism. Sage: Los Angeles, London, New Delhi, etc.

SAID, Edward [1977](2003): Orientalism. Penguin: London

SALM, Steven J.; FALOLA, Toyin [Eds.] (2005): African Urban Spaces in Historical Perspective. University of Rochester Press: Rochester, NY

SAUNIER, Pierre-Yves (2013): Transnational History. Palgrave Macmillan: Houndmills

SCHINZINGER, Francesca (1984): Die Kolonien und das Deutsche Reich: Die wirtschaftliche Bedeutung der deutschen Besitzungen in Übersee. Franz Steiner Verlag Wiesbaden: Stuttgart

SCHLER, Lynn (2007): The unwritten history of ethnic co-existence in colonial Africa: An example from Douala, Cameroon, pp 27-43. In: AHLUWALIA, Pal; BETHLEHEM, Louise; GINIO, Ruth [Eds.] (2007): Violence and Non-Violence in Africa. Routledge: London, New York

SCHMIDT, Wilhelm R. ; WOLCKE-RENK, Irmtraud D. (2001): Deutsch-Südwest-Afrika: Fotos aus der Kolonialzeit 1884-1918. Sutton: Erfurt

SCHOLZ, Wolfgang (2002): Stadtplanung in Afrika – Über den Umgang mit dem schwindenden Einfluss der Planung auf die Siedlungsentwicklung. In: RaumPlanung 101: pp 77-81. Dortmund

SCHOTT, Dieter (1997a): Energie und Stadt in Europa: Von der vorindustriellen 'Holznot' bis zur Ölkrise der 1970er Jahre: Einführung, pp 7-42. In: SCHOTT, Dieter [Ed.] (1997): Energy and the City in Europe: From Preindustrial Wood-Shortage to the Oil Crisis of the 1970s. Franz Steiner: Stuttgart

SCHOTT, Dieter (1997b): Power for Industry: Electrification and its strategic use for industrial promotion: The case of Mannheim, pp 169-193. In: SCHOTT, Dieter [Ed.] (1997): Energy and the City in Europe: From Preindustrial Wood-Shortage to the Oil Crisis of the 1970s. Franz Steiner: Stuttgart

SCHOTT, Dieter (1999): Die Vernetzung der Stadt: Kommunale Energiepolitik, öffentlicher Nahverkehr und die „Produktion" der modernen Stadt Darmstadt – Mannheim – Mainz 1880-1918. Wissenschaftliche Buchgesellschaft: Darmstadt

SCHOTT, Dieter (2006a): Wohnen im Netz: Zur Modernisierung großstädtischen Wohnens durch technische Netzwerke 1900-1939, pp 252-270. In: JANATKOVÁ, Alena; KOZIŃSKA-WITT, Hanna [Eds.] (2006): Wohnen in der Großstadt 1900-1939: Wohnsituation und Modernisierung im europäischen Vergleich. Franz Steiner Verlag: Stuttgart

SCHOTT, Dieter (2006b): Wege zur vernetzten Stadt – technische Infrastruktur in der Stadt aus historischer Perspektive, pp 249-257. In: Informationen zur Raumentwicklung 5.2006. Bonn

SCHOTT, Dieter (2009): Die Stadt als Thema und Medium europäischer Kommunikation – Stadtplanung als Resultat europäischer Lernprozesse. In ROTH, Ralf [Ed.] (2009): Städte im europäischen Raum: Verkehr, Kommunikation und Urbanität im 19. und 20. Jahrhundert. Franz Steiner Verlag: Stuttgart

SCHOTT, Dieter (2014a): Europäische Urbanisierung (1000 – 2000): Eine umwelthistorische Einführung. Böhlau: Köln, Weimar, Wien

SCHOTT, Dieter (2014b): Die Großstadt als Lebensraum des modernen Menschen, pp 71-94. In: MARES, Detlev; SCHOTT, Dieter [Eds.] (2014): Das Jahr 1913: Aufbrüche und Krisenwahrnehmungen am Vorabend des Ersten Weltkriegs. Transcript: Bielefeld

SCHOTT, Dieter; KLEIN, Stefan (1998): Mit der Tram ins 21. Jahrhundert: Geschichte, Gegenwart und Zukunft der Straßenbahn, pp 9-27. In: Idem [Eds.] (1998): Mit der Tram ins nächste Jahrtausend: Geschichte, Gegenwart und Zukunft der elektrischen Straßenbahn. Klartext: Essen

SCHRÖDER, Rainer (1992): Das Gesinde war immer frech und unverschämt: Gesinde und Gesinderecht vornehmlich im 18. Jahrhundert. Keip: Frankfurt

SCHUBERT, Dirk (1997): Stadterneuerung in London und Hamburg: Eine Stadtbauge-schichte zwischen Modernisierung und Disziplinierung. Vieweg: Braunschweig

SCHUBERT, Dirk (2000): The Neighbourhood Paradigm: From Garden Cities to Gated Communities, pp 118-138. In: FREESTONE, Robert [Ed.] (2000): Urban Planning in a Changing World: The Twentieth Century Experience. E&FN Spon: London

SCHUBERT, Michael (2003): Der schwarze Fremde: Das Bild des Schwarzafrikaners in der parlamentarischen und publizistischen Kolonialdiskussion in Deutschland von den 1870er bis in die 1930er Jahre. Franz Steiner Verlag: Stuttgart

SCHÜTZLER, Heiko (2000): Die BVG wird gegründet, pp 118-23. In: Berlinische Mo-natsschriften 6/2000

SEIER, Andrea (2001): Macht, pp 90-107. In: KLEINER, Marcus S. [Ed.] (2001): Michel Foucault: Eine Einführung in sein Denken. Campus: Frankfurt

SILVA, Carlos Nunes (2015a): Introduction, pp 1-7. In: SILVA, Carlos Nunes [Ed.] (2015): Urban Planning in Sub-Saharan Africa: Colonial and Post-Colonial Planning Cultures. Routledge: New York, London

SILVA, Carlos Nunes (2015b): Urban Planning in Sub-Saharan Africa: An Overview, pp 8-40. In: SILVA, Carlos Nunes [Ed.] (2015): Urban Planning in Sub-Saharan Africa: Co-lonial and Post-Colonial Planning Cultures. Routledge: New York, London

SIMON, David (1983): Aspects of Urban Change in Windhoek, Namibia, during the tran-sition to independence. PhD dissertation at Linacre College: Oxford

SIMON, David (1984): The End of Apartheid? Some Dimensions of Urban Poverty in Windhoek. Conference paper: Cape Town

SIMONE, AbdouMaliq: Sacral spaces in two West African cities, pp 63-83. In: AHLUWALIA, Pal; BETHLEHEM, Louise; GINIO, Ruth [eds.] (2007): Violence and Non-Violence in Africa. Routledge: London, New York

SINGARAVÉLOU, Pierre [ed.] (2013): Les empires coloniaux: XIXe – XXe siècle. Points : Paris

SIPPEL, Harald (2004): Rechtspolitische Ansätze zur Vermeidung einer Mischlingsbevöl-kerung in Deutsch-Südwestafrika, pp 138-64. In: BECKER, Frank [ed.] (2004): Ras-senmischehen – Mischlinge – Rassentrennung. Zur Politik der Rasse im deutschen Ko-lonialismus. Franz Steiner Verlag: Stuttgart

SITTE, Camillo (1901, third edition): Der Städte-Bau nach seinen künstlerischen Grundsätzen: Ein Beitrag zur Lösung moderner Fragen der Architektur und monumentalen
Plastik unter besonderer Beziehung auf Wien. Carl Graeser & Co.: Wien

SPEITKAMP, Winfried (2005): Deutsche Kolonialgeschichte. Reclam: Stuttgart

SPEITKAMP, Winfried (2013): Kolonialdenkmäler, pp 409-21. In: ZIMMERER, Jürgen
[Ed.] (2013): Kein Platz an der Sonne: Erinnerungsorte der deutschen Kolonialgeschichte. Campus: Frankfurt

STADT FRANKFURT [Ed.] (2013): Gebäude- und Wohnungszählung 2011 in Frankfurt
am   Main: Erste   Ergebnisse   auf   einen   Blick.   Retrieved   at:
http://www.frankfurt.de/sixcms/media.php/678/11_GWZ2011.pdf   (retrieved   on
19.11.2015)

STANLEY, Benjamin W. (2012): An historical perspective on the viability of urban diversi-
ty: lessons from socio-spatial identity construction in nineteenth-century Algiers and
Cape Town. Journal of Urbanism: International Research on Placemaking and Urban
Sustainability, 5:1, 67-86

SUTCLIFFE, Anthony (1981): Towards the Planned City: Germany, Britain, the United
States and France 1780-1914. Blackwell: Oxford

SWANSON, Maynard W. (1977): The Sanitations Syndrome: Bubonic Plague and Urban
Native Policy in the Cape Colony, 1900-1909, pp 387-410. In: The Journal of African
History, Vol. 18, No. 3, 1977

SWANSON, Maynard W. [1977] (1995): The Sanitations Syndrome: Bubonic Plague and
Urban Native Policy in the Cape Colony, 1900-1909, pp 25-42. In: BEINART, William;
DUBOW, Saul [Eds.] (1995): Segregation and Apartheid in Twentieth Century South
Africa. Routledge: New York

TEUTEBERG, Hans-Jürgen; WISCHERMANN, Clemens (1985): Wohnalltag in Deutschland 1850-1914: Bilder – Daten – Dokumente. Coppenrath: Münster

TEUTEBERG, Hans-Jürgen (1986): Die Debatten der deutschen Nationalökonomie im
Verein für Socialpolitik über die Ursachen der „Wohnungsfrage" und die Steuerungsmittel
einer Wohnungsreform im späten 19. Jahrhundert, pp 13-59. In: Idem [Ed] (1986):
Stadtwachstum, Industrialisierung, sozialer Wandel: Beiträge zur Erforschung der Urbanisierung im 19. und 20. Jahrhundert. Duncker und Humblot: Berlin

THODE-ARORA, Hilke (2013): Hagenbeck: Tierpark und Völkerschau, pp 244-56. In:
ZIMMERER, Jürgen [Ed.] (2013): Kein Platz an der Sonne: Erinnerungsorte der deutschen Kolonialgeschichte. Campus: Frankfurt

THOMPSON, Susan (2000): Diversity, Difference and the Multi-Layered City, pp 230-248. In: FREESTONE, Robert [Ed.] (2000): Urban Planning in a Changing World: The Twentieth Century Experience. E&FN Spon: London

TOMLINSON, B. R. (1999): Economics and Empire: The Periphery and the Imperial Economy, pp 53-74. In: PORTER, Andrew [Ed.] (1999): The Oxford History of the British Empire: Volume III The Nineteenth Century. Oxford University Press: Oxford, New York

TURNBULL, Constance Mary (1989): A History of Singapore, 1819-1988. Oxford University Press: Oxford, New York

VAN LAAK, Dirk (2004): Imperiale Infrastruktur: Deutsche Planungen für eine Erschließung Afrikas 1880 bis 1960. Schöningh: Paderborn

VON PETZ, Ursula (1998): Robert Schmidt und die Grünflächenpolitik im Ruhrgebiet, pp 25-47. In: KASTORFF-VIEHMANN [Ed.] (1998): Die grüne Stadt: Siedlungen, Parks, Wälder, Grünflächen 1860-1960. Klartext: Essen

VON PETZ, Ursula (1999): Robert Schmidt and the public park policy in the Ruhr district, 1900-1930. In: Planning Perspectives 01/1999; 14(2), pp 163-82.

VON PETZ, Ursula (2016): Robert Schmidt 1869-1934: Stadtbaumeister in Essen und Landesplaner im Ruhrgebiet. Ernst Wasmuth Verlag: Tübingen, Berlin

VON SALDERN, Adelheid (1988): Neues Wohnen: Wohnverhältnisse und Wohnverhalten in Großwohnanlagen der 20er Jahre, pp 201-221. In: SCHILDT, Axel; SYWOTTEK, Arnold [Eds.] (1988): Massenwohnung und Eigenheim: Wohnungsbau und Wohnen in der Großstadt seit dem Ersten Weltkrieg. Campus: Frankfurt, New York

WALGENBACH, Katharina (2004): Rassenpolitik und Geschlecht in Deutsch-Südwestafrika (1907-1914). In: BECKER, Frank [Ed.] (2004): Rassenmischehen – Mischlinge – Rassentrennung. Zur Politik der Rasse im deutschen Kolonialreich. Franz Steiner Verlag: Stuttgart

WALLACE, Marion (2015): Geschichte Namibias: Von den Anfängen bis 1990. Basler Afrika Bibliographien/ Brandes & Apsel: Frankfurt am Main

WARD, Stephen V. (2000): Re-examining the International Diffusion of Planning, pp 40-60. In: FREESTONE, Robert [Ed.] (2000): Urban Planning in a Changing World: The Twentieth Century Experience. E&FN Spon: London

WARD, Stephen V. (2002): Planning the Twentieth-Century City. The Advanced Capitalist World. Wiley: Chichester

WARD, Stephen V. (2004): Planning and Urban Change. Second Edition. Sage: London, Thousand Oaks, New Delhi.

WARD, Stephen V. (2010a): Transnational Planners in a Postcolonial World, pp 47-72. In: HEALEY, Patsy; UPTON, Robert [eds.] (2010): Crossing Borders: International Exchange and Planning Practice. Routledge: London, New York

WARD, Stephen V. (2010b): What did the Germans ever do for us? A Century of British Learning About and Imagining Modern Planning. In: Planning Perspectives. Vol 25, no. 2, pp. 117-40

WARNER, Torsten (1996): Planung und Entwicklung der deutschen Stadtgründung Qingdao (Tsingtau) in China: Der Umgang mit dem Fremden. N/A: Hamburg

WASSER, Bruno (1993): Himmlers Raumplanung im Osten: Der Generalplan Ost in Polen 1940 – 1944. Birkhäuser: Basel, Berlin, Boston

WASSERSTEIN, Bernard (2002): Divided Jerusalem: The Struggle for the Holy City. Profile Books: London

WATSON, Peter (2010): The German Genius: Europe's Third Renaissance, the Second Scientific Revolution and the Twentieth Century. Simon & Schuster: London, New York, Sydney, Toronto, New Delhi

WENDT, Reinhard (2007): Vom Kolonialismus zur Globalisierung. Europa und die Welt seit 1500. Schöningh/UTB: Paderborn, München, Wien, Zürich

WERNER, Wolfgang (2002): Landreform und Landrechte in Namibia, pp 216-25. In: HESS, Klaus A.; BECKER, Klaus J. [Eds.] (2002): Vom Schutzgebiet bis Namibia 2000. Klaus Hess Verlag: Göttingen/Windhoek

WHITAKER, Charles Harris; ACKERMAN, Frederick L.; CHILDS, Richard S.; WOOD, Edith Elmer (1918): The Housing Problem In War and in Peace. The Journal of the American Institute of Architects: Washington D.C.

WHITAKER, Charles Harris (1920): The Joke about Housing. Marshall Jones Company: Boston

WITT, Peter-Christian (1979): Inflation, Wohnungszwangswirtschaft und Hauszinssteuer: Zur Regelung von Wohnungsbau und Wohnungsmarkt in der Weimarer Republik, pp 385-407. In: NIETHAMMER, Lutz [Ed.] (1979): Wohnen im Wandel: Beiträge zur Geschichte des Alltags in der bürgerlichen Gesellschaft. Hammer: Wuppertal

WOLPE, Harold [1977] (1995): Capitalism and Cheap Labour Power in South Africa: From Segregation to Apartheid, pp 60-90. In: BEINART, William; DUBOW, Saul

[Eds.] (1995): Segregation and Apartheid in Twentieth Century South Africa. Routledge: New York

WRIGHT, Gwendolyn (1991): The Politics of Design in French Colonial Urbanism. University of Chicago Press: Chicago, London

YEOH, Brenda S. A. (1996): Contesting Space: Power Relations and the Urban Built Environment in Colonial Singapore. Oxford University Press: Oxford, Singapore, New York

ZIMMERER, Jürgen (2001): Deutsche Herrschaft über Afrikaner: Staatlicher Machtanspruch und Wirklichkeit im kolonialen Namibia. LIT-Verlag: Münster, Hamburg, Berlin, London

ZIMMERER, Jürgen [2003] (2011): Krieg, KZ und Völkermord in Südwestafrika: Der erste deutsche Genozid, pp 45-63. In: ZIMMERER, Jürgen; ZELLER, Joachim [Eds.] [2003] (2011): Völkermord in Deutsch-Südwestafrika: Der Kolonialkrieg (1904-1908) in Namibia und seine Folgen. Weltbild: Augsburg

ZIMMERER, Jürgen; ZELLER, Joachim [Eds.] [2003] (2011): Völkermord in Deutsch-Südwestafrika: Der Kolonialkrieg (1904-1908) in Namibia und seine Folgen. Weltbild: Augsburg

ZIMMERER, Jürgen [Ed.] (2013): Kolonialismus und kollektive Identität: Erinnerungsorte der deutschen Kolonialgeschichte, pp 9-37. In: Idem (2013): Kein Platz an der Sonne: Erinnerungsorte der deutschen Kolonialgeschichte. Campus: Frankfurt

ZIMMERER, Jürgen [Ed.] (2013): Kein Platz an der Sonne: Erinnerungsorte der deutschen Kolonialgeschichte. Campus: Frankfurt

ZOLLMANN, Jakob (2010): Koloniale Herrschaft und ihre Grenzen: Die Kolonialpolizei in Deutsch-Südwestafrika 1894-1915. Vandenhoeck & Ruprecht: Göttingen, Oakville/CT

Websites

Berlin: http://www.berlin.de/geschichte/verbannte-buecher/ (retrieved on 24.04.2015)

Britannica: https://www.britannica.com/topic/Roman-Dutch-law (retrieved on 15.11.2017)

Hamburg: http://www.hamburg.de/geschichte/2207758/gross-hamburg-gesetz/ (retrieved on 06.08.2015)

Handelsblatt: http://www.handelsblatt.com/panorama/aus-aller-welt/pro-kopf-verbrauch-hier-leben-deutschlands-groesstestromverschwender/6140764.html?slp=false&p=2&a=false#image   (retrieved   on 19.08.2014)

Koloniale Rundschau: http://www.gaebler.info/ahnen/paul/johannes.htm#nation (retrieved on 07.04.2013)

RMD   Wasserstraßen:
    https://web.archive.org/web/20071008084609if_/http://www.rmdwasserstrassen.de/ (retrieved on 05.11.2017)

Spiegel Online: http://www.spiegel.de/wissenschaft/natur/impfkampagne-in-afrika-wiedie-rinderpest-besiegt-wurde-a-855594.html (retrieved on 17.09.2012)

Umweltbundesamt: http://www.umweltbundesamt.de/presse/presseinformationen/mehrengagement-bei-luftreinhaltung-bodenschutz (retrieved on 29.08.2014)

UNESCO: http://www.unesco.org/new/en/communication-and-information/flagshipproject-activities/memory-of-the-world/register/full-list-of-registeredheritage/registered-heritage-page-5/metropolis-sicherungsstueck-nr-1-negative-of-therestored-and-reconstructed-version-2001/ (retrieved on 25.05.2015)

Zeit-Online: http://www.zeit.de/politik/deutschland/2015-07/herero-nama-voelkermorddeutschland-norbert-lammert-joachim-gauck-kolonialzeit (retrieved on 10.07.2015)

Illustrations

Cover: "Windhoek, Old Location, family in front of hut, view toward Windhoek central" (NAN Photo-No. 08179). Reproduction by permission of National Archives of Namibia

Figure 1: Author's representation, based on
    https://upload.wikimedia.org/wikipedia/commons/7/7f/BlankMap-
    World_1935.png (retrieved on 19 August 2015)

Figure 2: Author's representation

Figure 3: Author's representation

Figure 4: Author's representation

Figure 5: Author's representation

Figure 6: Author's representation

Figure 7: Author's representation

Figure 8: TPR (1938) July: CONZEN, G.: Towards a Systematic Approach in Planning Science: Geoproscopy: p 9

Figure 9: "Plan of Windhoek and Klein-Windhoek and environs, 1892, by Curt von François" (NAN Photo-No. 09052). Reproduction by permission of National Archives of Namibia

Figure 10: Sketches by Joseph Eppeler (contained in NAN-File SVW B.2.a, sheet 13). Reproduction by permission of National Archives of Namibia

Figure 11: Author's representation

Figure 12: Author's representation based on

Left: https://upload.wikimedia.org/wikipedia/commons/7/7f/BlankMap-World_1935.png (retrieved on 19 August 2015),
Right: Google earth (retrieved on 23 August 2015)

Figure 13: Author's representation based on:
https://upload.wikimedia.org/wikipedia/commons/d/d1/Europe_in_1923.jpg (retrieved on 20 August 2015)

Figure 14: ADSWA II, No. 1 (1 April 1911)

Figure 15: "South West Africa showing Native Reserves / Drawn in the Surveyor General's Office, Windhoek 07.03.1924" (NAN Map-No. 00532). Reproduction by permission of National Archives of Namibia

Figure 16: "Prisoners of war, Nama / Herero prisoners of war concentration camp, Alte Feste in background, 1904" (NAN Photo-No. 11495). Reproduction by permission of National Archives of Namibia

Figure 17: Top: "Windhoek Old Location c. 1914, looking towards South. Wireless station and Kaiser-Wilhelm-Berg in background" (NAN Photo-No. 20074), bottom: "Windhoek Northern Residential Area, Villas, Leutwein Street" (NAN Photo-No. 02308). Reproduction by permission of National Archives of Namibia

Figure 18: "The Wonder Hut" (contained in NAN-File MWI 36/32/37). Reproduction by permission of National Archives of Namibia

Figure 19: "Coloured Township Windhoek", no scale (contained in NAN-File MWI 5/4). Reproduction by permission of National Archives of Namibia

Figure 20: "Coloured Township: Type C of houses; Haustype E; Plan of House F", all undated (contained in NAN-File MWI 5/4). Reproduction by permission of National Archives of Namibia

Figure 21: Author's representation based on map showing Tram System 08 July 1921, no scale (contained in NAN-File MWI 117/1/44). Reproduction by permission of National Archives of Namibia

Table 1: Author's representation based on Ward 2000: 44

Table A1: Author's representation

Table A2: Author's representation

Figure A4: "Old Location Windhoek, aerial view" (NAN Photo-No. 00868). Reproduction by permission of National Archives of Namibia

Figure A5: "Air photo of the Old Location, taken on 12.07.1948" (NAN Photo-No. 24625). Reproduction by permission of National Archives of Namibia

APPENDIX

A1: Statistics Der Städtebau

Der Städtebau

	1910	1911	1912	1913	1914	1915	1916	1917	1918	1919	1920	1921	1922	1923	1924	1925	1926	1927	1928	1929	1930	1931	1932	1933	1934	1935	1936	1937	1938	1939
Australia	0,3																													
Austria	0,5	1,3	0,3	6,3			0,3											2,2	1,7	2,7			5,7						6,5	
Belgium	5,8		2,6	0,3	7,4	1,9	2,7	5,2	1,5										1,4		5,5									
Brazil	0,5																					4,3								
Canada			0,3	0,3																										
Chile													2,3				3,1			3,7		7,6								
China																														
Cuba																										1,7				
Czechoslovakia	1	4,3		8,8	2,1	1,9													0,7		2,8	1,1								
Denmark	0,8										8,7							1,9			1,8			2,8						
Dutch East Indies																														
Estonia												10,4																		
Finland	8,6	9,4		2,6				1,6	0,3	7,9	8,1	12,5	6,2			3,8	5,2	6,5	1,5	2,2			5,8							
France																														
Germany	32	53,6	66,8	41,3	52,5	44,4	62,1	52,5	52,1	68,6	56,4	45,3	47,1			54,3	36,6	40,8	42	32	59	25,4	37,8	26,7	29,4	28,8	56,3		57	25,9
Greece		5,1																	0,7				4,7							
Hungary				0,3	1,8						4																			
India																														
Iraq																			1	0,4										
Italy	5					1,9	0,3									7,7	8,1		9	0,1	1,8			9,1		7,9			5,4	13,5
Japan																										2,5				
Luxembourg																		0,8	0,9			2,2		1,1						
Netherlands	4,8				0,5	3,9	5,5					5,2				4,7	2,4	0,5	1,4											
Norway																	6,8			0,3					1,5					
Persia																														
Poland						0,6	6,9	2,2																						
Romania								3	7,2				3,9								0,9					1,7				
Russia																						4,3		4,5	6					
Samoa												0,6													1,1					
Spain												1,8	1,6					0,5				6,5	10,5		5,3					
Sweden																0,9			4,8	0,6			0,5							
Switzerland			0,6	1,7	1,8	11,3	1,9		1,2	1,2	1,2					1,2	1,8	10,9		3,3	3,7								3,2	
Turkey																0,3														
United Kingdom												1,2				1,2	3,4			1	1,8				0,8	1,7	6,7		4,8	
United States	3,5	3,2	4	10,3	7,1	0,3	5,2	1,9	2,1	0,3	1,2						2,4	8,4	2,9	10,4	8,3	15,7		2,3	2,3	4,6				3,1
Yugoslavia						0,6	3,3			0,9			1,3													3,3	1,3		2,2	
International matters	27,5	11,5	3,7	3,1	3,4						7,5	6,1	4,5			23	10,7	3	5,5	12,5	14,3	33	20,9	22,2						
General matters	9,8	11,5	21,8	24,2	20,3	33,1	11,8	33,6	35,6	21	12,8	13,5	33,1			2,9	14,1	19,6	25,8	30,7			15,1	22,7	53,6	47,9	35,8		21	57,5
Subtotal	100	100	100	100	100	100	100	100	100	100	100	100	100			100	100	100	100	100	100	100	100	100	100	100	100		100	100

Coverage on countries and matters of particular relevance as shown in Figure 5

	1910	1911	1912	1913	1914	1915	1916	1917	1918	1919	1920	1921	1922	1923	1924	1925	1926	1927	1928	1929	1930	1931	1932	1933	1934	1935	1936	1937	1938	1939
Belgium	5,8	1,3	2,6	-	-	-	2,8	5,2	1,5	7,9	1,3	12,5	6,2	-	-	3,8	0,8	2,2	1,6	2,2	-	-	5,8	5,7	-	-	-	-	-	-
France	8,6	53,6	66,8	41,3	52,5	44,4	62,1	52,5	52,1	68,6	56,4	45,3	47,1	-	-	54,3	36,7	40,8	42	32	59	25,4	37,8	26,7	29,4	28,8	56,3	-	57	25,9
Germany	32,0	-	-	-	-	1,9	0,3	1,6	-	-	-	-	-	-	-	7,7	8,1	1,1	9	0,2	1,8	-	-	9,1	-	7,9	-	-	3,2	13,5
Italy	5	-	-	-	2,9	-	-	-	-	-	-	-	-	-	-	-	2,4	0,8	0,9	-	-	-	-	-	-	-	-	-	-	-
Netherlands	4,8	-	-	-	0,5	3,9	5,5	-	-	-	-	-	-	-	-	-	-	-	4,8	-	-	-	-	-	-	-	-	-	-	-
Sweden	-	-	-	-	-	-	-	-	-	-	-	-	-	-	-	-	-	-	-	0,5	-	6,5	-	-	5,3	-	-	-	-	-
United Kingdom	3,5	-	4	10,3	7,1	0,3	5,2	-	-	0,3	1,3	1,2	-	-	-	0,3	3,4	10,9	2,9	1	1,8	15,7	2,3	4,6	0,8	1,7	6,7	-	4,8	-
United States	27,5	-	-	0,9	3,4	0,6	-	1,9	2,1	0,9	7,5	6,1	4,6	-	-	1,2	10,7	3	5,5	12,5	8,3	-	20,9	22,2	-	3,3	1,3	-	3,3	-
International matters	9,8	11,5	21,8	24,2	20,3	33,1	11,8	33,6	35,6	21	12,8	13,5	33,1	-	100	14,1	19,6	25,8	25,8	30,7	14,3	33	15,1	22,7	53,6	47,9	35,8	100	2,2	3,1
General matters	-	11,5	-	-	-	-	-	-	-	-	-	-	-	-	-	-	-	-	-	-	-	-	-	-	-	-	-	-	21	57,5
Not specified	3	22	0,9	17,7	11,3	15,8	12,4	5,2	8,4	1,2	20,9	21,4	9,1	-	-	6,8	20,9	10,6	7,6	10,4	14,8	19,5	18	9,1	8,7	5,8	-	-	11,8	-
	97	78	99,1	82,3	88,7	84,2	87,6	94,8	91,6	98,8	79,1	78,6	90,9	-	-	93,2	79,1	89,4	92,4	89,5	85,3	80,6	82	90,9	91,3	94,2	100	-	88,2	100

iii

A2: Statistics The Town Planning Review

	1910	1911	1912	1913	1914	1915	1916	1917	1918	1919	1920	1921	1922	1923	1924	1925	1926	1927	1928	1929	1930	1931	1932	1933	1934	1935	1936	1937	1938	1939	1940	1941	1942	1943
Australia	0,3	-	3,1	-	0,1	-	-	-	-	-	0,3	2,3	-	-	-	-	-	-	-	-	-	-	-	-	6	-	-	-	-	-	-	-	-	-
Austria	6,7	9,8	-	-	-	-	-	-	-	-	-	-	-	-	-	-	-	-	-	-	-	-	-	-	-	-	-	-	-	-	-	-	-	-
Belgium	-	-	12,3	8,8	1,1	8,4	0,9	-	-	-	0,3	0,5	11,5	-	-	-	-	-	0,3	-	-	0,3	0,3	-	-	-	-	-	-	-	-	-	-	-
Canada	-	-	1,8	1,8	0,6	3,9	3,4	-	2,1	-	-	-	-	-	-	-	-	-	-	-	-	4	-	-	-	-	-	-	-	-	-	-	-	-
Egypt	-	-	-	-	-	-	-	21,2	-	-	-	-	-	-	-	-	-	-	-	-	-	-	-	12,6	-	-	-	-	-	-	-	-	-	-
France	1,6	7,1	7,1	4,8	6,5	3	0,9	-	2,5	-	9,1	11	5,1	0,4	0,2	14,2	-	-	-	-	-	-	-	-	-	-	-	-	-	15,6	-	-	-	-
Germany	3,7	0,2	0,1	-	-	3,4	1,5	-	-	-	-	4,2	5,7	-	4,2	-	-	-	-	-	-	-	-	-	-	-	-	-	3,5	-	-	-	35,5	-
Greece	-	-	-	-	-	-	-	-	-	-	-	-	-	5,2	-	-	-	-	-	-	1,3	-	-	-	-	-	-	-	-	-	-	-	-	-
India	-	-	-	-	-	-	1,1	-	1,1	1,3	-	4,2	1,2	-	-	-	-	-	-	-	0,7	-	-	-	-	-	-	2,5	-	-	-	-	-	-
Ireland	-	-	-	-	-	-	-	26,7	-	-	-	-	-	-	-	-	-	-	-	-	-	-	-	-	-	3,8	-	-	-	-	-	-	-	-
Palestine	-	-	-	-	-	-	-	-	-	-	-	-	-	-	-	-	15,1	-	-	-	-	-	-	-	-	-	15,4	4,1	0,3	-	-	-	-	-
Italy	-	0,2	1,8	-	-	-	-	12,4	7	-	-	1,6	-	21,3	14,5	22,3	22,3	38,9	12,2	22,4	8,9	24,9	16,1	0,6	7,1	-	-	-	-	-	-	-	-	-
Kenya	-	-	-	-	-	-	-	-	-	-	-	-	-	-	-	-	-	-	-	-	-	-	0,6	-	-	-	-	-	-	-	-	-	-	-
Malaysia	-	-	-	-	-	-	-	-	-	-	-	1,6	-	-	-	-	-	-	-	-	-	-	-	-	-	-	-	-	-	-	-	-	-	-
Malta	-	-	-	-	-	-	-	-	-	-	-	-	-	2,3	-	-	2,3	2,3	-	-	-	-	-	-	-	-	-	-	-	-	-	-	-	-
Myanmar	-	-	-	-	-	-	-	-	-	-	-	-	-	-	-	-	-	-	-	-	-	-	-	-	-	-	-	-	-	-	-	-	-	-
Netherlands	-	-	-	-	-	-	-	-	-	-	-	-	-	-	-	-	-	0,8	-	-	-	-	-	-	-	7,8	19,2	-	-	-	-	-	-	-
New Zealand	-	-	-	-	-	-	-	-	-	-	-	1,4	-	2,3	-	-	-	-	2,1	-	3,3	-	1,8	-	-	-	-	-	-	-	-	-	-	-
Norway	-	-	-	-	-	-	-	-	-	-	-	-	-	-	-	-	-	-	-	-	-	-	-	-	0,3	-	-	-	-	-	-	-	-	20
Poland	-	-	-	-	-	-	-	-	-	-	-	-	-	-	-	-	-	-	-	-	-	-	-	-	-	-	-	-	-	-	-	-	-	-
Portugal	-	-	-	-	-	-	6,2	-	-	-	-	-	-	-	-	-	-	-	-	-	-	-	-	-	-	-	-	0,8	-	-	-	-	-	-
Russia	-	-	-	-	-	-	0,4	-	-	-	-	-	-	-	1,7	-	-	-	-	-	-	-	-	-	-	-	-	-	-	-	-	-	-	-
Spain	-	-	-	-	-	-	-	-	-	-	-	-	-	-	-	-	-	-	-	-	-	0,5	-	-	-	-	-	-	-	-	-	-	-	-
Sudan	-	-	-	1,9	-	-	-	-	-	-	-	-	-	-	-	-	-	-	-	-	-	-	-	-	-	-	-	-	-	-	-	-	-	-
Sweden	-	-	-	-	-	-	-	-	-	-	-	-	-	-	5,7	-	-	6,5	-	-	-	-	-	-	-	-	-	-	-	-	-	-	-	-
United Kingdom	53,3	44,5	48,7	41,3	29,6	35,6	51,9	37,8	62,7	39,9	72,5	48,2	26,1	53,9	39,1	62,6	49,6	27,1	63,8	42	46,9	43	61,4	57,9	56,4	66,3	54,9	51,2	27	29,3	-	-	54,8	15,3
United States	11,1	20,4	0,2	2,5	35	5,9	4,7	1,8	1,1	5,2	2,6	7	14	4,6	10,9	3,9	4,4	4	16,3	33,7	15,5	22,4	12,8	16,7	13,1	14,4	2,2	4,1	21,2	15,6	-	-	-	2,4
International matters	19,8	9,5	16,2	33,7	28,1	10,3	12,6	-	5,6	51,6	1,5	10,1	28	6,3	2,9	3,9	3,8	-	-	0,3	7,9	1,1	1,8	4,7	10,5	2,5	1,6	21,2	44,1	1,8	-	-	-	1,2
General matters	3,5	8,2	10,5	5,2	-	17,9	16,4	-	18	2	13,7	13,6	9,6	6,1	20,8	15,5	1,7	17,8	5,6	1,6	15,5	0,5	0,9	7,6	2,8	6,6	6,6	16,2	3,9	1,8	-	-	9,7	61,2
Subtotal	100	100	100	100	100	100	100	100	100	100	100	100	100	100	100	100	100	100	100	100	100	100	100	100	100	100	100	100	100	100	-	-	100	100

Coverage on countries and matters of particular relevance as shown in Figure 4

	1910	1911	1912	1913	1914	1915	1916	1917	1918	1919	1920	1921	1922	1923	1924	1925	1926	1927	1928	1929	1930	1931	1932	1933	1934	1935	1936	1937	1938	1939	1940	1941	1942	1943
Belgium	-	-	12,3	8,8	1,1	8,4	0,9	-	2,1	-	0,3	0,5	-	-	-	-	-	-	-	-	-	-	0,3	-	-	-	-	-	-	-	-	-	-	-
Canada	-	-	1,8	0,6	-	3,9	3,4	-	-	-	-	-	-	-	-	14,2	-	0,3	-	-	-	-	4	-	-	-	-	-	-	-	-	-	-	-
France	1,6	7,1	7,1	-	4,8	3	-	-	-	-	9,1	11	5,1	-	0,2	-	-	-	-	-	-	-	-	-	3,7	-	-	-	3,5	15,6	-	-	35,5	-
Germany	3,7	0,2	0,1	6,5	7,7	3,4	1,5	-	1,1	-	-	-	5,7	0,4	-	-	-	1,2	-	-	1,3	-	-	-	-	-	-	-	-	-	-	-	-	-
India	-	-	-	-	-	1,4	1,1	-	1,1	1,3	-	-	-	5,2	4,2	-	-	1,2	-	-	0,7	-	-	-	-	-	-	-	-	-	-	-	-	-
Italy	-	0,2	1,8	-	-	-	-	12,4	-	-	-	-	-	5,2	14,5	-	22,3	38,9	12,2	22,4	8,9	24,9	16,1	0,6	7,1	-	15,4	4,1	0,3	-	-	-	-	-
United Kingdom	53,3	44,5	48,7	41,3	29,6	35,6	51,9	37,8	62,7	39,9	72,5	48,2	26,1	53,9	39,1	62,6	49,6	27,1	63,8	42	46,9	43	61,4	57,9	56,4	66,3	54,9	51,2	27	29,3	-	-	54,8	15,3
United States	11,1	20,4	0,2	2,5	1,5	5,9	4,7	1,8	1,1	5,2	2,6	7	14	4,6	10,9	3,9	4,4	4	16,3	33,7	15,5	22,4	12,8	16,7	13,1	14,4	2,2	4,1	21,2	15,6	-	-	-	2,4
International matters	19,8	9,5	16,2	33,7	35	10,3	12,6	-	5,6	51,6	1,5	10,1	28	6,3	2,9	3,9	3,8	-	-	0,3	7,9	1,1	1,8	4,7	10,5	2,5	1,6	21,2	44,1	1,8	-	-	-	1,2
General matters	3,5	8,2	10,5	17,9	28,1	16,4	6,6	-	18	2	13,7	13,6	9,6	6,1	20,8	15,5	1,7	17,8	5,6	1,6	15,5	0,5	0,9	7,6	2,8	2,8	6,6	16,2	3,9	37,7	-	-	9,7	61,2
Not specified	7	9,8	3,1	1,9	0,1	-	6,6	47,9	-	-	0,3	9,6	11,5	2,3	7,4	-	18,1	10,6	2,1	-	3,3	8,1	2,7	12,6	6,3	13,9	19,2	3,3	-	-	-	-	-	20
	93	90,2	96,9	98,1	99,9	100	93,4	52,1	100	100	99,7	90,4	88,5	97,7	92,6	100	81,9	89,4	97,9	100	96,7	91,9	97,3	87,4	93,7	86,1	80,8	96,7	100	100	-	-	100	80

A3: Transcript of Petition by Joseph Eppeler

(File SVW B.2.a, Baupolizei Allgemeines, Sheets 13-20)

<u>Anschrift</u>

Betrifft Eingabe des Technikers   Windhuk, 20. Okt. 1917

Eppeler betr. Bauwesen der

Stadt Windhuk

Unter höflicher Bezugnahme

auf die stattgefundene Bespre-

chung erlaube ich mir in der

Anlage 2 Aufsätze einzureichen

mit der Bitte um gefl. durchsicht
.
Hochachtend

Joseph Eppeler

Techniker des Hochbaureferats

An

den Herrn Bürgermeister

    der Stadt <u>Windhuk</u>.

Die Stadt Windhuk vom Standpunkt des Städtebaus.

In den folgenden Zeilen soll dargelegt werden, was ein
Städtebaukundiger über die Anlage und bisherige Entwicklung
des Windhuker Stadtbildes denkt und was in Bezug auf die gesetzmäßige
Weiterentwicklung desselben zu geschehen hat.

Zunächst, was versteht man unter „Städtebau"? Städtebau ist die Bezeich-
nung für eine Berufstätigkeit, die in Südwest so gut wie unbekannt ist.
Der Städtebauer ist ein Baukünstler, dessen Spezialstudium die Anlage
der Dörfer und Städte ist, die Anlage neuer Stadtteile und die Regulie-
rung, Erhaltung und Verbesserung schon bestehenden.

Die Kunst des Städtebaus besteht darin, die Technik des Geometers mit der
Kunst des Architekten und der Wissenschaft des Ingenieurs so zu vereinigen,
daß der entstehende Bebauungsplan technisch und künstlerisch vollkommen ist,
das heißt nicht nur das Verkehrsbedürfnis berücksichtigt, sondern auch den zahlreichen Forderungen gerecht wird, die sich ergeben z.B. aus der geschichtlichen
Entwicklung des Ortes, aus dem bestehendem Besitzstand, aus den mannig-
fachen Terrainverhältnissen, aus den geographischen und klimatischen Lagen,
aus den meteorologischen und hydrologischen Verhältnissen, aus der boden-
ständigen Bauweise und so fort.

Während man früher bei den Entwürfen von Stadtplänen sich hauptsächlich nach Verkehrsansprüchen richtete und daneben auf wirtschaftlichen, sozialen
und hygienischen Anforderungen gerecht zu machen fühlte, ist man heutzutage
bestrebt das Städtebild ästhetisch und wohnlich zu gestalten, ohne dabei das erst-
genannte zu vernachlässigen.

Die Aufgabe des Städtebauers greift also weiter als den bloßen Straßen-
plan festzulegen; die architektonische Charakteristik der entstehenden Bauwerke,
ihre Abstufung in der Steigerung vom Wohnbau zum Monumentalbau, die
künstlerische Fragen, wie die Aufstellung von Monumenten, öffentlichen
Brunnen, Anlage öffentlicher Gärten hingen gewissermaßen in freier Hand.
Sein Einfluß zeigt nicht nur bis über alle öffentlichen Stadtgebilde, wie Straßen,
Plätze und öffentliche Bauten sondern erstreckt sich auch auf die architektonische Gestaltung des privaten Hauses, des Mietprüfers sowohl wie der
Hilfe, damit diese Gestaltung harmonisch und den Augen wohltuend sich
einfügen in das künstlerisch durchdachte Städtebild, natürlich ohne daß die
Interessen der einzelnen in irgend einer Weise geschädigt werden.

Wer in den letzten Jahren vor dem Weltkriege in Deutschland war

und dort mit gesundem Auge ganz neue Stadtteile durchwandert hat, der
wird in so mancher deutschen Stadt sich gewundert haben über den ganz
anderen, viel wohnlicheren Struktur, den diese Stadtteile aufweisen
als z. B. jene, die vor 20-30 Jahren entstanden sind. Das liegt nicht allein
an dem Charakter des einzelnen Hauses, es liegt an ihrem Zusammen-
wirken der einzelnen Kräfte, die der Städtebauer in seinen Dienst ge-
zogen hat. Dies zur Einleitung.

Betrachten wir nun einmal vom Standpunkt des Städtebaus

unsere liebe Hauptstadt, wie sie entstanden ist, wie sie heute ist und was bei künstlerischer Leitung ihrer baulichen Entwicklung aus ihr werden kann.

Es gibt in Windhuk manches recht ansprechende Gebäude, das, vorzüglich in seiner Architektur, harmonisch in seinem Aufbau und zweckmäßig in seiner Gestaltung das Auge des Beschauers erfreut, ihn mit kritisch geschultem Blick es zu zergliedern sucht und dann mit innerer Befriedigung feststellt: „So ist es schön, so muß ein Bauwerk sein, um das Herz zu erfreuen!" – Auch manch Anblickes Straßenbild bewundert das Auge. Blicke von der Kaiserstraße zur Gartenstraße hinauf und du hast ein Beispiel, wie die Pflanze als Architektur wirkt und das Straßenbild ringsum sprießt. Kommst du von Kleinwindhuk auf die Leutweinstraße und wendest den Schritt der neuen evangelischen Kirche zu, so kannst du an einem praktischen Beispiel sehen, wie man einen guten Straßenabschluß erzielt, ohne den Verkehr zu behindern.

Ist man denn diesem Bestreben architektonisch gut zu bauen und durch durch [sic] das richtige Hineinsetzen des Hauses in das Landschaftsbild wohltuend auf Gemüt und Sinn zu wirken überall in Windhuk treu geblieben? Leider nein, eher ist das Gegenteil der Fall. Wie kommt das?

Zweifellos hat der unbekannte Schöpfer des Windhuker Stadtplanes schematisch durch eine regelmäßige Anlage mit breiten, geraden Straßen etwas Besseres schaffen wollen als die in den alten Städten vornehmen, winkeligen Gassen; praktisch hat er sich die Sache sehr leicht gemacht, indem er den Plan lediglich mit Schienen und Winkel auf das Reißbrett warf, ohne all die gewichtigen Momente zu beachten, welche bei einer falschen Anlage zu berücksichtigen sind, ein unverzeihlicher Leichtsinn, dessen Folgen sich durch alle zukünftigen Zeiten hinziehen werden.

Es war gewiß nicht nötig, Straßen mit so starkem Gefälle zu planen, wie der neben dem Postgebäude hochgehende Parkweg oder die von der Luisenstraße zur evangelischen Kirche hinaufführende Schulstraße. Es war ebenfalls nicht nötig, innerhalb des engeren Stadtbildes Straßen zu projektieren, die nach ihrer Durchführung auf beiden Seiten außerordentlich hohe Böschungen haben würden, wie die neben dem „alten Römer" abzweigende mitten durch den meteorologischen Hügel führende Straße. Sind nicht einige der auf die

östlichen und westlichen Höhen projektierten Straßen überhaupt unausführbar, andere nach ihrer Fertigstellung für den Fuhrmannsverkehr praktisch unbenutzbar! Zerbrich dir einmal den Kopf und gib Antwort auf die Frage, warum von einem imaginären Punkt vor dem „alten Römer" Straßen in sechs Richtungen führen. Vielleicht, um das Vorhandensein eines Platzes zu begründen, aber von einem Platz verlangt man Geschlossenheit und die mangelt diesem Platz. Die Wohnstraßen hätte man ruhig enger machen sollen, dafür aber mehr Plätze schaffen sollen, aber richtige Plätze.

viii

Wer beging dann in der Folge weiterhin Fehler, in dem man den Ausspannplatz, d. h. den Haupthandelsplatz an das eine Ende einer langen Straße legte und den Bahnhof an deren anderes Ende, wodurch natürlich ein in steter Verbindung miteinanderstehenden Verkehrszentren ungebührlich weit auseinandergezogen wurde. Man bedenke nur, welche Anzahl von Fuhrwerken zum Waren- und Personentransport zwischen diesen beiden Verkehrszentren ständig hin- und hergondeln und welche Unmenge von Geld, Zeit und Material diese unüberlegte Anlage im Lauf der Jahre schon gekostet hat. Auch ist dadurch die eigentliche Geschäftsstadt ein langer Bandwurm angeblich das Projekt den Güterbahnhof in die Gegend des Eingeborenenfriedhofs zu verlegen; mit welchem Resultat? Der vorgenannte geschäftliche Bandwurm verlängert sich um die Strecke Ausspannplatz - Eingeborenenfriedhof!

Als Gegenbeispiele, in dieser Hinsicht wenigstens, kann man Swakopmund und Karibib anführen. Wie kurz sind dort, bei der mehr kreisförmigen Stadtentwicklung alle Entfernungen gegen hier.

Fast macht es den Eindruck als habe man sich bemüht die öffentlichen Gebäude usw., wenn eben möglich dort zu errichten, wo sie auch den Grundsätzen vernünftigen Städtebaus nicht hingehören.

Sehe man eine Stadt wie Pretoria, sie sei als Beispiel nur genommen, weil sie ihre Entstehungsart und ihrem Werdegang nach unseren Verhältnissen näher kommt als eine deutsche Stadt. Dort gruppierten sich um den Ausspannplatz nach und nach Kirche, Regierungsgebäude, andere öffentliche Gebäude, Geschäftshäuser und so weiter der naturgemäße Mittelpunkt und die Verkehrszentrale gegeben, um welche herum die Stadt sich harmonisch entwickeln konnte, In diesem Falle wenigstens war das natürliche praktische Empfinden der Buren weitschauender als die vielgerühmte deutsche Gründlichkeit.

Hier hat man fast lauter Verkehrsstraßen geschaffen und fast garkeine Wohnstraßen. Die Folge ist: Die meisten der überbreiten Verkehrsstraßen müssen natürlich verkehrsarm bleiben und es bieten sich

keine für das öffentliche Leben notwendigen Sammelpunkte. Die schnurgerade verlaufenden Straßenzüge und die weiten offenen Plätze erwiesen sich sowohl in gesundheitlicher als künstlerischer Hinsicht als vollständig unzulänglich.

Als erste Zug- und Stauberzeuger vermögen sie nicht mehr wie die alten Stadtanlagen die klimatischen Differenzen auszugleichen und die Wetterunbilden zu mildern, und sie behindern endlich infolge ihrer gleichförmigen Grundlinigkeit jede künstlerische Entfaltung, die im alten deutschen Stadtbild unbeschränkte Möglichkeit besaß.

Fast überall schweift der Blick ins Ungewisse, Uferlose, man vermißt die Möglichkeit, wie ein die Städtebilder alter deutscher Siedlungen aufweisen – Bitte, um nur ein Beispiel anzuführen eine Nebenstraße der Sternstraße gerade auf die Gebäude der katholischen Mission zugeführt, so hätte man einen ähnlich schönen Abschluß erzielt, wie ihn in Swakop-

mund die protestantische Kirche bildet, die wirklich in jeder Hinsicht am
richtigen Platze steht und deren Architektur auf dem Standort angepaßt ist.

Solche scheinbar geschlossenen Straßen legte das Mittelalter in den
deutschen Städten systematisch an, war doch der Städtebau schon ein Lehr-
fach auf den Universitäten des Mittelalters, erst die später über Deutschland hereinbrechenden großen Umwälzungen ließen diese Wissenschaft
einschlafen, bis die neueste Zeit sie in modernem Sinne wieder
belebte.

Im alten Stadtbild gehen die Straßen in leichten Kurven aus und
ein und man gewann in wechselnden Bildern den Anblick der in-
dividuell belebten Häuserfronten – in Windhuk gleitet der Blick, von
keinerlei Augenruhepunkten unterstützt und erfrischt, die langdurch-
gehenden Straßenzeilen hinab.

Diese Öde zu beleben ist man auf den übrigens ebenfalls ganz
unkünstlerischen Ausweg verfallen die Häuser durch unsinnige Giebelaufbauten, durch ganz geschmacklose Blechtürmchen, Filigranwetterfähnchen und
Miniaturerkern und sonstigen Nichtigkeiten herauszuputzen, die dem
Scheinwesen unserer Zeit entsprechen.

Damit sind wir bei der Architektur angelangt. Eine gerechte
Kritik muß anerkennen, daß die Gouvernementsbauten der letzten Jahre
vor dem Kriege befriedigen, mag eine etwas allzuspitzfindige Kritik
sie noch so sehr herunterreißen. Um einige wenige Beispiele zu er-
wähnen, so muß doch jeder vorurteilsfrei denkende anerkennen, daß
das Gouvernementsgebäude, das Elisabethheim, das neue Pensionat,
die Gemeindeschule, der Bahnhof, die dahinter liegenden drei Doppel-
wohnhäuschen in ihrer Gesamterscheinung durchaus befriedigen. Von
den kürzlich durch die englische Eisenbahnverwaltung errichteten Wohn-
häusern kann das allerdings niemand behaupten.

Sheet 16

Gut, in jeder Hinsicht wirken die drei Burgen auf der Höhe; von anderen
Privatbauten ist architektonisch fehlerlos das Geschäftshaus der Firma Rudolf
Schuster. Diese Beispiele mögen genügen. Es sei hier von einer eingehenden
Kritik der einzelnen Bauten abgesehen, zumal man sich in neuerer Zeit
bemüht hat recht ansprechende Häuschen zu errichten, wenn auch nicht überall die
erwartete Wirkung erzielt worden ist. Was aber im allgemeinen die
Architektur der älteren Windhuker Wohn- und Geschäftshausbauten angeht,
leider auch mancher der neueren. Ja kann man sagen, man hat über der
Sucht einen südwestafrikanischen Stil zu finden (der sich hauptsächlich durch sinn-
lose Giebelaufbauten charakterisiert) die Hauptsache vollkommen vergessen
gehabt, daß nämlich nicht der neue Stil die absolute Notwendigkeit war,
sondern etwas ganz anderes, die Läuterung des Geschmacks, den Sinn für das
<u>an sich</u>[1] Schöne und Zweckmäßige.

---

[1] All emphases in original

x

Von den meisten Windhuker Häusern kann man behaupten, daß diese Klavierkisten mit dem unvermeidlichen 20 Grad-Dach anscheinend von irgend einem Maurerpolier ohne jedes tektonische Gefühl gleichgültig, nüchtern, charakter- und gedankenlos und unorganisch in das südwestafrikanische Landschaftsbild hineingebaut sind, und es hätten sich mit denselben Mitteln ohne Mehraufwand anheimelnd schöne und wohnliche Bauten errichten lassen. (Vergleiche hierzu die beiliegenden Skizzen)

Obwohl aus persönlichen Rücksichten sehr ungern muß hier im Interesse der Sache auch auf ein Beispiel hingewiesen werden, wie man ebenfalls nicht bauen soll. Das Genossenschaftsgebäude und das in gleichem Stil errichtete Nachbargebäude sind in der Front an der Kaiserstraße ausgezeichnet gut in der gesamten Architektur; obwohl verschieden im Aufbau harmonieren die Verhältnisse jedes Hauses in sich und mit denen des anderen. Stellt man sich nun aber auf die Höhen jenseits des Reviers und schaut sich Windhuk an, so wirkt nichts trauriger als gerade dieser Gebäudekomplex. „Ja, das ist ja die Rückseite", hört man entschuldigend sagen. Die moderne Architektur kennt aber keine Rückseite, ein Haus muß allseitig gut ausgebaut werden, zumal wenn, wie in diesem Falle, es so weit sichtbar ist und dadurch wesentlich zum gesamten Charakterbild des Ortes mit beiträgt.

Jeder der einmal in Ländern spanischer Zunge war und sei es auch nur auf der Durchreise in Teneriffa, weiß, daß dort gerade die Innenhöfe architektonisch wundervoll ausgebildet sind. Diese wohnliche Innenhofausbildung und der gleichzeitige reiche Pflanzen- und Blumenschmuck dieser Höfe machen sie zu kleinen Paradiesen. Damit vergleiche man einmal die umbauten Windhuker Höfe mit ihrer kahlen Nüchternheit und man wird nicht mehr sagen: „Das ist ja nur die Rückseite!"

Um es kurz zu sagen, was das Ergebnis der bisher gehandhabten Bauweise

ist: Die Stadt hat unter ihrem Einfluß von vornherein darauf verzichtet wohnlich zu sein, sowohl nach innen wie nach außen. Die überhastete Bautätigkeit hat Zustände geschaffen, die keineswegs den Anforderungen entsprechen, welche die Neuzeit an gesundes und Anmüt [sic] und Geist erhebendes Wohnen und an die Entwickelung des öffentlichen und geschäftlichen Verkehrs stellt.

Mehr oder weniger erwacht heute das Bewußtsein, daß man eine vollkommen verfehlte Stadtanlage erzielt hat. Unsere noch im Ausbau begriffene Stadt ist bisher so ziemlich in allen Punkten das schnurgerade Gegenteil von dem geworden, was man unter einer wohnlichen Stadt versteht, wie es die Städte der alten Zeit waren.

Daß ist gewiß, wenn Windhuk eine liebliche, reizvolle, wohnliche Stadt würde, so würde mancher der Leute, die ihren Reichtum hier erworben haben und ihn nun in Europa verzehren, wiedergekommen sein und hätte hier seinen Lebensabend erwartet; denn ihr Ort wäre ihm lieb geworden, er hätte sich hier heimisch gefühlt, und das ist genug; denn nach Vergnügungen jagt man nicht mehr, wenn man ein arbeitsreiches Leben hinter sich hat. Und die Gesamtheit hätte den Vorteil gehabt.

Die eigentlich technische Seite des gesamten städtischen Bauwesens, wie Straßenbau, Wasserleitungsanlagen, Hochbauwesen, Baupolizei usw. fällt zwar auch in das Gebiet des Städtebaus, ihre Besprechung ist jedoch nicht Zweck dieses Aufsatzes und sie soll deshalb hier nicht weiter erörtert werden. Lediglich der Bauberatung sollen einige Zeilen gewidmet sein. Sie in erster Linie soll uns Antwort geben auf die Frage: „Was ist da zu tun?"

Die offizielle behördliche Bauberatung ist eines der besten Mittel hier helfend einzugreifen. Kurz vor dem Ausbruch dieses Krieges war sie in Deutschland schon fast überall, selbst auf dem Land eingerichtet, und es ist sehr viel Gutes und Schönes durch sie geschaffen, Unzweckmäßiges und Unschönes durch sie verhindert worden.

Die Bauberatung wird in folgender Weise gehandhabt. Wird der Behörde ein neues Bauprojekt zur Genehmigung vorgelegt und es verstößt in irgend einer Hinsicht gegen die in diesem Aufsatz ent- wickelten Grundsätze oder es ist sogar so, daß es, wie das Gesetz sagt, eine „Verunstaltung des Landes" bedeutet, so wird der Bauherr oder evtl. dessen Bauleiter vorgeladen, und es wird dem Erschienenen klar entwickelt, aus welchen Gründen die Stadt die Errichtung des Gebäudes in der beabsichtigten Form nicht gern genehmigt.

Hat der Mann sich den Plan von einem unfähigen Maurer- polier oder einem auf diesem Gebiet nicht genügend bewanderten Techniker machen lassen, so wird ihm nahegelegt, den Entwurf von einem Architekten

umarbeiten zu lassen, der mehr Verständnis für eine gesetzmäßige und zugleich schöne Planung hat.

Ist das Projekt so klein, daß sich die Kosten der Bauzeichnung viel- leicht nicht lohnen, so fertigt auch der Bauberater selbst dem betr. Bauherrn eine bessere Skizze an. In den meisten Fällen sehen die Bauherren ihren bei der besseren Ausführung herausspringenden Vorteil ein und sind gefügig.

In Deutschland hat man für widerspenstige Bauherren, wie sie vielfach auf dem Lande, manchmal aber auch in der Stadt zu finden sind, das „Gesetz gegen die Verunstaltung des Landes", auf Grund dessen die Baugenehmigung verweigert werden kann. Ob man hier ohne das Gesetz auskommt, bleibt abzuwarten, es kann jedoch bei dem hier durchweg etwas höheren Bildungsstand unserer deutschen Bevölkerung gehofft werden.

An das Projekt selber aber sind folgende Ansprüche zu stellen:

Zweckmäßigkeit ist die erste Forderung des Bauherrn und sie muß
unter allen Umständen erfüllt werden;
Darstellung des Zweckes ist die erste Forderung der Baukunst. Diese
Darstellung erfolgt durch möglichst scharfe Herausgestaltung aus dem
Zwecke, nicht nur durch Erfüllung der sachlichen Forderungen, sondern auch
durch ein Mehr, durch Erfindung der für diese bezeichnenden für sie
würdigen Form.

Die Bauberatung ihrerseits gründet sich darauf, daß das schöne
Bauen nicht in der Fassadenkunst beruht, nicht in der Ziermacherei oder
in den Täuschungen, die seit einem halben Jahrhundert das Aussehen
der Städte und des Landes so heruntergebracht haben. Es gilt die Erkenntnis, daß das Bauen eine Kunst ist, die nicht länger bloßen
Unternehmern und Spekulanten überlassen bleiben darf, wenn das ganze
Lebensbild in der Stadt nicht für immer den Stempel der Verrohung
und der Lieblosigkeit tragen soll, der ihn von den Bauspekulanten auf-
gedrückt wird. Was darin zu leisten versucht wird, und wie es sich
besser machen läßt, dafür mögen die beiliegenden Skizzen mehr als
Worte sagen.

Die befriedigende Lösung der Städtebaufragen und Hausbau-
fragen nach künstlerischen und auch auf verkehrstechnischen Grundsätzen
hängt davon ab, ob die Stadtverwaltung und die Regierung die ihnen
zustehende Macht zum Wohle der Allgemeinheit ausnutzen oder nicht.
Das aber ist nur möglich, wenn die Regelung dieser Fragen in einer
Hand vereinigt werden. In Deutschland hat jede Stadt ihren Stadtbaumeister, ja jede größere Gemeinde, dem die hier erörterten
Fragen und damit das gesamte städtische und private Bauwesen unter-
stellt sind, an den natürlich gefordert wird, daß er die gesamten

in Frage kommende Gebiete des Straßen-, Hoch- und Tiefbaus usw.
technisch beherrscht und nicht zuletzt architektonisch Verständnis besitzt.

Eine Landeshauptstadt wie Windhuk begnügte sich bisher mit
der gelegentlichen technischen Aushilfe des Gouvernements! Was
der Mangel dieser städtischen Bauzentrale an ästhetischen Werten
gezeigt hat und welche Unsummen diese Ersparnis bisher gekostet
hat und leider in Zukunft noch kosten wird, dafür liegen wohl auf
allen technischen Gebieten hinreichende Beweise vor.

Die Folgerungen ergeben sich von selbst. Möge man auch hier
zur Erkenntnis kommen, daß Städtebau für das Gemeinwohl eine
der wichtigen Fragen ist, die nicht vernachlässigt werden dürfen.

Ende

Hierzu ein
Skizzenblatt

Die Aufgaben
eines in Windhuk einzurichtenden
Stadtbauamtes.

Übersicht.

Einleitung: Unhaltbarkeit der bisherigen Praxis.

Ausführung: Die verschiedenen Tätigkeitsgebiete:

      1.) Hochbau,   Neubauten,
                     Unterhaltung der Bauten,
      2.) Tiefbau,   Straßenbau,
                     Wasserleitung,
                     Kanalisation,
      3.) Wasserbau, Revierregulierungen,
                     Sperren,
      4.) Baupolizei, Eigentliche Baupolizei,
                     Prüfung der Baugefüge,
                     Einrichtung der Bauakten,
                     Vorbereitung der Baupolizei-Ordnung,
                     Bauberatung,
      5.) Innere Verwaltung.

Schluß: Prinzip der Einrichtung.

==================

  Es dürfte heute keine Meinungsverschiedenheit mehr darüber herrschen, daß die bisherige Handhabung des gesamten Bauwesens durch die Stadtverwaltung unhaltbar geworden ist und etwas vom verwaltungstechnischen Standpunkt geschehen muß, um bei dem ständig zunehmenden Ausbau der Stadt die Übersicht zu behalten.

  Die einzig mögliche Lösung dieser Frage ist die Errichtung eines angebrachten städtischen Bauamtes. In Folgendem soll nun mit Rücksicht auf die bestehenden Verhältnisse dargelegt werden, welche Aufgaben das Stadtbauamt zu erledigen haben wird. Die einzelnen in Betracht kommenden Gebiete sind in der Hauptsache: Hochbau, Tiefbau, Wasserbau, Baupolizei.

  Hochbau. In dieses Gebiet fällt die Projektierung und Neuerrichtung von Gemeindebauten, ihre Verwaltung, Erhaltung und Wiederinstandsetzung. Daß namentlich die Instandhaltungsarbeiten in Hinsicht auf Güte und Preis der in Betracht kommenden Lieferungen

xiv

für die Gemeinde vorteilhafter sein werden, wenn eine sachtechnische
Verwaltung diese Arbeiten ausführen läßt, liegt wohl auf der Hand.
Arbeiten von minimalem Umfang vergibt das Bauamt selbst
oder mit Genehmigung des Herrn Bürgermeisters, alle größeren Arbeiten
vom Bauamt ausgeschrieben und vom Gemeinderat vergeben. Das
gilt auch für die anderen Arbeitsgebiete des Stadtbauamtes.

Tiefbau: Dieses Gebiet gliedert sich in Straßenbau, Wasser-
leitungsbau, Normalbau.

Die historische Entwickelung und das schnelle Aufblühen der
Stadt, überhaupt die ganzen Zeitverhältnisse brachten es mit sich,
daß der Anlage von Straßen von vornherein nicht die genü-
gende Aufmerksamkeit geschenkt wurde. Ein sehr oberflächlich
gearbeiteter Bebauungsplan wurde von Landmessern ausge-
arbeitet, die ihr Fach vorzüglich verstanden haben mögen, jedoch
von den Anforderungen modernen Städtebaus und von Straßenbau im besonderen wenig Ahnung hatten. Wie von diesen Ge-
sichtspunkten aus die ganze Anlage verfehlt ist, ist in einem
besonderen Aufsatz dargelegt. Insbesondere vom Standpunkt
praktischen Straßenbaus sind einige projektierte Straßen infolge
der Geländeverhältnisse ganz unausführbar, zum wenigsten ver-
ursacht der Ausbau enorme Schwierigkeiten, da die Höhenlage nicht
mit der Situation in Einklang zu bringen ist; andere sind wohl
ausführbar, aber kaum für die Bebauung brauchbar.

Es ist unbedingt erforderlich von sämtlichen Straßen Flucht-
linien und Höhenpläne festzustellen, in denen die jetzigen und
zukünftigen Höhen genau festgelegt sind, sonst erlebt man später
unliebsame Überraschungen. Infolge des Mangels genauer
Höhenpläne sind schon des Öfteren unangenehme Erscheinungen
zutage getreten, es sei hier nur verwiesen auf die Höhenlage
des Schmerenbeckschen Hauses, auf die nachträgliche Abgrabung
der Stübelstr. vor dem Grundstück des Herrn Dr. Kannegiesser, auf
die Schadensersatzansprüche, welche Herr Lavrin daraus gegen die
Stadt geltend zu machen beabsichtigt, weil ihm bei Erbauung seines
Hauses die zukünftige Höhenlage der Straße unrichtig angegeben
worden sei. Der Beispiele sind gewiß noch mehr. Es sei auch
darauf hingewiesen, daß die Anfertigung der Höhenpläne gleich-
zeitig eine wundervolle Vorarbeit für die später anzulegende
Kanalisation bildet.

Daß auch augenblicklich leider niemand vorhanden ist, der
den Ausbau der Straßen fachtechnisch leitet, sieht jeder Fachmann
bei Beobachtung der Ausführung dieser Arbeiten sofort.

Wenn man sieht, wie die Arbeiten an der Kaiserstraße ausge-
führt werden, muß man annehmen, daß von derselben weder
genaue Längsprofile, viel weniger aber nach Querprofile
festgelegt sind, es scheint, daß alles aufs Geratewohl nach Augen-
maß gemacht wird. Vorschriftsmäßige Herstellung mit Park-
lage und richtiger Beschotterung sucht man vergebens. Die Folgen
dieser wohl etwas kurzsichtigen Sparsamkeit werden nicht ausbleiben.
Sie nach Möglichkeit zu mildern und unangenehmen Überraschungen vorzubeugen, wie sie vorstehend an einigen Beispielen gezeigt
sind, wird eine der Hauptaufgaben des Stadtbauamtes sein.

Hand in Hand mit dem Straßenbau hat die Anlage der Wasserleitung zu gehen.

Ursprünglich war eine Wasserleitung vom Gouvernement
für die damals noch nicht so dicht besiedelte Stadt angelegt worden. Bei
der Einfachheit der damaligen Anlage hielt man die Anfertigung
eines Planes für überflüssig. Später übernahm die Stadt die Anlage, baute Abzweige, Nebenleitungen, neue Leitungen, Über-
leitungen von einer Leitung in die andere; leider aber wurden
niemals Pläne über die nacheinander entstandenen Anlagen
angefertigt und die Sache steht heute so, daß sich kein Mensch mehr
durchfinden kann und dauernde gleichmäßige Versorgung aller
Nachteile trotz der vorhandenen Wassermengen nicht möglich ist.

Die einzige Rettung ist eine vollständige Neuprojektierung
der gesamten Anlagen unter möglichster Verwendung vorhandenen
Materials. Diese Arbeit ist aber so umfangreich, daß dazu ein
besonderer Techniker erforderlich ist. Da kein genügend weites
Rohr für die Hauptleitungen vorhanden ist, muß wohl oder übel die
Durchführung der Wasserleitungserneuerung bis nach dem
Kriege verschoben werden. Die Ausarbeitung der Pläne kann
dagegen schon jetzt erfolgen, was vielleicht zweckmäßig ist, damit
nachher keine übereilte Arbeit geliefert wird. Einwandfrei kann
aber die Arbeit nur werden, wenn vorher die zukünftigen
Straßenhöhen auf dem Papier eingehend festgelegt werden, da
sonst ein ewiges Aufreißen und Wiederverlegen die Folge sein
muß.

Wie bereits gesagt, sind die Höhenpläne auch für die Kanalisation
unbedingt erforderlich. Nötig wird ja, wenn auch in vielleicht noch
ferner Zukunft, die Kanalisation zweifellos schon allein aus dem
Grunde, weil bei dem jetzigen Senkgrubensystem auf die Dauer
eine für die allgemeinen Gesundheitsverhältnisse außerordentlich
schädlichen Verseuchung des Bodens eintreten muß.

<u>Wasserbau.</u> In dieses Gebiet fällt die Regulierung der Reviere
der Ent- und Bewässerungsanlagen, die Anlage öffentlicher und
privater Brunnen, die Errichtung von Rinnen und Talsperren,
Grundschwellen und Zisternen.

Zum weitaus größten Teile fällt die Projektierung, Be-
rechnung und Ausführung dieser Arbeiten in den Arbeitsbereich des Gouvernements.
Nehmen wir aber z.B. einen Fall, wie die endgültige Regulie-
rung des großen Windhuker Reviers, so liegt es zweifellos im
Interesse der Stadt hierfür selbst ein Projekt auszuarbeiten, wie es
den zukünftigen städtischen Interessen am dienlichsten ist, die das
Gouvernement niemals so machen kann, als die Stadt selber.

<u>Baupolizei.</u> Das Nichtvorhandensein einer technisch beratenen
Baupolizeibehörde, ja nicht einmal einer Baupolizei-Ordnung ist ein
in den Fachkreisen lange empfundener Mangel in Windhuk.
Gewiß mußte auch bisher stets eine Baugenehmigung einge-
holt werden. Die Prüfung des Baugesuches war praktisch jedoch nicht
viel mehr als eine rein bürokratische Maßnahme. Selbst wenn
auf Ersuchen der Gemeinde eine technische Prüfung des Gesuches
durch das Hochbaureferat der Regierung erfolgte, so kümmerte
sich nach erteilter Genehmigung meist kein Mensch mehr darum,
ob die Ausführung auch den Anordnungen genau entsprach.

Das ganze Baupolizeiwesen gewinnt praktisch erst dann Sinn,
wenn die Gemeinde eine technisch geleitete Bauzentrale hat, die
von jedem Grundstück genaue Bauakten einrichtet, somit dies
möglich ist. Das ist nicht nur wichtig, um jederzeit die Unterlagen
für Erweiterungsbauten, Umbauten, Straßenregulieren, Wasser-
leitungs- und Kanalanschlüsse usw. zur Hand zu haben, sondern auch,
weil auf diese Weise die anderen Dienstzweige entlastet werden
und das ewige Aktensuchen wenigstens in dieser Hinsicht wesentlich eingeschränkt wird.

Von großem Wert für die Wohnlichkeit des Ortes ist eine
Nebentätigkeit der Baupolizei, die Ausübung der sogenannten
Bauberatung. Hierüber ist mehr gesagt in dem beiliegenden Aufsatz
über „Windhuk vom Standpunkt des Städtebaus" und es wird höflichst
gebeten den entsprechenden Abschnitt dort gütigst nachzulesen und
dazu das beiliegende Skizzenblatt zu vergleichen.

<u>Innere Verwaltung.</u> An dieser kann das Stadtbauamt in
mancher Hinsicht mitwirken, z.B. es an der Verwaltung und dem
Verkauf der Grundstücke mitarbeitet, die Pläne derselben be-
wahrt für deren ordnungsmäßige Weiterführung durch das Vermessungs-

amt Sorge trägt, Zeichnungen für andere Verwaltungszweige
legen usw., anfertigt, alle Schriftstücke erledigt welche technische
Sachen angehen usw.

Die praktische Einrichtung aller dieser Dinge kann
natürlich nicht von heute auf morgen geschehen, sondern muß sich
nach und nach entwickeln.

Zunächst käme nur die Anstellung eines technisch allseitig gebildeten Technikers in Frage, der möglichst eine ähnliche
Stellung in Deutschland längere Zeit bekleidet, nicht eines
technischen Spezialisten, sondern eines Mannes der alle technischen Fragen des Hoch- und Tiefbaus genügend aus praktischer
Erfahrung kennt, sie vom verwaltungstechnischen Standpunkt
zu handhaben weiß und der nicht zuletzt auch etwas künstle-
risches Verständnis besitzt.

Diese Besetzung würde voraussichtlich auf lange Jahre genügen. Die Gehaltsauslagen für diesen Fachmann stehen in
keinem Verhältnis zu den Unkosten, welche die Stadt sich durch
die Vernachlässigung eines so wichtigen Verwaltungs-
zweiges bisher aufgeladen hat und - wenn es so weiter geht –
in Zukunft aufladen wird.

Schluß.

A4: Aerial photo of Old Location, Windhoek, circa 1930

A5: Aerial photo of Windhoek Location 1948

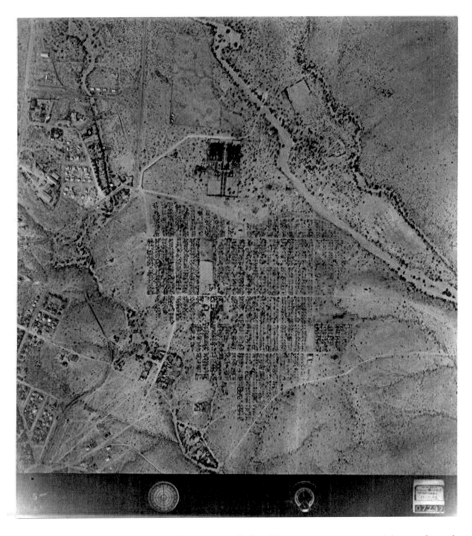

Note the relatively lush vegetation around the European cemetery (situated at the image's top/centre) as opposed to the ordered but barely green Indigenous Location extending to the cemetery's north (covering the image's central and bottom areas).

Matteo Landricina
Nkrumah and the West
"The Ghana Experiment" in British, American, German Archives and Ghanaian Archives
The developmental years of Ghana – the first state to become independent from colonialism in sub-Saharan Africa in 1957 – were marked by the United Kingdom's effort to showcase its former colony as a model of successful democracy export for the rest of Black Africa. They called it the "Ghana Experiment". Major Western powers like the United States and West Germany participated in the attempt to keep Ghana aligned with the West. As Ghana's President Kwame Nkrumah embarked on a bold anti-imperialistic, pan-African policy, Britain and the United States concerted a common strategy which accelerated Nkrumah's eventual downfall in 1966 and brought Ghana back into the Western sphere of influence.
Studien zur Afrikanischen Geschichte, vol. 34, 2018, 440 pp., 34,90 €, br., ISBN 978-3-643-90972-5

Lars-Christopher Huening
No Mistaken Identity
Kinshasa's Press and the Rwandophone 'Other' (c. 1990- 2005)
Studien zur Afrikanischen Geschichte, vol. 33, 2015, 360 pp., 39,90 €, pb., ISBN 978-3-643-90643-4

Daniela Dohr; Philipp Kumria; Jonas Metzger
Saatgut und Sozialsystem
Gender, Monetarisierung und bäuerliche Praktiken der Ernährungssicherung in Namibia und Tansania
Spektrum – Berliner Reihe zu Gesellschaft, Wirtschaft und Politik in Entwicklungsländern, Bd. 112, 2016, 200 S., 24,90 €, br., ISBN 978-3-643-13217-8

Martin Eberhardt
Zwischen Nationalsozialismus und Apartheid
Die deutsche Bevölkerungsgruppe Südwestafrikas 1915 – 1965
Periplus Studien, Bd. 10, 2007, 584 S., 39,90 €, br., ISBN 978-3-8258-0225-7

Diego Augusto Menestrey Schwieger
The Pump Keeps on Running
On the emergence of water management institutions between state decentralization and local practices in northern Kunene
Kölner Ethnologische Studien, vol. 36, 2017, 488 pp., 34,90 €, pb., ISBN 978-3-643-90838-4

Silke Tönsjost
Umverteilung und Egalität
Kapital und Konsummuster bei Ovaherero-Pastoralisten in Namibia
Kölner Ethnologische Studien, Bd. 35, 2013, 272 S., 29,90 €, br., ISBN 978-3-643-12240-7

Mathias Polak
Zwischen Haushalt und Staat
Lokale Water Governance im zentralen Norden Namibias
Forum Politische Geographie, Bd. 12, 2014, 256 S., 39,90 €, br., ISBN 978-3-643-12623-8

Salomé Ritterband
Tracking Indigenous Heritage
Ju/'Hoansi San Learning, Interpreting, and Staging Tradition for a Sustainable Future in Cultural Tourism in the Tsumkwe District of Namibia
Legal Anthropology and Indigenous Rights, vol. 3, 2018, 294 pp., 29,90 €, pb., ISBN 978-3-643-90976-3

Jürgen Zimmerer
Deutsche Herrschaft über Afrikaner
Staatlicher Machtanspruch und Wirklichkeit im kolonialen Namibia
Europa – Übersee. Historische Studien, Bd. 10, 3. Aufl. 2004, 344 S., 24,90 €, br., ISBN 3-8258-7473-7

LIT Verlag Berlin – Münster – Wien – Zürich – London
Auslieferung Deutschland / Österreich / Schweiz: siehe Impressumsseite